Trade and Protectionism

NBER–East Asia Seminar on Economics
Volume 2

National Bureau of Economic Research
Korea Development Institute
Chung-Hua Institution for Economic Research

Trade and Protectionism

Edited by Takatoshi Ito
and Anne O. Krueger

The University of Chicago Press

Chicago and London

TAKATOSHI ITO is professor of economics at Hitotsubashi University.
ANNE O. KRUEGER is Arts and Sciences Professor of Economics at Duke University. Both are research associates of the National Bureau of Economic Research.

The University of Chicago Press, Chicago 60637
The University of Chicago Press, Ltd., London

Printed in the United States of America

02 01 00 99 98 97 96 95 94 93   1 2 3 4 5

ISBN: 0-226-38668-6 (cloth)

Library of Congress Cataloging-in-Publication Data

Trade and protectionism / edited by Takatoshi Ito and Anne O. Krueger.
p. cm.—(NBER-East Asia seminar on economics: v. 2)
"Papers presented at the Second Annual East Asian Seminar on Economics, held in Taipei, Taiwan, June 19–21, 1991"—Intro.
Includes bibliographical references and index.
1. East Asia—Foreign economic relations—United States—Congresses. 2. United States—Foreign economic relations—East Asia—Congresses. 3. Protectionism—East Asia—Congresses. 4. East Asia—Commercial policy—Congresses. 5. United States—Commercial policy—Congresses. I. Ito, Takatoshi. II. Krueger, Anne O. III. Series.
HF1600.5.Z4U67 1993
382′.73—dc20   92-39852
CIP

♾ The paper used in this publication meets the minimum requirements of the American National Standard for Information Sciences—Permanence of Paper for Printed Library Materials, ANSI Z39.48-1984.

Since this volume is a record of conference proceedings, it has been exempted from the rules governing critical review of manuscripts by the Board of Directors of the National Bureau (resolution adopted 8 June 1948, as revised 21 November 1949 and 20 April 1968).

Contents

Introduction 1
Takatoshi Ito and Anne O. Krueger

PART I

1. **Discrimination, Regionalism, and GATT** 7
Richard H. Snape
Comment: Koichi Hamada

2. **American Bilateral Trading Arrangements and East Asian Interests** 25
Anne O. Krueger
Comment: Robert E. Baldwin
Comment: Kuo-shu Liang

PART II

3. **Forward Pricing versus Fair Value: An Analytic Assessment of "Dumping" in DRAMs** 47
Kenneth Flamm
Comment: Yun-Wing Sung

4. **Japan's Agricultural Policy and Protection Growth** 95
Masayoshi Honma
Comment: Joachim Zietz

5. **The Growth of Agricultural Protection** 115
Joachim Zietz and Alberto Valdés
Comment: Masayoshi Honma

PART III

6. **Economic Growth and Trade Relations: Japanese Performance in Long-Term Perspective** 149
Gary R. Saxonhouse
Comment: Takatoshi Ito
Comment: Yun-Wing Sung

7. **Protectionist U.S. Trade Policy and Korean Exports** 183
Chong-Hyun Nam
Comment: Shujiro Urata
Comment: Chia Siow Yue

8. **Access to the Japanese Market by Asian Countries: A Case Study of the Wool Textile Industry** 223
Motoshige Itoh and Kaori Hatanaka
Comment: Chong-Hyun Nam
Comment: Tan Eu Chye

PART IV

9. **Technology Transfer in the Asian Pacific Region: Implications of Trends since the Mid-1980s** 243
Tran Van Tho
Comment: Takatoshi Ito
Comment: Bih Jane Liu

10. **Japanese Foreign Direct Investment and Its Effect on Foreign Trade in Asia** 273
Shujiro Urata
Comment: Tran Van Tho
Comment: Yoo Jung-ho

PART V

11. **The Political Economy of U.S.-Taiwanese Trade and Other International Economic Relations** 307
Robert E. Baldwin and Douglas Nelson
Comment: Koichi Hamada
Comment: Richard H. Snape

12. **The Political Economy of Trade Protection in the Republic of China on Taiwan** 339
Tain-Jy Chen and Chi-ming Hou
Comment: Kenneth Flamm
Comment: Ching-huei Chang

13. **The Political Economy of Protection Structure in Korea** 361
Yoo Jung-ho
Comment: Anne O. Krueger
Comment: Chia Siow Yue

14. **Government Policy and Strategic Industries: The Case of Taiwan** 387
Ya-Hwei Yang
Comment: Yoo Jung-ho
Comment: Tan Eu Chye

15. **Export-Oriented Growth and Equity in Korea** 413
Wontack Hong
Comment: Motoshige Itoh
Comment: Richard H. Snape

Contributors 437

Author Index 439

Subject Index 443

Introduction

Takatoshi Ito and Anne O. Krueger

This volume contains the papers presented at the Second Annual East Asian Seminar on Economics, cosponsored by the National Bureau of Economic Research, the Korea Development Institute, and the Chung-Hua Institution for Economic Research, which was the conference host. The topic of the conference, held in Taipei, Taiwan, 19–21 June 1991, was "Trade and Protectionism," with special reference to issues of importance to trading relations between North America and East Asia.

The crosscurrents in the world trading system are of concern throughout the world. Over the first three decades after the Second World War, the increasingly open, multilateral international trading system served the entire world economy well. Successive GATT rounds of trade negotiations, unilateral liberalizations of trade on the part of the European countries, and falling costs of transport and communications served increasingly to integrate the world economy. The rate of growth of world trade was almost double that of world GNP and as such contributed to the enormous worldwide economic growth of the period.

In the 1980s, there have been some portents that this trend toward liberalization may be reversing. On one hand, the Uruguay Round of trade negotiations under GATT did not reach a satisfactory outcome on the planned timetable, and protectionist pressures in some of the major industrialized countries appeared to be increasing. On the other hand, there appeared to be pressures for regional trading arrangements. Europe 1992 was the first and most prominent. However, in the late 1980s, the U.S.–Canada Free Trade Agreement began coming into force, and it was announced that the United States and

Takatoshi Ito is professor of economics at Hitotsubashi University. Anne O. Krueger is Arts and Sciences Professor of Economics at Duke University. Both are research associates of the National Bureau of Economic Research.

Mexico would enter into a Free Trade Agreement. The specter of a Western Hemisphere trading bloc and a European trading bloc naturally alarmed those who believe in the importance of the multilateral trading system for the entire world economy.

These pressures are of particular concern to East Asian countries, both because trading relations with North America and Europe are important to their economies, and because the overall health of the world trading system is of vital importance to them. On the one hand, trade frictions over particular issues between the United States and East Asian countries have led to tensions. When these trade frictions are combined with the prospects of regional trading blocs, natural concerns arise in East Asia over future access to markets.

Because of the importance of trading relations to the East Asian economies, and because of the visibility of trade frictions with North America, it was natural to focus on various aspects of U.S.–East Asian trading relations, in the context of the global economy, at this year's conference. Research on the issues underlying trade frictions can make a significant contribution to narrowing areas of disagreement and to distinguishing protectionist rhetoric from reality.

The first two papers in this volume focus on the context in which East Asian trading relations with the United States take place. Richard N. Snape's paper focuses on the role of GATT, the importance of the open multilateral trading system, and the current threats to it. Anne O. Krueger's paper then provides an analysis of U.S. regional trading arrangements, with a focus on Mexico as a more important potential competitor with East Asian countries than is Canada. She concludes that, based on existing economic capacities, successful economic reforms and the opening up of the major Latin American countries should spur their growth sufficiently so that, over the intermediate-term future, East Asian countries may gain more trading opportunities from Latin American growth than they may lose through trade preferences. Krueger also points to the relatively small size of the Latin American economies contrasted with those in Europe and East Asia and concludes that the United States would incur significant losses were it to take actions that resulted in the United States being isolated in a Western Hemisphere trading bloc.

The second set of papers focuses on sensitive sectoral issues that have led to trade frictions. Kenneth Flamm analyzes semiconductor trade, and Masayoshi Honma and Joachim Zietz and Alberto Valdés focus on aspects of agricultural trade. Flamm emphasizes possible justifications of the "fair market price" determination in Japanese-American semiconductor trade. Both Honma's and Zietz and Valdés's papers show the rapid increase and high levels of agricultural protection in Japan, Korea, and Hong Kong and examine the political determinants of protection.

The third set of papers focuses on trade issues between East Asian countries and their trading partners. Gary R. Saxonhouse analyses U.S.-Japanese trade issues, while Chong-Hyun Nam examines the effect of U.S.-administered protection on Korean exports, and Motoshige Itoh and Kaori Hatanaka consider the openness of the Japanese market to exports from other Asian countries.

Next, aspects of international economic relations among Asian countries are considered. Tran Van Tho analyzes foreign direct investment relations between Japan and other Asian countries, with emphasis on the technology component of the investment, while Shujiro Urata examines the relation between Japanese foreign direct investment and trade flows among Asian countries.

In most of the papers, attention is paid to the political factors affecting trade policies. As already mentioned, Zietz-Valdés and Honma analyze political factors determining the level of protection to agriculture. The final group of papers, however, focuses on the overall political-economic interaction in affecting levels of protection. Robert E. Baldwin and Douglas Nelson apply the interest-group model of protection to U.S.-Taiwan trade relations, while Tain-Jy Chen and Chi-ming Hou examine the political economy of Taiwan's structure of protection. Yoo Jung-ho provides an analysis of the structure of Korea's protection from 1978 to 1988. Ya-Hwei Yang examines the effectiveness of Taiwan's effort to support industrial development through credit subsidies, and Wontack Hong examines the effect of Korea's export-oriented trade strategy on income distribution in Korea.

As will be seen in the papers themselves and in the discussants' remarks, these papers only begin to address the questions that arise from consideration of protection and trade relations in North America and East Asia.

Acknowledgments are in order. Our greatest thanks go to the National Bureau of Economic Research, which provided support in the logistical arrangements for the conference, as well as to the Starr Foundation for financing for the North American participants. The Chung-Hua Institution was a cosponsor and local host of the conference. We are indebted to the many fine scholars at the Institution who participated in the conference, and especially to the late Chi-ming Hou, who coordinated all the arrangements and to whose memory this volume is dedicated. Although Dr. Hou was very ill at the time of the conference, his enthusiastic participation and support contributed enormously to the success of the conference. We also thank the Korea Development Institute, the third cosponsor, for sending excellent Korean economists to the conference. We gratefully acknowledge financial support from the NIRA (National Institute for Research Advancement) for sending the Japan-based economists to the conference. Finally, we are indebted to Gail McKinnis, who efficiently and conscientiously undertook the thankless tasks of chasing down missing papers, ensuring that all discussants' comments were in, and handling referees' reports as well as the many other chores that are essential parts of transforming conference papers into a worthwhile volume.

I

1 Discrimination, Regionalism, and GATT

Richard H. Snape

Preferential trading agreements are back in fashion. The purpose of this paper is to survey briefly the background to discriminatory trading arrangements and the economic effects of some forms of them. It discusses some problems with departures from nondiscrimination and proposes a manner in which nondiscrimination may be pursued further through the General Agreement on Tariffs and Trade (GATT).

Following the creation of the European Economic Community (EEC) and the European Free Trade Area (EFTA) in the late 1950s, many new trading arrangements were formed among developing countries, but without any notable long-term successes. Meanwhile, the British Commonwealth preference system, which had been at the center of dispute during the negotiations over the International Trade Organisation (ITO) and the GATT at the end of the Second World War, withered. In the 1970s, more emphasis was given in international negotiations to preferences for developing countries and the creation of commodity cartels. In the 1980s and early 1990s, the pendulum has swung back to the formation of free trade and other preferential trading areas, mainly on a regional basis.

Of particular importance has been the change in attitude of the U.S. government. Having been discriminated against in the prewar period, during which German and British hub-and-spoke bilateral systems dominated much of world trade, the United States was firmly against allowing discrimination in the club that was to become the GATT. It compromised to the extent of agreeing to the continuation but not the extension of existing preferences and to preferential arrangements that involved essentially free trade among the participants: customs unions and free trade areas. The United States supported

Richard H. Snape is professor of economics at Monash University, Melbourne, Australia.
The author is indebted to the discussants and Doug Nelson for comments.

the formation of the EEC for essentially political reasons and in the late 1960s reluctantly agreed to the generalized system of preferences for developing countries, negotiated through the GATT.

In contrast to its earlier position—that of being clearly the leader in developing a nondiscriminatory trading system—the United States has been at the front in the new wave of preferential trading arrangements, having granted unilateral preferences to Caribbean countries in 1983 and concluding free trade agreements with Israel in 1985 and Canada in 1988. Now, in the early 1990s, the Bush administration is currently seeking a free trade agreement with Mexico, has indicated that other Latin American countries may be candidates for similar agreements, and has put out feelers in other directions also.

Over the last nine years, successive U.S. trade representatives have explicitly stated that bilateral and multilateral negotiations would proceed together. The position was well stated in the Reagan administration's statement on trade policy of 23 September 1985: "While our highest priority remains the improvement of the world trading system through a new round of multilateral trade negotiations, the United States is interested in the possibility of achieving further liberalization of trade and investment through the negotiation of bilateral free-trade arrangements such as the one recently concluded with Israel. We believe that, at times, such agreements could complement our multilateral efforts and facilitate a higher degree of liberalization, mutually beneficial to both parties, than would be possible within the multilateral context."

While still the secretary of the U.S. Treasury, James Baker added, "[Our] approach is idealistic in aim, but realistic and often incremental in method. It seeks to move nations toward a more open trading system through a strategy of consistent, complementary, and reinforcing actions on various international fronts, bilateral and multilateral. . . . [The trade agreement with Canada] is . . . a lever to achieve more open trade. Other nations are forced to recognize that we will devise ways to expand trade—with or without them. If they choose not to open their markets, they will not reap the benefits."[1]

This statement of Baker's threatens the EEC, Japan, and others: join in the multilateral negotiations, or the United States will discriminate against you by entering into more favorable trading relationships with other parties. Many observers question whether this two-track approach can be sustained. Do the threat, pursuit, and negotiation of preferential arrangements stimulate and complement multilateralism as claimed in Baker's statement, or do they undermine it?

Preferences can be explicitly negative as well as positive. Sanctions against South Africa, Iran, and Iraq are examples of negative preferences. Amendment of the main safeguard provision of the GATT against "fair" trade (Ar-

1. Remarks made by James Baker to the Canadian Importers and Exporters Associations, Toronto, 22 June 1988.

ticle XIX) to allow discrimination ("selectivity") against those countries whose exports triggered the safeguard action was pressed by some countries in the Tokyo Round of multilateral trade negotiations but was resisted. It has resurfaced in the Uruguay Round, and it could emerge from it, if the Round is completed. The draft of a Safeguards Code (interpretation of Article XIX) that was on the table at what was intended to be the final ministerial meeting of the Uruguay Round in Brussels in December 1990 contained square-bracketed sections that would have allowed such selectivity "in exceptional circumstances."

Probably the most important of explicitly negative preferences are the Section 301 and the now expired Super-301 provisions of the 1988 U.S. Omnibus Trade and Competitiveness Act (Bhagwati and Patrick 1990). Many of the provisions allow for explicit discrimination against other countries in a manner that is inconsistent with the GATT (both with respect to the nondiscrimination provisions and because the relevant tariffs have been bound) and with the position adopted so forcefully by the United States in the negotiations that established the post–World War II international economic institutions. Indeed, it is reminiscent of the German and British policies of the 1930s (Condliffe 1940, chaps. 4, 8).

In comparing nondiscriminatory multilateralism and trade discrimination in all its forms, it can be instructive to recall the role of the price system in a market economy. The market allows (to varying degrees, depending on the nature of the transaction) the depersonalization of trading. This has several consequences, the foremost economic one being efficiency. Nonmarket systems function through obligations, responsibilities, love, hate, threats, war, queues, cooperation, and favors. This occurs at both the micro level of individuals and at the macro level of nations. Personal and political relationships come to the fore: markets help depoliticize transactions nationally and internationally. A corollary is that nontariff barriers to international trade invite discrimination and in some forms make it inevitable. Managed trade is political trade.

It may be that international transactions can never be completely depoliticized—trade policy is intertwined with foreign policy, as Cooper (1987) reminds us. Trade is between "us" and "them" (Kindleberger 1986, 1). There is no doubt, however, that the level of politicization is lowest with nondiscriminatory trade. Preferences granted can be removed, and, to the extent that trade policy is seeking international political favor, it is likely not to be economically efficient.

1.1 Forms of Barrier Reduction

Trade preferences may be given by selectively reducing trade barriers against the preferred countries or by raising barriers against others. Both tactics were relevant in the discriminatory 1930s; they are both relevant in today's trading world also, with the threat of action by the United States in particular against countries that it judges not to be playing by the appropriate rules. But for the moment I focus on preferences granted by barrier reduction. Barrier reduction may be undertaken in a manner that discriminates against countries or does not; it may be undertaken as part of a negotiated international agreement or unilaterally. This gives four possibilities:

(i) unilateral nondiscriminatory reductions;
(ii) unilateral discriminatory reductions;
(iii) internationally negotiated nondiscriminatory reductions; and
(iv) internationally negotiated discriminatory reductions.

In this list, the GATT allows (i) and (iii), in the latter case provided that the reductions or concessions are passed on to all members of the GATT unconditionally. Except for preferences for developing countries, it does not permit (ii) and allows (iv) only if the negotiated agreement fulfills what on paper are stringent conditions, to which I shall return later.

Looking at the choice between (i) and (ii), why should a country discriminate among other countries if it is receiving nothing in return from those that it favors? Given the trade policy of other countries, a country will generally gain more in terms of real income from a nondiscriminatory reduction in its trade barriers than from a similar preferential barrier reduction: with nondiscrimination it could obtain all the trade creation gains (and more) without the trade diversion costs.[2] This statement should be qualified for a country that has market power with respect to its imports or exports and where the elasticities of supply or demand differ across its trading partners (and the markets can be segmented). But the optimal trade taxes necessary to exploit these terms of trade effects are difficult enough to calculate in practice where the rest of the world is treated as one market. Calculation of a set of discriminatory trade taxes that would increase a country's real income where the rest of the world is treated as a set of segmented markets is a problem of a much higher order. Further, the products for which such discrimination would be most relevant will generally be those over which the producing enterprise itself has market power and for which it will set prices on different markets that reflect the differential conditions on those markets. So any qualification of the general statement that, for given trade policies of other countries, a nondiscriminatory barrier reduction is likely to raise real income more than a discriminatory barrier reduction will probably be of minor importance in practice.

I now pass on to the choice between the unilateral and negotiated barrier reduction and then to that between discrimination and nondiscrimination.

2. Preferential reduction of nontariff barriers may result in trade diversion without any trade creation. This occurs, e.g., when a global import quota remains unaltered but preferential access is granted within this quota.

1.2 Unilateral or Negotiated Barrier Reduction?

The usual reason for undertaking liberalization in the context of *any* international agreement (preferential or not), rather than doing it unilaterally, is to obtain something in return from trading partners. To use the language of trade negotiation, such concessions not only provide a source of economic gain (including gain in the sense of reduced uncertainty) for the home country but also provide within that country the political balance of obvious and concentrated gainers, exporters, to be placed against the obvious and concentrated losers, producers of import-competing industries in which there is trade creation.

In addition to seeking concessions with respect to its exports, a government may choose to enter negotiated discriminatory or nondiscriminatory international agreements so as to constrain its own policies, even if little is obtained as "concessions" from abroad. There are times when governments are able to stand back and make assessments in the general interest relatively free from sectional pressures. External security considerations may provide such an opportunity, or the opportunity may occur soon after an election or after election debts have been paid. International commitments provide a bulwark against subsequent sectional pressures: they may be compared with the wax in the ears of Ulysses' sailors and the ropes that bound him to the mast so that they might all withstand the deadly temptations of the Sirens. A very important variation on the same theme occurs in the United States, where the authority has been granted by Congress to the administration to negotiate international agreements, which then must be passed or rejected by Congress in their entirety (the "fast track" authority). This process prevents the tariff-by-tariff logrolling by Congress of the sort that yielded the Smoot-Hawley tariff. Congress thereby has constrained itself (Destler 1986, chap. 2), and all tariff reductions since the early 1930s in the United States have come about through this process. More generally, the temptations referred to may not only be protectionist: they may also be manifest in loose monetary and fiscal policies that will be less sustainable in the presence of international commitments. Also, international negotiations themselves direct attention to an overview of economic policy that can also help keep pressures for inefficient policies at bay.

I address later the question of whether preferential or multilateral, nondiscriminatory negotiations are likely to provide the greater constraints.

1.3 Discrimination versus Nondiscrimination

The case for nondiscriminatory multilateralism as compared with preferential schemes can sound rather fundamentalist. It has been characterized as such recently by Rudiger Dornbusch in the *Economist* (Dornbusch 1991, 65). Part of the case for multilateralism and nondiscrimination is systemic and difficult to pin down in practice, much as it is difficult to pin on individuals the effects that their tax avoidance has on respect for (and compliance with) the taxation system as a whole. There are public good aspects to compliance with a nondiscriminatory world trading system as there are to compliance with a reasonable taxation system. The argument in favor of any particular preferential trading arrangement will thus appear to be stronger than the argument for preferential arrangements as a whole. Each has a systemic effect, to which reference was made earlier.

For the choice between discriminatory and nondiscriminatory barrier reduction, the question is whether the extra "something in return" in a preferential agreement compensates for the trade diversion costs; working on a larger canvas, however, governments can also consider the effect on the trading system as a whole of the development of preferential trading arrangements—the systemic effect—which can react on them adversely. While small countries may gain most from discrimination in their favor, they also stand to lose most from the collapse of a multilateral system. It was this systemic effect that was in the minds of those who pressed for tight constraints on preferential arrangements in the GATT, and I shall return to it later.

Usually the extra "something in return" for a preferential barrier reduction will be a greater decrease in the barriers against the home country's exports than could otherwise be achieved, although guarantees against increases in barriers against its exports are also important in some agreements. This has been so for Canada in its negotiations with the United States: it obtained special dispute settlement procedures in relation to antidumping and countervailing duty matters, selective exemption from restriction of its exports from safeguard action under the GATT's Article XIX unless the exports had themselves contributed "importantly" to the injury of an industry in the United States, and also exemption from any restriction that may be imposed on some exports from other countries, for example, meat and the enrichment in the United States of foreign uranium (Articles 704 and 1102, Chapter 19, and Annex 902.5 of the agreement; Snape 1988, 12; Snape 1989b, 194). Such guarantees are, of course, discriminatory: the provisions for meat and uranium discriminate against Australia. It can be expected that other countries that seek trade agreements with the United States will also seek preferential treatment with respect to contingent protection and dispute settlement.

Often preferential trading arrangements are part of larger preferential and political agreements—sometimes a key element of the larger picture as in the development of the EEC, sometimes rather incidental and minor as in ASEAN (the Association of Southeast Asian Nations). The assessment of the total gains and losses then may be beyond the calculus of economists, but this does not prevent this calculus being used to evaluate some of the economic effects of preferences.

Article I of the GATT does not permit any new preferential trading arrangement between members of the GATT and any other *country.*[3] Amendments to the GATT have qualified this by allowing preferences to be extended to developing countries without reciprocity, while Article XXIV qualifies it by permitting contracting parties to form preferential arrangements[4] provided that:

(i) they are in the form of customs unions (free trade internally and common barriers externally) or free trade areas (free trade internally and differentiated barriers externally) covering "substantially all the trade in products" or are interim arrangements leading to these ends;
(ii) they do not result in raised barriers against nonparticipants (the "general incidence" must not be raised in the case of customs unions); and
(iii) GATT is notified of the intention to form such arrangements.

The view taken is clearly that free trade areas and customs unions that cover most trade among the members will tend to be more trade creating than diverting so that on balance they are liberalizing. There is also a judgment implied that the multilateralism of the GATT as a whole is not undermined by such arrangements.

In fact, very few free trade areas or customs unions have been authorized by the contracting parties to the GATT. Schott (1989, annex A) lists sixty-nine preferential trading arrangements considered by the GATT under the provisions of Article XXIV up to late 1988. Of these, only four have actually been deemed compatible with the Article, although it should be pointed out that, if the conditions of the Article are met, approval is automatic and requires no special action (Jackson 1969, 582). The conditions in fact have seldom been met, but no proposed agreement has been prohibited. It can reasonably be said that surveillance has been ineffectual (Schott 1989, 24–26).

An attempt has been made in the Uruguay Round negotiations to strengthen the conditions and surveillance of free trade areas and customs unions. The "Draft Final Act Embodying the Results of the Uruguay Round of Multilateral Trade Negotiations" tabled for consideration by trade ministers in Brussels in December 1990 spoke of the "need to reinforce the effectiveness of the role of . . . [the GATT] in reviewing agreements notified under Article XXIV, by clarifying the criteria and procedures for the assessment of new or enlarged agreements, and improving the transparency of all Article XXIV agreements." One of the more significant provisions was that the "reasonable length of time" for interim arrangements prior to the adoption of free trade among members should not normally exceed ten years. Others were for calculating a common external tariff of a customs union to satisfy the provisions of Article

3. Often overlooked is that Article I provides that any trade concession granted to any other country (not just any other contracting party) by a contracting party must be extended unconditionally to all other contracting parties.

4. Article XXIV as written could appear to prohibit free trade or customs union agreements between members and nonmembers of the GATT. This is not the way it has been interpreted in practice (Jackson 1969, 582).

XXIV, for raising previously bound tariffs on the formation of a customs union, and for more effective review under GATT procedures of the proposed barrier reductions and their timetable. But, even if accepted, these provisions appear very weak given the flagrant disregard for some of the constraints of Article XXIV in the past. It is unlikely that the intended thrust of Article XXIV will be enforced unless a major player takes a lead. Such a lead has been advocated by Bhagwati (1990, 163), but at this juncture is appears unlikely—this being reflected in the weakness of the Brussels document—particularly in view of the current enthusiasm for free trade agreements which are unlikely to satisfy a reasonable interpretation of Article XXIV.

In section 1.2 above it was mentioned that international agreements and negotiations may have the useful role of constraining domestic policies for the general good. Following this line, a question arises whether preferential or nondiscriminatory agreements are more effective in providing the constraints on domestic policy. There does not seem to be a general answer to this. It depends very much on who the partners are in a preferential arrangement and on the nature of the agreements. It is probably easier to get tight, binding agreements between a small group of similarly minded and endowed countries than between a large number of diverse countries. Multilateral agreements are more likely to contain words that are intended to mean different things to different people. But a bilateral agreement between two countries that are not well matched politically or economically is unlikely to provide much of a constraint on the more powerful country.

Thus, when fully implemented, the U.S.-Israel Free Trade Agreement will constrain Israel's trade policy much more than it will that of the United States. The GATT provides a greater constraint on the trade policy of the United States than does or will the U.S.-Israel Free Trade Agreement; the opposite is probably the situation for Israel. On the other hand, there is not likely to be much pressure on most U.S. industries from imports from Israel (particularly as many agricultural products are effectively excluded from the agreement), and the pressure on the United States to break the agreement is therefore likely to be small.

Where there is a dominant party to an agreement, other parties are linked to an economy that may or may not prove to be dynamic. Nondiscrimination provides constraints on a country's industries and its policies from the world as a whole; preferential arrangements tie the parties to a significant extent to the efficiencies or inefficiencies of the dominant member. It is not clear that the tie to the British economy that the Commonwealth preference system provided for some countries was a net advantage to these countries in the two decades or so after World War II.

While the United States is at the center of current regional initiatives, regionalism is being advocated and preferential agreements formed between countries other than the United States. The Closer Economic Relations agreement between Australia and New Zealand is one of the freest of free trade arrangements, covering all commodities, factor movements, and many services, while it has no safeguard provisions.[5] It more than satisfies the GATT provisions and does not appear to encourage substantial trade diversion, partly because both countries have been lowering their external barriers significantly against the rest of the world. On the other hand, from a historical perspective it is difficult to believe that actual and proposed trade agreements between Latin American countries will come anywhere near satisfying the GATT provisions or will provide effective constraints on their policies. Further, there is likely to be costly trade diversion while external barriers in Latin America remain high.

Agreements among a small number of participants may be negotiated more quickly than multilateral agreements, although Schott (1989, 19–20) questions the strength of this point. Negotiations that appear to be going nowhere are unlikely to constrain policies, and this is a problem associated with the stalling of the Uruguay Round. While a nondiscriminatory agreement under the GATT may be better for Latin American countries than an agreement among themselves or with the United States, waiting for this option to firm may miss the bus of opportunity (Dornbusch 1991, 65). But the arrival of the GATT bus may not be exogenous: a substantial push by Latin American countries may get it moving. Regional negotiations divert negotiating attention and muscle from multilateral negotiations. But if the Uruguay Round is unsuccessful, a set of agreements (or, better, a single agreement) with the United States may be better for these countries than nothing, and better than a purely Latin American agreement.

The completion of the single market in Europe in 1992 far exceeds the requirements of the GATT with respect to internal trade, although some questions can be raised with respect to external trade, particularly in agriculture, textiles, clothing, automobiles, and some electronic products. But the formation of such a trading bloc, and the possibility that disputes between it and the United States or Japan may be solved on a political bilateral level, with little regard and unfortunate consequences for other less powerful countries, has worried many commentators.

The greater are the concentrations of power, the less likely is a general rules-based system to function effectively unless it is established in a hegemonic manner. Yet rules of general application protect the weak against the strong. The GATT as a *general* set of rules—general with respect to countries and commodities apart from specific exceptions—provides such protection. Effective constraints on the actions of powerful countries are likely to be achieved by international agreements only if these agreements incorporate other countries, or groups of countries, of comparable power. But between

5. There are no safeguard provisions with respect to dumping or "fair" trade (cf. Article XIX of GATT), and the parties have agreed to abolish all production subsidies that may promote exports to each other. (Direct export subsidies are already proscribed by the GATT's Subsidies Code.)

countries of comparable power there is always a temptation to settle outside the agreement: to preserve the agreement and the benefits it provides, this temptation needs to be resisted, particularly when the relevant countries are large.

1.4 Hub-and-Spoke "Free" Trade Agreements

It can be argued that what the architects of the GATT had in mind in framing Article XXIV were agreements like the European Common Market with respect to most industrial (although not agricultural) goods, in which the members have reduced barriers progressively without generally raising them against the rest of the world (except for voluntary export restraints on a number of sensitive products) and in which new members have been added from time to time. On the other hand, the arrangements for agriculture in the EEC are clearly not consistent with this intention.

While the U.S.-Canada Free Trade Agreement is one of the cleanest from a GATT perspective, it is most unlikely that the GATT architects envisaged a set of bilateral agreements between a central country and others: the hub-and-spoke model that could develop around the United States.[6] While Canada has sought to be included in the U.S. negotiations with Mexico, it appears unlikely that one agreement will cover the United States, Canada, and Mexico. The U.S. Congress has ensured that new countries will not be added to existing bilateral agreements without its explicit approval. Differing labor costs and conditions and environmentalist pressures in the United States, will make it very difficult to incorporate Mexico into the existing U.S.-Canada Free Trade Agreement or to negotiate an agreement with Mexico that is close in its provisions to that with Canada. While Canada may also negotiate a pact with Mexico, it is unlikely that the three deals could be covered by one agreement—or, if they could be, it would in all probability require different provisions covering at least some of the trade between the three pairs of participants, perhaps with lengthy transitional arrangements. Similar considerations arise with respect to Chile, which could be next in line for negotiations with the United States, and they would apply even more strongly with respect to other Latin American countries, particularly as their macroeconomic policies would make it more difficult for free trade with the United States to be sustained. A hub-and-spoke network appears more likely than a multicountry free trade agreement, at least for a lengthy transitional period.

The United States, along with Britain and Germany, was central to a network of bilateral arrangements in the 1930s, but, in sharp contrast to the others, the U.S. arrangements were clearly trade liberalizing, albeit from very high tariff levels. It is often stated that it was out of the U.S. arrangements that the GATT was born—"that GATT was the Trade Agreements Program writ

6. For analyses of hub-and-spoke systems, see Wonnacott (1990) and Park and Yoo (1989).

large" (Diebold 1988, 11)—although this perhaps gives insufficient credit to James Meade and others on the other side of the Atlantic.[7] These U.S. bilateral agreements differed in important ways from the current U.S. carrot-and-stick approach in that (i) they were not generally accompanied by negative discrimination, actual or threatened, and (ii) the barrier reductions were quite limited in product coverage but were nondiscriminatory. The negotiations covered products of which the United States and the partner country were principal suppliers, and there was careful product selection and specification to ensure that the parties were the principal suppliers. But then the barrier reductions were not restricted to the partners but were extended to all countries, unconditionally (Diebold 1988, 7–11).[8] Minor existing suppliers and, more important, new suppliers could then benefit from the opening of trade.

A hub-and-spoke model centered on the United States would differ from the EEC model in that it would comprise separate bilateral arrangements, and additional countries would not be expected to enter under the same conditions. It would differ from the 1930s U.S. model in that the negotiated concessions would not be extended to others on an unconditional most-favored-nation basis. Because of the careful product specification, new agreements in the 1930s did not tend to undermine significantly the preferences granted in existing agreements; in contrast, the hub-and-spoke model with wide product coverage involves significant undermining of this sort as new bilateral or multilateral agreements are negotiated. (This point has more force with respect to explicit positive preferences than to commitments not to impose restrictions.)

If countries B and C have free trade agreements with country A, what should their relations be with each other? If the agreements were truly and fully free trade agreements, then it would be relatively easy to have a free trade agreement embracing all three, and this would be GATT consistent. Again, if the agreement between A and B were an open agreement, C could join and have the same relations with both A and B. But where preferential agreements are not open and do not embrace all trade, it becomes much more difficult to devise agreements between parties.

While each of the partners with the United States, in a hub-and-spoke system may benefit from its own bilateral relationship, an important question is what effect such a network will have on the multilateral trading system as a whole. In considering the prospect of a free trade agreement between Mexico and the United States, Ron Wonnacott points out that there is a risk that, "in responding magnanimously to requests for bilateral agreements that are in its interests and, at least initially, in those of the applicant nations, the United States could inadvertently be creating a discriminatory, inefficient, hub-and-

7. See Meade's proposal for an International Commercial Union, reproduced as an appendix to Culbert (1987).

8. The United States did retaliate against Germany and Australia by withholding most-favored-nation extension of concessions negotiated with others (Diebold 1988, 9; Copland and Janes 1937, documents 173, 183, 186).

spoke trading structure that will be unnecessarily damaging to its partners and may erode prospects for future multilateral liberalization" (Wonnacott 1990, 2).

Each additional country added to a hub-and-spoke system lessens the gains for those already in it, with the exception of the hub country, for each new entrant reduces the advantage that the others have in trading with the hub country. It is only the hub country that does not have its sourcing, whether for industrial inputs or final products, distorted by trade barriers within the hub-and-spoke system. If "rim" countries wish to have a network of agreements among themselves to lessen the discrimination, the number of possible agreements increases rapidly as the number of countries increases: a system of six countries around one hub has a possible twenty-one bilateral agreements. But the more countries that are in the system, the greater the incentive for outsiders to join. This incentive for outsiders to join also applies to a single GATT-consistent free trade agreement covering several countries; however, while embracing a multicountry free trade arrangement probably moves the global system closer to multilateralism, in adding more spokes to the hub bilateralism is multiplied.[9]

The complexity of the system and of the relationships it would bring could be quite damaging. Each agreement would involve discrimination against outsiders, in a different manner, and rules of origin and content (which could differ in the various agreements, unlike a customs union or multicountry free trade agreement) would be of considerable importance. Furthermore, should a network develop, many if not most of the agreements are unlikely to satisfy a reasonable interpretation of Article XXIV of the GATT, but, as past experience has shown with respect to the enforcement of this Article, this is unlikely to prevent their adoption, particularly as the erstwhile leader of multilateralism, the United States, would be involved. If the requirements of the Article were truly met with respect to free trade covering "substantially all trade in products," it would be relatively easy to move to a multicountry free trade agreement: it is the deviations from a really free trade agreement that lead to separate bilateral agreements. One source of difficulty lies in the favored treatment that countries would seek (following the Canadian example) with respect to the U.S. safeguard provisions against both fair and unfair trade and dispute settlement. These provisions could well vary with each spoke. The hub-and-spoke model could well bring substantial damage to the multilateral system as it has developed over the last forty-odd years.

There is another factor involved. The ability of a country's administration to focus on various negotiations and the supply of trade negotiating staff are limited, even in the United States. Distraction of attention can only be harmful to the Uruguay Round of multilateral trade negotiations, which ground to a

9. For more extensive considerations of these points, see Wonnacott (1990) and Park and Yoo (1989).

halt last December in Brussels and need full attention if they are to be revived. This applies not only to the United States but also to its potential partners, who may see a deal with the United States as an alternative to Uruguay.

1.5 Regionalism without Discrimination?

I have stated above that there can be no trade preference for one country without discrimination against others.[10] Is there a role for trade agreements between groups of countries that fall short of the multilateral but that do not involve discrimination? Of course almost anything that facilitates trade between a restricted set of countries will imply some trade diversion as well as trade creation. This can apply to treaties of friendship, commerce, and navigation, which aim at facilitating trade between the signatories without discriminating against other countries. Similarly, many if not most of the actions being taken within Europe to complete the internal market, such as recognition of standards, removal of internal customs posts, and the like, will have incidental trade-diverting effects for the rest of the world even though their net effects will almost certainly increase global efficiency and diversion is not the intention (Emerson 1989; Snape 1989a). There will be diversion of existing trade even if existing (or threatened) negative discrimination is removed between countries. In this case, both the trade diversion and the trade creation would be economically beneficial for the country removing the discrimination, and it is again likely to improve global efficiency, but it would adversely affect those trading partners that had not been discriminated against. Australia and some other countries concluded agreements with Japan in the late 1950s that aimed at the removal of such discrimination.

But there is probably no advocate of multilateralism and nondiscrimination who would argue that there should be no agreements with economic implications between countries unless the benefits are extended to others. The line drawn by the GATT with respect to trade barrier agreements has been described above: free trade internally on most goods with unraised barriers against the rest of the world.

Bilaterally negotiated tariff reductions that are extended on an unconditional most-favored-nation basis to all other members of the GATT (or all countries) also clearly pass GATT rules of nondiscrimination. However, in practice, the product selection and specification that might be finely drawn to prevent free riding (as in the U.S. bilateral agreements in the 1930s) could run into GATT problems. It is no accident that Article I of the GATT refers to concessions that when granted to one contracting party must be granted to all contracting parties for "like products," rather than for "the same product" or for "identical products." Tariff classifications cannot be drawn so as to make

10. Regionalism without discrimination is a theme of Drysdale (1988, esp. 237ff.) and Drysdale and Garnaut (1989).

contrived distinctions between products from different sources.[11] Such agreements would be GATT consistent in their nondiscrimination between countries (and in this respect are less discriminatory than agreements under Article XXIV) but could fail on grounds of product specification and/or breadth of product coverage.

All the GATT rounds of multilateral trade negotiations until the Kennedy Round proceeded on this principal-supplier basis but within a multilateral context, the results of the whole set of bilateral agreements being generalized without discrimination except that implied by product selection, within that allowed by "like products." GATT would still appear to be the most appropriate forum in which to negotiate such nondiscriminatory deals. Effort devoted to stand-alone bilateral or regional negotiations is likely to be effort diverted from multilateral negotiations.

The discussions and negotiations that have been undertaken over the last two years under the Asia Pacific Economic Cooperation (APEC) initiative have been aimed at trade facilitation among the participants with a minimum of discrimination against others.[12] One of the principles adopted at the initial ministerial meeting in November 1989, as set out in the "Chairman's Summary" of that meeting, was that "consistent with the interests of Asia Pacific economies, cooperation should be directed at strengthening the open multilateral trading system: it should not involve the formation of a trading bloc." Much of the focus so far, apart from attempting to push the Uruguay Round along, has been on the exchange of information, marine resource conservation, and like matters; the adoption of common standards in some areas such as telecommunications equipment is also under consideration.

In some quarters, a "Pacific Round" of trade negotiations and barrier reductions has been proposed, the negotiated barrier decreases to be extended to others countries unconditionally. Drysdale and Garnaut (1989) argue that, provided Latin American countries are included, the trade patterns are such that free riding by other countries should not be a major problem, the "tendency [being] for barriers to intra-Pacific trade to be highest in commodities and markets in which other Pacific economies are competitive suppliers" (p. 251). They suggest that the "Pacific Round" negotiations take place at a "time of crisis." Collapse of the Uruguay Round and U.S. congressional protectionist pressure could provide the crisis; APEC could provide the forum.

11. In an important decision, a GATT panel concluded the Spain should not impose different tariffs on Arabica and Robusta coffee, a difference that discriminated against Brazil (GATT 1985, Article I, p. 4).

12. Those countries participating in the discussions are the ASEAN six (Brunei, Indonesia, Malaysia, the Philippines, Singapore, and Thailand) together with Australia, Canada, Japan, the Republic of Korea, New Zealand, and the United States; a formula for incorporating the Peoples Republic of China, Taiwan, and Hong Kong is under investigation.

1.6 Conclusion

The case for multilateralism and nondiscrimination, particularly for small countries, is as strong as ever. Discrimination implies politicization. If trade liberalization is to proceed through international negotiation and commitment—and for many countries there are reasons for it to do so—nondiscriminatory agreements and rules of general application protect the weak.

There is a strong temptation to attempt to settle particular trade disputes and concerns bilaterally with specific rather than generalized reciprocity. But whether these settlements involve the lowering of specific trade barriers or the giving of commitments not to raise them, the efficient multilateral trading system is best preserved by extending any concessions to other traders. Unconditional most-favored-nation status is the surest way to do this. For preferential arrangements, the least damage (or the most good) will be done to the multilateral system by trade agreements that follow the rules of Article XXIV of the GATT strictly *and* that are open to new participants on the same conditions as the old. The hub-and-spoke system that could develop around the United States should it pursue more preferential trading agreements could significantly damage the multilateral trading system that the United States has worked hard to develop over the last forty-odd years.

For matters and disputes that embrace a limited range of products, countries may be unwilling or politically unable to take the unconditional most-favored-nation path when the issues are treated in isolation. Here the best way may be to revive the procedures of early GATT rounds—to have modest objectives concerning a limited range of issues and to conduct negotiations primarily between pairs or among groups of countries that have strong interests in particular issues, but to do this in a multilateral context. With enough issues considered and a sufficient number of participants in attendance, the concessions negotiated could be extended to all on an unconditional most-favored-nation basis. GATT rounds do not have to encompass everything, nor do they have to last forever. A more modest but more frequent set of negotiations could complement the blockbusters like the Uruguay Round and help enforce the day-to-day application of nondiscrimination, on which the *general* agreement and its multilateral benefits ultimately depend.

References

Bhagwati, Jagdish. 1990. Multilateralism at risk: The GATT is dead. Long live the GATT. *World Economy* 13 (June): 149–69.

Bhagwati, Jagdish, and Hugh T. Patrick, eds. 1990. *Aggressive unilateralism: America's 301 trade policy and the world trading system.* Ann Arbor: University of Michigan Press.

Condliffe, J. B. 1940. *The reconstruction of world trade*. New York: Norton.
Cooper, Richard N. 1987. Trade policy as foreign policy. In *U.S. trade policies in a changing world economy,* ed. Robert M. Stern. Cambridge, Mass.: MIT Press.
Copland, D. B., and C. V. Janes. 1937. *Australian trade policy: A book of documents, 1932–1937*. Sydney: Angus & Robertson.
Culbert, Jay. 1987. War-time Anglo-American talks and the making of the GATT. *World Economy* 10 (December): 381–407.
Destler, I. M. 1986. *American trade politics: System under stress*. Washington, D.C.: Institute for International Economics; New York: Twentieth Century Fund.
Diebold, William, Jr. 1988. The history and the issues. In *Bilateralism, multilateralism and Canada in U.S. trade policy,* ed. William Diebold, Jr., Cambridge, Mass.: Ballinger, for the Council on Foreign Relations.
Dornbusch, Rudiger. 1991. Dornbusch on trade. *Economist,* 4 May, 65.
Drysdale, Peter. 1988. *International economic pluralism: Economic policy in East Asia and the Pacific*. Sydney: Allen & Unwin.
Drysdale, Peter, and Ross Garnaut. 1989. A Pacific free trade area? In Schott 1989a.
Emerson, Michael, et al. 1989. *The economics of 1992: The E.C. Commission's assessment of the economic effects of completing the internal market*. Oxford: Oxford University Press.
GATT. 1985. *Analytical index*. Geneva: General Agreement on Tariffs and Trade.
Jackson, John H. 1969. *World trade and the law of GATT.* Charlottesville, Va.: Michie.
Kindleberger, Charles P. 1986. International public goods without international government. *American Economic Review* 76 (March): 1–13.
Park, Yung Chul, and Jung Ho Yoo. 1989. More free trade areas: A Korean perspective. In Schott 1989a.
Schott, Jeffrey J., ed. 1989a. *Free trade areas and U.S. trade policy.* Washington, D.C.: Institute for International Economics.
———. 1989b. More free trade areas? In Schott 1989a.
Snape, Richard H. 1988. Is non-discrimination really dead? *World Economy* 11 (March): 1–17.
———. 1989a. External economic effects of Europe 1922. Seminar Paper no. 8/89. Monash University, Department of Economics.
———. 1989b. A free trade agreement with Australia? In Schott 1989a.
Wonnacott, Ronald J. 1990. U.S. hub-and-spoke bilaterals and the multilateral trading system. Commentary no. 23. Ottawa: C. D. Howe Institute, October.

Comment Koichi Hamada

This is an excellent paper, implemented with balanced judgment and rigorous logic. Economic, political, and legal aspects of the difficulties created by discriminatory practices and regionalism are carefully discussed, and the merit of the multinational approach through the GATT is forcefully presented. In my first reading, I felt as if I had found a trace of some possible Australian concern that it might become a potential outsider to various possible regional

Koichi Hamada is professor of economics at Yale University and a research associate of the National Bureau of Economic Research.

agreements. The author's presentation at the conference convinced me, however, that I had overstretched my imagination.

In the ideal world where neither negotiation costs nor domestic political constraints for trade representatives exist, it is easy to agree with the author on the importance of the overall approach based on the well-defined GATT rule. In this sense, I find many of his arguments quite convincing. Difficulties arise because we do not live in such an environment. Here, for the sake of argument, I would like to play the role of an antagonist and see how strong a case I can make for bilateral agreements and regionalism against multilateral agreements.

To begin with, I would like to distinguish between two types of bilateral agreements. The first type works to restrict trade at the expense of consumers. For example, voluntary export restraints (VERs), most ordinary market arrangements (OMAs), and compulsory import expansions (CIEs) between two countries fall into this category. Not only do they violate the principle of free trade, but they also represent a temptation to both countries because their incentive structure is such that both exporters and import competitors are eager to agree on these arrangements at the expense of consumers. We should be much concerned with this type of bilateralism.

On the other hand, in this paper the word *bilateralism* often refers to the creation of a free trade area that involves tariff reductions and the elimination of other trade barriers between two trading partners. This second type of bilateral agreement certainly exerts trade diversion effects on the rest of the world. In contrast to the first type, this type of regionalism has at least favorable efficiency consequences within the region. Hence, it can be regarded as a piecemeal approach to free trade. I think that there is something to be said for this kind of approach when the multinational way of achieving free trade is made difficult for political or other reasons.

My second point is about the number of negotiators. Multilateral negotiations and agreements often require many meetings or a creation of new institutions and therefore involve substantial costs. Often bilateral negotiations and agreements could save these costs. It would be an interesting study to compare the negotiation costs required for bilateral agreements with those required for multilateral agreements or agreements made through international organizations. Incidentally, the study of possible Parkinson's law effects in international organizations would be another research agenda.

Third, a thought experiment can be conducted by relying on the logic of the Coase theorem in law and economics. The theorem states that, if we have environmental problems, mutual negotiations seeking Pareto improvement would sustain the system. Suppose that there are only three countries—A, B, and C—in the world, and suppose that A and B first create a free trade area that is mutually beneficial. Is it possible to devise an international arrangement to compensate the loss to C? The answer to this question, however, would be that it is difficult. Another question to be explored is whether it is more difficult for C to join the agreement and for the system to create a free trade world than it is for the three countries to create such a system from the outset in the absence of the free trade area between A and B? The answers to these questions depend on the economic and political structures of these countries.

If we argue Snape's point in reverse, we may ask the following question. Suppose that there is a free trade area between A and B. Will it then be beneficial for country C if the free trade area is divided again into A and B? There are cases, as an analogy to dividing a monopoly firm, where dividing pays, but this would not always be the case.

Finally, we should keep in mind the distinction between the normative question of international lawmaking, that is, the question of what the ideal trade regime is, and the positive question of how the trade regime actually emerges or changes. For the normative question, Snape's argument may be mostly correct, but in the actual world we must negotiate under political constraints. Given such consequences, piecemeal policy-making could be a faster way of achieving integration as well as a more efficient world market economy. It is necessary, of course, to devise an incentive mechanism to keep any regional integration from developing into a protectionist region or a "fortress."

2 American Bilateral Trading Arrangements and East Asian Interests

Anne O. Krueger

One of the major success stories of the era since the Second World War has been the liberalization of the international trading system. Trade in goods and services among nations has grown at a rate more than one and a half times the rate of growth of world GNP. Partly in consequence of rapid growth of trade, growth rates of world real output reached sustained levels previously unattained in human history.

There is no question but that the open, multilateral trading system (the GATT system, for short) was a major factor in contributing to world economic growth and that future growth of trade and of the world economy is dependent on the maintenance of the system. However, one important reason why the GATT system flourished was American support for it. The U.S. commitment to the principle of most-favored-nation treatment of all trading partners and its support of GATT provided the leadership that enabled successive rounds of multilateral reductions in trade barriers and trade liberalization.

In recent years, the American commitment to an open multilateral system has been, at least to a degree, eroded, as U.S. policy has shifted to a "two-pronged" approach. On the one hand, the United States has continued to participate in the Uruguay Round of trade negotiations; on the other hand, the United States has indicated a willingness to bargain bilaterally for free trade areas with individual trading nations.[1]

Anne O. Krueger is Arts and Sciences Professor of Economics at Duke University and a research associate of the National Bureau of Economic Research.

The author is indebted to Rosalinda Quintanilla for helpful discussions and to David Orsmond for comments and valuable research assistance in the preparation of this paper.

1. It is outside the purpose of this paper to attempt to analyze the reasons for this shift in approach. Suffice it to say that there are several motives, and different parties undoubtedly place different weight on each of them. For some, frustration with the American inability to proceed further under GATT has been a factor, and this has certainly been the stated American position. For these individuals, bilateralism is intended as a supplement to GATT. For some others, bilateralism has appeared as an attractive alternative to multilateralism, even perhaps providing an

As a consequence of that willingness, the U.S.-Canada Free Trade Agreement has already been signed, and the U.S.-Canada free trade area is in its transition phase. The United States and Mexico have announced their intention to negotiate a free trade agreement (FTA), with Canada included in the bargaining, and President Bush has announced the Enterprise for the Americas, under which it is contemplated that the United States might enter into FTAs with other Latin American countries.[2]

The possibility of a hemisphere-wide trading area raises a number of important questions. The most significant issues concern the degree of commitment the United States maintains for the open, multilateral system. The United States has maintained that its free trade area arrangements will be consistent with GATT and, indeed, will constitute "super-GATT" arrangements among countries willing to pursue free trade beyond their commitments in GATT. Whether that contention is valid is itself a subject in need of considerable analysis, although the test will be in the evolution of the GATT system, the outcome of the Uruguay Round, and subsequent trading relations. A second major issue is the extent to which the world trading system may degenerate into trading blocks. Some fear that the European Community (EC) arrangements may turn into a "Fortress Europe," although events to date surrounding 1992 do not support that view. Were Europe and the Western Hemisphere each to evolve trading arrangements that gave strong preferences to regional trading partners, it would surely elicit responses from other trading countries. That possibility appears remote at the present time: not only are trading relations between Europe, North America, and East Asia important to all groups of countries, but the market forces emanating from lowered costs of communications and transportation continue to lead to incentives for increasing integration of the world economy and greater economic losses for countries that choose to erect protective barriers against imports.

On the assumption that the basic framework for international trade will remain the open, multilateral trading system, questions arise as to the likely effect of FTAs between the United States and other Western Hemisphere countries on East Asian countries. The purpose of this paper is to examine that question. It is assumed that American negotiations with other Western Hemisphere countries are and will continue to be GATT compatible. In that context, I examine the potential effects of such American bilateral Western Hemi-

umbrella under which protection for their interests might be increased. For still others, a foreign policy motive, especially regarding Canada and Mexico, has been important. For a discussion, see Schott (1989b).

2. The United States has taken other steps that indicate an erosion of the traditional commitment to multilateral trading arrangements. Bilateral bargaining over trade barriers is a prominent example. Perhaps best known, however, is the inclusion of "Super-301" in the 1988 Trade Expansion Act. Under that provision, the U.S. trade representative is authorized unilaterally to declare countries "unfair traders" without resort to GATT procedures. For a discussion of "Super-301," see Bhagwati and Patrick (1990) and Bhagwati (1988).

spheric trading arrangements on other American trading partners and especially the East Asian "superexporters," who have long relied on the relatively open American market in pursuing their strategy of export-led growth.

It is well known that preferential trading arrangements can be welfare improving or welfare reducing depending in part on whether they are "trade creating" or "trade diverting." Especially given the likelihood that the United States will sequentially enter into FTAs with other Western Hemisphere countries, there is the potential for trade diversion and rediversion throughout the hemisphere. In addition, there are significant questions about how those arrangements might affect East Asian trading partners.

I will argue that any assessment of existing economic conditions and trading patterns among Western Hemisphere countries suggests that the direct trade diversion resulting from these arrangements on East Asian trade will be minimal. Indeed, given the small share of East Asian exports in the Latin American markets at the present time, it can be argued that, *if* the Western Hemisphere FTAs are successful, they should stimulate more rapid economic growth in the Latin American countries. To the extent that they do that, East Asian countries may gain as the increased participation in international trade and the more rapid economic growth of the countries in question more than offset whatever small amount of trade diversion there may be.

The analysis proceeds as follows. The first section reviews the current status of Western Hemisphere bilateral trading arrangements. Even the prospective Mexican agreement has not yet been negotiated, and there are many questions pertaining to the extent that it will actually free trade between the United States and Mexico. The second section then analyzes the current patterns of trade between the relevant pairs of trading countries. The dominance of the United States in trade with Canada and Mexico is seen, which limits the possible order of magnitude of trade diversion from existing trade flows. The third section then considers the commodity composition of U.S. trade with East Asian countries and the possible initial order of magnitude of trade diversion of the current bilateral trading arrangements. The final section then assesses the relation of the current and prospective Western Hemisphere trading arrangements in the context of an open, multilateral trading system. It will be argued that U.S. tariffs are low enough that the potential for trade diversion from East Asia to Latin America is limited, although there are interesting questions concerning the effect of the FTA arrangements on the Multifiber Arrangement (MFA) and world trade in textiles and apparel. However, levels of protection in Latin American countries remain significantly higher. Should FTAs be negotiated, there would be an initial wide margin of preference for commodities from other FTA members. An offsetting consideration, however, is that businesses in FTA countries other than the United States would perceive themselves to be subject to higher costs than their U.S. counterparts because of these tariffs; pressures should therefore arise for reductions in protection throughout Latin America. If that happens, the growth potential from the FTA would be greater and the potential for trade diversion considerably weakened.

2.1 A Western Hemisphere Free Trade Area?

Although American officials spoke of their willingness to enter into bilateral agreements with "like-minded free trading countries" as early as 1983 and actually signed an FTA with Israel, it was not until the U.S.-Canada Free Trade Agreement was successfully negotiated in 1987 that these statements began to assume importance.[3] Even then, Canada and the United States have such a long border and sufficiently close trading relations that a Free Trade Agreement could be regarded as a natural "GATT-plus" arrangement under which barriers in addition to those negotiated away under GATT could be removed.

Even after it was negotiated, it was at least plausible that the U.S.-Canada arrangement would be the only major initiative under announced American policy and that it would be largely trade creating. During the period 1986–88, few thought that any Latin American country would seriously contemplate entering into such an arrangement, despite the fact that "framework agreements" had already been entered into by several Latin American countries.[4] Not only were most Latin American countries still highly protectionist, but many of them continued to experience severe macroeconomic instability; in these circumstances, it appeared highly unrealistic to think that a free trade area was a serious alternative.

However, all that changed when the president of Mexico announced in the spring of 1990 the intention of the government of Mexico to seek an FTA with the United States. Although Mexico had a long history of very high protection against imports (both through tariffs and, after 1982, through quantitative restrictions on imports) and was experiencing rapid inflation, in the mid- and late 1980s the Mexican government had already undertaken a series of steps designed to reform economic policies. Not only had quantitative restrictions on imports been almost entirely removed, but the average level of tariffs had

3. The U.S.-Israel Free Trade Agreement is not analyzed in this paper. Israel's trade with the United States is sufficiently small and different from that of Latin American and East Asian countries that it is not a major consideration for an analysis of potential effects of a North American free trade area on East Asian exporters. For an analysis of the agreement, see Rosen (1989). The Caribbean Basin Initiative, which was passed by Congress in 1983, was the first use of regional trade preferences under U.S. trade law. While not creating a free trade area, the Caribbean Basin Economic Recovery Act of 1983 (and subsequent amendments) provided duty-free access to the U.S. market for certain commodities not already covered by preferential treatment under the Generalized System of Preferences.

The U.S.-Canada Free Trade Agreement came into force on 2 January 1988 and provided for a ten-year phase-in of agreed-on liberalizing measures. To date, tariffs have been reduced at a rate more rapid than that envisaged in the agreement. The idea of a U.S.-Canada free trade area was not a new one. It had been seriously considered several times before, but rejected by Canada (see U.S. Council of Economic Advisers 1988, chap. 4).

4. For a listing of the countries with which the United States has signed framework agreements, see U.S. Council of Economic Advisers (1991, 253).

been sharply reduced. In addition, serious efforts to deregulate domestic economic activities (such as freight transport) and to privatize state-owned firms were under way. While inflation remained (and remains) a difficult problem, associated in part with heavy obligations for servicing internal as well as external debt, the idea of a free trade area with the United States did not appear as unrealistic as it would have had the policies of the 1960s and 1970s still been in effect.

At the time this paper was written (mid-1991), negotiations had not begun on the U.S.-Mexico FTA. Since the ultimate agreement may take a variety of forms, any judgment as to the effects of the agreement must be based on some assumptions regarding the outcome of the negotiations.[5] A number of significant questions remain to be addressed, including the key issue of the relation of the U.S.-Mexico FTA to the U.S.-Canada FTA and the subsequent linkages between Mexico and Canada and any further signatories of FTAs with the United States.[6] In addition, it is not known whether the agreement will be across the board or sectoral in nature.

From a Mexican perspective, major concerns arise over U.S. willingness to permit Mexican construction firms, trucking companies, and other labor-intensive services to operate in the United States. The United States, in turn, wants access to the Mexican market in high-tech services and liberal conditions governing direct foreign investment in Mexico. A key issue in all free trade agreements, but especially so when there is a long, open border, is what rules of origin will be adopted and what criteria and mechanisms will be established for their enforcement. There are also important questions regarding the treatment of Mexican imports into the United States (and possibly into Canada) of textiles and clothing in commodity lines for which MFA quotas are in force. Finally, as with the U.S.-Canada agreement, key issues concern the application of U.S. antidumping and countervailing duty provisions to Mexican exports to the United States.

How "trade creating" the U.S.-Mexico FTA will be will depend greatly on these provisions and the evolution of the agreement. As of the summer of 1991, that outcome is by no means clear. There are a number of issues that are politically contentious in the United States, and the opposition of American labor to any agreement has been vehement.[7] There will be especially difficult

5. There are also important questions regarding Mexican exchange rate policy and macroeconomic balance that will have an important effect on the evolution of any U.S.-Mexico FTA. Should the Mexican authorities attempt to control the nominal exchange rate in the face of domestic inflation, e.g., the probable outcome would be unsustainable current account deficits with the United States in the short run. The response to this event would have to be either to alter monetary/fiscal/exchange rate policy or to abandon the FTA. Which of these courses would be chosen is a matter for speculation.

6. For analyses of the potential difficulties with a series of bilateral agreements between the United States and individual trading partners, see Park and Yoo (1989) and Wonnacott (1990).

7. American labor has been joined in its opposition by some environmental groups, and it is unclear how the American administration will deal with these issues. The U.S. trade representative has provided Congress with assurances that these issues will be dealt with in the course of the negotiations (*New York Times*, 15 May 1991, 1, C2).

issues concerning Mexico's access to the American market for textiles and apparel, for many agricultural products (where phytosanitary regulations are the main trade barrier), and for overland and ocean shipping. On the Mexican side, there are questions as to macroeconomic policy, American access to Mexican petroleum resources and various parts of the services industries, regulations governing direct foreign investment, and other issues.

As a consequence of these uncertainties, one can well imagine a *de minimus* agreement, to be phased in over a long time period, with negligible effects on the flow of goods and services between Mexico and its northern neighbors for the foreseeable future. Alternatively, one can equally imagine an agreement that effectively removes most trade barriers within a reasonably short period of time and the consequent rapid expansion of flows. For purposes of this paper, it will be assumed that the FTA takes the latter form, providing virtually full mobility of goods, services, and capital within the foreseeable future.[8]

Subsequent to the announcement that there would be negotiations for a U.S.-Mexico FTA, President Bush announced the Enterprise for the Americas in June 1990. In effect, this was a statement of American willingness to enter into FTAs with any interested Latin American countries willing to meet certain conditions.[9] Again, the relationships of new FTA entrants to those already party to an FTA have not been clarified, and no negotiations have begun. To date, Chile has expressed serious interest in such negotiations. Given the low level of prevailing Chilean tariffs and Chile's stable macroeconomic situation, it is economically realistic to assume that such an FTA could be agreed on and implemented within a fairly short period of time.

For other Latin American countries, however, the situation is very different.

8. Even should the negotiated agreement itself be toward much freer trade, there are questions as to whether Mexico can achieve the stated goal of maintaining a fixed exchange rate vis-à-vis the dollar as the agreement enters force. There are two serious dangers. (1) The Mexican authorities might attempt to fix the nominal exchange rate at an unrealistic level. If this happened, the consequences for income and employment in Mexico would not be dissimilar to those for East Germany after reunification with West Germany in 1990, and it is questionable whether any Mexican government could continue with that policy stance. (2) The initial exchange rate might be established in such a way that the real exchange rate was initially realistic, but Mexican monetary and fiscal policy might be incompatible with the maintenance of that real rate at a fixed nominal exchange rate. A fixed exchange rate regime in conjunction with the FTA would not be sustainable in that circumstance. Should either of these dangers materialize, monetary/fiscal/exchange rate policy would have to change, or the FTA would have to be abandoned in the longer run.

9. These conditions included primarily the reliance on the private sector and market forces to guide the preponderance of economic activity and the existence of relatively open access for foreign direct investment. Inducements to join the Enterprise for the Americas included the promise of not only preferential access to the American market but also favorable consideration for debt-relief negotiations. A number of important questions remain unresolved. Chief among them is whether negotiations will be bilateral, with the result that many countries will have FTAs with the United States but not with each other, or whether a technique will be found for multilateralizing the FTA. The existence of a number of bilateral FTAs between the United States and individual Western Hemisphere countries would create a number of legal and administrative issues. For an analysis, see Wonnacott (1990).

Most of them retain very high walls of protection against imports, which implies that a move toward an FTA with the United States would require a major realignment of the existing trade regime.[10] In addition, a number of Latin American countries exhibit a high degree of macroeconomic instability. Despite repeated announcements of plans and programs to stabilize the economy and reduce inflation, success has been elusive in most countries.[11]

For that reason, analysis in this paper is largely confined to the potential effect of a U.S.-Mexico FTA under the assumption that the agreement is one that permits virtually free movement of goods, services, and capital across the border. On the one hand, it is not even clear whether the U.S.-Mexico FTA will be that liberalizing, and other FTAs are even further in the future. On the other hand, Mexico is a very large trading country, representing a sizable share of all U.S.–Latin America trade. An examination of the potential orders of magnitude of the effects of a U.S.-Mexico FTA provides, therefore, a reasonable basis for a judgment as to what may happen over the intermediate term for the entire Western Hemisphere trading arrangements.

2.2 Current Trading Patterns

It thus seems plausible to assume that, over the next five years, any Western Hemisphere integration that does occur will take place between Canada, the United States, and Mexico. Table 2.1 gives some salient data on their trade. As can be seen, the United States is the "giant" among the three. Although Mexico's population, at 85 million, is about one-third that of the United States, its per capita income is about one-tenth that of the United States.[12] Thus, Canada, with a much smaller population but a per capita income similar to that in the United States, has a GNP approximately one-quarter that of the United States, while Mexico's GNP in dollar terms in 1989 was about 3 percent that of the United States.

10. For many Latin American countries that still have highly restrictive trade regimes and countries that are in the process of removing trade barriers, there are significant questions as to why they should not liberalize unilaterally vis-à-vis the entire world, rather than joining a Western Hemisphere FTA. The issue is perhaps most important for those countries whose share of trade with the United States is smaller than that of Mexico and Canada. For an analysis, see Nogues (1990).

11. The macroeconomic instability issue is most pronounced in Argentina and Brazil—the two largest exporters in South America. Those two countries, along with Uruguay and Paraguay, recently entered an agreement to form an FTA among themselves within five years. That FTA was announced as a "first step" toward a hemisphere-wide arrangement. Even among those four countries, macroeconomic imbalances are large, and trade barriers are high. It is thus questionable whether they can achieve welfare-improving integration among themselves over the next five years and virtually certain that their entry into a hemisphere-wide FTA would not begin for the better part of a decade.

12. These proportions are not very different from those between East and West Germany at the time of German reunification. East Germany had a population of about 17 million and a per capita income estimated to be about one-eighth that of West Germany; West Germany's population was about 51 million.

Table 2.1 **Basic Data on the United States, Canada, and Mexico, 1989**

	U.S.	Canada	Mexico
Population (millions)	248.8	26.2	84.5
GNP (billions of U.S.$)	5,200.8	528.9	175.7[a]
GNP per capita	20,903.5	20,170.4	2,079.0
Total exports (billions of U.S.$)	364.0	121.4	24.8
Percentage exports of GNP	7.0	22.9	14.1
Percentage of exports to:	. . .	70.3	63.3
U.S.			
Canada	21.5	. . .	2.4
Mexico	6.9	.4	. . .
Total imports (billions of U.S.$)	492.2	118.2	25.1
Percentage imports of GNP	9.5	22.4	14.3
Percentage of imports from:			
U.S.	. . .	63.1	67.0
Canada	18.2	. . .	1.8
Mexico	5.6	1.2	. . .

Sources: International Monetary Fund, *International Financial Statistics Yearbook,* 1990; and *Direction of Trade Statistics Yearbook,* 1990.

Note: Exports are c.i.f.; imports are f.o.b.

[a]GDP for Mexico.

If attention turns to relative importance in trade, relative size is not dissimilar: Canadian exports represent more than one-fifth of GNP and were $121 billion in 1989; American exports were $364 billion and 7 percent of GNP. Absolutely, however, U.S. exports were much larger, at $364 billion, contrasted with Canada's $121 billion. Mexico's exports constituted just 14 percent of GNP, reflecting in part the residual effect of that country's half-century-long policy of protection. Total Mexican exports, at $24.8 billion in 1989, were about 8 percent of those of the United States. The figures for imports are roughly comparable.

Turning our attention to the relative importance of each of the countries as trading partners for the other two, asymmetry is immediately evident. The United States is the destination for 70 percent of Canada's exports and 63 percent of Mexico's; Canada obtains 63 percent of its imports from the United States and Mexico 67 percent. But when the U.S. trade pattern is examined, the relationship is very different. Although Canada is the United States's largest trading partner, only 21.5 percent of exports are destined for Canada and 6.9 percent for Mexico; on the import side, 18 percent of American imports originated in Canada and 1.8 percent originated in Mexico. Interestingly, also, trade relations between Canada and Mexico are symmetrically very small. Less than 1 percent of Canadian exports went to Mexico, and 2.4 percent of Mexico's exports went to Canada, with a similar pattern on the import side.

The United States is clearly the predominant trading partner for Canada and Mexico. Moreover, American protection levels for most imports are considerably lower than those of Canada and Mexico.[13] The average Canadian tariff level against imports from the United States was estimated to be 10.4 percent, while the average American tariff against Canada was 3.3 percent at the time the FTA went into effect (U.S. Council of Economic Advisers 1988). Mexico's average tariff level against U.S. imports is currently estimated to be about 10 percent, while the average U.S. tariff against Mexican imports is about 4 percent (U.S. Council of Economic Advisers 1991). Because of the large size of the American market and its general openness, it is reasonable to conclude that, for Canada and Mexico, the decision to enter an FTA with the United States is largely trade creating.

Given the low average U.S. tariff level, the margin of preference for Canadian and Mexican goods is and will continue to be fairly small. This fact, combined with the very low levels of trade between Mexico and Canada, on the one hand, and East Asia, on the other, suggests that the potential for trade diversion from East Asian sources to U.S. sources for Canadian and Mexican imports is fairly small.[14]

Table 2.2 gives data on Canada's commodity composition of exports. As can be seen, except for road vehicles (where the U.S.-Canada Auto Pact accounted for almost the entire volume of trade), Canada's comparative advantage is based strongly on its abundance of natural resources. Of the $29.6 billion of Canadian exports destined to countries other than the United States, $20 billion consisted of primary commodities. It is therefore unlikely that Canada will be able to use the small margin of preference under American tariffs to divert U.S. or Mexican imports from East Asian sources to Canadian sources. Likewise, Canadian imports of manufactured commodities from East Asian countries are small (and negligible from Mexico), and trade diversion in significant orders of magnitude does not appear to be a realistic possibility. The average Canadian tariff of 10.4 percent suggests that there may be scope for increased Canadian imports from the United States as tariff barriers are reduced. Those increases should, however, be largely trade creating.

Rather, it is with Mexico that East Asian exporters may be more concerned. Mexico's low wage rate and other advantages in manufacturing vis-à-vis the United States appear more similar to those historically held by East Asia. Canadian hourly compensation costs for production workers averaged $14.72 in 1989. This figure was above the U.S. average of $14.31 and the Japanese $12.73. Not only was Mexico's average $1.72 well below those in the industrialized countries, as would be expected, but it was also below average hourly

13. The important exception is textiles and clothing. See the discussion in sec. 2.3 below.

14. In 1985, the last year for which data are available from international sources, Japanese imports from Mexico were $1.7 billion, of which more than $1.5 billion was petroleum. Mexican imports from Japan were $842 million, of which more than half were machinery and transport equipment and much of the remainder chemical products. Data are from United Nations (1988).

Table 2.2 **Canadian Trade with the World and with the United States, 1990 (billions of U.S. dollars)**

	Exports to:		Imports from:	
	World	U.S.	World	U.S.
Total	119.4	89.8	116.1	74.8
0. Food and livestock	9.2	3.8	6.2	3.6
1. Beverages and tobacco	.7	.4	.6	.1
2. Crude materials	17.3	7.7	3.9	2.8
3. Mineral fuels	13.0	11.0	7.4	2.1
4. Animal fats	.2	.1	.1	.1
5. Chemical products	6.6	4.5	7.8	5.8
6. Manufactures based on primary commodities	20.1	16.1	14.8	9.6
6.4 Paper	7.7	6.5	1.6	1.3
6.5 Textiles	.6	.4	2.3	1.2
6.6 Mineral products	.8	.7	1.9	1.1
6.7 Iron and steel	2.0	1.6	2.3	1.3
6.8 Nonferrous metal products	5.5	4.0	1.7	1.3
6.9 Metal products	1.6	1.4	3.1	2.1
7. Machinery and transport equipment	45.6	41.0	58.7	41.9
7.1 Power machinery	3.4	2.7	5.3	4.0
7.2 Special machinery	1.9	1.4	4.8	3.0
7.5 Office machinery	2.4	1.9	5.2	3.3
7.6 Telecommunications	1.5	1.0	3.0	1.3
7.7 Electric machinery	3.7	3.4	8.8	6.3
7.8 Road vehicles	26.8	26.3	22.2	17.0
8. Miscellaneous manufactures	4.3	3.6	13.9	7.3
8.2 Furniture	1.3	1.2	1.1	.7
8.4 Apparel	.3	.2	2.4	.2
8.5 Footwear	.1	.1	.8	.1
8.7 Scientific equipment	.7	.5	2.4	1.9
8.8 Cameras and clocks	.2	.2	1.1	.5
9. Miscellaneous manufactures	2.4	1.3	2.6	1.5

Source: Organization for Economic Cooperation and Development, *Foreign Trade by Commodities,* ser. C, 1990, vols. 2 and 3 (Paris, 1991).

compensation for Korea ($3.57), Taiwan ($3.53), and other East Asian newly industrializing countries.[15]

2.3 Trade Diversion from Asia?

It thus appears that, if there is any quantitatively significant concern about trade diversion from East Asian countries resulting from the formation of a North American (and possibly, ultimately, a Western Hemisphere) free trade

15. U.S. Department of Labor, Bureau of Labor Statistics, Office of Productivity and Technology, Data Sheets, September 1990.

area, that concern should center on Mexico's ability to compete, primarily in the U.S. market, because of her margin of preference under the FTA. Even there, several considerations suggest that there may be significant, perhaps even total, offsets to any trade diversion that does occur. First and most important, Mexico encountered enormous economic difficulties in the 1980s, reflected in its debt crisis in 1982, stagnant per capita income over much of the decade, and high rates of inflation. In responding to these economic difficulties, the government has already shifted from a highly restrictive, inner-oriented trade regime to a much more liberalized one with relatively low tariffs, and growth has gradually resumed. Although inflation remains problematic for Mexico, there is some basis for optimism that it may be controlled, or at least its side effects suppressed. Should that happen, the potential for accelerated economic growth in Mexico is substantial and would be so even in the absence of an FTA. That growth would naturally be spearheaded by expanding exports, as producers respond to the altered incentives that a more liberalized trade regime and realistic exchange rates created. As such, Mexico might in any event become more competitive, especially in labor-intensive commodities as labor costs rise in the East Asian countries. To a degree, it might be more natural to consider Mexico as a competitor for the "next tier" of countries that may achieve rapid development through export-oriented growth—countries such as Sri Lanka, Turkey, and perhaps Brazil, where hourly compensation is also well below that in East Asian newly industrialized countries (NICs).

A second, equally important consideration is that Mexican export-led growth would naturally be accompanied by rising imports. Therefore, even should some trade diversion occur as a result of the FTA, it would be at least partially offset, from an East Asian perspective, by more rapid growth of total Mexican imports, a growth in which East Asia would doubtless share.[16]

The notion of trade diversion is static and refers to existing trade whose sources might be altered as a consequence of preferential trading arrangements. Any examination of the possible orders of magnitude should be based on the existing commodity composition of trade, in this case U.S. imports.

Table 2.3 gives data on U.S. imports from Mexico, other Latin American countries, and East Asian countries in 1990. A first significant characteristic to note is that almost half of U.S. imports from Latin America are from Mexico, reflecting the close ties that already exist between those two countries. The second phenomenon is equally important: American imports from East Asia are much greater than are those from Latin America. Mexico's total ex-

16. The argument is similar to one that can be made retrospectively for Europe: it is no doubt true that there was some trade diversion as the European Common Market was created. The more important reality, however, was that the EC was created in the context of overall trade liberalization and that liberalization spurred economic growth. On net, therefore, trade flows with third countries grew more rapidly than they would have in the absence of the Common Market and trade liberalization. Thus, U.S. trade with Europe increased rapidly during the period of European integration.

Table 2.3 U.S. Imports from Western Hemisphere and East Asian Countries, 1990 (billions of U.S. dollars)

	Mexico	Other Latin America	Japan	Korea	Taiwan	Singapore	Hong Kong
Total U.S. imports	30.8	36.0	93.1	19.3	23.8	10.1	9.9
0. Food & livestock	2.8	7.3	.3	.2	.3	.1	.1
1. Beverages & tobacco	.3	.3	.0	.0	.0	.0	.0
2. Crude materials	.8	1.8	.2	.1	.1	.0	.0
3. Mineral fuels	5.5	13.6	.1	.0	.0	.2	.0
4. Animal fats	.0	.0	.0	.0	.0	.0	.0
5. Chemicals	.7	1.2	2.5	.3	.4	.4	.0
6. Manufactures based on primary commodities	2.6	3.6	7.3	2.3	3.3	.1	.6
7. Machinery & transport equipment	13.8	2.5	71.6	7.8	9.4	7.8	2.3
8. Miscellaneous manufactures	3.1	4.9	9.6	8.6	10.0	1.0	6.5
9. Other	1.3	.5	1.4	.1	.3	.4	.3

Source: Organization for Economic Cooperation and Development, *Foreign Trade by Commodities,* ser. C, 1990, vol. 3 (Paris, 1991).

ports to the United States (including oil) are about the same in total magnitude as those from Taiwan and Hong Kong and less than one-third those from Japan. Moreover, almost all the East Asian exports to the United States consist of manufactured products, whereas more than one-third of Mexico's and about two-thirds of the rest of Latin America's exports to the United States are in commodity categories 0–4. Thus, if one eliminates those categories in which East Asia is not now exporting to the U.S. market, Latin America's total exports to the United States were $65.3 billion in 1990, contrasted with $156.2 billion from East Asia. While Latin American exports—most of which are Mexican—of manufactures to the United States are not negligible, they are small contrasted with those of East Asia.

Closer examination of the commodity composition of manufactured imports to the United States suggests that the scope for trade diversion out of existing trade flows is even smaller than that. Table 2.4 gives the commodity composition of American imports of manufactures by countries. As can be seen, the major commodity category in which there appears to be significant U.S. imports from both East Asia and Mexico is machinery and transport equipment. In that category, Mexico is a much larger exporter than the rest of Latin America combined, exporting $13.8 billion in 1990, contrasted with Japan's exports of $71.6 billion and exports from Singapore, Korea, and Taiwan of $7.8, $7.8, and $9.4 billion, respectively.

It should be noted, however, that the machinery and transport equipment category is the one with the greatest Mexican maquiladora exports.[17] Because

17. The maquiladora industries operate under special sections of the U.S. trade law that permit the export of parts and components for assembly abroad. Mexico has special legislation governing

Table 2.4 **U.S. Imports of Manufactures from Latin America and East Asia by Two-Digit Industries, 1990 (billions of U.S. dollars)**

	Mexico	Other Latin America	Japan	Korea	Taiwan	Singapore	Hong Kong
6. Manufactures based on primary materials	2.6	3.6	7.3	2.3	3.3	.1	.6
6.4 Paper	.2	.1	.3	.1	.1	.0	.0
6.5 Textiles	.3	.4	.6	.5	.5	.0	.2
6.6 Mineral products	.5	.4	.8	.1	.4	.0	.2
6.7 Iron and steel	.4	.9	2.3	.6	.2	.0	.0
6.8 Nonferrous metals	.5	1.0	.5	.0	.0	.0	.0
6.9 Metal products	.5	.2	1.7	.6	1.7	.0	.2
7. Machinery and transport equipment	13.8	2.5	71.6	7.8	9.4	7.8	2.3
7.1 Power mach.	1.1	.6	3.4	.1	.1	.1	.0
7.2 Special mach.	.1	.3	3.5	.1	.3	.0	.0
7.5 Office mach.	.7	.1	11.3	1.4	3.2	4.4	.8
7.6 Telecommunications	2.8	.0	9.6	1.7	1.5	1.3	.5
7.7 Electric machinery	4.6	.4	9.1	2.6	2.3	1.5	.8
7.8 Road vehicles	3.7	.5	28.7	1.4	.9	.0	.0
8. Miscellaneous manufactures	3.1	4.9	9.6	8.6	10.0	1.0	6.5
8.2 Furniture	.6	.1	.2	.1	1.1	.0	.0
8.4 Clothing	.7	2.6	.2	3.4	2.6	.7	4.2
8.5 Footwear	.2	1.4	.0	2.7	1.6	.0	.1
8.7 Scientific equipment	.5	.1	1.7	.1	.2	.1	.1
8.8 Cameras and clocks	.1	.0	2.8	.1	.4	.0	.6

Source: Organization for Economic Cooperation and Development, *Foreign Trade by Commodities,* ser. C, 1990, vol. 2 (Paris, 1991).

those exports are already duty free and compete head-on with East Asian exports (entering under the same provisions of the trade law) under current U.S. trade law, these activities are ones where an FTA is unlikely to provide any additional competitive advantage to Mexico. Even when U.S. imports do not originate in maquiladoras, the average tariff rate on machinery and equipment imports into the United States is 4.5 percent.

For Mexican exports outside maquiladoras, U.S. duties are low on most commodities, and there are few quantitative restrictions on manufactured imports except for textiles and apparel. As can be seen from table 2.4, Mexican exports to the United States in those commodity categories are currently very small, but it is conceivable that they are constrained by the Multifiber Arrangement, rather than by any lack of comparative advantage. Although Ja-

---

the operation of the maquiladora factories; their output has been a major part of the expansion of manufactures in recent years. For an analysis of maquiladora industries, see Zermaño (1987). It is estimated that 45 percent of Mexico's manufactured exports to the United States in 1988 originated in maquiladoras (U.S. Council of Economic Advisers 1991, 254).

pan's exports of these commodities are insignificant, Korea and Taiwan continue to export substantially under their MFA quotas, and *if* Mexican imports were permitted freely under the FTA, there could be trade diversion in that commodity category.

To examine how severe such trade diversion might be, U.S. imports under the Multifiber Arrangement were separately examined. The data are given in table 2.5. As can be seen, Mexico has been a relatively small exporter of textiles and apparel.[18] East Asian countries exported only $8.7 billion to the U.S. market in 1990 under the MFA, out of total U.S. imports under the MFA of $27.9 billion. It would thus appear that, at least as far as a U.S.-Mexico free trade area is concerned, any trade diversion in textiles and apparel would be likely to be relatively small and would have more effect on suppliers other than the East Asian NICS and Japan.

2.4 Implication of a North American FTA on the World Trading System

Despite the size of Mexico and Latin America in terms both of population and geography, the economic policies adopted by the countries of the region have left them very small and poor economically. The negative economic consequences of inner-oriented policies did not become evident until the 1980s, when economic growth ground to a halt in most of Latin America. Although efforts at policy reform are under way in a number of countries, there are many—including notably the biggest, Brazil and Argentina—where efforts have not as yet been able to reverse the decline in economic activity.

When policy reform is successful, economic growth can accelerate, based on export-led growth in response to altered incentives. This was demonstrated by the East Asian NICs several decades ago. As export-led growth accelerates, exporters in the countries whose policies have been successfully altered will no doubt increase their competitiveness and their share of world markets. That share is currently abnormally low in response to the highly protective policies that have been followed. To a considerable extent, policy reform in Latin America would increase Latin American competitiveness (as it already has for Chile), regardless of whether there are preferential trading arrangements with Canada and the United States.

Should policies be successfully reformed, there will be a major reduction in the overall level of protection that Latin American countries accord their domestic producers. Moreover, a successful FTA with the United States would result in pressure by Latin American exporters for even further tariff reductions: insofar as U.S. tariffs were lower than those of Latin American countries even after policy reform, those countries' producers would be confronted with higher costs of imports than would their American counterparts.

18. Indeed, Mexico is a net importer of apparel from the United States.

Table 2.5 **U.S. Imports of Multifiber Arrangement Products, 1990 (billions of U.S. dollars)**

	Total	Cotton	Wool	Man-Made	Other
All countries	27.9	12.0	2.4	12.0	1.6
Mexico	.7	.3	.0	.3	.0
Japan	.6	.2	.0	.4	.0
Korea	2.7	.5	.1	1.9	.2
Taiwan	3.0	.8	.0	2.1	.0
Singapore	.6	.3	.0	.3	.0
Hong Kong	3.8	2.1	.4	1.0	.3
Thailand	.6	.3	.0	.3	.0
Philippines	1.1	.5	.0	.5	.0
China, P.R.	3.5	1.4	.2	1.3	.7

Source: U.S. International Trade Commission, *U.S. Imports of Textiles and Apparel under the Multifiber Arrangement: Annual Report for 1990* (Washington, D.C., May 1991).

It thus must be concluded that the major change that can happen in Latin America is significantly trade creating, as previous walls of protection are significantly reduced. Latin American economic growth should then make Latin American countries more competitive in their export markets but also result in increased demand by Latin America for goods produced in North America and in the rest of the world.

When current trade flows and relative economic sizes of countries are examined, the overwhelming conclusion is that the small volume of trade emanating from Latin America at the present time implies little opportunity for trade diversion. To be sure, the cumulative consequences of trade preferences within North America over a ten- or fifteen-year period could be substantial. Moreover, it is to be expected that some foreign direct investment that might otherwise have been destined for East Asia will instead be directed to Mexico, if for no other reason than a smaller likelihood of actions under U.S.-administered trade provisions. There are already anecdotal reports of companies relocating from East Asia to Mexico in anticipation of an FTA (Hufbauer and Schott, 1992, 16). Even so, if the Western Hemisphere countries do open their economies and achieve more rapid economic growth, the total effect should be more like that of the European Communities over their first thirty years: overall expansion was sufficiently large that trade and investment flows increased externally and internally.

From the viewpoint of the United States, Latin American markets are simply too small relative to Asian and European markets for the United States to be able to afford to cut itself off from these other geographic areas. The important question is why the United States should be willing to enter into FTAs with Latin American countries. From an American perspective, any trade diversion that does occur will make the United States less competitive in world markets, while there are few benefits to an FTA that cannot be realized in an open, multilateral system. If American officials believe that a Western Hemisphere FTA for the United States represents a genuine economic alternative to the present U.S. position as a nondiscriminatory multilateral trader, examination of the volumes of trade possible with Latin American countries and their specializations should dissuade officials from those views.

If the Uruguay Round succeeds and existing tariff and nontariff barriers to trade are further reduced multilaterally, the potential for trade diversion would be minimized. In that context, a Western Hemisphere FTA might provide encouragement to Latin American countries to undertake the policy reforms that are in any event in their self-interest. Growth in Latin America could accelerate sufficiently to be a net benefit to the United States economically.

An examination of East Asian interests in any potential Western Hemisphere free trade arrangement, therefore, shows that they lie in ensuring the success of the Uruguay Round and the maintenance of an open, multilateral trading system. In that case, accelerated Latin American growth would constitute rapidly growing markets for imports, and East Asia should continue to be competitive in those markets. The smaller the margin of preference accorded by the United States to Latin American countries, the larger the trade-liberalizing effects of the Uruguay Round.

References

Bhagwati, Jagdish. 1988. *Protectionism.* Cambridge, Mass.: MIT Press.

Bhagwati, Jagdish, and Hugh Patrick, eds. 1990. *Aggressive unilateralism.* Hertfordshire: Harvester Wheatsheaf.

Hufbauer, Gary C., and Jeffrey J. Schott. 1992. *North American free trade: Issues and recommendations.* Washington, D.C.: Institute for International Economics.

Nogues, Julio. 1990. Unilateral trade liberalization or free trade areas for developing countries. Working paper. Washington, D.C.: World Bank.

Park, Yung Chul, and Jung Ho Yoo. 1989. More free trade areas: A Korean perspective. In Schott 1989a.

Rosen, Howard. 1989. The U.S.-Israel Free Trade Agreement: How well is it working and what have we learned. In Schott 1989a.

Schott, Jeffrey, ed. 1989a. *Free trade areas and U.S. trade policy.* Washington, D.C.: Institute for International Economics.

———. 1989b. More free trade areas? In Schott 1989a.

United Nations. 1988. *Commodity trade statistics.* New York.

U.S. Council of Economic Advisers. 1988. *Economic report of the president.* Washington, D.C.: U.S. Government Printing Office.

———. 1991. *Economic report of the president.* Washington, D.C.: U.S. Government Printing Office.

Wonnacott, Ronald J. 1990. U.S. hub-and-spoke bilaterals and the multilateral trading system. Commentary, no. 23. Ottawa: C. D. Howe Institute, October.

Zermaño, Mayra. 1987. The economic effects of the Mexican maquiladora industries. Ph.D. diss., University of Minnesota.

Comment Robert E. Baldwin

A major conclusion of Anne Krueger's paper is that the potential for trade diversion from East Asia to Latin America under U.S. free trade agreements with Mexico and possibly with other Latin American countries is quite limited. While I basically agree with this, I do think that there could well be somewhat greater trade diversion than she believes will occur. However, I agree completely with another of her conclusions, which is implicit in her paper, namely, that any trade diversion that does occur will not cause serious adjustment problems for East Asian exporters. It seems to me that this is the message of the numbers she cites concerning the small volume of U.S. imports from Latin America compared to U.S. imports from East Asia in those product lines where trade diversion is possible. Even if the Latin American countries are able to mobilize investment and labor resources quite rapidly and thus increase their exports to the United States at high annual rates in categories where trade diversion is possible, this still implies relatively modest rates of decline in the exports of these goods by the East Asian countries to the United States. Thus, any required adjustment should be handled quite easily.

As far as the extent of trade diversion is concerned, Krueger argues that it will be small because the level of U.S. protection against Mexican exports is already low. The average U.S. tariff against Mexican imports of only 4 percent is, of course, an average weighted by current trade volumes. For some low-volume imports from Mexico, tariffs are relatively high, namely, on footwear and various miscellaneous items like sporting goods. I would not be surprised to see a significant volume of trade diversion in these product lines, especially because rising wages in Taiwan and Korea are beginning to make these goods noncompetitive anyway. Investors from Taiwan and Korea may lead the way in shifting production to Mexico. As Krueger points out, apparel and textiles are other categories where significant diversion is possible if the United States permits free imports of these products from Mexico. I doubt that U.S. textile and apparel manufacturers will allow this, however.

In addition to the statutory levels of tariff protection, another condition that can significantly affect the extent of trade diversion in such products as chemicals and steel is the manner in which the antidumping and countervailing duty laws are enforced in a U.S.-Mexico Free Trade Agreement (FTA). If, as in the U.S.-Canada agreement, the antidumping and countervailing duty laws are not administered as strictly as against nonmember countries, the production of some of these goods could be shifted from East Asia to Mexico and other potential Latin American members.

The point that Krueger makes about the potential for trade diversion in the

Robert E. Baldwin is professor of economics at the University of Wisconsin—Madison and a research associate of the National Bureau of Economic Research.

machinery and transportation equipment category is a very good one. As she points out, U.S. imports from Mexico in this category are composed largely of products whose components are exported to Mexico from the United States and then assembled by Mexican labor. Duty is paid only on the Mexican value-added component in the final product. This means that the average implicit duty on these goods is quite low—a fact that does not leave much room for trade diversion. However, the extent to which East Asian and other exporters ship components to Mexico after the FTA will also depend crucially on the foreign-content rules in the agreement. If a product can have a high foreign content and still be regarded as a Mexican product with duty-free privileges, then diversion via this route could become important. But U.S. domestic interests are likely to block this.

Two other factors that Krueger touches on and that are likely to operate to keep both trade diversion and trade creation down are the rules concerning environmental conditions and labor standards that are likely to be included in the agreement. The president did have to make concessions on these matters in order to get Congress to extend the fast-track authority needed for negotiating a North American FTA. If new imports from Mexico (and perhaps existing imports) must be based on production conforming to stricter environmental and labor standards than now prevail, this will act as a new nontariff barrier to these imports. Conceivably, what is gained in trade terms by Mexico because of a zero-duty tariff on its exports to the United States could be offset by such new nontariff trade measures. For example, it is quite possible that imports from Mexico will be subject to countervailing duties if they are not produced in a manner that meets strict environmental and labor standards. I think that shortly we will see such environmental standards pushed strongly in multilateral forums as well as regional ones.

In conclusion, I think that, while there are some categories of goods where trade diversion may be important, it will have only a modest adjustment effect on East Asian countries, like Taiwan and Korea, that are already upgrading beyond labor-intensive manufacturers. The greatest effect of any trade diversion is, as Krueger points out, likely to be on countries like Indonesia and Sri Lanka, which like Mexico also abound in unskilled labor.

Comment Kuo-shu Liang

I read Anne Krueger's paper with great interest and relief. She pointed out that, "in recent years, the American commitment to an open multilateral system has been, at least to a degree, eroded as U.S. policy has shifted to a "two-

Kuo-shu Liang is chairman of the Bank of Communications in Taipei, Taiwan, and professor of economics at National Taiwan University.

pronged" approach. On the one hand, the United States has continued to participate in the Uruguay Round of trade negotiations; on the other hand, the United States has indicated a willingness to bargain bilaterally for free trade areas with individual trading nations." She concludes that "it . . . seems plausible to assume that, over the next five years, any Western Hemisphere integration that does occur will take place between Canada, the United States, and Mexico." However, "it is . . . unlikely that Canada will be able to use the small margin of preference under American tariffs to divert U.S. or Mexican imports from East Asian sources. . . . Likewise, Canadian imports . . . from East Asian countries are small (and negligible from Mexico), and trade diversion in significant orders of magnitude does not appear to be a realistic possibility. . . . Rather, it is with Mexico that East Asian exporters may be more concerned." "Mexico might in any event," she continues, "become more competitive, especially in labor-intensive commodities." But the Mexican rising imports would at least partially offset some trade diversion that may occur. If Mexican imports were permitted freely under a free trade agreement (FTA), there could be only a relatively small trade diversion in textiles and apparels.

Concerning the important question of "why the United States should be willing to enter into FTAs with Latin American countries," Krueger stresses that FTAs "might provide encouragement to Latin American countries to undertake the policy reforms that are in any event in their self-interest and that the effect on growth and living standards in Latin America could be sufficiently positive to be a net benefit to the United States economically." Krueger also stresses that the margin of preference accorded by the United States would be smaller the larger the trade-liberalizing effects of the Uruguay Round. Therefore, if one examines "East Asian interests in any potential Western Hemisphere free trade agreement," those interests "lie in ensuring the success of the Uruguay Round and the maintenance of an open, multilateral trading system."

I fully agree with Krueger's conclusion that, if the Uruguay Round crumbles, the barriers will become tougher. However, the important question that has to be answered is whether bilateral trade deals can coexist with GATT's multilateral body.

Reflecting multilateralism and nondiscrimination, GATT provides rules that would enable the contracting parties to gain from trade according to the principles of the theory of comparative advantage. However, GATT's success in reducing import quotas and tariffs has led nations to turn to other methods to obtain trade advantages, such as production subsidies, restrictive quality standards, and other barriers that are more difficult to identify and police. In accommodating the political objectives of powerful members, GATT also compromises on the most-favored-nation principle in dealing with the question of integration. Article XXIV legitimates the formation of customs unions and free trade areas to lower tariffs among participants without extending the privilege to other nonparticipating countries, thus denying them the benefits of most-favored-nation rights. The United States used Article XXIV to initiate a looser Western Hemisphere free trade area. By encouraging bilateral trade deals rather than GATT's multilateral sort, the 1988 Trade Act has given exporters a new, bilateral lever, the threat of trade retaliation, with which to open markets abroad.

However, even while Krueger and others may argue that the emerging Western Hemisphere free trade area will be trade creating and offer little opportunity for trade diversion, the East Asian countries have been concerned that the free trade area may replace the freer, multilateral trading system by a trade bloc, and they may take retaliatory actions under the pretext of unfair trade or antidumping protests. As a result, the politically powerful trade bloc will divert trade from less powerful but efficient rivals. In a bilateral confrontation, the weak will concede—resentfully—and the strong will retaliate. It is recommended that discriminatory trade agreements be put under the surveillance of GATT, with strict rules and effective measures for mediation.

Of Professor Krueger's argument that FTAs might encourage Latin American countries to undertake policy reform, the reasons why bilateral attempts will work better than multilateral attempts need to be elaborated. Trade policy may be utilized to secure a particular economic objective, but this will be related to a "policy assignment" problem. The bilateral "open foreign markets aggressively" policies, based on an exaggerated "I am more open than thou" presumption, may produce an atmosphere of mutual hostility, the suspicion of unfair manipulation, and charges of unfair trade (Bhagwati 1988, 126). Trade policy has to be used to secure gains from trade, and other policies have to be used to reform economic policies not related to trade.

Finally, Taiwan has shown a great interest in negotiating with the United States to form a U.S.-Taiwan free trade area. It is recommended that the United States and other major industrial powers support Taiwan's entrance into the General Agreement on Tariffs and Trade. In the past forty years, exceptionally high rates of economic growth have transformed Taiwan from an underdeveloped island into the fifteenth largest trading power in the world and one of the world's most dynamic economies. Taiwan's entrance into GATT will be a significant step toward ending its economic and diplomatic isolation and will enable it to play a more active role in the world economy.

Reference

Bhagwati, Jagdish. 1988. *Protectionism.* Cambridge, Mass.: MIT Press.

II

3 Forward Pricing versus Fair Value: An Analytic Assessment of "Dumping" in DRAMs

Kenneth Flamm

Since the mid-1970s, the concept of sales at a cost less than a constructed "fair value" has become an alternative standard for findings under the U.S. trade laws that imports are being "dumped" in the U.S. market.[1] It has been estimated that, since 1980, about 60 percent of all dumping cases have been based on charges of selling at a price below some constructed average cost (Horlick 1989, 136). Perhaps the most widely publicized application of this standard can be found in the case of imports of the largest category (by value) of semiconductor device sold, dynamic random access memory (DRAM) chips. A U.S. firm's petition for relief from dumping, brought against Japanese 64,000-bit (64K) DRAM imports in 1985, specifically acknowledges that prices for these chips in the U.S. market may actually have been marginally higher than prevailing prices in the Japanese market, the exact opposite of the traditional concept of dumping as sales abroad at less than home market prices.[2] Instead, the U.S. complainant charged that Japanese chips were being sold at prices not covering the full costs of production, the new definition of dumping in the U.S. trade laws.

The investigation of DRAM dumping was expanded by the U.S. govern-

Kenneth Flamm is senior fellow in the Foreign Policy Studies Program at the Brookings Institution in Washington, D.C.

The views expressed in this paper are the author's alone and do not represent those of other staff, officers, or trustees of the Brookings Institution. The author thanks Yuko Iida Frost for her very helpful research assistance and Ann Ziegler for wrestling the mathematical appendices into WordPerfect's equation format. Without implicating them in his errors, the author thanks Dan Hutcheson, Takatoshi Ito, Motoshige Itoh, Anne Krueger, Douglas Nelson, Gary Saxonhouse, and Yun-wing Sung for helpful comments and suggestions.

1. A brief history of the origins of this new standard may be found in Nivola (1990, 229–30) and Horlick (1989, 133–34).

2. See the Micron Technology (1985, 11–14) petition to the U.S. Commerce Department and the U.S. International Trade Commission.

ment to include 256K and 1 megabit (1M) DRAMS and, folded into investigations of U.S. industry charges of dumping of erasable programmable read only memory (EPROM) chips, ultimately culminated in the controversial U.S.-Japan Semiconductor Trade Arrangement (STA) of 1986. One of the outcomes of the STA was a system of floor prices for Japanese DRAM and EPROM imports administered by the U.S. Commerce Department, based on the calculation of something called "foreign market value" (FMV), derived from the "fair value"–constructed cost comparisons enshrined in the dumping provisions of U.S. trade law.

Although the FMV calculations have been dropped from the 1991 successor to the STA, Japanese producers are required to continue to collect the same data, in order to facilitate a "fast response" dumping investigation. Thus, one may surmise that the implicit threat of a dumping investigation continues to give the FMV calculation a significant—if shadowy—role in determining lower bounds on pricing of Japanese chip exports to U.S. (and possibly third-country) markets.

While the idea of requiring producers always to maintain a price at or above some concept of full long-run average cost is hard to defend, either as a positive description of what a profit-maximizing producer in a "competitive" market would choose to do or as a normative guide for efficient resource allocation, it is possible to construct an economically coherent argument that pricing below *marginal* cost can serve as a warning signal of "strategic" behavior by producers that in some circumstances can justify policy intervention by the government. However, in an industry subject to so-called learning economies (where unit production cost falls with cumulative production experience), it is possible that producers may rationally choose to "forward price," that is, sell at a price below current marginal cost, for completely "competitive," nonstrategic reasons.

Is below-marginal-cost pricing for nonstrategic reasons empirically relevant in the semiconductor industry? Is it reasonable to defend even some revised version of a constructed cost test for dumping, based on a constructed *marginal* cost, as a reasonable trip wire for government scrutiny of possible strategic behavior by foreign producers? Perhaps the most interesting question is, What can we deduce about the relation between price and production costs using a minimally realistic model of the product life cycle when large up-front investments in capacity constrain output, large and relatively fixed investments in research and development (R&D) create economies of scale, and learning economies are likely to be significant? How is an "FMV-like" system likely to constrain producer behavior in these circumstances? Because these characteristics are typical not just of semiconductor manufacture but of a broad range of high-technology products, the answers to these questions, and the methodology used in the inquiry, are of some importance.

This paper is intended to provide a simple analytic framework that can be used to compare the time path of output and prices in a nonstrategic, competitive (open-loop Cournot-Nash equilibrium) semiconductor industry with various variants of constructed "fair value" that would be associated with the same path for output. The model is applied with empirically based parameters associated with 1M DRAM chip production, in order to explore how pricing of semiconductors is likely to be constrained, over the product life cycle, by constructed values—FMV-type pricing rules. The basic model should also prove useful in analyzing many other interesting questions about the potential effect of public policies affecting high-technology industries with scale and learning economies.

3.1 Economic Rationality of Below-Marginal-Cost Pricing

To a first approximation, stripped of a variety of practically important cost allocation and accounting issues, the U.S. Commerce Department's procedures for constructing FMVs resemble an economist's concept of average cost of production, plus a fixed 8 percent markup that ostensibly reflects "normal" profit. (This completely arbitrary 8 percent markup is ignored in further discussion.) A result taught in most any introductory economics course is the fact that, under some circumstances (e.g., a downturn in demand), it can be economically rational for a producer in a competitive industry to sell at a price less than full average cost, just as long as short-run marginal cost is covered by price. As long as a firm at least covers the variable costs of running a production line and the marginal cost of producing an incremental unit on that line, it makes economic sense to continue operating a factory, even if revenues received are insufficient to recover the full historical cost of an initial investment in developing the product and building the factory.

Thus, most economists would find it entirely normal that over at least some periods, observed prices would fall short of the full (long-run) average cost of production.[3] Any policy measure that prohibits marginal cost pricing by foreign exporters, while leaving domestic producers unaffected, will—if it actually affects market outcomes—increase domestic production at the expense of domestic consumers and (possibly) foreign producers. It will also arguably deny foreign producers national treatment, forbidding them the right to economic behavior permitted domestic firms.

If price falls short of the full average cost of production continuously, of course, one may safely predict that some firms will exit the industry and that the industry will shrink to the point that full average costs are at least recovered over the life of sunk investments by the remaining firms. Thus, if sustained constructed "fair value" dumping (pricing below long-run average cost) is observed in a competitive industry, one may generally infer that excess ca-

3. For further elaboration on this point, see, e.g., Deardorff (1989, 30–33).

pacity exists and that exit will follow. But observed pricing behavior may still reflect "normal," competitive behavior on the part of the firms pricing below FMVs.

Can one imagine any economic justification for remedial policies triggered by selling below a constructed FMV? The point at which many economists would agree that something other than "competitive," nonstrategic behavior might be suspected is when a firm's price falls short of its short-run marginal cost or, even more obviously, average variable cost (which bounds short-run marginal cost from below over the relevant range).[4]

In considering why a firm might rationally choose to produce and sell a product at a price not covering the current marginal cost of production, it is helpful to distinguish between "strategic" and nonstrategic behavior. I shall label a firm's behavior "strategic" when it explicitly takes account of effects of its decisions on the behavior of other economic agents. This contrasts with what I will call "nonstrategic" behavior, decisions taken considering the actions or choices of other agents as fixed, unaffected by one's own.

One possible explanation for producers pricing below marginal cost, consistent with nonstrategic behavior, is that current production may lower a firm's future production costs. In this case, measured current marginal cost overstates "true" marginal cost, which should take into account the cost-reducing effects of current production on future output.[5]

But another possible explanation for behavior of this sort is a strategic motive on the part of the "dumper": either predation (actions intended to encourage other firms to exit from the industry), limit pricing (intended to discourage entry by others), or a defensive response against predatory behavior by others.[6] In this case, the rents received from the exercise of monopoly power later must be forthcoming to justify absorption of a temporary loss on output shipped now.

Many forms of strategic behavior by firms, like predation, are regulated within a national market by antitrust laws. Thus, a constructed cost test, used

4. For a detailed survey of the literature on tests for predatory behavior, see Ordover and Saloner (1989, 579–90).

5. Note that such learning economies can also be used as a strategic instrument, with a firm's production decisions taking into account the effect of its learning on the actions of its rivals. For such a model, see Fudenberg and Tirole (1983). Deardorff (1989, 37–38) points out that low-priced sales designed to build brand loyalty or otherwise alter consumer preferences might also rationally lead a producer to sacrifice current profitability for future rents and price below marginal cost. In effect, greater current output shifts future demand schedules, and current marginal revenue understates "true" marginal revenue. Such "demand-side learning effects," however, may be considered a form of "strategic" behavior since they are designed to alter the behavioral response to price of other economic agents (i.e., consumers).

6. The modern rehabilitation of the theory of predation focuses on its effect on rival firms' expectations about future profitability: as an exit-inducing investment in "disinformation" about the predator's cost structure, e.g., or as the consequence of asymmetric financial constraints among competing firms created by imperfections in capital markets. The basic references are Milgrom and Roberts (1982) and Kreps and Wilson (1982); useful interpretations are found in Milgrom (1987) and Tirole (1988, 367–80).

in the framework of the dumping laws, might be interpreted as a second-best attempt to remedy behavior by foreign firms that, if carried out on a purely domestic basis, would be considered the domain of antitrust policy. Lacking the ability to impose domestic policy standards on a foreign firm's behavior outside the national market, a national government can instead impose controls on the manifestations of that behavior—that is, pricing of sales to importers—in the domestic market.

Since, absent learning effects, pricing below short-run marginal cost is sufficient (but not necessary)[7] to conclude that a firm is acting strategically in its pricing policies, it may seem reasonable at that point to review its activities and to take corrective action if the intent is deemed to be predation and the potential effect significant. It is at least possible that increased monopoly rents paid out later by national consumers to foreign producers, and deadweight losses, could more than offset the windfall to national consumers created by a temporary episode of low import prices, justifying some policy intervention (as noted by Deardorff [1989, 35–36]).

From this point of view, the economic problem with cost-based definitions of dumping is not necessarily their existence but their use of the wrong cost concept (long-run average cost instead of short-run marginal cost) as the prima facie trigger for consideration of possible intervention. This perspective also leads one to focus on the close relation between "fair trade" laws and competition and antitrust policy. It might be argued that some binding international standards for competitive business behavior (and their enforcement) might be offered as a constructive alternative to national fair value dumping tests based on constructed costs, as remedies for predation.

This paper will not attempt to evaluate whether predation is a plausible description of what was going on in the DRAM marketplace in the 1980s. I merely note that predatory behavior was one of the allegations made by the U.S. industry in pressing its case for protection. However, the modern theory of predation has been interpreted to suggest that high-technology industries are particularly important places to look for such behavior.[8]

3.2 Costs and Pricing in the Semiconductor Industry

High-technology industries, facing large sunk costs in research and development relative to sales, along with highly capital-intensive industries, are by nature particularly prone to trade friction involving charges of dumping based

7. Criticism of a short-run marginal cost test for predation generally argues that the rule is not stringent enough; prices above short-run marginal cost may still be associated with socially costly predatory activity (see Tirole 1988, 372–3; Ordover and Saloner 1989, 579–80).

8. Paul Milgrom argues that "policymakers should be especially sensitive to predatory pricing in growing, technologically advanced industries, where the temptation to discourage entry is large, and the costs of curtailed entry even larger" (1987, 938). For further consideration of the plausibility of strategic behavior in semiconductor competition, see Flamm (in press, b).

on constructed cost tests. When fixed investments in R&D or factories are very large in relation to a firm's sales, a significant gap between average variable cost and long-run average cost will exist, and short-run marginal cost may fall significantly below long-run average cost for a substantial range of economically rational output levels. In such a case, perfectly competitive behavior may often trigger pricing below long-run average cost—and dumping charges—in a downturn.

High-tech industries are also particularly prone to dumping cases because of the peculiar way in which R&D investments are treated by trade law (and many companies') accounting principles. An investment in a capital facility, for example, is not charged immediately against company revenues when construction is begun, or completed, but spread over the period in which it is to be used through the use of depreciation charges. One may argue that accounting depreciation is at least an attempt to approximate the profile of true economic depreciation charges. An R&D investment, by way of contrast, is generally charged against revenues at the moment it is incurred, not spread over its economically useful life.

It is sometimes argued that, when processed through constructed cost calculations, this "front loading" of R&D leads to artificially high prices for high-tech imports (like DRAMs) when initially shipped, in effect retarding technological progress. Defenders of this practice argue that, since R&D charges are often allocated on the basis of sales rather than identified with some particular product, the practical effect is to spread R&D charges over generations of products, through time (although it clearly remains true that a company just entering an industry after making a fixed R&D investment will necessarily have to charge an initially high price).

The semiconductor industry is both technology intensive and capital intensive: it spends almost 15 percent of sales on R&D; it also typically spends an even larger fraction of sales (15–20 percent annually) on capital investments. Demand for semiconductors is also notoriously cyclical, and it is not, therefore, surprising to find that constructed cost tests for dumping were invoked in the 1985 industry downturn.

In addition, semiconductor production is believed to be characterized by so-called learning economies. Unit production costs are believed to fall sharply with accumulated production experience. This further complicates our discussion of the borderline between nonstrategic pricing behavior and strategic activities. The key result due to Spence (1981) is that, with learning economies but no strategic interactions with its rivals, a rational firm will generally equate marginal revenue to a value below its current short-run marginal cost of production, as it takes into account the cost-reducing effect of current production on future production costs.

While the Spence model is rather unsuitable for analyzing production decisions in the semiconductor industry, the point it makes greatly complicates the issue of whether constructed cost-dumping tests—amended perhaps to use short-run marginal cost rather than long-run average cost as the trip wire for possible intervention—can be justified as a reasonable safeguard against predation by foreign producers. For in the Spence model, even with nonstrategic behavior—that is, with a firm taking production decisions by competitors as given, independent of its actions—economically rational firms will engage in "forward pricing," that is, choose output levels where marginal revenue lies below their current short-run marginal cost.

3.3 Modeling the Semiconductor Product Life Cycle

In my somewhat stylized depiction of the industry, a DRAM producer will be assumed to produce a homogeneous commodity, perfectly substitutable for that of other producers.[9] Difficult issues concerning the timing of the switch-over from one generation of DRAM to another, and intergenerational externalities, are ignored by assuming that a DRAM producer faces a fixed period over which the DRAM is sold and that costs for developing and producing his product are relevant to that generation of DRAM alone. The product life cycle begins at time 0 and ends at time 1 (hence, the unit of time is the "product life cycle"). Every producer faces revenue function R, giving total revenues at any moment t as a function of his own production, $y(t)$, and the aggregate output of all other producers, $x(t)$. All revenues and costs are measured in constant dollar terms. Following Spence, for simplicity, I ignore discounting on the grounds that product life cycles are short (typically, a new generation of DRAM is introduced every three years) and the additional complexity introduced by discounting over time substantial.

In semiconductor production, plant capacity may be measured in terms of "wafer starts," the number of slices of silicon, on which integrated circuits are etched, that can be processed per unit time. At any moment t, $w[E(t)]$ functioning chips are yielded per wafer processed, where w is an increasing function of $E(t)$, "experience" through time t. How one defines relevant "experience" is a subject explored below. I will parametrize the effect of output, y, on relevant experience, E, as

$$\dot{E} = \frac{dE}{dt} = \frac{y}{K^{\gamma}},$$

where K is capacity, and γ is a parameter taking on a value between zero and one. For notational simplicity, time will sometimes be suppressed as an argument of time-varying variables.

Some of the variable cost of producing a chip is incurred with every wafer processed, and some of the cost is incurred only with good, yielded chips (assembly and final test, e.g.). If a wafer-processing facility is utilized at rate

9. This is not an unreasonable approximation. For more detailed discussion of this issue in the context of semiconductor price indexes, see Flamm (in press, a).

$u(t)$ (u between 0 and 1), total variable costs at any moment are $dy + cuK$; d is manufacturing cost per good, yielded chip, c processing cost per wafer start. Note that $y(t, K) = w[E(t)]u(t)K$.

Up-front, sunk costs independent of output levels (like R&D) are equal to F, and fixed capital investment costs required for a facility processing K wafer starts are equal to r per wafer start. For the moment, take K (wafer-processing capacity) as a given. The producer's problem is to maximize

$$\max_{u(t),K} \int_0^1 \{R[x(t), y(t)] - dy(t) - cu(t)K - rK\}dt - F,$$

$$\text{(1)} \qquad \text{with} \quad y(t) = w[E(t)]u(t)K,$$

$$\text{s.t.} \quad \dot{E} = \frac{y}{K^{\gamma}} = w[E(t)]u(t)K^{1-\gamma}.$$

Firms will be assumed to simultaneously choose initial capacity investments K and a time path for utilization rates, which give rise to a path for output over time, which they then proceed to follow. My assumption that capacity investments in DRAMs are committed at the beginning of the product cycle is not terribly unrealistic: it typically takes a year or more to get a new fabrication facility up and running, and a new generation of DRAM is introduced roughly every three years.[10]

For the moment, take γ to equal zero (i.e., absolute cumulative production is the relevant measure of experience). The model that I present in appendix A will, like the Spence model, assume a Nash equilibrium in output paths; that is, given rivals' actual choices of output paths, (1) is maximized by every firm. Firms' behavior in this static game is *nonstrategic* since they take their rivals' output choices as given.[11]

3.3.1 Spence's Model

If wafer-processing capacity K is not fixed over the life cycle but is continuously variable, as is implicit in Spence's formulation, then we have a special case of the above model in which r is zero (capital costs are included in wafer-

10. The world record for bringing a new fabrication facility on line seems to be held by NMB Semiconductor, which claims that it took only nine months to go from initial ground breaking for a new factory to initial production of 256K DRAMs in 1985 (see Waller 1988).

11. An alternative would be to set up a two-stage competition among rival firms, with capacity investment as the initial phase, followed by a second stage in which firms choose output paths subject to capacity constraints. The solution of the static game presented here corresponds to the open-loop (nonstrategic) equilibrium of this two-stage game, in which a firm's first-period choice of capacity takes its rivals' choices in both periods as given. An alternative equilibrium concept would assume second-period subgame perfectness, i.e., that firms take into account the effect of their first-period capacity choices on their rivals' second-period output paths. This creates *strategic* interactions among firms (see Dixit 1986, 114; Shapiro 1989, 383–86). Flamm (in press, b) extends the model presented in this paper to include strategic capacity investments by firms. Note that, despite its nonstrategic nature, the present model is developed using the conjectural variations framework—which (somewhat controversially) permits strategic behavior—to allow greater generality in its application and to preserve comparability with the Baldwin-Krugman model.

processing cost c and some arbitrary initial scale for capacity K is set), capital is a completely variable input, and a producer is free to choose any nonnegative u—that is, u is unbounded above, not bounded by one—and produce any yielded chip output desired. Under these circumstances, as is easily shown in appendix A, formal maximization of objective function (1) yields the first-order condition

(2) $$R_y = d + \frac{c}{w} - \frac{\delta}{K^{\gamma}};$$

that is, u is chosen so that marginal revenue is set equal to current marginal cost $(d + c/w)$ less a term proportional to nonnegative adjoint variable δ, which captures the future cost-reducing effects of current production. Adjoint variable δ, in turn, is determined by the transversality condition,

(3) $$\delta(1) = 0,$$

and equation of motion,

(4) $$\dot{\delta} = -\frac{c}{w}uKw_E.$$

By differentiating both sides of equation (2) with respect to time, we immediately see that marginal revenue, R_y, must be constant over time and therefore, by (3), equal to current marginal cost at the end of the product cycle, $d + c/w[E(1)]$.

In short, with continuously variable capacity, a profit-maximizing producer will choose his output so that marginal revenue equals his terminal (not current!) marginal cost. This is so-called forward pricing. With a constant elasticity and autonomous demand, a constant price proportional to terminal marginal cost will result.

Now this does not necessarily mean that price falls below current marginal cost since price will in general exceed marginal revenue. Whether constructed "fair values" based on current marginal cost will serve as binding constraints on pricing will depend on many factors, including market structure and the elasticity of industry demand.

While this model provides an appealing explanation of the phenomenon of forward pricing, a notable empirical feature of business practice within the semiconductor industry, the actual trajectory of pricing suggested by this model (with a constant elasticity demand, price is fixed at some constant level over the entire product cycle) is quite inconsistent with observed behavior.[12] Chip prices typically drop very quickly over the first part of the product cycle, drop less quickly as the product approaches maturity, and fall very slowly, if

12. Dick (1991), e.g., invokes the Spence model to motivate his assumptions about the time path of semiconductor prices over the product life cycle but ignores the constant pricing prediction of the Spence model.

at all, at the end. As shall be seen in a moment, a more realistic treatment of capacity constraints yields a more plausible trajectory for prices.

3.3.2 The Baldwin-Krugman Approach

The pioneering attempt to incorporate learning economies into a stylized, empirical model of the semiconductor industry is that of Baldwin and Krugman (B-K) (1988).[13] The B-K focuses on regional segmentation of the U.S. and Japanese semiconductor markets, in order to simulate the effect of market closure policies, and takes an approach to producer behavior that differs significantly from that of Spence. B-K constrain firms to operate at full capacity over the entire product cycle; the choice variable for the firm is initial capacity, which, once set, determines output levels over the entire product life cycle. The first-order condition for an optimum is that the life-cycle revenue created from the addition of a marginal unit of wafer-processing capacity just equals the cost of building and operating that marginal unit of wafer-processing capacity (since all capacity is always fully utilized, the distinction I am drawing between investment costs and wafer-processing costs is immaterial).

Firms in the Spence model are never capacity constrained; firms in the B-K model always operate at their capacity constraint. The Spence model has firms forward pricing—maintaining marginal revenue constant over the life cycle, equal to their terminal marginal cost. The B-K model has marginal revenue—and price—falling smoothly over the life cycle. Thus, while the striking forward pricing behavior of the Spence model has disappeared, a more empirically plausible path for prices has replaced it.

As Krishna (1988) notes, however, the algebraic tractability created by the simplicity of the B-K specification of firm behavior has been purchased by excluding the possibility of some interesting forms of strategic competition. (Because B-K empirically calibrate conjectural variations, strategic interactions among firms exist.) Investments in capacity may be undertaken with strategic objectives, to convince rivals to exit or dissuade them from entering an industry, creating additional monopoly power that can then be exploited. Constraining firms to operate at full capacity over the entire product life cycle may restrict them to suboptimal output paths, where monopoly power is not fully exploited. It also hinders analysis of interesting policy questions regarding the potential welfare effect of strategic government policies that may foster the creation and exercise of monopoly power.

A variant of the B-K model can be fit into the framework outlined above for the Spence model, after suitable amendments. Utilization rate u is constrained

13. A somewhat different exposition of this model is given in Helpman and Krugman (H-K) (1989, chap. 8). This later interpretation differs in some significant respects from B-K. For example, the learning curve in B-K has yields improving with cumulative wafers processed (i.e., faulty chips have the same yield-enhancing effects as good ones), while H-K presents a more conventional view of the learning curve, with yield rates rising with cumulative output of *yielded* (i.e., good) chips. While the B-K assumption on yields is not the accepted approach to modeling yield improvement within the industry, it simplifies the mathematical structure of the model.

to equal one at all times, and objective function (1) is maximized with respect to K alone The right-hand side of equation (4) is replaced by the more complex variant shown in appendix A (corresponding to $u = 1$), and a new question determining optimal capacity choice is added:

$$(5) \qquad \int_0^1 \left[\left(R_y - d - \frac{c}{w} + \frac{\delta}{K^\gamma} \right) uw - \gamma \frac{\delta}{K^\gamma} uw - r \right] dt = 0,$$

where the B-K specification fixes u equal to one and γ equal to zero.

3.3.3 A More Realistic Model of the Semiconductor Product Cycle

It is possible to create a more realistic model of firm behavior, in which firms can continuously adjust output, as in the Spence model, yet also face capacity constraints on output, as in the B-K model.

I briefly summarize the more detailed exposition laid out in appendix A to this paper. The firm's problem is to maximize (1) by choosing both an initial level of capacity K and time-varying utilization rates $u(t)$ for that capacity that determine output at any moment in time. The optimal level of capacity chosen satisfies equation (5) above; the left-hand side of this equation can be interpreted as the net marginal return on additional investment in capacity. It also must be true that the optimal path must be capacity constrained over some interval (i.e., $u[t] = 1$).

In general, the optimal path for $u(t)$ will be made up of three types of segments: interior segments, where $0 > u > 1$; lower-boundary segments, where $u = 0$; and upper-boundary segments, where $u = 1$. Within an interior segment, equations (2) and (4) will hold, as in the Spence model, as will a form of forward pricing: marginal revenue will be held constant, set equal to current marginal cost less δ/K^γ—the marginal cost-reducing value (over the remainder of the product life cycle) of an additional unit of output—at the endpoint of this interval.

With additional assumptions, one can further sharpen the characterization of the optimal behavior of a profit-maximizing firm. I shall assume a symmetric industry equilibrium with N identical firms, an autonomous demand (i.e., not an explicit function of time), and concavity of total industry revenues in industry output (as would be the case, e.g., with a constant elasticity demand function and price elasticity exceeding unity). Although a nonstrategic, Nash equilibrium in output paths is assumed for the remainder of this paper, for expositional purposes I will parametrize a firm's perceptions of other firms' reactions to changes in its output in terms of a constant, nonnegative conjectural variation. (The two interesting cases that motivate this parametrization are Cournot-Nash equilibrium [conjectural variation equal to zero] and a collusive, constant market share cartel [conjectural variation equal to $N - 1$.)[14]

14. The major behavioral assumption excluded by a nonnegative conjectural variation is Bertrand competition in prices. Because DRAMs are essentially a homogeneous commodity sold in

Under these assumptions, optimal u must decline over an interior segment, and u must be continuous in time. Therefore, the optimal path of the utilization rate must look like an upper-boundary segment, possibly followed by an interior segment, possibly then followed by a lower-boundary segment. Along lower-boundary segments, where $u = 0$, δ will be constant and therefore equal to its terminal value. Thus, the Spence forward pricing result of marginal revenue being set equal to terminal marginal cost will hold whenever we are producing but are not capacity constrained (i.e., $0 < u < 1$, along an interior segment).

If we further assume that firm marginal revenue exceeds the initial value of current marginal cost (so some production will always be profitable) as industry output approaches zero (as must be the case with a constant elasticity demand), we can exclude the possibility of lower-boundary segments occurring along the optimal path. Note that nothing about the specific shape of the learning curve (function w) beyond the fact that it is increasing in experience ($w_E > 0$) has been assumed in arriving at this characterization of optimal policy.

In short, with this simple description of the semiconductor product life cycle, we derive a more realistic specification of firm behavior that captures both the importance of capacity investments and the ability of firms fully to exploit what monopoly power they enjoy by varying utilization rates over time. It is simple enough to be empirically tractable. Firms will make some capacity investment, run at that capacity full blast for some period of time, then possibly switch to a constant output path (with constant marginal revenue but decreasing utilization of capacity as yields rise) over the remainder of the product life cycle.

3.4 Preliminary Observations

Even with its relatively general structure, the analysis presented above provides a couple of insights into the question of "dumping" over the product life cycle. First, below-current-marginal-cost pricing will *never* be observed near the end of the product cycle among competitive, nonstrategic, profit-maximizing firms. This follows immediately from the fact that, if any output is being produced, marginal revenue will never be less than the right-hand side of equation (2) (see app. A), which at time 1—the end of the product cycle—equals current marginal cost ($d + c/w$). Since price exceeds marginal revenue, price must also exceed current marginal cost in some neighborhood of time 1, the end of the product cycle.

well-developed secondary spot markets, specifying that producers sell at a single market price and choose quantities sold is the natural assumption. Moreover, Kreps and Scheinkman (1983) have shown that, in a two-stage game, where first-stage capacity investments are followed by a second-stage Bertrand game in prices and a particular ("efficient") rationing rule, the outcome is a Cournot equilibrium in output.

3.4.1 Closing the Model

Can we say anything about the relation between price and long-run average cost? The model sketched out thus far takes the number of firms in the industry—which will affect profitability and pricing—as given. One "natural" way to close the model is to specify that firms enter the industry until rents earned by producers, that is, the integrand in equation (1), just equal zero. The zero-profit condition then determines N, the number of firms entering the industry (I will ignore the difficulties created by insisting that N be an integer).

Zero profits mean that total life-cycle revenues just equal total life-cycle costs. Therefore (after dividing both concepts by total output over the product life cycle) average "life-cycle" price must equal average "life-cycle" cost per unit.

But is there any clear relation between current price and current "fully allocated" average cost at any given moment? Current short-run marginal cost (SRMC) is a relatively clear concept: the additional current cost saved by producing one less unit at any given moment. This is the incremental cost saved when output is reduced by one unit.[15] In my model, current short-run marginal cost—$d + c/w$—is constant at any moment and equal to current average variable cost.

To define a current average cost, however, it is first necessary to define an intertemporal cost allocation rule to spread fixed entry costs F and capital costs rK over the product life cycle. Dividing the capital and entry costs allocated to some instant in time by output produced at that moment yields a current average fixed cost per unit produced. If this current average fixed cost is added to current average variable cost (identical to short-run marginal cost in my model), we have a long-run average cost (LRAC) concept that satisfies the basic requirements of a long-run average cost: when multiplied by output at that moment and summed over all moments, total costs of production over the entire product life cycle are given.

Now, because my assumption about entry means that total life-cycle costs are exactly equal to total life-cycle revenues, price less the fully allocated long-run average cost defined above (i.e., profit per unit), multiplied by output, and summed over every moment of the product cycle must be exactly equal to zero. Thus, if price exceeds the fully allocated average cost concept at any instant, it must fall below fully allocated average cost at some other instant over the product cycle, and vice versa. Therefore, if my assumption that entry drives long-run profits to zero is a realistic one, below-LRAC "dumping" *must* be occurring sometime during the product cycle, unless the cost allocation rule for fixed costs defines an average fixed cost that, when added to current average variable cost, is exactly equal to actual price *at every moment*.

15. When a firm operates at less than full capacity, this is identical to the increased cost incurred in producing one more unit. When operating at full capacity, the incremental cost of an additional unit is effectively infinite; marginal cost is "L-shaped" with a kink at full-capacity output.

It is easy to see that, for a cost allocation rule to satisfy this requirement, with learning economies present, it must generally be a function of *all* the parameters of the control problem and will, in general, take on negative values as well as positive values. Since the cost allocation rules actually used to spread fixed costs over the product cycle—by firms or by the U.S. Commerce Department—are generally functions only of the size of the fixed costs and time and produce only nonnegative values, it is essentially guaranteed that there will be an episode of below-LRAC dumping if learning economies are present and the industry is in a symmetric, zero-profit equilibrium.[16]

3.5 Some Further Assumptions

My next step is to take this simple control model and solve it to explicitly derive an individual firm's behavior over time. Let the time at which a firm switches from full blast production to constant output production be t_s (with full blast production over the entire product life cycle an important possibility). To sharpen my characterization of a profit-maximizing firm's optimal policy, I must address some additional issues.

16. Define a cost allocation rule $g(Z, t)$, where Z is a vector of arguments, t is time, such that

$$\int_0^1 g(Z, t)dt = F + rK.$$

Define fully allocated average cost (FAAC) by

$$\text{FAAC} = \frac{c}{w} + d + \frac{g}{y},$$

i.e., current average variable cost plus average fixed cost. We know that the optimal path must contain a capacity-constrained segment and that along this portion of the optimal path

$$\dot{P} = P'N\dot{y} = P'NKw_E\dot{E}$$

in symmetric industry equilibrium. If price P is always to equal FAAC along this segment, however, differentiating the expression for FAAC with respect to t, and setting this equal to the last expression, we must at every moment of this interval have

$$\begin{aligned}\frac{dg}{dt} &= w_E\dot{E}(P'NK + \frac{c}{w^2} + \frac{g}{Kw^2})y \\ &= Kw_E\dot{E}[(1 + \beta)P - d].\end{aligned}$$

Since equilibrium N, and therefore P, will generally be functions of all the parameters of the optimal control problem, a function g that satisfies this last equation must generally include all parameters of the control problem as arguments, unless $w_E = 0$, in which case g is constant. (In this latter case, I note at the end of app. A that all capacity is utilized and output is constant over the entire product life cycle.) Thus, if there are learning economies (w_E not equal to zero), a cost allocation rule g varying only with F, r, K, and t cannot satisfy the requirement that P = FAAC, for arbitrary values of the parameters of the control problem, over this capacity-constrained interval.

Also, we have already noted that it is possible for P less than current marginal cost to be optimal in the presence of learning economies. (Indeed, the simulations reported below contain examples of such behavior.) Reexamining the definition of FAAC, it is clear that g must be negative for P = FAAC to hold true over such an interval.

3.5.1 Learning Economies

I shall approximate the learning curve by specifying that

$$w(E) = \phi E^{\varepsilon}, \quad \text{with } E(0) = E_0,\ 0 \leq \varepsilon \leq 1.$$

This gives yielded chips per wafer as a function of experience, E. This functional form is best regarded as an approximation: mass production typically starts at initially low yields; yields then rise quickly and flatten out at the end of the product cycle in a pattern closer to a logistic curve. Analytic tractability is the grounds for selecting this approximation. Note that a "dummy" value E_0 is used as an argument in the function to specify some initial nonzero yield—without this constant, yields would stay "stuck" at zero forever.[17]

This approximation to the "true" learning curve is shown in figure 3.1. If (as is believed in the industry) the "true" learning curve behaves more like a logistic function in its early stages, my approximation somewhat distorts yields, output, and pricing in the very earliest portion of the product cycle.

Defining *experience* raises additional issues. It is customary to use cumulative output as a proxy for experience in empirical studies, and most published empirical studies of learning economies have taken this approach. But using absolute, company-wide production experience as the determinant of any single facility's productivity implies that running, say, ten facilities in parallel produces the same yields at the end of a period as running a single facility to produce the same output over a much longer period. In the semiconductor industry, it is widely believed that improved manufacturing yields come from two main sources—iterative refinements of the operation of the production line (with each new refinement building on previous experience) and "die shrinks" (reductions in the feature size for chip designs made possible by improved use of existing process equipment)—that are iterative and sequential in nature. That is, lessons learned from running a line over some period of time are then applied to refine the operation of that line over a subsequent period.

However, by this logic, if numerous identical production lines are run in an identical fashion over the same period of time, then the same "lessons" are being learned, in parallel, on each line, and yields at the end of the period should be no higher than if only a single line were being run. Of course, if a new line (one with less experience and lower yields) were put into operation after an older line had been running for some time and it were possible completely to transfer the fruits of greater experience across facilities, then the maximum experience on any one line would be the "experience" variable determining production yields. Because all investment occurs at a single initial moment in my simple model, all lines will have identical amounts of produc-

17. B-K use the same functional form but do not face the "stuck" yield problem because the argument in their learning curve is gross wafers processed, not net good chips yielded. The latter specification is generally industry practice in estimating learning curves.

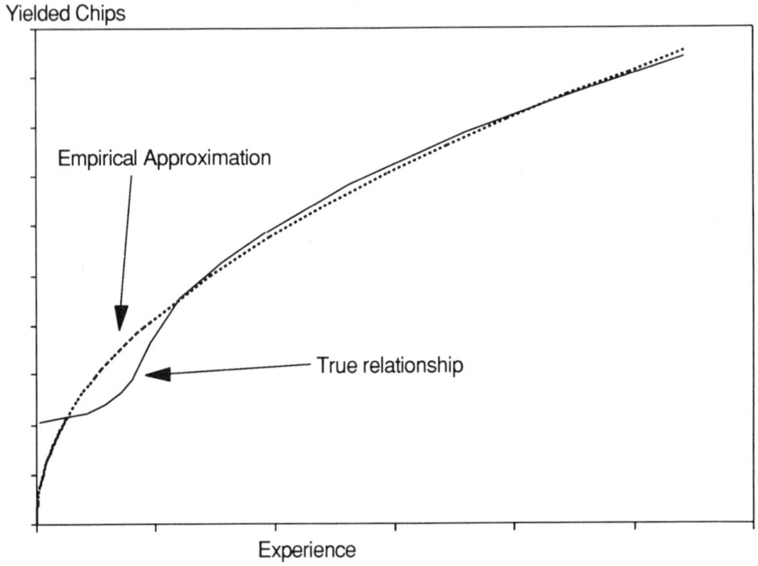

Fig. 3.1 Empirical approximation to hypothetical true yield curve

tion experience at any subsequent moment in time, and cumulative output per facility is the desired measure of experience.

It is possible that the lessons learned on different lines are not the same ones if completely different "experiments" in production refinement are being conducted at every production facility. If, once again, experience can be completely transferred across facilities and there is no duplication in "lessons learned" in different facilities, then it might be argued that company-wide, absolute cumulative output, rather than cumulative output per unit capacity, is the relevant experience variable.[18]

One way to parametrize these differences in the conceptualization of how learning economies work is to define *experience* as cumulative output divided by K^{γ}, where γ takes on value 0 if absolute, company-wide cumulative output is the correct experience variable, 1 if experience per facility (or unit capacity) is what is relevant. This means that

$$\dot{E} = \frac{y}{K^{\gamma}} \quad \text{with some initial } E(0) = E_0 \tag{7}$$

defines $E(t)$.[19] My approach will be an agnostic one: I will solve the model using both 0 and 1 as possible values for γ and then ask which seems to predict

18. Or perhaps even industry-wide cumulative output, if complete cross-company diffusion of the lessons of production experience occurs.

19. Note that an alternative specification might make cumulative output, or cumulative output per unit capacity, the state variable, subject to some initial value, and make this alternative state

more empirically plausible behavior. While the "true" value almost certainly lies somewhere between these two extremes, it is my prior belief that it should be substantially closer to one. With plausible empirical assumptions, it turns out that parameter γ plays a critical role in defining the nature of an industry equilibrium.

Note that the existing empirical literature on learning curves gives us little help in deciding the correct specification. If data on cumulative output from a given facility, or aggregate data from a group of facilities with fixed capacities, are used to estimate the relation $y = wK$ using (6), we get an equation like

$$\ln[y(t)] = a + \varepsilon \ln[Q(t)],$$

that is, giving the natural log of total output as a linear function of the natural log of cumulative output Q, even if cumulative output per unit capacity is the relevant experience variable. The effects of capacity size, K, have been absorbed into constant a. Data from different facilities of varying size within a single company, or from different companies, along with an additional variable controlling for capacity size, are required to identify and estimate γ.

An exact solution for $E(t)$ will be useful in what follows. Substituting (6) into the above differential equation giving $\dot{E}$, and solving for E as a function of time (assuming capacity-constrained output),

(8) $$E(t, K) = [E_0^{1-\varepsilon} + K^{1-\gamma}\phi t(1 - \varepsilon)]^{1/1-\varepsilon}$$

describes the time path of $E(t, K)$ through time t_s, the endpoint of the period of full blast production.

3.5.2 Final Test and Assembly Yields

A tested, just-fabricated "good" die is not yet a finished integrated circuit (IC). The dice produced on the wafer fabrication line must then be assembled into a sealed package, then subjected to a rigorous final testing process. While yields of good, tested chips assembled from "good" dice may also show some evidence of a "learning curve," the effect of learning in this stage of the IC production process is thought to be quite small relative to learning economies in the wafer fabrication phase of IC manufacturing.

I will model assembly and final test yields by assuming a fixed yield of final good chips from "good" dice produced on the wafer fab line; that is, $v = \xi y$; where v is "net" good, assembled and tested ICs produced from quantity y of "gross" good dice yielded by wafer fabrication. If we denote DRAM consumers' inverse demand function for finished chips by $\tilde{P}(\xi x, \xi y)$, then the produc-

variable times K to some power the argument of w, the function giving yield per wafer. Such a specification, however, makes initial yield (with no experience) a function of the scale of capacity investment, which is undesirable. (In that case, increasing or decreasing capacity simply to raise initial yield on every line will play an entirely artificial role in determining optimal capacity.)

er's maximization problem, taking into account assembly and final test yield losses, is to

$$\max_{u(t),K} \int_0^1 \tilde{P}[\xi x(t), \xi y(t)]\xi y(t) - \frac{d}{\xi}\xi y(t) - \frac{c}{w\xi}\xi y(t) - rK,$$

$$\text{with} \quad \xi y(t) = \xi uwK,$$

$$\dot{E} = uwK^{1-\gamma}.$$

Now, if we define an inverse demand function for "gross" chips (including product ruined in assembly and final test) by

$$P[x(t), y(t)] = \tilde{P}[\xi x(t), \xi y(t)]\xi$$

and substitute, we get exactly the maximization problem given earlier in equation (1), where

$$R[x(t), y(t)] = P[x(t), y(t)]y(t).$$

Thus, after converting net, finished IC demand to a gross (defect-inclusive) demand for fabricated chips, we can pose the optimization problem in terms of choosing a time path for wafer fab output y (as opposed to net output ξy) and otherwise ignore the additional yield losses in the assembly and final test stages of production.[20] In interpreting the results, we must only remember to divide all "gross" per unit cost and revenue measures (like price, marginal revenue, marginal cost, etc.) emerging from the optimization analysis by ξ, in order to get the "net" cost and revenue measures per good unit observed in the chip marketplace.

3.5.3 DRAM Demand

We must specify a demand function for DRAMs, and an industry structure, in order to calculate marginal revenue R_y. I shall assume a constant elasticity demand function of the form

(9) $$z = \alpha P^{\beta},$$

with z aggregate demand for DRAMs, P DRAM price, and an industry made up of N identical firms. With this specification, we have

(10) $$R_y = \left(\frac{Ny}{\alpha}\right)^{1/\beta}\left(\frac{\sigma}{\beta} + 1\right),$$

where parameter σ equals the conjectural variation plus one, divided by N, the number of firms. With Cournot competition, σ is $1/N$; with a constant market share cartel, it is 1.

20. The critical assumption is that all "good" chips coming off the wafer fab line incur all the costs of assembly and final test before being culled.

3.6 Model Solution

Next, I briefly summarize the method used to solve numerically for an optimal policy. Full details are given in appendix B. It is useful to categorize optimal policies in terms of two possibilities. One possibility is that full blast production is followed by an "interior segment" where a firm is producing at less than full capacity. In this case, an optimal policy boils down to picking both an optimal capacity K and some optimal time t_s to switch from full blast production to constant output production. The other possibility is that the firm runs at full capacity throughout the product cycle. In this latter regime, necessary conditions for the firm determine only an optimal capacity.

3.6.1 Optimal Output Decisions—with Interior Segments

Appendix B shows that, when the firm produces at less than full capacity, an optimal, profit-maximizing policy must set the difference between marginal cost and marginal revenue equal to δ/K^{γ}, the value of an additional unit of current production in reducing future production costs over the remainder of the product cycle. Therefore, at the optimal switchpoint t_s to an interior segment, we can solve a differential equation determining δ and derive an equation giving t_s as a function of K, N, and other parameters of the control problem.

A second equation giving optimal capacity may be derived from equation (5). After solving for δ over both interior and boundary segments and substituting into (5), we have an expression implicitly giving K as a function of optimal t_s and N. Together with the previous equation, for given N, and various other parameters, we have two equations in two unknowns. An optimal t_s and K pair must solve these two equations.

3.6.2 Optimal Capacity—with No Interior Segment

In many important cases, the optimal path may not contain an interior segment. In this case, $u(t)$ will always equal one. The transversality condition will still hold, and, using this boundary value, we can solve the equation of motion for δ given in appendix B.

Since, however, this expression gives us optimal K conditional on full-capacity utilization over the entire product cycle, we must be careful to ensure that such a path is in fact a Cournot equilibrium. In searching for Cournot equilibria, then, attempts were made to solve both the two-equation system characterizing an optimal policy with interior segments, for a t_s and K pair, and the single equation giving optimal K assuming full-capacity utilization throughout the product cycle. Solutions found were then checked as possible Cournot equilibria, by perturbing both firm capacity K and switching time t_s (if relevant) by .01 in all feasible directions, while maintaining the hypothesized equilibrium output path for all other firms, and calculating the effect on firm profitability (which should necessarily be negative in a Cournot equilibrium).

3.7 Plausible Parameter Values

The final step in this simulation of firm behavior is to decide on empirically plausible parameter values to be used in this model.

3.7.1 Learning Economies

While I am unaware of any published studies of experience curves in the semiconductor industry that control for the effects of varying facility capacities (i.e., estimate γ), there are numerous published estimates of learning curve elasticity ε based on the relation between log output (or log cost) and log cumulative output. In DRAMs, there are several published reports of an empirical 72 percent "learning curve," meaning that current unit cost drops by 28 percent with every doubling of output, corresponding to $\varepsilon = .47$.[21]

To specifically estimate the parameters of the learning curve for 1M DRAMs, estimates of "typical" wafer yields based on historical data and projections for the last four years of a five-year product life cycle were used to derive nonlinear least squares estimates of parameters corresponding to E_0, ϕ, and ε in equation (6).[22] Parameter γ was assumed to equal one; because the unconstrained estimate of E_0 was a small number very close to zero, I imposed a value of .01 for E_0. This was the largest power of ten, which substituted into (8) to constrain parameter estimation, left other parameter estimates unchanged from values produced by the unconstrained estimation procedure. Learning elasticity ε was estimated to be .49, while ϕK^{γ} had an estimated value of 31.[23]

To further check whether this critical parameter seems to reflect the reality of 1M DRAM production accurately, actual company-specific quarterly production estimates for the six largest 1M DRAM manufacturers were used to estimate learning elasticity ε. "Experience" at time t is given by

21. With a constant wafer-processing cost as the only cost element (the model that underlies these studies), we have

$$\text{unit cost} = \frac{c}{w} = \left(\frac{c}{\phi}\right)E^{-\varepsilon}.$$

A learning elasticity ε equal to .47 is solved from the 72 percent learning curve, since $2^{-\varepsilon} = .72$ (see Noyce 1977; U.S. Congress 1983, 76). On the basis of studies of production costs for IBM bipolar integrated circuits in the 1960s and 1970s, engineers at IBM derived a virtually identical 71 percent learning curve (see Harding 1981, 652). Webbink's 1977 survey of the integrated circuit industry notes that interviewed companies believed ε to lie generally in the .32–.52 range, depending on type of devices (Webbink 1977, 52). Note that Baldwin and Krugman appear to have erred in interpreting the report in U.S. Congress (1983) of a 72 percent learning curve—their basis for assuming that $\varepsilon = .28$ when it actually corresponds to $\varepsilon = .47$!

22. Since the unit of time is the (assumed five-year) product cycle, yields after two years correspond to time .4, after three years .6, etc. The data are given in VLSI Research (1990, addendum A). The data in this addendum correspond to a "typical" wafer fab running twenty-five hundred wafer starts per week, run at full capacity over the product life of the 1M DRAM (conversation with Dan Hutcheson, 19 August 1991).

23. If instead γ was set equal to zero, the estimate of ϕ would have risen from thirty-one to thirty-six, but the estimated ε would not have changed.

$$E(t) = E_0 + \frac{Q(t)}{K^\gamma},$$

where $Q(t)$ is cumulative production through time t, and K is capacity. If E_0 is small relative to $Q(t)/K^\gamma$, then

$$\ln[y(t)] = \ln[\phi K^{1-\gamma\varepsilon}] + \varepsilon \ln[Q(t)] + (\varepsilon E_0 K^\gamma)\frac{1}{Q(t)}$$

must hold true.[24] If we choose a period of time in which capacity is approximately constant and fully utilized, then the expressions in K in the above equation may be regarded as part of firm-specific coefficients on two variables—a constant and the inverse of cumulative output—and ε as the coefficient of the log of cumulative output in a regression equation. The equation also provides a simple test for the hypothesis that γ equals zero since, in that case, the coefficient of inverse cumulative output should be constant across firms.

The above equation was estimated using data on cumulative output and current production for the six largest 1M DRAM producers (Toshiba, Hitachi, Fujitsu, NEC, Mitsubishi, and Samsung) over the quarters from 1988:3 to 1989:2, a period of booming demand when trade press accounts suggest that DRAM output was capacity constrained. The point estimate of ε was .65, corresponding to a 36 percent learning curve, confirming other evidence suggesting substantial learning economies.[25] Constraining the coefficient of inverse cumulative output to be the same for all companies reduced the estimate of ε to .51, but a formal statistical test of the corresponding hypothesis that $\gamma = 0$ was inconclusive.[26] In summary, all available data seem to point to a

24. Making use of the fact that $\ln(1 + x) = x$ approximately, for x small.

25. The data used are Dataquest estimates of quarterly output. Reported shipments by Motorola have been added to Toshiba's output and reported shipments by Intel to Samsung's output (since it is believed that most Motorola chips were fabricated by Toshiba and Intel chips "private-labeled" Samsung output during this period). The regression estimated was $\ln y = a_i + \varepsilon \ln Q + b_i 1/Q$, with coefficients a and b varying by producer. The estimate of ε was .52, with a standard error of .07.

26. The results were as follows:

Variable	Unconstrained		With Constraints	
	Estimated Coefficient	Standard Error	Estimated Coefficient	Standard Error
Ln cum. output	.67	.17	.52	.07
Inverse cum. output:				
Toshiba	−.77	1.62	−.13	.05
Hitachi	.27	.42		
NEC	.21	.46		
Fujitsu	.13	.30		

(*continued*)

large yield elasticity with respect to production experience, close to .5, and at least some evidence suggests that absolute cumulative output is not an appropriate choice of "experience" variable.[27] I shall use .49 as my estimate of ε, 31 as my estimate of φ.

3.7.2 The Demand for 1M DRAMs

There is little reliable information on the price elasticity of demand for DRAMs. Wilson, Ashton, and Egan (1980, 126–27) estimate that this price elasticity ranges between −1.8 and −2.3 on the basis of a graph of log bit price versus log bits sold. Finan and Amundsen (1986a, C-18; 1986b, 321) report a −1.8 price elasticity on the basis of a simple regression of log bit price on log bits sold worldwide. Neither of these estimates makes any attempt to control for the effect of variation in the overall level of economic activity on chip demand. Flamm (1985, 130–31) estimates an overall price elasticity of demand for semiconductors used in the computer industry of −1.6, assuming a quality adjustment equivalent to the improvement in bit density observed in DRAMs and chip use in computers fixed in proportion to computer output.

To get as reliable an estimate as possible for 1M DRAM demand, I estimated a loglinear demand function giving quantity shipped of 1M DRAMs as a loglinear function of real 1M DRAM price, real prices for 64K and 256K DRAMs (as possible substitutes), real GNP, and a linear trend included to capture intergenerational "transition" effects.[28] The implicit GNP price defla-

Mitsubishi	.75	.44		
Samsung	−.06	.09		
Constant terms:				
Toshiba	2.69	2.04	4.33	5.78
Hitachi	2.21	1.83	3.94	5.78
NEC	2.42	1.85	4.12	5.99
Fujitsu	2.40	1.79	4.06	6.05
Mitsubishi	2.02	1.84	3.96	5.78
Samsung	2.94	1.62	4.42	6.66
	R^2 = .99, SE = .083		R^2 = .98, SE = .094	

The test statistics for the hypothesis of a common coefficient on inverse cumulative output—F-statistic = 1.89 with 5 and 11 df; Wald chi-square statistic = 9.45 with 5 df—lead us to reject the hypothesis at the 10 percent, but not reject at the 5 percent, significance levels.

27. Estimation of a learning elasticity requires data on either current and cumulative output or current average variable cost and cumulative output. The dubious practice of using price as a proxy for current unit cost—as in Dick (1991)—will almost certainly lead to incorrect results since the simple models of pricing behavior reviewed above suggest that market prices will diverge from either current average or marginal cost.

28. The data on quantity cover quarterly worldwide shipments from 1985:2 to 1989:4 by "merchant" producers and are unpublished Dataquest estimates. Data on DRAM prices are also unpublished quarterly Dataquest estimates of average sales price over this same period. Real (deflated) GNP and the implicit GNP price deflator are taken from Council of Economic Advisers, *Economic Report of the President* (various years).

tor, rebased so that the fourth quarter of 1989 was equal to 1, was used to deflate all monetary values to "real" 1989:4 levels. Deflated GNP and substitute DRAM prices were converted to indices taking on value 1 in 1989:4; as a result, the constant in a regression equation may be interpreted as the "level" of DRAM demand corresponding to 1989:4 values for these variables. The estimated regression equation (with estimated standard errors underneath the various coefficients) was

$$\begin{aligned}\ln(Q) = \underset{(1.02)}{22.97} + \underset{(2.43)}{1.23}\ln(P_{64K}) + \underset{(1.68)}{.63}\ln(P_{256K}) - \underset{(.49)}{1.47}\ln(P_{1M}) \\ + \underset{(.27)}{.29}T - \underset{(36.26)}{1.75}\ln(\text{GNP})\end{aligned}$$

and the estimated price elasticity about -1.5. Dropping the linear time trend variable as a proxy for transitional "generational shift" effects had little effect on the estimated own price elasticity, raising it to -1.55. Interestingly, dropping both GNP and the time trend substantially raised the estimated price elasticity, to -2.1.

On the basis of these results, -1.5 was used as an estimate of 1M DRAM own price elasticity β, and the value 190,000 was used as an estimate of product life-cycle demand "level" α.[29] To transform this demand function to a demand for "gross" fabricated dice (prior to test and assembly losses), it was assumed that net output of tested and finished chips equals .9 times good dice produced in wafer fab.[30] With the functional form assumed, a simple transformation of α is merely substituted for its original value in order to derive the appropriate inverse demand function.[31]

3.7.3 Cost Parameters

Based on estimated 1989 values found in VLSI Research (1990), I estimated r (capital cost per unit product cycle wafer capacity) to be \$240. Variable cost per wafer processed (including materials, labor, and wafer probe test) was estimated to be \$390.[32] Test and assembly costs were assumed to equal \$0.23 for the IC package and about \$0.52 for assembly and final test, for a total of \$0.75 per device produced.[33]

29. Exp(22.97) multiplied by 20 (= 190,000 million) gives demand that would be observed at a 1M DRAM price of \$1.00 over a twenty-quarter (five-year) product cycle, given real output and substitute price levels prevailing in 1989:4.

30. For estimated test and assembly yields in this general neighborhood, see VLSI Research (1990, addendum A) and ICE (1988, 7-16–7-17).

31. That is, $P(\xi z)\xi = (\xi Ny/\alpha)^{1/\beta}\xi = (Ny/\alpha')^{1/\beta}$, where $\alpha' = \alpha\xi^{-(1+\beta)}$.

32. VLSI Research (1990, addendum A) puts material and labor cost at \$380 per wafer processed; I add on a \$10.00 wafer probe test cost based on ICE (1988, 7-9).

33. The package cost comes from conversations with Dan Hutcheson of VLSI Research; the assembly cost is estimated to range from \$0.07 to \$0.20 offshore, or from \$0.10 to \$0.50 per device onshore (in the United States, Europe, and Japan), in ICE (1988, 7-16–7-18). I have used a "typical" value of \$0.32. Final test cost is estimated to be \$0.20 per unit in ICE (1988, 7-18), for a grand total of \$0.75 for package, assembly, and final test.

Overhead is normally a significant part of semiconductor cost. On the basis of aggregate historical data for the period 1981–87, I have assumed \$0.36 in general, administrative, and selling costs for every dollar of direct manufacturing cost.[34] Thus, the estimates for *c, d,* and *r* given above were marked up an additional 36 percent. Table 3.1 shows the assumed empirical parameter values used.

3.8 Baseline Simulations

Table 3.2 gives the optimal values of t_s and K derived from numerical solution of the optimal control problem described above. The roots of a system of two nonlinear equations in two unknowns (eqq. [B1] and [B2] in app. B), or one equation in one unknown (in the case where "full blast" production over the entire product life cycle is the optimal policy, eq. [B2′] in app. B), were sought. Table 3.2 also shows a "gross rent," that is, profits net of all costs other than fixed entry cost *F*, received by each producer. The columns of table 3.2 correspond to different assumed numbers of firms in the industry, the rows to differing assumptions about parameter gamma (γ), which defines the experience variable relevant to learning economies.

Since identical firms are assumed to make up the industry in equilibrium, one may "close" the model by assuming free entry, that firms enter the industry up to the point where gross rent per firm just covers the fixed cost of entry (F). Because we are restricted to an integer number of firms, I define the *equilibrium* as the number of firms where one more entrant reduces rent per firm below entry cost *F*. As a consequence of the integer number of firms, the symmetric equilibrium so defined will generally be characterized by some small, positive rent (net of entry cost F).

I shall assume that the fixed entry cost (primarily total R&D costs for the 1M DRAM) that must be invested prior to mass production of the 1M DRAM runs between roughly \$250 and \$500 million. Thus, for $\gamma = 1$, if entry costs F amounted to \$250 million, we would expect to find fourteen identical firms in the industry, each with facilities capable of producing 4.66 million wafer starts over a five-year product life cycle. With entry costs F of \$500 million, we would expect nine producers, each with the capacity to produce 6.94 million product cycle wafer starts. In either case, the optimal policy would involve full blast production over the entire life cycle. Thus, one immediate observation that emerges from table 3.2 is that, with $\gamma = 1$ (which I argued earlier is a heuristically appealing specification), small differences in fixed entry costs can make a large difference in the industrial structure of the industry (number of firms observed). The same cannot be said for γ much less than 1.

34. The data on which this calculation is based are found in ICE (1988, 7-20). I have excluded R&D and interest expense as elements of "overhead."

Table 3.1 **Empirical Parameter Values**

Parameter		Assumed Value
α_0	"Level" of life-cycle demand for assembled and tested units at $1.00 per chip	190,000 million units
β	Price elasticity of demand	-1.5
ξ	Share of good, yielded chips as fraction of good dice after assembly and final test	.9
α	Level of demand for "gross" fabricated dice (including units rejected at final test)	$\alpha_0 \xi^{-(1+\beta)}$
ϕ	Learning curve wafer fab yield "level" parameter	31
E_0	Initial "experience" at time 0	.01
ε	Experience elasticity of wafer fab yield	.49
γ	(Gamma) parameter determining experience variable	0–1
m	Overhead expense per dollar direct manufacturing cost	.36
d	Package, assembly, and final test cost per fabricated unit	$0.75 $\times$ (1 + m)
c	Fabrication cost per processed wafer	$390 $\times$ (1 + m)
r	Capital cost per unit life-cycle wafer-processing capacity	$240 $\times$ (1 + m)

Table 3.3 summarizes some characteristics of industry equilibria derived from table 3.2 under differing assumptions about fixed entry costs *F.* I have taken *F* as either $500 or $250 million; these values are best interpreted as bracketing a range of feasible values. Alongside the equilibrium number of firms, the Hirschman-Herfindahl index of concentration is also shown.[35]

In order to get at the issue of whether "dumping" is observed, I have calculated observed prices and various cost concepts at one hundred equally spaced points over the product life cycle. One useful cost concept is current short-run marginal cost (SRMC), which in my model happens to be constant at any moment in time, coincides with average variable cost, and is equal to $d + c/w$. This is the incremental cost saved when output is reduced by one unit. Another important cost concept is fully allocated, long-run average cost (LRAC). To define this concept, I have assumed straight-line depreciation in spreading capital and fixed entry costs over the product life cycle: an equal amount of these fixed costs is allocated to every moment in time. Capital and fixed entry costs per unit are then calculated by dividing fixed costs corresponding to time t by the number of units $y(t)$ produced at that moment. Adding average variable cost to average fixed cost, I then have LRAC $= d + c/w + F/y + r/uw$. Multiplying LRAC by output at any instant, and summing these costs at every instant over the product cycle, gives the total cost of producing some time-varying path of output over the entire product cycle.

Table 3.3 shows that, assuming $\gamma = 1$, price falls short of short-run mar-

35. This index is defined as $HHI = \sum_{i=1}^{n} s_i^2$, where s_i is the market share of company i. The index ranges in value from 1, with monopoly, to 0, with a competitive industry composed of an infinite number of equally sized firms. In the special case of N identical firms, this index is just equal to $1/N$.

Table 3.2 **Baseline Simulation Results**

	Number of Firms															
	1	2	3	4	5	6	7	8	9	10	11	12	13	14	15	16
gamma = 1																
K (mil. wafer starts)	13.49	19.08	16.03	13.34	11.31	9.79	8.62	7.69	6.94	6.32	5.8	5.36	4.98	4.66	4.37	4.11
ts	1	1	1	1	1	1	1	1	1	1	1	1	1	1	1	1
Gross rent (mil. $)	29,370	10,380	4,985	2,902	1,894	1,332	988	761	604	491	407	343	293	253	221	195
gamma = .9																
K (mil. wafer starts)	15.46	21.92	18.4	15.73	12.95	11.19	9.84	8.77	7.91	7.2	6.6	6.09				
ts	1	1	1	1	1	1	1	1	1	1	1	1				
Gross rent (mil. $)	32,360	10,370	4,360	2,180	1,191	676	382	204	90	15	−36	−70				
gamma = .8																
K (mil. wafer starts)	16.96	23.91	20.12	16.76	14.23	12.32	10.86	9.68	8.74	7.96	7.3	6.74				
ts	1	1	1	1	1	1	1	1	1	1	1	1				
Gross rent (mil. $)	35,570	10,410	3,752	1,455	477	5	−240	−371	−442	−479	−496	−500				
gamma = .7																
K (mil. wafer starts)	17.683	24.59	20.84	17.48	14.94	13	11.492	10.291								
ts	1	1	1	1	1	1	1	1								
Gross rent (mil. $)	38,840	10,630	3,296	846	−151	−601	−811	−907								

gamma = .68						
K (mil. wafer starts)	17.73	24.56	20.86	17.53	15	13.07
ts	.98	.95	.96	.98	1	1
Gross rent (mil. $)	39,480	10,700	3,232	747	−258	−707
gamma = .6						
K (mil. wafer starts)	17.77	24.4	20.81	17.57	15.11	13.22
ts	.86	.82	.84	.86	.88	.9
Gross rent (mil. $)	41,950	11,050	3,061	428	−619	−1,074
gamma = .5						
K (mil. wafer starts)	17.57	23.82	20.45	17.39	15.04	13.23
ts	.72	.68	.7	.72	.75	.77
Gross rent (mil. $)	44,820	11,630	3,029	197	−924	−1,406
gamma = .3						
K (mil. wafer starts)	16.69	22.06	19.18	16.53	14.46	12.86
ts	.51	.47	.49	.51	.53	.55
Gross rent (mil. $)	49,660	13,020	3,414	187	−1,120	−1,697
gamma = 0						
K (mil. wafer starts)	14.88	19.02	16.82	14.76	13.12	11.83
ts	.31	.28	.29	.31	.33	.34
Gross rent (mil. $)	54,880	15,140	4,492	782	−796	−1,543

Table 3.3 **Characteristics of Symmetric Industry Equilibria**

	F = \$500 Mil.				F = \$250 Mil.			
			Segments of Product Cycle				Segments of Product Cycle	
	No. Firms	Hirschman-Herfindahl	$P < SRMC$	$P < LRAC$	No. Firms	Hirschman-Herfindahl	$P < SRMC$	$P < LRAC$
gamma = *1*	9	.1111	0–.03	0–.32	14	.0714	0–.03	0–.35
gamma = *.9*	6	.1667	0–.03	0–.29	7	.1429	0–.03	0–.29
gamma = *.8*	4	.2500	0–.02	0–.19	5	.2000	0–.02	0–.24
gamma = *.7*	4	.2500	0–.01	0–.17	4	.2500	0–.01	0–.15
				.93–1				.97–1
gamma = *.68*	4	.2500	0–.01	0–.16	4	.2500	0–.01	0–.15
				.87–1				.91–1
gamma = *.6*	3	.3333	0–.01	0–.07	4	.2500	0–.01	0–.12
								.71–1
gamma = *.5*	3	.3333	0–0	0–.05	3	.3333	0–0	0–.05
gamma = *.3*	3	.3333	0–0	0–.02	3	.3333	0–0	0–.02
				.48–.50				.49–.49
gamma = *0*	4	.2500	0–0	0–.01	4	.2500	0–0	0–.01
				.24–.63				.25–.58

ginal cost over the first 3 percent of the product life cycle and falls short of average cost over roughly the first third of the product cycle. With $\gamma = 0$, by way of contrast, price is less than marginal cost only at the very beginning of the product cycle; price is less than average cost over two distinct periods—at the very beginning and over roughly the second quarter of the product life cycle. Indeed, given my assumptions about other parameter values, for all values of γ price falls short of marginal cost only at the very beginning of the product cycle. Further perusal of this table makes clear, however, that the timing of periods of sales at less than average cost is quite sensitive to the specification of the experience variable—depending on γ, such episodes can occur at the beginning of the product cycle, the middle, or the end or in some combination of these sequences.

Table 3.3 also shows that the value of γ makes a big difference in the structure of a symmetric industry equilibrium. With cumulative output per facility ($\gamma = 1$) the relevant experience variable, a relatively large number of firms (nine to fourteen) populate the industry. With γ much below .9, no more than three or four firms make up the industry.

Figure 3.2 shows the path of price, marginal revenue, marginal cost, and average cost over time in the case where entry costs are $250 million and $\gamma = 1$. Figure 3.3 shows the time path for these variables over the product cycle when $\gamma = 0$ instead.

Ironically, the specification of firm behavior in the B-K model—full blast production over the entire product cycle—turns out to be optimal if parameter γ is close to 1 (see table 3.2). The irony arises because the B-K model also specifies absolute cumulative output ($\gamma = 0$) as the experience variable, and, given realistic choices for other parameters, optimal behavior would then require cutting back production to levels below capacity after about the first third of the product cycle.

3.8.1 Reality Checks

How plausible are these simulations, and do they suggest anything about the realism of various assumptions about parameters? One straightforward way to evaluate the model is to compare the predicted industry structure with observed industry structure. Figure 3.4 shows Hirschman-Herfindahl concentration indexes constructed from Dataquest estimates of annual producer shipments of various generations of DRAMs.[36] For virtually all generations of

36. These indexes are calculated from unpublished Dataquest estimates of DRAMs shipped from 1974 through the end of 1989. Note that there were two distinct varieties of 16K DRAM, one with a single-voltage power source, the other requiring dual voltages; each is treated as a separate product in this figure. In calculating concentration indexes for 1M DRAMs, I have allocated Motorola-labeled product to Toshiba (since virtually all Motorola's product over this period is believed to have been assembled from Toshiba-fabricated dice or produced by a Toshiba-Motorola joint venture); 1M DRAMs bearing the Intel label have been assigned to Samsung since it is believed that virtually all Intel's sales over this period were "private labeled" Samsung product. Neither of these adjustments has a particularly significant effect on the pattern of concentration.

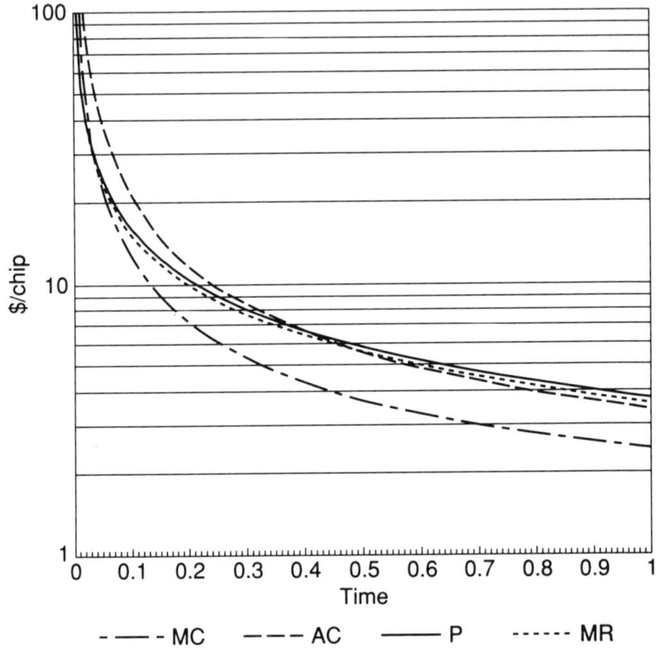

Fig. 3.2 Time profile of costs and prices, simulated equilibrium with gamma = 1 (MC = short-run marginal cost; AC = long-run average cost; P = price; MR = marginal revenue).

DRAM, the concentration index declines sharply from an initially very high level, as one producer after another comes on line with volume production. The index then levels off near .1, rising sharply at the end of the product cycle as producers drop the product line one after another. Although the early phases of the 256K and 1M DRAM may have been somewhat more concentrated than in earlier generations' life cycle, they too seem destined to follow this pattern eventually.

Comparing the Hirschman-Herfindahl indexes associated with my simulations to the pattern depicted in figure 3.4, only the results associated with the specification of cumulative output per facility ($\gamma = 1$) as the experience variable fit reasonably closely. Note that my assumption of symmetric firms means that the associated Hirschman-Herfindahl index of concentration must be constant over time. While conceding that my model is at best an approximation to reality, I conclude that only a γ close to 1 yields predicted behavior that is reasonably close to industrial reality.

Another cut at this question may be had by comparing predicted with actual paths for DRAM prices over time. To do so, I have assumed that a five-year product cycle for the 1M DRAM effectively began in 1988 (although small quantities were produced as far back as late 1985, quantity production did not

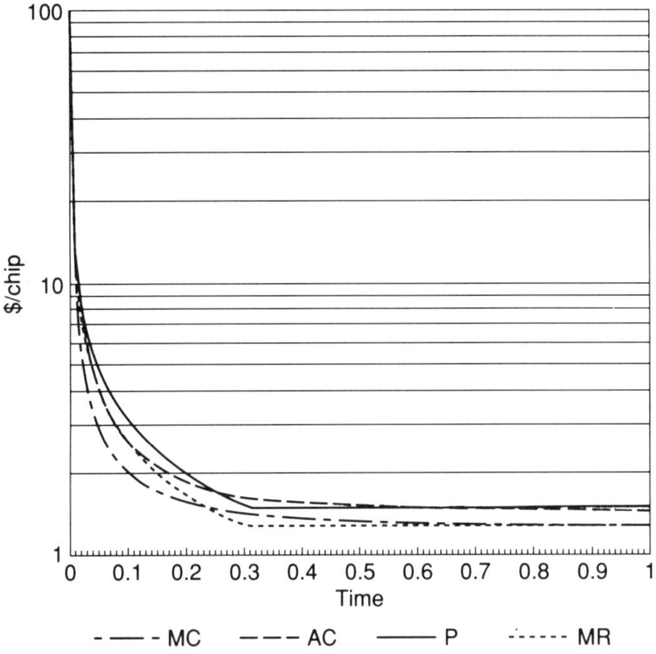

Fig. 3.3 Time profile of costs and prices, simulated equilibrium with gamma = 0 (MC = short-run marginal cost; AC = long-run average cost; P = price; MR = marginal revenue).

really ramp up until 1988). Figure 3.5 charts the actual behavior of one set of estimates of large volume contract prices for 1M DRAMs in the U.S. and Japanese markets through September 1991, along with simulated 1M DRAM price levels associated with an assumed γ equal to 1 and 0, respectively.[37] Note that the period from 1988 through the first quarter of 1989 was a period of extreme shortage in real-world DRAM markets, while the period after late 1989 was one marked by lackluster demand. Given that the early portion of my empirical approximation to the learning curve is probably poorer than in later periods (see the discussion above) and that my assumption of symmetric firms is probably least appropriate in the early stages of the product cycle, I am not surprised to find that the very earliest part of the predicted time path for prices seems least accurate. All things considered, the simulation with $\gamma = 1$ seems to do a reasonable job of tracking real 1M DRAM prices! The simulation with $\gamma = 0$ clearly does not.

Thus, two pieces of evidence—observed and predicted concentration indexes and the time path of DRAM prices—seem to suggest that a value of γ close to 1 provides significantly more realistic predictions than a value close to 0.

A final point to consider is that, historically, the industry folklore holds that

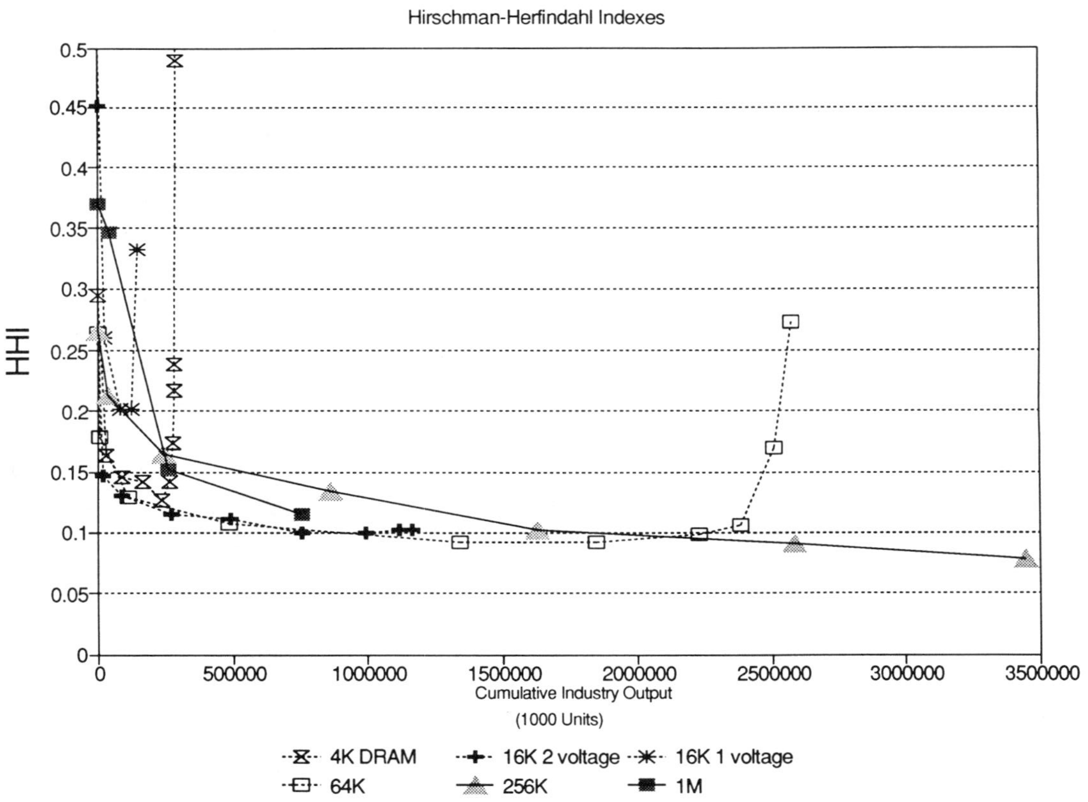

Fig. 3.4 Historical pattern of concentration in DRAM supply

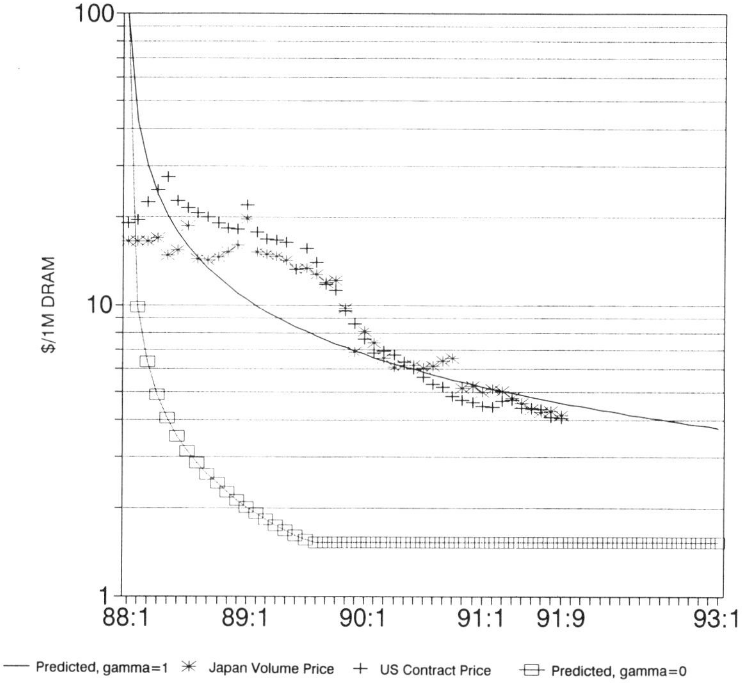

Fig. 3.5 Historical pricing compared with simulated equilibria

DRAM producers have traditionally run their plants at full blast while keeping them in operation, a behavior that is consistent with the simulations presented here. However, beginning in mid-1989, Japanese DRAM producers have announced production cutbacks for DRAMs. This raises three issues that I mention but do not explore in this paper. First, DRAM capacity may be shifted, at some cost, to production of other types of integrated circuits, a possibility not explicitly incorporated into my model. Second, DRAM demand is notoriously cyclical, and the consequences of shifts in demand for optimal producer behavior is, again, not explicitly explored here. Third, production of DRAMs after the conclusion of the 1986 Semiconductor Trade Arrangement was clearly affected by political constraints, may have led to a degree of collusive behavior among producers, and otherwise involved political economic factors not incorporated into my model.

3.8.2 The Dumping Issue

Given empirical values deemed to be plausible in the case of 1M DRAMs, the exercises portrayed in tables 3.2 and 3.3 suggest that a short-run marginal cost test for dumping, as a screening test for potentially predatory behavior, is likely to give only "false positives" (pricing below current marginal cost absent strategic behavior) in the very earliest stages of the product cycle. One might interpret this to mean that a marginal-cost-based dumping test might be defensible if some sort of "exception" to a marginal-cost-based pricing standard is granted when a new product is first introduced. But it is not clear how robust this conclusion is to changes in empirical parameters used in my simulations; further sensitivity analysis might shed greater light on this question.

The same cannot be said for an average cost test for predation. Depending on parameter values, episodes of below-average-cost pricing can pop up in virtually any part of the product life cycle, even when producer behavior is entirely nonstrategic.

Indeed, while the simulations depicted in tables 3.2 and 3.3 all show an episode of below-average-cost pricing at the beginning of the product cycle, possibly followed by a later episode, it would be incorrect to assert that below-average-cost pricing will always necessarily be observed at the beginning of the product life cycle.[38] Figure 3.6 shows that, by artfully changing a single parameter (in this case, by greatly raising initial yields, making $E_0 = 500$), assuming $\gamma = 1$ and F = \$250 million, one arrives at a symmetric industry equilibrium where price *never* falls below marginal cost and price falls below average cost only during the last half of the product cycle.[39]

3.9 Conclusions

In recent years, pricing below a constructed long-run average cost has become the principal grounds for applying the "dumping" laws to U.S. imports of foreign products. While this practice has little obvious economic defense, it is possible to argue that a test based on marginal cost might serve as a useful screen for potentially predatory behavior by foreign exporters. However, in the presence of learning economies, such as are thought to be present in many high-tech industries, including semiconductors, below-marginal-cost pricing can be rational even in the absence of strategic behavior, such as predation.

In this paper, I have developed a more realistic model of pricing over the life cycle of a product in which both fixed costs and learning economies are significant. Using empirically plausible parameters for production of 1M DRAMs, and assuming nonstrategic producer behavior, I have found that below-marginal-cost pricing is likely to be observed only in the very earliest stages of the product cycle.

The analysis has also shed considerable light on other facets of pricing and production over the product life cycle. A specification of learning economies

37. These data are monthly averages of Dataquest estimates of average contract prices in these markets. The data are reported in *Computer Reseller News* (various issues). For more on the strengths and weaknesses of these data and a thorough discussion of the segmented spot and contract markets in which DRAMs are sold, see Flamm (in press, a).

38. Dick (1991, 144–46) proposes this behavior.

39. The symmetric equilibrium depicted in this figure corresponds to eighteen producers, each with a capacity of 3.88 million life-cycle wafer starts, producing full blast over the entire product cycle.

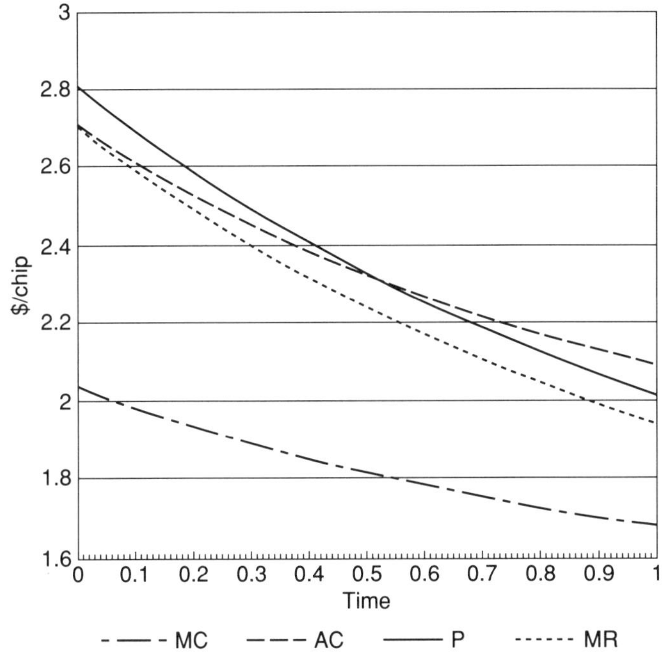

Fig. 3.6 Time profile of costs and prices, simulation with very high initial yield (MC = short-run marginal cost; AC = long-run average cost; P = price; MR = marginal revenue).

based on cumulative output per facility as the "experience" variable was found to yield results that were considerably more realistic than other possible—and popular—specifications. Contrary to popular belief, below-average-cost pricing does not necessarily have to occur near the beginning of the product cycle.

The model presented here appears to produce fairly realistic predictions of industry structure and pricing behavior when used with empirically plausible parameters. Interesting extensions of this work include considering the possibility of strategic, noncooperative behavior on the part of producers as well as cooperative or collusive behavior. Policy issues that might be explored include the effect of various government policies on industry structure and some measure of aggregate national welfare.[40]

Appendix A

Let $y(t)$ be company's output at time t, $x(t)$ output of other companies, F fixed cost of entry, $R[y(t), x(t)]$ company's revenues at time t, d assembly and test

40. These issues are explored in Flamm (in press, b).

cost per chip, c wafer-processing cost, $u(t)$ utilization rate at time t, K fixed capacity, r capital cost per unit capacity, w yielded good chips per wafer, Q cumulative company output, γ experience specification parameter $(0 \leq \gamma \leq 1)$, and E "yield relevant" experience $(E_0 + Q/K^\gamma)$.

1. The general problem described in the text is

$$\max_{u(t),K} \int_0^1 \{R[y(t), x(t)] - F - dy(t) - cu(t)K - rK\}dt,$$
$$\text{where } y(t) = u(t)w(E)K,$$
$$\text{s.t. } \dot{E} = \frac{y(t)}{K^\gamma} = u(t)w(E)K^{1-\gamma}, \quad w_E > 0,$$
$$u \in [0, 1], \quad w > 0.$$

Form the Hamiltonian (suppressing the arguments of functions for notational simplicity)

$$H = R - F - dy - cuK - rK + \delta\frac{y}{K^\gamma},$$

with

$$\dot{\delta} = -\frac{\partial H}{\partial E} = -\frac{\partial H}{\partial y}\frac{\partial y}{\partial E} = -(R_y - d + \frac{\delta}{K^\gamma})uw_E K,$$

where R_y denotes $\partial R/\partial y$, marginal revenue. By the maximum principle, choose $u(t)$ to maximize H, given $u \in [0, 1]$, with $\delta(1) = 0$ (transversality condition). There are three possible cases to consider.

$$0 < u < 1, \quad \frac{\partial H}{\partial u} = \left(R_y - d + \frac{\delta}{K^\gamma}\right)\frac{\partial y}{\partial u} - cK = 0,$$

(A1a)
$$\left(R_y - d + \frac{\delta}{K^\gamma} - \frac{c}{w}\right)Kw = 0,$$
$$R_y - d - \frac{c}{w} + \frac{\delta}{K^\gamma} = 0, \quad \dot{\delta} = -\frac{c}{w}uw_E K < 0.$$

At an interior maximum, we also have a second-order necessary condition:

$$\frac{\partial^2 H}{\partial u^2} = R_{yy}(Kw)^2 \leq 0.$$

(A1b)
$$u = 1, \quad R_y - d - \frac{c}{w} + \frac{\delta}{K^\gamma} \geq 0,$$
$$\dot{\delta} = -\left(R_y - d + \frac{\delta}{K^\gamma}\right)w_E K < 0,$$

(A1c)
$$u = 0, \quad R_y - d - \frac{c}{w} + \frac{\delta}{K^\gamma} \leq 0, \quad \dot{\delta} = 0.$$

Together with the transversality condition, this implies that $\delta \geq 0$ everywhere.

Along an interior segment, that is, possibility (A1a),

$$R_y = d + \frac{c}{w} - \frac{\delta}{K^{\gamma}},$$

(A1d) $$(\dot{R}_y) = \left(-\frac{c}{w^2}w_E\frac{y}{K^{\gamma}}\right) - \frac{\dot{\delta}}{K^{\gamma}} = -c\frac{w_E}{w^2}uwK^{1-\gamma} - \left(-cu\frac{w_E K^{1-\gamma}}{w}\right) = 0,$$

which means that R_y is constant along an interior segment.

The above analysis holds for any given K. Full optimization requires that optimal parameter K must be chosen to satisfy (see Leitmann 1966, 98–100):

$$\int_0^1 \frac{\partial H[\delta(t), K, u^*(t), E^*(t)]}{\partial K} dt = 0,$$

where $u^*(t)$ is the optimal utilization rate and E^* the trajectory of experience variable E corresponding to $u^*(t)$. Then

$$\int_0^1 \left[\left(R_y - d + \frac{\delta}{K^{\gamma}}\right)\frac{\partial y}{\partial K} + R_x\frac{\partial x}{\partial K} - \gamma\frac{\delta}{K^{1+\gamma}}y - cu - r\right]dt = 0.$$

I will assume nonstrategic behavior—the firm perceives $\partial x/\partial K = 0$—so

$$\int_0^1 \left[\left(R_y - d - \frac{c}{w} + \frac{\delta}{K^{\gamma}}\right)uw - \gamma\frac{\delta}{K^{\gamma}}uw - r\right]dt = 0.$$

The expression in brackets above $= 0$ if u interior, ≥ 0 if $u = 1$, and ≤ 0 if $uz = 0$.

Note that this shows that the expression in brackets must be positive, and $u = 1$, over some interval if optimal $K > 0$ (and any output is produced). The identical trajectory of output (and variable profit) could otherwise be produced at lower cost by choosing some smaller $\bar{K}$, then choosing utilization rate $\bar{u}(t) = (K/\bar{K})u(t) < 1$.

2. The above is perfectly general. To explicitly solve for an optimal path, I add additional structure and make the following further assumptions: (i) Industry inverse demand (and firm revenue function R) and learning function w are twice continuously differentiable functions in all their arguments. (ii) There are N firms. (iii) Industry revenues are an autonomous, strictly concave function of industry output.

Let $\bar{R}(z)$ be industry revenues, $z(t)$ industry output ($z[t] = x[t] + y[t]$). Then $\bar{R}(z) = P(z)z$, where $P(z)$ is industry inverse demand.

I will assume $\bar{R}_{zz} = P''z + 2P' < 0$ for $z \geq 0$ (i.e., $\bar{R}$ strictly concave). So

(A2a) $$P'' < -\frac{2P'}{z} \quad \text{for } z \geq 0.$$

I have also assumed that $R[y(t), x(t)]$ is autonomous, not a function of time other than through $x(t)$ and $y(t)$. Since output is a perfectly homogeneous commodity, with a single market price assumed,

$$R[y(t), x(t)] = P(x + y)y,$$
$$R_y = P'\frac{dz}{dy}y \text{ p}+ P = P'(1 + \lambda)y + P,$$

with λ (= dx/dy) the conjectural variation perceived by the firm. I shall regard λ as a constant varying between 0 and $N - 1$. These limits parametrize λ as lying between two useful limiting cases of industrial organization: (i) $\lambda = 0$ with Cournot competition; (ii) $\lambda = N - 1$ with a constant market share cartel made up of N identical firms.

I will be assuming $\lambda = 0$ for the moment, but I will develop my analysis of optimal utilization rates including the case of a constant market share cartel.

Note that

$$R_{yy} = P''\left(\frac{dz}{dy}\right)^2 y + 2P'\frac{dz}{dy} = (1 + \lambda)[P''(1 + \lambda)y + 2P']$$
$$< (1 + \lambda)2P'\left[1 - \frac{y}{z}(1 + \lambda)\right],$$

using (A2a). Now, consider two cases: (i) Under Cournot competition, $\lambda = 0$, since

$$\frac{y}{z} \leq 1, \text{ then } 1 - \frac{y}{z}(1 + \lambda) > 0, \quad \text{and} \quad R_{yy} < 0.$$

(ii) Under N identical firms in a collusive, fixed-market-share cartel, $\lambda = N - 1$,

$$\frac{y}{z} = \frac{1}{N}, \quad 1 - \frac{y}{z}(1 + \lambda) = 0, \quad \text{and} \quad R_{yy} < 0.$$

In these two cases, firm revenue R is strictly concave in y, with $R_{yy} < 0$ everywhere. Now, since functions R and w are assumed twice continuously differentiable in their arguments, so too will be the Hamiltonian H, with $H_{uu} = R_{yy}(Kw)^2 < 0$. H is strictly concave in u. For given K, then, the necessary conditions for optimal u are also sufficient to guarantee that we are maximizing H. More important, the strict concavity of H in u and the constant bounds constraining feasible u mean that we may invoke an appropriate theorem to conclude that optimal u is continuous in other arguments of H.[41] Since

41. For example, a result proved by Debreu, found in Lancaster (1987, 349–50), or a theorem due to Fiacco, cited in McCormick (1983, 245–46). More directly, we may note that the strict concavity of H in u means that, at every moment, the $u(t)$ that maximizes H is unique. Since the set of feasible values from which $u(t)$ is chosen is compact, we may invoke a theorem (6.1) from Fleming and Rishel (1975, 75) to conclude that $u(t)$ is a continuous function of time.

the other arguments of H are continuous functions of time, u must also be a continuous function of time as well.

Note also that $u(t)$ is a continuously differentiable function of time within an interior segment. This is a consequence of the linearity of $\dot{E}$ in u and the strict concavity of the Hamiltonian.[42]

Next I restrict discussion to symmetric industry equilibria, that is, with the industry made up of identical firms. In this case, I will show that, along an interior segment of such an equilibrium, $\dot{u} < 0$.

We already know (see [A1d]) that, along an interior segment,

$$\begin{aligned}(\dot{R}_y) &= 0 \\ &= \frac{d}{dt}[P'(1 + \lambda)y + P] \\ &= \dot{y}[P''(1 + \lambda)Ny + P'(1 + \lambda) + P'N].\end{aligned}$$

Is it possible that the expression in brackets equals zero? If

$$P''(1 + \lambda)Ny + P'(1 + \lambda) + P'N = 0,$$

$$P'' = -\frac{P'\left(1 + \dfrac{N}{1 + \lambda}\right)}{z} > -\frac{P'}{z}(2)$$

since $1 + N/(1 + \lambda) \geq 2$. But this contradicts (A2a) and our assumption that $\bar{R}_{zz} < 0$. So we must have $\dot{y} = 0$.

Now

$$y = uKw, \quad \dot{y} = \dot{u}Kw + uKw_E\frac{y}{K^\gamma} = 0,$$

which can only be true if $\dot{u} < 0$.

Since u is continuous over time, when $u = 0$, it cannot jump to 1. Indeed, u cannot even become positive since $\dot{u} < 0$ as soon as $u > 0$. So, when $u = 0$, the optimal policy must remain $u = 0$.

If we add the further assumption that $\bar{R}_z(0)$ exceeds current marginal cost at time 0 (as must be true with constant elasticity < -1), then, because $y/z = 1/N$,

42. Consider optimal control $u^*(t)$ over some interior segment $t_1 < t < t_2$. Because of the strict concavity of the Hamiltonian, a local interior maximum of H must also be a global maximum of H with no constraints on control $u(t)$. That is, optimal control $u^*(t)$ over this interval must also be the optimal control for the problem

$$\max_{u(t)} \int_{t_1}^{t_2} [R(x, y) - F - dy - cuK - rK]dt,$$

subject to the initial and terminal conditions that $E(t)$ take on the values at times t_1 and t_2 associated with optimal control $u^*(t)$ in the original problem, but with no bounds on control $u(t)$. As Fleming and Rishel (1975, corollary 6.1, p. 77) note, the linearity of the equations of motion in the control variable and the concavity of the Hamiltonian are sufficient to guarantee that the optimal control is a continuously differentiable function of time for this subproblem (with no constraints on $u[t]$).

$$R_y = \bar{R}_z - P'z\left[1 - \frac{y}{z}(1 + \lambda)\right] \geq \bar{R}_z,$$

and (A1c) cannot hold, it can never be optimal for $u = 0$.

Note the role of learning economies in this model. If $w_E = 0$ everywhere, (no learning) δ must be constant and equal to zero and optimal u constant over the product cycle. Optimal capacity choice implies that $R_y - d - c/w$ must be greater than zero, and therefore $u = 1$. The first-order conditions then require that K be chosen so variable profit generated by a marginal unit of capital $[R_y - d - c/w]w$ just covers the cost of capital (r), and all available capacity is fully utilized over the entire product life cycle.

Appendix B

Specification of the Demand Curve

Let inverse demand be given by $P = (z/\alpha)^{1/\beta}$ with $z = x + y$ total industry output and β the price elasticity of demand. Consider industry sales, given by

$$\bar{R} = \left(\frac{z}{\alpha}\right)^{1/\beta} z, \quad -1 < \frac{1}{\beta} < 0,$$

$$\bar{R}_z = \left(\frac{1}{\beta} + 1\right)\left(\frac{z}{\alpha}\right)^{1/\beta} > 0,$$

$$\bar{R}_{zz} = \left(\frac{1}{\beta} + 1\right)\frac{1}{\beta}\alpha^{-1/\beta} z^{1/\beta - 1} < 0,$$

and note that $\lim_{z \to 0} \bar{R}_z = \infty$.

Now, marginal revenue for any individual firm is given by

$$R_y = P'\left(1 + \frac{dx}{dy}\right)y + P = P\left[\frac{P'zy}{Pz}\left(1 + \frac{dx}{dy}\right) + 1\right]$$

$$= P\left[\frac{1}{\beta}\frac{y}{z}(1 + \lambda) + 1\right],$$

with $\lambda = \frac{dx}{dy}$ defining the conjectural variation:

if $\lambda = N - 1$, we have a constant market share cartel;
if $\lambda = 0$, we have Cournot competition.

In addition, I assume that the industry is made up of N identical firms. In symmetric industry equilibrium, each firm has market share $y/z = 1/N$. Let $\sigma = (1 + \lambda)/N$. So

$$R_y = P\left(\frac{\sigma}{\beta} + 1\right),$$

$$\text{where} \quad \sigma = \begin{cases} 1, \text{ cartel;} \\ 1/N, \text{ Cournot.} \end{cases}$$

Thus, in an industry made up of N identical firms,

$$R_y = \left(\frac{N\,y}{\alpha}\right)^{1/\beta}\left(\frac{\sigma}{\beta} + 1\right).$$

Specification of Learning Economies and Output

Let $w = \phi E^{\varepsilon}$, with

$$\dot{E} = \frac{y}{K^{\gamma}}, \quad E(0) = E_0, \quad 0 \leq \varepsilon \leq 1, \quad 0 \leq \gamma \leq 1.$$

Initial yield (ϕE_0^{ε}) is independent of capacity choice. We are mainly interested in two specific cases: $\gamma = 0$ (learning depends on absolute production experience) and $\gamma = 1$ (learning depends on experience per unit capacity, or facility). Then $y = \phi E^{\varepsilon} u K$.

a) Over the interval from 0 to t_s, where $u = 1$,

$$\dot{E} = \frac{y}{K^{\gamma}} = \phi E^{\varepsilon} K^{1-\gamma}.$$

Solving this differential equation, we have

$$E(t, K) = \left[E_0^{1-\varepsilon} + K^{1-\gamma}\,\phi t(1 - \varepsilon)\right]^{1/1-\varepsilon},$$
$$y(t, K) = \phi E(t, K)^{\varepsilon} K.$$

We also know

$$\dot{\delta} = -\frac{\partial H}{\partial E} = -\left(R_y - d + \frac{\delta}{K^{\gamma}}\right) w_E K = -\left(R_y - d + \frac{\delta}{K^{\gamma}}\right)\varepsilon\phi E^{\varepsilon - 1} K,$$

which can be rewritten as the linear monic differential equation

$$\dot{\delta} + f_1(t, K)\delta = f_2(t, K),$$

with

$$f_1(t, K) = \varepsilon\phi E(t, K)^{\varepsilon - 1} K^{1-\gamma}, \quad f_2(t, K) = -[R_y(t, K) - d] f_1(t, K) K^{\gamma}.$$

Solving for δ, for some t in the interval $(0, t_s)$, given boundary value $\delta(t_s) = \delta_{ts}$, we have

$$\delta(t) = \frac{\delta_{ts} + \int_{ts}^{t} f_2(\tau) e^{\int_{t_s}^{\tau} f_1(\mu) d\mu} d\tau}{e^{\int_{t_s}^{t} f_1(\tau) d\tau}}.$$

Define function $\delta_B(t, t_s, K, \delta_{ts})$ by the right-hand side of this equation. With some difficulty, and a great deal of tedious algebra, we can then integrate this expression and have

$$\delta_B(t, t_s, K, \delta_{ts})$$

$$= \frac{\delta_{ts} + \frac{\beta + \sigma}{\beta + 1}\left(\frac{\phi K N}{\alpha}\right)^{1/\beta} E(t_s, K)^{\varepsilon/\beta}\left\{1 - \left[\frac{E(t, K)}{E(t_s, K)}\right]^{\varepsilon/\beta + \varepsilon}\right\} K^{\gamma}}{\left[\frac{E(t, K)}{E(t_s, K)}\right]^{\varepsilon}}$$

$$- \frac{d\left(1 - \left[\frac{E(t, K)}{E(t_s, K)}\right]^{\varepsilon}\right) K^{\gamma}}{\left[\frac{E(t, K)}{E(t_s, K)}\right]^{\varepsilon}}$$

b) Over the interval from t_s to 1, optimal u is set such that $y(t, k) = y(t_s, k)$, that is, constant output. $E(t_s, k)$ and $y(t_s, k)$ are given by expressions in the last section. Over the interval from t_s to 1, then,

$$\dot{E} = \frac{y(t_s, K)}{K^{\gamma}}, \quad \text{so } E(t, k) = (t - t_s)\frac{y(t_s, K)}{K^{\gamma}} + E(t_s, K);$$

$$E(t, K) = (t - t_s)\phi E(t_s, K)^{\varepsilon} K^{1-\gamma} + E(t_s, K) = E(t_s, K)[1 + Q(t, t_s, K)],$$
$$\text{where} \quad Q(t, t_s, K) = \phi E(t_s, K)^{\varepsilon - 1} K^{1-\gamma}(t - t_s),$$

incremental experience from time t_s to time t, relative to experience at t_s;

$$\dot{\delta} = -\frac{cuw_E K}{w} = -\frac{cyw_E}{w^2} = -c\frac{\phi^2 E(t_s, K)^{\varepsilon} K \varepsilon E(t, K)^{\varepsilon - 1}}{\phi^2 E(t, K)^{2\varepsilon}} = f_3(t; t_s, K),$$

$$\text{where } f_3(t; t_s, K) = \frac{-c\varepsilon E(t_s, K)^{\varepsilon} K}{E(t, K)^{\varepsilon + 1}}$$

Conditional on assumed switchpoint t_s, the solution to this differential equation can be written as

$$\delta(t) - \delta(1) = \int_1^t f_3(\tau; t_s, K) d\tau,$$

or, making use of the fact that $\delta(1) = 0$ (transversality condition), define function δ_E as

$$\delta_E(t;\, t_s,\, K) = \int_1^t f_3(\tau;\, t_s,\, K)d\tau$$

$$= \frac{cK^\gamma}{\phi[E(t_s,\, K) + \phi K^{1-\gamma}(t - t_s)E(t_s,\, K)^\varepsilon]^\varepsilon}$$

$$- \frac{cK^\gamma}{\phi[E(t_s,\, K) + \phi K^{1-\gamma}(1 - t_s)E(t_s,\, K)^\varepsilon]^\varepsilon}$$

$$= \frac{cK^\gamma}{\phi E(t_s,\, K)^\varepsilon}\left\{\frac{1}{[1 + Q(t,\, t_s,\, K)]^\varepsilon} - \frac{1}{[1 + Q(1,\, t_s,\, K)]^\varepsilon}\right\}.$$

In particular, we can solve for $\delta_E(t_s;\, t_s,\, k)$, that is, the value of δ at t_s, which, given some assumed t_s, solves the equation of motion over an interior segment and the transversality condition at time 1. In this special case, we have

$$\delta_E(t_s;\, t_s,\, K) = \frac{cK^\gamma}{\phi E(t_s,\, K)^\varepsilon}\left\{1 - \frac{1}{[1 + Q(1,\, t_s,\, K]^\varepsilon}\right\}.$$

Solution of the Model

Our specification has ruled out the possibility that optimal $u = 0$. The optimal path for u will consist of a capacity-constrained ($u = 1$) segment through time t_s, possibly followed by an interior segment. For the moment, assume that $t_s < 1$.

Case 1: $t_s < 1$

At t_s, we also know that $u(t)$ will be entering an interior segment, so

$$\frac{\delta}{K^\gamma} = -\left[R_y(t_s,\, K) - d - \frac{c}{\phi E(t_s,\, K)^\varepsilon}\right]$$

must be true at t_s. Thus, for given K, optimal t_s must satisfy

$$\frac{\delta_E(t_s;\, t_s,\, K)}{K^\gamma} + \left[R_y(t_s,\, K) - d - \frac{c}{\phi E(t_s,\, K)^\varepsilon}\right] = 0,$$

or, substituting,

$$\text{(B1)}\quad \frac{-c}{\phi[E(t_s,\, K) + \phi K^{1-\gamma}(1 - t_s)E(t_s,\, K)^\varepsilon]^\varepsilon} + \left[\frac{N\phi E(t_s,\, K)^\varepsilon K}{\alpha}\right]^{1/\beta}\left(\frac{\sigma}{\beta} + 1\right) - d = 0.$$

This is just the condition that marginal revenue equal current marginal cost at terminal time 1. If K is chosen to nonstrategically maximize profits, optimal K must satisfy

$$\int_0^1 \left\{ \left[R_y(t, K) - d - \frac{c}{\phi E(t, K)^{\varepsilon}} + \frac{\delta}{K^{\gamma}} \right] u\phi E(t, K)^{\varepsilon} - \gamma \frac{\delta}{K^{\gamma}} u\phi E(t, K)^{\varepsilon} \right\} dt - r = 0.$$

Since the expression in brackets is 0 after t_s and u is 1 before t_s, this can be written as

$$\int_{ts}^{1} -\gamma \frac{\delta}{K^{\gamma}} u\phi E(t, K)^{\varepsilon} dt + \int_0^{ts} \left\{ [R_y(t, K) - d] \phi E(t, K)^{\varepsilon} + \frac{\delta}{K^{\gamma}} \phi E(t, K)^{\varepsilon} (1 - \gamma) \right\} dt - ct_s - r = 0.$$

We may substitute for δ with the function δ_B and δ_E, described earlier. Noting that

$$u(t) = \frac{y(t_s, K)}{K\phi E(t, K)^{\varepsilon}} = \frac{\phi E(t_s, K)^{\varepsilon} K}{K\phi E(t, K)^{\varepsilon}} = \frac{E(t_s, K)^{\varepsilon}}{E(t, K)^{\varepsilon}} = \frac{1}{[1 + Q(t, t_s, K)]^{\varepsilon}}$$

over the interval from t_s to 1, we can solve analytically for the first integral above, so, substituting,

$$\text{(B2)} \qquad -\frac{c\gamma(1 - t_s)}{(1 - \varepsilon)} \left\{ \frac{\dfrac{1}{Q(1, t_s, K)} + \varepsilon}{[1 + Q(1, t_s, K)]^{\varepsilon}} - \frac{1}{Q(1, t_s, K)} \right\} + \int_0^{t_s} \left([R_y(t, K) - d] \cdot \phi E(t, K)^{\varepsilon} + \delta_B \left\{ t, t_s, K, -\left[R_y(t_s, K) + d + \frac{c}{\phi E(t_s, K)^{\varepsilon}} \right] K^{\gamma} \right\} \cdot (1 - \gamma) \frac{\phi E(t, K)^{\varepsilon}}{K^{\gamma}} \right) dt - ct_s - r = 0.$$

An optimal t_s and K choice, then, must solve equations (B1) and (B2).

Case 2: $t_s = 1$

The other possibility is that $t_s = 1$ and producers fully utilize available capacity throughout the product life cycle. Since there is no interior segment, equation (B1) does not have to hold at t_s. Instead, the transversality condition means that $\delta(t_s) = 0$, so $\delta_B(t, 1, K, 0)$ gives the value of $\delta(t)$ at any time t. Incorporating this into the first-order condition for optimal K, I then have

$$\text{(B2}'\text{)}\quad \int_0^1 \left\{ [R_y(t,\, K) - d] \cdot \phi E(t,\, K)^{\varepsilon} + \delta_B(t,\, 1,\, K,\, 0) \cdot (1 - \gamma)\, \phi \frac{E(t,\, K)^{\varepsilon}}{K} \right\} dt - c - r = 0,$$

which can be solved for optimal K.

In searching for Cournot equilibria, then, attempts were made to solve (B1) and (B2) for optimal (t_s, K) and (B2′) for optimal K (assuming $t_s = 1$).

Industry Profits

Total rents per firm, gross of fixed entry cost F, earned in an industry made up of N identical firms can be calculated as (for given optimal t_s and K)

$$\int_0^1 \left(\left\{ \left[\frac{Ny(t,\, K)}{\alpha} \right]^{1/\beta} - d \right\} y(t,\, K) - cu(t)K - rK \right) dt$$

or

$$\int_0^{ts} \left(\left\{ \left[\frac{Ny(t,\, K)}{\alpha} \right]^{1/\beta} - d \right\} y(t,\, K) \right) dt + \left\{ \left[\frac{Ny(t_s,\, K)}{\alpha} \right]^{1/\beta} - d \right\} y(t_s,\, K)(1 - t_s)$$

$$- cKt_s - \frac{cK(1 - t_s)}{(1 - \varepsilon)} \left\{ \frac{\dfrac{1}{Q(1,\, t_s,\, K)} + 1}{[1 + Q(1,\, t_s,\, K)]^{\varepsilon}} - \frac{1}{Q(1,\, t_s,\, K)} \right\} 3 - rK.$$

References

Baldwin, Richard E., and Paul R. Krugman. 1988. Market access and international competition: A simulation study of 16K random access memories. In *Empirical methods for international trade,* ed. Robert C. Feenstra. Cambridge, Mass.: MIT Press.

Deardorff, Alan V. 1989. Economic perspectives on antidumping law. In *Antidumping law and practice: A comparative study,* ed. J. H. Jackson and E. A. Vermulst. Ann Arbor: University of Michigan Press.

Dick, Andrew R. 1991. Learning by doing and dumping in the semiconductor industry. *Journal of Law and Economics* 34 (April): 133–59.

Dixit, Avinash K. 1986. Comparative statics for oligopoly. *International Economic Review* 27 (February): 107–22.

Finan, William F., and Chris B. Amundsen. 1986a. An analysis of the effects of targeting on the competitiveness of the U.S. semiconductor industry. Study prepared for the Office of the U.S. Special Trade Representative, the U.S. Department of Commerce, and the U.S. Department of Labor by Quick Finan & Associates, Washington, D.C.

———. 1986b. Modelling U.S.-Japan competition in semiconductors. *Journal of Policy Modeling* 8(3): 305–26.

Flamm, Kenneth. 1985. Internationalization in semiconductors. In *The global factory: Foreign assembly in international trade,* ed. J. Grunwald and K. Flamm. Washington, D.C.: Brookings.

———. In press, a. Measurement of DRAM prices: Technology and market structure. In *Price measurements and their uses,* ed. M. F. Foss, M. Manser, and A. Young. Chicago: University of Chicago Press.

———. In press, b. *Mismanaged trade? Strategic policy and the semiconductor industry.* Washington, D.C.: Brookings.

Fleming, Wendell H., and Raymond W. Rishel. 1975. *Deterministic and stochastic optimal control.* New York: Springer.

Fudenberg, Drew, and Jean Tirole. 1983. Learning by doing and market performance. *Bell Journal of Economics* 14 (Autumn): 522–30.

Harding, William E. 1981. Semiconductor manufacturing in IBM, 1957 to the present: A perspective. *IBM Journal of Research and Development* 25 (September): 647–58.

Helpman, Elhanan, and Paul R. Krugman. 1989. *Trade policy and market structure.* Cambridge, Mass.: MIT Press.

Horlick, Gary N. 1989. The United States antidumping system. In *Antidumping law and practice: A comparative study,* ed. J. H. Jackson and E. A. Vermulst. Ann Arbor: University of Michigan Press.

Integrated Circuit Engineering (ICE). 1988. *Mid-term 1988.* Scottsdale, Ariz.: ICE.

Kreps, D. M., and J. A. Scheinkman. 1983. Quantity precommitment and Bertrand competition yield Cournot outcomes. *Bell Journal of Economics* (Autumn): 326–37.

Kreps, D. M., and R. Wilson. 1982. Reputation and imperfect information. *Journal of Economic Theory* 27:253–79.

Krishna, Kala 1988. Market access and international competition: A simulation study of the 16K random access memories: Comment. In *Empirical methods for international trade,* ed. Robert C. Feenstra. Cambridge, Mass.: MIT Press.

Lancaster, Kelvin. 1987. *Mathematical economics.* New York: Dover.

Leitmann, George. 1966. *An introduction to optimal control.* New York: McGraw-Hill.

McCormick, Garth P. 1983. *Nonlinear programming: Theory, algorithms, and applications.* New York: Wiley.

Micron Technology. 1985. Petition for the imposition of antidumping duty. Submission to the U.S. Department of Commerce and the U.S. International Trade Commission, Washington, D.C., 21 June.

Milgrom, P. 1987. "Predatory pricing." In *The new Palgrave: A dictionary of economics,* ed. J. Eatwell, M. Milgate, and P. Newman. London: Macmillan.

Milgrom, P., and J. Roberts. 1982. Limit pricing and entry under incomplete information. *Econometrica* 50:443–59.

Nivola, Pietro S. 1990. Trade policy: Refereeing the playing field. In *A question of balance: The president, Congress, and foreign policy,* ed. Thomas E. Mann. Washington, D.C.: Brookings.

Noyce, Robert N. 1977. Microelectronics. *Scientific American* 237 (September): 62–69.

Ordover, Janusz A., and Garth Saloner. 1989. Predation, monopolization, and antitrust. In *Handbook of industrial organization,* vol. 1, ed. R. Schmalensee and R. D. Willig. Amsterdam: North-Holland.

Shapiro, Carl. 1989. Theories of oligopoly behavior. In *handbook of industrial organization,* vol. 1, ed. R. Schmalensee and R. D. Willig. Amsterdam: North-Holland.

Spence, A. Michael. 1981. The learning curve and competition. *Bell Journal of Economics* 12:49–70.

Tirole, Jean. 1988. *The theory of industrial organization.* Cambridge, Mass.: MIT Press.
U.S. Congress. Office of Technology Assessment. 1983. *International competitiveness in electronics.* Washington, D.C.: U.S. Government Printing Office.
VLSI Research. 1990. *Megabit manufacturing economics.* San Jose, Calif.: VLSI Research.
Waller, Larry. 1988. DRAM users and makers: Shotgun marriages kick in. *Electronics,* November, 29–30.
Webbink, Douglas W. 1977. *Staff report on the semiconductor industry.* Washington, D.C.: Federal Trade Commission, Bureau of Economics.
Wilson, Robert W., Peter K. Ashton, and Thomas P. Egan. 1980. *Innovation, competition, and government policy in the semiconductor industry.* Lexington, Mass.: Lexington.

Comment Yun-Wing Sung

During my flight to the conference, I was reading *Newsweek* magazine, in which I came across Michael Boskin's comment on potato chips and computer chips: "Potato chips, computer chips, they're all chips. What's the difference?" I agree wholeheartedly with Boskin because I know nothing about computer chips, and I beg your forgiveness if I mix them up with potato chips.

I enjoy Kenneth Flamm's paper very much. Flamm's model has the advantages of both the Spence model, which explains forward pricing, and the Baldwin and Krugman model, which gives a realistic time path of prices. In Flamm's model, firms first make some optimal capacity investment. Initially, they run that capacity full blast and then switch to a policy of maintaining constant output but decreasing utilization of capacity. In other words, firms exploit their monopoly power at the latter stages of the product cycle. The driving force behind the time paths of falling prices and decreasing capacity utilization is learning economies.

Although Flamm's model undoubtedly represents a big step forward in modeling, it does not take into account the effects of entry, and this is a significant weakness. According to the product-cycle theory, firms producing high-tech products typically enjoy temporary monopoly powers at the first stage of the product cycle, and they earn substantial economic profits. Such profits attract imitators, and the economic profits are competed away. In contrast to Flamm's model, firms exploit their monopoly powers at the initial rather than the latter stages of the product cycle. The fall in prices over time is a result of entry as well as learning economies.

In the case of the time path of prices, the effects of entry and learning economies work in the same direction: both factors lead to a fall in prices. How-

Yun-Wing Sung is senior lecturer in economics at the Chinese University of Hong Kong.

ever, in the case of the time paths of capacity utilization and exploitation of market power, the two factors work in opposite directions. Entry leads to a weakening of market power and increasing capacity utilization over time, but learning economies have the opposite effects.

It might be argued that, unlike potato chips, entry in the computer chips industry is much more difficult and learning economies in the computer chips industry much more significant, with the result that the effects of learning economies on capacity utilization and exploitation of market power predominate over those of entry. However, this is an empirical matter that cannot be presumed. Moreover, both casual empiricism and the product-cycle theory suggest that entry is an extremely important factor that cannot be ignored.

Besides entry, temporal optimization on the part of buyers would also counteract the decrease in capacity utilization over time. Buyers expect the prices of chips to fall over the product cycle, and they postpone their purchase as a result. This shifts purchases from the initial stages to the latter stages of the product cycle and tends to increase capacity utilization over time. It should be noted that Flamm's model assumes a constant elasticity of demand over time and thus cannot take into account the postponement of purchases on the part of buyers.

4 Japan's Agricultural Policy and Protection Growth

Masayoshi Honma

In recent years, agriculture has attracted worldwide attention in the political arena, such as the summit meetings and the OECD's council meetings at the ministerial level. Also, agriculture is one of the most important areas of the current Uruguay Round of GATT negotiations. The main focus of agricultural issues is the high level of agricultural protection in such industrial countries as EC member states and Japan. Even the United States, which insists on drastic reductions in agricultural support, does not do its duty and liberalize trade in several agricultural commodities, in violation of the ideal of the GATT.

It is commonly observed that the agricultural sector is strongly protected in those developed economies in the advanced stage of economic development, where the urban population shows less resistance to high food prices and farmers are more powerful in lobbying for protection. As several studies show, it is true that Japan's level of agricultural protection has been one of the highest in the world in recent years (e.g., OECD 1987; Webb, Lopez, and Penn 1990). While among the developed countries Japan is not unique in protecting agriculture, it is, however, unique in the relations existing there between agricultural protection and agricultural trade and production. Even though its domestic agriculture is highly protected, Japan has increased agricultural imports sharply and become increasingly less food self-sufficient (as shown in table 4.1)—in contrast with the EC countries, which maintain high levels of food self-sufficiency under the protection of the Common Agricultural Policy. Japan is now one of the largest food importers and the country most open to agricultural trade if measured in terms of food self-sufficiency.

Masayoshi Honma is professor of economics at Otaru University of Commerce, Hokkaido, Japan.

The author acknowledges with gratitude the permission of Yujiro Hayami for the use in this paper of the materials that are part of the results of a series of research studies of Japan's agricultural policies conducted jointly with him.

Table 4.1 Food Self-Sufficiency Rates in Japan, 1960–89 (%)

	1960	1970	1980	1989
Grains	82	46	33	30
Food grains	89	74	69	68
Rice	102	106	100	100
Wheat	39	9	10	16
Legumes	44	13	7	9
Vegetables	100	99	97	92
Fruits	100	84	81	67
Eggs	101	97	98	98
Dairy products	89	89	82	80
Meat	91	89	81	72
Beef	96	90	72	54
Pork	96	98	87	77
Sugar	18	22	27	35
Total final food consumption	91	81	75	68

Source: Japanese Ministry of Agriculture, Forestry, and Fisheries, *Shokuryo Jukyu Hyo* (Food balance sheets).

Another feature of Japan's agricultural protection that is different from other developed countries is its rapid growth in the protection level. In other words, the strong protection accorded agriculture in Japan is a relatively recent phenomenon. As we will see in section 4.2, Japan's level of agricultural protection in 1955 was much lower than that of European countries. However, that level rose rapidly and became the highest among industrial countries by 1970.

These characteristics of Japan's agricultural policy are strongly related to the fast decline in comparative advantage in agriculture in the course of the high industrial productivity growth that followed the recovery from World War II. The decline in comparative advantage in agriculture was coupled with rapid increases in the demand for highly valued foodstuffs such as meat and milk as per capita income rose. To increase domestic production of those products, imports of feed grains and soybeans were liberalized in the 1950s and the early 1960s, respectively, and thereafter Japan's agricultural imports sharply increased.

At the same time, the decline in comparative advantage in agriculture created a demand for agricultural protection. The rapid change in comparative advantage created a serious intersectoral adjustment problem requiring reallocation of agricultural resources to industry. In order to decrease the cost of intersectoral adjustment that rural people had to shoulder in such forms as rural depopulation and rural-urban income disparity, farmers lobbied for protection in order to shift a part of the intersectoral adjustment cost to the general public.

Agricultural protectionism in a rapidly growing economy appears to have a strong logic if we examine the domestic political market in which the level of protection is determined. Japan's protection policy for agriculture has been persistent and is not likely to cease because it has been domestically at an equilibrium in the political market. However, there is another player emerging on the political scene—the foreign pressure demanding agricultural trade liberalization in Japan in exchange for the flood of exports of manufactured goods from Japan. Japan is now facing a sharp conflict between the internal resistance to and the external pressure for agricultural trade liberalization.

This paper examines the development of Japan's agricultural policy and the process of growth of agricultural protection, focusing on the political market. In the following sections, I first review briefly the background of current food and agricultural policies in Japan. Then I examine the level of Japan's agricultural protection in an international comparison. The growth in agricultural protection is next related to political and economic factors to determine the level of protection, and the relation is tested by a regression analysis. Finally, some implications of Japan's growth of agricultural protection are drawn.

4.1 Review of Agricultural Policies in Japan

4.1.1 Two Institutional Bases

Current Japanese agricultural policies are implemented mainly through two institutions: the Food Control Law of 1942 and the Agricultural Basic Law of 1961. The Food Control Law was originally designed to control food distribution during the war, when food was in very short supply. After the war, agricultural and nonagricultural economies were reconstructed, and the food supply recovered. The Food Control Law has been adjusted to account for the increasing food supply, and few food items remain under direct government control—with the notable exception of rice.

Only agents designated by the Food Agency within the Ministry of Agriculture, Forestry, and Fisheries may participate in the marketing of rice, and prices are regulated from the farm gate to the wholesale level. In administrative practice, however, those regulations have gradually been relaxed. For example, producers now sell high-quality rice, which is an important factor in rice consumption, directly to wholesalers through cooperatives at a negotiated price, although the quantities of rice that producers can sell through this channel and through the government agency at a fixed price are limited by quotas. Officially, producers cannot sell rice through any other channels, but it is said that about two million tons, or nearly one-fifth of total output, are marketed illegally, through private channels. In addition, two auction markets were established by the government in 1990, and about 1 million tons of rice are sold at regular auctions at more flexible prices, reflecting demand and supply by variety of rice.

The Food Control Law, originally instituted to protect consumers during the war, works currently to support agricultural producers. The high support price stimulated an expansion of domestic production in excess of consumption, resulting in an accumulation of surplus rice in government storage, which made the adoption of an acreage-control program in 1969 inevitable. The acreage-control program was strengthened under the continuous pressure of the ever-accumulating surplus stock and escalating government deficit. The acreage diverted from production is currently 830,000 hectares, almost one-third of the paddy fields in Japan.

In the course of economic development that followed Japan's postwar recovery, farmers' incomes tended to lag behind those of urban workers. In an attempt to prevent the rural-urban income gap from widening, the Agricultural Basic Law, a national charter for agriculture, was enacted in 1961. The law declared that it was the government's responsibility to raise agricultural productivity and thereby close the gap in income and welfare between farm and nonfarm people. Among the measures identified as necessary for this purpose were incentives to expand the production of the high-income-elasticity agricultural commodities and to enlarge the scale of the production unit. In order to improve farming efficiency, it was considered essential to increase the scale of farm operations by reducing the number of inefficient farm units and promoting cooperative operations among the remaining farms.

Despite such attempts at structural adjustment, the rate of agricultural productivity growth was not raised sufficiently, and the rural-urban income gap continued to widen. The reaction of farmers was to organize political lobbying for protection by means of government intervention in agricultural product and input markets. When the increasing demand of farmers for protection was coupled with the decreasing resistance of the nonfarm population as a result of the increasing per capita income and the decreasing Engel coefficient, the result was a level of agricultural protection that remains among the highest in the world.

4.1.2 Means of Agricultural Protection

Japanese agriculture is protected by such policy instruments as border protection, direct supports on farm product prices, and subsidies on agricultural production inputs. A major source of criticism of Japanese trade practices has been quantitative restrictions on imports of agricultural commodities. Until 1988, twenty-two agricultural and marine products were subject to an import quota (IQ). However, the quotas on ten types of agricultural products were removed after a GATT multinational panel declared them illegal in 1988. Further, the quotas on beef and oranges, which used to be held up as symbols of the closed nature of Japan's market, were removed in April 1991 as a result of bilateral negotiations with the United States.

Besides the IQ restrictions, the imports of six agricultural commodities are controlled by trade monopolies of governmental or semigovernmental agencies: rice, wheat, and barley by the Food Agency; butter and powdered milk by the Livestock Industry Promotion Corporation; and silk by the Silk and Sugar Price Stabilization Corporation.

While quantitative restrictions are strong in Japan, border protection by means of tariffs and levies seems to be relatively modest (Johnson, Hemmi, and Lardinois 1985). In Japan, the variable levy of the EC type is not commonly used, but a somewhat similar system is used for pork, in the form of a differential tariff, and for sugar and silk, in the form of an adjustable surcharge.

In addition to such indirect supports as border protection, various agricultural products are subject to direct government price support. The largest price support program is applied to rice under the Food Control Law. The price of rice that the government purchases from farmers is determined at a fixed level each year on the bases of production costs, nonfarm wages, general price level, and other economic conditions. This government rice price influences the price of rice distributed through other channels. Currently, the price of rice in Japan is not only far above the world price but also above the market equilibrium price under autarky (Otsuka and Hayami 1985). Wheat and barley produced domestically are purchased by the Food Agency, if their market prices decline below floor prices.

The so-called price stabilization programs for meat, dairy products, and silk involve buffer stock operations to support domestic wholesale prices between certain ceiling and floor prices. The deficits from the programs are financed partly by levies on imports and partly by transfer from the general budget. The same applies to the government purchase at floor prices of sugar cane, sugar beets, and potatoes for starch making.

Deficiency payments from the government apply to a limited number of products such as soybeans, canola, and milk for processing. A variation of the deficiency payment scheme used in Japan is the Price Stabilization Fund, to which the government and producers pay contributions and from which producers receive deficiency payments if market prices decline below target prices. This scheme is applied to calves, fruit for processing, and some vegetables.

Production subsidy is also a major policy instrument for agricultural protection. Japanese agricultural policy depends heavily on subsidies, which are spread across a large number of items, each receiving a relatively small disbursement. In Japan, subsidies have substantially contributed to agricultural capital formation, especially to investment in land infrastructure. It may appear that subsidies allocated to land infrastructure for such public-good projects as irrigation and drainage facilities are not protectionist in nature. However, only about 20 percent of land infrastructure investment is allocated to major canals and water-control facilities, the rest going to farm ditches and farm consolidation and reshaping, for which individual beneficiaries can be easily specified.

4.2 Growth in Agricultural Protection

4.2.1 Japan's Level of Agricultural Protection

Japan's agricultural policy is now aimed mainly at protecting domestic agriculture. However, such a high level of agricultural protection is a relatively recent phenomenon. This can be clearly demonstrated by an international comparison over time. The measure used for comparison is the average nominal rate of protection (NRP), calculated by subtracting the value of agricultural output in border prices from the value of agricultural output in domestic prices and dividing the remainder by the value of agricultural output in border prices; this is equivalent to the weighted average of the NRPs of individual commodities using their shares in the total output value at border prices as weights.

Table 4.2 summarizes the average NRPs estimated for fourteen industrial and newly industrializing countries by comparing producer and border (im-

Table 4.2 **Comparison of the Nominal Rates of Agricultural Protection between East Asian Countries and Eleven Other Developed Countries, 1955–87 (%)[a]**

	1955	1960	1965	1970	1975	1980	1985	1987
East Asia:								
Japan	18	41	69	74	76	85	108	151
Korea	−46	−15	−4	29	30	117	147	160
Taiwan	−17	−3	−1	2	20	52	28	74
European Community:								
Denmark	5	3	5	17	19	25	34	69
France	33	26	30	47	29	30	37	81
German, F.R.	35	48	55	50	39	44	40	79
Italy	47	50	66	69	38	57	72	127
Netherlands	14	21	35	41	32	27	38	57
United Kingdom	40	37	20	27	6	35	39	79
Average[b]	35	37	45	52	29	38	43	84
Nonaligned Europe:								
Sweden	34	44	50	65	43	59	65	131
Switzerland	60	64	73	96	96	126	181	218
Food exporters:								
Australia	5	7	5	7	−5	−2	−7	5
Canada	0	4	2	−5	−4	2	0	19
United States	2	1	9	11	4	0	11	23

Sources: Data for 1955–80 are from Anderson and Hayami (1986, 26). Data for 1985 and 1987 are estimates by the author.

[a]Defined as the percentage by which the producer price exceeds the border price. The estimates shown are the weighted averages for twelve commodities, using production valued at border prices as weights. The twelve commodities are rice, wheat, barley, corn, oats, rye, beef, pork, chicken, eggs, milk, and sugar.

[b]Weighted average for all six countries shown for 1975, 1980, 1985, and 1987 but excluding Denmark and the United Kingdom for earlier years.

port c.i.f. or export f.o.b.) prices for selected years between 1955 and 1987. Producer prices are used because they include the effects not only of border protection but also of more direct agricultural support policies such as deficiency payments. However, the use of producer prices leads to an underestimation of protection to the extent that there are costs of marketing from the farm gate to a point in the marketing chain equivalent to the internationally traded product. This bias is obvious in the case of the food-exporting countries such as Australia and the United States, for which the estimates of nominal protection rates are negative in some years when in fact no policy was exercised to exploit agriculture or, rather, modest protective policies were adopted. However, insofar as this bias is similar across countries and over time, it does not present a serious problem for the purpose of making broad comparisons.

As seen in table 4.2, average NRPs in recent years show a high level of agricultural protection in Japan. In 1987, the average NRP of Japan (151 percent) is much higher than the EC average (84 percent) and is lower than that in only Switzerland (218 percent) and Korea (160 percent). The U.S. dollar was sharply depreciated in 1987, especially in comparison to 1985, when the dollar was still high relative to other currencies owing to the money supply control of the Reagan administration, with the effect of lowering domestic agricultural prices in other countries relative to the import prices in dollar terms. Therefore, not only in Japan but also in most countries that apply insulation policies to prevent domestic agricultural markets from being tied to fluctuations in world prices, average NRPs rose sharply between 1985 and 1987. It is also noted that even the United States itself and other food exporters raised their agricultural protection levels from 1985 to 1987, reflecting the increases in export subsidies and other government expenses for agricultural support programs in recent years.

In any case, there is no doubt that the level of agricultural protection in Japan, as measured by average NRP, is among the highest in the world. However, the average NRP of Japan in 1955 was 18 percent, only half the EC average of 35 percent. It rose rapidly thereafter, reaching the EC level in 1960 and the Swiss level in 1965. This was the period when Japan's economic growth was especially rapid. More dramatic were the cases of Korea and Taiwan. Before the mid-1960s, when their spurt of industrial development began, their average NRPs were negative, reflecting the practice of agricultural exploitation policies common to low-income countries. During the 1970s, the protection level rose sharply, and Korea caught up with Japan by 1980.

4.2.2 Hypotheses on the Determinants of Agricultural Protection

Underlying the growth in agricultural protection is the change in equilibrium of the political market. The political market for agricultural protection is stylized in the framework of the neoclassical economic theory of politics (Hayami 1988, app. A). In this framework, the demand and supply schedules of a policy that changes the level of agricultural protection are essentially the marginal evaluations of changes in political support for politicians by those who demand and those who oppose, respectively, agricultural protection. Therefore, the level of protection is determined at a subjective equilibrium by politicians to maximize their net revenue in the form of political support.

In a consideration of the factors that affect the demand and supply schedules of agricultural protection policies, there are two important variables that act to shift each schedule. One is the comparative advantage of agriculture, and the other is the share of agriculture in the total economy.

The comparative advantage of agriculture is inversely related to the stage of a country's industrial development and the need of reallocating resources from agriculture to industry. In the process of economic development based on industrial growth, agriculture loses its comparative advantage, and the income position of farmers deteriorates, unless resources are reallocated smoothly from agriculture to industry. Most of the resources in agriculture, however, are specialized and not easily transformed for other uses. Thus, farmers demand protection so that they can stay in farming despite the fact that their productivity growth lags behind that of industry. With economic development, a declining farming population finds it easier to organize and create political pressure. Correspondingly, the farmers' marginal political support for politicians or the demand schedule of agricultural protection is shifted upward.

The share of agriculture in the total economy indicates the degree of resistance to agricultural protectionism. As the importance of agriculture in an economy declines in the course of economic development, resistance to agricultural protectionism tends to decline. A relative contraction of the agricultural sector in the total economy reduces the burden of agricultural protection per capita of the nonagricultural population. Consumers' resistance to agricultural protection is reduced as their incomes rise and the Engel coefficient decreases; hence, the effect of rising food prices on the cost of living diminishes. People become more tolerant of the high cost of agricultural protection as their nostalgia for the pastoral life increases, and their interest in environmental conservation grows as the agricultural sector shrinks. Correspondingly, the marginal cost to politicians or the supply schedule of agricultural protection declines.

Therefore, I hypothesize that the level of agricultural protection is inversely associated with the comparative advantage of agriculture and the share of agriculture in the total economy. Not only the historical experiences of Japan, Korea, and Taiwan on NRPs but also the cross-sectional observations of NRPs in table 4.2 suggest the association of agricultural protection with comparative advantage. These countries with large endowments of agricultural land per capita, like Australia, Canada, and the United States, show low levels of NRPs, whereas Switzerland, Japan, and Korea, which are characterized by very meager endowments of natural resources for agricultural production relative to both physical and human capital for nonagricultural production, show the highest levels of NRPs in recent years. Even within the EC, the NRP is low for Denmark and the Netherlands, which have traditionally been efficient agricultural producers, but high for Italy, which is known for its low agricultural productivity. At the same time, the general tendency of increases in NRPs over time observed in table 4.2 may support the hypothesis that the level of agricultural protection is associated with the share of agriculture, which has been contracting in most of the countries under study here.

Another factor that obvious influences changes over time in the level of agricultural protection is the international terms of trade between agricultural and industrial commodities. It is common for national governments in developed countries to intervene in agricultural markets so as to stabilize domestic prices at the expense of instability in international prices (Johnson 1975), whereas industrial commodities are traded relatively freely with international price fluctuations pervading domestic markets. Therefore, the inverse correlation between the level of agricultural protection and the international terms of trade, defined as agricultural export prices divided by industrial export prices in the world market, is expected. Indeed, the increase in NRP in most countries during the period between 1955 and 1970 corresponded to changes in the international terms of trade, which turned against agriculture under the pressure of accumulated surpluses of agricultural commodities in the United States and other major exporters. On the other hand, precipitous drops in NRPs were experienced from 1970 to 1975, corresponding to the sharp increases in world agricultural prices relative to industrial prices during the so-called world food crisis period.

Other than the three major factors outlined above, I also consider some country- or region-specific factors that explain the variations in the level of agricultural protection in table 4.2. The first factor is that EC member countries may have a different basis from other countries for agricultural protection because the EC acts as a regional bloc under the Common Agricultural Policy. The second is that Sweden and Switzerland have sought to be self-reliant and neutral militarily and have therefore preferred to maintain food self-sufficiency as a part of national security with a high level of agricultural protection. The third is that Korea and Taiwan have taken a similar course in that their level of agricultural protection has grown as their economies have developed. Finally, it is worthwhile to raise the question as to whether Japan's agricultural protection level, which is now among the highest in the world, is unique or can be explained by factors common to industrial countries.

4.3 Regression Analysis of Agricultural Protection Level

4.3.1 Specification

In order to test the hypotheses in the previous section, a multiple-regression analysis is conducted. The dependent variable representing the level of agricultural protection in the regression is the average nominal protection coefficient (NPC) for agriculture, which is obtained by adding one (100 percent) to NRP. NPC, the ratio of the value of agricultural output in domestic prices to its value in border prices, is used instead of NRP because NPC is consistent with the explanatory variables that are defined as an index setting the base point at 100, as explained below. Also, the logarithmic transformation of NPC represents a rate of difference between the output valued in domestic and in border prices, and it is therefore easy to interpret the estimated coefficients in equations with variables transformed into logarithms.

The explanatory variables are three fundamental variables representing (i) the comparative advantage of agriculture, (ii) the share of agriculture in the total economy, and (iii) the international terms of trade between agriculture and industrial commodities and four dummy variables representing the country- or region-specific factors of (i) the EC (six EC countries), (ii) nonaligned Europe (Sweden and Switzerland), (iii) Asian newly industrializing economies (NIEs) (Korea and Taiwan), and (iv) Japan.

As a variable to represent the comparative advantage of agriculture, I use an index of the productivity ratio, which is the ratio of labor productivity in agriculture to labor productivity in industry. Intercountry cross-sectional data on labor productivity in agriculture in real terms, as measured by total agricultural output per male worker, are available from Hayami and Ruttan ([1971] 1985) for 1980 and previous years. They are updated using agricultural production indexes (FAO, *Production Yearbook*) and data on male agricultural labor (ILO, *Yearbook of Labor Statistics*). As labor productivity in industry, average GDP per male worker for the whole economy at 1975 constant prices converted into U.S. dollars by purchasing-power-parity exchange rates in 1975 (OECD, *National Accounts of OECD Countries*) is used because of the lack of comparable labor productivity data for the industrial sector. It seems reasonable to assume that labor productivity in the industrial sector and labor productivity in the total economy are closely correlated in industrial countries. The productivity ratio thus calculated is expressed as an index, with the U.S. value in 1975 set at 100.

Two alternative variables are used to represent the relative share of agriculture in the total economy: agriculture's share in the labor force and agriculture's share in total GDP at 1975 constant prices. These data are obtained from ILO and OECD statistics.

The international terms of trade are specified as the ratio of the index of world export unit value of agricultural products (FAO, *Trade Yearbook*) to the export unit value index of manufactured goods from market economies (United Nations, *Statistical Yearbook*), with the 1975 value set equal 100.

Detailed explanations of and data for the variables listed above are given in Honma and Hayami (1986, 1991). The variables other than dummies are transformed into logarithms, and the regression equation is specified as follows:

(1) $$\ln P = b_0 + b_1 \ln C + b_2 \ln S + b_3 (\ln S)^2 + b_4 \ln T + b_5 E + b_6 N + b_7 A + b_8 J + e,$$

where P is the nominal protection coefficient, C is the index of comparative advantage in agriculture, S is the share of agriculture in the total economy, T is the international terms of trade, and E, N, A, and J are dummies representing the EC, nonmilitarily aligned countries, Asian NIEs, and Japan, respectively, taking a value of 1 if the observation is for the region or country and 0 otherwise. Specifically, the EC dummy is designed to be 1 from 1965 for the original EC member countries, 1 from 1975 for Denmark and the United Kingdom, and 0 otherwise to capture the effect of the Common Market correctly. The notation ln refers to natural logarithms, and e is the error term. The square of ln S is included to test for the possibility that the level of agricultural protection does not increase monotonically as the agricultural sector shrinks; the political influence of the farm sector may begin to decline beyond a certain threshold.

The model specified in the form of equation (1) is estimated by the ordinary least squares (OLS) method. Data for the dependent variable are available for fourteen countries at eight points in time for the period 1955–87, as observed in table 4.2. Thus, the regression analysis is conducted with 112 observations pooling fourteen countries at eight points in time between 1955 and 1987. It must be cautioned that some of the explanatory variables used in this analysis are not independent of the level of protection. For example, increased protection may exacerbate inefficiency in agricultural production and possibly block improvements in agriculture's comparative advantage. Likewise, protection increases inhibit the decline in the share of agriculture in the total economy. Considering the possibility of bias due to such simultaneity, the estimated regression parameters must be interpreted with caution.

4.3.2 Results of Estimation

The results of estimating regression equations are summarized in table 4.3. Regressions (1) and (2) represent the model, which includes only fundamental variables as explanatory variables; dummies are included in regressions (3) and (4). All the coefficients of fundamental variables satisfy the sign conditions postulated and are highly significant statistically. It is noteworthy that about 70 percent of the variations in NPC among countries and over time are explained in regressions (1) and (2) by only three fundamental variables—comparative advantage, share of agriculture, and international terms of trade—as the coefficients of determination adjusted for the degrees of freedom indicated. The results support my hypothesis that the level of agricultural protection rises as the comparative advantage shifts away from agriculture and as the international terms of trade turn against agricultural commodities.

The coefficients of the linear and square terms of agriculture's share are

Table 4.3 **Estimates of Regressions to Explain Nominal Agricultural Protection Coefficients in Fourteen Industrial Countries for 1955–87**

	Regression			
	(1)	(2)	(3)	(4)
Explanatory variables				
Comparative advantage:				
Productivity ratio	−.381**	−.337**	−.350**	−.291**
(ln *C*)	(−11.99)	(−11.51)	(−7.62)	(−7.42)
Share of agriculture:				
In labor force (*A*)	.345**		.306*	
($\ln S_1$)	(3.24)		(2.59)	
In GDP (*B*) ($\ln S_y$)		.290**		.309**
		(2.80)		(3.17)
Square of *A* $(\ln S_1)^2$	−.117**		−.098**	
	(−5.65)		(−3.82)	
Square of *B* $(\ln S_y)^2$		−.125**		−.111**
		(−5.10)		(−4.54)
Terms of trade (ln *T*)	−.946**	−1.078**	−.951**	−1.033**
	(−7.26)	(−8.39)	(−6.80)	(−8.01)
Dummy variables				
EC (*E*)			.096*	.126**
			(2.58)	(3.42)
Nonalliance (*N*)			.160**	.234**
			(2.83)	(4.42)
Asian NIEs (*A*)			−.029	−.039
			(−.34)	(−.48)
Japan (*J*)			−.017	.064
			(−.23)	(.86)
Intercept	10.481	10.937	10.321	10.417
Adjusted coefficient of determination ($\bar{R}^2$)	.702	.673	.734	.744
Standard error of estimate	.155	.162	.146	.144
Threshold value of S[a]	4.4	3.2	4.8	4.0

Note: Student *t*-values are in parentheses, with levels of statistical significance shown as ** (1 percent) and * (5 percent). Equations with variables transformed into logarithms are estimated by the ordinary least squares method.

[a]The threshold value in the share of agriculture was obtained by solving $b_2 + 2b_3 \ln S = 0$.

positive and negative, respectively, in any case. This means that NPC is a concave function of agriculture's share and, therefore, that there is a specific point in agriculture's share that maximizes the level of agricultural protection with other things held constant. Thus, NPC continues to increase at a diminishing rate until the share of agriculture declines to a certain point, beyond which NPC decreases at a rate corresponding to further decreases in agriculture's share. This threshold point in agriculture's share is calculated by solving the following equation for *S*:

$$\partial \ln P / \partial \ln S = b_2 + 2b_3 \ln S = 0.$$

The calculated threshold value for each equation is shown in the last row of table 4.3. The threshold is reached when agriculture's share in the male labor force is 4–5 percent or when its share in GDP is 3–4 percent. These levels have already been reached in most European countries and those countries that are major food exporters, while Korea and Taiwan are still approaching the threshold. Japan, whose agricultural share is 5.7 percent in the male labor force or 2.3 percent in real GDP in 1987, is just passing the threshold. In other words, the farm bloc in Japan is at the height of its political strength today, having reached the optimal size for effective lobbying. This may partly explain why neither the ruling Liberal Democratic Party (LDP) nor any opposition party could say anything in favor of agricultural trade liberalization during the recent general elections for fear of losing farm votes. At the same time, the results outlined above suggest that the political strength of farmers in Japan may weaken gradually if Japan's agricultural share declines further. However, the share of agriculture, especially in the labor force, is unlikely to decline significantly in the short run because of the generally slow movement of labor out of agriculture. Moreover, the high level of agricultural protection itself plays a role in keeping agriculture's share from declining. Such resistance of agriculture's share to a further decline, combined with a high level of protection, results in a stalemate of domestic agricultural policies not only in Japan but also in other developed countries. Agricultural issues were brought onto the stage of international politics at, for example, summit meetings and the GATT multilateral negotiations as a way out of this stalemate was sought.

Another implication of the threshold values in table 4.3 is that agricultural protection may well increase further in newly industrializing countries such as Korea and Taiwan as their agricultural sectors continue to decline toward the present levels of Western Europe and Japan. This experience of Asian NIEs may be repeated in other newly industrializing areas such as ASEAN countries. Therefore, international collaborative efforts to prevent the spread of agricultural protection need to be intensified.

The coefficients of dummy variables in regressions (3) and (4) show the effects of country- or region-specific factors. The coefficients of the EC dummy are positive and statistically significant in both regression (3) and regression (4) at a conventional level. This supports the hypothesis that the EC acts as a regional bloc to provide more protection for agricultural producers in member countries than they would have without the Common Market. The coefficients of the nonalliance dummy are also positive and statistically significant, with a greater value than the EC dummy. Therefore, the hypothesis that the Swedes and the Swiss, who wish to remain nonaligned, are willing to shoulder the high cost of agricultural protection in order to increase their level of food self-sufficiency for reasons of national security is strongly supported.

An important finding from regressions (3) and (4) is that the coefficients of the Japan dummy and the Asian NIEs dummy are not significantly different from zero, even at a very low level of statistical significance. Such results imply that the agricultural protection level of Japan and Asian NIEs may be neither exceptional nor unique in view of determinants of agricultural protection postulated in this study. The high rates of agricultural protection growth in Japan and two other East Asian countries may be the results, not of factors specific to the region, such as extreme agricultural fundamentalism, but of factors common to all industrial countries, such as the high social costs of intersectoral adjustment arising from the decline in agriculture's comparative advantage and the decrease in the nonagricultural population's resistance to agricultural protection in the process of industrial development.

4.4 Accounting for Agricultural Protection Growth

In order to identify the contributions of the three fundamental variables to Japan's growth in agricultural protection for the period 1955–87, the growth rate of NPC is decomposed by using the following growth-accounting equation derived from equation (1):

$$(2)\qquad (\dot{P}/P) = b_1(\dot{C}/C) + (b_2 + 2b_3\,\overline{\ln S})\,(\dot{S}/S) + b_4(\dot{T}/T) + U,$$

where $(\dot{P}/P)$, $(\dot{C}/C)$, $(\dot{S}/S)$, and $(\dot{T}/T)$ are the annual compound rate of growth in NPC, the index of agricultural comparative advantage, the share of agriculture, and the international terms of trade, respectively; the b's are the regression coefficients estimated; $\overline{\ln S}$ is the mean of $\ln S$; and U is the unexplained residual. Each item on the right-hand side of equation (2) represents the contribution of each factor to the growth of NPC.

The results of the growth-accounting analysis for Japan based on the estimated coefficients of regressions (1) and (2) in table 4.3 are summarized in table 4.4. Japan's NPC rose at the rate of 2.4 percent per year on average for the period 1955–87. Roughly speaking, about half this growth of Japan's agricultural protection is explained by changes in the international terms of trade, about one-third by decreases in agriculture's share, and about one-sixth by declines in the agricultural comparative advantage, while the negative contribution of an unexplained residual of about 10 percent is recorded.

However, if the period under consideration is divided into two subperiods, 1955–75 and 1975–87, the following differences between the two periods can be seen. In the period 1955–75, which includes the era of rapid economic growth in Japan, the contributions of comparative advantage and agricultural share were much larger than in the second period, 1975–87. About 80 percent of the growth in agricultural protection for the first period is explained by the factors of comparative advantage and agricultural share, which are related to the costs of intersectoral adjustment and the changes in the political strength of the agricultural sector in the course of industrial growth.

Table 4.4 Accounting for Agricultural Protection Growth in Japan

	Year and Regression Used					
	1955–87		1955–75		1975–87	
	(1)	(2)	(1)	(2)	(1)	(2)
Growth in NPC (% per year)[a]	2.39	2.39	2.02	2.02	3.00	3.00
	(100)	(100)	(100)	(100)	(100)	(100)
Contribution due to:[b]						
Comparative advantage	.40	.35	.46	.40	.30	.26
	(17)	(15)	(23)	(20)	(10)	(9)
Agriculture's share	.97	.73	1.36	1.20	.31	−.04
	(40)	(31)	(67)	(59)	(10)	(−1)
Terms of trade	1.29	1.47	.41	.46	2.75	3.13
	(54)	(62)	(20)	(23)	(92)	(104)
Unexplained residual	−.27	−.17	−.20	−.05	−.35	.35
	(−11)	(−8)	(−10)	(−2)	(−12)	(−12)

[a]Numbers in parentheses represent the sum of contributions in percentages.

[b]Contribution is calculated on the basis of eq. (2) using the estimated coefficients in table 4.3 and the per annum growth rate of the related variable for each period. The percentage of the total growth of NPC due to each factor is shown in parentheses.

On the other hand, the growth in agricultural protection in the second period is explained mostly by the international terms of trade. This seems to imply that there was no longer strong pressure for further agricultural protection attributed to rapid industrial growth, which ended in the mid-1970s. However, the farmers were still politically strong enough to maintain the protective measures established in the previous period. With border protection measures that block the penetration of price fluctuations in the world market into the domestic market, the protection level rises automatically owing to this insulation of the domestic market from outside competition, when the international terms of trade turn against agricultural products, especially in the 1980s. Such irreversibility of agricultural policy has been a growing source of trade friction between Japan and the food-exporting countries. The large contribution of the terms of trade to the growth in agricultural protection for 1975–87 resulted from the gap between domestic and international prices that widened as the world food market became increasingly depressed in the 1980s. As a result, external pressure on Japan to liberalize agricultural trade has increased in recent years. Concomitantly, such external pressure has become a more dominant player in the political market for agricultural protection in Japan, while domestic consumers have been tolerant of protection growth.

4.5 Conclusion

A source of agricultural protectionism in an industrializing economy is the difficulty of reallocating resources, especially labor, from the agriculture to the nonagricultural sector in the face of relative declines in demand for food as per capita income increases. As an economy reaches an advanced stage of development, the political environment favors the agricultural sector for protection because the relative contraction of agriculture in the total economy reduces consumers' resistance to agricultural protection, on the one hand, and makes political lobbying by farmers more efficient, on the other. Thus, agricultural protectionism tends to be accepted in the process of economic development, and protectionist policies for agriculture are commonly observed in most industrial countries.

I examined the growth of agricultural protection in Japan in this political market framework. Japan's level of agricultural protection was much lower than the European level in 1955, when Japan's economy was still relatively undeveloped. But protection increased rapidly thereafter in the course of Japan's rapid industrial growth in order to ease the problem of a widening urban-rural income disparity, which was caused by the difficulty of reallocating resources. A multiple regression analysis using observations from fourteen countries at eight points in time from 1955 to 1987 found that the growth in agricultural protection in Japan was not based on a unique bias toward strengthening agricultural protectionism but could be explained by the decline in agriculture's comparative advantage, the contraction of agriculture's share in the total economy, and the worsening international terms of trade, all of which are factors common to all industrial countries as determinants of the agricultural protection level.

However, the way in which the level of agricultural protection is raised has been changed. Japan's growth in agricultural protection by 1975 was attributed mostly to changes in the comparative advantage and the share of agriculture that were related to the rapid industrial growth. But its growth in the 1980s was explained mainly by changes in the international terms of trade. This implies that, even when the intersectoral adjustment problem became less serious after the Japanese economy entered a slower growth era, the farm bloc remained strong enough politically to maintain the established protection measures, with the result that the protection level continued to rise in response to declines in the world market prices of agricultural products.

It is time for Japan's policymakers to consider efficient ways of real intersectoral adjustments along with substantial decreases in the agricultural protection level, in order to avoid progressive decay under increasing foreign pressure and to harmonize agricultural policies internationally while seeking economic prosperity based on freer trade with international cooperation.

References

Anderson, K., and Y. Hayami, eds. 1986. The political economy of agricultural protection: East Asia in international perspective. London: Allen & Unwin.

Hayami, Y. 1988. *Japanese agriculture under siege: The political economy of agricultural policies*. London: Macmillan.

Hayami, Y., and V. W. Ruttan. [1971] 1985. *Agricultural development: An international perspective*. Rev. ed. Baltimore: Johns Hopkins University Press.

Honma, M., and Y. Hayami. 1986. The determinants of agricultural protection levels: An econometric analysis. In *The political economy of agricultural protection: East Asia in international perspective,* ed. K. Anderson and Y. Hayami. London: Allen & Unwin.

———. 1991. Causes of agricultural protection. In *Agricultural development of Japan: A century perspective,* ed. Y. Hayami and S. Yamada. Tokyo: University of Tokyo Press.

Johnson, D. G. 1975. World agriculture, commodity policy and price variability. *American Journal of Agricultural Economics* 57:823–28.

Johnson, D. G., K. Hemmi, and P. Lardinois. 1985. *Agricultural policy and trade.* New York: New York University Press.

OECD. 1987. *National policies and agricultural trade*. Paris.

Otsuka, K., and Y. Hayami. 1985. Goals and consequences of rice policy in Japan, 1965–80. *American Journal of Agricultural Economics* 67:529–38.

Webb, A. J., M. Lopez, and R. Penn. 1990. Estimates of producer and consumer subsidy equivalents: Government intervention in agriculture, 1982–1987. USDA/ERS Statistical Bulletin no. 803. Washington, D.C.: USDA.

Comment Joachim Zietz

Masayoshi Honma's paper is a commendable effort at testing, for the case of agriculture, two implications of Downs's (1957) model of the political market for protection: (i) as comparative advantage declines for agriculture, the demand for protection rises; (ii) as the agricultural sector shrinks in size, the supply of protection rises.

At least two important results emerge, one methodological and one substantive. As for methodology, the paper's results lend support to Downs's model of the political market for protection. This is comforting since this model is a popular point of departure in studies of agricultural protection. The substantive contribution of the paper is to relate the size of the agricultural sector to average protection in agriculture. It is suggested that agricultural protection reaches a maximum when agriculture reaches about 3–4 percent of GDP. The latter result suggests some interesting applications for predicting future levels of agricultural protection.

Some of the paper's technical details require some comments. The average rates of nominal protection calculated for grains and livestock in table 4.2 have to be interpreted with some care. They are weighted averages, with the weights representing the adjustment of markets to the change in relative prices caused by protection. Since both the intensity of the adjustment response and the length of the adjustment period may be quite different among various commodities, weighted averages may lead to some peculiar results, for example, to relatively low average nominal rates of protection for livestock in Japan. Unweighted averages may avoid some of these problems, although they can also introduce others.

The regression model is subject to some caveats.

1. The choice of the dependent variable in the model, the nominal rate of protection (NRP), raises some interesting questions. First, does the NRP adequately capture the protective effort of the government? The answer to this question can only be a qualified yes. Border measures are surely captured, regardless of whether they come in the form of tariff or nontariff barriers to trade. This does not apply, however, to other government interventions, such as government support measures (e.g., explicit or implicit input subsidies) that work on the input side. The measure known as producer subsidy equivalent (PSE) combines these subsidies with the NRP and, therefore, is a more complete measure of government support. But even PSEs do not capture the protection afforded to value added. Hence, effective rates of protection that model the true production incentive effect more closely can still be underestimated for certain products. The relatively low NRP for beef in Japan, for example, hides a very high effective rate of protection that is induced by the low tariff on feed grain imports.

Joachim Zietz is professor of economics at Middle Tennessee State University.

Second, the NRP may not be tied very closely to the variables that are targeted by agricultural policymakers and the farming lobby. For example, the NRP for a particular commodity can change dramatically from year to year without a change in government policy because of changes in world price. A similar problem arises from the need to convert all prices into a common currency, mostly the U.S. dollars. The recent changes in the value of the dollar cause fluctuations in the NRP that cannot be attributed to changes in government policy. In sum, the use of the NRP may induce a significant amount of noise in the regression equation, that is, variation that cannot be attributed to government policy. If the latter is what is the focus of the research, the NRP may not be an ideal candidate for the dependent variable.

2. In an apparent effort to reduce the noise introduced into the NRP measure by world price fluctuations, Honma introduces into the regression equation the international terms of trade between agriculture and industry. One wonders to what extent this variable is exogenous. There may be a good case for believing that it is endogenous, especially in a regression that explains the NRP of the majority of industrialized countries. Agricultural protection by industrialized countries is well known to depress world prices quite significantly and, hence, to deteriorate the terms of trade for agricultural exporters. If this is the case, however, the agricultural terms of trade make little sense as an explanatory factor. Being the consequence of high NRPs, they cannot serve, at the same time, as an explanation of high NRPs.

3. The evidence on the dummy variables is used to conclude that Japanese protection is not fundamentally different from that of other industrialized countries. This conclusion holds for the set of dummy variables presented. However, those dummy variables assume a standard fixed-effects model: they modify the intercept term for various classes of observations. This is not the only model one can think of. Dummy variables may be used with equal justification to modify any of the slope parameters. In a general interaction term model, Japan may turn out to be fundamentally different after all, for example, with regard to its response to a decline in comparative advantage.

4. A number of measures, such as productivity, are defined with respect to the male labor force. This may introduce some unwanted noise into the regression for countries that have experienced a strong increase in female labor force participation over the sample period, such as the United States. A more general definition of the labor force would probably be preferable.

5. The unexplained part in table 4.4 suggests an overestimate of NRPs for the period 1955–70 and an underestimate for 1970–87. In a straight time-series analysis, this would be indicative of positive autocorrelation. How can that be explained in this context? Has there been a structural change over time in the behavior of governments, or is it an indication of a problem with statistical model adequacy? The reader may be more convinced of the merits of the model if some statistical adequacy tests were performed. For example, a RESET test may be useful not only as a check on general error orthogonality

but also to see whether the nonlinearity in the size of agriculture is the only one in the model.

Overall, the model provided by Honma provides a good starting point for investigating some additional questions regarding the political economy of agricultural protection. One interesting next step could be to disaggregate the model further. One may ask, for example, why ruminant meat and dairy is so much more protected than nonruminant meat in most countries. Does this pattern develop over the course of a country's development, or does it hold at any stage of development? Similar questions can be posed about the differences in the pattern and degree of protection provided to staple food products versus nontraditional agricultural products, such as fruit and vegetables.

Reference

Downs, Anthony. 1957. *An economic theory of democracy.* New York: Harper & Row.

5 The Growth of Agricultural Protection

Joachim Zietz and Alberto Valdés

Agricultural protectionism in industrialized countries is well known to heavily burden consumers and/or taxpayers. But it also reaches far beyond a country's borders. It negatively affects actual or potential agricultural exporters. Among them are industrialized countries such as Canada, Australia, and New Zealand, but also numerous developing countries, including some of the poorest. Since agriculture is the sector of comparative advantage for many developing countries, now and for some time in the future, agricultural protection does materially impair their potential for economic growth (Valdés and Zietz 1980; Valdés 1987; Goldin and Knudsen 1990).

Agricultural protection is not only important quantitatively, in the sense of imposing heavy costs on developing countries as well as on consumers and taxpayers in industrialized countries. Agricultural protection also has significant qualitative effects. Because agriculture is hardly under any of the disciplines of the General Agreement on Tariffs and Trade (GATT), it is the cause of continual trade friction among the major industrialized countries. It has also been at the heart of many of the problems encountered in international trade negotiations under the aegis of the GATT. Overall, agriculture has helped discredit the GATT process and may yet prevent true progress in opening up international trade (Zietz and Valdés 1988).

Finally, agricultural protection is not confined to the old industrialized countries. On the contrary, it appears to spread to developing countries in the process of industrialization. Korea and Taiwan are two prominent examples. The two countries have experienced a dynamic growth of agricultural protection that is unprecedented in history, thus providing them with protection levels not unlike those of Japan or the European Community (EC).

Joachim Zietz is professor of economics at Middle Tennessee State University. Alberto Valdés is an economist with the World Bank.

The determinants of agricultural protection and its growth over time have been investigated in previous studies. Among the contributions are Anderson (1983), the papers in Anderson, Hayami, et al. (1986), Anderson and Tyers (1989), Krueger, Schiff, and Valdés (KSV) (1988), and Lindert (1991). Most of these studies, however, are conducted at a fairly high level of aggregation.[1] By contrast, this paper's perspective is somewhat more disaggregate in nature. This allows one to address more readily such important issues as the commodity composition of protection, the type of protective measures being used, and the intrinsic dynamics of agricultural protection. A more detailed understanding of how agricultural protection develops, in turn, permits one to provide more specific predictions of the future course of protection and to suggest ways to halt or slow its growth.

The paper is organized as follows. To provide a framework for the subsequent discussion, the first section surveys the pattern and extent of agricultural protection in East Asia relative to other industrialized countries. The following section identifies the rationale for the observed pattern of agricultural protection and its growth over time. The concluding sections supply both some predictions of how agricultural protection may spread to other developing countries and some ways to contain its spread.

5.1 The Pattern of Agricultural Protection in East Asia Compared to Other Industrialized Countries

Table 5.1–5.3 provide some detail on the extent of protection for some important traded agricultural commodities in East Asian countries and other industrialized countries. Table 5.1 uses producer subsidy equivalents (PSEs) as the method to measure the level of support to producers. PSEs have become a popular measurement instrument at least since the publication of the OECD (1987) report on agricultural policies in industrialized countries. PSEs include direct assistance to farmers via border measures that keep the domestic producer price above the import price and nonborder government assistance financed through the budget, such as input subsidies. For the EC and East Asia, border measures are the major cause behind the high PSEs.[2] For most, although not all, agricultural commodities in the United States, subsidies and direct payments to farmers are the dominant form of assistance.[3] Hence, in general, it is the taxpayer who finances the support to farmers in the United States, whereas it is the consumer who does the same in other countries. The trade effect of a particular PSE figure can differ depending on what makes up the PSE (Zietz and Valdés 1988). Even if this were not the case, the PSE still

1. An exception is KSV (1988), which is also unique in putting into perspective the relative importance in terms of incentives to farmers of direct sectoral (agricultural) protection and the indirect effects resulting from economy-wide policies, such as overvalued exchange rates.

2. The PSEs are therefore close in value to the nominal rates of protection.

3. PSEs can therefore diverge significantly from nominal rates of protection.

Table 5.1 Average Producer Subsidy Equivalents for Major Commodities, 1982–87

	Wheat	Rice	Sugar	Beef
Australia	6.7	11.2	13.8	6
Canada	36.2		37.7	10.3
EC	31	47.5	32.8	43.5
New Zealand				12
U.S.	40.7	46.5	68.4	9
Japan	99.7	89.4	69.7	61.9
South Korea		74.0		64.4
Taiwan	65.9	31.4	43.4	18.5

Source: Webb, Lopez, and Penn (1990).

provides only the support level provided to producers. If one is interested in measuring the trade effect of government assistance, one has to look also at the consumer subsidy equivalents (CSEs). CSEs tend to be negative for most countries with positive PSEs and with border measures making up the bulk of the PSEs. Consumers are, in other words, taxed by agricultural support measures and, therefore, consume less than in the absence of agricultural support measures. As a consequence, imports are lower.

In Korea and Japan, protection for the major food staples such as rice is mainly rationalized, at least officially, with food security arguments, an objective for which border measures are not optimal in the sense of minimizing the associated welfare losses.[4] Assuming that the governments are not acting irrationally, there appears to be a need for explaining this particular choice of intervention. In this context, a natural ancillary question is to what extent the motivation for protection in East Asia is different from that for the European Community (EC). The EC's main objective for protecting the agricultural sector is, quite openly, to achieve income parity for its farmers. Again, border measures do not provide the welfare-maximizing tool to achieve this objective. Hence, the question for choosing border measures also arises with regard to the EC. The discussion in the following section will also try to shed some light on this choice.

As demonstrated in table 5.1, support levels in Korea and Taiwan have surpassed those in the EC and are closing in on those in Japan. This is quite remarkable given that producers of agricultural products were still taxed in the early 1960s. This unusually fast shift from taxing agriculture to protecting it has been the subject of several studies (Anderson, Hayami, et al. 1986). A question that arises in this context is whether the East Asian experience with

4. This is an optimal tool of intervention only if self-sufficiency (reduction in or elimination of imports) is desired. To simply achieve food security or income parity, more efficient measures are available. For a discussion of border measures from the perspective of GATT, see Snape (1987).

agricultural protection is an exception or whether one could expect other developing countries on the verge of industrialization to follow suit. Needless to say, the latter would have significant implications for world agricultural markets. This point will be explored in some detail in the following sections.

It is well documented that protection in industrialized countries extends to product groups other than the major staples of table 5.1. Fruit and vegetables, that is, higher-value agricultural products similar to beef, are also heavily protected (Islam 1988). Japan has some of the highest tariff levels among industrialized countries for these products. For most countries, there exists a significant degree of tariff escalation for this product category. Products are less heavily protected when they are fresh compared to when they are processed. Nontariff barriers (NTBs), such as discretionary import licensing procedures as well as sanitary and phytosanitary regulations, tend to be widespread for these product groups. They materially restrict trade, especially for developing countries without the legal expertise and political power to cut through the bureaucratic maze associated with these measures.

Table 5.2 provides some more detail on the import regime for agricultural products for East Asian countries. One observes that both South Korea and Taiwan follow the pattern of Japan rather closely: high tariffs on the major staples and on high-value products combined with restrictive import licensing, customs clearance, and sanitary regulations. The NTBs in these three East Asian countries appear to be particularly effective in restricting trade, even with other industrialized countries (U.S. Trade Representative 1991). What makes these NTBs so effective is the fact that they are often administered by lower-level bureaucrats with significant discretionary power to interpret rules and guidelines that are intentionally left rather vague.

5.2 Agriculture's Response to a Loss of Comparative Advantage

5.2.1 The Loss of Agricultural Comparative Advantage

The point of departure for our discussion is a structural change of the economy of the type that occurs during the development process. For a low-income agriculture-based country, such a structural change is typically the emergence of a rapidly growing manufacturing sector. This development is of interest for the discussion of agricultural protection insofar as industrial earnings tend to jump ahead of those in agriculture. The resulting sectoral income disparity, in turn, increases the opportunity cost of traditional farming and, hence, eventually eliminates its comparative advantage.

The economic reasons for a loss in comparative advantage can be found on both the input and the output side of the agricultural production process.[5] On

5. A common way to think of agriculture's loss in comparative advantage is in terms of an appreciation of the real sectoral (agricultural) exchange rate.

Table 5.2 **Import Protection for Agricultural Products in East Asia**

Country	Protective Measure
Japan	A. High tariffs on agricultural products relative to industrial products (12.1 vs. 2 percent)
	B. Extensive quantitative import restrictions on cereals (ban on rice imports); planned phasing out of quotas on beef and oranges
	C. Restrictive phytosanitary restrictions on fresh fruit and vegetables
South Korea	A. High tariffs (up to 50 percent) on high-value agricultural products such as fresh fruit, nuts, juices, and processed foods
	B. Restrictive import licensing regime for agricultural products (none for industrial products) covering, among others, rice (effective import ban), beef (effective import ban from 1985 to 1989), feed grains, soybeans, and fruit and vegetables; beef liberalization in progress
	C. Slow and arbitrary customs clearance procedures, including excessive and discretionary phytosanitary regulations
Taiwan	A. High tariffs on agricultural products relative to industrial products (23.2 vs. 9.7 percent) in 1989
	B. Very high tariffs (40–50 percent) on high-value agricultural products such as fresh fruit and processed foods
	C. Strict import licenses for most agricultural products, with effective bans on wheat flour, chicken, and peanuts
	D. Restrictive phytosanitary standards and testing requirements for meats, fruit juices, and other products

Source: U.S. Trade Representative (1991).

the input side, rising unit production costs are to blame. They have their origin in two developments. First, urban migration and wage competition with industry tend to raise rural wages above the rate of productivity growth in the traditional agricultural sector. Second, industrial inputs, such as farm machinery or fertilizer, rise in price if a policy of import substitution is followed for the industrial sector. On the output side, the reasons for a lower income growth rate in agriculture relative to industry can be found in (i) a changing demand pattern and (ii) the indirect effects of general trade and macroeconomic policies that affect the exchange rate.

There are a number of reasons for demand to shift away over time from traditional agricultural products or agricultural products in general. One important reason for a relative decline in demand derives from Engel's law.[6] Products with an inelastic income elasticity will experience less sales growth than products with an income elasticity above unity. Hence, their share in total product will decline in a closed economy that grows over time. Ceteris paribus, the relative decline in demand will deteriorate the internal product or sectoral terms of trade, raise the opportunity cost of production, and, hence, lower or possibly eliminate any existing comparative advantage.

6. Other reasons for changing demand patterns clearly exist, e.g., changing preferences. But we will abstract from them at this point to streamline the discussion.

An overvalued exchange rate, as caused, e.g., by a fixed nominal exchange rate combined with domestic inflation, can have a similar effect. It tends to lower the border price of agricultural tradables and, therefore, depresses the demand for domestically produced commodities, hurting the producers of both exportables and import-competing products. Industrialization through a policy of import substitution has the similar effect of implicitly taxing exports and subsidizing imports. The economics of these effects has recently been subjected to a thorough investigation for agricultural products, particularly in KSV (1988), Schiff and Valdés (1992), and several studies at the International Food Policy Research Institute (see, e.g., Dorosh and Valdés 1990; Mundlak, Cavallo, and Domenech 1989; Bautista 1987; and Garcia 1981).

5.2.2 Responses Other than Protection to a Loss in Comparative Advantage

In the process of losing its comparative advantage, traditional agriculture is put under pressure to adjust, that is, to identify ways to avoid the negative income effects that accompany a loss in comparative advantage. Protection, or, more generally, government support programs, is clearly one way to avoid these income effects. However, there may be alternative viable responses.

Take first the loss in comparative advantage that results from a relative decline in revenue. To simplify the discussion, let us assume that farmers can do little to materially affect overall macroeconomic or trade policies and thus eliminate the pressure on revenue that may originate from this side. Low income elasticities for traditional staple food products such as cereals[7] are then the main reason for declining product or sectoral terms of trade. To escape their consequences, productivity can be raised. This may be done by switching to large-scale production and/or the adoption of input-saving production technologies. Alternatively, farmers can switch to agricultural products with high income elasticities of demand. Products that fit into this category include such high-value commodities as beef and veal; other livestock, such as poultry and pork (nonruminant meats); fresh fruit and vegetables; processed foods, such as preserved fruit and vegetables, jams and jellies, and fruit juices; and, last but not least, items that satisfy the demand for healthier products, such as biologically grown foods. The common theme is to move from homogeneous commodities that are sold under conditions of perfect competition into product groups with a high value-added content, for which product innovation, differentiation, and identification allow for some degree of imperfect competition.

The latter has been a quantitatively important response in East Asia. The share of gross value of cereals in agricultural production has declined by one-third or more in Japan, Korea, and Taiwan since the 1950s. During the same time, the share in agricultural production of livestock (in particular nonrumi-

7. Compare, e.g., the collection of elasticity estimates in Carter and Gardiner (1988).

nant meats) and fruit and vegetables has doubled or tripled (Anderson 1986, 12). This move toward high-value products with high income elasticities, however, can avoid the need for government assistance only as long as adequate resource endowments exist for the latter products. For beef and veal, for example, which are classic high-value high-elasticity commodities, this means the availability of cheap feed, either in the form of extensive pasturelands or low prices for feed grains. An alternative to beef production for countries endowed with little land is the production of nonruminant meats, that is, pork and poultry. These livestock products offer income elasticities similar to that of beef without the need for extensive grazing land. This is why a country like Thailand, with a very low pasture per capita figure (see table 5.4 below), can be a very significant and competitive exporter of nonruminant meats. It may also explain why Korea and Taiwan, both with similarly low pasture per capita levels, have relatively low support levels for pork.

If rising unit costs endanger comparative advantage, an increase in productivity is a vital response. Eventually, as wages continue to rise disproportionately in industry, rising unit costs are of concern also in the production of high-value products. This will happen the sooner the more labor intensive their production is. Many horticultural products fit into this category. It is interesting to note in this context that much of the fruit and vegetable production in the United States depends for its competitiveness on cheap migrant labor that is hired on a seasonal basis. The absence of cheap labor in addition to high land prices may explain the considerable protection afforded to high-value fruits documented for Japan, Korea, and Taiwan in table 5.2.

From the discussion above it follows that, in the long run, sufficient productivity growth and/or low labor costs are essential to avoid a loss in comparative advantage for agriculture. Whether sufficient productivity growth can be achieved depends on a number of variables. A very important one is the resource base of the country. A few examples will illustrate the role of the resource base in this context.

Raising productivity sufficiently may be difficult to achieve for countries with little arable land relative to the population size. Better production technology alone is certainly insufficient for staple food products such as cereals because these products will likely remain very land intensive regardless of any foreseeable improvement in production technology. The key to productivity increases, in particular for staple foods, would therefore appear to rest on the ability to make use of economies of scale in production. This in turn requires sufficient land resources. Tables 5.3 and 5.4 illustrate the implications of this simple idea with some numbers on the endowments of countries with agricultural land. Table 5.3 refers to industrialized countries and table 5.4 to developing and newly industrialized countries. Both tables rank the included countries by two criteria: (i) hectares of permanent pastureland per one thousand inhabitants and (ii) hectares of arable and permanent cropland per one thou-

Table 5.3 Industrialized Countries' Endowment of Land Useable for Agriculture

Country	Permanent Pastures (in hectares) per 1,000 Inhabitants	Country	Arable and Permanent Cropland (in hectares) per 1,000 Inhabitants
Australia	26,939.9	Australia	2,994.3
New Zealand	4,337.8	Canada	1,826.6
USSR	1,343.1	USSR	833.5
Ireland	1,335.1	United States	793.6
Canada	1,230.2	Spain	530.3
United States	1,009.1	Denmark	502.7
Greece	530.8	Hungary	499.3
Yugoslavia	275.1	Finland	491.8
Spain	267.4	Romania	467.9
Austria	261.3	Bulgaria	464.2
Switzerland	247.5	Poland	399.1
Bulgaria	228.7	Greece	398.0
France	221.1	Sweden	355.2
United Kingdom	203.6	France	343.0
Romania	193.7	Yugoslavia	336.8
EC-12	176.4	Czechoslovakia	332.5
Hungary	117.5	Germany, East	297.8
Poland	109.4	Ireland	294.9
Czechoslovakia	105.9	Portugal	270.6
Italy	87.2	EC-12	245.3
Netherlands	77.7	Italy	212.1
Germany, East	75.0	Norway	204.3
Germany	74.9	Austria	200.7
Germany, West	74.9	Germany	159.9
Belgium/Luxemburg	69.7	New Zealand	159.7
Sweden	68.1	United Kingdom	124.6
Portugal	52.0	Germany, West	122.2
Denmark	42.3	Israel	102.4
Israel	37.8	Belgium/Luxemburg	79.7
Finland	26.9	Switzerland	63.4
Norway	23.6	Netherlands	61.5
Japan	5.1	Japan	39.4

Source: Calculated from information given in U.S. Department of Agriculture (1990).

sand inhabitants.[8] A high value for the first criterion can be interpreted as being indicative of a comparative advantage in ruminant meat production. This is borne out by the fact that, of the six countries with values in excess of one thousand in table 5.3, five are net exporters of ruminant meat, with the one exception being the former Soviet Union. In addition, four of the coun-

8. Arable land includes mainly land under temporary crops, whereas permanent cropland refers to land that is not planted after each harvest (e.g., fruit, rubber, and other trees) (see U.S. Department of Agriculture 1990).

Table 5.4 **Endowment of Land Useable for Agriculture: Developing Countries and Newly Industralized Countries**

Country	Permanent Pastures (in hectares) per 1,000 Inhabitants	Country	Arable and Permanent Cropland (in hectares) per 1,000 Inhabitants
Somalia	5,342.6	Argentina	1,182.0
Zambia	5,223.9	Senegal	791.7
Argentina	4,678.7	Zambia	774.3
Uruguay	4,521.7	Tunisia	693.4
Paraguay	4,498.8	Cameroon	681.9
Bolivia	4,195.3	Sudan	569.8
Madagascar	3,333.3	Brazil	559.0
Mozambique	3,188.4	Niger	551.6
Sudan	2,557.1	Turkey	548.4
South Africa	2,511.7	Paraguay	544.0
Tanzania	1,576.6	Bolivia	539.8
Peru	1,458.1	Syria	535.5
Niger	1,445.3	Uganda	443.0
Algeria	1,440.2	Uruguay	442.0
Colombia	1,391.9	South Africa	406.5
Burkina Faso	1,265.8	Burkina Faso	384.2
Brazil	1,224.2	Thailand	383.9
Chile	1,095.0	Morocco	383.7
Ethiopia	1,067.4	Chile	359.0
Venezuela	1,008.7	Ivory Coast	354.5
Morocco	954.3	Iraq	347.1
Mexico	945.4	Algeria	343.0
Iran	934.2	Malawi	339.4
Senegal	863.6	Ethiopia	329.3
Cameroon	813.7	Zimbabwe	325.5
Syria	793.1	Iran	314.9
Panama	590.9	Mexico	313.5
Zimbabwe	578.1	Malaysia	312.8
Ecuador	521.7	Nigeria	311.8
Zaire	490.2	Madagascar	298.0
Guinea	483.9	Ecuador	276.1
Tunisia	426.8	Burma	272.8
Uganda	335.6	Panama	258.2
Dominican Republic	326.9	Zaire	254.9
China	306.7	Tanzania	233.8
Ivory Coast	297.0	Dominican Republic	229.7
Ghana	269.3	Guatemala	229.4
Malawi	262.9	Mozambique	223.9
Iraq	254.8	Ghana	222.0
Nigeria	210.2	India	220.9
Kenya	183.3	Venezuela	217.9
Turkey	177.3	Pakistan	214.2
Guatemala	168.8	Peru	198.7
Nepal	116.4	Somalia	189.8
Haiti	84.4	Colombia	185.9
Indonesia	73.1	Rwanda	184.5

(continued)

Table 5.4 (continued)

Country	Permanent Pastures (in hectares) per 1,000 Inhabitants	Country	Arable and Permanent Cropland (in hectares) per 1,000 Inhabitants
Rwanda	70.0	Haiti	153.4
Pakistan	52.0	Philippines	144.4
Sri Lanka	27.8	Nepal	136.4
Taiwan	21.9	Indonesia	128.7
Philippines	21.2	Sri Lanka	118.7
India	15.6	Guinea	116.9
Thailand	14.1	Kenya	116.2
Burma	9.8	Vietnam	111.6
Bangladesh	6.0	China	93.6
Vietnam	5.2	Bangladesh	90.8
South Korea	1.9	South Korea	52.2
Malaysia	1.7	Egypt	51.3
Egypt	.0	Taiwan	45.8

Source: Calculated from information given in U.S. Department of Agriculture (1990).

tries are reported with low PSE values in table 5.1, which suggests that their export performance is not the result of government intervention. It is also interesting to see Japan at the very bottom of the list of countries in table 5.3. Again, this corresponds well with the very high PSE values in table 5.1. The second criterion used in tables 5.3 and 5.4, arable land per capita, is intended to show that countries with high values are likely to be able to produce and export cereals or other land-intensive crops competitively. It comes as no surprise that the countries with large, sparsely populated land masses, such as the United States, Canada, and Australia, tend to be net exporters of cereals. Again, Japan is at the bottom of the list, with PSE levels on cereals that are far in excess of those of other industrialized countries. The message of table 5.4 is fairly similar to that of table 5.3. Argentina, an important exporter of both ruminant meat (beef) and cereals, is very close to the top of the list of countries, suggesting a strong comparative advantage, whereas Korea and Taiwan are close to the bottom.

One may note in this context that a large land endowment is certainly not sufficient for a country to be a competitive exporter of meats or cereals.[9] Other factors can reduce or eliminate the advantage of a large land endowment. Examples are ill-defined property rights or heavy taxation of the agricultural sector. The latter factors largely explain why countries such as the former Soviet Union and Romania are net importers of cereals despite their favorable land endowments.

9. The EC, e.g., is an exporter of beef only because of very high levels of government assistance (table 5.1) and very low costs for feed grain substitutes (soybeans, cassava, etc.).

To the extent that productivity cannot be increased sufficiently and cheap labor is not available, two choices remain to farmers to avoid the negative income effects associated with a loss in comparative advantage. They can (i) raise their off-farm labor supply or (ii) invest in political activity with the objective to obtain government help through either input subsidies or higher output prices. Which route is taken depends ultimately on the perceived cost-benefit ratios associated with each option.

Sufficient nonfarm employment opportunities within reach of the rural household can prevent negative income effects when comparative advantage declines. Nonfarm employment has certainly been a significant factor for East Asian farmers. As reported by Anderson (1986, 13), the share of income from nonfarm sources has risen for Japanese farm households from 49 percent in the early 1960s to more than 80 percent in the early 1980s.[10] An even stronger increase has been observed for Taiwan, with the share going from 34 to 74 percent. Lagging somewhat behind in this respect is Korea, with the share moving from 20 to 35 percent. The main reason for the slower pace of change in Korea is likely the slow growth of off-farm employment opportunities in rural areas compared to Taiwan and Japan (Otsuka 1989).[11] The continued relatively strong dependence of farm households on farm income in Korea clearly raises their exposure to negative income effects. One would expect this to lead, ceteris paribus, to a relatively strong preference for the last option to avoid negative income effects: lobbying for government assistance. The figures in table 5.1 appear to support this view. Comparing the PSEs for Korea and Taiwan, two countries of a similar level of development, Korea has indeed significantly higher government support levels than Taiwan.

5.2.3 Protection as an Alternative Response to a Loss of Comparative Advantage

A Demand/Supply Framework of the Political Market for Government Assistance

For farmers in East Asia, Europe, and, partly, the United States, government support through subsidies and/or import protection has been an important way to minimize income reductions resulting from a loss in comparative advantage. For example, general equilibrium calculations by Vincent (1989) for Korea show that protection has raised farm incomes more than 40 percent in real terms for producers of cereals, about 20 percent for producers of other crops, and 12 percent for livestock producers. The success of farmers in East

10. This, combined with high government support levels, has managed to make farmers one of the most well-off segments of the population (Otsuka 1989, 442).

11. Anecdotal evidence also supports the importance of off-farm employment opportunities in much of Europe. The demand for protection appears to be strongest in regions with little or no industry. Many of these regions tend to be mountainous, with high production costs and little scope for achieving economies of scale.

Asia and the EC in securing government assistance stands in strong contrast to the implicit taxation that farmers in many developing countries are subjected to (KSV 1988). Some straightforward political economy considerations may help explain why farmers differ in their ability to obtain government assistance (including import protection).

Downs's (1957) neoclassical economic theory of politics provides a simple starting point.[12] The model allows one to think of protection as the result of demand and supply forces. Downs's model assumes that politicians adopt policies that maximize their chances of staying in office. The beneficiaries of a particular policy, such as government assistance, invest in lobbying effort up to the point where an additional investment of resources is expected to have no net benefits (Baldwin 1982). The expected losers of a particular policy also invest in lobbying effort, similarly balancing marginal cost and expected marginal benefit. One can think of the beneficiaries of government assistance as on the demand side for protection, whereas politicians are on the supply side. Politicians supply protection up to the point where the marginal cost of lost support from those opposing government assistance or protection is just equal to the marginal gain in support from those groups demanding assistance or protection.

The emphasis of Downs's model on marginal changes clearly entails one problem: it is ill equipped to deal with large changes, such as major structural shifts or regime switches. In those instances, political coalitions tend to break down or are realigned, and formal models based on marginal changes can therefore predict little. However, the loss of comparative advantage in agriculture tends to occur gradually rather than at distinct points in time. Hence, sufficient political stability may be maintained, at least in principle, even though not in each case, for Downs's model to remain a useful framework for thinking about the growth of agricultural protection.

The Determinants of Demand

From the earlier discussion it followed that the basic demand of farmers for protection or, more generally, government intervention results from the high cost, relative to investing in political lobbying, of avoiding income losses through (i) raising productivity growth, (ii) diversifying into products with high income elasticities, or (iii) more off-farm employment. According to Downs's theory and Olson's (1965) work, the demand for protection gains political clout with a decline in group size and the consequent cost of organization. The empirical work by Honma and Hayami (1986) and Honma (in this volume) has provided support for this hypothesis for agriculture. As agriculture shrinks in the development process, the demand for protection becomes more effective ceteris paribus, reaches a maximum, and eventually declines again as the size of the agricultural sector shrinks under a critical level. In

12. Downs's theory is also at the heart of numerous previous studies, including Anderson, Hayami, and Honma (1986) and Anderson and Tyers (1989).

addition to smaller group size, there are other changes taking place as employment shrinks in agriculture that help organize a farming lobby and that raise the demand for government support. Education levels rise, and, as information and transportation become more easily accessible, better and lower-cost communication links are established with the city centers. The lower cost of information, in turn, allows the rural sector to identify more quickly and more reliably any emerging income disparity in relation to other groups in the country. It also reduces the cost of becoming informed and taking part in and organizing political activity. In addition, as agriculture becomes more commercialized, agricultural support services establish themselves in the rural sector.[13] These too can be counted on investing lobbying effort that is directed at the survival of the farming sector.

The Determinants of Supply

The supply of protection depends on (i) the perceived costs of protection to individuals or groups inside or outside the sector and (ii) the power of the bureaucracy that is charged with overseeing the particular sector demanding protection. The latter point is of particular importance for agriculture. Agriculture is one of the few sectors that has managed in most countries to establish a separate ministerial bureaucracy for itself. These bureaucracies tend to be massive and powerful in most industrialized countries, with a keen understanding that additional government programs for their clientele, the farmers, translate into job security and added prestige (Messerlin 1981).[14]

High perceived costs of protection are likely to generate resistance or countervailing power. For politicians, this is equivalent to a rise in their supply curve of protection. Higher bribes are required from the sector seeking protection, while less protection is provided at the same time. One can identify a number of factors that tend to shift the supply curve for agricultural protection or support.

1. An agricultural sector that is large relative to other sectors tends to raise the supply curve for agricultural support measures, in particular income transfers. To provide support to agriculture under this scenario, politicians would have to impose heavy costs on the sectors outside agriculture. Hence, as long as agriculture dominates the economy, protection or government support is quite unlikely. There are exceptions, however, for example, if a country happens to be an oil exporter. Oil revenue can be used to subsidize agriculture even if it is still large in size. This has been done, for example, in Indonesia starting in the 1970s (Barichello 1989).

2. As income increases, food items take up an increasingly smaller budget

13. These range from the agricultural machine industry, transportation, banking, insurance, and marketing services to research and development facilities specializing in agriculture.

14. An agricultural bureaucracy is often established early on in the development process. Its first task may be to tax the agricultural sector. Later on in the development process, however, as the focus switches to assisting agriculture, these bureaucracies tend to grow along with the extent of assistance and protection granted to the sector.

share. This consequence of Engel's law ensures that consumers do not have much of an incentive to get informed or organized to oppose agricultural protection. The cost associated with becoming active are simply much higher than the expected benefits. We have a case of rational indifference. On this account, the supply curve of agricultural protection tends to decline over time. Poor consumers with a relatively large share of their budget going to food products should of course have more of an interest in opposing protection. Poor consumers, however, are generally also those with the least knowledge and political power.

3. Industry resistance to agricultural protection has the potential to shift up the supply curve for protection. There are at least three factors that can provide industry with a rationale to oppose agricultural protection. During the earlier stages of development, agricultural protection may translate into higher wage costs and, hence, reduced profitability.[15] As the budget share that workers have to devote to food declines over time, this factor decreases in importance. Later on in the development process, industry's foreign export markets may become jeopardized as other countries threaten to or do retaliate against the country's agricultural protection. This factor has been growing in importance recently for the East Asian countries: the United States has started to link, at least informally, access to the U.S. market in manufactured products to exporting countries' ability to contain or reduce their level of agricultural protection in product groups of interest to the United States. Finally, the international competitiveness of an export-oriented industry may be threatened by the currency appreciation that regularly follows a rise in protection (Clements and Sjaastad 1984). Clearly, either of the last two factors can operate to contain agricultural protection only if there is a sufficient degree of export orientation in industry.

4. In the longer run, as income levels reach a certain critical level, resistance to agricultural protection may also arise out of environmental concerns of the public. In much of the EC, for example, intensive land utilization by agriculture, with its heavy emphasis on the use of environmentally damaging chemicals, has been associated by organized environmental groups with agricultural protection. Since environmental concerns appear to have a high income elasticity of demand as well as organized and vocal lobbying groups, they may eventually grow to develop into a credible countervailing power against the farming lobby.[16]

5. Resistance against agricultural protection may also arise from within agriculture itself. Two factors that have already been mentioned separately com-

15. Real wage rigidity may be the result of strong trade unions, such as those common in parts of Latin America.

16. However, there also appears to be the distinct possibility of environmental concerns operating on the demand side for protection. An example would be restrictions on imports of agricultural products grown with the help of chemical agents that are known to be harmful to the environment.

bine to bring this about. First, agricultural protection raises land prices, that is, the return to the fixed factor. Second, more land is needed by farmers to achieve economies of scale for such land-intensive products as cereals. In sum, agricultural protection actually makes it more difficult for farmers to halt the decline in comparative advantage. Whether this factor is sufficient to contain protection depends on the structure of the affected farms. Many small farms, none able to reap economies of scale with any reasonable increase in size, will not be able to contain protection. On the contrary, they are likely to demand protection. What is needed, then, are farms that already have a critical size.

6. A tight government budget is likely to shift upward the supply curve of protection. This is particularly true if agricultural protection is provided in the form of support prices, as for many commodities in the EC, or when government support of the agricultural sector is provided mainly through budgetary expenses, as in the United States. Resistance can then be expected by (i) taxpayers and (ii) the recipients of government support programs, who compete with agriculture for funds.[17] Budgetary considerations also appear to play an increasing role in East Asia (Moon 1989, 440). The increasing importance of budgetary pressures is not an accident. If an increasing number of countries follow a policy of agricultural support and protection, world prices become artificially depressed. Lower world prices, however, tend to increase, ceteris paribus, the budgetary cost of government support programs. Hence, ever higher budgetary expenditures will be necessary just to maintain the initial level of real support to farmers. This vicious circle has become quite significant during the 1980s, at least for the United States and the EC. Its importance can be measured by the fact that it is generally credited with being one of the driving forces behind the Uruguay Round and its focus on agriculture (Zietz and Valdés 1988).

7. Protection can be contained by credible pressure from outside the country. This point has already been touched on in the context of industry resistance to agricultural protection. Outside pressure can take the form of (i) bilateral pressure applied by a powerful trading partner that is negatively affected by agricultural support programs or (ii) legal obligations such as those deriving from GATT.

If bilateral pressure is brought to bear on a country, it can arouse national resentment that the groups benefiting from protection may be able to capital-

17. The fact that most developing countries tax agriculture at the beginning of their development process (KSV 1988) can also be interpreted, in a wider sense, as reflecting budgetary pressures. Since there are few organized activities that can be taxed, taxes would be unacceptably high for those that can, such as the fledgling manufacturing sector. Resistance to high taxes would be strong, however, because the persons involved tend to be well informed and small in number. Taxes on trade (in particular exports) and through marketing boards remain as alternatives with less political fallout because of their relatively broad base, their indirect nature, and the problems of the agricultural sector to organize effectively. In sum, agriculture is taxed by default at low levels of development as much as by design.

ize on in their effort to prevent or slow a policy change. This may have played some role, for example, in the case of the long-standing Japanese resistance to U.S. demands that the Japanese market be opened up for agricultural products. However, if a country stands to lose significantly in areas outside agriculture, the support for continued protection that derives from growing national resentment may not be sufficient to neutralize the internal pressure for moderating agricultural protection that comes from outside agriculture, mainly industry. The supply curve of politicians for agricultural protection would therefore likely shift up. This mechanism has been behind (i) Korea's agreement to raise beef imports from the United States in 1988 and 1989 following a complete import ban in 1985 and (ii) Korea's acceptance of the unfavorable 1989 GATT panel ruling on its beef import regime (U.S. International Trade Commission 1990). Another example of the effectiveness of this type of outside pressure in changing the outcome in the political market for protection is Japan's recent agreement to phase out quotas on beef and oranges.

Legal obligations under the GATT can be another effective way to stem a rise in protection (Hudec 1987, chap. 9). In agriculture, however, GATT has not been able to serve this function because of the loose discipline it puts on this sector. One of the primary objectives of the Uruguay Round is to change this.

Decisions on the Type of Protection

If the political market for government assistance actually leads to protection, the question arises of how this protection is administered. What methods of protection are used, subsidies or border measures, and, if border measures, tariffs or nontariff barriers? From the discussion in the last section, it is clear that measures that are transparent in their protective intent, whose costs to the public are easily identified, and that require little manpower to administer cannot be the preferred tools for politicians. Measures that have to be preferred from an economic point of view, in the sense that they minimize welfare losses, are likely to raise the resistance level of both the public and the agricultural bureaucracy and are therefore not preferred from a political point of view. For that reason, uniform tariffs may be as unacceptable to politicians as direct income transfers to farmers that are uncoupled from production.[18] Measures that require annual budget appropriations will likely fall in the same category. Border measures, by contrast, whether in the form of tariffs or NTBs, fare better on this account, in particular as long as the GATT continues to force little discipline on agriculture. And since the public has to be kept in the dark about the level and extent of protection and the agricultural bureaucracy kept busy, politicians prefer more obscure border measures to more transparent ones. Hence, we tend to observe in agriculture more restrictions, such

18. A full discussion of this issue is provided in Miner and Hathaway (1988, 111–65).

as variable levies, seasonal quotas, sanitary regulations, burdensome customs clearance procedures, and discretionary import licensing, than uniform tariffs. Obfuscation is clearly not limited to border measures but is also the leading principle in the design of domestic agricultural support measures in most industrialized countries. These tend to be excessively complex, difficult for the public to understand, and often difficult to administer. A good recent overview of the many domestic measures being applied in various countries is given in Webb, Lopez, and Penn (1990).

Budget pressures and international obligations constrain the choice of protectionist tools. The former tend to slow down the growth of government assistance and import protection measures with high budget outlays, in particular support prices defended by variable import levies as in the EC or deficiency payments as in the United States. With few international constraints on their choice of measures, however, governments retain the option to switch to a less costly alternative with an equivalent effect. In agriculture, this can mean, for example, the increased use of health and sanitary regulations and standards,[19] discretionary import licensing (table 5.2), voluntary export restraints (VERs),[20] political pressure to gain voluntary import expansions,[21] or more exotic schemes such as the sale of surplus food tied to the sale of high-technology products or arms. More stringent international legal obligations may prevent this switch to measures with equivalent effect. However, they are effective only insofar as they minimize loopholes and vague rules. The latter are easily spotted by the protectionist lobby, and, once they are identified, politicians will face significant pressure to make use of them. This explains, in part, the rise in gray-area measures such as VERs and the tactical use of antidumping and countervailing duty investigations in sectors other than agriculture that are subject to GATT rules.

The Trend Growth of Protection Levels

Once a mechanism for government assistance is in place, the question arises of how to set and adjust support levels over time. For example, government-defended support prices for staple food products are seldom kept at their initial level but tend to rise over time. What is the operating target that governments, and the agricultural lobby, use in this case to adjust the level of assistance? In the EC, with its elaborate system of support prices, the level of government assistance is set in a process that resembles the centralized annual wage bargaining between unions and employer associations that are typical of most major member countries of the European Community. Support price de-

19. Take, for example, the EC directive on the hormone content of meats that restricted U.S. exports to the EC (U.S. International Trade Commission 1990).

20. Although less prevalent in agriculture so far, VERs are by no means unknown. An example is the VER the EC has negotiated with Thailand on cassava exports, a feed grain substitute.

21. These have become a favorite tool of the United States, in particular following the passage of the "Super-301" legislation in 1988.

cisions, for example, boil down to a bargaining game between the European Commission and the farming lobby as represented by the national ministries of agriculture in the Council of Ministers.[22] In this process, the level of assistance tends to get tied to wage increases outside agriculture, with income parity of farmers being the overriding concern.

A natural question in this context is to what extent the East Asian practice is similar to that in the EC. Do developments in industry also drive agricultural output prices in East Asia? Figures 5.1 and 5.2 provide some graphic evidence for Korean rice and beef prices, respectively. Figure 5.1 reveals that the relation between the domestic and the world price of rice appears to have changed over time in Korea.[23] Both prices move in parallel through 1968. Starting in 1969, however, the domestic price of rice follows a strong upward trend, whereas the world price rises only moderately. Yet there appears to remain some relation between the two, although of a different nature than before 1969. In particular, it is now the growth rate of the domestic price rather than its level that starts to move in parallel with the world price. For example, the world food shortage in 1973–74, with its sharp rise in world food prices, induces an increase in the growth rate of the domestic rice price. The world commodity price boom of 1980 again accelerates the growth rate of the domestic price; the downturn in world price in 1982 slows it down. By contrast, the level of the domestic rice price appears to be tracked rather closely by the level of industrial productivity, which, in turn, is closely associated with real industrial wages.

The situation for beef prices is fairly similar (fig. 5.2). Domestic price equals world price through 1966. After that, the domestic price increases sharply relative to the world price. The year-to-year movements of the domestic price, however, follow the world price rather closely throughout the three decades, without the break observed for rice. By contrast, the level of industrial productivity predicts beef prices much less accurately than it does rice prices, although it provides the general trend for domestic beef prices.

Figures 5.1 and 5.2 suggest at least two tentative conclusions. First, government price policy and hence the government's decisions on protective measures can differ among commodities, a point that has also been forcefully made by KSV (1988) and Schiff and Valdés (1992).[24] Second, Korean experience suggests that agricultural policymakers in East Asia tie their level of agricultural assistance to productivity growth in industry, an outcome that is fairly close to that of the agricultural protection game in the EC. This supports the general conclusion derived in earlier, more formal work that the history of

22. Petit (1985) provides a detailed discussion of the political economy of decision making on agricultural issues in the EC and the United States.

23. The figure depicts the price for a traditional variety of rice.

24. KSV (1988) and Schiff and Valdés (1992) mainly differentiate between agricultural exportables that tend to be heavily taxed, through direct and indirect methods, and imported food products that are generally protected.

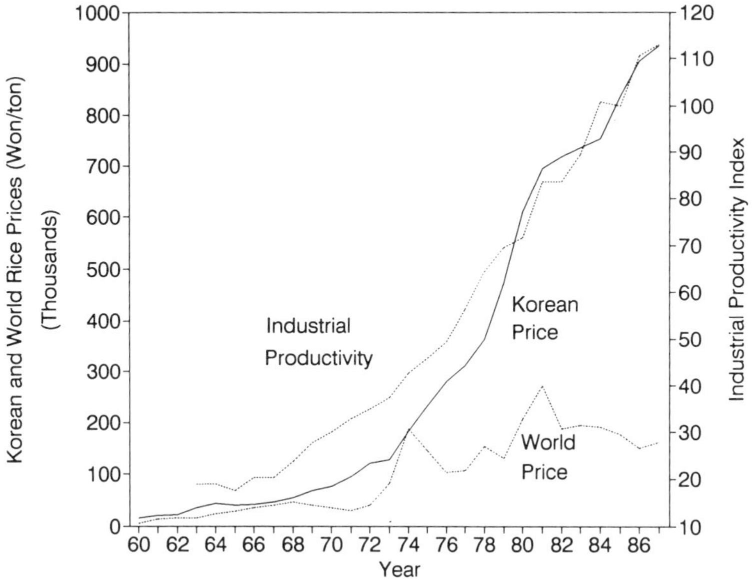

Fig. 5.1 The development of Korea and world rice prices relative to industrial productivity in Korea, 1960–87

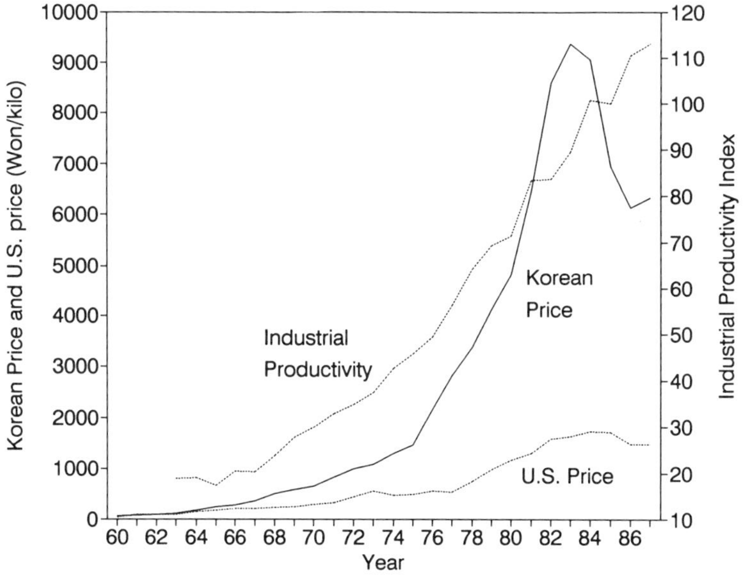

Fig. 5.2 The development of Korean and world beef prices relative to industrial productivity in Korea, 1960–87

agricultural protection in East Asian countries is similar to that observed elsewhere (Honma and Hayami 1986; Honma, in this volume). East Asia is not a special case. What appears to be certain from figures 5.1 and 5.2 is that the changes in nominal protection coefficients or producer subsidy equivalents, which are the focus of international attention, are not the focal point of domestic policy decisions. Rather, these measures of protection follow as a residual from the interplay of domestic decisions on import protection and the changing conditions on the world market.

5.3 The Future of Agricultural Protection

5.3.1 Some General Trends

Where will the forces of demand and supply carry agricultural protection in the future? In some of the major industrialized countries, in particular the United States and the EC, budget pressures appear to have reached a critical point, forcing governments to engage in negotiations aimed at limiting at least a further growth in agricultural protection. This does not yet apply to many developing countries that are on the verge of industrialization. One can therefore not exclude the possibility that such rapidly industrializing countries as Malaysia, Thailand, and Indonesia or such energy-exporting countries as Mexico, Nigeria, Saudi Arabia, and Yemen may repeat the Korean and Taiwanese experience with agricultural protection. To provide some feeling for the likelihood of this development, we will try to identify some general tendencies of government behavior toward agriculture.

A particular agricultural commodity will likely receive different treatment in the following three groups of countries: (i) importers with little import-competing production, such as Egypt for cereals; (ii) importers with a sizable import-competing sector, such as Korea for rice; and (iii) actual or potential exporters, such as Argentina for cereals. Countries in the first group are unlikely to introduce significant protection. The import-competing sector will be below the critical size to lobby effectively relative to other special interest groups. This is quite different for the second group of countries. Hence, ceteris paribus, we are very likely to see a significant growth of protection for this group. The third group, which consists of countries with a comparative advantage in the particular agricultural product, will be unlikely to introduce protective measures. The main issue for these countries is rather the removal of export taxes. In Latin America, agricultural interests appear to have gained sufficient strength in the 1980s to slowly eliminate the taxation of agricultural exportables.[25] A similar observation holds for Thailand. The long-standing

25. Export taxes have traditionally been a very important source of government revenue in many Latin American countries. Their removal and substitution by other taxes has raised difficult technical as well as political economy problems.

tax on rice exports was finally eliminated in 1986. However, there is also an opposing trend. Export taxes on agricultural raw materials, such as coffee beans and oranges, are a way to induce the domestic production of high-value processed products, such as soluble coffee and orange juice. Export taxes on the inputs used in the food-processing industry may therefore become more popular in the future. To ensure the success of the processing industry, the export tax on inputs may be combined with "infant industry" protection of the output. A recent example of this is provided by Indonesia (Barichello 1989). Table 5.5 provides some evidence for other Asian countries.

5.3.2 A Geographic Breakdown

From a geographic perspective, Asia appears to be the region with the most significant potential for agricultural protection. Most countries in this region have relatively little agricultural land relative to the size of the population. In addition, many countries have significant domestic production levels for staples, in particular rice and coarse grains. Recent evidence provided by KSV (1988), for example, suggests a growing trend in direct protection for these agricultural importables in such countries as Malaysia and the Philippines. Similar developments are under way in Indonesia (Barichello 1989). The experience of the latter country is particularly interesting because agricultural protection has gained momentum at a much lower per capita income level than in Taiwan or Korea. This has been made possible by the inflow of oil export revenue in the 1970s. Table 5.5 provides some background on the

Table 5.5 **Import Protection for Agricultural Products in Several Asian and African Countries**

Country	Protective Measures
Thailand	A. High tariffs (60 percent and more) on high-value agricultural products such as fresh fruit, beef, and processed foods
	B. Restrictive import registration and licensing procedures
Malaysia	A. High tariffs (30–50 percent) on high-value agricultural products such as fresh fruit, juices, and processed foods
	B. Sales tax serving as discriminatory excess import surcharge
Philippines	A. High tariffs (50 percent and more) on high-value agricultural products such as fresh fruit and processed foods
	B. High tariffs (20 percent) on meat imports, strict import licensing for beef and pork
	C. Restrictive state trading practices in rice and feed grains
Indonesia	A. High tariffs up to 50 percent
	B. State trading for wheat and soybeans, effective import ban for rice
Nigeria	A. Import bans on wheat, rice, maize, vegetable oils, and other products
	B. High tariffs on certain coarse grains (100 percent)

Source: U.S. Trade Representative (1991).

type and level of agricultural protection found in the Asian countries discussed above.

On the basis of table 5.4, a number of countries in sub-Saharan Africa have a likely comparative advantage in ruminant meat production. Exports of these products are indeed quite important for Somalia, Mali, and Botswana, to name just three. The region is a large exporter of tropical beverages, fibers, and sugar. Yet the level of implicit and explicit export taxes tends to be high (Schiff and Valdés 1992). One would expect that there will be a growing tendency in the future for the protection of processed products, such as those derived from coffee or cocoa beans. Export taxes on the raw products may remain in place to further nurture the development of an indigenous processing industry. To counteract the implicit import subsidy provided by exchange rate overvaluation, some countries, for example, Ghana, have erected very high import barriers for import-competing products, in particular basic staples, such as rice (KSV 1988). Nigeria, the most populous country in the region, also falls into this category (table 5.5). As an oil exporter, it appears to follow policies that are similar to those of another oil exporter, Indonesia.

The countries in North Africa and the Middle East are net importers of cereals, many with low self-sufficiency ratios. Protection is therefore relatively unlikely except for those countries with significant domestic production, such as Morocco and Syria, or oil exporters. Saudi Arabia, for example, has used a heavy dose of protection and has spent vast sums to produce cereals domestically. By the end of the 1980s, these policies had managed to more than double its self-sufficiency ratio (58 percent) compared to 1970. Other oil exporters in the region may follow this pattern, especially in the aftermath of the Gulf War and the trade embargo imposed on Iraq. Yemen, for example, appears to be well on its way. Since numerous countries in the region have the potential for the production of fruit and vegetables, one may also see protection evolve for these products, in both their fresh and their processed forms.

Latin American countries have recently made great strides toward liberalizing their trade regimes. Following the example of Chile, most have discarded import licensing and quantitative restrictions or are in the process of doing so (table 5.6). Differences among countries appear to result mainly from the speed with which they are adopting a system of tariffs only (tariffication) or are reducing tariff levels within that system. The ongoing push for trade liberalization should help remove the remaining trade bias, allowing the countries to take full advantage of their export potential. Exports are likely to grow in most products, including those that are land intensive. Land does not appear to be a constraining factor for many Latin American countries (table 5.4). So there is scope for production under economies of scale similar to that in Australia and other large agricultural producers. Anecdotal evidence suggests that there is already a growing tendency toward increasingly large agricultural production units that are managed much like a business firm. This represents somewhat of a reversal from earlier times, when large, inefficiently

Table 5.6 **Import Protection for Agricultural Products in Several Latin American Countries**

Country	Protective Measures
Argentina	A. Three-tiered tariff structure with 0, 11, and 22 percent, respectively
	B. Phasing out of import licensing in 1991
Brazil	A. Tariff rates between 0 and 40 percent by 1994, with average tariff rate of 20 percent
	B. Automatic import licensing within five days
Chile	A. 11 percent uniform tariff rates, some specific tariffs left
Colombia	A. Tariffs of 0–50 percent, additional surcharges of around 10 percent on wheat imports; by 1994 tariffs targeted to be between 0 and 15 percent
	B. Import licensing phased out in 1991
Mexico	A. Maximum tariff rates of 20 percent, with a trade-weighted average of 10 percent
	B. Import licensing left for 6 percent of tariff categories, mainly agricultural products, including cereals and fruit

Source: U.S. Trade Representative (1991) and information obtained from countries.

managed estates were split up into smaller units. A point other than economies of scale that works against agricultural protection in Latin America is the virtual absence compared to Europe and Asia of farming establishments in remote disadvantaged regions. The farmers in these regions appear to have a more than proportionate influence on the formulation of agricultural policies in Asia and Europe.

5.4 Containing the Spread of Agricultural Protection

The discussion presented above suggests that a continuation of current trends is likely to raise agricultural protection among developing countries that are on the verge of industrialization, especially in Asia. If this is to be avoided, the protectionist forces have to be checked. Three main approaches appear promising in this respect.

First, governments of developing countries have to be induced early on in the development process to prepare for structural adjustment. Policies have to be devised that moderate the negative income effects that result from a loss in comparative advantage for agricultural products. In this way, demands for protection may not come up or may be moderated. Among the possible adjustment policies are (i) efforts to raise off-farm employment opportunities in rural areas[26] and (ii) incentives for farmers to switch to high-value products that use less of the scarce factor (e.g., land or labor). To be successful, these policies require an accompanying set of appropriate policy instruments. Chief

26. One may note that raising off-farm employment has a dual purpose. Not only can it reduce the demand for protection, but it is also a cornerstone of a policy aimed at alleviating rural poverty. For this latter point, see Johnson et al. (1991).

among those would be better primary education in rural areas, improved infrastructure, support for research and development, and extension services.[27]

Second, on the basis of the recent Latin American experience and, in particular, the Chilean experience, it appears that a policy change to tariffs only (tariffication) can be a powerful way to contain the forces of protection. The strength of the tariffication system lies in its transparency. It makes it difficult for special interest groups to obtain special treatment without other groups in society noticing or fully understanding the extent of that special treatment. Tariffication is clearly most powerful in constraining protectionist demands when it is coupled with a commitment to uniformity in tariffs. In fact, a quasi-constitutional commitment to uniform tariffs can provide politicians with a shield against protectionist demands that is similar to that envisioned by the GATT. The Chilean experience of the last decade has shown this point quite forcefully. However, to change from a system with no constraints on the type and extent of protectionist policies to one of uniform tariffs is unlikely to be easy. From the Latin American experience, it appears that such a switch in policy is easier to achieve if a country has gone through an economic crisis that has lasted long enough or was deep enough to thoroughly discredit the old economic system and to sufficiently weaken the established special interest groups. To be successful, the reform process also has to be credible. A new political leadership that is unburdened by the policies of the past and the example of other countries being successful with economic policy reform may help induce such credibility. The timing of the reform process may also be of importance in this context. In particular, a swift change in the policy regime may induce more credibility in the commitment to the reform process than a slow reform pace. A quick change may also take better advantage of any temporary disorganization of special interest groups. A slow change, by contrast, could allow protectionist forces sufficient time to reorganize and eventually bring the whole reform process to a halt.

Third, the forces potentially opposing agricultural protection have to be strengthened. Outside pressure through the GATT appears to be a promising way to achieve this objective. However, there are two important preconditions: (i) agriculture has to be fully incorporated in the GATT; (ii) the GATT disciplines have to be extended to developing countries.[28]

The first point implies that there must not be different trade rules governing different sectors. No sector must be able to claim special treatment. This applies to agriculture as well as to textiles and clothing and services. Without equal treatment of sectors, GATT cannot inspire much confidence. After all, why should an exporter of agricultural products have to export under differ-

27. Many of the same policy instruments have also been recommended to alleviate rural poverty (Johnson et al. 1991).

28. A more detailed discussion of these and similar points is contained in Zietz and Valdés (1988). A generalization can be found in Zietz (1989).

ent rules than an exporter of chemicals? A corollary is that the large industrialized countries have to give up (i) exempting sectors from GATT disciplines once they lose their comparative advantage in them (agriculture, apparel) and (ii) demanding at the same time new disciplines for those sectors that their comparative advantage is moving to (high-tech industries and services). In other words, industrialized countries cannot be summarily exempted from the need for structural adjustment, while this is demanded from developing countries.

Extending the GATT disciplines to developing countries essentially means discontinuing the rules on special and differential treatment (S&D). S&D has exempted developing countries from any meaningful GATT disciplines (Hudec 1987). The GATT has, therefore, been unable to fulfill one of its most important objectives for developing countries, that is, to serve politicians as a shield against domestic demands for protection. From the perspective of the GATT and its survival as a guarantor of free trade, S&D treatment is likely to be counterproductive in the future. Developing countries are moving rapidly into areas such as light industries and heavy manufacturing and areas where intellectual property rights play a major role. Exempting them from the disciplines that apply to industrialized countries in these areas erodes and eventually destroys the credibility of GATT as an institution. The growth of bilateral pressure tactics on the part of industrialized countries, such as "Super-301"-type arrangements, is the likely result in the short run. Full-fledged managed trade would loom in the longer run. This would spell the end of GATT and of a multilateral trading system based on the principle of comparative advantage. Developing countries can be expected to be the biggest losers under such an arrangement.

To bring about the suggested changes is a most difficult task. However, the Uruguay Round has offered the best hope as of now to move in the right direction. The basic reason is that developing countries have, for the first time, some substantive offers to make to industrialized countries in the negotiations. This allows them, in principle, to take part in the negotiations as true negotiators and not just as observers. This was not the case in prior rounds. Developing countries could be found only on the request side of negotiations. As a consequence, they could not take part in any substantive negotiations and so concentrated on S&D instead. To take full advantage of the different role of developing countries, however, some changes are required in the way GATT negotiations are taking place.

Since countries are at different levels of development at any given point in time, successful GATT negotiations require cross-sectoral deals. Balanced give and take within sectoral boundaries is impossible to achieve for the set of all countries. Insisting on this older GATT negotiating scheme means restricting meaningful negotiations to take place only among countries at the same stage of development or concentration of their main economic activity. In practice, that implies negotiations between Europe, the United States, and

Japan. It is impossible to balance the offers and requests of all potential participants by sector. Table 5.7 provides an illustration of this for the case of agriculture. A possible balancing of offers and requests within agriculture is theoretically possible if an entry other than a question mark appears for each country or group of countries. This is the case only for the United States and the EC.[29] All other parties approach the negotiations only from one side or not at all. Hence, there is little substance that they can contribute to the negotiations if the negotiations are conducted on the traditional sector basis. Meaningful requests and offers are possible between all participants if cross-sectoral agreements are allowed. That way, requests of the three major blocks of industrialized countries for new GATT agreements on services, trade-related investment measurements (TRIMs), and trade-related intellectual property rights (TRIPs) can be balanced by the requests of the Cairns group members, newly industrialized countries (NICs), and other developing countries for liberalization in agriculture, textiles, and apparel (MFA), as well as more discipline in the use of voluntary export restraints (VERs), countervailing duties (CVDs), and antidumping measures (ADs). It remains to be seen to what extent these opportunities can be exploited in the future.

5.5 Summary and Conclusions

The paper has investigated the determinants of agricultural protection and its growth over time, as it relates to developing countries in general and the newly industrialized countries of East Asia in particular. One conclusion is that a loss of comparative advantage in agriculture can be prevented only if productivity growth in agriculture matches that in industry. For most agricultural products, however, productivity growth ultimately hinges on sufficient endowments with arable land and cheap labor, a condition not met by the newly industrialized countries of East Asia. In the absence of adequate factor endowments, farmers can avoid income losses relative to industry only if they are able to engage in off-farm employment or if they lobby for protection.

The demand for protection tends to grow strongly as the farming sector shrinks in size, education levels rise, and information costs decline. The supply of protection by politicians rises as the farming sector declines in size and income levels rise. Factors that can potentially limit the supply of agricultural protection are (i) resistance by industry, (ii) environmental concerns, (iii) a tight government budget, and (iv) international obligations coupled with credible enforcement mechanisms.

The objective of agricultural protection in East Asia appears to be very similar to that of the European Community and other industrialized countries.

29. The entry "harmonize" in table 5.7 means that the United States allows the EC to remove the zero tariff binding on feed grain substitutes, while at the same time EC protection levels on grains are reduced somewhat.

Table 5.7 **Potential Offers and Requests for Agriculture**

	U.S.	EC	Japan	Cairns	NICs	Importers
Offer	harmonize	liberalize	liberalize	?	liberalize	?
Request	liberalize	harmonize	?	liberalize	?	?

Note: Cairns stands for the members of the Cairns group, which are nonsubsidizing food exporters; NICs represents those food-importing newly industralized countries that are not part of the Cairns group, e.g., Korea and Taiwan. Importers denotes developing country net food importers such as Egypt. The offers and requests are potential, not actual. A question mark denotes the absence of a meaningful offer or request, even potentially.

The emphasis is on maintaining income parity with industry. The methods that are employed to achieve this objective can be predicted from a simple demand and supply framework of protection. They tend to be border measures, often of an obscure nature and difficult to understand or to predict.

The paper suggests that many Asian countries that are on the verge of industrialization have considerable potential for agricultural protection because most of them have a significant amount of domestic production but lack the natural comparative advantage in agriculture that is typical of many Latin American countries. To contain a further spread of agricultural protection, more emphasis has to be put on off-farm employment in rural sectors and firm GATT disciplines that apply to agriculture in developed and developing countries alike.

References

Anderson, Kym. 1983. The growth of agricultural protection in East Asia. *Food Policy* 8 (4): 327–36.

———. 1986. Economic growth, structural change, and the political economy of protection. In Anderson and Hayami 1986.

Anderson, Kym, and Yujiro Hayami, with Aurelia George et al., eds. 1986. *The political economy of agricultural protection: East Asia in international perspective.* Sydney: Allen & Unwin.

Anderson, Kym, Yujiro Hayami, and Masayoshi Honma. 1986. Growth of agricultural protection. In Anderson and Hayami 1986.

Anderson, Kym, and Rod Tyers. 1989. Agricultural protection growth in advanced and newly industrialized countries. In Maunder and Valdés 1989.

Baldwin, Robert E. 1982. The political economy of protectionism. In *Import competition and response,* ed. Jagdish N. Bhagwati. Chicago: University of Chicago Press.

Barichello, Richard R. 1989. The political economy of agricultural policy in Asia: The case of Indonesia. In Maunder and Valdés 1989.

Bautista, Romeo M. 1987. *Production incentives in Philippine agriculture: Effects of trade and exchange rate policies.* Research Report no. 59. Washington, D.C.: International Food Policy Research Institute.

Carter, Colin A., and Walter H. Gardiner. 1988. *Elasticities in international agricultural trade*. Boulder, Colo.: Westview.

Clements, Kenneth W., and Larry A. Sjaastad. 1984. *How protection taxes exporters*. Thames Essay no. 39. London: Trade Policy Research Centre.

Dorosh, Paul, and Alberto Valdés. 1990. *Effects of exchange rate and trade policies on agriculture in Pakistan*. Research Report no. 84. Washington, D.C.: International Food Policy Research Institute.

Downs, Anthony. 1957. *An economic theory of democracy*. New York: Harper & Row.

Garcia, Jorge Garcia. 1981. *The effects of exchange rates and commercial policy on agricultural incentives in Colombia, 1953–1978*. Research Report no. 24. Washington, D.C.: International Food Policy Research Institute.

Goldin, Ian, and Odin Knudsen, eds. 1990. *Agricultural trade liberalization: Implications for developing countries*. Paris: OECD and World Bank.

Honma, Masayoshi, and Yujiro Hayami. 1986. The determinants of agricultural protection levels: An econometric analysis. In Anderson and Hayami 1986.

Hudec, Robert E. 1987. *Developing countries in the GATT legal system*. Thames Essay no. 50. London: Trade Policy Research Centre.

Islam, Nurul. 1988. *Horticultural exports of developing countries: Past performance, future prospects, and policy issues*. Research Report no. 80. Washington, D.C.: International Food Policy Research Institute.

Johnson, D. Gale, Alberto Valdés, Dennis McCaffrey, and Jo Anne Yeager, 1991. Guidelines for developing a strategy for agricultural and natural resources. Bethesda, Md.: ABT Associates for U.S. AID, June.

Krueger, Anne O., Maurice W. Schiff, and Alberto Valdés. 1988. Agricultural incentives in developing countries: Measuring the effect of sectoral and economywide policies. *World Bank Economic Review* 2 (3): 255–71.

Lindert, Peter H. 1991. Historical patterns of agricultural policy. In *Agriculture and the state: Growth, employment, and poverty in developing countries*, ed. Peter Timmer. Ithaca, N.Y.: Cornell University Press.

Maunder, Allen, and Alberto Valdés, eds. 1989. *Agriculture and governments in an interdependent world: Proceedings of the Twentieth International Conference of Agricultural Economists*. Aldershot, England: Dartmouth.

Messerlin, Patrick A. 1981. The political economy of protectionism: The bureaucratic case. *Weltwirtschaftliches Archiv* 117 (3): 469–96.

Miner, William M., and Dale E. Hathaway, eds. 1988. *World agricultural trade: Building a consensus*. Halifax, N.S.: Institute for Research on Public Policy and Institute for International Economics.

Moon, Pal-Young. 1989. Agricultural policy reforms in South Korea: Motivations, features, and effects. In Maunder and Valdés 1989.

Mundlak, Yair, Domingo Cavallo, and Roberto Domenech. 1989. *Agriculture and economic growth in Argentina, 1913–84*. Research Report no. 76. Washington, D.C.: International Food Policy Research Institute.

OECD. 1987. *National policies and agricultural trade*. Paris.

Olson, Mancur. 1965. *The logic of collective action*. Cambridge, Mass.: Harvard University Press.

Otsuka, Keijiro. 1989. Discussion opening. In Maunder and Valdés 1989.

Petit, Michel. 1985. *Determinants of agricultural policies in the United States and the European Community*. Research Report no. 51. Washington, D.C.: International Food Policy Research Institute.

Schiff, Maurice W., and Alberto Valdés. 1992. *A synthesis of the economics in developing countries*. Vol. 4 of *The political economy of agricultural pricing policy*. Baltimore: Johns Hopkins University Press.

Snape, Richard H. 1987. The importance of frontier barriers. In *Protection and competition in international trade: Essays in honor of W. Max Corden,* ed. Hendryk Kierzkowski. Oxford: Basil Blackwell.
U.S. Department of Agriculture. Agriculture and Trade Analysis Division. Economic Research Service. 1990. *World agriculture: Trends and indicators, 1970–89.* Statistical Bulletin no. 815. Washington, D.C., September.
U.S. International Trade Commission. 1990. *Operation of the trade agreements program: 41st report, 1989.* Publication no. 2317. Washington, D.C., September.
U.S. Trade Representative. 1991. *1991 national trade estimate report on foreign trade barriers.* Washington, D.C., March.
Valdés, Alberto. 1987. Agriculture in the Uruguay Round: Interests of developing countries. *World Bank Economic Review* 1 (4): 571–93.
Valdés, Alberto, and Joachim Zietz. 1980. *Agricultural protection in OECD countries: Its cost to less developed countries.* Research Report no. 21. Washington, D.C.: International Food Policy Research Institute.
Vincent, David. 1989. Domestic effects of agricultural protection in Asian countries with special reference to Korea. In *Macroeconomic consequences of farm support policies,* ed. Andrew B. Stoeckel, David Vincent, and Sandy Cuthbertson. Durham: Duke University Press.
Webb, Alan J., Michael Lopez, and Renata Penn, eds. 1990. *Estimates of producer and consumer subsidy equivalents: Government intervention in agriculture, 1982–87.* Statistical Bulletin no. 803. Washington, D.C.: Agriculture and Trade Analysis Division, Economic Research Service, U.S. Department of Agriculture, April.
Zietz, Joachim. 1989. Negotiations on GATT reform and political incentives. *World Economy* 12 (1): 39–52.
Zietz, Joachim, and Alberto Valdés. 1988. *Agriculture in the GATT: An analysis of alternative approaches to reform.* Research Report no. 70. Washington, D.C.: International Food Policy Research Institute.

Comment Masayoshi Honma

Joachim Zietz and Alberto Valdés presented us a good summary of a general framework in which to consider the growth of agricultural protection in industrializing economies. They derived meaningful implications of such agricultural protectionism for developing countries and for the current GATT system. Their insight into the process of the political market is useful for sharpening our understanding of the disarray into which world agricultural policies have fallen today. Since their approach to agricultural protectionism is based on the same framework as my approach in Honma (in this volume), I found nothing with which to disagree regarding the substance of their paper. My remarks, therefore, will be complimentary and serve mainly to open discussion.

As Zietz and Valdés have shown, the pattern of agricultural protection in the world as revealed by cross-country and longitudinal observations lends

Masayoshi Honma is professor of economics at Otaru University of Commerce, Hokkaido, Japan.

itself readily to an explanation in terms of political market factors. The political market approach is an attempt to explain why government interventions are persistent and not likely to cease despite the fact that they are economically less efficient and usually lead to high-cost solutions to stated objectives. The solution in the political market is not economically efficient. Therefore, an analysis of the political market explains the discrepancy between political and economic solutions.

Zietz and Valdés neatly summarize the development of agricultural protectionism in international comparisons, and they explain the pattern of agricultural protection that follows changes in the political environment as an economy develops. As they indicated, the high level of agricultural protection in industrial countries is at a political equilibrium with the high demand for and high supply of protection policies. Therefore, there is less incentive to change this political equilibrium domestically. One way to break down this equilibrium is to introduce another player into the political market, which is foreign pressure. Foreign pressure comes from foreign producers, not consumers, so that foreign pressure becomes a strong countervailing force working against the domestic demand for protection. The recent removal of import quotas for beef and oranges in Japan is a good example of the importance of foreign pressure in determining a country's level of protection. In other words, political markets are now internationally linked, and we need to analyze a new equilibrium of the political market in an international setting.

In a consideration of the political equilibrium at a high level of agricultural protection domestically, it is important to indicate that such an equilibrium is sustained by the asymmetry of information on the costs and benefits of agricultural protection. The benefits are well recognized by farmers, who, therefore, can calculate the benefits when they demand protection. However, the costs of protection are generally vague and not so visible. Politicians always prefer more obscure measures of protection. The indication by Zietz and Valdés that protection measures tend to be well hidden and less straightforward, for example, nontariff barriers (NTBs), is very important. Therefore, another step toward breaking down the persistent political equilibrium of protection is to make the costs of protection visible to the general public. For example, the calculations of producer subsidy equivalents (PSEs) by the OECD are appreciated to take into account costs of agricultural protection whether they are used in multilateral negotiations or not.

In calculating the costs of protection, not only the costs burdening consumers and taxpayers but also the cost of political lobbying should be considered. In order to influence politicians, interest groups invest in lobbying, but the outcome is not economically productive. Lobbying activities clearly absorb scarce resources, and the social value of these resources should be counted in the total welfare costs as well as the conventional deadweight loss arising from government intervention. If the cost of rent-seeking activities becomes large, it seriously disturbs economic development and delays the takeoff of developing economies.

Following the use of foreign pressure and more information on the real cost of protection, the third factor to break through the stalemate of protectionism is reorienting policy measures to support farmers. The root of agricultural protection is the rural-urban income disparity, or "negative income effects," in Zietz and Valdés's terms, in the process of economic development. As they mention, there are four ways for farmers to escape from the income disparity problem. First is to increase agricultural productivity. Second is diversifying production toward more income-elastic products. Third is raising off-farm labor supply. And fourth is lobbying for protection. Farmers generally choose lobbying to avoid the income gap because the other ways are more costly. Therefore, a desirable policy to eliminate the income gap encourages farmers to use methods other than lobbying, which is not efficient in the macroeconomic sense. Government assistance in developing new technologies for higher productivity, providing better market information and demand analyses for farmers' production diversification, and offering job training to improve both job opportunities and job skills are all effective ways to reduce the cost of farmers' attempts to avoid negative income effects. These government services strongly resemble public goods and may be acceptable to the general public as a way of supporting farmers. And those who lag seriously behind in income earnings because, for example, there is little job opportunity in their area should be supported by direct payments from a social security program—support that comes not because they are farmers but because they are poor. In other words, agricultural policy should be reoriented toward so-called decoupling. Assisting or supporting agriculture itself is not a bad policy, but the means of assistance is the problem.

The concept of "decoupling" should also be applied to the treatment of developing countries in the GATT system. Zietz and Valdés discuss the special and differential treatment of developing countries in section 5.4, which is the most important part of their paper. They propose that, ideally, special and differential treatment should be phased out altogether. They also state that it has done little good to developing countries but a lot of harm to the GATT process. I agree on both points. Developing countries should not be exempted from the GATT disciplines for the same reason that agriculture should not be exempted. Any exemptions erode and jeopardize the credibility of the GATT as an institution. If agriculture should be incorporated fully into the GATT, why not incorporate developing countries fully into the GATT? The GATT disciplines should be applied without exemptions regardless of sector or country. If some assistance is needed, it should be directed toward that need in the most efficient way. For example, assistance for development should come from official development aid or some other direct means rather than through interventions or special and differential treatment in trade. Even exemption from the GATT disciplines for balance-of-payments reasons should be eliminated. This exemption appears to play a role in increasing import restrictions in developing countries. If a country faces a difficulty in its international balance of payments, it should be financed directly through the IMF on behalf of the GATT. Better yet, the GATT itself should have such a financing function to serve countries that have temporary difficulties in international balance of payments. In other words, collaborations between the GATT and the IMF that differ from those under the current system are required. These strict applications of the GATT principles are essential if the growth of the world economy through international trade is to be maintained. I hope that the current negotiations of the Uruguay Round will be successful in this regard.

III

6 Economic Growth and Trade Relations: Japanese Performance in Long-Term Perspective

Gary R. Saxonhouse

Since the second half of the nineteenth century, Japan's productivity growth has outstripped that of every other major industrialized economy. This impressive achievement rested on 250 years of growth and structural change prior to the opening of Japan to international trade in the nineteenth century. Japan's superior performance is not the exotic product of a small cluster of distinctive economic institutions. Japan's rapid economic growth has coexisted with labor markets, capital markets, and product markets whose structure and organization have changed radically over time. Japan's economic performance has been successful for far too long for it to be attributable to any one particular configuration of its economic institutions.

The invariance of Japan's economic record to a wide variety of institutional circumstances is important to keep in mind when considering Japan's distinctive trade structure. Japan's rapid economic growth over the past century has gone hand in hand with a very distinctive performance in international trade. What Japan sells to the rest of the world has changed continuously and dramatically over time. At the same time, Japan has long imported a distinctively low level of manufactured imports. There have been facile attempts to link Japan's controversial trade performance with some of Japan's distinctive economic institutions. As with Japan's economic growth, so Japan's trade performance has also been distinctive for too long to be the product of any specific configuration of Japan's product markets and/or factor markets or any particular style of state intervention.

None of this should suggest that Japan's superior economic performance is so deep rooted as to defy economic explanation. Rather, it is important to focus on the real continuities in Japan's experience. In particular, Japan's geography is much different from that of the world's other major industrialized

Gary R. Saxonhouse is professor of economics at the University of Michigan.

economies. Throughout the past century, relative to these other economies, Japan, while uniquely poorly endowed with natural resources, has also been well endowed with a high-quality labor force and with unusually thrifty households. These distinctive Japanese circumstances may go a long way toward explaining its superior economic growth performance, its meager level of manufactured imports, and its lack of participation in intraindustry trade.

Throughout modern Japanese history, Japan's international trade has been based on the sharp differences in its circumstances from those of the rest of the industrialized world. In recent years, this has put Japan at odds with the rest of the major actors in the global economy. Increasingly, international trade between most major economies is governed by their similarities, not by their differences with each other. Similarities-based trade has none of the politically contentious income redistribution consequences of differences-based trade. Similarities-based trade builds alliances for the further reduction of trade barriers. By contrast, while differences-based trade is the traditional substance of international trade theory, nonetheless it taxes the legitimacy of the international economic system.

In the first two sections of this paper, Japan's distinctive economic performance will be reviewed. In a third section, how well traditional and newer theories of international trade explain Japan's performance will be examined and new statistical tests will be presented. Finally, the implications of the changing pattern of Japanese trade for the past, present, and future of Japan's international economic relations will be discussed.

6.1 Productivity Growth: Prewar and Postwar

It is all too easy to forget that the various national economic performances as presently observed may be surprisingly deep rooted. For example, relatively poor American productivity performance is arguably an old, old story and not the result of a sudden loss in American know-how. U.S. productivity growth has been relatively poor, not only for the past fifteen or twenty years, but for the better part of the past century (Maddison 1982, 98; Baumol, Blackman, and Wolff 1989).[1] Between 1899 and 1913, the U.S. growth rate was already lower than that of Sweden, France, Germany, Italy, and Japan. The U.S. rate of productivity growth was again below all these countries (except for Germany) between 1913 and 1939. While U.S. productivity grew relatively rapidly during both world wars, this is in good part a result of the slowdown in the growth of other countries. And the American experience relative to other countries in the four decades after the Second World War seems to differ only in detail from its experience in the four pre–Second World War decades (see table 6.1).

If there are continuities in American performance, there are certainly con-

1. For a more skeptical view, see Williamson (1991).

Table 6.1 Comparative Levels of Productivity, 1890–1986 (U.S. GDP per manhour = 100)

	1890	1938	1950	1986
France	55	64	44	89
Germany	58	56	33	79
Italy	44	49	32	74
Japan	23	33	14	51
Sweden	44	59	55	76
United States	100	100	100	100

Source: Maddison (1982, 98) and Maddison (1989, 89).

tinuities also present in Japanese economic performance. Between the late 1940s and the mid-1980s, Japan's productivity growth exceeded the performance of every other major economy (World Bank 1986). Not only did Japan's productivity grow faster than each of the OECD economies, but it also grew faster than any of the Latin American economies and faster than such Asian economies as Hong Kong, Korea, Taiwan, and Singapore.

Like the United States, however, Japan's prewar experience resembles its postwar experience. Japan grew faster than any other economy in the postwar period, but it also grew faster than all other major economies during the seven decades between the Meiji Restoration (1868) and 1938 (Maddison 1982). Indeed, Japan's distinctive position can be pushed back still further. Already in the 1870s and 1880s Japan's level of economic accomplishment was well above the rest of Asia. Only in the 1950s and 1960s would other Asian economies reach the levels of performance that Japan had achieved eighty years earlier (Ohkawa 1978). This impressive achievement, in turn, rested on almost three hundred years of growth and structural change prior to the opening of Japan to international trade in the 1850s. While Tokugawa Japan missed the scientific and industrial revolutions of the seventeenth and eighteenth centuries, this by no means necessitated economic stagnation. For example, between 1600 and 1870, Japanese agricultural output grew at an impressive average annual rate of 0.33 percent (Umemura 1973).

It is no simple matter to account precisely for these long-standing differences in U.S. and Japanese productivity performance. There is some reason to believe that, among the countries with the capacity to learn from foreign experience elsewhere, productivity bears a negative relation to the level of productivity performance (Baumol, Blackman, and Wolff 1989).[2] Following the mid-1890s, the United States had a lower rate of productivity growth than Sweden, France, Germany, Italy, and Japan, but, in the mid-1890s, it already had the world's highest level of productivity. By contrast, among these countries, Japan had by far the lowest level of productivity in the mid-1890s but followed with by far the highest rate of productivity growth.

2. For a contrary view, see De Long (1988).

With hindsight, it is not surprising that there should be substantial convergence in U.S. and Japanese economic performance. American wealth in the late nineteenth century rested on an abundance of natural resources and a skilled population capable of economically exploiting the latest scientific and technological achievements within the framework of largely accommodating policies of local, state, and national governments (Wright 1990). Despite economic improvement during the Tokugawa period, and despite the comparatively high basic literacy and numeracy of Japan's male population in the late nineteenth century, Japan's familiarity with Western science and technology was still much too limited to overcome its relative dearth of natural resources (Dore 1965).

Over the course of the late nineteenth century and the twentieth century, however, these conditions have changed dramatically. During this period, there has been no significant growth in the size or importance of American natural resource wealth relative to the American population. Growth in natural resource wealth could not push America forward relative to the rest of the world as had happened earlier in the nineteenth century. Quite the contrary. New mineral discoveries in the Middle East, Africa, Latin America, and Australia and transportation improvements in these regions and elsewhere have tangibly diminished natural resources as the basis of twentieth-century American prosperity.

While natural resource wealth has long since ceased to provide the basis for American productivity growth, productivity growth has not stagnated. The growth of America's physical capital stock and new investments in research and development and human resources have continued to raise American productivity. Despite nine decades of relatively slow productivity growth, America's high late nineteenth-century level of productivity and the happy absence of wartime destruction have left the United States, at least as late as the end of the 1980s, with the highest level of aggregate productivity among the world's major economies.

The declining importance of natural resource wealth could only help Japan's relative performance in the twentieth century. Increasing Japanese thrift and increasing Japanese capacity to make use of hitherto remote or unknown foreign advances in science and technology have helped Japan to achieve the twentieth century's highest rate of productivity growth (Ohkawa and Rosovsky 1973). Unhappily, in part because of its very low level of productivity in the late nineteenth century (and hence the very great potential to benefit from foreign information), and in part because of the destruction resulting from Japan's disastrous Pacific war, nine decades of relatively rapid productivity growth have still left Japan with the lowest level of productivity among the world's major industrialized economies (Maddison 1989, 89).

It is useful to be reminded of the persistence of relative national economic performance. For all the fascination that social scientists may have with institutions, relative performance for many economies often seems independent of all but the most radical institutional change. Long before permanent employment was a significant element in Japanese management strategy, long before semiannual bonuses were a significant element in Japanese employee compensation, long before stability was the hallmark of Japanese macroeconomic management, and long before high quality was a familiar attribute of Japanese goods, Japanese productivity growth rates were the envy of the world.[3]

When Japanese labor turnover rates in manufacturing were far higher than what was ever experienced in Europe or the United States, when Japanese industry exhibited great creativity in producing unprecedentedly poor-quality products, and when Japanese macroeconomic management bordered on the chaotic, Japan was still able to raise its rate of productivity improvement above what was experienced by other major industralized countries (Saxonhouse 1976; Saxonhouse and Ranis 1985). The available historical evidence suggests that Japan's longtime rapid rate of economic improvement does not rest on a few distinctive institutional arrangements. Japan's superior economic performance has persisted even as its most basic economic institutions have changed markedly. Japan is under pressure in negotiations such as the Structural Impediments Initiative (SII) to harmonize its economic institutions with those of its trading partners (Saxonhouse 1991). On the basis of the past record, there is certainly considerable reason to believe that Japan can absorb such adjustment without much damage to its capacity for continued superior economic performance.

6.2 Trade and Economic Growth

It is hard to think about the determinants of long-term national economic performance without considering the role of international economic relations. The classical economics of Smith, Ricardo, and Mill stressed the intimate link between the size of markets and productivity improvement.[4] At an aggregate level, the evidence of the past century is mixed. With the radical exception of Japan, and possibly France, foreign trade declined in importance between the late nineteenth century and the Second World War. During this period, exports grew far more slowly than GNP for most major economies. It is significant that Japan, the country with the highest rate of productivity growth, also experienced continued rapid growth in the role that foreign trade played within its economy. By contrast, as seen in table 6.2, for the rest of the major industralized countries, a decline in the importance of foreign trade did not mean a decline in the rate of productivity growth. Quite the contrary. For example, as noted in table 6.3, during the interwar years, even as foreign trade dropped sharply, productivity growth actually accelerated.

In the decades since 1945, international trade's importance once again re-

3. For an interpretation of Japanese economic performance that stresses bonus payments, permanent employment, and macroeconomic stability, see Weitzman (1984) and Freeman and Weitzman (1987).

4. Smith's pin factory is the most famous example.

Table 6.2 **Trade and Overall Economic Activity, 1890–1986 (1890 = 100)**

	1890		1938		1986	
	Exports	Output	Exports	Output	Exports	Output
France	100	100	220.9	184.4	3,585.3	916.4
Germany	100	100	193.0	347.2	2,938.1	1,575.4
Italy	100	100	161.8	242.6	7.721.7	1,282.8
Japan	100	100	4,426.5	468.8	93,278.0	5,341.3
Sweden	100	100	351.8	406.5	4,108.1	1,982.8
United States	100	100	310.4	369.2	2,555.2	2,108.7

Source: Maddison (1982, apps. A, F) and Maddison (1989, app. B).

Table 6.3 **Productivity, 1870–1979, GDP per Manhour in 1970 U.S. Relative Prices ($)**

	1870	1890	1913	1938	1950	1979
France	.42	.59	.90	1.69	1.85	7.11
Germany	.43	.62	.95	1.47	1.40	6.93
Italy	.44	.47	.72	1.28	1.37	5.83
Japan	.17	.24	.37	.87	.59	4.39
Sweden	.31	.45	.83	1.55	2.34	6.71
United States	.70	1.06	1.67	2.62	4.25	8.28

Source: Maddison (1982, 212).

versed course. Instead of declining, international trade has grown much faster than GNP for all the major industrialized economies. For some but not all of the major industrialized economies, this explosive growth in international trade has gone hand in hand with an acceleration in the rate of productivity increase. This has been true most notably for Japan but also for such countries as France, Germany, and Italy.

What accounts for the varied relation between international trade and economic growth over the course of the last century? In view of the experience since 1945, it may surprise some to learn that, for much of both the nineteenth and the twentieth centuries, many economists believed that, as nations experienced economic growth, trade would grow less important (Cooper 1964). In 1821, Robert Torrens wrote, "As the several nations of the world advance in wealth and population, the commercial intercourse between them must gradually become less important and beneficial" ([1821] 1965, 288). Torrens found that trade resulted from the exchange of manufactures and raw materials. He argued that, as land became scarcer as a result of population growth, the basis for trade would disappear.

At the turn of the century, Werner Sombart formulated the so-called law of the declining importance of export trade. Sombart claimed that the gradual industrialization of the agricultural countries and the increasing capacity to consume on the part of the home market would lead to a reduction of the growth of foreign trade relative to the growth of internal trade and production (Sombart 1903).

Sombart's general outlook was shared by other major figures in economics in the first half of the twentieth century. For all their celebrated differences in macroeconomics, Dennis Robertson and John Maynard Keynes both agreed that foreign trade would be relatively less important in future years. In a widely read essay entitled "The Future of International Trade" written in the 1930s and reprinted approvingly by the American Economic Association a decade later, Robertson wrote that trade would become increasingly less important, partly because economic growth would make it less rewarding, and partly because it would be stifled by restrictive commercial policy introduced to reduce the risks inherent in dealing with foreigners (Robertson 1938). Keynes emphasized demand considerations in his own analysis. Keynes observed that the income elasticity of demand for nontradables is much higher than it is for imported goods. This means that, as incomes rise with economic growth, an ever greater share will be spent on locally produced services (Keynes 1933).

In the postwar period, economists have spent a great deal of theoretical energy investigating how the sources of economic growth, such as technological change and capital accumulation, affect the volume of trade.[5] Much of this research has been conducted for the elementary case where two countries producing two goods with two inputs trade with each other. In this simple world, as a country accumulates more of its relatively scarce factor of production, its interest in trade declines. Similarly, technological change in an import-competing industry that saves on the use of a scarce factor of production should also encourage a decline in trade. Technological change that saves on a scarce factor in an export industry gives a more complicated result. The factor-saving effect of the technological change should encourage a decline in trade. This effect is opposed, however, by the cost-reducing effect of technological change, which should encourage an expansion of the more efficient export industry. The relative strength of these two forces will in any particular instance determine the net effect on trade of technological change.

The simple framework just presented can be adapted to help examine the role of trade within the American and Japanese economies over the past century. For much of the period before the Second World War, the United States was an importer of products that used unskilled labor intensively and an exporter of products that used natural resource products intensively (Crafts and Thomas 1986; Wright 1990). If technological change was generally labor saving during this period, this should have worked to diminish the significance of trade for the American economy. This trend might have been reinforced by the natural resource–using bias that American technological change in all likeli-

5. Much of this early literature is reviewed in Bhagwati (1964).

hood also exhibited during this same period (Wright 1990). As before, this would have happened if the factor-using bias of this technological change was more significant than its cost-reducing effect. Further reinforcement might have come from the historical antitrade bias of demand noted by Keynes.

Unlike the United States during the period before the Second World War, Japan had an abundance of relatively unskilled labor and exported labor-intensive products (Yamazawa 1978). During the same period, however, Japan's increasing capacity to make use of imported Western technology resulted in Japanese technological change being strongly labor saving (Ohkawa and Rosovsky 1973). This by itself is probably enough to explain the distinctive role that international trade played within the Japanese economy during the early decades of the twentieth century. Despite international trade becoming relatively less important for all major economies, and despite a dramatic increase in global protectionism, trade became much more important for the Japanese economy during these years. Technological change that made Japan's most abundant resource still more abundant surely accelerated this trend.

6.3 Intraindustry Trade

The simplest factor-endowment-based theories of international trade are able to provide some insight into early twentieth-century trends. They are of much less help, however, in explaining the explosion in international trade that has occurred in the four decades since the end of the Second World War. The convergence in income levels and in the availability of capital, skills, and technology among the world's major market economies should have worked to continue to diminish the relative significance of international trade in the postwar period. If countries trade to substitute for what is relatively scarce at home, the more similar countries become, the less basis there is for trade.

Assuming that the sharp reversal of the protectionist trends that dominated international commercial policy in the early decades of the twentieth century is insufficient to explain postwar performance, what significant considerations have been left out of the preceding analysis? In the last decade or so, economists have increasingly appreciated that a large share of international trade is driven by considerations other than simple differences in local scarcities of factors of production such as land, labor, and capital (Helpman and Krugman 1985). In particular, within many industries that are important for international trade, a great variety of goods is produced. Because of scale economies, no country is able to produce the full range of differentiated products within any industry by itself. In this case, two countries could be identical, but there is still a basis for trade. Quite in contrast with interindustry trade, with similar tastes, the more countries resemble each other in their size and their factor endowments, the more differentiated products mutually desired will be produced, and the more beneficial trade will be.

This new perspective on trade does help explain why international trade has grown more rapidly than production during the postwar period (Helpman 1987). As noted in table 6.4, during the postwar period, the economic conditions of the sixteen nations that dominate international trade have become more equal. This decline in the dispersion of the level of economic performance has gone, as theory predicts, hand in hand with growth in intraindustry trade as a proportion of total trade (Grubel and Lloyd 1975). At least this is true if intraindustry trade is measured at the three-digit or four-digit SITC or ISIC levels (Lipsey 1976).

Data on the dispersion of economic performance is also consistent with the prewar experience in international trade. During the early decades of the twentieth century, there was no pronounced trend in the dispersion of economic performance among the major economies, and the relative importance of international trade declined. Intraindustry trade was not growing fast enough to offset the relatively slow growth of interindustry trade (Hirschman 1945, chap. 7).

A postwar world characterized by intraindustry trade might have been expected to be relatively free of international commercial policy disputes. If the vast majority of international trade is undertaken by countries that are quite similar to each other and are primarily exchanging different varieties of similar goods produced using similar technologies, such trade is most unlikely to have the income redistribution implications associated with factor-endowment-based trade. The new exchange of capital-intensive products for labor-intensive products between two countries will change the distribution of income between capital and labor in each country. Two-way trade in electrical machinery, however, is much less likely to produce this result. Perhaps this does explain why industrialized countries in the postwar world have had such great success in removing barriers among themselves and why this success has been confined to trade in manufactures. As will be seen, it may also explain the distinctively contentious relations that Japan has had with other industrialized economies.

For all the importance of intraindustry trade in the past four decades, such trade has not been an important element in Japan's postwar growth. As table

Table 6.4 **Coefficient of Variation GDP per Capita of Sixteen Major Economies, 1870–1987**

1870	.279	1950	.383
1900	.297	1973	.171
1913	.345	1987	.142
1929	.329		

Sources: Maddison (1982) and Maddison (1989).

Note: The economies in this dispersion index include Australia, Austria, Belgium, Canada, Denmark, Finland, France, Germany, Italy, Japan, the Netherlands, Norway, Sweden, Switzerland, the United Kingdom, and the United States.

6.5 indicates, Japan is distinctive among major industrialized countries for its very limited participation in intraindustry trade. Despite experiencing a rate of growth of foreign trade since the late 1930s that among industrialized countries is exceeded only by France and Italy, Japan's intraindustry trade has lagged.

Japan's experience has been exceptional because its postwar trade has probably grown rapidly for much the same reasons that its prewar trade also grew rapidly. Japan's continuing capacity to make use of foreign advances in science and technology and increasingly also its capacity to make efficient use of its own research and development resources has continued to make labor-saving innovations an important source of cost reduction in Japanese export industries. Where in the prewar period labor-saving innovations in export industries meant an unambiguous bias toward more trade, in postwar Japan, with labor increasingly scarce, this bias has attenuated. This may help explain why in the last decades of the twentieth century, despite a rapid stream of productivity-enhancing technological innovations, Japanese trade has not outstripped the growth of the Japanese GNP to anywhere near the extent of what was experienced in the prewar decades. Among the major industrialized economies examined here, Japan has experienced the smallest rise in its trade-to-GNP ratio.

While economic theory suggests that, given Japan's distinctive geography and factor endowments, it is not surprising that Japan is a relatively meager participant in intraindustry trade, there remains a strong suspicion among Japan's trading partners that Japanese government policies are somehow responsible.[6] In this event, the conjecture that Japan's meager participation in intraindustry trade might be explained by Japan's distinctive factor endowments certainly needs to be subjected to a careful empirical test.

6.4 A Factor-Endowment-Based Theory of Intraindustry Trade[7]

Assume that all manufactured goods are differentiated by country of origin. Given the same homothetic preferences usually assumed in empirical work making use of Heckscher-Ohlin-style trade models, each economy will consume identical proportions of each variety of each good.[8] This means that country j's import and export of good i will be given by[9]

$$M_{ij}^{+} = S_j(\overline{Q}_i - Q_{ij}); \tag{1}$$

$$X_{ij}^{+} = (1 - S_j)Q_{ij}, \tag{2}$$

6. Concern about Japan's meager participation in intraindustry trade dates from the late 1960s (Saxonhouse 1972). Helpman and Krugman (1985) show that, the more different are two countries' factor endowments, the less the role that intraindustry trade will play in their total trade.

7. This paper extends earlier research on this subject (Saxonhouse 1989). See also the survey on earlier empirical work on Japanese trade structure in Saxonhouse and Stern (1989).

8. See, e.g., the analysis in Leamer (1984) and Saxonhouse (1983).

9. Lawrence (1987) makes use of variants of (4) and (4′).

Table 6.5 Intraindustry Trade Indices for Manufacturing, 1975–88

	1975	1980	1985	1988
Japan	26	28	26	33
United States	62	66	61	60
France	78	82	82	81
Germany	58	66	67	69
Korea	36	40	49	N.A.

Sources: Iwata (1991, 333–69); and Tsushosangyōsho (1990, 208).

where $M_{ij}^{+} \equiv$ imports of good i by country j, $Q_{ij} \equiv$ production of good i in country j, $\bar{Q}_i \equiv \Sigma_j Q_{ij} \equiv$ global production of good i, $\Pi_i \equiv \Sigma Q_{ij} \equiv$ GNP of country j, $\Pi \equiv \Sigma_j \Pi_j \equiv$ global GNP and $S_j \equiv \Pi_j/\Pi \equiv$ share of country j in global GNP; but

$$(3) \qquad S_j = \frac{\Pi_j}{\Pi} = \frac{\Sigma_s W_{sj} L_{sj}}{\Sigma_i \bar{Q}_i},$$

where $L_{sj} \equiv$ endowment of factor of production s in economy j, and $W_{sj} \equiv$ rental for factor of production s.

Following the approach taken in interindustry trade analyses based on the Heckscher-Ohlin framework, if factor price equalization is assumed, then, by Hotelling's lemma, if Π_j is differentiated with respect to output price,[10]

$$(4) \qquad Q_{ij} = \sum_{s=1}^{N} R_{is} L_{sj},$$

where R_{is} is a function of the parameters of Π_j and output prices, which are assumed to be constant.

Substituting (3) and (4) into (1) and (2), we get

$$(5) \qquad M_{ij}^{+} = \sum_{s=1}^{N} B_{is}^{+} L_{sj} - \sum_{s=1}^{N} \sum_{r=1}^{N} D_{isr}^{+} L_{sj} L_{rj}, \quad i = 1, \ldots, N,$$

and

$$(6) \qquad X_{ij}^{+} = \sum_{s=1}^{N} R_{is} L_{sj} - \sum_{s=1}^{N} \sum_{r=1}^{N} D_{isr}^{+} L_{sj} L_{rj}, \quad i = 1, \ldots, N,$$

where B_{is}^{+} and D_{isr}^{+} are functions of parameters of Π_j, and where output prices will be constant under the assumptions already made. The linear factor-endowment terms in (5) represent economy j's demand for good i, while the

10. The GNP function Π_j has been defined to allow for differentiated products and economies of scale. Following Helpman and Krugman (1985), this can be done by including optimal firm scale in Π_j. Provided that optimal firm scale is small relative to market size, change in industry output can be achieved by changes in the number of firms in the industry. Firms are assumed to be identical. This means that, at an industry level, there will be constant returns to scale.

linear terms in (6) represent economy j's supply of good i. The interaction terms in equations (5) and (6) represent economy j's demand for its domestically produced variety j of good i. M_{ij}^{+} in (5) can be interpreted as that part of economy j's demand for good i that cannot be satisfied by the domestically produced variety j. X_{ij}^{+} in (6) is the supply of variety j of good i available after domestic demand has been met. Neither M_{ij}^{+} nor X_{ij}^{+} can be negative. If (5) is subtracted from (6), net exports will be given by[11]

$$(7) \qquad (X_{ij}^{+} - M_{ij}^{+}) = \sum_{s=1}^{K}(R_{is} - B_{is}^{+})L_{sj}, \quad i = 1, \ldots, N.$$

Net exports reflect the balance between the domestic demand for and supply of good i by economy j. Since domestic demand for the domestic variety of good i appears in both equation (5) and equation (6), these terms cancel out in equation (7).

By contrast with (5) and (6), (7) is the traditional Heckscher-Ohlin interindustry trade equation with net exports as a linear function of factor endowments (Saxonhouse 1983; Leamer 1984). Within the Heckscher-Ohlin framework, the nonlinear terms in (5) and (6) cancel out.[12]

The presence of factor-endowment interaction terms in equations (5) and (6) presents a number of estimation problems. Given the desire to use a relatively homogeneous country sample, which means that only a relatively small number of observations are available, and given the large number of interaction terms, precise estimation of (5) and (6) would be difficult. Alternatively, recall from (3) and (5) that

$$\begin{aligned} M_{ij}^{+} &= \sum_{s=1}^{K} B_{is}^{+} a_s L_{sj} - \sum_{s=1}^{K}\sum_{r=1}^{K} D_{isr}^{+} a_s L_{sj} L_{rj} \\ &= \frac{\Pi_j}{\Pi}\overline{Q}_i - \frac{\Pi_j}{\Pi}\sum_{s=1}^{K} R_{is} a_s L_{sj}. \end{aligned}$$

11. In the common case that the number of goods exceeds the number of factors ($N > K$), trade will likely be indeterminate. In theory, this should mean that empirical work using such cross-national models should fare poorly (Petri 1991). In practice, such models do very well in explaining cross-national trade patterns (Leamer 1984; Saxonhouse 1983). How can this paradox be resolved? One convention might allow that in the limit there are approximately the same large number of factors as commodities and that trade patterns are determinate. Missing data present problems for estimation, but not problems for actual trade flows. If these missing factor endowments are statistically orthogonal to the factor endowments for which data are available, their absence will not bias estimation of the model. If this view is wrong, and if there are many more goods than factors of production in the international economic system, production and trade should be highly specialized. In fact, what is generally observed, at the level of disaggregation relevant for empirical work, is just the kind of incomplete specialization suggested by a system where the numbers of goods and factors are the same.

12. Since (7) can be derived from the intraindustry gross trade equations (5) and (6), this should demonstrate the compatibility of these two approaches. Contrary to what authors such as Zysman and Tyson (1983) allege, the incorporation of scale economies and product differentiation into conventional models of international trade in order to account for intraindustry trade need not invalidate the Heckscher-Ohlin interpretation of intraindustry trade.

Dividing through by Π_j we get

$$(8)\qquad \frac{M_{ij}^{+}}{\Pi_j} = \frac{\overline{Q}_i}{\Pi} - \frac{1}{\Pi}\sum_{s=1}^{K} R_{is}a_sL_{sj} = F_i - \sum_{s=1}^{K} R_{is}^{*}a_sL_{sj},$$

where $F_i \equiv \overline{Q}_i/\Pi \equiv$ global sector i as a proportion of global GNP and $R_{is}^{*} \equiv R_{is}/\Pi$.

Equation (8), like equation (7), is a simple linear function of factor endowments. When estimated together with equation (7), it can be used to test the hypothesis that the variation of intraindustry trade participation across countries is caused, not by government trade policies, but by differences in factor endowments.

The structure embodied in equations (7) and (8) results from relaxing many of the strictest assumptions of the Heckscher-Ohlin model in order to incorporate hitherto neglected phenomena. Still further relaxation of assumptions is possible. Following earlier work (Saxonhouse 1983, 1989; Bowen, Leamer, and Sveikauskas 1987), suppose that the assumption that strict factor price equalization across countries is dropped. Suppose rather that international trade equalizes factor prices only when factor prices are normalized for differences in quality. For example, observed international differences in the compensation of ostensibly unskilled labor may be accounted for by differences in labor quality. Instead of (7) and (8), we have

$$(7')\qquad (X_{ij}^{+} - M_{ij}^{+}) = \sum_{s=1}^{N}(R_{is} - B_{is}^{+})a_sL_{sj}, \quad i = 1, \ldots, N,$$

and

$$(8')\qquad \frac{M_{ij}^{+}}{\Pi_j} = F_i - \sum_{s=1}^{K} R_{is}^{*}a_sL_{sj}, \quad i = 1, \ldots, N,$$

where $a_s \equiv$ quality of factor s.

6.5 Estimation Procedures

Equations (7′) and (8′) can be estimated for N commodity groups from cross-national data. a_s is not directly observable but can be estimated using (7) and (8) (Saxonhouse 1983, 1989). Formally, the estimation of (7′) and (8′) with a_s differing across countries and unknown is a multiplicative errors in variables problem. Instrumental variables methods will allow consistent estimation of the $(R_{is} - B_{is}^{+})$ and the R_{is}^{*}. For any given cross section, the a_s will not be identified. In the particular specification adopted in (7′) and (8′), however, at any given time, there are $2N$ cross sections that contain the identical independent variables. This circumstance can be exploited to permit consistent estimation of the a_s.[13] Since the same error will recur in equation after equation owing to the unobservable quality terms, it is possible to use this recurring error to obtain consistent estimates of the quality terms. These estimates of a_s can then be used to adjust the factor endowment data in (7′) and (8′) to obtain more efficient estimates of the $(R_{is} - B^{+}_{is})$ and the R^{+}_{is}.

6.6 Estimating Interindustry Trade Equations and Import Share Equations

Earlier work with a related empirical framework (Saxonhouse 1989) has been criticized because the sample used in its estimation included many poorer countries that had substantial levels of protection (Tyson 1989). The estimated coefficients of a framework such as (7′) and (8′) will embody the average level of protection of the sample used in its estimation. It is useful to know that, after due allowance has been made for its distinctive factor endowment, Japanese trade structure differs little from that of other advanced countries that are thought of as having relatively low levels of protection. It may be quite a different matter if Japanese trade structure differs little from that of mixed samples of countries, some with low levels of protection, others with extremely high levels.[14] With this in mind, equations (7′) and (8′) are estimated with data taken from the relatively homogeneous sample of twenty-four economies listed in table 6.6 for 1983 for each of the sixty-one trade sectors listed in table 6.7.

The six factor endowments used in this estimation include directly productive capital stock, educational attainment, labor, petroleum reserves, coal, and arable land. Unlike the interindustry trade equation (7′), the dependent variables in the import share equation (8′) will never be negative, but they will occasionally be zero. As seen in table 6.8, some of the import share equations will contain some zero observations. As suggested (Saxonhouse 1989), equation (8′) should be specified as a Tobit model.[15]

The results of estimating equations (7′) and (8′) are given in tables 6.9–6.12. Note that thirty-eight of the sixty-one net trade equations and thirty-four of the sixty-one import share equations are statistically significant. When all 122 trade equations are taken jointly as a system, they are statistically signifi-

13. For further explanation of the statistical techniques used here, see Saxonhouse (1989).

14. In general, less advanced economies impose more protection than the most advanced economies (Honma and Hayami 1986). As noted (Saxonhouse 1989), this development-related protection can be explained by changes in the levels of the factor endowments. Typically, the less scarce the factor endowments, the less the protection. Under these conditions, using a mixed sample of advanced and developing economies will not pose much of a problem for interpreting findings about Japan because development-related protection in the sample will not be incorporated into the estimated coefficients.

15. The Tobit estimation methods used for equation (8′) are described in Greene (1981, 1983) and in Chung and Goldberger (1984).

Table 6.6 Country Sample for Empirical Work

Australia	Italy
Austria	Japan
Belgium and Luxembourg	Netherlands
Canada	New Zealand
Denmark	Norway
Finland	Portugal
France	Singapore
Germany	Spain
Greece	Sweden
Hong Kong	Switzerland
Iceland	United Kingdom
Ireland	United States

Table 6.7 Trade Sectors in Sample

Petroleum, petroleum products (PETRO33)
Crude materials, crude fertilizer (MAT27)
Metalliferous ores, metal scrap (MAT28)
Coal, coke briquettes (MAT32)
Gas, natural and manufactured (MAT34)
Electrical energy (MAT35)
Nonferrous metals (MAT68)
Wood, lumber, cork (FOR24)
Pulp, waste paper (FOR25)
Wood, cork manufactures (FOR63)
Paper, paperboard (FOR64)
Fruit, vegetables (TROP5)
Sugar, sugar preparations, honey (TROP6)
Coffee, tea, cocoa, spices (TROP7)
Beverages (TROP11)
Crude rubber (TROP23)
Live animals (ANL0)
Meat, meat preparations (ANL1)
Dairy products, eggs (ANL2)
Fish, fish preparations (ANL3)
Hides, skins, furskins, undressed (ANL21)
Crude animal, vegetable minerals (ANL29)
Animal, vegetable oils, fats, processed (ANL45)
Animals, n.e.s. (ANL94)
Cereals, cereal preparations (CER4)
Tobacco, tobacco manufactures (CER12)
Oil seeds, oil nuts, oil kernels (CER22)
Textile fibers (CER26)
Animal oils, fats (CER41)
Fixed vegetable oils (CER42)
Nonmetallic mineral manufactures (LAB66)
Furniture (LAB82)
Travel goods, handbags (LAB83)

(continued)

Table 6.7 (continued)

Clothing (LAB84)
Footwear (LAB85)
Miscellaneous manufactured articles n.e.s. (LAB89)
Postal pack not classified according to kind (LAB91)
Special transactions not classified according to kind (LAB93)
Coins, nongold, noncurrent (LAB96)
Leather, dressed furskins (CAP61)
Rubber manufactures, n.e.s. (CAP62)
Textile, yarn, fabrics (CAP65)
Iron and steel (CAP67)
Manufactures of metal (CAP69)
Sanitary fixtures, fittings (CAP81)
Machinery, other than electrical (MACH71)
Electrical machinery (MACH72)
Transport equipment (MACH73)
Professional goods, watches, instruments (MACH86)
Firearms, ammunition (MACH95)
Chemical elements, compounds (CHEM51)
Mineral tar and crude chemicals from coal, petroleum, and natural gas (CHEM52)
Dyeing, tanning, coloring matter (CHEM53)
Medicinal, pharmaceutical products (CHEM54)
Essential oils, perfume matter (CHEM55)
Fertilizers, manufactured (CHEM546)
Explosives, pyrotechnic products (CHEM57)
Plastic materials, cellulose (CHEM58)
Chemical materials, n.e.s. (CHEM59)

cant, with $F(53, 2753)_{.05} = 3.61$.[16] For individual factor endowments, out of sixty-one estimated net trade equations, capital has significant coefficients in twenty-seven, labor has nineteen, education has twenty, oil has thirteen, coal has sixteen, and land has twenty. By marked contrast with the net trade results, the sixty-one import share equations have a great many more significant coefficients. What are the determinants of import shares? Capital once again has the most significant coefficients with thirty-six, labor and education have twenty-nine, oil has twenty-eight, coal has twenty-four, and arable land has thirty-four.

Consistent with earlier findings from a diverse set of economies (Saxonhouse 1989), the determinants of import shares do appear quite similar to the determinants of net trade.[17] Physical capital is a source of comparative disadvantage in the net trade in natural resources and a source of comparative advantage in the net trade of capital-intensive manufactures, machinery, and

16. The joint test used here is described in McElroy (1977).
17. Lawrence (1987) suggests the contrary.

Table 6.8 **Proportion of Zero Observations in the Import Share Equations**

PETRO33	0	CER26	0
MAT27	0	CER41	0
MAT28	0	CER42	0
MAT32	0	LAB66	0
MAT34	.075	LAB82	0
MAT35	.525	LAB83	0
MAT68	0	LAB84	0
FOR24	0	LAB85	0
FOR25	0	LAB91	.125
FOR63	0	LAB93	.175
FOR64	0	LAB96	.025
TROP5	0	CAP61	0
TROP6	0	CAP62	0
TROP7	0	CAP65	0
TROP11	0	CAP67	0
TRP23	0	CAP69	0
ANL0	.575	CAP81	0
ANL1	0	MACH71	0
ANL2	0	MACH72	0
ANL3	0	MACH73	0
ANL21	.025	MACH95	.075
ANL29	0	CHEM51	0
ANL43	0	CHEM52	0
ANL94	0	CHEM53	0
CER4	0	CHEM54	0
CER8	0	CHEM56	0
CER9	0	CHEM57	0
CER12	.025	CHEM58	0
CHER22	0	CHEM59	0

chemical products. Endowments of capital also encourage the imports of natural resource products and labor-intensive products while again discouraging the imports of capital-intensive manufactures, machinery, and chemical products.

By contrast with physical capital, labor's role as a determinant of trade patterns is more complex. Generally speaking, labor is a source of comparative advantage in the net trade of capital-intensive manufactures, labor-intensive manufactures, and chemical products. At the same time, endowments of labor also discourage the imports of most nonnatural resource–related manufactures. Human capital's role is also quite complicated. While human capital is a source of comparative disadvantage in net trade in natural resource–related products and a source of comparative advantage in the net trade of most nonnatural resource–related manufactures, its role as a determinant of import shares is subtle. Endowments of human capital encourage import of tropical products, animal products, labor-intensive manufactures, and

Table 6.9 **Estimation of Equation (7′):**
$(X^{+}_{ij} - M^{+}_{ij}) = N_0 + N_1$ Capital $+ N_2$ Labor $+ N_3$ Educ. $+ N_4$ Oil $+ N_5$ Coal $+ N_6$ Land Ara.

	R_2	$F(6,17)$		R^2	$F(6,17)$
PETRO33	.891	23.2**	CER42	.103	.033
MAT27	.615	4.53**	LAB66	.621	3.92**
MAT28	.702	5.72**	LAB82	.317	1.32
MAT32	.593	4.13**	LAB83	.581	5.08**
MAT34	.367	1.64	LAB84	.394	1.85
MAT35	.198	.700	LAB85	.461	2.42
MAT68	.602	4.29**	LAB89	.623	4.68**
FOR24	.591	4.09**	LAB91	.595	4.16**
FOR25	.361	1.60	LAB93	.618	4.58**
FOR63	.400	1.89	LAB96	.307	1.25
FOR64	.253	.96	CAP61	.671	5.78**
TROP5	.331	1.40	CAP62	.754	8.68**
TROP6	.526	3.14**	CAP65	.612	4.47**
TROP7	.585	3.99**	CAP67	.808	11.9**
TROP11	.463	2.44	CAP69	.744	8.23**
TROP23	.251	.95	CAP81	.406	1.94
ANL0	.196	.69	MACH71	.646	5.17**
ANL1	.361	1.60	MACH72	.915	30.5**
ANL2	.105	.33	MACH73	.863	17.8**
ANL3	.711	6.97**	MACH86	.684	6.13**
ANL21	.439	2.21	MACH95	.933	39.5**
ANL29	.362	1.61	CHEM51	.709	6.90**
ANL43	.401	1.90	CHEM52	.412	1.99
ANL94	.386	1.78	CHEM53	.583	3.96**
CER4	.689	6.28**	CHEM54	.526	3.14**
CER8	.514	3.00**	CHEM55	.671	5.78**
CER9	.390	1.81	CHEM56	.396	1.86
CER12	.733	7.78**	CHEM57	.519	3.06**
CER22	.721	7.07**	CHEM58	.591	3.77**
CER26	.642	5.08**	CHEM59	.717	7.18**
CER41	.762	9.07**			

**$F(6,17)_{.05} = 2.70$.

capital-intensive manufactures. At the same time, endowments of human capital strongly discourage imports of machinery and chemical products.

Surprisingly, oil and arable land appear to have quite the opposite effect from coal on trade structure. While encouraging the net export of natural resource products, factor endowments of oil and arable land are a source of comparative disadvantage for most nonnatural resource manufactures and encourage the import, in particular, of labor-intensive manufactures, capital-intensive manufactures, and chemical products. Coal's effect is much the opposite. Endowments of coal are a source of comparative advantage for net

Table 6.10 **Number of Significant Coefficients in Equation (7′) by Sectoral Grouping, Factor Endowment, and Sign**

	Capital		Labor		Education		Petroleum		Coal		Land	
	+	−	+	−	+	−	+	−	+	−	+	−
(7) Petroleum and raw materials (PETRO33, MAT27–68)	a	3	a	1	a	a	2	a	1	a	3	a
(4) Forest products (FOR24–64)	a	1	a	a	a	a	a	a	a	1	1	a
(5) Tropical products (TROP5–23)	a	1	1	a	a	2	a	1	a	1	a	a
(8) Animal products (ANLO–94)	a	2	a	1	a	1	a	a	1	a	2	a
(8) Cereals (CER4–12)	2	2	2	a	a	3	2	a	1	a	1	1
(9) Labor-intensive manufactures (LAB66–96)	2	1	2	a	2	1	a	2	a	2	a	1
(6) Capital-intensive manufactures (CAP61–81)	4	a	2	1	4	a	a	3	1	1	a	3
(5) Machinery (MACH71–95)	4	a	2	2	4	a	1	a	3	a	a	4
(9) Chemical products (CHEM51–59)	4	1	3	2	2	1	a	2	4	a	a	4

Note: Numbers in parentheses at the left of sectoral grouping rows indicate the number of equations in each sectoral grouping.
[a]No significant coefficients in this cell.

Table 6.11 Estimation of Equation (8′):

$$\frac{M_{ij}^{+}}{\Pi_j} = P_0 + P_1 \text{ Capital} + P_2 \text{ Labor} + P_3 \text{ Educ.} + P_4 \text{ Oil} + P_5 \text{ Coal} + P_6 \text{ Land Ara.}$$

	R^2	$F(6,17)$		R^2	$F(6,17)$
PETRO33	.871	19.1**	CER42	.601	4.27**
MAT27	.293	1.17	LAB66	.578	3.88**
MAT28	.116	.13	LAB82	.409	1.96
MAT32	.068	.21	LAB83	.663	5.57**
MAT34	.071	.22	LAB84	.436	2.19
MAT35	.096	.30	LAB85	.399	1.88
MAT68	.507	2.91**	LAB89	.676	5.91**
FOR24	.414	2.00	LAB91	.173	.59
FOR25	.394	1.84	LAB93	.451	2.33
FOR63	.173	.59	LAB96	.432	2.15
FOR64	.512	2.97**	CAP61	.671	5.78**
TROP5	.594	4.15**	CAP62	.754	8.68**
TROP6	.390	1.81	CAP65	.635	4.93**
TROP7	.619	4.60**	CAP67	.764	9.17**
TROP11	.563	3.65**	CAP69	.631	6.65**
TROP23	.714	7.07**	CAP81	.611	5.99**
ANL0	.430	2.14	MACH71	.698	6.55**
ANL1	.526	3.14**	MACH72	.861	17.6**
ANL2	.511	2.96**	MACH73	.903	26.4**
ANL3	.922	33.5**	MACH86	.869	17.7**
ANL21	.095	.30	MACH95	.090	.28
ANL29	.537	3.29**	CHEM51	.453	2.35
ANL43	.845	15.4**	CHEM52	.314	1.30
ANL94	.573	3.80**	CHEM53	.672	5.80**
CER4	.362	1.61	CHEM54	.539	3.31**
CER8	.411	1.98	CHEM55	.663	5.57**
CER9	.551	3.48**	CHEM56	.081	.25
CER12	.372	1.68	CHEM57	.703	6.71**
CER22	.177	.61	CHEM58	.426	2.10
CER26	.540	3.33**	CHEM59	.598	4.21**
CER41	.136	.45			

**Significant at the .05 level, $F(6,17)_{.05} = 2.70$.

trade in capital-intensive manufactures, machinery, and chemical products. Coal endowments also discourage the imports of most nonnatural resource manufactures in addition to discouraging the imports of oil.[18]

18. Despite a sample restricted to relatively high-income countries, the findings presented here are quite similar to the results obtained when a more comprehensive sample of countries is used (Saxonhouse 1989).

Table 6.12 **Number of Significant Coefficients in Equation (8′) by Sector Grouping, Factor Endowment, and Sign**

		Capital		Labor		Education		Petroleum		Coal		Land	
	F_i	+	−	+	−	+	−	+	−	+	−	+	−
(7) Petroleum and raw materials (PETRO33, MAT27–68)	3	1	1	1	1	[a]	1	[a]	2	[a]	1	[a]	3
(4) Forest products (FOR24–64)	2	1	[a]	2	1	[a]	1	[a]	2	[a]	[a]	2	[a]
(5) Tropical products (TROP5–23)	4	2	1	1	2	2	1	2	1	[a]	[a]	1	2
(8) Animal products (ANL0–94)	5	3	1	1	2	2	1	3	1	3	2	1	3
(8) Cereals (CER4–12)	6	3	2	[a]	2	2	2	1	2	1	1	[a]	5
(9) Labor-intensive manufactures (LAB66–96)	6	3	2	[a]	4	2	1	2	2	2	2	1	3
(6) Capital-intensive manufactures (CAP61–81)	5	1	3	1	2	3	1	2	2	1	3	4	1
(5) Machinery (MACH71–95)	4	1	3	1	3	1	4	1	1	[a]	4	2	2
(9) Chemical products (CHEM51–59)	7	2	6	1	4	1	4	3	1	[a]	4	3	1

Note: Numbers in parentheses at the left of sectoral grouping rows indicate the number of equations in each sectoral grouping.

[a]No significant coefficients in this cell.

6.7 Is Japanese Trade Behavior Distinctive?

Tables 6.9–6.12 report results where equations (7′) and (8′) have been estimated using 1983 data but without using Japanese observations. Equations (7′) and (8′) have also been reestimated including Japan but successively excluding Canada, the United States, and Singapore from the sample. In an effort to test whether Japanese trade patterns are distinctively different from the patterns observed by other countries, and following suggestions from Srinavasan and Hamada (1989), tolerance intervals have been constructed for Japanese trade flows using the trade equations that were estimated without Japanese observations. Unlike forecast intervals (Saxonhouse 1989), which focus on particular parameters, tolerance intervals, by indicating the probability with which a given proportion of a population distribution will fall within a particular range, provide a conceptually sound test of whether Japanese trade patterns are distinctively different from the patterns observed by other countries.[19] Observations on Japanese import shares and Japanese net trade that lie outside the tolerance interval can be considered out of line with what might be expected given the experience of other countries.

To the extent that tolerance intervals constructed with non-Japanese evidence can capture Japan's trade structure, it is difficult to argue that Japan's sectoral policies are yielding distinctive outcomes. It is very important to note here that this does not necessarily mean that Japan has a liberal trade regime. If all countries with relatively small amounts of arable land protect their wheat growers, Japan can protect its wheat growers, but its behavior will not appear distinctive. At the same time, a change in Japanese trade policy will yield an increase in Japanese wheat imports. It is also important to note that, even if observations on Japanese import shares and Japanese net trade lie outside the tolerance interval, this result need not be attributed to the presence of Japanese trade barriers. There may be other important variables, for example, foreign trade barriers that have also been excluded from the model being employed here.

The tolerance interval results are presented in tables 6.13–6.16. Of the 122 actual observations on Japanese net trade and Japanese import shares, only seventeen lie outside the constructed tolerance intervals. This is virtually identical to the finding for Canadian net trade and import shares. By contrast, ten observations on U.S. net trade and import shares and no less than twenty-three observations on Singaporean net trade and import shares lie outside the tolerance intervals. These findings appear broadly consistent with earlier re-

19. Saxonhouse (1989) uses forecast intervals to test whether Japanese trade patterns are distinctive. For any given probability, forecast intervals will almost always be narrower than tolerance intervals. Using forecast intervals instead of tolerance intervals biases any test in favor of accepting the hypothesis that Japanese performance is distinctive. To the extent that this hypothesis is largely rejected when forecast intervals are used, it will also be rejected when tolerance intervals are used (Christ 1966).

Table 6.13 Extreme Observations on Net Trade, 1983

Japan	United States
Fruit, vegetables	Plastic materials, cellulose
Cereal, cereal preparations	Clothing
Wood, cork manufactures	Dairy products, eggs
Pulp, waste paper	Transport equipment
Leather, dressed furskins	
Crude materials, crude fertilizers	
Manufactures of metal	
Nonmetallic mineral manufactures	
Professional goods, watches, and instruments	
Canada	**Singapore**
Fish, fish preparations	Wood, lumber, cork
Wood, lumber, cork	Wood, cork manufactures
Wood, cork manufactures	Fruit, vegetables
Pulp, waste paper	Crude animals, vegetable, minerals
Paper, paperboard	Hide, skins, furskins, undressed
Manufactures of metal	Rubber manufactures
Nonmetallic mineral manufactures	Manufactures of metal
	Machinery other than electrical
	Electrical machinery
	Professional goods, watches, instruments
	Plastic materials, cellulose

Table 6.14 Does $(X^{\dagger}_{ij} - M^{\dagger}_{ij})$ Lie Outside the Estimated Tolerance Interval? Test Statistic for Case where 95 Percent of Population Distribution Is Included in Tolerance Interval with Probability .95

	Japan	U.S.	Canada	Singapore
PETRO33	.75	2.32	1.05	.82
MAT27	3.78*	.92	1.88	1.67
MAT28	2.15	2.88	1.72	1.61
MAT32	1.91	3.03	2.14	2.61
MAT34	1.45	1.22	1.52	1.38
MAT35	1.16	2.36	2.45	1.99
MAT68	2.12	1.52	2.10	.92
FOR24	2.70	2.35	3.88*	4.01*
FOR25	3.72*	1.97	1.54	2.79
FOR63	21.58*	2.62	4.41*	4.67*
FOR64	3.25	1.74	3.85*	3.24
TROP5	4.68*	.41	2.44	3.86*
TROP6	.62	1.81	.92	2.07
TROP7	1.14	1.92	2.63	1.68
TROP11	.83	.77	1.56	.92
TROP23	.41	1.76	2.04	2.33
ANL0	.36	.62	.92	1.36
ANL1	2.87	1.63	1.76	1.14

(continued)

Table 6.14 (continued)

	Japan	U.S.	Canada	Singapore
ANL2	3.06	3.69*	2.14	1.17
ANL3	2.88	.87	4.15*	2.14
ANL21	3.21	1.51	2.11	6.12*
ANL29	1.42	.12	.78	4.06*
ANL45	.33	1.26	1.98	.54
ANL94	.93	1.58	1.03	1.36
CER4	4.62*	3.67*	1.40	1.64
CER8	2.15	2.26	1.52	.38
CER9	2.76	1.21	.75	1.63
CER12	3.20	.93	1.58	.19
CER22	.84	.67	3.14	2.78
CER26	1.34	.42	3.11	3.36
CER41	.82	.63	1.57	1.01
CER42	1.13	1.67	1.42	1.22
LAB66	3.78*	3.26	3.68*	2.94
LAB82	2.56	2.89	2.44	2.62
LAB83	1.31	2.29	1.94	2.35
LAB84	2.50	4.33*	1.73	3.32
LAB85	3.21	2.84	2.27	2.86
LAB89	1.78	1.63	.67	1.55
LAB91	.62	.73	.95	1.24
LAB93	.45	.85	1.36	1.55
LAB96	.41	.53	1.28	.89
CAP61	3.71*	1.48	3.00	1.46
CAP62	.97	.58	3.34	3.92*
CAP65	.70	3.19	1.09	1.85
CAP67	1.72	1.88	2.51	2.63
CAP69	4.32*	3.15	3.98*	4.66*
CAP81	.44	1.23	.99	1.54
MACH71	1.19	1.07	2.54	5.93*
MACH72	1.36	.68	3.50	3.39
MACH73	3.15	4.02	3.26	3.20
MACH86	3.89*	1.74	1.45	5.43*
MACH95	.57	.82	1.76	1.63
CHEM51	.60	1.98	1.17	.88
CHEM52	1.31	.85	1.94	1.56
CHEM53	.33	1.52	1.00	1.43
CHEM54	.59	.26	.75	1.62
CHEM55	1.16	1.03	1.35	1.27
CHEM56	.76	2.35	1.87	2.04
CHEM57	.54	1.19	2.16	.70
CHEM58	.96	5.12*	1.30	4.53*
CHEM59	1.16	2.28	.43	3.16

* ≡ observation lies outside tolerance interval.

Table 6.15 Extreme Observations on Import Shares, 1979

Japan	United States
Wood, cork manufactures	Metalliferous ore, metal scrap
Meat, meat preparations	Clothing
Cereal, cereal preparations	Footwear
Feedstuff for animals	Textile yarn, fabrics
Tobacco, tobacco manufactures	Rubber manufactures
Footwear	Transport equipment
Rubber manufactures, n.e.s.	
Textiles, yarn, fabrics	
Canada	**Singapore**
Wood, lumber, cork	Coal, coke briquettes
Paper, paperboard	Wood, cork manufactures
Oil seeds, oil nuts and nut kernels	Fruit, vegetables
Leather dressed furskins	Sugar, sugar preparations
Rubber manufactures	Cereal, cereal preparations
Manufactures of metal	Oil seeds, oil nuts, oil kernels
Machinery, other than electrical	Textile fibers
	Crude animals, vegetables and minerals
	Leather, dressed furskins
	Rubber manufactures
	Machinery other than electrical
	Transport equipment
	Medicinal pharmaceutical products
	Plastic materials, cellulose

Table 6.16 Does M^*_{ij}/Π_j Lie Outside the Estimated Tolerance Interval? Test Statistic for Case Where 95 Percent of Population Distribution Is Included in Tolerance Interval with Probability .95

	Japan	U.S.	Canada	Singapore
PETRO33	.83	1.79	.76	1.32
MAT27	.74	2.31	2.07	1.44
MAT32	1.55	3.10	1.04	4.77*
MAT28	1.26	4.14*	.76	2.62
MAT34	1.21	1.36	2.52	3.16
MAT35	.66	2.12	2.80	1.95
MAT68	2.15	1.47	3.13	1.73
FOR24	3.01	2.68	3.90*	2.89
FOR25	1.92	.63	1.71	2.14
FOR63	4.36*	2.94	3.39	3.72*
FOR64	2.83	2.51	4.04*	2.11
TROP5	3.17	.62	1.86	4.23*
TROP6	1.62	2.24	.73	3.91*
TROP7	.82	1.47	1.65	1.80
TROP11	.51	2.76	1.32	.92
TROP23	.73	1.05	.97	1.58

(continued)

Table 6.16 (continued)

	Japan	U.S.	Canada	Singapore
ANL0	.17	1.62	1.34	1.76
ANL1	5.14*	2.49	.93	2.14
ANL2	2.86	1.77	2.13	.91
ANL3	2.65	.82	.34	1.53
ANL21	1.07	1.38	2.40	.69
ANL29	.94	1.26	1.73	3.01
ANL45	1.17	1.94	1.68	2.15
ANL94	.42	1.23	.28	1.37
CER4	6.38*	2.60	2.15	4.76*
CER8	3.66*	2.82	3.21	3.25
CER9	2.26	.89	1.43	1.87
CER12	4.10*	1.04	1.26	.92
CER22	.88	.71	3.91*	4.43*
CER26	1.83	2.47	1.60	5.00*
CER41	.65	.98	2.26	1.93
CER42	.78	1.19	2.68	1.55
LAB66	2.09	1.86	1.13	2.14
LAB82	1.38	1.22	2.39	1.52
LAB83	.92	.57	1.84	1.99
LAB84	2.84	4.15*	1.92	2.35
LAB85	4.32*	3.69*	2.34	1.92
LAB89	1.51	.72	.97	1.36
LAB91	.79	.42	.93	.62
LAB93	.45	.39	.62	1.14
LAB96	.76	.41	.53	.96
CAP61	1.63	2.15	4.54*	5.32*
CAP62	3.67*	4.79*	5.27*	6.03*
CAP65	4.38*	4.87*	3.24	3.41
CAP67	1.36	.74	3.13	2.37
CAP69	1.53	1.32	4.12*	2.80
CAP81	.37	1.98	1.44	1.26
MACH71	3.07	3.14	3.82*	6.35*
MACH72	2.17	1.31	1.04	2.96
MACH73	.94	3.64*	1.77	6.82*
MACH86	1.26	1.06	2.58	3.27
MACH95	2.15	1.68	.85	2.00
CHEM51	1.76	.88	.73	1.21
CHEM52	.33	.76	1.52	1.93
CHEM53	.65	.84	1.25	2.62
CHEM54	1.15	1.62	.29	3.67*
CHEM55	1.09	.90	.76	.94
CHEM56	1.84	1.35	.92	.67
CHEM57	1.55	.58	2.67	1.53
CHEM58	2.14	2.86	3.42	5.38*
CHEM59	.75	1.11	.92	2.74

* ≡ observation lies outside tolerance interval.

search that used more a heterogeneous sample of countries (Saxonhouse 1989). Whatever Japanese trade policies (and/or informal barriers) may have been, more than likely, with the possible exception of a number of agricultural sectors, they have not been a major determinant of what is distinctive about Japanese trade patterns.

Following a suggestion by Bowen (1989), the significance of this finding can be further explored by using estimated equations (7′) and (8′) to replicate intraindustry trade indices similar to those presented in table 6.5 By successively reestimating equations (7′) and (8′) and a related GNP equation, each time excluding a different country, not just Japan, Canada, the United States, and Singapore, but also each of ten other countries, it is possible to examine how the factor-endowment-based explanation of net trade and import shares can also account for intercountry variations in intraindustry trade. The results of replicating intraindustry trade indices for 1979 and 1986 using export and import values that have been forecast from equations (7′) and (8′) and the associated GNP function are presented in table 6.17.

While it could hardly be expected that intraindustry trade indices using forecasted trade flows would exactly match the indices constructed using actual data, as seen in table 6.17 the general patterns of cross-national participation in intraindustry trade in both 1979 and 1988 are clearly captured. Countries such as Canada, France, the Netherlands, and the United Kingdom that are very active participants in intraindustry trade are forecast as active

Table 6.17 Intraindustry Manufacturing Trade Indices, 1979 and 1988 (36 sectors)

Country	1979		1988	
	Actual	Forecast	Actual	Forecast
Australia	.38	.43	.40	.42
Belgium and Luxembourg	.85	.69	.88	.75
Canada	.74	.66	.78	.73
Finland	.59	.60	.62	.58
France	.79	.73	.83	.75
Germany	.68	.64	.69	.64
Italy	.60	.61	.64	.67
Japan	.35	.32	.39	.37
Netherlands	.71	.83	.73	.85
Norway	.57	.61	.63	.62
Sweden	.73	.59	.70	.56
United Kingdom	.82	.80	.84	.84
United States	.65	.58	.69	.63
Singapore	.48	.42	.58	.54
Switzerland	.67	.71	.64	.75

Note: Index $j = \sum_{n=1}^{n} [(X_{ij} + M_{ij}) - |X_{ij} - M_{ij}|]/\sum_{i=1}^{n} (X_{ij} + M_{ij})$.

participants. The behavior of countries such as Australia, Singapore, and Japan that have been much less active participants in such trade are also accurately forecast. The substantial changes in the participation in intraindustry trade for many countries between 1979 and 1988 are also accurately forecast. The results for Japan are particularly instructive. Consistent with the new theory of intraindustry trade, they demonstrate that Japan is a relatively meager participant because, with its very distinctive pattern of factor endowments, it does remain quite unlike its trading partners. As shown in table 6.17, in the late 1980s Japan's participation in intraindustry trade has been increasing. This primarily reflects the increasing capital intensity and skill intensity of many of Japan's substantial trading partners in East and Southeast Asia.

6.8 Finale

Regardless of its determinants, Japan's distinctive pattern of trade has posed a continuing dilemma for Japanese international economic policy. There have always been important political constituencies in the major industrialized nations supporting trade in otherwise unavailable natural resource products. There has also been great support in the postwar period for the highly beneficial and minimally disruptive trade based on intraindustry specialization. A large proportion of the total volume of post–World War II trade has been of these two types. Together, constituencies supporting these two types of trade have successively pushed the almost unprecedented liberalization of the postwar international commercial system.[20]

Japan is neither a natural resource products–based exporter nor a major participant in intraindustry trade. Japan's focus on interindustry specialization has meant that, at the best case, expansion of Japanese trade improves foreign welfare on net while altering the almost always politically sensitive foreign income distribution. At worst, an expansion of Japanese trade can reduce foreign welfare by undermining the economic rents embodied in the profits and in the high wages of foreign industries producing tradable goods (Krugman 1984; Katz and Summers 1989). While there is very good reason to believe that, on net, the growth in Japanese trade has been beneficial, to date Japanese trade has not created powerful liberal trade constituencies within its trading partners. Rather, the faster-than-desired structural adjustment imposed on its trading partners has nurtured protectionist interests. As long as the Japanese economy was relatively small, complaints were localized, confined to particular sectors and, at the general level, relatively easily overwhelmed by the constituencies favoring more liberal trade. As Japan has become a much larger force in the global economy, and with its influence magnified by needless mismanagement of the American economy, attention has come to focus on

20. The remarkably prescient discussion in Hansen (1945) is very instructive on this point.

the disruptive features of international trade at the expense of trade's many benefits.

As discussed earlier, mutual beneficial interindustry trade is based on the existence of differences among countries. By contrast, mutually beneficial intraindustry trade is based on similarities among countries. From the traditional Japanese perspective, it is doubtless puzzling that foreign diplomats continually request that Japan become ever more like its trading partners. It is often argued that removing what is distinctive about Japan might diminish the basis for trade. Ironically, foreign diplomats, however, are approaching Japan from a different perspective. By asking Japan to harmonize a wide array of its domestic economic practices with foreign practices, they are hoping to create a basis for greatly expanded, mutually beneficial intraindustry trade between Japan and its trading partners. If harmonization by itself helps to shore up the tattered legitimacy of the international trading system, then the hard diplomacy required to achieve this end may well be worth the great effort that has been expended. If, however, the only criteria for success are major changes in trade structure and trade volume, the research presented here continues to support the position that increased frustration and ill will may be the only outcome of such efforts. Japan will become a major participant in intraindustry trade only as the rest of natural resource–poor East and Southeast Asia converge to the Japanese level of development.

References

Baumol, William, Sue Anne Blackman, and Edward Wolff. 1989. *Productivity and American leadership*. Cambridge, Mass.: MIT Press.

Bhagwati, Jagdish. 1964. A survey of the pure theory of international trade. *Economic Journal* 74 (March): 1–84.

Bowen, Harry P. 1989. Comment. In *Trade policies for international competitiveness*, ed. Robert Feenstra. Chicago: University of Chicago Press.

Bowen, Harry P., Edward E. Leamer, and Leo Sveikauskas. 1987. Multicountry, multifactor tests of the factor abundance theory. *American Economic Review* 77 (September): 791–809.

Christ, Carl F. 1966. *Econometric models and methods*. New York: Wiley.

Chung, Ching-Fan, and Arthur S. Goldberger. 1984. Proportional projections in limited dependent variables models. *Econometrica* 52 (March): 531–34.

Cooper, Richard N. 1964. Foreign trade and economic growth. *Journal of Economic History* 23 (December): 609–28.

Crafts, N. F. R., and Mark Thomas. 1986. Comparative advantage in UK manufacturing trade. *Economic Journal* 96 (September): 629–45.

De Long, J. Bradford. 1988. Productivity growth, convergence and welfare: Comment. *American Economic Review* 78 (December): 1138–54.

Dore, Ronald. 1965. *Tokugawa education*. Berkeley: University of California Press.

Freeman, Richard B., and Martin Weitzman. 1987. Bonuses and employment in postwar Japan. *Journal of the Japanese and International Economies* 2:168–94.

Greene, William H. 1981. On the asymptotic bias of the ordinary least squares estimator of the Tobit model. *Econometrica* 49 (March): 505–14.

———. 1983. Estimation of limited dependent variable models by ordinary least squares and the method of moments. *Journal of Econometrics* 21 (February): 195–212.

Grubel, Herbert C., and P. J. Lloyd. 1975. *Intra-industry trade*. New York: Wiley.

Hansen, Alvin H. 1945. *America's role in the world economy.* New York: Norton.

Helpman, Elhanan. 1987. Imperfect competition and international trade: Evidence from fourteen industrial countries. *Journal of the Japanese and International Economies* 1 (March): 62–81.

Helpman, Elhanan, and Paul Krugman. 1985. *Market structure and foreign trade.* Cambridge, Mass.: MIT Press.

Hirschman, Albert O. 1945. *National power and the structure of foreign trade*. Berkeley: University of California Press.

Honma, Masayoshi, and Yujiro Hayami. 1986. Structure of agricultural protection in developed countries. *Journal of International Economics* 20 (February): 115–31.

Iwata, Kazumasa. 1991. Japan's intra-industry trade and intra-firm trade in the 1980's. In *The Asia Pacific region in the 1990's,* ed. Yoshida Taroichi. Tokyo: Foundation for Advanced Information and Research.

Katz, Lawrence, and Lawrence Summers. 1989. Can interindustry wage differentials justify strategic trade policy. In *Trade policies for international competitiveness,* ed. Robert Feenstra. Chicago: University of Chicago Press.

Keynes, John M. 1933. National self sufficiency. *Yale Review* 22 (June): 755–69.

Krugman, Paul R. 1984. The U.S. response to foreign industrial targeting. *Brookings Papers on Economic Activity,* no. 1:77–121.

Lawrence, Robert A. 1987. Does Japan import too little: Closed minds or markets? *Brookings Papers on Economic Activity,* no. 2:517–54.

Leamer, Edward E. 1984. *Sources of international comparative advantage.* Cambridge, Mass.: MIT Press.

Lipsey, Robert E. 1976. Review of Grubel and Lloyd. *Journal of International Economics* 6 (November): 312–14.

McElroy, M. B. 1977. Goodness of fit for seemingly unrelated regressions. *Journal of Econometrics* 6 (November): 381–87.

Maddison, Angus. 1982. *Phases of capitalist development.* Oxford: Oxford University Press.

———. 1989. *The world economy in the 20th century.* Paris: OECD.

Ohkawa, Kazushi. 1978. Initial conditions: Economic level and structure. In *Japan's historical development experience and the contemporary developing countries: Issues for comparative analysis,* ed. Kazushi Ohkawa and Yujiro Hayami. Tokyo: International Development Center of Japan.

Ohkawa, Kazushi, and Henry Rosovsky. 1973. *Japanese economic growth.* Stanford, Calif.: Stanford University Press.

Petri, Peter. 1991. Market structure, comparative advantage, and Japanese trade under the strong yen. In *Trade with Japan,* ed. Paul Krugman. Chicago: University of Chicago Press.

Robertson, Dennis. 1938. The future of international trade. *Economic Journal* 48:1–14.

Saxonhouse, Gary R. 1972. Employment, imports, yen and the dollar. In *Discord in the Pacific,* ed. Henry Rosovsky. Washington, D.C.: Columbia.

———. 1976. Country girls and communication among competitors in the Japanese cotton spinning industry. In *Japanese industrialization and its social consequences,* ed. Hugh Patrick. Berkeley: University of California Press.

———. 1983. The micro- and macroeconomics of foreign sales to Japan. In *Trade policy for 1980's,* ed. William R. Cline. Cambridge, Mass.: MIT Press.
———. 1989. Differentiated products, economies of scale, and access to the Japanese market. In *Trade policies of international competitiveness,* ed. Robert Feenstra. Chicago: University of Chicago Press.
———. 1991. Japan, SII and the international harmonization of domestic economic practices. *Michigan Journal of International Law* 12 (Winter): 450–69.
Saxonhouse, Gary, and Gustav Ranis. 1985. Technology and the quality dimension in Japanese cotton textile industry. In *Japan and the developing economies,* ed. Kazushi Ohkawa and Gustav Ranis. Oxford: Basil Blackwell.
Saxonhouse, Gary, and Robert M. Stern. 1989. An analytical survey of formal and informal barriers to international trade and investment in the United States, Canada, and Japan. In *Trade and investment relations among the United States, Canada, and Japan,* ed. Robert M. Stern. Chicago: University of Chicago Press.
Sombart, Werner. 1903. *Die deutsche Volkswirtschaft in neunzehnten Jahrhundert und Anfang des 20. Jahrhunderts.* Berlin: G. Bondi.
Srinavasan, T. N., and Koichi Hamada. 1989. The United States–Japan problem. Yale University. Typescript.
Torrens, Robert. [1821] 1965. *Essay on the production of wealth.* Reprint. New York: A. M. Kelley.
Tsushosangyōsho. 1990. *Tsushōhakushō heisei ni-nen.* Tokyo.
Tyson, Laura. 1989. Comment. In *Trade policies for international competitiveness,* ed. Robert Feenstra. Chicago: University of Chicago Press.
Umemura, Mataji. 1973. A note on economic development in the Tokugawa period. In *The Japanese experience since the Meiji period,* ed. Kazushi Ohkawa and Yujiro Hayami. Tokyo: Japan Economic Research Center.
Weitzman, Martin. 1984. *The share economy.* Cambridge, Mass.: Harvard University Press.
Williamson, Jeffrey G. 1991. Productivity and American leadership: A review essay. *Journal of Economic Literature* 29 (March): 59–68.
World Bank. 1986. *World bank tables.* Washington, D.C.
Wright, Gavin. 1990. American industrial leadership success, 1879–1940. *American Economic Review* 80 (September): 651–68.
Yamazawa, Ippei. 1978. Industrialization and external relations: Comparative analyses of Japan's historical experience and contemporary developing countries' performance. In *Japan's historical development experience and the contemporary developing countries: Issues for comparative analysis,* ed. Kazushi Ohkawa and Yujiro Hayami. Tokyo: International Development Center of Japan.
Zysman, John, and Laura Tyson. 1983. *American industry in international competition.* Ithaca, N.Y.: Cornell University Press.

Comment Takatoshi Ito

The ground that this paper covers is very broad, ranging from 1600 to 1991, from macro to micro, and from economics to politics. The paper is extremely

Takatoshi Ito is professor of economics at Hitotsubashi University and a research associate of the National Bureau of Economic Research.

informative, reflecting Saxonhouse's long history of academic work on the Japanese economy and his recent experience on the Council of Economic Advisers dealing with Japan politically. Saxonhouse discusses various interesting topics, but I will limit my comments to two, intraindustry trade and the Structural Impediments Initiative (SII).

Intraindustry trade issues have been hotly debated by Robert Lawrence and Gary Saxonhouse. They do not disagree on the fact that Japan, along with Australia, is an outlier among industrial countries, with a very low intraindustry trade index. Lawrence argues that, with various factors controlled, the index remains low, explaining the fact as a reflection of either the Japanese market being closed or the Japanese minds being "closed." Saxonhouse argues that a special endowment pattern, a strong comparative advantage of manufacturing sectors, and a geographic location far away from other similar economies explain the low index. For the purposes of this debate, the recent rise of other Asian economies provides a good opportunity to judge which side is right. Because of geographic proximity, similarity in resource endowments, and close affinities among cultural heritages, Asian nations will leave Japan with no excuse for not increasing intraindustry imports, once these Asian economies become strong industrial powers, which should be some time in the not-too-distant future.

Put simply, it is not surprising not to see Lincoln Continentals on Japanese streets, but it would be surprising not to see Hyundai Excels and Sonatas; it is not surprising not to see Compaq computers in Japan, but surprising not to see any by Leading Edge; and it is not surprising not to see Philips color televisions, but surprising not to see GoldStars.

Japan placed itself in two dilemmas in the 1980s. First, Japanese policymakers like to deal with "free traders" in Washington. On the other hand, Japanese policymakers believe in long-term relationships, nonmarket (internal) labor markets, industrial policies, a no-bankruptcy policy, and policy interventions in general. Second, Japan has defended some policy measures on the grounds of its own "uniqueness." Rice should not be imported because rice for the Japanese is "unique." The Japanese are "unique" in their thrift and in the relationship between a paternalistic firm and its loyal employees. The uniqueness produced a high saving rate, high labor quality, and a stable relationship. These arguments were used against Japan by revisionists: "If you are so unique, why don't we treat you differently."

Regarding SII, it is puzzling why the United States asks Japan to become better and more efficient. It is not quite true that SII make Japan more efficient. From the Japanese point of view, U.S. demands are often treated as "foreign pressure" to shift from producer's surplus to consumer's surplus.

Comment

Yun-Wing Sung

I very much enjoyed Gary Saxonhouse's wide-ranging paper, which argues that the contrast in U.S. and Japanese productivity performance is extremely persistent and is independent of all but the most radical institutional change. While the paper gives plenty of historical evidence on the persistence of national economic performance, the case is overstated. Although the paper argues that national economic performances "may be surprisingly deep rooted," it does not elaborate on what those roots are from a theoretical standpoint. Without a theory of productivity growth, arguments based on historical evidence alone leave much to be desired. Saxonhouse seems to have an implicit theory of productivity in mind, although he does not spell out what it is. For example, the paper argues in the closing sections that the Structural Impediments Initiative (SII) is likely to improve Japan's competitiveness. If Saxonhouse is right, SII clearly represents a case where institutional change does affect competitiveness, and economic performance is not really so independent of institutional changes.

The closest that Saxonhouse comes to stating a theory of productivity is his statement that, "among the countries with the capacity to learn from foreign experience elsewhere, productivity bears a negative relation to the level of productivity performance," and he explains the contrast in U.S. and Japanese productivity growth performance by the countries' difference in productivity levels. However, such an explanation of productivity growth contradicts the central theme of the paper, that productivity performance is extremely persistent and deep rooted because differential productivity growth will converge over time and the superior productivity growth of Japan will disappear. In this case, Japan's superior productivity growth is only a historical accident: the destruction of World War II prevented the convergence of productivity levels of Japan and the United States.

It should also be noted that the East Asian newly industrialized countries (NICs) can certainly be classified as "countries with the capacity to learn from foreign experience elsewhere." However, according to Saxonhouse's data, Japan's productivity performance is superior to that of the East Asian NICs despite the fact that Japan's level of productivity is much higher. Productivity levels thus may not be a decisive factor in explaining productivity growth.

Saxonhouse cited his earlier work that Japan's lack of intraindustry trade can be explained by "Japan's distinctive factor endowments." For readers unfamiliar with Saxonhouse's previous work, it would have been much better if he had elaborated on what those material and human endowments are. Besides Japan's own endowments, it must be stressed that the lack of neighboring countries with a similar level of development also hampers Japan's intraindus-

Yun-Wing Sung is a senior lecturer in economics at the Chinese University of Hong Kong.

try trade. A substantial portion of intraindustry trade is intrafirm trade: the shipping of parts and components back and forth across borders of adjacent countries among subsidiaries of the same firm. Land access is a crucial element in the coordination of production across borders because turnaround time in transportation by land is much faster than that by sea. Japan's geographic insularity and the absence of highly developed economies adjacent to Japan combined to hamper Japan's intrafirm trade and intraindustry trade. It should be noted that Japan's recent wave of investment in the East Asian NICs has increased its intraindustry trade. However, the lack of land access between Japan and the East Asian NICs will continue to be an obstacle to intraindustry trade.

7 Protectionist U.S. Trade Policy and Korean Exports

Chong-Hyun Nam

Since the end of World War II, tariff barriers to trade in manufactures have been almost eliminated in most of the advanced industrial countries (AICs) through successive rounds of trade negotiations in the GATT. The shift into a more open international trading system, which was chiefly led by the United States, not only brought about unprecedented growth of the world economy but also produced an environment in which some developing countries emerged as significant exporters of labor-intensive manufactures, the newly industrializing economies (NIEs). The Republic of Korea is well known as a successful front-runner among the NIEs in that regard.

As the world economic climate changed for the worse, however, beginning with the first oil crisis in 1973–74 and culminating with the second oil price increase in 1979–80, protectionist pressures grew tremendously in most of the AICs. Because the already low tariffs in the AICs are mostly bound by the GATT, nontariff barriers (NTBs) have become the main method of protection in the AICs. Recent studies indicate that the United States has been one of the leading nations in applying the NTBs, and the major export items of the developing countries, notably of the NIEs, have been the prime target of those actions (see, e.g., Nogues, Olechowski, and Winters 1985; Finger and Nogues 1987; and Nam 1987). In this paper, the nature and extent of trade restriction measures undertaken by the United States and their effects on Korean exports to the United States during the 1980s are examined.

The paper will begin with a brief description of the development of trade between Korea and the United States. This will be followed by the review of protectionist elements embedded in the current U.S. trade laws. Then an attempt will be made to examine the pattern of the U.S. NTBs and their effects

Chong-Hyun Nam is professor of economics at Korea University.

on Korean exports. Finally, policy implications for Korea will be considered in a concluding section.

7.1 Trade Development between Korea and the United States

During the past quarter century, Korea's strong performance in exports has been the principal factor behind its successful growth and industrialization. As can be seen from table 7.1, exports exploded from $119 million in 1964 to $62.4 billion in 1989, with an average annual growth rate of 28.5 percent in nominal value. The ratio of exports to GNP was only 4.3 percent in 1964 but rose rapidly to 29.7 percent in 1989. As a result, Korea has become a major exporting nation, ranking eleventh in the world with a share of 2.1 percent in total world exports in 1989.

Rapid expansion of exports has accompanied the rapid growth of real GNP, and this in turn has brought fundamental changes in all sectors of the economy. Real GNP in Korea increased nearly thirteenfold between 1964 and 1988, with an annual growth rate of 10.7 percent. The rapid expansion of

Table 7.1 **Major Economic Indicators of the Korean Economy, 1964–89**

	1964	1974	1989	1964–74[a]	1974–89[a]	1964–89[a]
Population (million)	28.0	34.7	42.4	2.2	1.3	1.7
GNP (in billion won)[b]	9,449	24,207	119,577	9.9	11.2	10.7
Per capita GNP:						
in thousand won[b]	337	698	2,822	7.6	9.8	8.9
in U.S. dollars[c]	102	540	4,968			
Sectoral value added (share of GNP, %):						
Primary industry	47.6	25.7	10.8			
Manufacturing	10.5	27.4	31.3			
Services and social overhead	41.9	46.9	57.9			
Sectoral employment (share of total labor force, %):						
Primary industry	62.5	48.4	20.1			
Manufacturing	8.2	17.3	27.6			
Services and social overhead	29.3	34.3	52.3			
Exports and imports:						
Commodity exports, f.o.b.						
(in million U.S. dollars)	119	4,460	62,377	43.7	19.2	28.5
Ratio of exports to GNP	4.3	28.5	29.7			
Commodity imports, f.o.b.						
(in million U.S. dollars)	365	6,852	61,465	34.1	15.7	22.8
Ratio of imports to GNP	13.3	43.8	29.3			

Source: Economic Planning Board, *Major Statistics of Korean Economy* (various years).

[a]Based on current prices.

[b]Average annual growth rate.

[c]Based on 1985 prices.

exports was achieved mainly by the increase in production of manufactured goods since the early 1960s. Exports of manufactured goods accounted for only 51.1 percent of total exports in 1964 but increased to 94.5 percent by 1989. As a result, the manufacturing sector's share in GNP increased from 10.5 percent in 1964 to 31.3 percent in 1989, whereas the share of agriculture decreased from 47.6 to 10.8 percent for the same period.

Ever since Korea began its outward-oriented economic development in the mid-1960s, access to the U.S. market has been critical to Korea's export success. The United States took as much as 47.3 percent of Korea's total exports in 1970 but only 26.3 percent in 1980 (see table 7.2). The absorption by the United States of Korea's exports rose again to 29.8 percent in 1990. At the same time, the United States was the second largest supplier of imports, next to Japan, in the Korean market in 1970 with a share of 29.5 percent of Korea's total imports. The U.S. share in Korea's import markets steadily declined to 21.9 percent in 1980, but rose again to 24.3 percent in 1990.

The relative importance of Korea to the United States both as a purchaser of U.S. exports and as a supplier for the U.S. market is not nearly as great, but that is changing rapidly. Korea took less than 1 percent of total U.S. exports in 1970, but it took 3.9 percent in 1990. Meanwhile, although Korea supplied less than 1.4 percent of total U.S. imports in 1970, it supplied more than 4.3 percent in 1990. As a result, the bilateral trade volume between the two countries has increased from a mere $980 million in 1970 to more than $36 billion in 1990, surpassing the volume between the United States and

Table 7.2 **Trade Dependency between Korea and the United States, 1970–90 (million U.S. dollars)**

	1970	1980	1990	1970–80[a]	1980–90[a]
Korea's exports to the U.S.[b]	395	4,607	19,360	27.8	15.4
Share (%) in Korea's exports	47.3	26.3	29.8		
Share (%) in U.S. imports	.9	1.8	3.9		
Korea's imports from the U.S.[b]	585	4,890	16,942	23.7	13.2
Share (%) in Korea's imports	29.5	21.9	24.3		
Share (%) in U.S. exports	1.4	2.2	4.3		
Korea's trade balance against the U.S.[b]	−190	−284	2,418		
Korea's trade balance against world[b]	−1,149	−4,787	−4,828		

Source: Korea Foreign Trade Association, *Major Statistics of Korea Economy,* 1990.

[a]Average annual growth rates are given in percentages.

[b]All measures are in customs clearance base.

France and between the United States and Italy early in the 1980s. Since 1983, Korea has been the seventh largest trading partner of the United States, standing behind only Canada, Japan, Mexico, West Germany, Taiwan, and the United Kingdom.

The relative dependence between Korea and the United States in trade is, therefore, quite a contrast. When measured by the ratio of bilateral trade volume to each country's total trade volume, Korea's dependence on the U.S. market represented more than 27 percent in 1990, whereas the U.S. dependence on Korea's market was merely 4.1 percent. The relative dependence of each country can be contrasted even more when measured by the ratio of bilateral trade volume to GNP in each country. The ratio is estimated at 16.2 percent for Korea but only 0.7 percent for the United States. This vividly illustrates how much each country can hurt the other by introducing new protectionist measures. This also indicates how much bargaining leverage each country may have when each other's market is being held hostage in bilateral trade negotiations.

The dependence of Korean exports on the U.S. market has been more critical in some of the leading export sectors than in others. Table 7.3 presents the shares of Korea's major export items going to the United States. In 1988, the United States took more than 50 percent of Korean exports in road vehicles, footwear, and data-processing machines. The United States also received more than 30 percent of Korean exports in apparel and clothing, metal products, telecommunications apparatus, and electrical machineries. On the other hand, Korea relied on the United States to supply more than 60 percent of its imports of transport equipment (including aircraft), cereal, furskins, and pulp products. Korea also relied on imports from the United States for more than one-quarter of its imports of electrical machinery, organic chemicals, metalliferous ores, and textile fibers. Thus, Korean exports to the United States tend to be mostly labor-intensive consumer goods, whereas Korean imports from the United States comprise mostly resource-based raw materials, including agricultural products and highly sophisticated capital goods.

While bilateral trade between the two countries grew tremendously in size, the bilateral trade balance was persistently in favor of the United States until 1981. It shifted into Korea's favor beginning in 1982 and has since grown to a significant magnitude, reaching a peak at $9.7 billion in 1987. Since then, however, Korea's bilateral trade surplus against the United States decreased significantly to $2.4 billion by 1990. Partly owing to its rising bilateral trade surplus against the United States, and partly owing to an accelerated increase in the domestic savings rate as a result of rapid economic growth, Korea began to register an overall trade surplus beginning in 1986. Such a successful transformation into a trade surplus economy from a long debt-ridden deficit economy has, however, been met by industrial countries, notably by the United States, with an increased level of protection. The overall trade balance of Korea moved into the red again in 1990.

Table 7.3 Korea's Major Exports to and Imports from the United States, 1988 (million U.S. dollars)

Ranking	Exports: Commodity[a]	Exports Value: Total (A)	Exports Value: To U.S. (B)	Exports Value: B/A (%)	Imports: Commodity[a]	Imports Value: Total (A)	Imports Value: From U.S. (B)	Imports Value: B/A (%)
1	Road vehicles	4,525	3,452	76.3	Electrical machinery and apparatus	5,526	1,454	26.3
2	Apparel and clothing accessories	8,693	3,236	37.2	Transport equipment, excluding road vehicles	1,691	1,017	60.2
3	Footwear	3,801	2,336	61.5	Organic chemicals	3,162	816	25.8
4	Telecom. sound recording apparatus	6,210	2,234	36.0	Cereal and cereal preparations	1,151	790	68.6
5	Electrical machinery and apparatus	6,416	2,176	33.9	Raw hides, skins, and furskins	1,141	770	67.5
6	Office and automatic data-processing machines	2,574	1,310	50.9	Metalliferous ores and metal scrap	1,887	593	31.4

(continued)

Table 7.3 (continued)

	Exports				Imports			
		Value				Value		
Ranking	Commodity[a]	Total (A)	To U.S. (B)	B/A (%)	Commodity[a]	Total (A)	From U.S. (B)	B/A (%)
7	Miscellaneous manufactured articles	3,959	1,701	43.0	Machinery for particular industries	2,593	556	21.5
8	Manufactures of metals	1,973	783	39.7	Textile fibers and their waste	1,484	524	35.3
9	Textile yarn, fabrics, made-up articles	4,847	624	12.9	Pulp and waste paper	838	522	62.2
10	Iron and steel	3,186	577	18.1	General industrial machinery and equipment	2,602	485	18.6
Subtotal		46,184	18,429	39.9		22,075	7,527	34.1
Total exports/imports		60,696	21,404	35.3		51,811	12,757	24.6

Source: Korea Foreign Trade Association.

[a]Commodity classification is based on the Standard Korea Trade Classification at the two-digit level.

7.2 Protectionist Elements in U.S. Trade Policy: A Developing Country's Perspective

During the postwar period, the United States emphasized international cooperation to strengthen the multilateral trading system based on the GATT's framework. However, beginning in the 1970s, and especially during the 1980s, the United States has increasingly pursued an aggressive bilateral approach to protect certain domestic interests and to increase its access to foreign markets. Both the growing trade deficits of recent years and a heightened sensitivity to so-called unfair foreign trade practices are often cited as major factors behind such a policy shift in the United States.

According to a recent IMF (1988) report, over the period 1980–87, the United States initiated a total of 411 antidumping (AD) investigations, 283 countervailing duty (CVD) investigations, 60 safeguard investigations, and 60 investigations of "unfair" trade practices abroad under Section 301 of the U.S. Trade Act of 1974. Of these, about 40 percent were directed at exports from developing countries, whereas their share in total U.S. imports represented only 26 percent. The recent trend contrasts with the total of 196 AD and 125 CVD investigations and 20 Section 301 investigations conducted by the United States during the postwar period until 1980. Furthermore, as of May 1988, the United States maintains 62 voluntary export restraints (VERs) out of a total of 261 known to exist worldwide. These affect mainly textile and steel products that are major export items of developing countries, especially NIEs.

There is considerable evidence indicating that such actions based on U.S. trade laws have been used more as a form of "administered protection" or "process protectionism" rather than to counter "unfair" foreign trade practices (see, e.g., Finger, Hall, and Nelson 1982; and Schott 1989). A number of VERs that protect the domestic market are, for instance, the result of AD or CVD investigations or safeguard actions.[1]

Since the 1979 trade legislation, the scope of U.S. trade laws has been steadily broadened to cover almost any foreign trade and industrial policy as a potential candidate for retaliation, and the criteria and requirements for granting import relief in particular situations have been significantly eased. The recently passed Omnibus Trade and Competitiveness Act of 1988 is one such example. According to the law, the scope for which AD or CVD actions could be applied was significantly extended and the criteria relaxed. Further, the U.S. administration was given enough discretionary power to eliminate any foreign trade practices that are deemed to be "unfair" according to the criteria set by U.S. government officials. Threats to restrict access to its domestic market have been used as a major bargaining chip by the United States.

1. It is striking to learn that such administered protection is cited as one of the serious reasons why Canada recently entered into a free trade agreement with the United States (see IMF 1988, 12).

The increased use of a bilateral approach to settle trade disputes by the United States appears to have worked adversely, especially against developing countries, whose bargaining leverage is relatively weak. For instance, once a charge is successfully filed, the burden of proof falls entirely on exporters. Such proof, however, requires not only a large amount of information but also expensive legal costs, which may be too burdensome for many developing countries to bear.[2] Hence merely filing a petition itself can be a powerful means of harassing developing country exporters.

In the following section, a brief review will be made of major U.S. trade laws and practices, examining protectionist elements inherently embedded in those laws and practices, mainly from the perspective of developing countries.

7.2.1 Safeguard Actions (Section 201)

The objective of Section 201 of the Trade Act of 1974, as amended, is to provide an industry temporary relief from import competition for structural adjustment. Hence, it is not necessarily related to any potentially "unfair" foreign trade practices. Its principles are embodied in Article XIX of the GATT, the escape clause that, under the appropriate circumstances, permits contracting parties to escape temporarily from GATT commitments and take measures to protect an injured domestic industry.

Under Section 201, the U.S. International Trade Commission (ITC) is required to report its findings on injuries to the president; if the finding is affirmative, the ITC's report includes a remedy recommendation that the president may consider to alleviate the injury. Relief may be provided through any combination of tariffs and quotas, trade adjustment assistance to the injured domestic industry, or negotiated orderly market agreements (OMAs) with relevant foreign nations. Relief may last for a maximum of eight years.[3]

Import relief under Section 201 is supposed to be applied to all imports rather than those from a selected number of countries or firms; hence, it is nondiscriminatory. Furthermore, Article XIX of the GATT authorizes member countries to retaliate if the country undertaking safeguard actions does not compensate its trading partners for the increased protection provided for its domestic industry.

When properly enforced, therefore, Section 201 seems to provide an appro-

2. For example, in June 1988, a Korean firm producing industrial belts was petitioned by U.S. firms on AD and CVD charges, but the CVD charge was dropped in April 1989 for *de minimus* benefits, and the AD charge was closed with no injury finding in June 1989. In the meantime, however, it cost the firm nearly $300,000 in legal expenses (for U.S. lawyers) alone to defend itself against the invalid charges. The firm's exports to the U.S. market were $4.3 million in 1988. An UNCTAD (1984, 16) study also reports that the cost of a fairly routine AD or CVD proceeding in the United States easily exceeds $100,000.

3. Prior to the 1988 Trade Act, the maximum period was five years, with a possible extension of three more years.

priate route for temporary protection while causing less friction to its trading partners, especially developing countries. Unfortunately, however, this route has been used infrequently, compared to other means of administered protection, for several reasons. First, the standard used in determining injury under Section 201 is in general higher than that used for AD or CVD cases since Section 201 investigations include imports from all sources that are not allegedly unfair trade (see Stern and Wechsler 1986). Second, even if injury to a domestic industry has been found, the president is not legally bound to follow the ITC's recommendation to remedy the situation. Finally, the president may be, in fact, reluctant to authorize protection measures because that could provoke retaliation unless compensation is adequate. In an effort to avoid such retaliation, the president frequently resorts to negotiated settlements through VERs or OMAs with certain key suppliers that limit their exports to the United States.

7.2.2 Antidumping and Countervailing Duties

United States antidumping laws[4] are designed to raise the price of foreign goods sold in the United States at "less than fair value" (LTFV) or "dumped." The U.S. countervailing duty law[5] aims to offset the price advantage of imported goods due to subsidies provided by foreign governments. According to these statutes, import relief is to be automatically granted on the finding of material injury, or threat of material injury, inflicted on the domestic industry by foreign imports and the finding that the imports causing the injury are either sold at LTFV or subsidized.

These unfair trade laws are consistent with GATT rules as they appear in Articles VI and XVI. GATT rules require, for instance, that the importing country's industry has been injured and that that injury was caused by either LTFV or government subsidies, but under the GATT each importing country sets up its own specific criteria for such findings. For the past decade, these criteria have been constantly revised to make it easier to raise protectionist barriers using the U.S. AD and CVD laws. There is considerable evidence to indicate that these unfair trade laws have been abused in the United States as anticompetitive or antitrade instruments, reducing the general welfare of both exporting and importing countries. The abuse is made possible, especially against developing countries, partly because the laws fail to reflect modern economics and partly because there is a lot of leeway for government officials to interpret and enforce the laws. Some of the notable features will be discussed briefly below.

First, under the current U.S. AD laws or GATT rules, any price discrimination between the home market and abroad due to exporting at a price lower

4. Tariff Act of 1930, Sec. 731, as amended.
5. Tariff Act of 1930, Sec. 701, as amended.

than that charged on the home market, regardless of the cost of production, may be subject to AD charges. In many developing countries, however, domestic prices may be set higher than their export prices, for a variety of reasons.[6] For instance, in developing countries where imports are protected and the domestic market size is not large enough to warrant perfect competition, a domestic monopoly or oligopoly may sell its products on the domestic market at prices higher than internationally competitive levels. In these circumstances, foreign competitors are not harmed because their export prices are normally set at least at or above international levels. In fact, sales in domestic markets are favored more than sales abroad in such cases. Nonetheless, such a price difference is normally subject to an AD charge. It is believed that such price discrimination is most common in developing countries, especially where a policy shift from inward to outward orientation has yet to be made.

Even in outward-oriented developing countries, it is not uncommon to maintain relatively high import barriers. This is because the extent of liberalization of their import regime is often dictated by policy options open to them at the time they shift from inward to outward orientation. For example, economies like Korea or Taiwan, which are unlike Hong Kong or Singapore, pursued their outward orientation without wholesale dismantling of their import barriers, at least until very recently. In these economies, outward orientation was achieved through the use of export subsidies to offset the antiexport bias of their import barriers (an "export-subsidy" route to outward orientation), instead of an outright liberalization of trade with currency adjustments (a "free trade" route to outward orientation).[7]

The export-subsidy route is a close substitute for the free trade route, at least in theory, since a 10 percent tariff on all imports, together with a 10 percent subsidy on all exports, would be equivalent to no tariff and no subsidy and a 10 percent depreciated exchange rate. Unless the export-subsidy route leads to a balance-of-payments surplus, therefore, foreign competitors should not consider it harmful compared to a free trade situation. In fact, developing economies like Brazil, Mexico, and Korea have, until recently, all been experiencing balance-of-payments deficits despite subsidies provided for their exports, indicating that their subsidies were not enough to offset their currency overvaluation. Nonetheless, their import protection policies have frequently led to AD charges, and, at the same time, their export subsidies have been frequently countervailed by the United States.

6. Providing import protection for an export industry may sound ironic, but it is often done as part of an overall incentive system or under infant-export arguments. Or exports may be differentiated products, which may differ slightly from products for domestic sales.

7. The export-subsidy route has often been preferred to the free trade route, mostly for political reasons: because of the political influence of vested interest groups benefiting from import protection, because of the fear of the inflationary effect of a required devaluation, and because of the erroneous belief on the part of policymakers that exports and import substitution could be better promoted under the export-subsidy route.

Second, the GATT fails to provide a general definition of the export or domestic subsidies to be banned. It does take, however, a somewhat more lenient view of domestic subsidies while strictly banning any form of export subsidies, providing a positive list of objectives for which domestic subsidies may be used.[8] However, U.S. CVD law forbids any domestic subsidies as long as they are industry specific, irrespective of their objectives.[9] Therefore, even domestic subsidies aimed at compensating externalities or offsetting other domestic distortions are banned under current U.S. CVD law. This amounts to depriving developing countries of some of the more efficient means of supporting their industrialization efforts.

Third, both the GATT and the U.S. AD (or CVD) laws require an injury test as a prerequisite for imposing AD duties (or CVDs) on dumped (or subsidized) imports, yet the meaning of *material injury* is not clearly defined.[10] The concept of material injury is increasingly problematic, particularly for developing countries. Aside from the unclear definition of material injury, the loose requirement of a causal link between dumping (or subsidies) and injury in the GATT rules as well as in U.S. law[11] can lead to the abuse of AD (or CVD) measures by blurring the distinction between subsidies and shifts in comparative advantage as a major cause of the material injury. In fact, this view is partly supported by the evidence that recent U.S. countervailing actions have been heavily concentrated in a few industries, such as iron and steel, textiles, and metal products, in which comparative advantage has already been established in favor of developing countries (see, e.g., Nam 1987, 739).

Finally, when the ITC's preliminary determination of injury is positive, the Department of Commerce (DOC) calculates dumping margins by comparing the adjusted "U.S. price" of the imported product to its "fair value" or "foreign market value." The fair value is normally estimated on the basis of the home market price of exporting nations. But the DOC can determine the fair value on the basis of the export price to third countries when the sales volume in the home market is small. The DOC can also use a "constructed value" for the fair value when neither the home market price nor the export price to third countries is deemed adequate for the fair value. The "constructed value" appears to be the most abused concept in calculating dumping margins, however. It is based on the estimated cost of production using the best information available, often information provided by petitioners. The constructed value also includes general expenses of at least 10 percent of the estimated produc-

8. For detailed GATT rules on subsidies, see Nam (1987).

9. See Sec. 771[5][B] of the U.S. Trade Agreement Act of 1979.

10. According to the U.S. Trade Agreement Act of 1979, *material injury* is defined as "harm which is not inconsequential, immaterial or unimportant" (Sec. 771[7][A]).

11. When the ITC determines the existence of injury, that determination is based on the cumulative effect on the U.S. industry of imports from all sources in the aggregate, rather than the imports from the country in question.

tion costs, plus a profit of at least 8 percent of the sum of such general expenses and the production cost, and the cost of packing for shipment to the United States. The value, so constructed, may be sufficiently elastic to meet any protectionist purpose of government officials.

7.2.3 Unfair Import Practices (Section 337)

Section 337 of the Tariff Act of 1930, as amended, is designed to provide relief to firms suffering from the infringement of intellectual property rights by foreign competitors and from unfair methods of competition or unfair acts in the importation of merchandise into the United States. The violations of intellectual property rights include import practices that infringe on valid and enforceable U.S. patents, copyrights, or trademarks. Other unfair import practices include methods or acts (such as antitrust violations, false designation of origin, or improper interference with contractual obligations) that destroy, threaten, or substantially injure a U.S. industry or prevent its establishment.

Section 337 is administered by the ITC. The ITC investigates any alleged violation of the law under Section 337 and reports its findings to the president, along with a statement of the action to be taken as a result of the investigation. The president can reject the ITC's findings, but such presidential action is rare.

The penalties in Section 337 cases can be very severe. A violation can result in a general exclusion of the concerned product, and all other goods containing it as an intermediate input, from the U.S. market. In addition, or alternatively, the ITC may issue a cease-and-desist order to the exporters committing the unfair act or practice. The 1988 Trade Act has significantly reinforced the penalty scheme for the enforcement of Section 337. At the same time, the 1988 Trade Act amended Section 337 so that U.S. petitioners need not prove injury to win an affirmative ITC determination in cases involving infringement of U.S. intellectual property rights. No doubt, these amendments significantly increase the chance that this law will be abused. The abuse is more likely against exports from NIEs like Korea since the structure of their exports is rapidly shifting into technologically more sophisticated products.

Recently, at the request of the EC, a GATT panel was formed to investigate Section 337. The panel reported in January 1989 that Section 337 violated the GATT rule (Article III, 4) of national treatment for imports. The panel found that Section 337 treated imported goods charged with patent infringement less favorably than domestic goods would be treated under U.S. domestic law. The United States, however, has not yet indicated whether it will revise its laws to accommodate the panel's recommendation.

7.2.4 The National Security Clause (Section 232)

Recently, U.S. firms or industries have even tried to have the U.S. government invoke trade restrictions against imports from Japan and other countries for reasons of national security. According to Section 232 of the Trade Expansion Act of 1962, as amended, the U.S. president is allowed to "adjust" imports so that they will not be a threat to or impair national security. Of course, this law is backed up by the GATT in principle.[12]

In the past, many U.S. industries have sought relief from import competition under the national security clause, but the U.S. government has been very cautious in granting it. The danger of misuse of the national security argument is quite obvious because it could readily be applied to all kinds of economic activities. Also, such misuse could readily call for the escalation of retaliation. For that reason, perhaps, only one industry, the powerful oil industry—and no manufacturing industry—has been successful so far in getting import relief under Section 232 (see Saxonhouse 1986, 234). The abuse of this law is not, however, unthinkable in the future.

7.2.5 Section 301

Section 301 of the Trade Act of 1974, as amended in 1988, is designed to enforce U.S. rights under international agreements and to effectively counter foreign unfair trade practices. Unfair trade practices include any act, policy, or practice of a foreign government that is found to violate an international trade agreement or anything that is construed to be "unjustifiable, unreasonable, or discriminatory."[13] Section 301 requires the U.S. trade representative (USTR) to take all appropriate and feasible actions to eliminate such unfair foreign trade practices.

Section 301 was considerably strengthened by requiring tougher reciprocity in market access as amended in the 1988 Omnibus Trade and Competitiveness Act. The meaning of *unreasonable practices* was further elaborated to include, for example, the failure of effective protection of intellectual property rights, the denial of fair and equitable market opportunities, toleration of private anticompetitive schemes, export targeting, and the persistent denial of workers' rights. The 1988 Trade Act made retaliatory action mandatory in cases involving "unjustifiable" acts[14] and at the USTR's discretion in cases involving "unreasonable or discriminatory" practices.

The 1988 Trade Act also amended Section 301 by adding a provision that is known as "Super-301." This provision requires the USTR to identify "prior-

12. Article XXI of the GATT states, e.g., that "nothing in this agreement shall be construed . . . (b) to prevent any contracting party from taking any action which it considers necessary for the protection of its essential security interests."

13. Unjustifiable practices are those that are inconsistent with international legal rights; unreasonable practices are unfair or inequitable practices, although they may not be inconsistent with international legal rights; and discriminatory practices are the denial of most-favored-nation (MFN) treatment to U.S. goods, services, or investments (see Sec. 301[d]).

14. Mandatory retaliation has certain exceptions, however. For instance, the USTR need not retaliate when the United States receives an unfavorable determination or ruling by the GATT, when a foreign country is taking specific measures to eliminate the problem, or when U.S. action is likely to affect the U.S. economy adversely.

ity foreign unfair practices" and "priority foreign countries" and to conduct bilateral negotiations with designated countries over a three-year period to reduce, eliminate, or compensate for these practices, or to retaliate. The Super-301 provision was only a temporary measure, however, lasting two years and expiring in 1990.

During the 1980s, and especially since the mid-1980s, the United States accelerated the use of Section 301 at an unprecedented rate, often directing it against developing economies. The aggressive use of Section 301 is particularly worrisome for developing countries, for several reasons.

First, Section 301 is neither covered by the GATT nor consistent with the GATT's principle of nondiscrimination. This law can be used highly selectively in choosing target countries or target practices, and there are no certain rules for retaliation. Therefore, the uncertainties that traders face under the threat of 301 actions can be unbearably high, particularly for developing countries whose trade dependency on the U.S. market is relatively high.

Second, any retaliation or threats of retaliation can quickly generate amplified political responses from trading partners. In particular, developing countries may feel that any unilateral liberalization effort needs to be reserved for future trade negotiations with the United States.

Finally, to enforce Section 301 properly, the United States has to constantly play the role of an international police force against all economic policies in all countries, which would require an exorbitant amount of resources. Resources certainly could be used more efficiently.

7.2.6 Voluntary Export Restraints

Beginning in the late 1970s, VERs became a popular means of import restriction in the United States. VERs are often negotiated when other GATT-consistent trade remedies are found to be ineffective or have difficulties controlling the flow of imports. Since VERs pretend to be voluntary and are bilateral in nature, they escape both U.S. laws and the GATT. While VERs give U.S. trade negotiators greater flexibility in providing protection for domestic producers, they reduce the pressure for domestic industries to adjust to changing conditions.

Since VERs allow foreigners to administer the export controls, they implicitly compensate the exporting country by transferring quota rents to the exporters at the cost of domestic consumers. Furthermore, VERs tend to provide more stable and certain trade environments, with secure market-sharing arrangements, than would alternative trade measures. Mostly for these reasons, exporting countries often easily yield to pressure to accept a VER.

However, there are reasons to worry about the rising trend of VERs. First, once a VER is instituted, it is not easy to get out of the trap since both exporters and importers have shared interests in maintaining it. Further, there is a great temptation to expand it to a global scale, thus contributing to the erosion of an open world trading system. As a result, the smooth industrial transformation to a changing comparative advantage would be significantly disturbed or delayed in both countries. The life of sunset industries may be prolonged, but the sunrise industries may stop growing long before they reach a peak. The damage will certainly be greater for countries with the potential for more rapid growth.

7.3 The Pattern of U.S.-Administered Protection as Applied to Korean Exports

7.3.1 Recent Trends

Korean exports have been facing increasingly adverse market situations in industrial countries, particularly since the mid-1970s. Of Korean exports going to nineteen industrial countries, the share of exports under import restrictions rose from 27.8 percent in 1976 to a peak of 45.8 percent in 1981, as shown in table 7.4. According to the table, however, the share has declined since then, to 22.3 percent by 1989.

A similar pattern holds for Korean exports to the United States: the share of Korean exports under restrictions rose from 37.5 percent in 1976 to a peak of 43.3 percent in 1985 but declined to 19.7 percent in 1989. The recent decline in the export coverage of NTBs, however, may be attributed more to the rapid growth of Korean exports than to the increased liberalization of import restric-

Table 7.4 Korean Exports under NTBs by Major Trading Partners

	1976	1981	1985	1987	1989
Exports to the U.S.:					
Total exports (million U.S. dollars)	2,493	5,661	10,754	18,311	20,639
Exports under NTBs (million U.S. dollars)	935	2,412	4,656	4,855	4,072
Share (= B/A) (%)	37.5	42.6	43.3	26.5	19.7
Share (%) of exports under NTBs to other industrial countries:					
Canada	39.3	45.6	31.1	42.9	23.9
EC	31.6	39.3	29.5	41.0	22.3
Japan	14.5	48.5	32.0	19.4	23.7
19 industrial countries[a]	27.8	45.8	36.6	31.0	22.3[b]

Source: Korea Foreign Trade Association, *Overview on Import Restrictions of Major Industrialized Countries* (various issues).

Note: NTBs here include VERs, ADs, CVDs, safeguard actions, and other import restriction under administrative or unfair trade regulations in force or under investigation.

[a]The nineteen industrial countries are the United States, Canada, Japan, Australia, New Zealand, Germany, the United Kingdom, France, the Netherlands, Belgium, Luxembourg, Denmark, Italy, Greece, Ireland, Finland, Norway, Sweden, and Austria.

[b]Of the nineteen industrial countries, New Zealand is omitted.

tions on the part of the United States: Korea's overall exports to the United States increased more than threefold, from $5.7 to $20.6 billion for the period 1981–89, while its exports to the United States under import restrictions increased about twofold, from $2.4 to $4.1 billion for the same period. The recent decline of Korean exports to the United States under NTBs, particularly during the later half of the 1980s, could also have been induced partly by a U.S. policy shift from raising protection of domestic industries to increasing access to foreign markets.[15] Nevertheless, 20 percent of Korean exports to the United States were still taking place under various forms of administered protection as of 1989.

Table 7.5 presents estimates of Korean exports going to the U.S. market under various types of administered protection. Over the period 1984–89, Korea exported a total of $27.1 billion to the U.S. market under various measures of administered protection. Of this total, nearly 77 percent was covered by VERs, 11.5 percent by ADs or CVDs, 4.5 percent by safeguard actions, and the remaining 6.7 percent by other unfair trade laws like Section 337 or the National Security Clause of Section 232.

VERs, therefore, appear to be the most important import-restricting instrument in force against Korean exports to the United States as far as their export coverage is concerned. Two of them were particularly notable during the later half of the 1980s. One is the VER on textile and clothing products under the Multifiber Arrangement (MFA) quotas, and the other is a VER agreement on iron and steel products.

International trade in textiles and clothing has long been regulated by restrictive trading systems. At first, the Short Term Cotton Textile Arrangement (STA) came into effect in 1961, and this was followed by a more comprehensive agreement known as the Long Term Arrangement on Cotton Textiles (LTA) in 1962. The LTA evolved into the first Multifiber Arrangement (MFA I) in 1974, in which coverage was expanded to noncotton products, especially synthetic fiber products. Since then, there have been several renewals: currently, MFA IV (1986–91) is in effect.

The main objective proclaimed in these agreements were to foster the expansion of world trade in textiles with the reduction of barriers to such trade while, at the same time, preventing disruptive effects in individual markets. But, each time the MFA was renewed, it was accompanied by an increase in coverage as well as in intensity to regulate international trade in textile products. According to a recent study by Kim (1989), for example, the number of

15. In recent years, e.g., the United States has launched a number of Section 301 investigations mainly to increase its access to Korean markets, beginning with cases for the liberalization of the insurance market and the protection of U.S. intellectual property rights in Korea in 1985. U.S. interests moved to cases of import liberalization of cigarettes, beef, and wine in 1988 and more recently to such areas as the opening up of the domestic telecommunications industry and removing restrictions on direct foreign investments. So far, most of these cases have been concluded to the satisfaction of the United States, and no Section 301 threat has yet been transformed into retaliatory action.

Table 7.5 Korean Exports Going to the United States under Restrictions, by Type of Administrative Protection, 1984–89 (million U.S. dollars)

Year	VER: Textile (1a)	VER: Steel (1b)	ADs[a] (2)	CVDs (3)	Safeguard (4)	Section 337 & Section 232[b] (5)	Exports under Restrictions[c] (6)	Total Exports to U.S. (7)	Share ([6]/[7]) (8)
1984	2,166	975	1,106	249	0	35	4,662	10,479	44.5
	(46.5)	(20.9)	(23.7)	(5.3)	(0)	(.8)	(100)		
1985	2,191	869	412	11	1,157	15	4,656	10,754	43.3
	(47.1)	(18.7)	(8.8)	(.2)	(24.9)	(.3)	(100)		
1986	2,510	731	397	10	17	965	4,621	13,880	33.3
	(54.3)	(15.8)	(8.6)	(.2)	(.4)	(20.9)	(100)		
1987	2,944	735	354	0	23	799	4,855	18,311	26.5
	(60.6)	(15.1)	(7.3)	(0)	(.5)	(16.5)	(100)		
1988	3,065	846	310	0	7	4	4,239	21,404	19.8
	(72.3)	(20.0)	(7.3)	(0)	(.2)	(.1)	(100)		
1989	3,135	652	270	0	11	4	4,072	20,639	19.7
	(77.0)	(16.0)	(6.6)	(0)	(.3)	(.1)	(100)		
Total	16,011	4,787	2,849	270	1,215	1,822	27,105	95,467	28.4
	(59.1)	(17.7)	(10.5)	(1.0)	(4.5)	(6.7)	(100)		

Source: See table 7.4.

Note: Numbers given in parentheses represent the share of exports under respective restriction in total exports under all restrictions.

[a]Exports that were subject to ADs and CVDs at the same time were included in AD cases.

[b]Section 337 refers to unfair importing practices, and Section 232 refers to National Security Clause.

[c]Exports under restriction = (1) + (2) + (3) + (4) + (5), including exports under investigation.

product categories of Korean exports in textile and clothing products going to the U.S. market under restrictions increased from twenty-seven during the MFA II period (1978–81) to seventy-five during the MFA IV period (1987–91), out of a maximum of 111 categories. When the MFA restriction ratio was measured by the share of MFA-restricted exports to total exports of textile and clothing products going to the U.S. market, it showed an increase from 73 to 97.3 percent between the two periods. It is, therefore, evident that most of the Korean exports of textile and clothing products going to the U.S. market are now subject to MFA quotas. Amazingly enough, however, Korea was able to increase its exports of textile and clothing products to the United States from $1.1 to nearly $4 billion for the period 1981–88, largely through product diversification and quality upgrading, whereas total Korean exports of textiles and clothing to all markets increased from $5.5 to $14.1 billion for the same period.

VERs on iron and steel products have a long history as well. The first one came into effect in 1968 when the United States negotiated VERs with Japanese and European exporters of steel to the United States. These were phased out with the worldwide steel boom in 1973. But, as steel market conditions continued to deteriorate in the late 1970s, the U.S. government introduced the trigger-price system (TPS) in 1978. Under the TPS, any imports priced below the trigger price were to be automatically retaliated against by AD duties, where the trigger prices were determined by Japanese unit costs of production plus freight from Japan to the United States.

As import penetration continued in the early 1980s, despite the TPS, U.S. steel producers began to file AD or CVD suits, and the U.S. government had to suspend the TPS in 1982. These unfair-trade-law suits, however, were not enough to control imports. The import penetration ratio reached over 20 percent of apparent domestic consumption in 1983 and over 25 percent in 1984. In early 1984, Bethlehem Steel and the United Steel Workers filed a petition under Section 201 to limit the share of imports to less than 15 percent of the U.S. market, and the ITC recommended quotas to keep the import share less than 18.5 percent of the domestic market. The U.S. government, however, opted for the VER approach in place of imposing worldwide quotas under section 201 to limit steel imports. The stated purpose of the VER was to control "unfairly traded" steel. But bilateral negotiations on VERs were concluded with major steel suppliers, including countries that trade fairly. For this VER program, Congress passed the Steel Import Stabilization Act, which enabled the president to enforce the steel VER for a five-year period ending on 30 September 1989. Under this VER program, Korea reached an agreement with the United States to limit its steel exports to less than 1.9 percent of U.S. domestic consumption on average. Recently, the steel VER was extended for another two and a half years.

Since the steel VER came into effect in late 1984, Korean exports of steel products have showed a declining trend in value despite the price-raising effect of VERs, indicating that Korean steel exports declined more rapidly in volume in recent years (see table 7.5: further discussion follows in sec. 7.4 below).

Excluding VERs, table 7.6 presents data on the frequency of various types of administered protection initiated by the United States against Korean exports or industries for the period 1980–89. According to the table, the number of initiations began to surge especially after 1982, when Korea began to record a trade surplus vis-à-vis the United States while the overall trade deficit of the United States began to grow at an unprecedented rate. The frequency reached a peak of eleven initiations in 1985 and since then has declined to six initiations in 1988.

Of the various types of administered protection, ADs have been most frequently employed, with a total of twenty-five cases for the period 1980–89. CVD cases and safeguard actions have been relatively infrequent, with a total of eight and eleven cases, respectively, for the same period. It is interesting to observe that initiations under Section 337 of the Tariff Act of 1930 have risen significantly, especially in the later half of the 1980s, with a total of sixteen cases for the period 1980–89. During the same period, three cases were initiated under Section 232 of the Trade Expansion Act of 1962. This contrasts with the number of administered protection cases that were registered during the 1970s. There were only six AD charges, four Section 337 cases, and no Section 232 cases during the 1970s. Administered protection, however, more

Table 7.6 Frequency of U.S.-Administered Protection Initiated against Korean Exports, 1980–89

	ADs		CVDs		Safeguard		Section 337		Section 232		Total	
Year	Ini.	Aff.	Ini.	Aff.	Ini.	Aff.	Ini.	Aff.	Ini.	Aff.	Ini.	Aff.
1970s	6	2	9	4	10	6	4	2			29	14
1980					1	1					1	1
1981	1	1			1	1					2	2
1982	2	. . .	1	1							3	1
1983	5	3			1	. . .	3	2	1	. . .	10	5
1984	3	. . .	2	1	3	. . .					8	1
1985	5	3	3	1	3	. . .					11	4
1986	4	3	1	1			4	3			9	7
1987					1	. . .	5	3	1	. . .	7	3
1988	2	1	1	. . .	1	. . .	1	. . .	1	. . .	6	1
1989	3	2					3	2			6	4
Total, 1980–89	25	13	8	4	11	2	16	10	3	. . .	63	29

Source: See table 7.4.

Note: Ini. = number of cases initiated. Aff. = affirmative determination, including alternative arrangements. Figures represent numbers of cases.

often took the form of CVD or safeguard actions during the 1970s, with nine and ten initiations, respectively.

The probability that such charges could obtain import relief appears to have been small, however. On average, roughly 46 percent of those charges made during the period 1980–89 ended up with some form of import relief, but the probability varies highly depending on the type of charge made. For example, nearly 70 percent of the Section 337 cases were able to obtain import relief either by an exclusion order or by a negotiated settlement through arrangements. But no case under the National Security Clause of Section 232 was successful in obtaining import relief. Petitions under Section 201 also had difficulty in obtaining import relief. However, more than half the AD or CVD cases obtained import relief with affirmative final determination.

LTFV charges, especially ADs, therefore, appear to have been the most important instrument of administered protection applied to Korean exports during the 1980s, and charges under Section 337 for the infringement of intellectual property rights showed a rapid rise during the later half of the 1980s. It is likely that charges under Section 337 will increasingly become a source of harassment in the future since U.S. producers no longer need to prove injury before the ITC to win the case. Some aspects of administered protection regarding the LTFV cases will be examined in more detail below in light of the Korean experience.

7.3.2 LTFV Cases

According to current LTFV case laws in the United States, the ITC is given the authority to determine the existence of injury on a case-by-case basis, and the DOC is in charge of determining the existence and the magnitude of dumping (or subsidization) brought by exporting firms (or governments). When the U.S. government receives a LTFV petition, the ITC is required to complete its preliminary investigation on injury within forty-five days, and the DOC is required to complete its preliminary determination on dumping (or subsidization) within 160 days (with a possible extension of fifty days).

If the preliminary determination of injury is negative, the case ends there. But if it is positive, the investigation continues to final determination, irrespective of the outcome of the DOC's preliminary determination on dumping (or subsidization). If the DOC's preliminary determination on dumping (or subsidization) is positive, however, "suspension of liquidation" of imports becomes necessary, and the concerned importers must post a bond with the government to pay ADs (or CVDs) if the final determination is also positive. Both the ITC and the DOC are required to complete final determination on injury and dumping (or subsidization), respectively, within seventy-five days of DOC's preliminary determination on dumping (or subsidization).

Table 7.7 provides information on the actual disposition of AD or CVD investigations conducted by the United States against Korean exports during the 1980s. Several features are worth noting. First, out of a total of thirty AD

Table 7.7 Disposition of AD and CVD Investigations by the United States against Korean Exports, 1980–88

	No. of Investigations	Average AD Margins	Average Subsidy Margins
Preliminary disposition	30 (100)		
A. Affirmative dumping (or subsidy) determination	16 (53)	14.64 (2.27–64.37)	5.45 (1.75–12.5)
B. Alternative arrangements negotiated	0 (0)		
C. Restrictive, total (A + B)	16 (53)		
D. Negative injury determination[a]	3 (10)		
E. Negative dumping (or subsidy) margin determination,[b] including *de minimus*	6 (20)		
F. Case withdrawn or terminated	3 (10)		
G. Not restrictive, total (D + E + F)	12 (40)		
H. Pending or under investigation	2 (7)		
Final disposition	30 (100)		
A. ADs or CVDs imposed	8 (27)	18.10 (1.91–64.81)	2.60 (.78–4.42)
B. Alternative arrangements negotiated	5[c] (16)	3.34 (1.26–5.00)	1.71 (1.62–1.8)
C. Restrictive, total (A + B)	13 (43)		
D. Negative injury determination	1 (3)		.53
E. Negative dumping (or subsidy) margin determination,[d] including *de minimus*	4 (13)		
F. Case withdrawn or terminated	8[e] (27)		
G. Not restrictive, total (D + E + F)	13 (43)		
H. Pending or under investigation	4 (13)		

Source: See table 7.4.

Note: The percentage of dispositions is shown in parentheses.

[a]Investigation ends. There is no preliminary subsidy (or dumping-margin) determination in such cases.

[b]Investigation continues without suspension of liquidation.

[c]Includes five agreements reached after an affirmative final decision.

[d]If the final subsidy (or dumping margin) is negative, there is no final injury determination.

[e]Includes one case withdrawn after an affirmative subsidy determination.

or CVD cases initiated during the period 1980–88, sixteen cases (53 percent) received a positive determination on dumping (or subsidization) in their preliminary investigations. But, in their final determination, only eight cases ended up with the imposition of ADs or CVDs, whereas alternative arrangements were reached in five cases to limit exports or raise export prices. It appears, therefore, that preliminary determinations have been slightly biased toward affirmative outcomes, as compared with final determinations. Second, more important is that in only three cases was the preliminary injury finding negative; investigations went on to final determination in 90 percent of the cases, even though only 53 percent of the cases were successful in obtaining a positive determination in the DOC's preliminary investigation. This must have increased both the burden of concerned exporters' legal expenses and the uncertainty faced by both exporters and importers. In the process, many financially squeezed exporters would have been pressured into negotiated settlements through "arrangements."

Finally, calculations show that average dumping margins for AD cases were much greater than average subsidy rates for CVD cases, roughly 10 percent versus 2 percent, indicating that ADs have been a more powerful instrument than CVDs to control Korean exports. Also, in some cases, wide variation in dumping margins was observed between preliminary and final determinations, notably in the notorious color television (1983 to the present) and album (1985 to the present) cases. For example, according to U.S. *Federal Register* reports for the color television case, in 1983 the dumping margin was calculated at 2.9 percent in the preliminary determination but 15.8 percent in the final determination. In an expedited review for the same case in 1984, however, the dumping margin was calculated at 32.4 percent in the preliminary determination but at only 11.5 percent in the final determination. In the album case, in 1985 the dumping margin was calculated at 4.0 percent in the preliminary determination but jumped to 64.8 percent in the final determination. The final dumping margin was based on the so-called constructed value. The same 64.8 percent dumping margin continued to survive even in the administrative review conducted in 1989 because the DOC still relied on the "best" information available to calculate the "constructed value." In fact, Korean album exporters have long since given up their struggle to export to the U.S. market in the face of harassment by AD charges.[16]

7.3.3 Industry Incidence of U.S.-Administered Protection

Table 7.8 presents frequency data on the industry incidence of administered protection initiated against Korean exports during the period 1980–89. According to the table, the metal products industry has been most frequently affected by administered protection, with a total of sixteen initiations during

16. Korean exports of album products to the U.S. market amounted to over U.S. $36 million in 1984. Since 1986, however, that figure has never reached more than U.S. $0.33 million per year.

Table 7.8 Industry Incidence of U.S.-Administered Protection on Korean Exports, 1980–89

Industry	ADs	CVDs	Safeguard	Unfair Trade Practice (Sec. 337)	National Security Clause (Sec. 232)	Total
Agricultural and marine products			2 (1)			2 (1)
Textiles	2 (1)			1 (1)		3 (2)
Footwear		2	1 (1)			3 (1)
Iron and steel	6 (5)	2 (2)	2 (1)			10 (8)
Metal products	4 (2)	5 (2)	3	3 (1)	1	16 (5)
Machinery					2	2
Electrical and electronic products	5 (3)		1	5 (4)		11 (7)
Transport equipment	1		1			2
Chemicals	4 (1)	1		2 (1)		7 (2)
Miscellaneous	3 (1)			4 (2)		7 (3)
Total	25 (13)	8 (4)	11 (2)	16 (10)	3	63 (29)

Source: The same as in table 7.4.

Note: Figures represent number of cases. Number of affirmative determinations including alternative arrangements is shown in parentheses.

the period 1980–89, but the chance to obtain import relief was only 30 percent. The iron and steel industry has also frequently suffered from administered protection with a total of ten initiations for the same period. The success rate for obtaining import relief, however, was very high for the iron and steel industry, with an 80 percent chance. The major instruments of administered protection applied to these two industries include AD and CVD charges, with nine and eight cases, respectively, during the period 1980–89.

Various forms of administered protection that were initiated against the iron and steel industry in the early 1980s were eliminated in return for the steel VER that was agreed on in 1984. The 1984 steel VER agreement also stipulated that, if any Korean steel exports were to encounter new investigations under Section 201, Section 232, Section 301, or AD or CVD laws, Korea was entitled to terminate the VER agreement with respect to some or all of the products covered by the steel VER. This illustrates vividly how alternative forms of administered protection can be exchanged to ensure a desired level of protection of the U.S. steel industry.

Exports of electrical and electronic products, which has emerged as Korea's number one export category in recent years, were also frequently met by AD charges or patent infringement charges, with four cases each for the period 1980–89.

Unlike AD or CVD actions, safeguard actions were dispersed more widely across industries, but the probability of their obtaining import relief was very slim: less than 20 percent. Out of a total of eleven initiations made during the period 1980–89, only two cases—stainless steel products and canned mushrooms—were able to obtain import relief. Neither import relief action lasted more than three years, however.

Under the National Security Clause of Section 232, there were three investigations during the period 1980–89, concerning machine tools, bearings, and certain plastic molding machines, but none led to any positive action for import relief.

In recent years, more technologically sophisticated Korean export products have been increasingly charged by U.S. industries with patent infringement under Section 337 of the Trade Act of 1930. These include, for example, such products as computer memory chips, car phones, metallic balloons, microwave-oven timers, and plastic bags. Since the punishment for patent infringement can be as severe as banning entry of the concerned articles into the United States, most cases tend to be settled through negotiated arrangements. For instance, of a total of sixteen cases initiated under Section 337 during the period 1980–88, ten were resolved through negotiated arrangements such as royalty payments or price or export quantity undertakings, three were dismissed or negatively determined, and two were put under an exclusion order by the ITC. Of the remaining two cases, one was unilaterally withdrawn by the petitioner, and the other remains under investigation.

7.4 Effects of U.S.-Administered Protection on Korean Exports

As seen in table 7.5 above, of the various forms of administered protection that have been applied against Korean exports by the United States, VERs have been the most important instrument so far as their coverage of Korean exports is concerned. Combined exports under the MFA quotas and the steel VER quotas, for example, constituted more than 70 percent of Korean exports that were going to the U.S. market under various forms of administered protection during the period 1984–88.

The economic effect of such VERs on Korean exporters or the Korean economy, however, has been analyzed infrequently. For one thing, VERs are a relatively less painful instrument of administered protection from the exporter's point of view. For another, any sensible analysis of VERs on an exporting country needs to be based on a global, instead of a bilateral, trade model since the United States makes bilateral VER agreements with many different major exporters at the same time. Any numerical exercise with such a global model, however, requires many ad hoc assumptions on various elasticities and may therefore be subject to a relatively large margin of error.

Nonetheless, the recent study by Tarr (1987) may be suggestive of the possible effects of such VERs on an exporting economy. Using a global trade model, Tarr estimated the welfare effects on Korea of the recent steel VERs imposed by the United States and the EC. According to Tarr's estimates, Korea is better off under the steel VERs than it would have been in the absence of them, with a net welfare gain of $32.4 million as a result of the steel VERs. The steel VERs were estimated to increase Korea's export price of steel products by $23.3 per ton on average and to reduce Korea's export volume of steel products going to U.S. and EC markets by 312,000 metric tons. This would result in a quota-rent transfer of $41.9 million to Korean exporters at the expense of U.S. and EC consumers. This would also incur a loss of $9.8 million for Korean exporters in inframarginal rents on their sales to the rest of the world.

Tarr's estimates of the welfare effects of the steel VERs on Korea, however, require cautious interpretation. First, the estimated welfare gain for Korea is based on an extremely short-run and static model. The analysis, therefore, fails to consider any dynamic consequences of the steel VER such as the welfare loss due to its investment-deterring effect on the steel industry in a dynamic economy like Korea's with the lowest steel-making costs in the world.[17] Partly because of delayed domestic investments in the steel industry, which was characterized by scale economies, Korea has not even been able to fill its VER quotas granted by the United States in recent years.[18] As can be seen in table 7.9, the share of Korean steel exports in U.S. steel consumption peaked in 1984 with a 2.3 percent share but declined to a 1.4 percent share in 1987, well below the 1.9 percent limit set by the Korea-U.S. steel VER agreement of 1984. Second, while the quota rents due to the steel VER are transferred to Korean exporters, some of them are bound to be dissipated by various forms of rent-seeking activities. Further, the quota rents help inefficient firms survive owing to reduced competitive pressures, while potentially more efficient firms are prevented from entering the industry.[19]

17. For a detailed analysis of the international competitiveness of the Korean steel industry, see Nam (1986).

18. Another important reason why Korea has been unable to fill its export quotas in recent years can be found in the dramatic recovery of the U.S. steel industry in terms of its international competitiveness, making home or other export markets more profitable for Korean steel makers. According to a recent report from the International Business and Economic Research Corporation (1989), e.g., the U.S. steel industry has significantly reduced its production costs by eliminating obsolete capacity and modernizing its facility. Between 1983 and 1988, according to the report, the U.S. steel industry closed down 39 million tons of obsolete capacity (about 25 percent of its total capacity), resulting in an increase in its capacity utilization rate from 56.2 to 88.7 percent and in cost reductions of at least 35 percent per ton of steel production. As a result, the U.S. steel industry was able to turn its losses of $2.2 billion in 1983 into profits of $1 billion by 1987.

19. In allocating VER quotas among exporters, the Korean Ministry of Trade and Industry sets up the basic rules and guidelines, and the Korea Iron and Steel Association oversees their actual implementation. According to the rules, VER quotas are divided into basic and open quotas, of which basic quotas are to be allocated to individual firms on the basis of their previous year's export performance in the U.S. market of VER-quota items, whereas open quotas are determined on the basis of their export performance in the U.S. market of nonquota items and in non-U.S.

Table 7.9 Korean Exports of Steel Products under the Steel VER (%)

	$t-3$	$t-2$	$t-1$	t	$t+1$	$t+2$	$t+3$
Exports to the U.S.							
Volume	63.7	45.2	91.0	100.0	76.6	61.3	62.7
Unit price	111.2	108.0	88.4	100.0	121.4	125.2	123.2
Share in U.S. consumption	1.2	1.4	2.1	2.3	2.0	1.7	1.4
Exports to third countries:							
Volume	198.2	128.3	99.5	100.0	102.8	105.3	109.6
Unit price	44.8	84.2	93.6	100.0	96.9	93.5	102.1
Exports to all countries:							
Volume	153.8	100.8	96.7	100.0	93.7	90.8	94.1
Unit price	53.6	86.5	91.7	100.0	103.1	100.0	105.9

Source: Adapted partly from Barks (1989, table 21, p. 54) and American Iron and Steel Institute, *Annual Statistical Report* (various years).

Note: t = 1984, when the Korea-U.S. steel VER went into effect.

Table 7.9 provides data on Korean steel exports going to the U.S. market as well as to third-country markets before and after the Korea-U.S. steel VER agreement of 1984. Korean exports of steel products going to the U.S. market declined sharply—by nearly 40 percent in volume—within the next two years after the 1984 steel VER agreement was reached. The unit export price rose by 25 percent over the same period. But it is not clear how much of this price rise may be attributed to the U.S. steel VER since the prices of Korean steel exports may be affected by such other factors as changes in the product composition of Korean exports and other cyclical factors as well. But the unit price of Korean steel exports to third-country markets did show a decline of 6.5 percent for the same period, due, perhaps, to the intensified competition in these markets.[20] Overall, Korean steel export volume declined 6 percent for the ensuing three years after the 1984 steel VER went into effect, but Korean exports to third-country markets increased 10 percent, suggesting that there was a substantial shift from U.S. to third-country markets for the disposition of Korean steel exports.

The MFA restrictions on the trade of textiles and clothing have long been in force, but relatively little is known about their economic consequences on exporters. One may be tempted, however, to conjecture that effects would

areas of all steel products. Until 1989, about 90 percent of total VER quotas took the form of basic quotas, while the remaining 10 percent were open quotas. However, as Korea's quota-filling rate dropped to as low as 60 percent of the VER quotas granted by the United States in 1989, the Ministry of Trade and Industry readjusted the distribution of basic and open quotas by reducing basic quotas to 70 percent and raising open quotas to 30 percent of total VER quotas in 1990. In principle, quota trading among exporters is not allowed in Korea.

20. It is puzzling that Korean steel exports to third countries were halved in volume while their export price doubled in the three years prior to 1984, as seen in table 9.10 below. They may reflect the severity of the worldwide recession in the steel market in the early 1980s with actual existence of dumping in third-country markets, while the U.S. market was sheltered under the TPS.

occur in the MFA case similar to those already seen in the steel VER case. In fact, according to Tarr and Morkre's (1984) estimates, tariff equivalents of MFA quotas on U.S. imports of apparel from Hong Kong turned out to be 20.2 percent on average in 1980. Recently, Kim et al. (1986) recalculated the average quota rent of apparel using the composition of Korean exports to the United States: it turned out to be 17 percent. According to Kim's experiments with a simple model, in 1983 Korean exports of textiles and clothing to the U.S. market would have increased by 16.7 percent in value if the MFA quotas of the United States were lifted, despite the resulting export price reduction of 17 percent for MFA-regulated products. The net welfare effect on Korea of the MFA quotas of the United States is unknown, however.

Unlike the VER cases, other measures of U.S.-administered protection, directed at Korean exporters only, are not likely to affect the U.S. domestic prices of the concerned products in any significant way.[21] This is mainly because Korean exports constitute only a portion of U.S. consumption of the concerned products, and they are likely to be highly standardized, with an ample substitution possibility from other supply sources. Therefore, any price-raising effect of U.S.-administered protection could be a fatal blow to the Korean exporters of the concerned products, and any reduction of Korean exports could be readily replaced by increased domestic production or imports from other competitors, leaving the domestic prices and quantity consumed in the United States relatively intact. In such cases, the welfare loss borne by Korean exporters due to U.S.-administered protection will be directly proportional to the extent of their export loss in the U.S. market. Korean exporters facing this type of U.S.-administered protection, therefore, will make an extra effort to divert their exports to third-country markets, in order to maintain a certain operational rate and salvage some of their losses in the U.S. market.

The changes in export value of goods subject to various forms of U.S.-administered protection, except for VERs, are summarized at an aggregate level in table 7.10.[22] A few notable features appear. First, for all cases with all outcomes, export value to the U.S. market declined by 10 percentage points on average between the year before and the year after the initiation of the investigation. There is also, clearly, export diversification from the U.S. market to third-country markets after the initiation of the investigation. Within a three-year period after the initiation of the investigation, export value to third-country markets increased by 50 percentage points, whereas it showed only a 5 percentage point increase during the three-year period prior to the initiation

21. According to an estimate by Messerlin (1988, 36), when facing AD measures by the EC, exports from NIEs do not enjoy any price increases, whereas exports from industrialized countries enjoy a 12 percent price increase.

22. Table 7.10 and tables 7.11 and 7.12 below are based on export value data classified by Korean CCCN or HS codes, which were converted from the U.S. import trade codes by the Korea Foreign Trade Association. Hence, errors might have been committed in calculating export values to the extent that Korean CCCN or HS codes do not match the U.S. International Trade Classification codes.

Table 7.10 **Effects of U.S.-Administered Protection on Korean Exports, 1980–88 (%)**

	$t-3$	$t-2$	$t-1$	t	$t+1$	$t+2$	$t+3$
All cases with all outcomes (50 cases):							
Exports to the U.S.	56.9	75.5	103.1	100.0 (5,806)	93.4	115.7	125.9
Exports to third countries	95.2	99.7	97.2	100.0 (6,084)	123.6	141.6	150.2
Exports to all countries	78.4	87.6	104.5	100.0 (11,889)	113.1	128.0	131.3
Cases with affirmative determination:							
Cases with positive government action (10 cases):							
Exports to the U.S.	41.8	76.3	80.5	100.0 (475)	54.2	46.7	92.9
Exports to third countries	86.2	108.4	112.0	100.0 (377)	156.2	192.1	187.1
Exports to all countries	60.4	88.4	99.5	100.0 (851)	123.4	158.2	110.8

Cases with alternative arrangement (11 cases):							
Exports to the U.S.	90.3	91.9	90.9	100.0 (2,759)	120.2	129.8	116.7
Exports to third countries	83.1	98.2	91.3	100.0 (2,976)	128.8	94.7	126.2
Exports to all countries	76.1	88.6	85.8	100.0 (5,735)	121.0	106.6	119.4
Cases with negative determination (25 cases):							
Exports to the U.S.	52.2	74.9	109.8	100.0 (2,458)	100.7	139.1	142.4
Exports to third countries	108.9	100.7	101.6	100.0 (2,339)	107.5	138.8	151.1
Exports to all countries	90.5	91.4	118.0	100.0 (4,797)	105.8	124.4	141.8

Source: Author's calculation based on the trade data provided by the Korea Foreign Trade Association.

Note: Administered protection includes here AD and CVD, Section 201, Section 337, and Section 232 cases. t = the year when the cases were initiated. The numbers given in parentheses represent actual export values in million U.S. dollars.

of the investigation. Second, a breakdown of all cases based on the final outcome of the investigation shows a more pronounced difference in their export responses. For the cases facing some form of positive action on the part of the U.S. government to restrict imports, for example, exports to the United States declined sharply, by some 50 percentage points in value, within the two years after the initiation of the investigation, while exports diverted to third-country markets from the U.S. market showed quite substantial growth. However, the cases facing affirmative determination but settled by alternative arrangements seem to have been relatively mildly affected in their exports to the United States. Finally, the mere threat of initiating an investigation may also have some effect on exports: export value declined by 10 percentage points in the cases with a negative final determination between the prior and the subsequent year of the initiation of the investigation. In this case, export value did not grow any in the first year after the initiation of the investigation, at a time when definitive measures were still not decided on.

The various types of administered protection have very different effects on Korean exports, as shown in table 7.11. When the cases with a final affirmative determination, including arrangement cases, are considered, AD or safeguard actions appear to have had the most significant effect on export value. Within one year after the initiation of the investigation, exports to the U.S. market declined in value by 40 percent on average in AD cases and by more than 50 percent in a safeguard case. However, exports to the U.S. market appear to have been least affected in the CVD cases and only mildly so in the unfair-trade-practice cases (Section 337 cases). This was, perhaps, because the two CVD cases considered in table 7.11 included steel products, for which a very low CVD rate—less than 2 percent on average—was initially applied, and these actions were subsequently dropped in return for the 1984 steel VER agreement. On the other hand, most of the Section 337 cases—six of eight cases facing affirmative determination—were resolved by alternative arrangements such as royalty payments and other compensation methods, rather than by accepting an exclusion order from the ITC. Such arrangements may not necessarily lead to a decrease in exports.

The breakdown by industry of the export decline, in response to U.S.-administered protection, is shown in table 7.12. As can be seen, the iron and steel industries showed no systematic response in their exports, except for the first year after the initiation of the investigation. This was, perhaps, due to the fact that most of the charges made against the iron and steel industries were concentrated in the early 1980s, just before the 1984 steel VER agreement was reached. The metal products industry also showed an expected pattern of export decline in the first year after the initiation of the investigation. The most significant effect on exports with an expected pattern can be found in the electrical and electronics industry, which has emerged as the number one export industry of Korea in recent years. The export value of this industry declined by over 35 percent within the two-year period after the

Table 7.11 **Effects of U.S.-Administered Protection on Korean Exports, by Type of Measures: Cases with Affirmative Determination (%)**

	$t - 3$	$t - 2$	$t - 1$	t	$t + 1$	$t + 2$	$t + 3$
ADs (10 cases):[a]							
Exports to the U.S.	73.6	95.8	82.3	100.0	59.7	61.1	93.7
				(822)			
Exports to third countries	77.6	97.5	120.9	100.0	151.0	180.7	207.1
				(588)			
Exports to all countries	65.9	92.9	102.1	100.0	123.0	156.3	130.5
				(1,409)			
CVDs (2 cases):							
Exports to the U.S.	60.3	71.5	117.1	100.0	168.0	216.5	162.4
				(453)			
Exports to third countries	90.4	119.0	84.5	100.0	66.3	69.0	64.3
				(808)			
Exports to all countries	66.2	84.4	89.8	100.0	95.5	111.3	92.5
				(1,260)			
Safeguard (1 case):							
Exports to the U.S.	87.1	121.4	142.4	100.0	48.7	34.3	46.0
				(18)			

(continued)

Table 7.11 (continued)

	$t-3$	$t-2$	$t-1$	t	$t+1$	$t+2$	$t+3$
Exports to third countries	376.1	345.2	211.9	100.0 (10)	123.1	91.0	24.0
Exports to all countries	188.8	200.2	166.9	100.0 (28)	74.9	54.3	38.2
Unfair trade practice (8 cases):[b]							
Exports to the U.S.	58.5	69.1	75.6	100.0 (1,941)	127.1	125.2	139.5
Exports to third countries	55.3	75.8	66.8	100.0 (1,947)	147.2	100.8	137.7
Exports to all countries	57.5	70.2	71.4	100.0 (3,889)	135.6	111.2	138.6

Source: See table 7.10.

Note: Affirmative determination includes alternative arrangements. The numbers given in parentheses represent actual export values in million U.S. dollars.

[a]Two cases that were subject to ADs and CVDs at the same time were included in AD cases.

[b]Unfair trade practice refers to Section 337 cases.

Table 7.12 **Effects of U.S.-Administered Protection on Korean Exports to the United States, by Industry and Final Outcome**

	$t-3$	$t-2$	$t-1$	t	$t+1$	$t+2$	$t+3$
Iron and steel [9]:							
Affirmative [7][a]	98.5	119.5	104.7	100.0	91.3	115.8	111.1
				(833)			
Negative [2]	67.3	75.3	105.4	100.0	109.2	89.4	82.0
				(117)			
Metal products [9]:							
Affirmative [3][a]	51.6	65.7	52.9	100.0	78.0	112.7	139.1
				(127)			
Negative [6]	49.1	47.3	50.7	100.0	97.6	92.2	63.0
				(549)			
Electrical and electronics [8]:							
Affirmative [5][a]	37.6	51.8	65.5	100.0	78.2	64.4	92.8
				(2,011)			
Negative [3]	74.4	144.7	263.4	100.0	124.6	228.8	
				(373)			
Others [20]:							
Affirmative [6][a]	63.2	80.3	97.5	100.0	86.6	57.7	92.9
				(264)			
Negative [14]	46.6	71.7	102.8	100.0	95.7	145.8	185.0
				(1,420)			

Source: See table 7.10.

Note: Administered protection includes here AD and CVD, Section 201, Section 337, and Section 232 cases. The number of cases involved is shown in square brackets. The numbers given in parentheses represent actual export value in million U.S. dollars.

[a]Affirmative determination includes alternative arrangements.

initiation of the investigation, for the cases faced with an affirmative determination. A similar pattern of export responses is observed for the remaining industries.

7.5 Concluding Remarks

This paper provides evidence that recent U.S. trade policy shows a strong drift toward protectionist bilateralism, endangering the international trading system based on the GATT rules. Evidence follows both from the review of protectionist elements embedded in current U.S. trade laws and from the examination of the pattern of U.S.-administered protection as applied to Korean exports during the 1980s.

However, the Korean experience indicates that greater and safer access to the U.S. market has been critical to Korea's economic success, and it will be no less so in the future, too. The key concern of Korea regarding U.S. trade policy is, therefore, how to help the United States stop or turn back its drift toward protectionist bilateralism. It appears that Korea may serve that purpose most effectively through the new round of multilateral trade negotiations that is currently under way, possibly in collaboration with other developing countries. Several ways to do so may be suggested.

First, Korea (or developing countries in general) should be ready to negotiate away its privilege of so-called special and differential treatment in the GATT—which has been largely ineffective or even served adversely in many developing countries by encouraging them to adopt an inward-oriented development path—in return for the dismantling of NTBs and protection-oriented legislation in the United States (or AICs). In other words, Korea (or developing countries) would be better off accepting the principle of full reciprocity in return for free and secured access to the U.S. market (or AICs' markets). The timetable for this to occur should be one of the main subjects of negotiation at the multilateral trade negotiations.

At the same time, Korea (or developing countries) should demand the rewriting of the current GATT rules on the AD or CVD process, and, accordingly, of national laws, in order to better reflect the merits of modern economics. The rules should be amended, for example, to accommodate economically meaningful tax-cum-subsidy measures to compensate for externalities or other market imperfections. Also, the possibility of the abuse of such statutes needs to be minimized, by making the rules more strict and possibly by having petitioners bear at least part of the legal costs for invalid charges.

Korea should also actively seek a multilateral agreement on the rules governing protection of intellectual property rights so that those rights are adequately protected but at the same time the free flow of technical know-how is not disturbed. In recent years, the fear of abuse of Section 337 in the United States has been of growing concern to Korean exporters. Korea (or developing countries) should demand that an injury test be required before the ITC makes a decision about the infringement of intellectual property rights.

Finally, it would be in Korea's (or developing countries') interests for the escape clause of the GATT (Article XIX) to be amended by relaxing the requirement for compensation so that Section 201 can become a main route for temporary import relief for structural adjustment in the United States (or AICs). Import restrictions would be at least more transparent and nondiscriminatory under Section 201 than they would be under other means of administered protection.

References

Bark, Taeho. 1989. The history, institutional framework and economic consequences of VERs in Korea. Working Paper no. 8917. Seoul: Korea Development Institute, June.

Finger, J. Michael, H. Keith Hall, and Douglas R. Nelson. 1982. The political economy of administered protection. *American Economic Review* 72 (June): 452–66.

Finger, J. Michael, and Julio Nogues. 1987. International control of subsidies and countervailing duties. *World Bank Economic Review* 1 (September): 707–25.

International Business and Economic Research Corporation. 1989. VRAs and steel: Fair trade or protection. Report prepared for the Korea Iron and Steel Association. Washington, D.C.

International Monetary Fund (IMF). 1988. Issues and developments in international trade policy. Occasional Paper no. 63. Washington, D.C.

Kim, Chungsoo. 1989. The Multi-Fibre Arrangement and structural adjustment of the Korean textile industry. Paper presented at the Workshop on International Textile Trade, the Multi-Fibre Arrangement, and the Uruguay Round, Stockholm, 20–21 June.

Kim, Chungsoo, et al. 1986. *Effects of neo-protectionism on the Korean exports.* Seoul: Korea Institute for Economics and Technology, May.

Messerlin, Patrick. 1988. Antidumping laws and developing countries. WPS 16. Washington, D.C.: World Bank, June.

Nam, Chong-Hyun. 1986. Changing comparative advantage and trade and adjustment policies in the steel industry. In *Industrial policies for Pacific economic growth,* ed. Hiromichi Mutoh, Sueo Sekiguchi, Kotaro Suzumura, and Ippei Yamazawa. Sydney: Allen & Unwin.

———. 1987. Export-promoting subsidies, countervailing threats, and the General Agreement on Tariffs and Trade. *World Bank Economic Review* 1 (September): 727–43.

Nogues, J. Julio, Andrzej Olechowski, and L. Alan Winters. 1985. The extent of nontariff barriers to industrial countries' imports. Report no. DRD 115. Washington, D.C.: World Bank, January.

Saxonhouse, Gary R. 1986. The national security clause of the Trade Expansion Act of 1962: Import competition and the machine tool industry. In *Law and trade issues of the Japanese economy,* ed. Gary R. Saxonhouse and Kozo Yamamura. Seattle: University of Washington Press.

Schott, J. Jeffrey. 1989. US trade policy: Implications for US-Korean relations. In *Economic relations between the United States and Korea: Conflict or cooperation?* ed. Thomas O. Baynard and Soo-Gil Young. Washington, D.C.: Institute for International Economics, January.

Stern, Paula, and Andrew Wechsler. 1986. Escape clause relief and recessions: An economic and legal look at Section 201. In *Law and trade issues of the Japanese economy*, ed. Gary R. Saxonhouse and Kozo Yamamura. Seattle: University of Washington Press.

Tarr, G. David. 1987. Effects of restraining steel exports from the Republic of Korea and other countries to the United States and the European Economic Community. *World Bank Economic Review* 1 (May): 397–418.

Tarr, G. David, and Morris E. Morkre. 1984. *Aggregate costs to the United States of tariffs and quotas on imports: General tariff cuts and removal of quotas on automobiles, steel, sugar, and textiles.* Staff Report to the Federal Trade Commission. Washington, D.C.: Bureau of Economics, December.

UNCTAD (United Nations Conference on Trade and Development). 1984. Protection and structural adjustment: Anti-dumping and countervailing practices. TD/B/979. January.

Comment Shujiro Urata

The purpose of Chong-Hyun Nam's paper is twofold—to examine the changing pattern of U.S. import protection policies and to investigate quantitatively the effect of such policies on Korean exports to the United States. The paper finds that U.S. import protection policies, mainly in the form of nontariff barriers (NTBs), were intensified in the early 1980s, when the problem of the U.S. trade deficit became serious. Nam argues that types of NTBs such as antidumping (AD) charges and countervailing duties (CVDs) are adopted in order to obtain voluntary export restraints (VERs), by pressuring exporting countries. VERs, which escape GATT illegality, are one of the most preferred forms of import protection as they provide benefits not only to import-competing producers in importing countries but also to exporters in the form of rents, at the cost of consumers in importing countries.

The paper finds that the NTBs applied by the U.S. government on Korean exports worked effectively to reduce the volume of Korean exports to the United States. Facing restrictions on their exports to the U.S. market, Korean producers adopted mainly two measures: a shift in export destinations away from the U.S. market and an upgrading of exports to high-value-added items.

On the basis of these findings, and recognizing the importance of the U.S. market for Korean exports, Nam presents a number of interesting and important policy recommendations for Korea. These recommendations may be grouped into two types—those that could be pursued unilaterally by Korea and those that seek a change in GATT trading rules and/or in U.S. trade laws.

Among the policy recommendations included in the first group, the most important one is the abolishment of the special and differential treatment extended to Korea and other developing countries in the GATT since such treatment adversely effects the economic development of these countries. As for changing international trading rules, the most important proposal is to revise tax-cum-subsidy measures to compensate for inefficiency caused by external-

Shujiro Urata is associate professor of economics at Waseda University, Tokyo.

ities or other market imperfections, which are not regarded as "legal" in international rules. Justification for such policy, according to Nam, may be found in the teachings of modern economics.

The examination of changes in U.S. import protection policies was well conducted and the description of the findings succinct. Moreover, the method of analysis used to measure the effect of NTBs on exports of the targeted products is interesting, and the results reveal that U.S. import protection measures were effective in limiting Korean exports in some products, as noted above.

The paper addresses some of the most important trade policy issues confronting us at present: proliferation of NTBs and the problem of North-South trade. The findings may be regarded as evidence supporting an argument against import protection in the form of NTBs from the point of view not only of exporting countries but also of importing countries. The main problem of import protection is, as correctly argued by Nam, its retardation effect on industrial transformation, which in turn deters the economic growth of both exporting and importing countries.

Although I agree with most of the arguments presented by Nam for the liberalization of foreign trade, I have different opinions on a few points. The first is Nam's suggestion for the revision of tax-cum-subsidy measures in the GATT and U.S. trade rules. While in theory tax-cum-subsidy measures may be justified to correct for the problems caused by market imperfections, the application of such measures is not without difficulties. Take the case of scale economies, for example, which is usually considered as warranting government intervention. Production subsidy for an industry subject to scale economies such as chemicals is often argued to be justified in order to overcome the infant stage and to achieve a minimum efficient scale of production. However, there are potential problems with the application of such measures. First, it is not so simple to identify the presence of scale economies in production, let alone the level of production corresponding to the minimum efficient scale. Second, such measures may provoke retaliation from trading partners, thereby leading to trade wars. Finally, rents may be created, with the result that removal of the subsidy may become difficult when such action is called for.

I now turn to a point that I think needs some empirical evidence in order to justify the argument. Referring to AD charges caused by lower export prices in relation to domestic prices, Nam asserts that, even in such cases, foreign competitors are not harmed because the export price is normally set at least at or above international levels. This observation must be supported by empirical evidence. In addition, this assertion points to the existence of import barriers in exporting countries because, without such barriers, exporters cannot maintain higher prices in the local market. Accordingly, import liberalization in developing countries may be called for.

Turning to the effect on Korean exports of U.S. import protection policies against Korean exports, Nam identifies a shift in export destinations and a quality upgrading of exports. I would be interested to know the effect of these changes on Korean foreign investment. As is often pointed out, faced with similar restrictions, Japanese producers shifted their location of production from Japan to the United States and to other countries that were free from such restrictions. This type of reaction from Korean producers may not have been so prevalent yet; however, such corporate strategy is likely to be carried out more actively in the future.

Finally, a few observations on the issue of trade liberalization, especially in relation to the Uruguay Round of multilateral trade negotiations are in order. The world is currently witnessing new and contrasting developments in the orientation of international trade policies pursued by developed countries, on the one hand, and by developing countries, on the other. Developed countries, especially those in Western Europe and North America, have been actively adopting protectionist policies since the mid-1970s, which had been preceded by substantial liberalization since the end of World War II. In contrast, the number of developing countries adopting liberalization policies has increased since the mid-1980s. Developing countries opened up their economies not only because of the pressure by developed countries but also because of their recognition that such policies would improve resource allocation, thereby increasing their exports and outputs as well as their consumers' welfare.

Recognizing the fact that developing countries, which were opposed to liberalization, are finally ready to open up their markets, the world must not miss this opportunity to promote expansion of world trade, which would lead to further expansion of the world economy. The results of Nam's analysis indicate clearly the unfavorable effect of protectionism by developed countries on developing countries, and in his paper Nam suggested proposals that could be carried out by developing countries. What is needed now is to convince developed countries of the unfavorable effect of protectionism on their economic performance. For that purpose, a detailed analysis of the effect of protectionism, in particular that in the form of NTBs, on developed countries is required.

Comment Chia Siow Yue

This is an excellent and highly informative paper. My comments are on three aspects of Chong-Hyun Nam's presentation, namely, the characteristics of U.S.-Korea bilateral trade, the rise in bilateral trade friction, and Korean policy responses.

Chia Siow Yue is associate professor in the Department of Economics and Statistics, National University of Singapore.

First, since Korea embarked on export-oriented industrialization in the 1960s, it has been and remains extremely dependent on the U.S. market. Bilateral trade has seen very rapid growth, but Korea remains a relatively small market for U.S. exports. As noted by Nam, this asymmetry in bilateral trade also characterizes U.S. trade relations with the other Asian newly industrialized economies (NIEs). This has led to unequal bargaining strength in trade negotiations, much to the aggravation of Korea (and other Asian NIEs).

Second, the growing trade deficit of the United States with Korea and the latter's growing competitiveness in high-tech sectors has led to a rise in trade friction as the United States seeks to redress Korean "unfair" trade practices, achieve greater access to the Korean market, and protect its intellectual property. The United States is no longer a benevolent hegemonic power and trading partner but is increasingly insisting on a level playing field. Korean exports to the United States are increasingly subject to U.S. NTBs and no longer eligible for GSP (Generalized System of Preferences) benefits, and the United States has demanded that Korea improve its enforcement of intellectual property rights and appreciate its currency. While Nam's paper emphasizes the negative developments in U.S. trade policy, it should also be noted that many restrictive U.S. trade practices were adopted in response to the perception that Korea has been guilty of "unfair" trade practices in the first place. It should also be noted that, in spite of these U.S. measures, Korean exports to the United States have continued to maintain high levels of growth, as Korean exporters diversify and upgrade. And while Korea (and other Asian NIEs) complain about the growth of protectionist measures by the United States, they face even more difficulties in penetrating the markets of Western Europe and Japan. Korea and the other Asian NIEs cannot expect to continue to depend heavily on the U.S. market and record growing surpluses. Bilateral trade will have to be more balanced to avoid further U.S. trade policy offensives.

Third, the final section of Nam's paper focuses on Korea's strategy in GATT to promote multilateralism and to reverse U.S. protectionist bilateralism. I would like to expand on this and discuss in broader terms the Korean policy responses to U.S. pressure for a level playing field as well as to domestic developments. Korea is rapidly undertaking structural adjustments, making trade policy changes, and seeking outward investments. There is less emphasis on government intervention in industrial and export targeting, a reflection of the adverse experience in the 1970s in promoting heavy and chemical industries, and a greater emphasis on promotion of domestic research and development to offset the problem of technology acquisition and on the promotion of small and medium-sized enterprises to promote equity and countervail the power of business conglomerates. In an effort to ensure continuing market access for its exports, Korea has resorted to the use of lobbyists and economic diplomacy. It is not clear, however, whether the use of paid lobbyists in the United States has been effective; critics argue that Korea's lobbying efforts have not been as effective as those of Japan and Taiwan.

In GATT negotiations, Korea appears prepared to give up the privilege of special and differential treatment and accept the principle of full reciprocity. It is also participating actively in Asia-Pacific forums such as the Pacific Economic Cooperation Conference (PECC) and the Asia-Pacific Economic Conference (APEC). Korea has also embarked on import liberalization and the enforcement of intellectual property rights, policy changes facilitated by the improved current account balance and by domestic inflationary pressures. It should be noted, however, that import liberalization by Korea will not necessarily improve U.S. export competitiveness and the bilateral trade balance. To ensure that its market-opening measures will benefit the United States, Korea has thus resorted to buying missions in the United States, and giving preferential market access to U.S. industries. However, there is a Korean perception that its efforts at import liberalization are not appreciated by the United States. Korea is also emphasizing further market and product diversification—market diversification to the EC, Japan, other Asian NIEs, and developing countries and reduced product concentration through technological upgrading and a shift to the production of parts and components. Finally, Korea has embarked on defensive outward investment—in the United States and other industrial countries, to counter the growing trade friction and to gain access to technology—and in Southeast Asia and other developing countries, in order to remain cost competitive in the face of rapidly rising domestic wages and currency appreciation.

8 Access to the Japanese Market by Asian Countries: A Case Study of the Wool Textile Industry

Motoshige Itoh and Kaori Hatanaka

The industrial structure and trade pattern of Japan have been undergoing substantial changes since 1985. The appreciation of the yen since the Plaza agreement is an important factor inducing these structural changes. Not only has the amount of imports increased substantially, but the content of imports has also changed drastically. In spite of the fact that Japan had experienced large changes in its terms of trade several times during the postwar period, the share of manufactured goods imports had remained quite stable (at low levels) until 1985. Japanese imports had been dominated by primary goods.

The share of manufactured goods imports has been increasing rapidly since 1985. This increase is closely associated with the transformation of the distribution and production system in Japan. Products imported from foreign countries do not go directly to consumers or to final users. They go through distribution channels—through traders, wholesalers, and retailers—and a considerable amount of value is added to the products in the process. Therefore, the way in which the distribution system is structured has a significant effect on the way goods are imported. Similarly, imports of intermediate goods are affected by the production structure within Japan and by the interfirm transactions therein. Of course, there is also a reverse relation. The growth of Japan-Asia trade becomes a driving force in altering these domestic structures.

The Structural Impediments Initiatives (SII) talks between Japan and the United States that were held from 1989 to 1990 were important in this respect. These trade negotiations were different in character from earlier talks. The focal points of discussion were business practices and regulation inside Japan. The specific issues examined in the SII negotiations were the various types of

Motoshige Itoh is associate professor of economics at the University of Tokyo. Kaori Hatanaka is a graduate student at the Faculty of Economics, the University of Tokyo.

practices in the Japanese distribution system, regulations such as the Large-Scale Retail-Store Law, land-regulation and tax systems that cause high real estate prices, and so called *keiretsu* transactions such as the cross-holding of stocks and exclusive business relations. Although the SII negotiations were between Japan and the United States, the topics on the SII agenda are important to any examination of trade between Japan and other Asian countries.

The purpose of this paper is to examine the relation between Japan's domestic economic structure and the pattern of its imports. We consider imports of both final consumption goods and intermediate goods since the mechanisms behind the importation of these two types of goods are somewhat different. This issue cannot be easily approached by means of a general theory or an empirical study covering various industries. Rather, we take a very micro approach. We choose a particular industry for a case study. The industry we choose is the textile industry—in particular, the wool textile industry, which has many of the features that we are interested in. Both intermediate goods (such as raw materials, yarn, and fabrics) and final consumption goods are traded across the border in this industry. Thus, the structure of the distribution system in Japan, the interfirm relations in the transactions of intermediate goods, and the way goods are produced affect the pattern of trade in this industry.

Although most of the discussion in this paper is restricted to the wool textile industry, the results obtained from such a case study do provide some insights into more general cases. We mention these general insights at various places.

The paper continues as follows. Section 8.1 provides some basic data on the structural change of the pattern of Japan's imports from other Asian countries. Section 8.2 then explains the basic structure of the wool textile industry and its trade pattern. In this section, we also discuss the factors that make it difficult for Asian goods to obtain ready access to the Japanese market. Section 8.3 then discusses the structural change in the domestic Japanese economy that will affect the market accessibility of the Asian products to the Japanese imports market. Section 8.4 provides brief concluding remarks.

8.1 Some Facts

One of the most important changes in the trade pattern of Japan since 1985 is a drastic increase in the share of manufactured goods to total imports. Table 8.1 shows the shares of manufactured goods imports of some major industrial countries. A large portion of Japan's imports consists of primary goods, and manufactured goods imports are only a small portion. It is commonly believed that that low level of manufactured goods among Japan's imports reflects the so-called processing-trade character of Japan.

Table 8.2 shows the decomposition of the share of manufactured goods imports to each exporting country. We can confirm that the shares of the manufactured goods imports from Asian countries have increased substantially during this period. Although many kinds of goods are involved in this change,

Table 8.1 **The Share of Manufactured Goods Imports to Total Imports of Various Regions (%)**

	Japan	U.S.	EC	Excluding intra-EC Trade
1970	30.3	68.0	61.6	46.8
1971	28.6	70.0	61.4	46.0
1972	29.6	70.8	62.0	46.6
1973	30.6	67.4	60.9	45.6
1974	23.7	57.4	55.5	39.1
1975	20.3	55.8	56.7	41.2
1976	21.5	54.1	57.5	41.6
1977	21.5	60.7	58.5	43.2
1978	22.5	56.8	61.5	48.1
1979	26.0	54.0	60.6	47.3
1980	22.8	56.8	58.2	43.5
1981	24.3	57.4	55.8	41.2
1982	24.9	62.6	57.0	42.5
1983	27.2	66.3	58.8	45.8
1984	29.8	71.0	59.4	47.0
1985	31.0	76.5	61.0	48.6
1986	41.8	80.7	69.4	59.5
1987	44.1	79.6	71.9	63.4
1988	49.0	81.5	. . .	. . .
1989	50.3			
1990	50.3			

Source: White Paper on International Trade and Industry (various years).

Table 8.2 **The Ratio of Imports of Manufactured Goods to Total Imports of Japan by Each Area (%)**

	U.S.	EC	NIEs	ASEAN
1985	55.2	84.2	57.8	9.2
1986	60.7	85.5	62.3	12.6
1987	56.1	85.7	66.2	15.7
1988	56.0	86.3	72.9	20.4
1989	58.3	86.1	75.5	25.8
1990	62.0	88.1	73.4	26.1

Source: Trade statistics from the Ministry of Finance.

we can demonstrate the increase in the importation of manufactured goods by examining the trends of the importation of several goods. In figure 8.1, we show the trends of imports from Asian countries of such goods as textiles and apparel, automobile parts, and electrical equipment. We can see that imports of these goods have increased substantially in the 1980s.

The types of commodities we pick up in figure 8.1 can be classified into

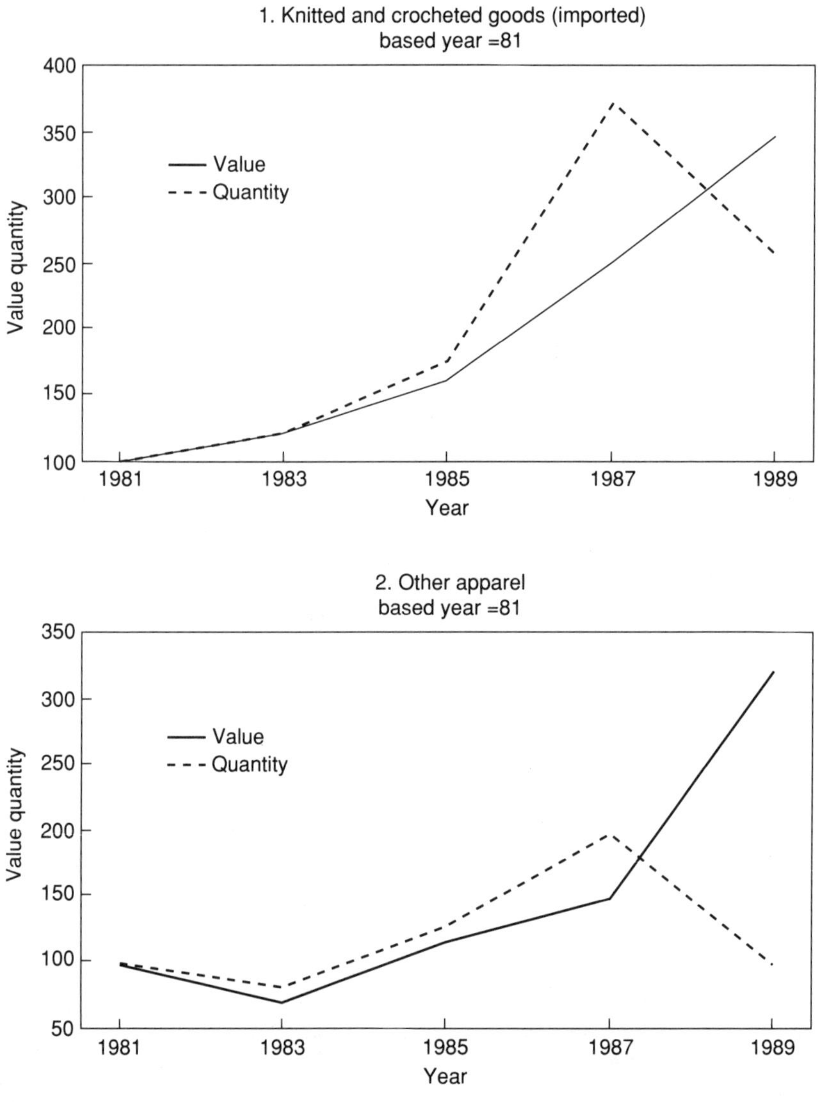

Fig. 8.1 Imports from Asian countries
Note: Electrical equipment (panel 3) includes switches, fuses, lighting arresters, etc.

two categories—final consumption goods and intermediate goods. For both types, the domestic economic structure is important in determining the amount of imports. In the case of final consumption goods, the structure of the distribution system is a crucial factor, and, in the case of intermediate goods, the domestic production system and interfirm transactions are crucial factors.

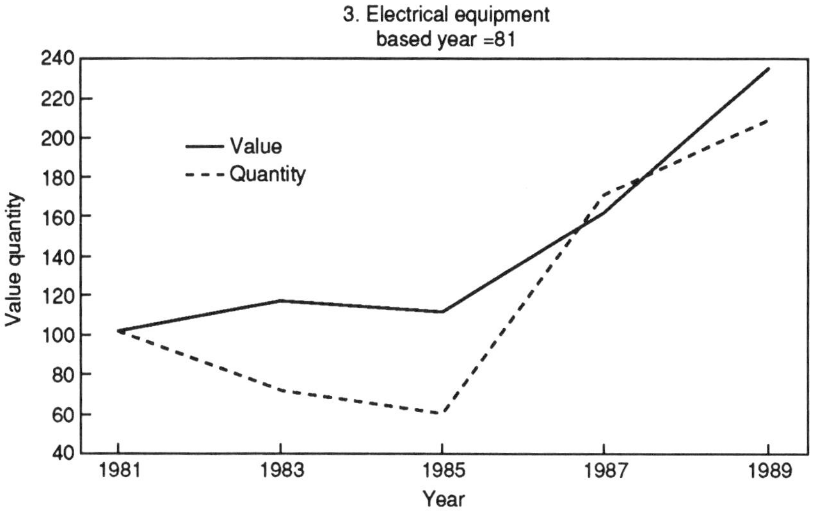

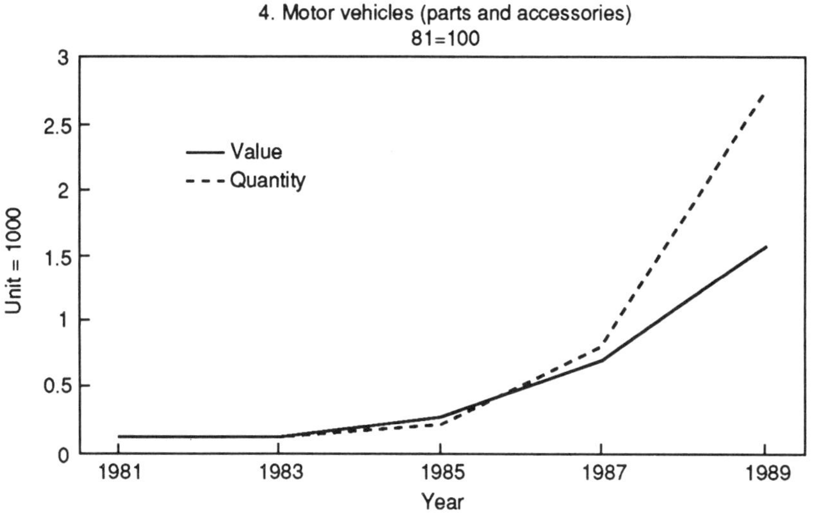

8.2 Production and Trade Structures of the Wool Textile Industry and the Factors That Become Barriers to Imports

In order to make the point clear that production structure and distribution channels are important factors in determining the pattern of Japan's imports, we examine the production and trade patterns of wool textile products. The wool textile industry has many of the features that are important for the issue of market access.

Figure 8.2 is a rough overall picture of this industry. One of the characteristics of this industry is that there are many firms involved in each stage of production. This industry begins with raw wool materials production, which is a typical agricultural sector. After raw materials come yarn production, fabric making, apparel making, and the distribution process. Along this vertical chain, various transactions are conducted, and the way in which these transactions are conducted affects the pattern of international trade.

We can think of various patterns of international trade in this industry. If raw materials are imported directly to Japan and all other processes are conducted within Japan, the trade pattern becomes that of imports of raw wool materials. Japan may import yarn, fabric, or apparel. In these cases, we observe manufactured goods imports. But the trade pattern can often be more complicated. There are cases where yarn and fabrics are produced within Japan but the fabrics are then sent to other Asian countries for cutting and sewing, with the final product being reimported to Japan.

If the transactions of any of these intermediate goods are simple ones, that is, if the quality of the products is homogeneous, if complicated coordination between sellers and buyers is not necessary, and if transport costs are not large, then a simple logic of comparative advantage determines the pattern of trade at each stage. The production of goods at each stage will be conducted at the place where the production cost is the lowest.

However, there are various factors that make it difficult for the above-mentioned simple international division of labor to be realized. Among these factors, the following three are the most important: the first is the quality of the intermediate goods; the second is the delicate coordination between sellers and buyers that is required to achieve high-quality final products; and the third is transport costs including not only shipping costs but also, and more important, the costs resulting from the difficulty of matching demand and supply. Let us discuss these three factors in more detail.

For transactions of yarn and fabric, the quality of the product often becomes a crucial factor. Table 8.3 compares the amounts of imports, exports, and domestic production of wool yarn and fabrics with those of cotton and knitted products. The share of imported wool yarn used for domestic production of wool fabrics and the share of imported wool fabrics used for domestic production of apparel are much lower than the corresponding figures in the cotton and knitted products industry.

We have conducted interviews that have provided us with some explanation of the low share of imported intermediate goods. Figure 8.3 gives some rough numbers for the vertical value-added structure of high-quality men's suits that are based on our field study.[1] Material costs represent a very small portion of the final retail price, as do the cost of yarn, which is less than 3 percent, and

1. Suits priced at 75,000 yen are not inexpensive products in the Japanese market, but they are not the top of the line either. Most imported European brands cost more than 100,000 yen.

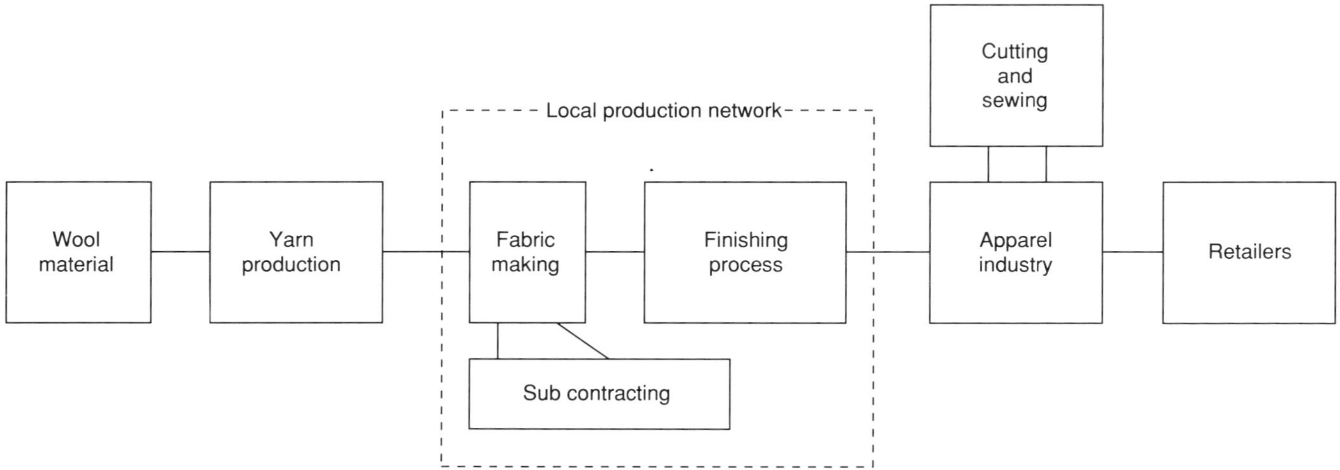

Fig. 8.2 An overall picture of the wool textile industry

Table 8.3 Trade and Domestic Production of Textile Products

	Domestic Production	Import	
		Value (million ¥)	Quantity
Wool for textiles:			
Yarns (t)	82,048	10,448	4,839
Fabric (thousand m^2)	295,975	46,260	23,590
Cotton:			
Yarns	459,160	79,848	208,881
Fabrics	1,914,634	80,716	798,084
Wool for knitting:			
Yarns	36,066	1,858	1,066
Fabrics	55,016	19,344	9,340

Source: Ministry of International Trade and Industry, *Year Book of Textiles Statistics, 1989.*
Note: For yarns, t = tons; for fabric, m^2 = square meters.

¥1,000 Raw material
↓
¥2,000 Yarn
↓
¥5,000 Fabrics
↓
¥25,000 Wholesale price
(cf. production [cutting and sewing] cost)
↓ ¥10,000
¥75,000 Retail price

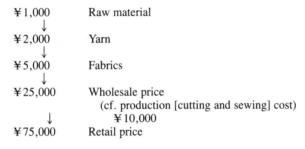

Fig. 8.3 The value-added structure of men's suits

the cost of fabric, which is less than 7 percent. Under this cost structure, a small change in material cost does not mean much for the price of the final product. More important is the quality of the intermediate goods (yarn and fabric). If there is any damage to the material, the final product will lose its whole value; in other words, poor-quality intermediate goods create a bottleneck in the whole production process.

The quality of the intermediate goods (yarn and fabric) is not restricted simply to quality in the usual sense, as discussed above. Design and fashion trends are also crucial. Product differentiation is quite important in the yarn sector. Fashion trends change quite frequently. According to our interview, about 60 percent of the sales of a leading Japanese wool yarn producer come from products not in the standard classification. In other words, they are special products. The company also puts great emphasis on the introduction of new products every year. Fashion trends are an important factor determining the demand pattern for yarn. Therefore, there are various kinds of interactions, such as information exchange and coordinated research on demand trends among yarn producers, fabric producers, and apparel makers, during the process of designing and producing new yarn. There are very few cases in which Japanese firms go abroad for yarn production. A Japanese producer operating in Asian countries such as Malaysia is producing only less expensive basic products.

A similar phenomenon can be observed in the transactions between fabric producers and apparel makers. Design is important to fabric producers. They supply new designs every year, and new design products are the main source of their profits. It is often the case that the best products are sold to apparel companies with whom they have a special relation, without any public exhibition.

The importance of quality and of coordination between buyers and sellers makes the importation of these intermediate goods difficult. In order to maintain good communication and cooperative coordination, the geographic distance and a long-term relation are important.[2]

Coordination between apparel makers and retailers is not simple either. The relation is not that of simple buying and selling. Owing to various reasons, such as dead stock risks, externalities of sales effort of the retailers to apparel makers, and the necessity of information exchange, various kinds of complicated transactions have emerged in the distribution system. The pattern of transactions differs depending on the type of retailers involved. It is not possible to discuss all the major cases.[3] So we restrict our discussion here to the case of the traditional department store, which has many of the characteristics of the typical traditional Japanese distribution system.

The distinctive feature of department stores is the diversity of products kept in a relatively small number of shops. To secure such diversity of products in one store, the retailer must seek the cooperation of the wholesaler and the manufacturer (wholesalers and manufacturers are often the same companies in apparel products). For this reason, products sold at a department store may be placed on consignment sale (with the wholesaler responsible for accepting unsold items), or they may be returned to the wholesaler. A considerable number of salesclerks working inside department stores are not employees of the store but are assigned to these retailers by the manufacturers or the wholesalers. The prices are also often defined by the manufacturer/wholesaler. To put it in extreme terms, the department store is very much a space-leasing business.

The system of division of labor between the retailer and the manufacturer is a natural result of marketing a wide range of products in a limited floor space. In addition, such a system cannot be founded only on a contract basis but must instead be nurtured as a long-term business relationship. When dis-

2. There is a growing literature on this issue. See, e.g., Williamson (1985) and Hart and Holmstrom (1987). Itoh (1991b) discuses this issue in the context of the Japanese distribution system.

3. On this issue, see Itoh (1991a).

tribution relies on a long-standing relationship between retailer and wholesaler/manufacturer, products from overseas find it difficult to obtain access. Even when high-quality products can be produced at a low cost in Asia, retailers are not inclined to increase their imports unless they can enjoy the same type of service as provided by domestic manufacturers/wholesalers. The manufacturer or the wholesaler may procure such products in Asian countries and channel them through established routes. For example, very expensive European-brand products are imported in this way. However, the makers may harbor great resistance to shifting procurement to other countries owing to the heavy commitment to manufacturing.

Finally, let us briefly mention transportation costs. By *transportation costs* we mean not only shipping costs but also the costs of matching supply and demand. In our interviews with people in the business, the importance of the size of the shipment was often emphasized. When importing from Asian countries, it is necessary to import the same type of goods on a large scale.

The size of imports affects the costs of retailers in the following ways. The first is dead stock risk. If retailers buy the same type of goods in large amounts, the dead stock risk will become larger. Retailers prefer to order a small amount and adjust the order after observing market demand. The second is inventory costs. Japanese retailers prefer to maintain as small an inventory as is possible. The reduction of dead stock risk and inventory costs was made possible traditionally by coordination between manufacturers and retailers. The so-called just-in-time delivery system is a way to minimize the amount of inventory in the hands of retailers. However, it is not easy for sellers and buyers to organize just-in-time delivery systems when they are not located close to one another, and a just-in-time delivery system is based on small-lot delivery, which is difficult for imported products. The spread of the just-in-time delivery system in the Japanese distribution system makes it difficult for Asian products to penetrate the Japanese market.

8.3 Domestic Structural Change and Access to the Japanese Market

We have seen the factors that become barriers to the importation of foreign products. We next consider what kind of structural changes are necessary for these barriers to be removed and whether these changes are actually taking place in Japan.

8.3.1 Structural Changes in the Distribution System

If the importation of final products is to increase, the structure of domestic distribution becomes a critical factor. As we discussed briefly in the previous section in the case of department stores, retailing activities are closely related to the way that products are purchased. Therefore, changes in the distribution system will have a significant influence on the accessibility of Asian products to the Japanese market.

The key element if Asian (apparel) products are to achieve better access is the size of imports. If a retailer can sell goods in large amounts, there will be more room on the market for inexpensive Asian goods. However, the Japanese system has no structure by means of which goods can be imported in large amounts. As we discussed in the case of department stores, the dependence of retail stores on wholesalers or manufacturers for dead stock risk taking, pricing, and other services made it difficult for retailers to take the initiative in purchasing Asian goods. So-called just-in-time delivery systems also made it difficult for foreign goods to penetrate the Japanese market.

There are also reasons why wholesalers have difficulty buying Asian apparel goods. The average size of Japanese wholesalers is quite small. This small size is a result of the small size of retailers. The Large-Scale Retail-Store Law restricted the entry of large-scale retail stores. Other factors such as population structure and the transportation system are also important, and we will comment on these points below. Therefore, wholesalers are not in a position to enjoy scale economies importing inexpensive foreign products.

As regards this point, there are some important structural changes that have emerged in the Japanese distribution system in recent years. The price gap between Japan and other Asian countries that has become marked since the appreciation of the yen has some influence on the Japanese distribution system. Distribution structure is transforming in order to pave the way for the access of inexpensive Asian products.

An example of this adjustment in the Japanese distribution system to inexpensive Asian goods is the rapid growth of the direct marketing business. The strength of the direct marketing business lies in its ready access to all consumers through the mail. Thus, the direct marketing business is in a position to sell large numbers of the same goods. Some of the most successful direct marketing companies in Japan are heavily concentrated in the sales of such goods as less expensive underwear, socks, and stockings, for which mass purchase and mass sales are easy. This new distribution channel is heavily biased toward Asian products. The traditional distribution channels are not in a good position to import these products in large amounts since they have a relatively small number of retail outlets. Even the largest retail chain stores in Japan do not have as many stores as those in the United States. The Large-Scale Retail-Store Law was one of the most important barriers to the increase in the numbers of stores.

Perhaps more important factors behind the structural changes in the Japanese distribution system are domestic. One of the major elements that triggered the changes in distribution is urbanization, that is, the concentration of the population in urban areas and advances in transportation spearheaded by motorization. These two elements expanded the commerce range (such as the number of consumers who can reach a shop in thirty minutes) covered by retail shops. The spread brought greater specialization of retail marketing in various forms. This is in stark contrast to the "one-stop shopping" characteristic that retailers possessed in the older distribution system to satisfy general consumer needs.

A typical new-type retailer growing rapidly under this structural change in the commerce range is the so-called chain specialty store. The distinctive characteristics of apparel specialty chain stores are a limited range of products and the opening of identical (both in business scale and in product variety) outlets in buildings adjacent to railway stations, shopping malls, and roadside sites. These specialty chain stores often have hundreds of outlets all around the nation. In this way, the store chain strives to achieve scale economies. Each outlet is not necessarily large. But even when each store is small, the large number of such outlets generates efficiency of scale in procurement. Business scale aids in reducing the store chain's risks in dead stock and merchandise procurement stock. This feature contrasts sharply with the case of department stores discussed in the previous section.

The recent deregulation of the Large-Scale Retail-Store Law will accelerate this structural change. It now becomes much easier for large-scale retail shops to expand their outlets. By increasing the number of shops, large-scale retail stores will be in a better position to enjoy scale economies of mass purchases and mass sales.

8.3.2 Coordination of Production Networks

Another important structural change taking place in the Japanese distribution system involves the vertical, upstream integration of retailers. Specialty retail chains and big national chain stores, which are in a position to utilize scale economies of mass merchandising, do not stop at just buying commodities from other Asian countries. They are moving in the direction of organizing a production network.

Figure 8.4 shows how toddlers' trousers sold in an apparel specialty chain store are manufactured in Asian countries.[4] The fabric was purchased in China and dyed and pressed in Japan, and accessories were produced in Hong Kong. These materials were next brought to Thailand for cutting and then to Vietnam for sewing. The finished merchandise was inspected in Thailand and marketed in Japan.

Such a scope of production involving many countries denotes the diversity of Asian countries in wages and labor characteristics. There is no capital flow behind these transactions; that is, Asian producers in this production network are independently owned. This type of coordination of production initiated by retailers is widely observed in various kinds of commodities. Naturally, some companies set up plants in Asian countries, which involves direct investment and intrafirm trade.

The case of apparel distribution applies to the trade and production of other

4. This is a case involving cotton products, not wool products.

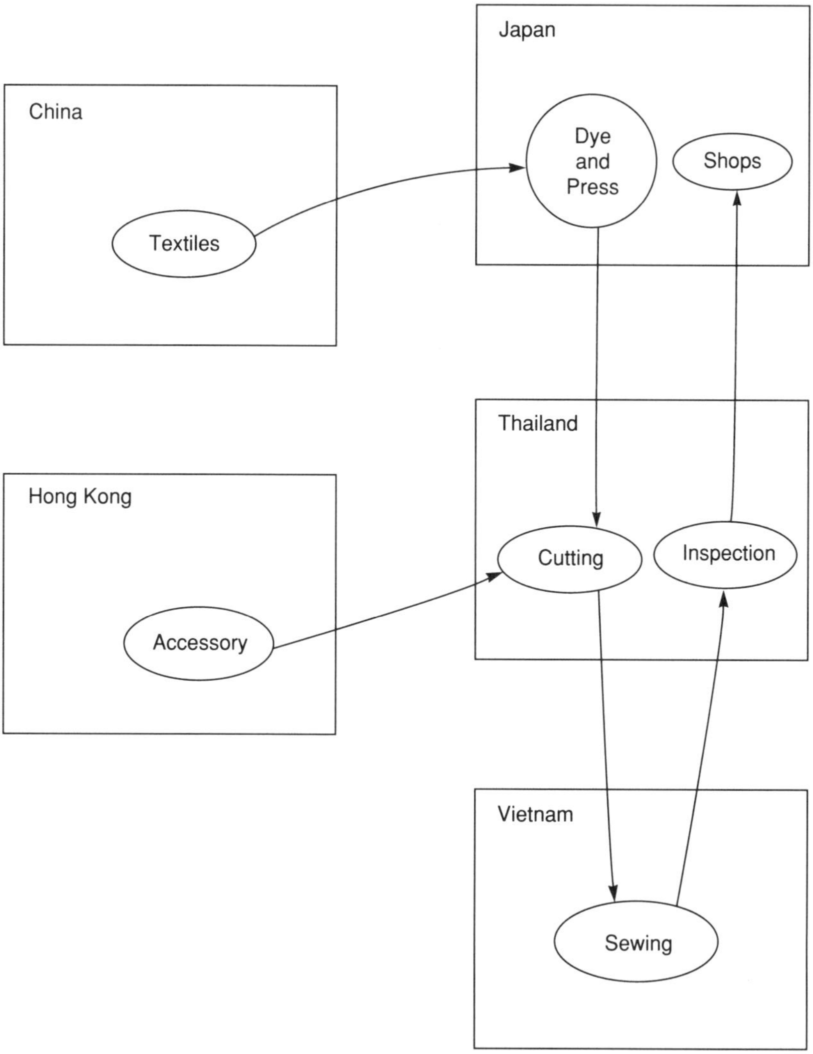

Fig. 8.4 The production route for toddlers' trousers

consumer goods as well as intermediate goods. In figure 8.1 above, a drastic rise was seen in imports of such products as textiles and electrical equipment and auto parts. In the food and sundries business, the growing market share of the general merchandise store operating on a national scale has made many companies avid importers of Asian products. The shift from conventional procurement routes via wholesalers to the development of product importation from Asian nations is believed to be accelerating in this area as well.

The concurrent transformation of domestic trading patterns and Asian trade is occurring in the production and distribution of various types of machinery and parts. Typified by auto parts procurement, the automobile industry grew by sustaining physical proximity and close business ties between manufacturer and parts maker. Production systems such as the *kanban* (just-in-time) system were founded on these continuing business relations.

Nonetheless, the production network, which has been concentrated in a single geographic area in the past, has begun to spread outside Japan into other parts of Asia. The expansion of manufacturing provides the advantage of low labor cost in parts procurement but also the impediment of maintaining intimate business relationships, which are best realized with proximity. The presence of high-quality and inexpensive labor in other Asian countries is magnifying the positive element and minimizing the negative.

These developments are causing automobile, electrical machinery, and other assembly-based industries to bypass Japan and build networks extending into all parts of Asia. Increased direct investment in Asia is a reflection of this outward movement. The rise in the parts trade shows the same structural change in consumer goods distribution mentioned earlier. Both were strictly domestic systems but have undergone major structural transformations. The speed of change is a major factor affecting Japan's Asian trade.

In light of the current situation, an examination of distribution and business among affiliated companies in the SII takes on special meaning. Future developments in trade between Japan and other Asian countries (as well as the world at large) are closely connected to how distribution and manufacturing in Japan will change.

It must be noted, however, that these structural changes did not take place because of the SII. It is more likely that they are the product of changes in the Japanese consumption structure and of the price gap with rest of Asia. The SII talks appear to be following the path paved by the changes.

8.4 Concluding Remarks

The imports of Asian goods by Japan have increased considerably since the appreciation of the yen of 1985. This change in imports is reflected not only in the aggregate amount of imports from Asian countries but also in the change in the contents of Japan's imports. As we have already mentioned, the share of manufactured goods imports in total imports has risen from a level of around 30 percent in the mid-1980s to 50 percent at the end of the 1980s.

The domestic structure of the distribution network and intermediate transactions has also changed significantly in the course of this import expansion. In fact, the change in import pattern and the change in the domestic distribution networks are interrelated. As we have seen in the case of wool textile products, and as is true with many industries, there is a long vertical chain of firms from raw materials upstream to distribution downstream. There are a large number of firms involved at each link in the chain. Thus, even for those products that are imported from abroad, there are still some domestic firms involved either in production (when imported goods are intermediate goods) or in distribution (when imported goods are final consumption goods) before the goods reach the final consumers. Thus, the structure of the distribution network and interfirm transactions affect considerably the way Japan imports Asian goods.

We have seen that the Large-Scale Retail-Store Act, by which the expansion of big chain stores was retarded, became a barrier to imports from Asian countries. The reason why the act has been an import barrier is rather complicated. As we have explained in this paper, the transactions between traditional retail stores and domestic wholesalers/manufacturers of apparel products is quite different from the transactions between chain-store-type retailers and producers. Traditional retail stores rely on wholesalers and manufacturers and on such services as just-in-time delivery, dead stock risk sharing, the provision of various information on the products, and the like. Such relations are in this case a far cry from simple buying and selling. It is not easy for Asian goods to penetrate this complicated network, even though their goods are priced to be strongly competitive. In the case of chain stores, the situation is very different. Since chain stores can enjoy economies of scale because they can sell large amounts of each good (so-called mass merchandising), they depend less on the wholesaler/manufacturer and on such services as just-in-time delivery and risk sharing.

We can learn from our case study how import activities are related to domestic interfirm transactions and the structure of distribution networks. It is thus vital for any discussion of market access to examine the domestic market structure. In Japan, there still remain various barriers in the distribution network. But we can also observe many changes in the domestic market that will accelerate the expansion of imports.

References

Hart, O., and B. Holmstrom. 1987. The theory of contract. In *Advances in economic theory: Fifth world congress,* ed. T. Bewley. Cambridge: Cambridge University Press.

Itoh, M. 1991a. The Japanese distribution system and access to the Japanese import market. In *Trade with Japan: Has the door opened wider?* ed. Paul Krugman. Chicago: University of Chicago Press.

———. 1991b. The distribution system as "network." In *Networks and society,* ed. Y. Oishi and M. Komai. Tokyo: Institute for Posts and Telecommunication Policy.

Williamson, O. E. 1985. *The economic institution of capitalism: Firms, markets, relational contracting.* New York: Free Press.

Comment Chong-Hyun Nam

As was discussed at length in a earlier session this afternoon, a larger question that relates to Motoshige Itoh and Kaori Hatanaka's paper is that the extent of import penetration of manufactured goods into Japanese markets is not only exceptionally low but also not increasing. For example, between 1975 and 1986, the average import penetration ratio for manufactured goods, which was measured as a percentage share of imports in apparent domestic consumption (= production + imports − exports), rose from 7.0 to 13.8 percent in the United States and from 24.3 to 37.2 percent in Germany but declined from 4.9 to 4.4 percent in Japan (Takeuchi 1990, 103).

An important question is why Japan imports so little. Apparently, Japan has the lowest import barrier as far as formal tariff or nontariff barriers (NTBs) are concerned among the major industrial nations. Therefore, the answer must be sought elsewhere. Many argue, for example, that Japanese institutions, legal frameworks, and business customs are all biased not only against consumers vis-à-vis producers but also against imports vis-à-vis domestically produced goods, constituting the so-called informal barriers to trade. Most frequently cited forms of informal barriers to trade include, for example, administrative guidance, customs procedures, technical barriers (such as product standards, testing and certification requirements), and the complicated distribution system. No one knows, however, how important each one is in accounting for the low import penetration ratio into the Japanese market.

This paper addresses the importance of the distribution system as an actual and potential barrier to imports in Japan. It is based on a case study of the wool textile industry at a micro level and illustrates very well how the Large-Scale Retail-Store Law has prevented large-scale distributors, at both the wholesale and the retail levels, from being established. The paper also points out that, as a consequence, manufacturers often merged with wholesale distributors and that retailers often became too small to bear the risk of ending up with dead stock. This often led to a kind of vertical collusion between wholesalers and retailers, which tended to maximize joint profits. Under these circumstances, it appears that there is little room for foreign suppliers to penetrate the Japanese market unless foreign suppliers or importers develop their own distribution channels inside Japan.

This paper does not, however, give any indication of the degree of restrictiveness of the distribution channels for foreign imports, that is, the extent to which those channels limit imports. This will depend on the price-raising effects of the distribution system on imports and supply and demand responses to price changes. An international comparison of markups at each stage of the distribution channel for both imports and domestically produced goods would therefore be useful.

Chong-Hyun Nam is professor of economics at Korea University.

At any rate, I am glad to learn that the Large-Scale Retail-Store Law has recently begun to be dismantled in Japan. Nonetheless, the reform process may be a very slow one, mainly because it will be very much subject to economic, political, and social interactions in the country and because the tradition cannot change overnight. However, the reform process can be accelerated if foreign competition is allowed into the distribution system itself. This would require opening up distribution business to foreign investments. Are there any serious obstacles to that now? Perhaps this is an issue that is being discussed at the moment at the U.S.-Japan Structural Impediments Initiatives (SII) talks. Certainly, many developing countries, particularly newly industrializing economies, have a keen interest in the outcome of the reform plan.

Reference

Takeuchi, K. 1990. Problems in expanding Japan's imports of manufactures from developing economies: A survey. *Asian Economic Journal* 4 (March): 103.

Comment Tan Eu Chye

Motoshige Itoh and Kaori Hatanaka's paper is of great significance for developing countries interested in penetrating the Japanese market, providing as it does a greater understanding of the difficulty involved in gaining significant market access into Japan. A number of factors that determine market access that I would regard as structural factors have been identified by Itoh and Hatanaka. These are factors beyond the traditional tariff and formal and informal nontariff barriers and exchange rate policies that ought to be looked into if one intends to address the issue of market access. These structural factors could restrict trade more than tariff and nontariff barriers do.

Nonetheless, the purpose of the paper—to examine the relation between the domestic economic structure and the pattern of Japan's imports—could have been better served by studying a number of industries rather than the wool textile industry alone. So would the overriding issue of the paper—access to the Japanese market by Asian countries—have been better dealt with by an analysis of both tariff and nontariff barriers in Japan that considered them separately from other structural factors. An estimation of the extent of changes in tariff and nontariff barriers since 1935 would have been especially useful, as it would have enabled a broader range of goods to be taken into account. Such an estimation could then have been supplemented by a computation of the import trade intensity index of Japan and market penetration ra-

Tan Eu Chye is an economics lecturer at the University of Malaya, Kuala Lumpur.

tios in order to gauge the extent of improvement in access to the Japanese market.

At any rate, the paper does indicate that access of Asian developing countries' products to the Japanese market is gradually improving with a proliferation of direct marketing activities, the deregulation of the retail system, urbanization, the mushrooming of chain speciality stores, and the increasing resort to global subcontracting. These recent developments, as mentioned by Itoh and Hatanaka, coupled with growing environmental concerns and the aging Japanese population, would in my opinion augur well for the industrial development of Asian developing nations.

IV

9 Technology Transfer in the Asian Pacific Region: Implications of Trends since the Mid-1980s

Tran Van Tho

In the past quarter century, the Asian Pacific region has experienced rapid economic growth characterized by rapid industrialization. Not only Asian newly industrialized economies (NIEs) but also many Association of Southeast Asian Nations (ASEAN) countries and China have shown a substantial rise in the manufacturing sector as a percentage share of GDP or total exports.

These facts imply that the structure of comparative advantage of each country and thus the pattern of specialization in the region have changed over time. In fact, for example, Taiwan and Korea have increasingly penetrated Japan's domestic market for capital and technology-intensive products, and two-way trade in manufactured products between Japan and ASEAN and between Japan and China has increased substantially. The share of manufactured products in Japan's total imports from ASEAN-4 (Indonesia, Malaysia, the Philippines, and Thailand) has risen from 6 percent in 1980 to 14 percent in 1987 and 23 percent in 1989. The corresponding figures for Japanese imports from China in the same years were 22, 40, and 52 percent, respectively.[1]

Behind the process of catching up by Asian Pacific developing countries in manufacturing production and exports have been changes in the factor endowments of each country. For latecomers to industrialization, this means that capital/labor ratios and technological levels have risen over time. In addition to the domestic accumulation of capital and technological development, capi-

Tran Van Tho is professor of economics at Obirin University, Tokyo, and senior economist at the Japan Center for Economic Research (JCER), Tokyo.

The author is grateful for helpful comments by Takatoshi Ito and Anne O. Krueger. Fruitful comments by Bih Jane Liu (National Taiwan University) and other participants at the second annual East Asian Seminar on Economics in Taipei are also highly appreciated. Thanks are due as well to Hal Hill of the Australian National University for providing helpful comments prior to the final revision of the paper.

1. Calculated from the December 1980, December 1987, and December 1989 issues of *The Summary Report Trade of Japan*, published by the Japan Tariff Association (Tokyo).

tal movement and technology transfer from other countries have promoted changes in the factor endowments of Asian Pacific developing countries. In particular, since the mid-1980s, factor movement from Japan to these countries has accelerated, and Asian NIEs have increasingly participated in the supply of capital and technology in the region.

This paper focuses on the role of technology transfer in the industrialization of the Asian Pacific region. It will provide some observations on the trends in the second half of the 1980s and discuss their implications for the future industrialization and division of labor in the region. In this paper, the Asian Pacific region is defined as including Japan, Asian NIEs, ASEAN, China, and Vietnam, but the last two countries will not be examined in detail. I will also confine my discussion to the manufacturing sector.

In what follows, section 9.1 will summarize the characteristics and effects of the channels through which technologies are transferred. In particular, some controversial issues regarding the relationship between foreign direct investment (FDI) and technology transfer will be discussed. In section 9.2, the pattern of Japan's technology transfer in the region since the mid-1980s will be analyzed. The "push factors" for the expansion of Japanese FDI as well as other channels of technology transfer will also be discussed. Section 9.3 highlights recent trends in the role of Asian NIEs as new transmitters of technology in the region via the channel of direct investment. The factors pushing firms in NIEs to expand FDI will also be mentioned. Section 9.4 will discuss the nature of the Asian Pacific region as a market for technologies from Japan and NIEs. In other words, the "pull factors" accounting for the expansion of direct investment and other flows of technology will be analyzed. In section 9.5, the implications of new trends in technology transfer will be discussed in the dynamic context of the Asian Pacific economies. Finally, section 9.6 will summarize my major conclusions.

9.1 Channels of Technology Transfer

In this paper, *technology* is defined in a broad sense to include not only production technology (hardware of production or knowledge about machines and processes) but also management expertise, marketing skills, and other intangible corporate assets.

Technologies can be internationally transferred through many channels. Broadly speaking, these channels can be divided into two categories, public and private. In the first category, technologies can be considered as public goods, and the transfer is conducted by public organizations, such as governments of advanced countries and international agencies. Such technologies are seen in fields such as agriculture and government administration, where markets for technologies do not exist. The transfer is conducted as a part of the technical assistance or economic cooperation provided to developing countries. By contrast, private channels of transfer relate to technologies that are developed by private firms and transferred on a commercial basis. The owners or suppliers of technologies are usually, but not always, multinational corporations (MNCs). The scope of this paper is limited to private channels of technology transfer.

Technology transfer by MNCs or other private firms is conducted through the following channels: (foreign) direct investment (FDI), licensing arrangements, plant export, original equipment manufacturing (OEM), and others.[2] FDI involves the transfer of a package of managerial resources including production technology, management know-how, and marketing skills. Other channels of transfer do not involve such packaging and have drawn wide attention since the late 1970s as "new forms" of MNCs' involvement in developing countries (Oman 1984).

The importance of each channel varies, depending on the strategy of the MNC supplying the technologies, the characteristics of the technologies themselves, and the policies, absorptive capacity, and managerial resource endowments of the recipient countries.

The preference of MNCs for one channel or another depends on many factors. If the technologies are newly developed, MNCs prefer direct investment with majority ownership to an arm's length transaction because majority ownership allows them to control use of the technologies, preventing the leakage of technology to third parties. Another determinant of the channel used is the firm's perception of the environment in the recipient country. If the environment is considered risky, licensing arrangements may be chosen since, with this channel, the MNC's level of commitment in the market is much lower than in the case of direct investment. In the case of OEM, the technological levels of the recipient firms are crucial since the products made by the latter as a result of technology transfer will be sold under the brand name of the transferring MNC.

From the standpoint of developing recipients, FDI may be the most effective channel for the development of a new industry since developing countries tend to be poorly endowed with management and marketing skills. However, if the technology is standardized and product markets are stable, recipient countries may prefer other channels that do not involve control by foreign firms. When the preferences of MNCs and recipients do not coincide, their respective bargaining power will determine which channel of technology transfer is ultimately used.

Since the remainder of this paper will focus on FDI, it seems fitting to discuss here the relation between FDI and technology transfer and the various controversies surrounding this issue.

In Asia, there have been complaints that Japan is passive in transferring

2. Other channels of technology transfer not dealt with in this paper include turn key contract, franchising, and international subcontracting. For a more detailed discussion of channels of technology transfer and related issues, see, e.g., UNCTC (1987).

technology to the region's developing countries. The complaints can be divided into two types. In the first type, Japanese firms are said to be unwilling to transfer technology (the technologies that Asian countries want); that is, no technology is transferred under any channel. This is a complaint often heard in Korea regarding the passive attitude of Japanese firms toward the transfer of recent high-technology developments in Japan. It is true that Japanese firms prefer to keep new technologies at home and serve foreign markets by exporting products from Japan. But, when Japanese firms decide to provide or transfer the technology to foreign countries, they will choose one of the channels discussed above. FDI is one of those channels. It can thus be implicitly assumed that FDI represents technology transfer. This leads to the second type of complaint from Asia, namely, that, even when Japanese firms do undertake FDI, they do not really transfer technology. This complaint is often heard from Thailand, Malaysia, and other Southeast Asian countries.

More concretely, firms affiliated with Japan are said to be reluctant to train local employees, with the result that there is no smooth transfer of technology. Japanese companies allegedly staff their affiliates with too many Japanese managers, thus depriving local staff of the opportunity to acquire management skills.[3] However, these claims are often confused by the lack of a clear definition of concepts, and thus, in many cases, friction between Japan and other Asian countries results from a gap in perception. Let me provide a simple framework to understand this problem and summarize the evidence shown by a number of surveys, including my own.

We may divide technologies into three types: production technology, administration technology, and management skills (Ogawa 1976). Accordingly, we may divide technology transfer into three levels. Suppose that an MNC undertakes an FDI project in a developing country to produce a manufactured product. First, a factory is built. The factory is a form that embodies both production technology and administration technology. Production technology is the combination of equipment and the knowledge to operate that equipment. The transfer of this technology requires the transfer of both equipment and knowledge—and therefore the training of local operators.

In the production process, there are many forms of administration: inventory, quality control, schedule control, facility administration, and so on. The transfer of these administration technologies involves the training and education of engineers and managers at middle levels (section chief, department head, etc.).

The third type of technology is the management skills embodied in the head office. The head office is usually located in the capital of the host country and manages the operations of a factory or a number of factories, and it also directs all planning, marketing, finance, and other similar activities. High-level managers at the head office have to follow the trends in product markets, tech-

3. See, e.g., the papers written by Southeast Asian scholars in Sekiguchi (1983).

nological change, and other areas and devise strategies that can cope with new situations. The transfer of such management skills requires the training of high-level managers, who are gradually allowed to fill the top-class managerial posts initially held by staff from the MNC's home country.

The behavior of MNCs regarding the transfer of the three types of technology discussed above can be hypothesized as follows. Regarding production technology and administration technology, MNCs have two incentives to transfer to the host country. First, since the employees and staff at these stages are large in number, most of them must be recruited from the local labor market; only a few, if any, are sent from the MNC's home country, except during the initial stage of the operations. Second, in order to run affiliated firms efficiently, MNCs have to train employees and middle managers so that they can operate or manage the factory smoothly.

Transferring management skills is more complicated. The persons in charge of planning or conducting financial and marketing strategies must have high levels of managerial knowledge and sometimes must be aware not only of the situation of the affiliated firm but also of the global strategy of the MNC as a whole. These persons therefore are frequently in contact with headquarters, and it is essential that they be able to communicate effectively with the headquarters. If these conditions are not met, MNCs have the incentive to send staff from the parent headquarters to fill the top managerial posts of the affiliates.

The evidence so far has confirmed the point that there is a relatively large number of Japanese expatriates in the joint ventures or subsidiaries of Japanese firms. However, this does not necessarily mean that there is a lack of technology transfer. In many cases, it may mean the reverse, particularly in the initial stage of the investment project. The important problem here is whether the number of Japanese staff has declined steadily over time as a result of the transfer of technology to local staff.

The results of my field surveys (Tran 1992) on the operation of Japanese affiliates in the synthetic fiber industry in Korea, Taiwan, Thailand, and Indonesia can be summarized as follows. First, in the case of production and administration technologies, Japanese firms have been active in training local employees, for example, by sending middle managers to Japan for training courses, by conducting on-the-job training, and by other activities. With these efforts, the transfer has been quite smooth. The number of Japanese staff at various managerial levels in the factory has been reduced steadily without interruption or major trouble in the operations. Second, there has, however, been no significant progress evinced in the transfer of management skills. This is particularly true for Thailand and Indonesia.

A survey by MITI (1989a, 21–22) also shows that, in the Japanese-affiliated firms in Asia, a substantial reduction in the number of Japanese staff was recorded at middle-management levels but not at higher levels.

What are the reasons for the differential transfer rates between the factory (the transfer of production and administrative technologies) and the head office (the transfer of management skills)? The quick transfer of production and administrative technologies can be explained by the cost and efficiency considerations of MNCs, as discussed earlier. The slow transfer of managerial posts may be attributed to the following four factors.

First, as noted earlier, communication between affiliated firms and the parent headquarters must be conducted smoothly. Because of language barriers, Japanese firms are reluctant to give high-level managerial posts to local staff.

Second, one of the major features of the Japanese management style is to grant managerial posts only to those employees who, after entering the company as university graduates, have worked their way up through the ranks, serving in various positions within the company for many years. Under such a system of intrafirm training and promotion, it takes about twenty years or more for an employee to reach a high managerial post.

Third, in the case where Japanese firms modify their management style and are willing to recruit qualified persons from the local labor market, it is essential that the supply side of that market meet the demand. However, in many developing countries, the shortage of qualified high-level managers is still a serious problem.

Fourth, in some Asian countries, the efforts of local partners to catch up (using local replacements for foreign managerial resources) have been weak. In many cases, local shareholders simply prefer to maximize the dividends from the joint ventures and thus discourage the localization of management since local managers are usually thought to be less efficient than Japanese ones.

In the case of Korea and Taiwan, the third and fourth factors have been small; that is, the local supply of human resources has expanded over time, and local efforts to catch up by replacing foreign managerial resources have been strong (Tran 1988). In addition, owning to historical factors, linguistic similarity, and educational access, Koreans and Taiwanese have an advantage in studying and learning the Japanese language. This point, together with many common cultural values in Far East Asia, has lowered the communication barriers between Japan and the two Asian NIEs. For these reasons, so long as FDI is undertaken, the transfer of management skills from Japan to Korea and Taiwan has been considerable. It is interesting to note that the claims that Japanese firms undertake FDI but do not transfer technology (management skills) have been heard from Southeast Asian countries but almost never from Asian NIEs.

Given the scope of this paper, I shall go no further on this point. I simply need to confirm here that FDI is a channel of technology transfer. When FDI is undertaken, it involves technology transfer, at least at the factory level.[4] As

4. According to MITI (1986, 591), in 1983 about 95 percent of production technologies used in Japanese affiliates in Asia were supplied by Japan. For affiliates in electronics and other machinery-related industries, such figures were in the range of 97–99 percent.

far as management skills are concerned, even when FDI does not involve a localization of such technology, management operations must nevertheless be moved from the MNC's home country to the host country. Therefore, FDI results in an increase in the production capacity in host countries, changes in the location of industrial activities, and, consequently, a change in the division of labor among home and host countries of MNCs.

9.2 Trends in Japan's Technology Transfer in Asia: Pattern and Factors

9.2.1 Foreign Direct Investment

Since late 1985, when the value of the yen began to increase sharply, Japan's FDI has rapidly expanded. Japanese manufacturing firms have ventured overseas at high speed. On a reported (to the Ministry of Finance) basis, Japanese FDI in world manufacturing industries reached U.S. $3.8 billion in fiscal 1986 (an expansion of 62 percent over the previous fiscal year), U.S. $7.8 billion in 1987 (an expansion of 106 percent), U.S. $13.8 billion in 1988, and U.S. $16.3 billion in 1989.

Along with these general trends, investment in Asia has also shown a high rate of expansion since 1986. For all manufacturing industries as a whole, the cumulative investment in the most recent four years exceeded the cumulative investment from 1951 to 1985 (see Table 9.1). The rapid appreciation of the yen has significantly changed the structure of Japan's international competitiveness. Wages and other factor costs in Japan, in dollar terms, rose rapidly owing to the drastic change in the value of the yen. In 1986, Japanese wages, for instance, were about four times higher than the average level in Asian NIEs and about thirteen times higher than in ASEAN countries (MITI 1988, 13). Given the still higher value of the yen in subsequent years, factor costs in Japan in the late 1980s should have been much higher than in 1986. As a result, many industries have had to venture overseas in order to achieve lower production costs. Until mid-1986, Asian NIEs, particularly Taiwan and South Korea, were the major markets absorbing these new direct investments. Since mid-1986, the waves have spread to ASEAN, especially Thailand and Malaysia. Since 1987, Japanese direct investment in Indonesia has also risen substantially. These investments include not only the establishment of new wholly owned subsidiaries or joint ventures but also the expansion of production (including the addition of new product lines) by existing ventures.

Three features of the Japanese manufacturing sector's direct investment in Asia since the mid-1980s may be noted. First, the industrial structure of Japanese FDI in the region has been significantly upgraded in the sense that the weight of more technologically sophisticated industries has risen considerably. This is partially reflected in the increasingly strong presence of the electrical and electronics industries. In the most recent four years, those industries accounted for more than 30 percent of the total Japanese manufacturing direct

Table 9.1 Japanese Manufacturing Direct Investment in Asia (million U.S. dollars)

	Asia		ASEAN-4		Asian NIEs	
	1951–85	1986–89	1951–86	1987–89	1951–86	1987–89
All manufacturing	7,517 (100.0)	8,074 (100.0)	4,207 (100.0)	3,618 (100.0)	3,891 (100.0)	3,001 (100.0)
Foodstuffs	256 (3.4)	795 (9.8)	165 (3.9)	136 (3.8)	90 (2.3)	595 (19.8)
Textiles	1,182 (15.7)	387 (4.8)	825 (19.6)	176 (4.9)	366 (9.4)	67 (2.2)
Pulp and paper	191 (2.5)	260 (3.2)	163 (3.9)	223 (6.2)	31 (0.8)	21 (.7)
Chemicals	1,292 (17.2)	786 (9.7)	438 (10.4)	276 (7.6)	876 (22.5)	432 (14.4)
Steel and nonferrous metals	1,697 (22.6)	881 (10.9)	1,494 (35.5)	579 (16.0)	231 (5.9)	220 (7.3)
General machinery	580 (7.7)	806 (10.0)	133 (3.2)	409 (11.3)	585 (15.0)	242 (8.1)
Electrical machinery	833 (11.1)	2,515 (31.1)	245 (5.8)	1,200 (33.2)	829 (21.3)	807 (26.9)
Transport equipment	692 (9.2)	633 (7.8)	392 (9.3)	230 (6.4)	386 (9.9)	239 (8.0)
Others	796 (10.6)	1,010 (12.5)	352 (8.4)	387 (10.7)	548 (14.1)	381 (12.7)

Source: Calculated from data released by the Ministry of Finance (Japan).
Note: Attention should be paid to the differences in the periods covered under "Asia" compared with those covered under "ASEAN-4" and "Asian NIEs," differences due to data availability. Figures in parentheses are share of each industry in all manufacturing.

investment in Asia, compared with 11 percent for the preceding period (table 9.1). In contrast, labor-intensive industries, typically textiles, and resource-intensive industries, such as chemicals and steel and nonferrous metals, have shown a sharp decline in their share of Japanese FDI. The exceptional case is foodstuffs, an industry that is considered labor intensive. Its share rose sharply in the second period. This was due, however, to the merger and acquisition of a large firm in Singapore by a Japanese manufacturer of alcoholic beverages in 1989. In terms of statistical data, this case has biased the structure of the Japanese manufacturing sector's direct investment in Asian NIEs (table 9.1).

The steady expansion of direct investment by Japan's electrical/electronics industry has been increasingly accompanied by the transfer of high technology. Until the early 1980s, firms tended to transfer standardized or low-level technologies such as those relating to the assembly of black-and-white television sets or to simple electronics parts. In recent years, however, Japanese firms have increased the transfer of technologies relating to sophisticated electronic parts, the production of color televisions, videocassette recorders, and other areas.

FDI from other industries has also been characterized by the transfer of high technology. In the case of Japanese direct investment in Korea's chemical industry, for example, the number of such high-tech projects as biotechnology and pharmaceuticals has increased (JETRO 1991, 146). Somsak (1991) also documented the fact that Japanese direct investment in Thailand has markedly increased in the fields of capital goods and intermediate electronic and electrical products.

The second feature of Japan's manufacturing sector's direct investment in Asia in recent years has been the increasing export orientation of investment projects. The rapid appreciation of the yen has forced Japanese firms to locate their manufacturing production activities overseas as a substitute for exports, on the one hand, and for sourcing cheaper products to serve their domestic markets, on the other. According to a MITI survey (1989a) of the markets for the products of Japanese manufacturing subsidiaries in Asia, 15.8 percent of the sales of those firms were shipped back to the Japanese market in 1986, compared to 10.8 percent in 1983; furthermore, 29.5 percent were exported to third countries, compared to 22.3 percent in 1983. For electrical and electronic products, third-country markets have been much more important than for manufacturing industries as a whole. According to another survey by MITI (1987, 269) on the purposes of direct investment projects undertaken after 1985 in Asian NIEs by Japan's electrical/electronics industry, 14.8 percent of the outputs were shipped back to the Japanese market, another 41.6 percent were exported to third countries, and only 43.6 percent were sold in local markets. Data from recipient countries such as Thailand (Somsak 1991) and Indonesia (Thee 1990) also show the same trends.

The third feature is the increasing presence of small and medium-sized firms (SMSFs). As shown in table 9.2, SMSFs accounted for more than half the FDI projects undertaken by Japanese firms in recent years. The table also shows that about two-thirds of manufacturing FDI projects undertaken by SMSFs have been concentrated in Asia. In particular, the concentration of investment in Asia by four manufacturing sectors, namely, machinery, textiles, metals, and miscellaneous goods, is prominent (Adachi 1991). Because of the rapid appreciation of the value of the yen, many SMSFs have sought low-cost production sites in Asia. Some of them are subcontractors of large firms in Japan and have undertaken FDI at the request of their parent firms, which want to ensure the supply of parts and components in the latter's Asian assembly plants.

Since the technological gap between developing countries and SMSFs of advanced countries can be hypothesized to be smaller than that between developing countries and larger firms, the technologies of Japanese SMSFs can be easily transferred to and diffused throughout Asia. This point will be discussed in more detail in section 9.5 below.

Table 9.2 **Trends in Japanese FDI by SMSFs (%)**

	1980	1985	1988	1989
Share of SMSFs in all Japanese FDI projects	41.3	31.1	59.6	53.8
Share of manufacturing investment in all FDI projects by SMSFs	30.4	43.1	44.5	38.2
Share of Asia in all manufacturing FDI by SMSFs:	57.6	63.5	65.6	64.7
Of which:				
NIEs-3[a]	36.4	30.7	26.8	20.4
China	21.2	21.1	8.1	7.9
Other Asia		11.7	30.7	36.4

Source: Small and Medium Enterprises Agency, *White Paper on Small and Medium Enterprises* (Tokyo: Ministry of Finance, various years).
[a]Korea, Taiwan, and Hong Kong.

9.2.2 Other Channels of Technology Transfer from Japan

Direct investment has not been the only channel of technology transfer from Japan. Since the mid-1980s, other channels have been adopted, including licensing arrangements, production cooperation, and OEM. Japanese firms seem to adopt different channels of technology transfer depending on the general technological level as well as the degree of political or economic risk in host countries. Table 9.3 provides some evidence for this point. The table summarizes the forms (channels) of technology transfer by Japanese firms during the first two and a half years since the value of the yen started its sharp rise. The table suggests that direct investment is important in Asian NIEs and ASEAN countries while licensing arrangements and production cooperation have been chosen mainly for the Chinese market. OEM has so far appeared only in Asian NIEs. This may be explained by the relatively high technological levels of firms in NIEs, compared to those in other Asian developing countries. Along with the accumulation of managerial resources, many firms in NIEs have preferred OEM-type technology transfers over FDI, which results in management control by MNCs.[5] In terms of the cost of buying technology, OEM is also much cheaper than licensing arrangements are. From the point of view of Japanese firms, the attainment of a high technological level by firms in NIEs is a precondition for transfer through the OEM channel because of the need to ensure product quality, as mentioned in section 9.1 above. The reason why licensing arrangements have been the most important channel of technology transfer for China may be that China is considered by Japanese firms to be much riskier than NIEs or ASEAN countries because of the possi-

5. About 30 of the firms surveyed by MITI (1989a, 122–23) have conducted OEM in Asia and other regions. The most important reason for choosing this channel of technology transfer is said to have been "requests" from recipient firms.

Table 9.3 **Forms of Technology Transfer to Asia by Japanese Firms, 1986–June 1988 (no. of cases)**

	Local Production (direct investment)	Licensing Arrangement	Production Cooperation	OEM
Korea	127	98	44	9
Taiwan	209	51	43	8
Hong Kong	39	5	9	1
Singapore	113	3	4	0
Asian NIEs (A)	488	158	100	18
Thailand	129	21	6	0
Malaysia	62	5	2	0
Philippines	28	5	2	0
Indonesia	45	16	8	0
ASEAN-4 (B)	264	47	18	0
China (C)	85	107	38	1
Asian Pacific (A + B + C)	837	312	156	19

Source: Compiled from NEEDS system of the *Japan Economic Journal* (*Nihon Keizai Shinbun*).

Table 9.4 **Channels of Technology Transfer from Japan to Asia**

	N	%
Total projects surveyed	856	100.0
FDI	477	55.7
Licensing arrangements	347	40.5
Other channels	32	3.7

Source: Survey by Nikkei Research Institute of Industry and Markets, Tokyo, October 1990.
Note: The survey covered only four machinery-related industries: general machinery, electrical/electronic products, automobiles, and precision machinery.

bility of changes in foreign and domestic economic policies as a result of changes in the political situation.

Table 9.4 gives the results of a survey of 474 Japanese manufacturers in four machinery-related industries (general machinery, electrical/electronics, transport equipment, and precision machinery). According to the survey, 342 firms had conducted a total of 856 projects involving technology transfer in Asian countries (including NIEs, ASEAN, China, India, and Pakistan) by October 1990. Even though India and Pakistan were included in the survey, these two countries together accounted for only 10 percent of the total number of technology transfer projects. Table 9.4 shows that both FDI and licensing arrangements have been important channels of technology transfer by Japanese machinery-related producers to Asian countries. Most projects involving "other" channels have probably been conducted in recent years. Table 9.5 breaks down all projects according to transferee and timing of the transfer.

Table 9.5 **Technology Transfer from Japan to Asia**

	Total No. of Projects	Before 1970	1971–80	1981–85	1986–Oct. 1990
Korea	195	9	44	53	87
	(100.0)	(4.6)	(22.6)	(27.2)	(44.6)
Taiwan	155	25	28	40	59
	(100.0)	(16.1)	(18.1)	(25.8)	(38.1)
Hong Kong	14	4	3	2	5
	(100.0)	(28.6)	(21.4)	(14.3)	(35.7)
Singapore	47	0	28	9	10
	(100.0)	(.0)	(59.6)	(19.1)	(21.3)
Thailand	109	11	21	8	63
	(100.0)	(10.1)	(19.3)	(7.3)	(57.8)
Malaysia	89	3	21	17	43
	(100.0)	(3.4)	(23.6)	(19.1)	(48.3)
Indonesia	63	3	21	19	18
	(100.0)	(4.8)	(33.3)	(30.2)	(28.6)
Philippines	31	2	10	6	11
	(100.0)	(6.5)	(32.3)	(19.4)	(35.5)
China	68	0	2	36	29
	(100.0)	(.0)	(2.9)	(52.9)	(42.6)
Asia total	856	59	187	229	357
	(100.0)	(6.9)	(21.8)	(26.8)	(41.7)

Source: See table 9.4.

Note: "Asia total" includes India and Pakistan, which do not appear in this table. "Total no. of projects" includes some that were to be conducted in 1991 and some for which the time of transfer was unknown. Figures in parentheses show percentage share in total number of projects. See also table 9.4.

Three points emerge from this table. First, Korea, Taiwan, Thailand, and Malaysia have been the major markets for Japan's machinery-related technologies, followed by China and Indonesia. Second, for most countries, about 40 percent or more of the projects were conducted during the latest five-year period. This, again, confirms the aggressive behavior of Japanese firms regarding technology transfer to Asia following the sharp rise in the value of the yen. Third, the concentration of technology transfer in that period was more pronounced in ASEAN countries like Thailand and Malaysia than in NIEs such as Taiwan and Korea. Since machinery-related technologies can be considered to be more sophisticated than those found in other industries such as textiles and foodstuffs, this suggests that Japanese firms have an increasingly strong interest in exporting high technologies to ASEAN's growing economies.

In sum, since the latter half of the 1980s, technology transfer by Japanese firms of all sizes to the Asian Pacific region has been actively conducted through various channels. Among the technologies transferred, sophisticated technologies such as those relating to electrical and electronic products have played an increasingly important role.

9.3 Asian NIEs as the New Transmitters of Technology: Pattern and Factors

Along with the intensive movement of technologies from Japan, the Asian Pacific economy has also been characterized by the active transfer of managerial resources from Asian NIEs since the second half of the 1980s. To provide a simple picture of that phenomenon, this section will review the pattern of direct investment (the major channel of technology transfer) from Taiwan and Korea to ASEAN countries.[6]

9.3.1 The Pattern of Taiwan's Direct Investment in ASEAN

Taiwan started FDI as early as 1959, but until around 1980 the annual FDI level was very small. Substantial FDI occurred in the early 1980s, and annual direct investment abroad expanded rapidly after the middle of the decade. The cumulative FDI for the two decades between 1959 and 1980 was only U.S. $100 million, while the same figure for the period 1981–85 was U.S. $114 million. The sum of FDI conducted during the two subsequent years, 1986 and 1987, was an even higher U.S. $160 million. At the end of the decade, annual FDI from Taiwan experienced continuing jumps: from U.S. $219 million in 1988, to U.S. $931 million in 1989, to U.S. $1.6 billion in 1990.[7]

A number of factors have pushed Taiwanese firms to expand investment abroad in recent years. These include the rapid rise in wages and other factor costs in Taiwan, the increase in the value of the new Taiwan dollar, and trade friction with the United States. For these reasons, Taiwanese FDI has so far been conducted mainly by manufacturing firms and in the manufacturing sector of the recipient countries. In terms of capital stock at the end of 1990, about two-thirds of Taiwanese FDI was accounted for by manufacturing industries.

Since the 1980s, more than half of Taiwanese direct investment abroad has been concentrated in the United States. However, by 1987, the United States has been particularly important for Taiwan's electrical and electronics industry. In the area of light manufacturing (labor-intensive industries), for ex-

6. For a short review of other channels of technology transfer from Asian NIEs, see, e.g., Chen (1985). This reflects, however, only the situation until the early 1980s.

7. FDI data released by Taiwanese authorities have usually been underestimated. This has been due in part to the fact that some investments were not submitted to the government for approval. The government's review process is usually time consuming, so, in order to avoid possible delays in their investment schedules, firms may have bypassed government regulations whenever possible. This data problem, however, does not significantly affect the analysis here unless the unreported FDI has had a pattern quite different from that described in the paper. In fact, so long as the magnitude or the amount of FDI is concerned, the underestimation of the data tends to strengthen my argument.

ample, textiles, apparel, wood products, foodstuffs, and beverages, ASEAN countries have been much more important. As shown in table 9.6, light-manufacturing industries accounted for about half of Taiwanese direct investment in ASEAN, and the investment stock in this region has far exceeded that in the United States. In particular, Taiwan's direct investment in labor-intensive industries in Thailand, Malaysia, and the Philippines has shown a high rate of expansion. In the most recent period, from 1988 to 1990, Taiwanese electrical and electronics firms have also conducted substantial direct investment in ASEAN countries (table 9.7). However, Taiwanese electronics firms' direct investment in Thailand and other ASEAN countries seemed to be involved primarily in the production of highly standardized products such as lamps, transformers, and washing-machine motors (Ramstetter 1988, 118; JETRO 1991, 159). This is quite different from FDI by Japanese electronics firms.

Recently, Taiwanese light manufacturers have also been active in direct investment in Vietnam, which promulgated a new foreign investment law in January 1988.[8]

As a result of active direct investment since the latter half of the 1980s, Taiwanese capital and technology have now gained a significant position in most ASEAN countries. Until the mid-1980s, in terms of FDI, the position of Taiwan as a capital supplier was negligible in most ASEAN countries, except for Thailand. However, the cumulative investment in recent years shows that Taiwan has become the largest supplier of managerial resources in Malaysia, the second (but close to first) largest supplier in Indonesia, and the third (but close to second) largest supplier in Thailand (see table 9.8).[9]

Since FDI involves the transfer of a package of production technologies, management skills, and marketing skills, the growth and the industry composition of the Taiwanese direct investment in ASEAN has many implications for the pattern of technology transfer to Southeast Asian countries. I shall return to this point in section 9.5 below.

9.3.2 The Pattern of Korea's Direct Investment in ASEAN

South Korea began direct investment abroad in 1968 when it undertook a project to procure lumber in Indonesia. Until 1985, however, the levels of

8. Direct investment in Vietnam from Asian NIEs and other sources is analyzed in Tran (1991a).

9. In the case of the Philippines, data in table 9.8 unfortunately do not show investments from Taiwan. According to the data from JETRO (1992, 216), however, out of 50.8 billion pesos of cumulative FDI (on an approval basis) from 1988 to 1990, Taiwan ranked second, with 17.4 percent of the total, preceded by Japan (25.3 percent) and followed by the United States (14.8 percent).

In the data for Indonesia, FDI in the mining sector is not included. The result is that the shares of Taiwan and Korea in table 9.8 tend to be overestimated since they have undertaken almost no direct investment in the oil exploration and other mining industries in Indonesia. I owe this point to Hal Hill. For details, see Hill (1988).

Table 9.6 **Structure of Taiwan's FDI: Cumulative Investment from 1959 to 1987 (thousand U.S. dollars)**

	ASEAN	U.S.	Other Regions	Total
Primary industries	638	. . .	4,659	5,297
	(.7)		(8.4)	(1.4)
Manufacturing:				
Light industries	42,421	24,151	12,706	79,278
	(49.2)	(10.4)	(23.0)	(21.2)
Electrical and electronic prods.	9,738	116,406	6,293	132,432
	(11.3)	(49.9)	(11.4)	(35.4)
Other manufacturing	26,040	40,051	12,932	71,851
	(30.2)	(17.2)	(23.4)	(19.2)
Construction and tertiary industries	7,306	52,606	18,636	78,548
	(8.5)	(22.6)	(33.7)	(21.2)
Total	86,143	233,214	55,226	374,583
	(100.0)	(100.0)	(100.0)	(100.0)

Source: Compiled from Republic of China, Ministry of Foreign Affairs, Investment Commission, *Statistics on Overseas Chinese and Foreign Investment, Technical Cooperation, Outward Investment, Outward Technical Cooperation* (December 1988, 1989, 1990).

Note: Figures in parentheses are industry shares in total investment within each region. "ASEAN" excludes Brunei. "Light industries" includes food and beverages, textiles, garments and footwear, lumber and bamboo products, pulp and paper products, leather and fur products, and plastics and rubber products.

Table 9.7 **Structure of Taiwan's FDI: Cumulative Investment from 1988 to 1990 (thousand U.S. dollars)**

	ASEAN	U.S.	Other Regions	Total
Primary industries	5,738	0	300	6,038
	(0.6)	(.0)	(.0)	(.2)
All manufacturing	855,778	712,537	82,766	1,651,092
	(94.2)	(67.2)	(11.4)	(61.1)
Light industries	151,656	189,500	11,512	352,668
	(16.7)	(17.9)	(1.6)	(13.1)
Electrical and electronic products	356,150	173,067	56,031	585,259
	(39.2)	(16.3)	(7.7)	(21.7)
Other manufacturing	347,972	349,970	15,223	713,165
	(38.3)	(33.0)	(2.1)	(26.4)
Construction and tertiary industries	46,649	348,220	644,623	1,044,799
	(5.1)	(32.8)	(88.6)	(38.7)
Total	908,626	1,060,757	727,689	2,701,929
	(100.0)	(100.0)	(100.0)	(100.0)

Source: The same as table 9.6.

Note: See table 9.6.

Table 9.8 **Major Suppliers of Direct Investment in Asian Countries (million U.S. dollars)**

		Suppliers								
Recipient Countries	Total	Japan	U.S.	U.K.	Holland	West Germany	South Korea	Taiwan	Hong Kong	Singapore
Investment stock at the end of 1987:										
Thailand	11,536	2,773	1,910	651	422	19	9	675	445	351
	(100.0)	(24.0)	(16.6)	(5.6)	(3.7)	(.2)	(.1)	(5.9)	(3.9)	(3.0)
Malaysia	4,200	1,741	202	879	61	68	. . .	34	262	594
	(100.0)	(41.5)	(4.8)	(20.9)	(1.5)	(1.6)		(.8)	(6.2)	(14.1)
Indonesia	17,284	5,928	1,244	560	851	867	222	144	1,876	299
	(100.0)	(34.3)	(7.2)	(3.2)	(4.9)	(5.0)	(1.3)	(.9)	(10.9)	(1.7)
Philippines	2,830	377	1,620	102	130	. . .	. . .	. . .	. . .	. . .
	(100.0)	(13.3)	(57.2)	(3.6)	(4.6)					
Cumulative investment in recent years:										
Thailand (1988–89)	7,868	4,431	570	250	63	175	66	530	278	408
	(100.0)	(56.3)	(7.2)	(3.2)	(.8)	(2.2)	(.8)	(6.7)	(3.5)	(5.2)
Malaysia (1988–89/90)	3,690	967	179	207	. . .	57	49	1,314	138	231
	(100.0)	(26.2)	(4.8)	(5.6)		(1.6)	(1.3)	(35.6)	(3.7)	(6.3)
Indonesia (1988–89)	11,159	1,304	783	110	572	973	728	1,126	867	489
	(100.0)	(11.7)	(7.0)	(1.0)	(5.1)	(8.7)	(6.5)	(10.1)	(7.8)	(4.4)
Philippines (1988–89)	275	71	98	4	18	. . .	. . .	. . .	. . .	. . .
	(100.0)	(25.8)	(35.6)	(1.5)	(6.5)	. . .	. . .	. . .	. . .	. . .

Source: Calculated from JETRO data.

Note: Original data for Thailand and Malaysia are in local currencies. The following exchange rates have been used for conversion: U.S. $1.00 = 25.07 baht = 2.49 ringgit at the end of 1987; and U.S. $1.00 = 25.7 baht = 2.7 ringgit for 1989 (annual averages). For data on Indonesia, see n. 9 of the text. Ellipses points indicate marginal or zero.

Korean FDI were small, and investments tended to be concentrated in resource development and in commerce and other service sectors aimed at facilitating export activities.

Since the mid-1980s, Korean FDI has been characterized by rapid expansion and by the increasing participation of manufacturing industries. The cumulative FDI for the latest four years (1986–89) amounted to U.S. $968 million, which was twice the cumulative FDI from 1968 to 1985 (U.S. $476 million). The manufacturing sector accounted for only 17 percent of investment stock at the end of 1985, but this share rose to an average of 39 percent during the period 1987–89. As will be seen below, the share of the manufacturing sector has been even higher for Korean FDI in ASEAN countries.

The factors accounting for the expansion of Korean manufacturing FDI since the second half of the 1980s are almost the same as in the case of Taiwan: a sharp rise in real wages, a revaluation of the local currency against the U.S. dollar, and trade conflict with the most important export market, the United States.

Recent trends in Korean direct investment in ASEAN are summarized in tables 9.9 and 9.10. These data illustrate the following features. First, for most ASEAN countries, substantial Korean direct investment began in the most recent two years. In particular, Korea's investment in Thailand and Indonesia was marginal before 1987. Second, with the exception of Indonesia, almost all direct investment in ASEAN has been in manufacturing industries (table 9.9).

Third, within the manufacturing sector, Korean firms tend to invest either in labor-intensive industries, such as foodstuffs, textiles and apparel, footwear and leather, wood and furniture, and other miscellaneous products, or in resource-intensive products, such as chemicals, nonferrous products, and fabricated metals (table 9.10). The first group of industries accounts for about 54 percent of the investment in Thailand, 81 percent in Indonesia, and 60 percent in the Philippines. The share of the second group of industries is high in resource-rich Malaysia. None of the ASEAN countries have received substantial direct investment from Korea's electrical and electronics industry.

These observations suggest that the pattern of Korean FDI in ASEAN has been almost the same as that of Taiwan: expansion in recent years and concentration in labor-intensive and technologically standardized industries. In addition, the average size of investment projects undertaken in ASEAN by Taiwan, Korea, and other Asian NIEs has been much smaller than that of projects undertaken by Japan (Ramstetter 1988; Thee 1990).[10]

10. Some Korean and Taiwanese firms undertaking FDI in ASEAN countries may be Japanese affiliates in those two Asian NIEs. At the moment, however, I cannot confirm this point. However, whether they are Japanese affiliates or pure Korean and Taiwanese firms, my argument is not significantly affected. Even if these firms were Japanese affiliates, their technologies should have been adapted to fit the NIEs' factor endowments. In addition, the management style and other intangible assets of those affiliates may have been largely localized since Japanese ownership in joint ventures in Korea and Taiwan has generally been as a minority. For the case of Korea, see, e.g., Koo (1985, 186–88).

Table 9.9 **Korea's Manufacturing Direct Investment in ASEAN (thousand U.S. dollars)**

	Thailand	Indonesia	Malaysia	Philippines
1973–85	1,871	11,993	26,488	2,009
1986	45	. . .	588	. . .
1987	997	2,349	240	2,062
1988	16,098	23,744	3,301	4,529
1989	13,363	76,383	33,858	8,758
1973–89	32,374	114,469	64,475	17,358
% of total	99.1	33.0	97.1	98.8

Source: Compiled from data in Rhee (1990). Original data were released by the Bank of Korea.
Note: "% of total" means share of manufacturing in total direct investment in all industries.

Table 9.10 **Industry Composition of Korea's Manufacturing Investment in ASEAN (outstanding investment stock as of the end of 1989) (thousand U.S. dollars)**

	Thailand	Indonesia	Malaysia	Philippines
Foodstuffs	. . .	25,685	. . .	. . .
Textiles and apparel	2,903	22,432	. . .	6,723
Footwear and leather	3,684	22,840	. . .	2,809
Wood and furniture	. . .	8,120	2,754	. . .
Paper	. . .	1,520	. . .	. . .
Chemicals	2,118	10,190	10,383	. . .
Nonferrous products	. . .	. . .	25,062	1,000
Primary metals	45	1,278	565	. . .
Fabricated metals	12,770	8,852	25,145	5,894
Other	10,854	13,552	566	932
Total	32,374	114,469	64,475	17,358

Source: See table 9.9.

9.4 The Asian Pacific Region as a Market for New Flows of Technologies: The Pull Factors

The analysis in preceding sections showed that, since the latter half of the 1980s, the Asian Pacific countries have seen intensive flows of production technologies, management skills, and marketing skills. These flows of technologies have been due not only to push factors, such as rising factor costs and rapid appreciation of currencies in the home countries of suppliers (as mentioned in secs. 9.2 and 9.3 above), but also to pull factors in the host countries. In other words, the reasons why Japanese and NIE firms have chosen the Asian Pacific region as a market for their managerial resources are also important. The pull factors in this region can be summarized as follows.

First, the absorptive capacity in Asia has increased considerably. The capacity for technology absorption may be defined as a synthesis of the educational and skill levels of the labor force, the availability of local entrepreneurship, and the government's ability to maintain a stable political and macroeconomic environment.[11]

Table 9.11 suggests a steady improvement in the educational levels of most Asian Pacific countries. It is noteworthy that Korea has by now achieved the same educational level as Japan in terms of both high school and postsecondary enrollment ratios. And, by the mid-1980s, the high school enrollment ratios of most ASEAN countries reached the levels attained by Asian NIEs in the early 1970s. These achievements in education have undoubtedly boosted the capacity of Asian developing countries to absorb foreign technologies. As Rosenberg (1982, 247–49) argued, historically, the countries that were most successful at borrowing technology were those that had well-educated populations.[12]

For other indicators of absorptive capacity, no direct and objective evidence can be shown. However, the perception of technology suppliers itself can suggest to some extent the absorptive capacity of host countries. For example, the positive response of Japanese firms in providing technologies through the OEM channel to Asian NIEs shows their recognition of the technological and management levels of firms in those countries. Regarding the policies of host countries, the capacity continuously to provide a politically and economically stable market environment is critical since this ensures the firms that they are not operating in a risky market; thus, they are more willing to make long-term investments, including human resource development. This relates to the second pull factor.

Second, the investment climate in the Asian Pacific region has been much more attractive, in terms of political and economic stability, than that in other developing parts of the world. In addition, the environment of the region as a whole has been further improved since the mid-1980s, in the sense that the favorable market conditions for foreign investment have spread from one

11. The increase in absorptive capacity by grading up the educational and technological level of the labor force is emphasized by Sekiguchi (1986), among others. Tran (1988) analyzed how Korea's synthetic fiber firms have increased their absorptive capacity and gradually substituted their own capital and technology for foreign resources. At the firm and government levels, the statement made by Vernon (1989, 36–37) is suggestive: "Some of the most critical factors in the successful transfer and application of technology are internal to the receiver of the technology: Internal to the country in terms of the economic and regulatory environment, internal to the firms in terms of the capacities, incentives, and attitudes of managers and technicians, and internal to the industrial structure of the country."

12. In its issue of 27 March 1991, the *Japan Economic Journal* (*Nihon keizai shinbun*) conducted a survey on the perception of top management of Japanese, American, and European firms. According to the results of the survey, the Asian Pacific countries will be considered as a promising investment region in the future, owing mainly to the high quality of the labor force.

Table 9.11 Educational Level of Asian Countries

	1965	1970	1975	1980	1984	1986
Japan:						
A	86	91	91	93	95	96
B	12.9	17.0	24.6	30.5	29.6	28.8
Korea:						
A	34	41	56	76	91	95
B	6.2	7.9	9.6	15.0	29.4	32.9
Hong Kong:						
A	34	41	49	64	69	. . .
B	5.4	7.4	10.1	10.5	12.8	. . .
Singapore:						
A	49	46	52	58	71	. . .
B	9.9	6.8	9.0	7.8	11.8[a]	. . .
Thailand:						
A	11	16	26	29	31	29
B	1.5	2.7	3.4	13.1	22.5[a]	19.6[b]
Philippines:						
A	41	49	54	65	68	68
B	18.8	19.8	18.4	27.7	34.1	38[b]
Malaysia:						
A	27	34	44	48	53	54
B	1.9	1.6	2.8	4.3	6.1	6.0[b]
Indonesia:						
A	12	12	20	29	39	41
B	1.5	2.8	2.4	3.9[c]	6.5	. . .
China:						
A	. . .	. . .	46	46	37	42
B	. . .	.1	.6	1.3	1.4	1.7

Source: Compiled from Unesco, *Statistical Yearbook.*

Note: A: high school enrollment ratio; B: postsecondary enrollment ratio. Ellipses points indicate that figures are not available.

[a]1983.

[b]1985.

[c]1981.

country to another and the area with a favorable investment climate has been expanded. In the region under review, we have witnessed that this area has expanded from the NIEs to Thailand in the mid-1980s (Chee 1988) to Indonesia (Thee 1990), and to Vietnam toward the end of the decade (Tran 1991a).

Government efforts to improve the investment climate may stem from a type of demonstration effect in the Asian Pacific region. The successful introduction of foreign managerial resources in a country may encourage neighboring countries to adopt similar policies to improve market conditions. The changes in external economic policies in Indonesia and Vietnam in the late 1980s, for example, may in part be explained by the demonstration effect from NIEs and Thailand.

Third, the Asian Pacific economy has experienced a rapid growth in the past three decades, and, given its current political stability and economic potential, the region has been considered as a growth center of the world. This has generated strong expectations among investors about the opportunities the region will provide. In addition, research on and international conferences about the region's economy have been intensively conducted. These activities contribute to the diffusion of knowledge and information about the economic situation and potential of the region and thus reduce the uncertainties of investment.

Fourth, the cost of the transfer of technology among the countries in the Asian Pacific region can be considered as small. The cost of transfer is not the cost of technology (the licensing fee) itself but a cost generated in the process of transferring a technology from one country to another. This includes communication (telephone, telex, etc.) costs, travel costs (for personnel in charge of the transfer project), and wages paid to the engineers and experts who help the transferees until the project begins its operations. According to Teece (1977), such transfer costs amount to 19 percent of the total cost (including the licensing fee) of the project.

Owing to geographic proximity and cultural affinities, the transfer cost of technologies provided by Japanese and NIE firms to other countries in the region can be considered as small, when compared to transferring technologies to other regions. In addition, for Japanese firms such costs may have declined over time owing to the learning effects of their previous FDI and other technology transfers in the region. For Taiwanese investors, the overseas Chinese networks in Southeast Asia enable them to reduce transfer costs.

Among these pull factors, the most important may be the second one. Political and economic stability is a precondition for firms to undertake FDI. Other factors promote and accelerate such investment. That is why after the Tien-an-men Square incident (June 1989), FDI in China has declined.

To be sure, the United States and some Western European countries have also become major markets for Japanese and NIE direct investment. These countries have indeed provided many pull factors, attracting FDI from East Asia. However, the Asian Pacific region is the single developing area of the world that has absorbed intensive flows of technology and other managerial resources from Japan and the NIEs. What implications will this fact hold for future economic development in the region?

9.5 Technology Transfer and Asian Pacific Dynamism: Implications of Recent Trends

The analysis in preceding sections suggests that, since the latter half of the 1980s, the Asian Pacific countries have seen intensive flows of production technologies, management skills, and marketing skills. Not only has the amount of managerial resources increased substantially, but the types of these resources have also been highly diverse. They include high technologies from Japan's electrical/electronics and other machinery-related industries, managerial resources from Japanese SMSFs, and labor-intensive technologies from Asian NIEs. The NIEs have increasingly played the role of both suppliers (of labor-intensive and standardized technologies) and recipients (of relatively sophisticated technologies from Japan), while ASEAN countries have been in a position to absorb various types of managerial resources.

From the economic development perspective of the Asian Pacific region, we may draw two implications from the trends in technology transfer since the second half of the 1980s. The first implication relates to the quantity or the amount of the flows of technologies, and the second one relates to the content or the structure of those flows.

9.5.1 Promotion of Industrialization by Intensive Flows of Technologies

The industrialization or economic development of a country is the result of many efforts, efforts that are not only economic but also political and social. Considering only the economic aspects, we can identify many indicators that determine the rate of economic growth. Saving and investment may be the most direct and important factors, as the Harrod-Domer model suggests. Industrial and trade policies are other areas that determine the success or failure of economic development. However, the experience of Japan, as well as that of Korea and Taiwan, also suggests the important role of foreign technologies in the industrialization process, even though, depending on policies and general technological levels in each country, the extent of that role and the channels utilized have been different.

The scope of this paper does not allow a detailed analysis of this point. I simply argue as follows. The importation of foreign technologies contributes to the process and the product innovations of recipient countries. The innovations have the following effects on economic development. On the macro level, the innovations result in an upward shift of the production function, which increases the rate of growth more than that of production factors. Moreover, some studies of the Japanese experience showed that the importation of technologies has enhanced domestic investment. This relates to the microeconomic effect of innovations. The availability of technologies enables the start of new industries. The importation of management skills or new organizational methods contributes to improvements in the operation of existing industries.

With these qualifications, we may say that the technology transfers from abroad cannot be a starter, but they can be promoters of industrialization in a country. Therefore, given the increasing absorptive capacity of Asian Pacific countries, the intensive flows of technologies since the mid-1980s may further enhance industrialization in the region. In addition, given the new features of Japanese FDI discussed in section 9.2 above, two related implications can be drawn here. First, since most new Japanese FDI projects have been export oriented, the implication is that new direct investment from Japan will contribute to the development of internationally competitive industries for Asian countries.

Second, since the mid-1980s, Japanese firms have invested in a wide range of industries. In particular, capital goods, intermediate goods, and parts-producing investment projects have increased substantially. This new feature is expected to upgrade, deepen, and broaden the industrial structure of Asian Pacific countries. Their industrial structure is expected to be much more sophisticated, and further industrialization in the region will be facilitated by new investments from Japan.

9.5.2 Facilitation of Asia's Further Industrialization by Increasing Availability of Various Levels of Technologies

Trends since the latter half of the 1980s also suggest that a wide range of different technologies is increasingly available in the Asian Pacific region. In particular, for ASEAN countries and other latecomers to industrialization in the region, many options for technology transfer have been provided, in terms of both supply sources of technology and channels of transfer. In this context, the increasingly strong presence of SMSFs and Asian NIEs as new sources of technologies is particularly noteworthy. This point reminds us of the argument regarding South-South technology transfer in the context of "appropriate technology" or the concept of an "optimal technological gap" stressed by Chen (1985).

The South-South technology transfer hypothesis suggests that the technologies transferred—usually from advanced southern countries to less developed southern countries—are more appropriate since the gap in factor endowments among southern countries is much smaller than that between North and South. The technologies developed and transferred by northern SMSFs also have the same characteristics. Those technologies are usually labor intensive, standardized, and used in small-scale operations. Thus, technologies transferred from SMSFs tend to fit the factor endowments of recipient southern countries.

The concept of an optimal technological gap is a modification of the concept *technological gap* suggested by Gerschenkron (1962)'s "advantages of backwardness" hypothesis. According to the technological gap argument, the greater the relative disparity in development level between a less developed country and more advanced countries, the faster the rate at which the former can catch up. In other words, the rate of technical progress in a relatively backward country is an increasing function of the gap between its own level of technology and that of the advanced countries. However, if the gap is too large, catching up may be impossible since the difference in technological capability is so great that the backward country cannot possibly apply or diffuse the advanced technology. For this reason, Chen (1985) suggested the concept of an *optimal technological gap*. If the gap is within a certain appropriate range, the rate of technical change in the backward region tends to rise rapidly, but the rate will decline along with further expansion of the gap. The level at which the rate of catching up is maximized is the optimal level.

In explaining the continuous spread of industrialization in the Asian Pacific region in the past twenty-five years or so, Kosai (1990, 6–7) pointed to three factors, of which the second is, interestingly, similar to the "optimal technological gap" argument: "(1) The demonstration effect of one country's continuous and easy-to-follow development patterns contributed to that of neighboring countries. (2) *Reasonably varying degree of differences in economic levels* among countries in the region meant each country can easily set a goal, and that the chances of catching-up, and the benefits to be expected from catching up were high. (3) The countries being chased took the development of the late comers as a challenge, and the competition spurred them on to further their own development" (my italics).

From the above discussion, we may hypothesize that the increasing role of SMSFs and Asian NIEs as suppliers of technologies will facilitate further industrialization in the region. In particular, intensive transfer of such tech nologies will help the development of the wide range of small-scale, labor-intensive industries (parts, peripheral products, and other supporting industries) that support the development of large-scale, capital intensive, and technologically sophisticated industries. The promotion of the development of such supporting industries will strengthen the industrial foundation of ASEAN countries and other latecomers in the region.

At the microeconomic level, not all firms within a single country, particularly a relatively large economy that has reached some level of industrialization, have the same level of technology. Most of the members of ASEAN are now countries of this type. In these countries, some relatively large firms, which have accumulated substantial managerial resources, including a large, highly qualified labor force, can efficiently absorb high technologies transferred from large Japanese firms.

In a word, the Asian Pacific region now has access to various sources of technologies. Combined with the increasing absorptive capacity of the countries in the region, the new trends in technology transfer since the latter half of the 1980s are likely to facilitate and promote further industrialization in this region.

9.6 Concluding Remarks

This paper has not touched on some other important aspects of technology transfer in the Asian Pacific region, such as transfer from the United States and other non-Japanese advanced sources, licensing arrangements, plant export, and other non-FDI channels of technology transfer from Asian NIEs. The technology transfer from Japan and the NIEs to China has also not been dealt with in detail. However, the paper has highlighted some important new trends relating to the issues under review. These include the intensive flows of technology through various channels from Japan and more recently from Asian NIEs and the multilayered structure of technological flows involving Japan's technology-intensive industries, small-scale projects by Japanese SMSFs, and labor-intensive industries from Asian NIEs. Combined with the increasing absorptive capacity of recipient countries, the new trends in technology transfer serve to facilitate further industrialization in the Asian Pacific region.

Economic development in the Asian Pacific region in the past twenty-five years or so can be viewed as a catching-up process by latecomers to industrialization. Korea, Taiwan, and other NIEs have attempted to catch up with Japan since the 1960s, starting with labor-intensive industries and then expanding to capital and technology-intensive industries. ASEAN countries and China have more recently joined this process by attempting to catch up with Asian NIEs in industries producing labor-intensive products. With the new trends in technology transfer discussed above, we may expect that such a multilayered pursuit process will be further promoted in the 1990s. Given the current economic reforms and open-door policy in Vietnam and the positive response of Asian NIEs to the country's new foreign investment law (Tran 1991a), it is very likely that Vietnam will join this multilayered pursuit process as part of the lower stratum of the region's industrialization.

References

Adachi, Fumihiko. 1991. Small and medium-sized firms in Japan's foreign direct investment. In Tran 1991b.

Chee, Peng Lim. 1988. Foreign direct investment and the changing investment climate in the ASEAN region. Discussion Paper no. 16. Tokyo: Seikei University, Center for Asian and Pacific Studies.

Chen, Edward K. Y. 1985. The newly industrializing countries as exporters of technology in Asia-Pacific. Paper presented at the sixth meeting of the Association of Development Research and Training Institute of Asia and the Pacific (ADIPA), Bangkok, June.

Galenson, Walter, ed. 1985. *Foreign trade and investment: Economic growth in the newly industrializing countries.* Madison: University of Wisconsin Press.

Gerschenkron, Alexander. 1962. *Economic backwardness in historical perspective.* Cambridge, Mass.: Harvard University Press.

Hill, Hal. 1985. *Foreign investment and industrialization in Indonesia.* Singapore: Oxford University Press.

Japan External Trade Organization (JETRO). Annual. *Sekai to Nihon no chokusetsu toshi* (Direct investment by Japan and the world). JETRO White Paper on Investment. Tokyo.

Koo, Bohn Young. 1985. The role of direct foreign investment in Korea's recent economic growth. In Galenson 1985.

Kosai, Yutaka. 1990. Asian economic growth: An overview: Asia in the year 2050. Discussion Paper no. 14. Tokyo: Japan Center for Economic Research, November.

Ministry of International Trade and Industry (MITI). 1986. *Kaigai toshi tokei soran* (Comprehensive statistics on Japan's foreign direct investment). Tokyo: Ministry of Finance.

———. 1987. *Tsusho hakusho* (White paper on international trade). Tokyo: Ministry of Finance.

———. 1988. *Tsusho hakusho* (White paper on international trade). Tokyo: Ministry of Finance.

———. 1989a. *Kaigai toshi tokei soran* (Comprehensive statistics on Japan's foreign direct investment). Tokyo: Ministry of Finance.

———. 1989b. *Tsusho hakusho* (White paper on international trade). Tokyo: Ministry of Finance.

Ogawa, Eiji. 1976. Nikkei sen-i kigyou ni okeru gijutsu iten (Technology transfer in Japanese textile affiliates in Asia). *Ajia Keizai* 17 (November): 49–61.

Oman, Charles. 1984. *New forms of international investment in developing countries.* Paris: OECD Development Center Studies.

Ramstetter, Eric D. 1988. Taiwan's direct foreign investment in Thailand: The potential for technology transfer. *Development and South-South Cooperation* 4 (December): 113–27.

Rhee, Sungsup. 1990. ANIEs integration into the global economy and implications for ASEAN. Paper presented at the Roving Seminar on Industrial Transformation and Regional Development, jointly organized by the United Nations Centre for Regional Development (Japan) and the National Institute of Public Administration (Malaysia).

Rosenberg, Nathan. 1982. *Inside the black box: Technology and economics.* Cambridge: Cambridge University Press.

Sekiguchi, Sueo, ed. 1983. *ASEAN-Japan relations: Investment.* Singapore: Institute of Southeast Asian Studies.

———. 1986. Chokusetsu toshi o tsujiru gijutsuiten (Technology transfer through foreign direct investment). In Sekiguchi and Tran 1986.

Sekiguchi, S., and Tran V. T., eds. 1986. *Chokusetsu toushi to gijutsuiten* (Foreign direct investment and technology transfer). Research Report no. 56. Tokyo: Japan Center for Economic Research.

Somsak, Tunbunlertchai. 1991. The changing pattern of Japanese direct investment in Thailand. In Tran 1991b.

Teece, David J. 1977. Technology transfer by multinational firms: The resource cost of transferring technological knowhow. *Economic Journal* 87 (June): 242–61.

Thee, Kian Wie. 1990. *The investment surge from the East Asian newly-industrializing countries into Indonesia.* Paper prepared for the Economics of Trade and Development Seminars, Research School of Pacific Studies, Australian National University.

Tran Van Tho. 1988. Foreign capital and technology in the process of catching-up by the developing countries: The experience of the synthetic fiber industry in the Republic of South Korea. *Developing Economies* 26 (December): 386–402.

———. ed. 1991a. *Betonamu keizai to Ajia-taiheiyou* (The Vietnamese economy and the Asian Pacific region). Tokyo: Japan Center for Economic Research.

———. ed. 1991b. *Japan's direct investment in Thailand.* Tokyo: Japan Center for Economic Research.

———. 1992. *Sangyo hatten to takokusekigyo* (The international spread of industrial development and multinational corporations). Tokyo: Toyo Keizai.

United Nations Centre on Transnational Corporations (UNCTC). 1987. *Transnational corporations and technology transfer: Effects and policy issues.* New York.

Vernon, Raymond. 1989. Technological development: The historical experience. Seminar Paper no. 39. Washington, D.C.: World Bank, Economic Development Institute.

Comment Takatoshi Ito

Tran Van Tho's paper describes and analyzes technological transfers from Japan and from Korea and Taiwan to Asian countries. The paper serves four purposes. First, it describes "facts," namely, types of technological transfers (FDI, licensing arrangements, OEM), time series of FDI, destinations of FDI, FDI by industry, and size of firms. Second, the paper attempts to analyze reasons for those facts. Third, FDI from Korea and Taiwan to other Asian countries is documented. Fourth, the paper derives implications for economic growth from technological transfer. It is a nice paper, highlighting Japanese investment in Asia.

This paper documents FDI, licensing arrangements, and OEM, with an implicit assumption that they represent technological transfers. However, FDI etc. are only proxies of technological transfers and may not be necessary or sufficient for technological transfers in a rigorous sense: even if factories are built, the Japanese management may not be willing to train workers in a host nation (a frequently heard complaint); and, even if a factory is not built, technical assistance could be sent so that know-how may be provided. The reader should be reminded of this qualification.

Tran's paper invokes many interesting questions. I feel that the following issues deserve more attention in future research on Japanese foreign direct investment.

Obviously, there may be conflicts between Japanese firms and host countries. Japanese firms may want to limit technological transfers by not training managers or by refusing to reveal contents of key components. Japanese firms may also restrict the sales of assembled goods, preventing them from coming back to the Japanese market to harm the parent company. (An example is that a Japanese electronics company put restrictions on sales to the U.S. market when it provided technology for videocassette recorders.) On the other hand, recipient countries would want to maximize transfers by restricting the type of FDI. They may allow joint ventures, barring 100 percent subsidiaries; they may insist on a licensing agreement.

In other words, Japanese (or Korean and Taiwanese) parent firms maximize their profits by FDI (limiting the amount of transfers), while the recipient countries maximize their profits by learning (sometimes copying or stealing) technologies. Hence, technological transfers have to be placed in the context of a trade-off between these two possibly conflicting maximizing agents. How are these conflicts resolved in the actual cases of East Asian countries?

Reasons why FDI to Asia increased rapidly should be discussed in a separate section, carefully differentiating "pull factors" and "push factors": (i) looking for cheap and abundant labor; (ii) exchange rates; (iii) political stability; (iv) economic stability; (v) educational level; and (vi) changes in

Takatoshi Ito is professor of economics at Hitotsubashi University and a research associate of the National Bureau of Economic Research.

regulations concerning capital controls. The reader should ponder which ones were most important. Note that some of the push and pull factors may have a multiplier effect. Technological transfers enhance economic progress, which in turn yields political progress. Note that Japanese FDI to the United States increased more than FDI to Asian countries.

As an implication of technological transfers, the paper points out that technological transfers propel industrialization. However, technological transfers are only one factor in industrialization. Saving and investment and monetary and fiscal policies may be more important. One important question in the theory of economic development is how great a difference technological transfers make. Would such transfers make growth faster, allowing foreign capital to come in (with, one hopes, technological transfers)? Or would it be better in the long run to nurture domestic infant industries (avoiding "rents" being siphoned out)? Korea's development seems to have more of the former element than Japan's did.

Comment Bih Jane Liu

Foreign direct investment and technology transfer have not been the focus of my research for the past several years. Thus, as the commentator on this very interesting and informative paper, I shall only mention several points that might need further clarification.

The first question is related to the relation between foreign direct investment and technology transfer. In this paper, the author uses the amount of foreign direct investment as the proxy for the amount of technology transfer that comes along with foreign direct investment. This usage might create inaccuracy problems because the extent of technology transfer that could be brought up with foreign direct investment also depends on other factors such as the attitude of investors toward technology transfer.

According to table 9.6, the accumulated amount of foreign direct investment from Taiwan to Southeast Asia is U.S. \$86 million for the period 1959–87. But other data sources indicate that the investment in Thailand alone by Taiwan in 1987 had already reached U.S. \$299 million. This wide difference might imply that the investment data used in this paper are seriously underestimated. This underestimation, I suspect, comes from the utilization of the investment data collected by the Investment Commission of the Ministry of Economic Affairs, and the Investment Commission's data are widely believed to be underestimated. This is because, unlike large Taiwanese investors, who tend to report their foreign investments to the Investment Commission in order to get assistance for their foreign endeavors, small Taiwanese investors

Bih Jane Liu is professor of economics at National Taiwan University.

are reluctant to report such investments since the review process is time consuming.

Tran argues that, according to the South-South technology transfer hypothesis and the theory of the optimal technological gap, increasing participation in foreign direct investment by small and medium-sized Asian firms is to the advantage of Asian developing countries in their pursuit of technology transfer and industrialization. However, on the contrary, it could also be argued that small and medium-sized firms, when compared with large firms, are often more conservative in transferring technology, which, in any case, may not embody the latest standards and designs that host countries seek. This means that the increasing participation of small and medium-sized firms in foreign direct investment might not be as helpful as the author expected in speeding technology transfer and thus the industrialization of Asian developing countries. As a matter of fact, the increasing participation of small and medium-sized firms in foreign direct investment was driven by their smaller profit margins, and investment abroad seems to be the direct solution to their increasing labor costs and the appreciation of their own currencies.

It seems to me that the author has been quite optimistic about the contribution of technology transfer to the industrialization of host countries. However, this contribution depends not only on the labor quality of the host countries, as the author has emphasized in this paper, but also on the backward and forward linkage effects and dynamic externalities such as learning by doing or learning by producing. Without these linkage effects and dynamic externalities, we might have the case proposed by McCulloch and Yellen (1982). That is, when one country enjoys clear technological superiority in one sector while in others its technology is the same as other countries, then capital mobility between these two countries can serve as a substitute for technology transfer. This implies that, as long as capital is perfectly mobile internationally, the extent of technology transfer has no effect on employment, income distribution, or national welfare. In such an extreme case, intensive inflows of technology are neither a necessary nor a sufficient condition for further industrialization, that is, not as the author has asserted.

Finally, one issue that has not been mentioned clearly in this paper is the resemblance of foreign investment patterns between Japan and other Asian newly industrialized economies (NIEs). It was observed that Taiwan and South Korea were basically following the earlier patterns of Japanese foreign investments. However, we do not know whether such resemblances in investment patterns between Japan and Asian NIEs still exist in the 1980s. Another interesting phenomenon left unexplained in this paper is that, according to table 9.2, the share of foreign direct investment by Asian NIEs in manufacturing industries is decreasing while the share of Japan is increasing.

Reference

McCulloch, Rachel, and Janet Yellen. 1982. Can capital movements eliminate the need for technology transfer? *Journal of International Economics* 12:95–106.

10 Japanese Foreign Direct Investment and Its Effect on Foreign Trade in Asia

Shujiro Urata

The world has witnessed a rapid expansion of foreign direct investment (FDI) in the latter half of the 1980s. During the 1960s, world FDI grew at about the same rate as world trade. Although the annual average growth rate of world FDI during the 1970s increased to around 15 percent, it was lower than the corresponding rate for world trade, which was recorded at 19.9 percent. In the early 1980s, world FDI declined mainly owing to slow economic growth and a recession. In 1983, the growth of world FDI regained growth momentum. It was only in 1986, however, that world FDI started to experience an unprecedented increase. Between 1985 and 1989, world trade grew at an average annual rate of 12.5 percent; world FDI grew even faster, at the rate of 33.1 percent.[1]

Major investing countries have been the United States, the United Kingdom, Japan, Germany, and other developed countries. In particular, the increase of Japanese FDI has been remarkably high since the mid-1980s, and in 1989 Japan was the world's largest FDI supplier in terms of the value of annual flows. Most of the leading investing countries are also major recipient countries of FDI, with the notable exception of Japan. In spite of the relative decline of developing countries as recipients of FDI, FDI inflow to developing Asian countries has increased remarkably in the latter half of the 1980s.

The rapid world FDI expansion in the latter half of the 1980s can be attributed to various factors. Strong world economic performance provided a favorable environment for FDI. Changes in the policies concerning FDI and foreign trade contributed to the expansion of FDI in developing countries. Specifically, liberalization and promotion policies toward FDI, as well as restrictive

Shujiro Urata is associate professor of economics at Waseda University, Tokyo.

The author is grateful to Anne Krueger, Takatoshi Ito, Tran Van Tho, Yoo Jung-ho, and other participants at the conference for helpful comments and discussions.

1. International Monetary Fund, *International Financial Statistics* (various issues).

policies toward imports, promoted FDI in developed countries. The substantial realignment of the exchange rates of the major currencies also played an important role in precipitating FDI by changing the pattern of comparative advantage of a number of countries. Finally, technological progress in services such as transportation and communications provided an added impetus to the increase of FDI.

FDI has been argued to influence the economic and trade performance of the investing as well as the recipient countries. FDI promotes the economic growth of recipient countries by creating employment, by transferring foreign technology, and possibly by expanding exports. The effect on investing countries is more mixed. FDI may improve the allocation of resources by speeding up the process of structural adjustment, while it may deteriorate the economic situation by removing the industrial base out of the investing countries, a "hollowing out" of the industry.

The purpose of this paper is twofold. One is to examine the changing pattern of Japanese FDI over time. My analysis, which will be focused on Japanese FDI in Asia, attempts to identify the distinguishable characteristics that emerged in the latter half of the 1980s. The other objective is to examine empirically the behavior of the Asian affiliates of Japanese firms and their effect on foreign trade in the Asian region. Such analyses not only deepen our understanding of Japanese FDI but also provide policymakers with valuable information in formulating foreign economic policies.

The structure of the paper is as follows. In section 10.1, the changing patterns of Japanese FDI are discussed chronologically, and, in section 10.2, the effect of Asian affiliates of Japanese firms on Asian trade is analyzed by comparing the pattern of affiliates' trade and that of overall Asian trade. Finally, in section 10.3, some concluding comments will be presented.

10.1 The Changing Pattern of Japanese Foreign Direct Investment[2]

10.1.1 The Period before the Mid-1980s

After World War II, Japanese FDI had resumed by 1951, but its magnitude remained low until the late 1960s, for various reasons. First, government regulations on FDI, which were imposed strictly until the late 1960s to cope with the shortage of foreign exchange, discouraged Japanese firms from undertaking investment abroad. Second, abundant investment opportunities inside Japan provided by the rapidly growing economy reduced the attractiveness of overseas investment. Third, lack of experience in undertaking FDI as well as lack of firm-specific assets such as technology and management know-how of the Japanese firms led to a decision by the Japanese firms that overseas markets would be better served by exports rather than FDI.

2. This section expands the discussion in Urata (1990, 1991).

Until the late 1960s, Japanese FDI was concentrated mainly in natural resource sectors and in commerce. FDI in natural resource sectors was undertaken mainly in developing countries in order to secure a stable supply of raw materials for manufacturing production in Japan, whose endowment of natural resources is very limited. Examples of such FDI in Asia include petroleum drilling in Indonesia, iron ore mining in Malaysia, and copper mining in the Philippines. In contrast, FDI in commercial activities taking the form of setting up a distribution network for Japanese exports was undertaken mainly in developed countries, in order to promote Japanese exports. Of the limited amount of FDI in manufacturing during the 1960s, a large portion was undertaken in developing countries to capture their local market because the import protection policies pursued by these countries made exporting to these markets difficult; local production therefore proved to be the only means for serving the local market.

In the late 1960s, Japanese FDI started to increase rapidly, with a concentration in Asian newly industrializing economies (NIEs) (the NIEs hereafter) and in manufacturing activities such as textiles and consumer electronics. Indeed, FDI by Japanese firms was so active at that time that the period around 1970 was characterized as the "first FDI boom." Active FDI by Japanese firms may be explained by both internal factors in Japan and external factors in Asia. As for the internal factors, a decline in the competitiveness of Japanese products in the foreign market, which emerged in the late 1960s, played a crucial role in promoting Japanese FDI. Faced with a decline in competitiveness, Japanese producers shifted their production to the countries where production would be carried out at lower cost.

Several factors that led to a decline in the competitiveness of Japanese products may be identified. To begin with, an increase in the price of Japanese products in overseas markets, resulting from rising wages and appreciation of the yen, led to a loss of competitiveness of Japanese products, especially for labor-intensive products. The rising wages resulted from the shortage of labor, which in turn was attributable to rapid economic expansion, and the appreciation of the yen was the consequence of accumulated current account surplus. Furthermore, trade friction with developed countries made further expansion of Japanese exports difficult, forcing Japanese firms to seek to move production overseas. Finally, liberalization of Japanese policies toward foreign exchange transactions provided an added impetus to the outflow of FDI.

Turning to the factors in Asia that attracted Japanese FDI, one can identify the abundance of low-wage labor with good quality and FDI promotion policies, which were pursued by setting up export processing zones and by providing preferential tax treatment. The export promotion policies of the NIEs, especially strongly applied to foreign investors, led to an increase of Japanese FDI because one of the motives behind active FDI by Japanese firms was to secure an export base. Moreover, provision of GSP (Generalized System of Preferences) treatment by developed countries to a number of Asian developing countries including the Asian NIEs increased the attractiveness of these countries as an export base for Japanese firms.

The outbreak of the first oil crisis in 1973 brought an end to the first FDI boom by Japanese firms (figure 10.1). The balance-of-payments situation deteriorated precipitously not only in Japan but also in other oil-importing countries. Contractionary monetary policies adopted in the oil-importing countries to overcome the difficult economic situation discouraged FDI. In addition, anti-Japanese movements in some Asian countries caused by the "overpresence" of Japanese firms discouraged Japanese FDI as well.

With economic recovery in the aftermath of the first oil crisis, Japanese FDI started to increase slowly in the second half of the 1970s. The rate of increase was intensified in 1978, when the Japanese yen appreciated. Despite a slight recovery, however, Japanese FDI did not increase much until the early 1980s. One notable development during the latter half of the 1970s is the change in geographic distribution of Japanese FDI. The share of developed countries increased, as Japanese firms stepped up their efforts in increasing FDI in these countries to cope with intensified trade friction in products such as electronics. Among the Asian countries, Japanese FDI shifted from the NIEs to Association of Southeast Asian Nations (ASEAN) countries for the following reasons. The increase in wages in the NIEs resulting from the shortage of labor reduced the attractiveness of these economies as hosts to FDI. To deal with the unfavorable labor situation in the Asian NIEs, Japanese firms in search of lower wages shifted FDI from the Asian NIEs to ASEAN countries.

In 1981, Japanese FDI increased sharply, as a number of direct investments related to natural resources were undertaken in the developing countries in Asia and in Latin America. Because of a remarkable increase in Japanese FDI, the early 1980s was characterized as the "second FDI boom." The second FDI boom did not last long, however, as Japanese FDI declined in 1982 and remained at about the same level until 1986. The stagnation of Japanese FDI in the early 1980s can be attributed to the following factors. As for Japanese FDI in developed countries, depreciation of the yen vis-à-vis the U.S. dollar made exporting profitable for Japanese firms and thus reduced the incentive for them to undertake FDI. As for Japanese FDI in developing countries, a slowdown in their economic growth, caused mainly by the deterioration in their foreign debt situation, discouraged FDI. Deterioration in the foreign debt situation could in turn mainly be attributed to the expansionary development policies pursued by these countries in the 1970s and in the early 1980s.

10.1.2 The Period after the Mid-1980s

Japanese FDI started to increase rapidly in 1986, and the increase continued until 1989. In 1990, Japanese FDI declined for the first time in eight years. The speed of the increase during the period 1986–89 was unprecedentedly high, as the average annual growth rate for the period was as high as 53.3

percent.[3] As a result of rapid FDI growth, the ratios of FDI to GNP and to gross fixed investment in Japan increased from 1.0 and 0.2 percent, respectively, in 1980 to 5.9 and 1.7 percent in 1989.[4] The rapid increase of Japanese FDI at this time, which is described as the "third FDI boom," was precipitated by the rapid appreciation of the yen. In addition, protectionist policies and movements toward regionalization in developed countries, and liberalization policies and favorable economic performance in developing countries, contributed to the increase of Japanese FDI in both regions.

Several notable characteristics of Japanese FDI in the latter half of the 1980s can be identified. First, the share of developed countries increased, as the combined share of North America and Europe in overall Japanese FDI increased from 54.1 percent in 1980–85 to 73.9 percent in 1986–89. Second, following the pattern originated in the early 1980s, a large portion of Japanese FDI in the latter half of the 1980s was undertaken in the nonmanufacturing sector; for the period 1951–79, the share of nonmanufacturing in overall FDI was 65.8 percent, while the corresponding share for the period 1980–89 was 75.1. Below I discuss some of the characteristics of Japanese FDI in the latter half of the 1980s in more detail and examine the factors behind such development by focusing separately on Japanese FDI in developed countries and in developing countries, with a particular emphasis on the developing countries in Asia.

Among the recipient countries of Japanese FDI, the share of developed countries increased during the 1980s. Several reasons may be given for this development. First, yen appreciation increased the attractiveness of overseas production as it reduced the export competitiveness of Japanese products by increasing the prices of Japanese products in the foreign market. It should be noted that the appreciation of the yen facilitated overseas investment by Japanese firms as it lowered the value of foreign assets in terms of the yen. Second, continuing trade friction with the United States and European countries forced Japanese firms to undertake FDI in these countries in order to maintain their markets. Third, the anticipated integration of the European Community (EC) in 1992 accelerated the pace of Japanese FDI as Japanese firms are eager to secure a foothold in the enlarged EC. The industries that have undertaken FDI in developed countries acting on these motivations include automobiles and electronic machinery. Finally, Japanese firms with abundant liquidity have found such assets as real estate in the developed countries, especially in the United States, very attractive.

The share of the developing countries in overall Japanese FDI declined during the 1980s because Japanese firms expanded their investment in the devel-

3. Unless otherwise noted, the statistics on Japanese FDI used in the paper are based on data reported by firms to the Ministry of Finance.

4. These figures are on a balance-of-payments basis.

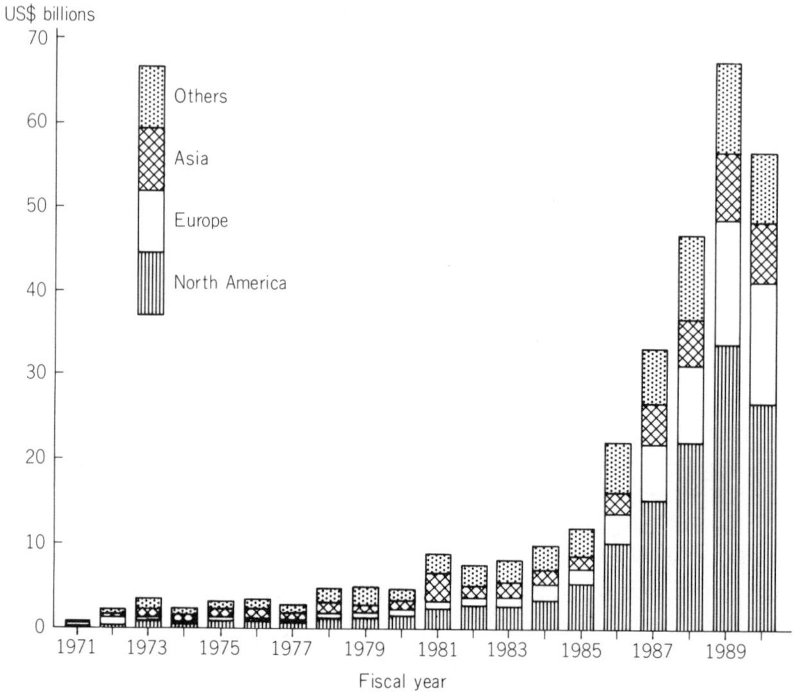

Fig. 10.1 Japanese foreign direct investment by region.
Source: Ministry of Finance statistics (reporting basis).

oped countries very rapidly. In spite of the relative decline in their shares, the magnitude of Japanese FDI in developing countries, especially the Asian developing countries, increased substantially. Annual reported Japanese FDI in Asia increased from $1.4 billion in 1985 to $8.2 billion in 1989. In 1989, the share of Asia in overall Japanese FDI stood at 12.2 percent. Among the countries in Asia, the Asian NIEs, the ASEAN countries, and China captured as much as 98.6 percent of Japanese FDI in 1989. As for the individual countries among the NIEs and ASEAN countries, the largest recipients in 1989 were Singapore, Hong Kong, and Thailand, in descending order in terms of the reported value of FDI; this pattern represents a shift away from Korea, Taiwan, and Indonesia, which captured substantial shares of Japanese FDI in the earlier period.

As a result of the rapid expansion of Japanese FDI in Asia since 1986, the Japanese share of overall FDI inflow for a number of Asian countries increased, although there are sizable year-to-year fluctuations. On an individual country basis, in 1989 Japan was the largest foreign investor in all Asian NIEs and ASEAN countries except Hong Kong.[5] These statistics indicate that the

5. Based on statistics published by official sources of the individual countries.

effect of Japanese FDI on the economic activities of the Asian countries is likely to be substantial. It should be noted, however, that the importance of the NIEs as an investor in Asia has been growing rapidly.

A large share of Japanese FDI in Asia has been in the nonmanufacturing sector. Indeed, the share of nonmanufacturing for Japanese FDI in Asia has been increasing over time; on the basis of the cumulative FDI since 1951, the share of nonmanufacturing increased from 56 percent in 1978 to 62 percent in 1989. The increase in the share of nonmanufacturing in Japanese FDI in Asia has been realized as a rapid increase of FDI in commerce, construction, finance, services, transportation, and real estate. The rapid expansion of Japanese FDI in nonmanufacturing in Asia can be attributed not only to such supply-side factors as the globalization of Japanese nonmanufacturing firms but also to such demand-side factors as the rapid increase of local demand for nonmanufacturing activities, resulting from remarkable economic expansion. Specifically, increased demand for final consumption by household has given rise to demand for retail services provided by supermarkets and department stores, while active fixed investment induced by favorable economic performance has led to an increase in demand for construction services. Moreover, liberalization and deregulation in the financial sector in a number of Asian countries resulted in active FDI in that sector.

Although the share of manufacturing in Japanese FDI in Asia has been declining over time, its share is still somewhat larger than the corresponding share for Japanese FDI in other parts of the world; the share of manufacturing in the cumulative Japanese FDI in Asia at the end of 1989 was 38.5 percent, whereas the corresponding share for the world as a whole was substantially lower, at 26.9 percent (see table 10.1). Among the manufacturing subsectors, the share of electrical machinery has been increasing rapidly for both the NIEs and ASEAN countries. For the manufacturing subsectors other than electrical machinery, there are wide variations in shares between the NIEs and ASEAN countries. For the NIEs, chemicals, general machinery, and food captured significantly large shares, whereas, for ASEAN countries, ferrous and nonferrous metals and textiles captured large shares. It should be noted here that, over time, the composition of Japanese FDI in the NIEs has been changing from such labor-intensive sectors as textiles to such capital intensive and technology-intensive sectors as machinery, while the composition of Japanese FDI in ASEAN countries shifted from such natural resource–based sectors as food and wood and pulp to labor-intensive sectors and then to capital intensive sectors.

Various factors contributed to the active FDI in the manufacturing sector in Asia by Japanese firms. Let us first discuss the factors mainly associated with the investor, Japan, and later those related to the recipients, the Asian countries. As already mentioned, the rapid appreciation of the yen deteriorated the competitiveness of Japanese products, thereby prompting Japanese producers to shift their production overseas. Moreover, rising wages due to the shortage

Table 10.1 **Japanese FDI in Asia: Cumulative Reported Amount (in million U.S. dollars), 1951–89**

	Asia		NIEs		ASEAN		World	
Sector	Amount	Share	Amount	Share	Amount	Share	Amount	Share
Food	1,049	2.6	685	3.4	301	1.7	3,266	1.3
Textiles	1,569	3.9	433	2.2	1,003	5.7	3,203	1.3
Wood and pulp	450	1.1	50	.3	385	2.2	2,654	1.0
Chemicals	2,077	5.1	1,307	6.6	712	4.1	8,649	3.4
Metals	2,578	6.4	449	2.3	2,072	11.8	9,261	3.6
General mach.	1,387	3.4	774	3.9	543	3.1	6,479	2.6
Electric mach.	3,348	8.3	1,637	8.2	1,447	8.3	14,676	5.8
Trans. mach.	1,326	3.3	625	3.1	622	3.5	9,009	3.5
Other manufac.	1,807	4.5	929	4.7	739	4.2	8,932	3.5
Manufac. total	15,591	38.5	6,891	34.6	7,824	44.6	66,127	26.9
Agri.-forestry	297	.7	46	.2	236	1.3	1,205	.5
Fishing	177	.4	8	.04	119	.7	678	.3
Mining	7,124	17.6	14	.07	6,997	33.9	15,211	6.0
Construction	643	1.6	375	1.9	257	1.5	2,089	.8
Commerce	2,575	6.4	2,077	10.4	439	2.5	25,159	9.9
Finance	3,588	8.9	3,054	15.3	514	2.9	57,271	22.6
Services	4,815	11.9	3,617	18.2	540	3.1	23,375	9.2
Transportation	982	2.4	901	4.5	58	.3	15,268	6.0
Real estate	2,351	5.8	1,957	9.8	297	1.7	34,742	13.7
Others	1,632	4.0	493	2.5	121	.7	7,515	3.0
Nonmanufac.	24,184	59.8	12,542	63.0	9,577	54.6	182,514	71.9
Branches	628	1.6	473	2.4	118	.7	4,659	1.8
Real estate	37	.1	14	.07	13	.07	595	.2
Total	40,465	100.0	19,919	100.0	17,531	100.0	253,896	100.0

Source: Ministry of Finance.

of labor and rising land prices in Japan provided an additional incentive for overseas production. Faced with changes in the cost of production between that in Japan and that in Asia, Japanese firms sought mainly three objectives from overseas production. One was to shift the sources of exports to developed countries by Japanese firms from Japan to Asian countries. Another was to substitute local production for exports to Asian countries. Finally, a number of Japanese firms set up a production base in Asia to supply products to the Japanese market; as such activity has become popular among Japanese producers, it has come to be called "reverse import" in Japan.

In addition to these cost factors, the factors associated with industrial organization, such as the behavior of rivals and customer firms, prompted some Japanese firms to undertake FDI. Specifically, a number of cases are reported in which some Japanese firms undertook FDI in order to keep up with rival firms that set up affiliates overseas. It is also rather common to observe that the motivation behind FDI by some Japanese firms is to follow their customers overseas in order to maintain their sales. This type of FDI is particularly noticeable in the machinery sectors, as the production of machinery products requires numerous components that are supplied by subcontractors. Indeed, one of the distinctive characteristics of Japanese FDI in Asia is the high share of small and medium-sized firms, a large portion of which supply components to large assembly firms.

Turning to the factors in Asia that promoted the inflow of FDI, it would be useful to divide Asia into the NIEs, on the one hand, and ASEAN countries, on the other. This is because the timing of active inflow of FDI differs in these two groups of countries and because the causal factors that induced FDI inflow differ between them. For the NIEs that attracted FDI notably until 1987, FDI promotion policies played an important role. Such policies were adopted in the hope that FDI would speed up the process of structural change required for their continued economic growth. Specifically, policymakers in Korea, Singapore, and Taiwan thought that the development of high-tech sectors, their targeted sectors, would be promoted by FDI because FDI brings in valuable technologies. In Hong Kong, such policies as the provision of technical training to factory workers were implemented to make Hong Kong a more desirable place for prospective FDI.

In the late 1980s, however, the NIEs became less attractive as hosts to manufacturing FDI for various reasons. For example, the appreciation of these currencies against the U.S. dollar and to some extent against the Japanese yen, as well as rising wages in the NIEs, increased the cost of production in these countries. Moreover, the abolition by the United States of the GSP status of the NIEs' exports in 1989 discouraged FDI inflow in the NIEs. Instead of the NIEs, the economies of the ASEAN countries, especially Thailand, attracted FDI in manufacturing, as they could provide the low-wage labor necessary for undertaking labor-intensive manufacturing processes. Liberalization policies toward FDI as well as foreign trade adopted by these countries also helped attract FDI. Behind the shift toward the outward-oriented development strategy of ASEAN countries, there must have been a recognition on the part of ASEAN governments that the economic success of the NIEs was achieved by an outward-looking strategy.

10.1.3 The Regional Strategy of Japanese Firms

So far we have examined the changing patterns of Japanese FDI and the factors behind such developments without explicitly analyzing the corporate strategy of Japanese firms. In this section, I attempt to identify the corporate strategy of Japanese firms that lies behind the patterns of FDI observed above, with a focus on Asia. It should be noted that a number of Japanese firms formulate global strategies, covering the following three regions: Asia (including Japan), North America, and Western Europe. Two notable developments should be mentioned. One is an increasing emphasis on regional strategy. Such a development is not only in response to regionalization movements in Western Europe and North America but also in recognition of the fact that it is advantageous to undertake production in the proximity of the market. The other development is that, within each region, different processes such as research and development and manufacturing are assigned to the areas where they may be performed most efficiently. As such, for a number of Japanese firms, corporate strategy toward the domestic market (i.e., the Japanese market) and that toward the overseas market (especially the Asian market) are formulated in close coordination.

Among various manufacturing subsectors, I examine the corporate strategy of the Japanese firms in the machinery sector for the following two reasons. One is the large share of the machinery sector in Japanese FDI, as described above. The other is because a new strategy has been adopted by some Japanese machinery firms, one whose characteristics are different from the characteristics of the corporate strategies employed by Japanese firms in other sectors or those observed in the earlier period.

Earlier, we found that the machinery sector, especially electrical machinery, has actively undertaken FDI. At least two reasons may be given for such a development. First, machinery products were frequently subject to trade friction. In order to get around the barriers imposed on Japanese exports, Japanese firms set up plants in developed countries as well as in developing countries. Second, machinery products are suitable for a production arrangement under which international division of labor is pursued within the firm. This is because the production process of the machinery products may be broken down into a number of subprocesses, and thus each process may be located in a country where that particular process may be performed most efficiently. Indeed, this is the strategy that a number of Japanese firms adopted in the latter half of the 1980s.

Specifically, the following kind of production arrangement has been adopted by some Japanese electronics producers. High-tech products such as semiconductors are produced by a parent company in Japan or by subsidiaries in other developed countries or in the NIEs, where high technological capability exists. These electronic components are then shipped to subsidiaries in ASEAN countries, where final products such as televisions or refrigerators are assembled by local labor. Such a division of the production process may be described as an interprocess, intrafirm production arrangement, and the type of international trade that such an arrangement gives rise to may be called interprocess, intrafirm, intraindustry trade. In the next section, I will examine empirically whether such production and trade patterns may be observed in Asia.

In a development somewhat related to the production arrangement just described, a number of Japanese firms have adopted a product differentiation strategy internationally by assigning the production of a product to the country where that particular product may be produced most efficiently or to a country where such a product is in great demand. For example, standard color televisions are produced by affiliates in ASEAN countries because their production requires only standardized technology and because they are in great demand in these countries. In contrast, large-screen televisions capable of receiving satellite broadcasts are produced in Japan because the sophisticated technologies necessary for their production exist in Japan and because there is a rapidly growing demand for such products in Japan.

New types of production arrangements under the new strategy discussed above are quite different from those under the old strategy. Under the old strategy, production is undertaken in the country where the market exists, without considering production efficiency. Several factors may be singled out as promoting the new strategy. One is the accumulated experience of Japanese firms in overseas business activities. Another is improvements in the quality of international communications and transportation services, which in turn were made possible by technological progress and liberalization policies. This factor played an important role, especially in the development of the interprocess, intrafirm, international production system. A number of firms have set up international procurement offices (IPOs) to manage the system efficiently. Singapore has been the most popular site for the IPOs because of its advantageous geographic location and its efficient and restriction-free communications and transportation services. It should be noted that Japanese FDI in these service sectors contributed significantly to setting up service networks throughout Asia.

10.2 Asian Affiliates of Japanese Firms and Foreign Trade in Asia

In the previous section, the changing patterns of Japanese FDI from the 1960s to the 1980s were discussed, and a number of hypotheses regarding the behavior of Japanese firms were presented without any statistical evidence being provided. In this section, I attempt to examine empirically the validity of some of those hypotheses with the objective of deepening our understanding of the behavior as well as the effect of Japanese firms in Asia.

10.2.1 Patterns of Sales and Procurement

Earlier, I argued that a main motive behind Japanese FDI in Asia is to set up an export base. In this section, I test the validity of this hypothesis by examining the pattern of sales of the Asian affiliates of Japanese firms. Moreover, I examine the pattern of procurement of intermediate goods and capital equipment of these affiliates. In the analysis, I compare the behavior of the affiliates in Asia with that of affiliates in other parts of the world to determine the special characteristics of the sales and procurement patterns of the affiliates in Asia.

Table 10.2 shows the geographic distribution of the sales of overseas affiliates of Japanese firms. The table shows the figures for the manufacturing sec-

Table 10.2 Sales and Procurement of Foreign Affiliates of Japanese Firms (percentage shares)

Affiliates	Local Market	Japan	Asia	N. America	Europe	Others
Sales destinations (1988):						
Asia	59.8	13.7	11.4	8.7	4.5	1.9
NIEs	56.1	15.1	11.7	9.8	5.3	2.1
ASEAN4	61.1	12.5	13.0	7.9	3.6	1.9
U.S.	95.0	3.4	.2	.9	.4	.1
EC	75.7	1.3	.7	1.3	20.3	.6
World	78.2	7.1	4.1	3.8	5.4	1.4
Procurement sources:						
Intermediate goods (1988):						
Asia	47.2	41.3	9.1	.6	.7	1.0
NIEs	49.6	41.9	6.9	.3	.3	1.1
ASEAN4	41.9	39.2	14.9	1.7	1.6	.9
U.S.	36.1	61.7	1.4	.2	.2	.4
EC	37.1	51.9	2.8	.6	7.5	.07
World	40.4	52.9	3.8	.6	1.7	.5
Capital equipments (1986):						
Asia	47.4	51.3				1.3
ASEAN5	24.9	75.1				.0
U.S.	66.4	33.6				.0
EC	81.4	18.6				.0
World	56.9	42.6				.5

Source: Wagakuni kigyo no kaigai jigyo katsudo (Survey of the overseas activities of Japanese companies), no. 19 (Tokyo: MITI, 1990). *Kaigai toshi tokei soran* (A comprehensive survey of foreign investment statistics), no. 3 (Tokyo: MITI, 1987).

Note: The figures are for manufacturing total. ASEAN4 are Indonesia, Malaysia, the Philippines, and Thailand; ASEAN5 are ASEAN4 plus Singapore. For the procurement of capital equipment, import sources are broken down into only Japan and others. Some numbers do not add to 100 percent, not only because of rounding, but also because of data inconsistency.

tor as a whole for 1988. In the table, one observes an interesting contrast in the geographic distribution of sales between affiliates in Asia and those in developed countries. For affiliates in Asia, the ratio of exports to total sales (the export-sales ratio) amounts to 40 percent, while the corresponding ratios for affiliates in the United States and in the EC are lower, at 5 and 25 percent, respectively. For affiliates in the EC, the export-sales ratio declines to less than 5 percent if intra-European trade is regarded as local sales. These observations indicate that the main motive behind Japanese FDI in Asia is to set up an export base, while the main motive behind Japanese FDI in the United States and in the EC is to maintain or capture the local market.

As for the destinations of the exports of Asian affiliates, Japan is the most important market as it absorbs 13.7 percent of their sales. Japan is followed by Asia (11.4 percent) and then by North America (8.7 percent). As the share of exports to Japan in total sales was significantly lower at 9.8 percent in 1980, the attractiveness of Japan as an export destination increased over time, mainly as a result of the following three factors: the appreciation of the yen, buoyant economic activity in Japan, and the import-promotion policies pursued by the Japanese government. Indeed, Japanese imports from overseas affiliates of Japanese firms—"reverse imports"—are growing rapidly. Among various kinds of products that are imported to Japan in the form of reverse imports, electrical products such as refrigerators, color televisions, and car stereos have grown rapidly in recent years (JETRO 1991).

Among the manufacturing subsectors, there are wide variations in the pattern of sales of the Asian affiliates of Japanese firms (table 10.3). The export-

Table 10.3 **Sales and Procurement of Asian Affiliates of Japanese Firms, 1988**

	Sales Destination (%)				Procurement Sources (%)			
		Exports to:				Imports from:		
Sector	Local Sales	Japan	Other Asia	Non-Asia	Local Procurement	Japan	Other Asia	Non-Asia
Manufacturing	59.8	13.7	10.9	15.6	47.2	41.3	9.0	2.4
Food	56.5	20.4	11.9	11.2	87.3	4.1	5.9	2.7
Textiles	52.3	10.8	7.7	29.2	48.8	19.1	6.7	25.4
Wood & pulp	31.2	41.4	18.5	8.9	82.4	2.7	13.2	1.8
Chemicals	81.6	3.8	9.8	4.8	59.6	23.1	2.9	14.4
Iron & steel	86.2	6.4	1.7	5.7	29.2	54.8	12.1	3.9
Nonfer. metals	60.1	14.4	14.0	11.5	69.1	22.6	.3	7.9
General mach.	64.0	17.3	6.9	11.9	44.2	52.3	3.0	.5
Elec. mach.	43.1	19.4	16.5	20.9	43.6	44.3	11.1	.9
Trans. mach.	93.2	1.7	1.4	3.7	47.7	44.4	7.6	.3
Precision mach.	40.3	26.7	20.9	12.1	28.9	60.1	10.6	.4
Petro. and coal prods.	98.7	.8	.2	.2	64.4	35.6	.0	.0
Others	72.4	10.6	4.3	12.7	58.7	29.1	8.4	3.8

Source: Wagakuni kigyo no kaigai jigyo katsudo (Survey of the overseas activities of Japanese companies), no. 19 (Tokyo: MITI, 1990).

sales ratio is high for wood and pulp, precision machinery, and electrical machinery, as more than 50 percent of their sales are exported. In contrast, petroleum and coal products, transport machinery, and iron and steel show low export-sales ratios, as less than 20 percent of their sales are exported.

The observed differences in the export-sales ratios for different subsectors can be attributed mainly to the differences in the motives behind Japanese FDI in these sectors, which in turn are influenced by the policies pursued by the host governments. For example, the main purpose of undertaking FDI in wood and pulp in Asia is to supply wood and wood products to Japan, where these products are in short supply. Therefore, a large part of wood and pulp sales goes to Japan. The remarkable difference in the export-sales ratios between electrical machinery and transport machinery appears to reflect different policies applied to these industries by host governments. For the development of the electrical machinery sector, a number of Asian countries adopted export-promotion policies and FDI-promotion policies. One of the notable developments in this regard was the setting up of export-processing zones. Responding to these incentives, Japanese firms have established an export base by FDI and exported a substantial portion of their sales. In contrast, import-protection policies are applied for the development of the transport machinery sector. As a consequence, as much as 93 percent of its sales were made locally.

There are notable differences in the pattern of export destinations among different manufactured products that are produced by Asian affiliates of Japanese firms. Japan is an important market for natural resource–based products such as wood and pulp and food. Japan is also an important market for precision machinery. For textile products, the market in non-Asia, consisting mainly of developed countries, is important.

Turning to the pattern of procurement of intermediate goods by overseas affiliates of Japanese firms, one finds that dependence on Japan is significantly higher than is observed in the case of sales (table 10.2 above). On the basis of the worldwide average, 50 percent of intermediate goods purchased by overseas affiliates of Japanese firms are imported from Japan. This high dependence in procurement is quite a contrast to the case of sales, where only 7.1 percent of sales were shipped to Japan. For the remaining portion of procurements, 40 percent are purchased locally, and 10 percent come from foreign countries other than Japan.

Despite a high level of dependence on Japan for the procurement of intermediate goods in general, there are variations in the geographic pattern of sources of procurement among affiliates in different regions. One distinctive characteristic of Asian affiliates is a high level of dependence on local markets. Specifically, for Asian affiliates, the local market is the most important source of procurement of intermediate goods, as 47.2 percent of procurement is made locally. Following local procurement, Japan is the next important source, as 41 percent of total intermediate goods are purchased in Japan. Far behind these two major sources of supply of intermediate goods is Asia, excluding Japan, as it supplies 9 percent of the intermediate goods procured by Asian affiliates of Japanese firms. As opposed to affiliates in Asia, for affiliates in the United States and the EC Japan is the most important source of intermediate goods, as Japan supplies 61.7 and 51.9 percent, respectively, of intermediate goods to these regions.

At least two reasons may be given for Asian affiliates' low level of dependence on Japan, in comparison with affiliates in the United States or the EC. One is that Japanese FDI in Asia has a relatively long history, compared to that in the United States or the EC. Consequently, a procurement network in Asia has been developed, and Asian affiliates therefore rely less on Japanese sources for the supply of intermediate goods. Another reason is that local content requirements have been imposed on FDI in Asia while such restrictions have not been formally applied in developed countries. These differences in FDI policy in Asia, on the one hand, and in the United States and the EC, on the other, have resulted in the different patterns of procurement identified above.

For affiliates in the NIEs and those in ASEAN countries, there is an interesting difference regarding the importance of the local market and that of Asian countries as sources of procurement. For affiliates in the NIEs, local procurement amounts to 50 percent of total procurement, and imports from Asia amount to only 7 percent. In contrast, for affiliates in ASEAN countries, local procurement is significantly smaller at 42 percent, and imports from Asia account for 15 percent of total procurement, significantly higher compared to the case of affiliates in the NIEs. In other words, for affiliates in ASEAN countries, the NIEs are important suppliers of intermediate goods, while, for affiliates in the NIEs, the local market supplies a significantly greater percentage of total procurement, and thus dependence on Asia is smaller. These differences reflect the differences in the production capability of intermediate goods in these two regions, which in turn can be mainly attributed to differences in the timing of Japanese FDI undertaken and in the level of economic development in these two regions. Compared to affiliates in ASEAN countries, affiliates in the NIEs have a longer history, and the level of economic development is significantly higher in the NIEs than in ASEAN countries. These two factors lead to high local capability in the NIEs in supplying intermediate goods.

The patterns of procurement of intermediate goods by Asian affiliates of Japanese firms differ substantially among different subsectors. As may be expected, the share of local procurement in total procurement is high for the natural resource–based sectors such as food, wood and pulp, and nonferrous metals (table 10.3 above). In contrast, for the machinery subsectors, which use manufactured intermediate goods as inputs, import dependence is high. Import dependence is particularly high for precision machinery, as more than 70 percent of intermediate goods are imported. One common characteristic concerning the procurement pattern among the machinery subsectors is a high level of dependence on Japan. This pattern is distinctively apparent for precision machinery, for which as much as 60 percent of intermediate goods is procured in Japan. It is interesting to note that, for textiles, non-Asia is an important source of procurements. Considering that a large share of sales in textiles is exported to non-Asia, one is led to the observation that Asian affiliates of Japanese textile firms appear to be involved in international production arrangements with non-Asian firms.

The pattern of procurement of capital equipment for overseas affiliates of Japanese firms presents quite a contrast to that observed for the procurement of intermediate goods (table 10.2 above). Unlike the case of intermediate goods, for capital equipment dependence on imports is significantly greater for Asian affiliates than for affiliates in the United States or the EC. Specifically, for affiliates in Asia, approximately half of capital equipment is supplied by local firms, while the other half is purchased from Japan. In contrast, for affiliates in the United States and for those in the EC, the local market supplies around 65–80 percent of total capital equipment, and the share of capital equipment imported from Japan in the total procurement of capital equipment amounts to around 15–35 percent.

The observed differences in the importance of the local market as a source of capital equipment in Asia, on the one hand, and in the United States and the EC, on the other, can be attributed to the differences in the capability of local firms in the production of capital equipment in these regions, which in turn largely reflect the differences in the level of economic development of these regions. As the production capability of capital equipment is rather limited in Asia, Asian affiliates depend on Japan for their supply, while affiliates in the United States and the EC face little difficulty in purchasing capital equipment in their respective local markets.

What is notable about the pattern of procurement of capital equipment by affiliates of Japanese firms is its remarkably high level of dependence on Japan among foreign sources. Indeed, for affiliates in ASEAN countries, the United States, and the EC, Japan is the only source of supply among foreign countries, while, for affiliates in Asia, including those in the NIEs, ASEAN countries, and the rest of Asia, some capital equipment, amounting to as little as 1.3 of total procurement, was imported from countries other than Japan. The extraordinarily high dependence on Japan for the procurement of capital equipment found in table 10.2 is consistent with the finding in Kreinin (1988), based on a survey of Australian affiliates of Japanese, American, and European firms, that, in sourcing capital equipment, dependence on the home country is notably high for Japanese firms. Kreinin argues that the purchasing pattern of affiliates of Japanese firms is explained mainly by their strong reliance on parent companies in making corporate decisions, including procurement decisions. Kreinin also found that the recent appreciation of the yen prompted some Japanese firms to consider diversifying their procurement sources. One of the problems of Kreinin's study is the small sample size, approximately twenty affiliates each for the Japanese, American, and European firms. In order to increase the confidence level of the findings, statistical information on procurement patterns of foreign affiliates of U.S. and European firms should be collected in a similar fashion as the data collected for Japanese firms in table 10.2, and then the information should be compared.

10.2.2 Foreign Trade Structure

In the previous section, I examined the geographic patterns of sales and procurement of Asian affiliates of Japanese firms. One of my main interests there was to analyze the degree of dependence on the foreign market for sales and procurement by Asian affiliates. In this section, I examine the effect of Asian affiliates on the trade structure of the Asian region. For the analysis, I examine the commodity trade statistics of Asian affiliates, on which information is available only for 1986.

Before pursuing the analysis, it is important to note the differences between the statistics based on industrial activities that I used for the analysis of the patterns of sales and procurement in the previous section and the commodity statistics that I use in this section. To be specific, there is no one-to-one correspondence between exports and overseas sales or between imports and overseas procurement. The lack of such correspondence is probably more serious for imports and procurements, as may be seen from the following example. Assume that we are interested in the value of imports of automobiles, which are obviously produced by the firms in the transport machinery sector. One may be tempted to use the value of procurements from foreign countries by transport machinery for the value of automobile imports, but such a practice is not appropriate since the procurements include imports not only of automobiles but also of those items not classified under "transport machinery," such as tires, which come under "other manufacturing" in the Ministry of International Trade and Industry (MITI) classification used in this study. In fact, most of the automobile imports may be classified under "procurements in commerce."

Table 10.4 shows the trade structure of Asia and that of Asian affiliates of Japanese firms (under the heads "overall" and "affiliates," respectively). For each trade structure, two types of trading partners are distinguished, the world and Japan. I first examine the export structure and then turn to the import structure.

Starting with Asian exports to the world, one finds that textiles and electrical machinery have large shares by capturing, respectively, 24.0 and 17.6 percent of total exports. The composition of exports to the world by Asian affiliates is not so different from that observed for Asian exports to the world. In spite of the similarity in the export structure of Asian affiliates and that of Asia, the differences in the magnitudes of the respective shares for some products reveal interesting characteristics of the activities of the affiliates of Japanese firms in Asia. The products whose compositional shares in affiliates' exports are larger than those in the overall Asian exports are electrical ma-

Table 10.4 The Trade Structure of Asian Countries and Asian Affiliates of Japanese Firms, 1986

	Exports (%)				Imports (%)			
	World		Japan		World		Japan	
Sector	Overall	Affiliates	Overall	Affiliates	Overall	Affiliates	Overall	Affiliates
Manufacturing	100.0	100.0	100.0	100.0	100.0	100.0	100.0	100.0
Food	5.4	1.5	23.7	3.6	4.3	2.8	1.1	.0
Textiles	24.0	20.6	17.7	13.0	10.1	6.5	5.7	1.5
Wood & pulp	4.0	.9	4.1	.7	3.5	.4	1.7	.03
Chemicals	4.6	7.0	6.4	2.6	14.9	15.4	11.3	12.1
Iron & steel	5.4	3.8	6.0	3.1	7.3	6.7	12.2	7.7
Nonfer. metals	1.2	6.6	3.2	14.0	2.4	2.8	1.8	2.1
Gen. mach.	8.0	3.7	3.5	9.5	15.7	6.0	20.1	6.7
Elec. mach.	17.6	27.9	9.2	41.7	19.2	37.0	24.0	43.2
Trans. mach.	4.6	11.8	1.1	4.7	6.6	12.1	8.7	15.4
Precision mach.	3.0	2.8	2.2	2.6	4.0	2.1	5.6	3.4
Petro. and coal prods.	4.0	.0	9.8	.0	3.5	.1	.4	.07
Others	18.3	13.5	13.0	4.6	8.5	8.1	7.3	7.8

Source: Computed from AIDXT, an international trade data base developed by the Institute of Developing Economies, Tokyo; and *Kaigai toshi tokei soran* (A comprehensive survey of foreign investment statistics), no. 3, (Tokyo: MITI, 1987).

chinery, transport machinery, chemicals, and nonferrous metals. Except for nonferrous metals, these products are so called high-tech products. The differential in the compositional shares is particularly large for electrical machinery, as its share in affiliates' exports is larger than the corresponding share in overall Asian exports by 10.3 percentage points. These observations indicate that the exports of Asian affiliates of Japanese firms are relatively more concentrated in high-tech products than in traditional products such as textiles and food. Based on these findings, one may argue that Japanese FDI contributes to the upgrading of the export structure of the Asian countries.

Let us now turn to Asian exports to Japan. The compositional structure of Asian exports to Japan differs somewhat from that of Asian exports to the world. The most distinctive characteristic associated with Asian exports to Japan is the high share of food products, as its share in total Asian exports to Japan amounts to 23.7 percent, significantly higher than 5.4 percent, which was recorded for Asian exports to the world. In contrast, the shares of four machinery products in Asian exports to Japan are much smaller, compared to the case for Asian exports to the world. These differences in the structure of Asian exports to the world and that of Asian exports to Japan reflect differences in the patterns of the comparative advantage of Japan vis-à-vis the rest of the world. Relatively speaking, Japan has a comparative advantage in machinery products and a comparative disadvantage in natural resource–intensive products such as food. Consequently, compared to Asian exports to the world, Asian exports to Japan are concentrated in natural resource–intensive products.

A comparison of the structure of Asian exports to Japan and the corresponding structure of Asian affiliates shows that the exports of Asian affiliates to Japan are heavily concentrated in electrical machinery, registering as high as 41.7 percent of total exports of Asian affiliates to Japan, indicating that Japanese FDI contributes to the export expansion of electrical products from Asia to Japan. This is not surprising once one recognizes the large magnitude of Japanese FDI that has been undertaken in the electrical sector and also that one of the main motives behind such FDI is to expand "reverse imports," as was pointed out earlier. Although accurate estimation of the proportion of exports by Asian affiliates to overall Asian exports to Japan is difficult because of data problems, the fact that the compositional share of electrical machinery in affiliates' exports to Japan is tremendously higher than that in Asian exports to Japan indicates that a significantly large portion of Asian exports to Japan in electrical machinery is conducted by Asian affiliates of Japanese firms.[6] In contrast, exports of food products and textiles, which are traditional exports of the Asian countries, appear to be undertaken largely by firms other than affiliates of Japanese firms.

6. Admitting data problems, Takeuchi (1990) estimates the proportion of Asian manufactured exports conducted by affiliates of Japanese firms in 1986 to be around 20 percent. Hirata and Yokota (1991) estimate the corresponding proportions for the NIEs and ASEAN countries to be 3.5 and 7.5 percent, respectively, in 1987.

Turning to Asian imports from the world, one finds that electrical machinery, general machinery, chemicals, and textiles have large shares. Compared to this, imports of Asian affiliates of Japanese firms are more concentrated in electrical machinery and transport machinery and less concentrated in textiles and general machinery. It must be noted here that the share of general machinery in the imports of affiliates is underestimated, possibly by a substantial margin. This is because their imports of capital equipment, most of which would be classified under "general machinery," are not included in the figures in table 10.4, as the figures in the table refer to the purchase of intermediate goods only. Incorporation of the imports of capital equipment into the imports of affiliates cannot be readily done as information on the imports of capital equipment is given only as the share of total fixed investment in the MITI sources, as presented in table 10.2 above. This problem should be kept in mind in interpreting the discussion of the import structure of Asian affiliates below.

The structure of Asian imports from Japan is not much different from the pattern observed for Asian imports from the world, although their imports from Japan are somewhat more concentrated in machinery products, especially in general machinery and electrical machinery, and less concentrated in textiles and natural resource–intensive products such as food, wood and pulp, and petroleum and coal products. The differences in the structure of Asian imports from the world, on the one hand, and those from Japan, on the other, reflect the differences in the pattern of comparative advantage of Japan vis-à-vis the rest of the world, which will not be repeated here, as it was discussed earlier.

Finally, an examination of the import structure of Asian affiliates in their trade with Japan reveals a significantly high concentration in electrical machinery, which accounts for 43.2 percent of total imports from Japan by Asian affiliates of Japanese firms. It is also worth noting that the share of electrical machinery in total imports from Japan by Asian affiliates is significantly higher than the share for imports from the world as a whole by Asian affiliates.

The findings from the analysis of the structure of foreign trade by Asian affiliates of Japanese firms show that their export and import activities are heavily concentrated in electrical machinery, pointing to the high degree of intraindustry trade in electrical products, in particular in their trade with Japan. To a lesser degree, a similar pattern may be observed for the trade in other machinery products. Moreover, the fact that a high proportion of trade in the machinery sector is conducted by Japanese firms suggests that a large portion of such trade takes the form of intrafirm transactions. In the next section, I examine these points in more detail.

10.2.3 Intrafirm, Interprocess, Intraindustry Trade

I have argued that the new pattern of foreign trade that emerged from the activities of Japanese firms in Asia in the latter half of the 1980s is intrafirm, interprocess, intraindustry trade. In this section, I examine whether such a trading pattern may be identified by focusing on the intraindustry, interprocess, and intrafirm aspects of Asian affiliates' trade in turn.

The large shares of machinery products in both manufactured exports and imports of Asian affiliates of Japanese firms found in table 10.4 suggest that a large portion of trade in machinery products by Asian affiliates may take the form of intraindustry trade.[7] Intraindustry trade takes two different forms: horizontal and vertical. Horizontal intraindustry trade involves trade in differentiated products. A typical example is trade in automobiles. Japan exports Toyotas to Germany, while Japan imports BMWs from Germany. This type of intraindustry trade, which arises because consumers have a taste for variety, tends to take place among developed countries. Vertical intraindustry trade involves trade in products that are at different stages in the production process. For example, Japan exports electronic components such as ICs to Thailand and imports finished products such as color televisions from Thailand, which are often produced with the integrated circuits (ICs) imported from Japan. This type of intraindustry trade may be classified as interindustry trade if detailed commodity classification is applied. Under a rough classification, such as the one used here, such trade falls into the category of intraindustry trade. Vertical intraindustry trade, or interprocess trade, tends to take place between developed and developing countries, where factor endowments or technological capabilities differ. Under such an arrangement, countries specialize in the process, which they can perform efficiently.

To see which type of intraindustry trade takes place in Asian trade with Japan by Asian affiliates, I examine the types of commodities traded between Japan and Asia by these affiliates. The types of commodities procured (imported) and sold (exported) in Asian trade with Japan by Asian affiliates are shown in table 10.5. Such statistics are available only for electrical machinery, transport machinery, and precision machinery. From the table, it is clear that vertical intraindustry trade, or interprocess trade, takes place in electrical machinery between Asia and Japan by Asian affiliates of Japanese firms; Japan exports electrical components to Asia and imports finished electrical products from Asia. A similar trading pattern is observed for precision machinery, but the presence of intraindustry, interprocess trade is hardly detected in transport machinery. For transport machinery, Asia imports not only parts and compo-

7. Intraindustry trade is of relatively little importance for Japan in comparison with other developed countries, but its importance as a factor in Japan's trade with Asian countries, especially with the NIEs, has been increasing since the mid-1980s. For more details, see MITI (1990). One should be reminded that, although several measures of intraindustry trade have been suggested and estimated, no single measure has been recognized as the best. Specifically, the level of commodity disaggregation and the treatment of trade surplus and deficit are shown to affect significantly estimates of intraindustry trade, making comparison of the estimates difficult. A lack of detailed data prevents me from estimating an intraindustry trade index for Asian affiliates of Japanese firms, although such estimates may prove helpful in examining the validity of the assertion given in the text.

Table 10.5 **Procurement and Sales of Asian Affiliates for Selected Products, 1986 (million yen)**

Products	Local Market	Japan	Other Countries	Total
Electrical machinery:				
Components:				
Procurement	45,076	79,591	17,376	142,043
Sales	74,269	20,182	46,759	141,210
Finished products:				
Procurement	8,634	26,634	393	35,661
Sales	97,758	48,192	58,752	204,702
Transport Machinery:				
Components:				
Procurement	7,518	16,473	6,204	30,105
Sales	41,715	5,937	25,059	72,711
Finished products:				
Procurement	6,754	21,326	0	28,080
Sales	66,569	1,808	4,497	72,874
Precision machinery:				
Components:				
Procurement	493	3,021	0	3,514
Sales	201	213	253	667
Finished products:				
Procurement	729	5,449	574	6,752
Sales	15,097	4,035	14,705	33,837

Source: Computed from *Kaigai toshi tokei soran* (A comprehensive survey of foreign investment statistics), no. 3 (Tokyo: MITI, 1987).

nents but also finished products from Japan, indicating that Asia has developed the necessary technological capability neither in the production of auto components nor in the efficient assembly of automobiles.

It was found above that Asian affiliates of Japanese firms, especially those in electrical machinery and precision machinery, are involved with vertical intraindustry trade with Japan. These findings tend to suggest that such trade takes place within a firm or in the form of intrafirm trade. This assertion is supported by the statistics on intrafirm trade by Asian affiliates of Japanese firms given in table 10.6. The figures in the table show the percentage share of intrafirm transactions in total transactions with various trading partners. According to the table, the average shares of intrafirm transactions in total transactions for sales and for procurement are, respectively, 24.0 and 37.3 percent.[8] The share of intrafirm trade is in general higher for foreign trade

8. Direct comparison of the importance of intrafirm trade in sales and procurement between affiliates of Japanese firms and those of non-Japanese firms is difficult because of a lack of comparable data. Affiliates of U.S. firms may be the only exception, as somewhat comparable statistics are reported. According to the U.S. Department of Commerce (1990), in 1988, for manufacturing, the share of U.S. imports shipped to U.S. parents by all affiliates in U.S. imports shipped by all affiliates was 79.9 percent, while the share of U.S. exports shipped by U.S. parents to all

Table 10.6 **Shares of Intrafirm Transactions in Sales and Procurement of Asian Affiliates of Japanese Parent Firms, 1986**

	Sales (%)				Procurement (%)			
		Exports to:				Imports from:		
Industry	Local Market	Japan	Others	Total	Local Market	Japan	Others	Total
Manufacturing	8.9	76.5	23.7	24.0	6.8	66.6	34.3	37.3
Food	.0	87.8	.0	27.5	.0	100.0	.0	3.1
Textiles	8.0	57.7	2.5	10.7	15.5	46.7	12.0	18.0
Wood & pulp	.0	27.7	.0	7.1	27.9	93.8	.0	23.5
Chemicals	2.6	83.9	1.5	5.8	5.5	24.4	67.5	20.9
Iron & steel	3.2	100.0	.0	8.2	16.5	40.2	3.5	32.1
Nonfer. metals	15.1	99.2	.6	36.3	.0	65.1	.0	6.9
Gen. mach.	29.9	94.7	46.6	54.3	15.8	80.0	96.8	52.7
Elec. mach.	9.6	73.0	32.1	31.6	6.2	78.1	55.9	49.9
Trans. mach.	9.1	46.0	62.8	22.0	4.0	56.1	67.9	42.0
Precision mach.	59.8	86.1	59.5	65.4	26.1	95.8	62.7	84.6
Petro. and coal prods.	.0	.0	.0	.0	.0	.0	.0	.0
Others	.0	88.5	13.8	8.9	7.9	81.5	9.7	33.2

Source: Kaigai toshi tokei soran (A comprehensive survey of foreign investment statistics), no. 3 (Tokyo: MITI, 1987).

than for local trade, and the share is very high for trade with Japan. The sectors with a high share of intrafirm trade in trade with Japan are food, general machinery, electrical machinery, and precision machinery.[9] It is also worth noting that the share of intrafirm transactions in total transactions with the regions other than Japan is also high for the machinery sectors.

Several reasons may be given for the prevalence of intrafirm trade. As for the high share of intrafirm trade in the exports of machinery, the distribution networks of Japanese firms are already well established, and it is therefore advantageous to export machinery products through these distribution networks, especially since machinery products may require after-sales services. The high share of intrafirm trade in imports may be attributable to the special characteristics of machinery production. For the production of machinery products, a great number of components, often those specifically made for certain products, are required. For the stable supply of such components, in-

affiliates in U.S. exports to all affiliates was 85.9 percent. These statistics are available only for affiliates in all the countries combined, not just for those in Asia. The comparable statistics for all affiliates of Japanese firms—the shares of intrafirm transactions in affiliates' exports and imports with Japan—were, respectively, 75.9 and 73.4 percent in 1986 (for data sources, see table 10.7 below). These findings suggest that the share of intrafirm trade in affiliates' trade for Japanese firms is somewhat lower than that for the U.S. firms.

9. According to a survey of Thai affiliates of Japanese electrical firms conducted by JETRO (1990), for 56.2 percent of the firms the motive behind FDI was to assemble the final products by utilizing intrafirm, interprocess trade.

trafirm procurement is regarded as more efficient than interfirm procurement. This is because production planning and coordination may be much easier within the firm. The importance of the quality of components also increases intrafirm transactions. Monitoring the quality of components is difficult if they are traded at arm's length. To avoid the problem of monitoring quality, which is especially important for machinery production, intrafirm transactions are preferred.[10]

The preceding discussion points to some of the problems associated with interfirm transactions, problems caused by market failure. To deal with the problem of market failure effectively, firms internalize these transactions. Before ending this discussion of the high share of intrafirm transactions of Asian affiliates of Japanese firms, it should be recalled that some Japanese firms initially undertook FDI in order to engage in interprocess, intrafirm division of labor and thus achieve efficient production. It may therefore be only natural to observe high rates of intrafirm transactions.

10.2.4 The Effect of Japanese Firms on Regionalization in Asia

Japanese firms have actively undertaken FDI as a means of globalizing their activities. However, international trade that emerges from globalization through FDI may lead to regionalization in foreign trade. Such a development may already have occurred in the EC and in North America: regional trading blocs have already been established there, and Japanese firms have undertaken FDI in these regions in order to maintain or capture local or regional markets. An interesting question, then, is the effect of Japanese FDI on foreign trade in Asia. Is it a force working toward the regionalization of Asia, or is it likely to increase the ties between Asia and the rest of the world? To answer this interesting question, I examine empirically the effect of Japanese FDI on intra-Asian as well as extra-Asian trade.

In table 10.7, for the NIEs and ASEAN countries, a comparison of the interregional patterns of foreign trade is made between the overall trade of the respective regions and trade conducted by affiliates of Japanese firms in each region. Several interesting points can be observed. To begin with, for both the NIEs and ASEAN countries, compared to their overall trade, trade by affiliates is heavily dependent on Japan. This tendency is particularly strong in imports. Second, because of affiliates' heavy reliance on the Japanese market for their imports, the shares other than Japan—in particular, those of North America and "others"—in the total imports of affiliates are much smaller than the corresponding shares for their overall trade. Finally, as is the case for imports, the exports of affiliates are concentrated in Asian countries other than Japan. These findings indicate that Japanese FDI in Asia is leading to the regionalization of foreign trade in Asia.

10. Caves (1982) presents a concise summary of the issue.

Table 10.7 **Interregional Dependence in Foreign Trade of Asian Affiliates**

	Trading Regions (%)				
	Japan	Asia	N. America	Others	Total
Exporting regions:					
NIEs:					
Overall trade	12.4	25.5	33.4	28.7	100.0
Affiliates	34.4	25.4	21.2	19.1	100.0
ASEAN 4:					
Overall trade	24.6	27.0	20.7	27.7	100.0
Affiliates	33.7	31.5	19.1	15.8	100.0
Importing regions:					
NIEs:					
Overall trade	23.8	27.4	18.0	30.8	100.0
Affiliates	83.1	13.2	.6	3.1	100.0
ASEAN 4:					
Overall trade	23.7	34.0	14.1	28.2	100.0
Affiliates	67.5	25.5	2.4	4.6	100.0

Sources: Computed from *Chosa,* no. 138 (Development Bank of Japan, February 1990); and *Wagakuni kigyo no kaigai jigyo katsudo* (Survey of the overseas activities of Japanese companies), no. 19 (Tokyo: MITI, 1990).

10.3 Conclusions

The history of Japanese FDI is relatively short, as it started to expand rapidly only in the 1980s. However, Japanese FDI has already affected the economies of the recipient countries as well as that of Japan since the speed and the magnitude of its increase have been quite substantial. For the recipient countries, Japanese FDI contributed to the expansion of employment, output, and exports: in 1988, Asian affiliates of Japanese firms employed more than 650,000 workers (580,000 in manufacturing), and their sales and exports amounted to 10,947 (5,541) billion and 2,384 (1,454) billion yen; export values amounted to U.S. $18.6 (11.4) billion. Net exports (exports-imports), which may be a better indicator of the net contribution of Japanese firms to the recipient countries, are estimated to be 308 billion yen, or U.S. $2.4 billion, for Asia. Despite positive net exports for Asia as a whole, there are substantial differences between the values for the NIEs and ASEAN countries—398 billion and −56 billion yen, respectively. These contrasting patterns appear to be mainly due to the differences in the lengths of the periods under operation of affiliates in the two different regions. Affiliates in the NIEs have longer histories, and thus their local procurement networks have been established, networks that rely less on imports. These observations indicate that the net export position for affiliates in ASEAN countries is likely to improve in the future.

In addition to the easily quantifiable benefits discussed above, Japanese FDI also produces benefits that are difficult to quantify. First, through FDI, technology is transferred from the investing country to the recipient. The kinds of technology transferred are not confined to technical technology, such as the production process, but also include management skills, such as the "just-in-time" production system. As technological progress is one of the most important factors in economic development, FDI could play a very important role in promoting the economic development of the recipient country. Second, through FDI, the recipient countries could gain access to various kinds of international networks, such as information networks and sales and procurement networks, affording them opportunities for further economic development. Needless to say, these unquantifiable benefits are closely related to the quanitifiable benefits discussed above, as, for example, better technology leads to export expansion.

Not only does Japanese FDI contribute to the economic development of the Asian countries, but it also improves resource allocation in Japan by speeding up the process of industrial adjustment. Given the labor shortage situation, the use of resources in Japan would be improved if labor-intensive production were reduced. Such a shift in the production structure would be facilitated by an outflow of FDI. As was found in this paper, labor-intensive processes have been shifted from Japan to Asian countries. These favorable effects of FDI in the recipient countries as well as those in investing countries are magnified through the interaction of economic growth and trade expansion. Such favorable interaction through FDI in Asia has been increasing recently, as the NIEs have joined Japan as important investors in the region.

The dynamic economic performance of the Asian region, which is partly propelled by Japanese FDI, undoubtedly contributes favorably to world economic growth. Balancing this favorable effect of Japanese FDI, however, the findings of the paper point to the closedness of the transactions involving Asian affiliates of Japanese firms as an area needing improvement. Two kinds of closedness were identified in these firms' behavior. One is an unusually strong orientation toward parent firms in affiliates' transactions. Although more studies have to be undertaken before bringing in a verdict on the validity of the hypothesis that the practices of Japanese firms are distinctly different from those of firms from other countries, diversification of trading partners should be sought by Japanese firms on at least two grounds: efficiency and fairness. With an opening up of trading opportunities, competition will be enhanced, leading to higher efficiency and minimizing unfair trading practices. The second kind of closedness of Japanese firms is their emphasis on regional trade. Such a pattern was realized partly in response to protectionism in the rest of the world. Recognizing the importance of free trade for world economic expansion, policymakers not only in Asia but also in other parts of the world should avoid protectionist or interventionist policies and a move toward regionalization so that FDI as well as trade flows will not be distorted.

References

Caves, R. 1982. *Multinational enterprise and economic analysis*. Cambridge: Cambridge University Press.

Hirata, A., and K. Yokota. 1991. Impact of industrial adjustment in Japan on developing countries. Paper presented at the conference on Industrial Adjustment in Developed Countries and Its Implications for Developing Countries, Tokyo: Institute of Developing Economies, 1–2 February.

Japan External Trade Organization (JETRO). 1990. *Kaigai toshi to Nihon kigyo no kigyonai bungyo* (Foreign direct investment and intrafirm trade by Japanese firms). Internal report. Tokyo, March.

———. 1991. *Sekai to Nihon no kaigai chokusetsu toshi* (White paper on overseas direct investment). Tokyo.

Kreinin, M. 1988. How closed is the Japanese market? Additional evidence. *World Economy* 11 (December): 529–42.

Ministry of International Trade and Industry (MITI). 1990. *Tsusho hakusho* (White paper on international trade). Tokyo.

Takeuchi, K. 1990. Does Japanese direct foreign investment promote Japanese imports from developing countries? PRE Working Paper on International Trade, WPS 458. Washington, D.C.: World Bank.

Urata, S. 1990. The rapid globalization of Japanese firms in the 1980s: An analysis of the activities of Japanese firms in Asia. Working paper. Paris: OECD Development Centre, Paris, 20–21 June.

———. 1991. The rapid increase of direct investment abroad and structural change in Japan. In *Direct investment in developing countries and structural change in the Asia-Pacific Region*, ed. E. Ramstetter. Boulder, Colo.: Westview.

U.S. Department of Commerce. 1990. *U.S. direct investment abroad: Preliminary 1988 estimates*. Washington, D.C.

Comment Tran Van Tho

The paper by Shujiro Urata can be divided into two parts. The first part describes the evolution of Japanese direct investment in Asia with an emphasis on trends since the latter half of the 1980s. The second part analyzes the effect of Japanese foreign direct investment (FDI) on Asian trade with Japan and other countries. It is in the second part of the paper that a number of important issues have been raised, and I have read this part with great interest. In particular, Urata raised the following important and interesting question: whether Japanese FDI is a force toward regionalism in Asia or whether it is likely to increase economic ties between Asia and the rest of the world. My comments will center on this question.

The question is of great importance and practical significance for at least

Tran Van Tho is professor of economics at Obirin University, Tokyo, and senior economist at the Japan Center for Economic Research (JCER), Tokyo.

two reasons. First, at present, the exports of most Asian countries must rely heavily on the American market, and protectionism in the United States is a serious problem for Asia. Thus, the current problem for Asia is how to diversify its export market away from the United States. In this regard, one of the important diversification strategies is to expand intraregional trade in Asia. In that sense, the question raised by Urata is very relevant. Second, at a time when we are concerned about the world trend toward the formation of trading blocs, the question of whether Asia will converge into a relatively autonomous economic region has many important implications. If Japanese FDI tends to strengthen economic ties between Asia and other regions, the trend is favorable in the sense that it contributes to a weakening of the world trend toward regionalism. In this case, however, if Japanese FDI tends to strengthen economic ties in a way that exacerbates the imbalance in Asian trade with the United States and other regions, Japanese FDI in Asia may also have a negative effect.

Let us see the empirical results of Urata's paper on the question raised above. Regarding this question, the paper concluded that Japanese FDI tends to regionalize trade in Asia. My first comment is that the paper should have gone further to discuss the implications of this conclusion. My second comment is on the empirical evidence, which is not sufficiently convincing. The evidence is provided only by the data in table 10.7, and, moreover, there are some problems with these data. These problems include the following. First, it is true that, in the trade of Asian NIEs or of ASEAN countries, Japanese affiliates tend to depend more heavily on Japan than is the case for overall trade. However, we cannot know whether affiliates' trade influences overall trade unless data on the share of affiliates' trade in overall trade are also provided. Second, looking at the data on Asian NIEs' imports from the rest of Asia excluding Japan (this appears as "Asia" in table 10.7) or ASEAN's imports from "Asia," we see that overall trade depends much more heavily on "Asia" than does trade by Japanese affiliates. Regarding exports by NIEs and ASEAN countries, "Asia" is almost equally important for the two types of trade. These observations tend to weaken the paper's conclusion on the issue under consideration. Third, the data in table 10.7 reflect the situation at only one point in time. We need time-series data to confirm or disprove the trends.

Finally, regarding table 10.7, let me point out an important problem that is not mentioned in the paper—the nonsymmetry of the Asian exports and imports of Japanese affiliates vis-à-vis North America. In both the NIEs and ASEAN countries, about 20 percent of Japanese affiliates' exports go to North America, while their imports from the same market are negligible. This trend tends to strengthen the overall imbalance of trade between Asia and North America. The trading behavior of Japanese affiliates in Asia has therefore had a negative effect on the economic relationship between Asia and North America. Such behavior is partially responsible for the increasing protectionism in the United States that is directed toward Asia's manufacturing goods.

Comment Yoo Jung-ho

Shujiro Urata's paper on Japanese foreign direct investment (FDI) is mostly about investments in Asia in the late 1980s, with some discussion of Japanese FDI in industrial countries and in earlier periods. It is highly informative, and the behavioral facts about Asian affiliates of Japanese firms are well documented. My comments on the paper are organized around the three issues that piqued economists' interest in FDI, namely, the determinants, the effects on the host and home economies, and the effects on the trade pattern.

The Determinants of Japanese FDI

As the reasons for Japanese FDI in developed countries, the paper mentions trade friction with the industrial countries, the formation of trade blocs such as EC 1992, and Japanese firms' newly acquired abundance of liquidity as the major reasons. While these are commonly cited, one wonders whether FDI has indeed been good insurance against import restrictions. One would also like to know whether Japanese firms have always made FDI when they had excess liquidity. The rapid increase in FDI could have been a response to a decline in the risk premium of the Japanese yen at the time, if there was such a decline. Aliber (1983) theorized that a decline in a currency's risk premium provides an advantage to firms located in the country of the currency in the form of the lowered cost of raising funds compared to firms elsewhere.

Regarding Japanese FDI to developing countries, the paper mentions as the major reasons the rise in the value of the yen, the rise in the wage rate at home, and the need to secure export bases to get around the industrial countries' import restrictions on Japanese goods and to supply to the host countries' domestic markets. Noting that Japanese investments in the late 1980s flowed relatively more to the member countries of ASEAN than to the newly industrializing countries (NICs), the paper mentions as reasons the appreciation of the NICs' currencies, the rise in the NICs' wage rates, and the economic policies of the Southeast Asian countries that became outward oriented.

Except for Japanese firms' desire to secure an export base, the reasons lead one to expect an increase in exports from the Southeast Asian countries to third markets such as the United States and Europe, replacing Japanese and NIC exports, and, perhaps, later on to Japan and the NICs. Since the Southeast Asian countries are technologically behind Japan and, in a few areas, behind the NICs, their rapid export increase would entail an increase in imports of technologically sophisticated parts and capital goods. Indeed, their exports and imports have been rapidly increasing. However, a large part of the increasing foreign trade was intrafirm trade between Japanese parent firms and their Asian affiliates.

Foreign direct investment as a firm's decision is a choice over the alterna-

Yoo Jung-ho is a senior fellow at the Korea Development Institute.

tive of, for example, exporting capital equipment and intermediate goods and purchasing the finished products under some arrangement. There must be reasons why the investing Japanese firms did not choose this alternative but decided that it is more profitable or advantageous to internalize the transactions that could take place through the market. This question is not explicitly addressed in this paper.

Some insights into the question may be gained by observing the corporate behavior of the affiliates of Japanese firms regarding sales and procurement and the effects on international trade, which are described in detail in the paper.

Some notable characteristics of their behavior are as follows. (1) For Asian affiliates, Japan was by far the largest among five procurement sources of the intermediate inputs outside the local market. The procurement from Japan was nearly four times as large as that from the other four sources combined, namely, Asia, North America, Europe, and "others." Only a negligible amount came from North American or European sources. (2) Among the same five regions besides the local market, Japan was again the most important as a destination of sales. However, sales were more evenly distributed among destinations than procurement was among sources. The combined sales to regions other than Japan were two times as large as sales to Japan. (3) Asian affiliates' exports to and imports from Japan were mostly intrafirm transactions, more than three-quarters for exports and two-thirds for imports on average for affiliates in the manufacturing sector.

The same pattern of procurement was observed for Australian affiliates of Japanese firms by Kreinin (1988), who also found that the counterparts of other countries' multinationals bought much greater proportions of procurement from other sources than the parent companies or the home countries. This pattern of procurement and sales of foreign affiliates of Japanese firms indicates a very close working relationship between the two. It seems more appropriate to call the affiliates plants or branch offices of the parent companies.

Thus, the close working relationship seems to be the key reason why Japanese firms make FDI, that is, why they choose to internalize the transactions that could take place through the market. The close working relationship may be needed to take full advantage of an invisible asset, which is often hypothesized to be the reason for FDI. That asset could be the Japanese management style, which demands exact specifications on parts, low defect rates, highly reliable delivery, and so on. If that were the case, the close working relationship between parent and affiliates may be necessary to achieve the high efficiency for which Japanese firms are renowned.

However, the current benefits from the Japanese investments may be likened to a good delivered now for which an unknown price has to be paid sometime in the future. The more closely affiliates are controlled by the parent firms, the more vulnerable would a host country find itself to foreign pressure.

The Effects of Japanese FDI

Regarding the effects on the home and host economies and the effects on the trade pattern of Japanese FDI, the paper notes that FDI tends to upgrade the export structure of the host countries. As supporting evidence, the paper points out that Asian affiliates' exports consist more of high-tech products than the total exports of the host countries. This cuts both ways. It can also be evidence that FDI did not upgrade the exports of the rest of the economy. The high proportion of high-tech products in affiliates' exports is really a consequence of Japanese parent firms buying the products of their affiliates, a reflection of the close working relationship between parent and affiliates. It is also a consequence of the nature of Japanese trade barriers that foreign firms find it much harder to overcome than Japanese firms and their affiliates.

Upgrading the export structure may have no beneficial effects if no technology transfer takes place or if the affiliates' interactions with indigenous firms are kept at a minimum in favor of interaction with parent firms. It simply represents a rise in the average high-tech content of the host country's exports as affiliates' exports are added to those of other firms in the host country. To be symmetric in evaluating the effect of Japanese FDI, the upgrading effect may be said to be accompanied by the "downgrading" effect on the host country's import structure since affiliates' imports consist more of the high-tech products than the total imports of the host country, thus raising the high-tech content of imports.

The paper observes that Japanese FDI in Asia had a positive effect on the regionalization of Asia's trade. It also claims that intrafirm, interprocess, intraindustry trade has evolved in Asia mainly through the activities of Japanese firms and that the expansion of such trade would promote the economic development of Asia. However, it is not clear why regionalization of trade is desirable. It should also be pointed out that expansion of trade need not take the form of intrafirm transactions and that not all trade expansion would have been lost had there been no Japanese FDI.

The Vulnerability of the Host Country

The beneficial effects derived from Japanese FDI in Asia are inseparable from the close working relationship that we have seen above. The paper observes that, against the favorable effect of Japanese FDI, the closedness of transactions involving Asian affiliates of Japanese firms becomes an important area in need of improvement. Urata goes on to say that the diversification of trading partners should be sought by Japanese firms for reasons of efficiency and fairness.

While the paper has identified the right issues, the problem is not just efficiency but the host country's vulnerability. The big question is whether the benefits of Japanese FDI last only as long as the FDI lasts. This will be the case if Asian affiliates' interactions with the host country's economy are kept at a minimum and cause no transformation of the economy. The employment created, exports, and flows of foreign exchange earnings will be gone when the Japanese parent firm decides to pull out in response to changed circumstances.

This vulnerability of the host country is not an inevitable price to be paid for the benefits of FDI since the alternative to Japanese FDI is not no FDI but FDI from other countries, foreign borrowing, or some combination of the two. Even though the loss in efficiency resulting from the lack of competition for affiliates' procurement may be more than compensated for by, say, the high efficiency of the Japanese management style, there still remains the question of the economy's vulnerability. This is the question that will be raised and examined over and over as the region is drawn closer together by Japanese FDI.

References

Aliber, Robert Z. 1983. Money, multinationals, and sovereigns. In *The multinational corporation in the 1980s,* ed. C. P. Kindleberger and D. B. Audretsch. Cambridge, Mass.: MIT Press.

Kreinin, Mordechai E. 1988. How closed is the Japanese market? Additional evidence. *World Economy* 11 (4): 529–42.

V

11 The Political Economy of U.S.-Taiwanese Trade and Other International Economic Relations

Robert E. Baldwin and Douglas Nelson

In most systematic work by economists on the political economy of trade policy, the primary causal mechanism is the competing demands for different trade policies by various domestic pressure groups, who are motivated by economic self-interest.[1] The supply side is modeled quite simply. Politicians also pursue their economic self-interest by seeking to be reelected and, consequently, supply the trade policies desired by the group or groups who, by providing votes and campaign contributions, give them the best opportunity for being reelected. This framework has led to a substantial body of theoretical and empirical work that has significantly improved our understanding of trade policy.

This model does, however, mainly emphasize the "demand" side since the demands of pressure groups are weighted to determine the equilibrium level of protection. In the typical political economy model of economists, the supplying of particular forms of trade policy by politicians, bureaucrats, and, more generally, the state, as part of their efforts to promote such collective goals as national security, is ruled out. Moreover, voters are portrayed as responding favorably only to policies that promote their short-run economic self-interests and not to the pursuit of such foreign policy goals. In this paper, we seek to show that this political economy framework is too narrow and to illustrate the fundamental role of the state in some circumstances by focusing

Robert E. Baldwin is professor of economics at the University of Wisconsin—Madison and a research associate of the National Bureau of Economic Research. Douglas Nelson is assistant professor of economics at Syracuse University.

The authors would like to express their gratitude for the assistance and encouragement given by the late Chi-Ming Hou, who was Charles A. Dana Professor of Economics at Colgate University and vice-president of the Chung-Hua Institution for Economic Research.

1. Baldwin (1984) and Marks and McCarthur (1990) provide overviews of the empirical research, while Nelson (1988) and Hillman (1989) provide overviews of the theoretical research on the political economy of trade policy.

on trade policy–making in the United States and Taiwan in the post–Second World War era.[2]

With the end of the Second World War, both the government of the United States and the government of the Republic of China (ROC) experienced major crises. In both cases, the appearance of an external threat caused a fundamental reassessment of the structural and institutional foundations of the state.[3] In both cases, the governments attempted to restructure the politics of trade policy by attaching trade policy to broader political goals. In both cases, the governments used their increased authority to pursue broadly liberal trade policies. Finally, in both cases the deterioration of the regimes erected in the postwar era has led to uncertainty about the sustainability of the commitment to a liberal trading order and greater unpredictability. Section 11.1 of the paper discusses the development of U.S. trade policy in general and its policy toward Taiwan in particular; section 11.2 discusses the development of Taiwan's trade policy in general and its policy toward the United States in particular; and section 11.3 summarizes our conclusions from the comparison of trade policy in the two countries.

11.1 External Threat, State Autonomy, and the Evolution of U.S. Trade Policy, 1945–91

11.1.1 Introduction

U.S. trade policies toward the Republic of China over the last fifty years illustrate very clearly the key shift in U.S. international economic policy in the post–World War II period, namely, the change from a pattern of policy-making largely shaped by foreign policy factors until the late 1960s (specifically, national security considerations) to one influenced mainly by domestic economic conditions.

Four features of this basic change are particularly relevant in analyzing U.S.-Taiwan trading relations. First, there has been a shift by the United States from an emphasis on reducing trade barriers in the world economy to achieving "fair" international trade. Today one frequently hears U.S. political leaders calling for "a level playing field," for foreign markets to be open as much as are U.S. markets, and for U.S. fair trade laws to be vigorously enforced. In recent years, there have been numerous charges of unfair trading practices against Taiwan by U.S. officials and leaders in the private sector,

2. In emphasizing the supply side, we recognize that voters and other political groups usually must approve of the policies initiated by the government if these policies are to be implemented successfully. The point we stress is that the government, rather than private pressure groups, sometimes initiates policy proposals and plays an important role in persuading the public of their merit.

3. The notion that external threats have been a significant force in the development of the nation-state is an old one. As examples of the large literature on this issue, see Hintze (1975), Lane (1958), and Tilly (1990).

including dumping and government subsidization, piracy of intellectual property rights, violation of worker rights, the maintenance of export requirements for foreign direct investors, and the manipulation of the exchange rate for export-promoting purposes.

A second major modification in U.S. trade policy is the greater use of unilateral and bilateral (or plurilateral) means, in contrast to multilateral mechanisms, to achieve its trading goals. For example, the number of antidumping and countervailing duties imposed unilaterally by the United States on other countries, including Taiwan, has increased dramatically since the early 1980s. Taiwan and other developing countries have also been pressured through such new measures as Section 301 of the 1974 Trade Act and Super-301 of the 1988 Trade Act. In recent years, the United States has also utilized bilateral negotiations as a means of resolving trade disputes with such countries as Taiwan to a much greater extent than in the early postwar period.

A third noteworthy characteristic of the "new" U.S. trade policy is a much greater willingness to use discriminatory nontariff measures, in contrast to most-favored-nation (MFN) tariffs, as a means of holding down imports. The orderly marketing agreement (OMAs) with Taiwan and Korea on nonrubber footwear put into effect in 1977, the more restrictive bilateral pact on exports of Taiwanese textiles and apparel to the United States agreed on in 1986, and the 1986 voluntary restraint agreement reached with Taiwan and Japan on machine tools are good examples.

The last change in U.S. trade policy that we wish to emphasize is the much greater role taken in recent years by Congress in shaping trade policy. Although the Constitution gives Congress the authority to regulate international commerce, beginning in 1934 Congress has authorized the president to enter into negotiations with other countries for the purpose of reducing tariffs by some maximum percentage (e.g., 50 percent) on a reciprocal basis. The president could decide which duties to cut. For many years after World War II, the president took the initiative in seeking additional tariff-cutting authority for new multilateral rounds of duty reductions and used his influence to secure congressional consent for this additional authority. However, this pattern changed drastically, beginning with the Trade Act of 1974. In that year, the administration proposed new authority for another GATT-sponsored multilateral round of trade negotiations, but Congress significantly altered the president's proposal. Since then, Congress has played the key role in writing trade legislation. In the 1988 Trade Act, for example, the role of the administration was reduced to one of trying to prevent the inclusion of some provisions that it strongly opposed. Congress has "taken charge" of U.S. trade policy in recent years, although the president still has considerable influence through veto power.

In an effort to understand better the difficulties faced by Taiwan and other newly industrializing nations in recent years in their economic relations with the United States, this paper analyzes the economic and political factors that first caused U.S. trade policy to be largely shaped by foreign policy considerations and then led to domestic economic considerations becoming the major force influencing trade policy. This analysis is undertaken in section 11.1.2. Section 11.1.3 then examines the various trade policy actions initiated by the United States against Taiwan over the last five years or so. Section 11.1.4 discusses specific trade policy actions brought by the United States against Taiwan in recent years.

11.1.2 The Brief Period of U.S. Hegemony after World War II

In understanding U.S. trade policy during the early post–World War II years, it is important to emphasize that the United States was thrust into the leadership position of the non-Communist states rather than actively seeking it. Control of the three key international economic institutions agreed on even before the end of the war, namely, the International Monetary Fund (IMF), the International Bank for Reconstruction and Development (the World Bank), and the ill-fated International Trade Organization, which became the General Agreement on Tariffs and Trade (GATT), is based on the notion of collective leadership by a small number of industrial powers. U.S. political leaders wished to participate actively in the process of creating a prosperous world economy, however. For example, in a 26 March 1945 message to Congress asking for an additional 50 percent duty-cutting authority, President Roosevelt stated, "If the economic foundations of peace are to be as secure as the political foundations, it is clear that this effort [the trade liberalization process associated with the reciprocal trade agreements program] must be continued vigorously." The $3.75 billion U.S. loan to the United Kingdom in 1946 is a financial illustration of this commitment.

Two developments prevented the new international organizations from operating in the manner intended by their founders. The first was the much greater economic destruction in the major countries than had been anticipated, while the second was the emergence of a new struggle for political and economic domination in the world. Restoring prewar production levels in such victorious countries as the United Kingdom and France as well as in countries such as Germany and Japan, who were on the losing side, proved to be a much more difficult task than imagined. The resources of the World Bank and the IMF were much too small to meet the reconstruction and balance-of-payments problems of these countries, to say nothing of the development needs of the less developed nations. Only the United States, whose industrial capacity at the end of the war was much larger than at the beginning, was capable of meeting even the most essential needs of these countries. Most U.S. political leaders argued that it was necessary to assist these countries to ensure the economic as well as the political benefits of the victory of the Allies.

Another, more compelling reason why the United States assumed a leadership role in the immediate postwar period was the political threat posed by the Soviet Union. The expansion of Soviet political influence into Eastern Europe, Manchuria, and northern Korea and the threat of Communist takeover in such nations as Turkey and Greece endangered the political benefits of the military victory.

As those political scientists who stress the importance of the state in explaining international relations (e.g., Krasner 1978, 1984; Evans, Rueschemeyer, and Skocpol 1985) point out, some political and economic actions of political leaders cannot, it seems, be explained in terms of the popular political economy model in which politicians, who wish to remain in office, shape their policies to reflect the interests of various pressure groups, who provide the funds and votes needed to ensure a high probability of reelection. Some policies, especially those related to national security, are taken well before the various political pressure groups are fully aware of the nature of the problem and have determined what policy action furthers their self-interests. The chief executive is invariably given the prime responsibility for initiating such decisions and, by the very nature of such matters, is provided information needed for decision making at a much earlier time than the general public. As Nelson (1990) states, the nature of these executive decisions and the extent to which they are accepted by others depends on the degree of the government's autonomy from direct social pressure, the degree of unity among government officials, and the degree of legitimacy granted to the government by society.

President Truman's first effort to counter the perceived threat by the Soviet Union to peace and stability was to provide military and economic assistance to Greece and Turkey, where there was a strong possibility of a Communist takeover. The president and his secretary of state, George Marshall, also moved on the economic front by initiating a massive foreign aid program aimed at strengthening Western European countries so that they could better resist internal and external pressures from the Communists. At the same time, the United States began to enter into a series of defensive military alliances, such as the Atlantic Treaty, with countries around the world in order to carry out a policy of containment of Soviet expansion. These policies toward the Soviet Union were accepted by leaders of both the Republican and the Democratic parties.

U.S. policy toward the Communists in China was quite different, at least until the Korean War. The decision had been made in World War II to concentrate on achieving victory in Western Europe first. Furthermore, the plan selected to defeat the Japanese was one involving island-hopping procedures led by U.S. forces rather than one based on defeating the Japanese forces in China and Korea and then invading Japan. Consequently, military and economic aid to the Nationalist government in China was modest in comparison with other theaters of operation. The view also seemed to be widely held in the U.S. government that corruption in Chiang Kai-shek's government was widespread and that aid from the United States was not effectively used (Koen 1974).

As it became apparent that the Communists were likely to be victorious in China against the Nationalist government, a decision was apparently made in the U.S. government to cease further military assistance to the Nationalist government and to try to reach an accommodation with the Chinese Communists.[4] After the victory on the mainland of Mao Tse-tung's forces in 1949, there were also apparently a number of important officials in the executive branch who wanted to recognize the new regime. But there was also an influential group in Congress and in the private sector, the so-called China Lobby, who strongly opposed any accommodation efforts. President Truman did, however, state in January 1950 that the U.S. government would not provide military aid or advice to the Chinese forces on Taiwan.

The Korean War, which started in June 1950 with the invasion of South Korea by North Korean forces, and especially the entrance of the People's Republic of China into the war after UN forces had reached the border of North Korea and China, dramatically changed U.S. policy toward the Republic of China (ROC) on Taiwan. The president took the lead under UN sponsorship in resisting this aggression by committing U.S. forces to combat in Korea and ordering the U.S. Seventh Fleet to patrol the Taiwan Strait to protect Taiwan from invasion by Red China. A large-scale program of both military and economic aid to Taiwan was also initiated in the latter part of 1950. The shift in policy was readily accepted by most voters, and Red China was lumped with the Soviet Union as a hostile power.

This incident again illustrates the autonomy of the state in international economic matters under some circumstances as well as the theme that international economic policy is sometimes shaped by foreign policy considerations. However, political pressure from the China Lobby also quite likely led to more economic assistance than otherwise would have been forthcoming. This economic aid lasted until 1965.

As far as trade policy is concerned, Taiwan did not receive any special treatment in the early postwar years. However, since part of the U.S. strategy of strengthening non-Communist countries was to engage in trade-liberalizing negotiations through the GATT process, and since developing countries were not required to make reciprocal cuts in their duties, Taiwan and other developing countries enjoyed improved access to U.S. markets without having to open up their own markets. Beginning in 1976, developing countries were also given duty-free treatment in the United States on many manufactured goods.

One important indirect U.S. influence on Taiwan's trade policy operated through the technical assistance provided by the U.S. AID Mission. As the easy phase of the import-substitution approach adopted in the early 1950s came to an end in the mid-1950s and growth began to slow down, U.S. AID officials pressed for liberalization of the trade and exchange rate regimes and for greater emphasis on private enterprise as the source of growth (Jacoby

4. This statement and the ones that follow are based on material in Koen (1974) and Davis and Hunter (1963).

1966, chap. 10; Ho 1978, chap. 10). Financial aid provided under the program was also important in facilitating this shift in policy.

U.S. hegemony in economic matters manifested itself in many ways in the late 1940s and the 1950s. The dollar became the main currency used in making international payments and replaced gold as the main means of holding reserves for balance-of-payments purposes. Between 1946 and 1949, U.S. exports were about twice as large as U.S. imports as a so-called dollar shortage emerged after the war, requiring the imposition of exchange controls in most countries. The U.S. share of total exports of the industrial countries rose to 35.2 percent in 1953, compared to 25.6 percent in 1938 (Baldwin 1958). In contrast, the combined share of Germany and Japan fell from 24.0 percent to 11.4 percent between those years.

U.S. economic dominance in the early postwar years was based to some extent on technological leadership but, more fundamentally, on the fact that the industrial capacity of most of its international competitors had been destroyed to a considerable extent or become obsolete. These countries still possessed the human skills and organizational abilities to restore their industrial capacities and adopt new technologies, however. With the help of the United States through its aid program, most industrial countries regained their prewar export shares by 1960 and were able to lift exchange controls by that date. The U.S. export share had fallen from its 35.2 percent level in 1953 to 29.4 percent in 1959. For manufacturing alone the decline was from 29.4 percent in 1953 to 18.7 percent in 1959. By 1971, the U.S. share of world exports of manufactures had fallen to 13.4 percent.

Another indication of the end of U.S. economic hegemony was growing dissatisfaction with the international monetary system based on the dollar. Countries' unwillingness to hold an increasing supply of dollars led to the collapse of the Bretton Woods system in the early 1970s and the introduction of a flexible exchange rate system.

11.1.3 U.S. Trade Policy after Hegemony

By the late 1960s it became clear that U.S. dominance in the trade area had come to an end. There was a sharp increase in import penetration ratios in such important product lines as wool and man-made textile products, footwear, automobiles, steel, and electrical consumers goods (e.g., television sets, radios, and phonographs). In view of this increasing import competition, Congress and important parts of the private sector were less willing to open U.S. markets for foreign policy reasons. Furthermore, it was apparent that the dangers of Communist expansion from both internal and external takeovers had decreased greatly from the late 1940s and 1950s. The aid and trade policies had been highly successful not only in strengthening the non-Communist nations so that they could better resist Communist expansionary pressures but also in turning some of these nations into very effective economic competitors to the United States.

When, for example, President Johnson proposed a new trade bill in 1968 extending the duty-cutting authority granted for the Kennedy Round of trade negotiations until 1970 and eliminating the American selling price (ASP) provision of U.S. trade law, not only was the request rejected, but the administration had to work hard to prevent the passage of legislation that would establish import quotas in such sectors as textiles, dairy products, steel, leather, and petroleum.[5] However, under the threat that Congress would pass legislation mandating import quotas for steel, the administration did negotiate a voluntary export restraint program with European and Japanese steel producers. Another general quota bill was approved by the two key committees in the House and Senate in 1970 and failed only because of a threat by some free trade–oriented members of Congress to filibuster against it on the floor of the Senate. The major national labor organization, the AFL-CIO, which had supported a liberal trade policy since the early 1930s, joined the ranks of those supporting this protectionist bill. Arguing, as the 1962 Trade Expansion Act did, that a major purpose of continuing multilateral trade liberalization is "to prevent Communist economic penetration" was no longer effective in persuading Congress to go along with the president's goal of using trade policy for foreign policy purposes.

Thus, when for the first time in the postwar period the United States began to face significant import competition over a wide range of commodities, it responded by rejecting increased protectionism. Instead, a new theme began to gain support, especially within the private sector and in Congress, namely, that unfair trade practices by foreign countries were the source of most of the competitive problems of U.S. industry. When in 1973 the Nixon administration requested broad authority to engage in reciprocal tariff-reducing negotiations and conclude international agreements on nontariff trade barriers, Congress completely reshaped the proposal, making its objective the tightening of GATT provisions dealing with unfair trade practices. These covered unfair practices leading both to increased U.S. imports and to reduced U.S. exports. Among the purposes of the legislation that emerged, namely, the Trade Act of 1974, are "to harmonize, reduce, and eliminate barriers to trade on a basis which assures substantially equivalent competitive opportunities for the commerce of the United States" and "to establish fairness and equity in international trading relations, including reform of the General Agreement on Tariffs and Trade."

In the GATT multilateral trade negotiations that followed the Tokyo Round, six major GATT codes were agreed on, covering customs valuation practices, government procurement policies, import licensing procedures, technical bar-

5. Under ASP, imports of benzenoid chemicals, rubber-soled footwear, canned clams, and certain woolen knit gloves were valued for duty-levying purposes, not at the export value of the goods (as stipulated under the GATT), but at the selling price of similar goods produced in the United States.

riers to trade, subsidies and countervailing duties, and dumping and antidumping duties. Tariffs on industrial products were also cut another 30 percent on the average.

The U.S. objective of bringing cases based on the new codes before GATT panels and gradually building up a body of "case law" that would curtail unfair practices by foreign countries did not work out as planned. In order to obtain agreement among the major participants, the codes were phrased in such a general and, sometimes, seemingly contradictory manner that the panels did not reach the strict decisions desired by U.S. trade negotiators. Other aspects of the dispute settlements procedures, especially those relating to the ability of a single GATT member to prevent adoption of a panel report and to the ability of a member to refrain from implementing a panel's decision, even if adopted, also proved to be very disappointing to the United States.

There was one feature of the U.S. legislation implementing the Tokyo Round codes that has proved to be very important in shaping U.S. trade policy. Congress insisted that the administration of the antidumping and countervailing duty laws be taken away from the Treasury Department, and the president agreed to shift these responsibilities to the Commerce Department. This change illustrates how institutional changes can sometimes have significant effects on economic policy. Because the secretary of the Treasury deals extensively with international financial matters, such as exchange rate and international tax policy, he generally must be acceptable to international business and financial groups, who tend to want as little regulation of trade and financial flows as possible. Consequently, the Treasury secretary usually favors a liberal trading system. The secretary of commerce, in contrast, is more oriented toward domestic business interests and is more likely to have protectionist leanings.

Although U.S. officials were disappointed with the way the Tokyo codes were administered by the GATT, they still emphasized the multilateral route as the main means of achieving their trade objectives. Under the urging of the United States, a GATT ministerial meeting was held in November 1982. At this meeting, the United States proposed a new round of negotiations to deal not only with such well-known issues as agriculture, safeguards, and dispute settlement procedures but also with new issues involving liberalizing trade in services, preventing trade-related investment measures from distorting trade, and expanding trade in high-technology products. Unfortunately, partly because of inadequate preparation and consultation with other participants by the United States, the meeting was a failure, with no new round of trade negotiations being agreed on.

There is considerable evidence to indicate that this failure marked a turning point in U.S. trade policy (Richardson 1991). U.S. trade policy officials decided to emphasize to a greater extent bilateral and plurilateral negotiations as a means of achieving U.S. trade policy objectives, although they did not abandon the multilateral approach. In particular, they decided to use some of the broad powers that Congress had previously granted the president to undertake more bilateral negotiations with such countries as Japan and the newly industrializing nations in order to gain greater access to their markets for U.S. exports and to begin to negotiate special regional agreements.

Significant macroeconomic developments also emerged in the 1980s that provided additional incentives for pursuing nonmultilateral means of achieving trade policy goals. A massive trade deficit emerged in the 1980s with the excess of merchandise imports over exports rising from $25 billion in 1980 to $160 billion in 1987. The causes are so well known that they need not be spelled out in detail here. In essence, the main cause was the rapid rise in government expenditures relative to tax revenues as the Reagan administration increased defense spending significantly while reducing tax rates. The rise in interest rates as the government bid for funds and the Federal Reserve pursued a tight monetary policy to control inflation attracted a substantial inflow of foreign funds, thereby bidding up the price of the dollar in terms of foreign currencies by about 55 percent in real terms between 1980 and 1985. The drop in private savings in the United States and the elimination of certain controls over foreign investment by the Japanese government contributed to the dollar appreciation.

The dollar appreciation made both U.S. exports much more expensive and imports from foreign countries much cheaper. The outcome was the massive trade deficit. Not only were industries that traditionally found it difficult to compete against foreign producers hurt badly, but many sectors that were usually highly competitive were faced with profit problems. Since the administration seemed unwilling to deal with the complaints from import-competing and export-oriented industries, these sectors turned to Congress for assistance. Raising taxes and reducing government expenditures were not popular, so more and more members of Congress and business leaders began to blame foreigners for their problems. In particular, they claimed that unfair trade practices by foreign producers caused imports to be excessive and reduced U.S. export opportunities significantly.

With its tightening of the countervailing duty and antidumping laws, special provisions for the steel and wine industries, authorization of a free trade agreement with Israel, and emphasis on reducing barriers to trade in services, the 1984 Trade Act was a product of an environment of congressional dissatisfaction with the operation of the fair trade laws and the administration's frustration with the multilateral approach. The 1988 Trade and Competitiveness Act is also a manifestation of the dissatisfaction by Congress with the way members of Congress perceived the trading system to be operating. Pressure on the president to retaliate against unfair trade actions was increased through the strengthening of Section 301 of the 1974 Trade Act and the enactment of the so-called Super-301 provision, which requires the administration to identify priority countries in terms of having policies that constitute significant barriers to U.S. exports and then to undertake negotiations with these countries aimed at eliminating or reducing these barriers. The countervailing duty and antidumping laws were further tightened.

The administration did succeed in obtaining authority to negotiate multilaterally on the various new and old issues they had raised in the 1982 GATT ministerial meeting, plus several more. Most of the countries who had opposed the 1982 initiative agreed in 1986 to undertake new multilateral negotiations, the Uruguay Round. Their acceptance of such negotiations appears to have been influenced by a fear that the United States would use unilateral, bilateral, and plurilateral means to achieve their objectives more than these other countries wished to see.

11.1.4 U.S. Trade Actions against Taiwan

Taiwan and such other countries as Korea and Brazil have taken the brunt of the aggressive unilateralism and bilateralism practiced by the United States against developing countries in recent years with regard to trade matters.[6] The elimination of the zero-duty status of Taiwan, Korea, Hong Kong, and Singapore in 1988 is a good example of the efforts to curtail imports from the industrializing developing countries. Another important example is the stricter enforcement of the countervailing duty and antidumping laws. After the Trade Act of 1979, these cases increased dramatically. In 1980 alone, U.S. industries filed petitions leading to sixty-eight countervailing duty (CVD) cases and thirty-seven antidumping (AD) cases. Between 1 January 1980 and the end of 1990, 313 CVD and 469 AD investigations were undertaken. In this period, there were seven CVD and twenty-nine AD cases filed against Taiwan. The number of CVD and AD cases against Korea were seventeen and twenty-eight, respectively, while the CVD and AD cases against Brazil during this period were thirty-six and twenty-five, respectively. The cases against these three countries constituted 76 percent of all CVD investigations against developing countries and 41 percent of the AD investigations against these countries. However, a statistical analysis of the economic factors influencing International Trade Commission injury determinations in these cases does not indicate that Taiwan is being treated differently than other countries (Baldwin 1991).

Another import-reducing measure used against Taiwan that illustrates U.S. policy very well is the bilateral textile agreement reached in 1986. Imports of textiles into the United States that had been growing at about 15 percent annually were projected to increase at only about one-half of 1 percent under the

6. Much of the following account of trade policy actions is taken from various issues of the weekly *International Trade Reporter* published by the Bureau of National Affairs, Washington, D.C.

two-year agreement. In announcing the agreement, the U.S. negotiator stated that it was only for two years because Taiwan maintained high duties on textiles. He also hinted that, if these were lowered, the growth rate of imports from Taiwan might be increased. In 1987, the agreement was extended for another year after Taiwan did cut its textile tariffs.

Much of the pressure has been directed at further opening Taiwanese markets to U.S. exports. Section 301 has been effectively used for this purpose. For example, in one instance, President Reagan stated in 1986 he would retaliate under Section 301 as long as Taiwan maintained a valuation process for duty-levying purposes that was based on an administrative valuation of goods rather than on their actual export prices. Taiwan quickly changed its customs valuation procedures (it had promised earlier to do so but had not met the date initially set), and the case was dropped. In 1991, a Section 301 case covering distilled spirits was dropped after Taiwan agreed to open this market to the United States and the European Community. The threat of a 301 action also hastened the opening of the Taiwanese market for beer, wine, and cigarettes to U.S. exporters.

The first case brought under Section 307 of the 1984 Trade Act, which aimed at preventing countries from imposing export performance requirements, was brought against Taiwan in 1986. A Japanese automobile firm investing in the country had been assigned an export requirement that U.S. negotiators thought could rise from 12.5 percent to 50 percent. Taiwan responded by dropping this requirement.

Using the threat of retaliation, the United States also pressed Taiwan to tighten its laws protecting intellectual property rights, to open its market for such services as insurance and construction, and reduce its duties on various manufactured and agricultural products. U.S. negotiators have praised the country's response on the intellectual property front but are still pressuring in the services area. Taiwan has significantly lowered its duties on many products in recent years, but the United States would like to see much greater liberalization in agriculture.

U.S. officials have also expressed dissatisfaction on many occasions with the exchange rate policy of Taiwan. The global current account surplus of Taiwan reached almost $14 billion in 1987, and its export surplus with the United States in that year was over $15 billion. Rather than allowing the Taiwanese dollar to appreciate, the monetary authorities increased their reserves holdings. These reached $65 billion in 1987 and made the country one of the largest holders of international reserves in the world. In response to U.S. pressure, Taiwanese authorities have allowed their currency to appreciate somewhat, but U.S. officials still believe the Taiwanese dollar to be significantly undervalued.

11.2 External Threat, State Building, and the Evolution of ROC Trade Policy

11.2.1 Introduction

Where the U.S. government faced what might be thought of as an "identity crisis" in the immediate postwar years, the government of the ROC and the dominant Kuomintang (KMT) party were threatened with total destruction. From outside, the KMT was threatened by the Communist government of the Peoples' Republic of China (PRC), while inside it perceived a threat from the Taiwanese people, who had good reason to consider the KMT a foreign conqueror. An understanding of this situation, and of the lessons that the KMT drew from its failure on the mainland, is essential to understanding ROC economic policy–making. Thus, before considering the evolution of Taiwanese trade policy, we briefly discuss the broader political-economic context.

11.2.2 The Foundations of State Autonomy in Postwar Taiwan

With the collapse of the Ch'ing empire in 1911, China entered a period of internal turmoil, the final outcome of which is still unclear. In the immediate aftermath of the revolution, central authority disappeared completely as warlords established local authority that was politically unresponsive to the center. Following the Northern Expedition and the establishment of a new government at Nanking by the KMT in 1927, and despite the brutality of their earlier purge of Communists, there was a brief period of high expectations.[7] Unfortunately, corruption, incompetence, foreign invasion, and civil war combined to render such expectations unachievable. While its failures in political discipline and social mobilization are of considerable interest in themselves, their relation to the economic policies (or lack thereof) of the KMT during the Nanking decade are of more immediate concern.

The Nationalist government in Nanking was in a constant state of fiscal crisis. On the one hand, the ROC faced the substantial costs of defense against foreign aggression and suppression of domestic rebellion. On the other hand, as part of the attempt to buy the allegiance of the KMT "warlords," the Nanking government ceded the proceeds of most of the land tax to the regional governments. Furthermore, until 1930, the revenues from customs and the salt tax were directly controlled by foreign governments. As a result, the central government relied heavily on foreign borrowing and virtually expropriatory taxation of the urban formal sector. Even after the government gained control of customs and salt tax revenues, the need to fund its borrowing costs as well as its military costs led the government to pursue a policy of revenue maximization via import and export taxes rather than a development-oriented policy of infant-industry protection. Thus, although the KMT was rhetorically

7. For excellent treatments of the KMT on the mainland, see Eastman (1974, 1984).

committed to industrial development, and although its policies of unifying both money and weights and measures did lower the transaction costs of business, it is difficult to avoid the conclusion that the overall effects of KMT economic policy were negative.[8]

It is particularly notable that, although the KMT (and Chiang Kai-shek in particular) commanded broad support during the war with Japan, the end of the war and the emergence of civil war with the Communists revealed that virtually no significant segment of society strongly supported the Nationalists. In the cities, while attempts to mobilize urban labor had effectively ended with the anti-Communist purges of 1927, shared anti-Communism was insufficient to overcome the fundamental distrust between Chinese capitalists and the KMT, as Coble (1980) demonstrates. In the countryside, land reform, like tax reform, was impossible if provincial "warlords" were to be kept in the Nationalist coalition. This left the peasants to the Communists without developing any strong commitment on the part of the rural elites. Thus, in retrospect, it is hardly surprising that, with the removal of the external threat, the KMT's popular support and its capacity to resist the Communist forces collapsed.

With the end of the war in the Pacific, Taiwan, which had been ceded to Japan in 1895 (making it Japan's first colony), was retroceded to the ROC in 1945. As a colony, although it was economically and politically dominated by Japan, Taiwan experienced considerable social and economic development. In an effort to impose order and increase agricultural productivity, the Japanese authorities undertook a cadastral survey followed by a modest land reform, the introduction of improved production techniques, and the organization of farmers into farmers' associations. In the more urban areas, the Japanese extended education, developed the processing and shipping industries to support the export of rice and sugar, and, with the onset of the Second World War, began to develop heavy industry for export to the Japanese market and a wide range of import-substituting goods. Although Taiwan sustained heavy damage toward the end of the war, it was probably the most agriculturally and industrially advanced province in China.[9] Furthermore, it was an economy with a strong orientation to modern market relations.

When the Nationalist government took control of Taiwan in 1945, it was not with the expectation that it might be a safe haven. Thus, instead of moving to integrate Taiwan politically and economically with the mainland, the ROC treated Taiwan as captured, hostile territory. Politically, the Japanese admin-

8. For a useful review of the basic economic data of the period 1912–49, see Feuerwerker (1977). For a more systematic discussion of economic performance in these years, see Hou (1965) and Young (1971). The negative effects of KMT monetary policy are too well known to require additional comment.

9. Amsden (1979) and Gold (1986, chap. 3) provide useful short accounts of the effects of Japanese colonialism on Taiwanese development.

istration was replaced by a Mainlander administration, and a nascent reform movement was brutally repressed (Mendel 1970).[10] Economically, ROC/KMT officials systematically dismantled what remained of the Japanese/Taiwanese industrial plant and seized the stocks of sugar and rice, generally for shipment to the mainland. Neither the political nor the economic actions of the ROC/KMT officials appear to have been intended to lay the foundation for complete economic integration or even efficient colonial administration. On the contrary, contemporary accounts stress their corruption, vindictiveness, and brutality (Kerr 1965; Peng 1972). That is, the ROC/KMT acted in Taiwan more or less as it did in the rest of China. The result was that, to use Gold's (1986, 49) felicitous description, "Taiwan's formal retrocession to China on October 25, 1945 inaugurated a period of rapid underdevelopment."

By the end of 1949, the ROC and the KMT were clearly faced with destruction by the Red Army. The Nationalists had been steadily pushed back and were preparing to retreat to Taiwan to make their last stand. Contrary to the politically self-serving rhetoric in both the United States and Taiwan to the effect that the United States was somehow responsible for the "loss of China," it appears to have been clear to Chiang Kai-shek that the most fundamental problem was the incompetence, lack of discipline, and corruption of the ROC army and the KMT (Eastman 1984, chap. 9). It also appears to have been clear to Chiang Kai-shek that dramatic changes were necessary in the ROC and KMT institutions and policies if they were going to survive. Thus, in 1948, Chiang Kai-shek entrusted the tasks of preparing Taiwan politically, militarily, and economically to a trusted comrade (General Ch'en Ch'eng) and to his son (Chiang Ching-kuo). Although these efforts continued to involve the ruthless suppression of political dissent, unlike the period from 1945 to 1947, internal reform of political and party institutions was equally important.

In broad outline, then, by 1950 the KMT had established itself on Taiwan, apparently with the genuine expectation of launching a counterattack on the now Communist-controlled Mainland. Ironically, the fact that the KMT had no organic relationships to the political structures of Taiwan (such as they were after half a century of Japanese rule combined with the recent KMT excesses) meant that it was now possible to implement the microeconomic and macroeconomic reforms that had been politically impossible on the mainland. Chiang Kai-shek implicitly proposed a classic state-building gamble: the external emergency would be used to justify direct repression of political dissent, while legitimacy was built on a foundation of rapid economic development. Absolutely essential to the success of this gamble was the transformation of the KMT into a disciplined, honest, and efficient instrument of Chiang's will.

10. This repression was to have long-term consequences for the politics of Taiwan since a substantial proportion of Taiwanese political activists were among the ten to twenty thousand Taiwanese people killed by ROC troops in the aftermath of the "28 February 1947 Incident."

Perhaps the greatest irony of all was the indirect role of the PRC in bringing the U.S. government back as a major player in the political-economic development of Taiwan. The U.S. government had been a substantial supporter of the Nationalist war effort against Japan. With the end of the war, however, the continued commitment of the United States was in substantial doubt. Not only was it not clear whether the United States would choose to pursue a hegemonic role in the postwar era or, following its historical traditions, revert to a more isolationist stance, but, even after that battle had been won by what Yergin (1977) calls the cold war realists, there was continuing doubt about America's commitment to the Nationalists. In fact, by 1949, the U.S. government had concluded that, short of a massive military effort on the part of the United States, the KMT could not be saved. Furthermore, many believed that, as a result of internal corruption and incompetence, it was not worth saving. Finally, some members of the administration thought that a Chinese Communist regime might eventually be a valuable ally against the Soviet Union and that continued support of the KMT would simply make such a strategy harder to realize.[11] As a result, by late 1949, the United States had decided not to reinstitute military aid and not to undertake a massive economic aid program, and it had secretly informed embassy officials to expect the fall of Taiwan. By the end of January 1950, both President Truman and Secretary of State Acheson had publicly announced that the United States would not become militarily involved in the defense of Taiwan. All this changed on 25 June, when North Korean troops invaded South Korea and any hope of normalized relations with the PRC ended when Chinese "volunteers" entered the conflict in November.

The decision by the United States to support the KMT government on Taiwan did nothing to change its dubious opinion of that government. As a result, the U.S. government sought to stiffen Chiang Kai-shek's resolve with respect to both political and economic reforms. Given the large commitment of economic and military aid and the large number of U.S. government personnel associated with that aid, the United States was a significant force for reform. It is important to recall, however, that, unlike, say, Vietnam, the ROC under Chiang Kai-shek appears to have been genuinely committed to reform.

Thus, for a variety of historically unique reasons, the government of the ROC on Taiwan was able to adopt and implement economic (as well as social and political) policy relatively free from direct pressure by Taiwanese economic interest groups. The modifier *relatively* should be taken very seriously. The point is certainly not that corruption, incompetence and internal conflict disappeared overnight. The point is that, within the government, the external threat and the experiences of the preceding twenty or so years made it possible to impose the sort of internal discipline that had been lacking on the mainland.

11. Barrett (1988) gives an excellent short account of the various positions in the postwar U.S. government with respect to Taiwan.

Similarly, in the relation between the state and civil society, there were no effective elites outside the state: the rural elites had been eliminated in the land reform (1949–53); Taiwanese industrial elites were few in number, tarred by their association with the Japanese, and dependent on the state; Taiwanese political elites had been either murdered or driven from political activity; and Chinese industrial elites had a long history of enmity toward the KMT, most having chosen not to follow the KMT to Taiwan but to relocate in Hong Kong and other overseas Chinese communities. As a result, there was an unusual degree of separation between the state and the civil society. With the exception of the parts of the economy under the direct control of the government, the military, and the party (a nontrivial part of the economy), the links between the economy and the various parts of the state tended to be informal and based on personal relationships (Winckler 1981, 1987, 1988). Furthermore, as a result of the genuine attempts to maintain internal discipline, these relationships, while locally significant, did not dominate policy in broad outlines (again, the state sector is an exception).

11.2.3 State Autonomy and Trade Policy in the ROC on Taiwan[12]

The previous section argued that, as the result of a unique conjuncture of domestic and international events, the government of the ROC on Taiwan possessed an unusually high level of autonomy that could be applied to economic policy. In this section we consider the particular case of international trade policy. As with most treatments, we will consider major stages in the development of Taiwan's trade policy: first-stage import-substituting industrialization (ISI); first-stage export-led growth (XLG); second-stage ISI; and second-stage XLG. The following section will then consider the effects of recent political developments on the future directions of Taiwan's trade policy.

Taiwan's experience with import-substituting industrialization was classic.[13] In the late 1940s and early 1950s, the Taiwanese economy was in a state of profound disequilibrium: hyperinflation, large trade deficits, a severe shortage of foreign exchange, an increase in population of nearly 30 percent, shortages of producer and consumer goods, and a devastated private and social physical plant. As part of the response to this disequilibrium, the government of the ROC adopted the ISI policy that was the standard policy recommendation of the period: strict licensing of imports; multiple exchange rates; high tariffs; and discrimination in favor of capital and intermediate good imports.

12. Given the dramatic success of Taiwan's trade and development policies, it is not surprising that these policies are well studied. Useful sources on the economics of trade and development in Taiwan are Ho (1978), Hou (1988), Hou and Chen (1989), Kuo and Wea (1988), Kuo (1983, pt. 3), Kuo and Fei (1985), Lee and Liang (1982), Li (1988), Liang and Liang (1982, 1988), Lin (1973), Schive (1990), Scitovsky (1986), and Tsiang (1984). On the politics and political economy, see Chen (1990), Chu (1989); Deyo (1987), Gereffi (1990), Gold (1986), Haggard (1990, chap. 4), Koo (1987), and, esp., Wade (1990).

13. Balassa (1980) gives an excellent short account of the received version of trade and development policy.

As with all programs of this sort, the existence of strong government controls and the rationing of scarce goods meant allocation on the grounds of political accommodation and/or direct venality. Without denying the existence of corruption, the need of the KMT to develop a new image (for both the Taiwanese civil society and the increasingly important U.S. aid establishment) restricted pure venality to relatively low levels.

In this period, however, the ROC government did find it necessary for political reasons to accommodate two important classes of person. The most important class was the 1–2 million Mainlanders (both military and civilian) that followed Chiang Kai-shek and the KMT to Taiwan. In addition to a dramatic expansion in the state apparatus per se, the ROC government absorbed a large number of Mainlanders in the state/party-owned enterprise sector (accounting for 50 percent of industrial production) and granted privileged access to the main ISI sectors (especially textiles). The other, much smaller group was the large landlords and comprador capitalists of the Japanese colonial era. The small number of these that were willing and able to form some relationships with the KMT state tended to gravitate to the four previously Japanese state enterprises whose shares had been allocated to landlords in partial compensation during the third stage of the land reform ("land to the tiller").[14]

A couple of patterns characteristic of the Taiwanese political economy were emerging even at this early stage. First, the weak political organization of economic interests permitted government officials and technocrats to dominate the policy process. Even potentially powerful groups (e.g., the Chinese military and Taiwanese landlords and capitalists) were related to the KMT state in a clearly subordinate way. Second, large-scale firms, both state owned and new or newly private, tended to be oriented to the local market. In addition to using these firms for political purposes, state planners sought to maintain control of sectors with significant linkage effects.

By the late 1950s, first-stage ISI entered a textbook crisis characterized by excess capacity in the main import-substitution sectors due to saturation of the small protected domestic market, a severe foreign exchange shortage due to the disincentives to export, and continuing balance-of-payments problems. Although the ROC government had pursued some export promotion in the context of its overall strategy of ISI, the end of the "easy" period of ISI led to a fundamental reorientation of strategy toward XLG. In addition to simplifying the exchange rate system, a variety of export-promotion measures were adopted, including subsidized credit for exporters; the liberalization of import restrictions for inputs to the export-producing sectors; a variety of tax exemptions and rebates granted to export production; the provision of information on foreign markets (thus reducing the transaction costs of exporting); and the liberalization of the foreign investment environment, permitting a wide range

14. The four state-owned firms were Taiwan Cement, Taiwan Agricultural and Forestry Products, Taiwan Industrial Machinery and Mining, and Taiwan Pulp and Paper.

of relationships between foreign (especially Japanese and U.S.) and Taiwanese firms engaged in production for export.[15] Like many XLG programs, however, the policy thrust was clearly toward export promotion, not general liberalization of the import control regime.[16] Tariffs and other controls on consumer goods remained high (in fact, many tariffs were increased for revenue reasons), while government policy continued to protect state- and KMT-owned enterprises from domestic and foreign competition.

Compared with export-promotion programs in many countries, the most notable aspect of the Taiwanese program was the relatively strong reliance on general promotion schemes (as opposed to firm and sector targeting). By creating a mechanism that was sensitive to market signals, Taiwan's export promotion schemes tended to select for global comparative advantage. The results were clear and dramatic. Where exports grew by 4.4 percent during the period of ISI (1952–60), the growth rate of exports was 25.3 percent from 1961 to 1970 and 27.1 percent from 1971 to 1981 (Kuo and Fei 1985). Perhaps more significant, on the basis of input-output data Kuo and Fei estimate that export expansion's contribution to the expansion of total output was 22.5 percent in 1956–61, 35 percent in 1961–66, 45.9 percent in 1966–71, and 67.7 percent in 1971–76.

As comparative research on the evolution of trade and development strategies suggests, the end of first-stage ISI need not have resulted in either liberalization or XLG. In Taiwan, the crisis of first-stage ISI generated substantial support for a package of policies that would stabilize the existing import-substitution sectors while moving directly to second-stage ISI. Particularly prominent among the policies suggested were the creation of government cartels and the identification and promotion of second-stage import-substitution sectors. The potential members of the coalition supporting some form of continued commitment to state-led ISI constitute an impressive list: many state technocrats charged with financial and banking policy were concerned about the effects of liberalization on price stability; managers and workers in the state/party sector were worried about the effect of reforms (there was talk of privatization among reformers); the military was committed to a fairly strong form of self-sufficiency; and, finally, some KMT leaders were concerned about the effects of liberalization on the creation of a Taiwanese (as opposed to Mainlander) business class, and some were worried about the creation of an independent capitalist class of any kind. These are precisely the groups that rent-seeking/endogenous policy theory suggests should dominate the policy-making process: they had concentrated benefits from resisting the policy, and they were already well organized within the state apparatus. Not only were

15. The major government programs implementing the XLG program were the Regulations for the Rebate of Taxes on Export Products (1955), the Program for the Improvement of Foreign-Exchange and Trade Control (1958), and the Statute for the Encouragement of Investment (1960).

16. Krueger (1978) is a standard source on liberalization programs.

the gainers from the switch to XLG diffused, but they were also virtually excluded from the political system.

The decision by the government of the ROC on Taiwan to respond to the crisis of ISI by a switch to XLG can be understood only in terms of *raison d'état,* both domestic and international.[17] It will be recalled that part of the strategy of the KMT on Taiwan was to develop political legitimacy via a policy of economic growth with political exclusion. When we recall that the highly concentrated power structure of the state makes persuasion potentially effective in struggles over policy, the notion that the intellectual arguments for export orientation and liberalization dominated those in favor of ISI deepening as a means of growth maximization seems quite plausible.[18] At the same time, U.S. representatives were promoting both XLG and expansion of the economic role of Taiwanese nationals. This was a nontrivial consideration in a period when U.S. military might was protecting Taiwan from a bellicose PRC and U.S. aid was funding both projects and macroeconomic imbalances. Furthermore, even if Chiang Kai-shek and his intimates had already decided to pursue XLG, U.S. preferences for that policy could be used to restrain the proponents of ISI deepening (especially the military).

In the event, as we have already noted, the policy was something of a compromise between ISI deepening and generalized liberalization. The structural features we identified with respect to the ISI policy are even clearer after the adoption of the XLG policy. Continued support/protection of import-substitution sectors meant large (especially state- and party-owned) firms serving the domestic market for consumer and intermediate goods. This support reflected not only a continuing need to provide a livelihood for Mainlanders who had followed Chiang Kai-shek in retreat but also a continuing belief in the need to control certain "strategic" sectors. On the other hand, the use of general instruments with relatively small industrial targeting meant expansion of small, Taiwanese-owned firms in the export sector. This reflects the second point, that the major beneficiaries of the XLG program were not the more effectively organized groups (Mainlanders and compradors) but local Taiwanese. This is consistent with a state-building view of policy, but not with a mechanical "rent-seeking" view.

By the early 1970s, the international political-economic environment of Taiwan's XLG policy was becoming increasingly uncertain: protectionism

17. We have already explained the state's *capacity* to take independent action in terms of the external and internal threats to KMT hegemony over the Taiwanese political system. These threats were used to justify a highly centralized power structure with tight discipline over the incumbents of both state and party positions and the application of tight control on the political activity of Taiwanese civil society. The issue here is why the individuals controlling the state (i.e., Chiang Kai-shek and his closest colleagues) chose to use this capacity for independent action to pursue XLG instead of ISI "deepening."

18. For the argument that intellectual persuasion was significant in this policy decision, see, among others, Haggard (1990) and Chen (1990). If this argument is accepted, the role of S. C. Tsiang and T. C. Liu would seem to be particularly important.

seemed to be on the rise in major export markets, as was actual protection; a second generation of newly industrialized countries (NICs) was beginning to compete for the same export markets; oil and other commodity prices that were inputs to Taiwan's production process rose dramatically; Taiwan was expelled from the United Nations in 1971; major-trading-partner Japan derecognized Taiwan in 1972; and improved relations between the United States and the PRC made Taiwan's "special relationship" with the United States appear increasingly uncertain. On the home front, the very success of the XLG policy tended to undermine comparative advantage in labor-intensive manufactures via its labor-market effects. In this situation, the government of the ROC on Taiwan opted for a period of second-stage ISI, including the expansion of state investment in both infrastructure and key intermediate products,[19] a brief flirtation with industrial rationalization and domestic content schemes for the automobile sector, and some attempts to micromanage the tariff structure and the foreign exchange market.

Once again, this decision is difficult to understand from a social demand point of view. By comparison with the previous period, it seems reasonable to assume that the proponents of ISI had grown relatively weaker. On the one hand, economic development and the passage of time were reducing the need for policies to ease the adjustment of Mainlanders to life on Taiwan. With respect to the military, while the diplomatic situation was uncertain, it is difficult to conceive of the PRC in the 1970s as a greater military threat than at the beginning of the previous period, when the U.S. navy was necessary to forestall an imminent invasion. On the other hand, the dramatic increase in the export sector should surely have increased the stake of that sector in a continuation of the policy of XLG. Nonetheless, diplomatic isolation and (the risk of) economic isolation appear to have been sufficient to induce the government to adopt the second-stage ISI policies characteristic of the other small, semiopen "pariah" states: Israel and South Africa.

11.2.4 Domestic Political Liberalization and the Politicization of Trade Policy

To this point we have argued that the central fact in the political economy of Taiwanese trade policy was the capacity of the ROC/KMT state to act independently of political pressure from Taiwanese civil society. The very genuine state of emergency permitted the KMT leadership to maintain discipline within the state/party apparatus and to restrict the political activity of Taiwanese civil society. Furthermore, the KMT state chose to use its autonomy to override effectively organized interests seeking broadly protectionist trade and development policies. The most recent phase in the political economy of trade and development policy is ushered in by a devastating external shock in

19. This involved heavy state involvement in petrochemicals as well as the creation of large, public-sector firms like China Steel and China Shipbuilding.

the context of fundamental change in the domestic political environment. The shock, of course, was derecognition by the United States on 15 December 1978. In this section, we consider the effects of the current trends toward political liberalization on the future of Taiwan's trade policy.

The domestic political implications of derecognition in Taiwan were profound, not so much because of any increased risk of aggression by the PRC or even of a dramatic worsening of relations with the United States,[20] but because of the politicizing effect of the change on Taiwanese civil society. It has been suggested that Taiwanese civil society in general, and business in particular, drew three important lessons from derecognition: "We can't trust the United States, we can't trust the government, so we must 'trust ourselves.' "[21] That is, there was a perceived need for direct, self-interested, collective political action by economic (as well as other) interest groups. This realization occurred in an environment of increasing liberalization both within the KMT and in Taiwanese civil society.[22]

The initial implication of the politicization of those parts of Taiwanese business that had not been previously directly organized by the state (i.e., primarily the Taiwanese nationals involved in exporting) in the context of a political opening was a move back toward export orientation. Specifically, the government of the ROC pursued a more substantial liberalization of the trade control regime (especially tariffs and licensing); a liberalization of exchange controls, considerably easing the process of foreign direct investment by Taiwanese firms; and a substantial financial liberalization. This outcome begins to look very much like demand-based politics of the familiar sort: Taiwanese export interests become organized and active, while the state/party-connected sectors are still frozen by the centralized state/party structure.

The end of martial law (1987), the death of Chiang Ching-kuo (13 January 1988) without a clearly dominant successor, and the end of the state of emergency all imply the emergence of genuinely competitive politics in Taiwan. At the same time, the conditions that gave rise to the dramatic separation of the Mainlander-dominated government from Taiwanese civil society have also substantially eroded: increasing numbers of native Taiwanese have entered the highest levels of the state (including, of course, the presidency); in addition, with the passage of time, native Taiwanese have developed closer relations with the KMT government; and most Mainlanders, especially of younger gen-

20. It is important to recall that it took Congress less than a week to pass the Taiwan Relations Act (1 January 1979), maintaining in existence all treaties between the United States and the ROC and ensuring continued equal treatment of the ROC under all relevant law.

21. Any residual hope that the election of a president from the right wing of the Republican party (traditional supporters of the Nationalist government as part of its strong anti-Communist, Asia-oriented foreign policy) would improve matters was quickly dashed by Reagan administration decisions not to export advanced military hardware to Taiwan.

22. For useful treatments of political liberalization in Taiwan, see Chen (1989), Tien (1989), and Winckler (1984).

erations, have adjusted to being, at least geographically, Taiwanese.[23] This has meant that it is increasingly difficult to maintain the kind of internal discipline within the state that characterized the Emergency years.

At least as important as the decrease in internal discipline, however, is the increase in competitive politics. Given the continuing differences in the concentrations of Mainlanders and native Taiwanese in import-substitution versus export-orientation sectors, this suggests that the politics of trade and development policy could become embroiled in communal politics. In the context of increasingly competitive politics, the development of multiparty competition and increased participation of the legislative Yuan in the trade policy process becomes quite significant. Without a strongman at the top of the political hierarchy to manage the system, and with increasingly organized and active interest groups, the capacity of the state to control trade policy is substantially reduced. While the export interests are better organized now than at previous points in the modern history of Taiwan, they will increasingly face political competition from the well-organized import-substitution sector. As in all competitive political systems, competition for office is costly and tends to breed close relations between suppliers of campaign finance and interests with money to give. The legislative Yuan is already becoming more active on trade policy issues.

Perhaps the safest conclusion is that, as with the United States, trade policy in Taiwan will become increasingly dominated by the politics of special interests, more prone to large and unpredictable changes, and more prone to politically driven protectionism reflecting the inherent biases in the politics of protection. At a time when Taiwan has a massive trade surplus in its major export market, this certainly suggests the potential for increasing conflict between the United States and Taiwan. As a response to this, the government of the ROC is pursuing a two-track strategy. The first track is an attempt to diversify export markets, especially with respect to Europe and the oil-exporting nations. The second track is the attempt to gain admission to the GATT. In an increasingly uncertain political-economic environment, the GATT is seen as some insurance for a country that relies extensively on trade. As part of this strategy, the most recent trend in Taiwan's trade policy is a move toward genuine liberalization: reduction of tariffs; dismantling of licensing schemes; and adoption of GATT-compatible domestic regulations. The stability of this strategy in the face of increasingly competitive politics is an interesting question.

23. The last of these should not be taken to mean that the distinction between Mainlander and native Taiwanese has lost political significance. In fact, with the realization that Mainlanders will not be going back to the mainland, both sides have recognized that their political struggles are of a longer-run sort. Furthermore, because these two groups have, to this point, been organized (politically and economically) in different ways, this suggests the possibility of increased communal conflicts in the future.

11.3 Conclusions

The United States and the Republic of China are paradigm cases of different types of trade liberalization (the United States as a hegemonic leader and the ROC as a peripheral or semiperipheral client). We have argued that, in both cases, the successful implementation of such a policy rested, at least in part, on historically unusual degrees of state autonomy from direct social pressure. This should not be a surprising conclusion. A fundamental part of the standard account of the political economy of protection is the asymmetry of protection-seeking forces vis-à-vis liberalization-seeking forces. While this balance may change at the margin, the underlying asymmetry is unlikely to change.[24] Thus, the discontinuous shift to liberalization in both the United States and the ROC must be accounted for, at least in part, by something outside simple pressure politics. An argument of this sort requires an answer to two questions: How did the state develop substantial autonomy with respect to trade policy (an area that had not been characterized by such autonomy in the past in either country)? Why did it choose to apply its autonomy to liberalization? We have focused primarily on the first question in this paper because it seems to be logically prior, but the second question is also of considerable significance. After all, a number of countries have experienced crises producing a substantial, if not quite equal, level of state autonomy without generating a commitment of liberalization (an obvious hegemonic example is the Soviet Union in the cold war era, while Tanzania and Ghana in the postindependence era are examples of peripheral states). An answer to the second question is well beyond the limits of this paper but would seem to be a research question of considerable importance.

A question of more immediate policy importance is raised by the argument developed in the paper. If liberalization rests on a political foundation of state autonomy, what happens when that base is eroded? In both the United States and the ROC, the emergence of increasingly democratic politics in the institutions controlling trade policy suggests, at a minimum, that trade policy will become decreasingly predictable in the future. In both countries, politicians have begun to recognize that international trade and competition are potent public political issues. This has reopened trade as a public issue in a way that we have not seen for nearly half a century. Whether we are interested in the positive or the normative implications of these changes, it seems clear to us that we will not make much progress until we begin a more serious, systematic study of the "supply side" of the political market and the way in which it interacts with demand.

24. Nelson (1989) develops this argument in detail for the case of U.S. trade policy since 1930.

References

Amsden, A. 1979. Taiwan's economic history: A case of *étatisme* and a challenge to dependency theory. *Modern China* 5 (3): 341–80.

Balassa, B. 1980. *The process of industrial development and alternative development strategies*. Essays in International Finance, no. 41. Princeton, N.J.: Princeton University, Department of Economics.

Baldwin, Robert E. 1958. The Commodity structure of trade: Selected industrial countries, 1900–1954. *Review of Economics and Statistics* 40:50–68.

———. 1984. Trade policies in developed countries. In *Handbook of international economics*, ed. R. Jones and P. Kenen. Amsterdam: North-Holland.

———. 1991. Recent changes in U.S. trade policy toward the Republic of China and other newly industrializing countries. In *R.O.C.-U.S.A. relations, 1979–1989*. Taipei: Institute of American Culture; Academia Sinica.

Barrett, Richard E. 1988. Autonomy and diversity in the American state on Taiwan. In Winckler and Greenhalgh 1988.

Chu, Y. -H. 1989. State structure and economic adjustment of the East Asian newly industrialized countries. *International Organization* 43 (4): 647–72.

Chen, T. -J. 1989. Democratizing the quasi-Leninist regime in Taiwan. *World Politics* 41 (4): 471–99.

———. 1990. Political regimes and development strategies: South Korea and Taiwan. In Gereffi and Wyman 1990.

Chung-Hua Institution for Economic Research (CIER). 1988. *Conference on successful economic development strategies of the Pacific rim nations*. Taipei: CIER.

Coble, P. 1980. *The Shanghai capitalists and the nationalist government, 1927–1937*. Cambridge, Mass.: Harvard University Press.

Davis, Forrest, and Robert A. Hunter 1963. *The Red China lobby*. New York: Fleet.

Deyo, F., ed. 1987a. *The political economy of the new Asian industrialism*. Ithaca, N.Y.: Cornell University Press.

Deyo, F. 1987b. State and labor: Modes of political exclusion in East Asian development. In Deyo 1987a.

Eastman, L. 1974. *The abortive revolution: China under nationalist rule*. Cambridge, Mass.: Harvard University Press.

———. 1984. *Seeds of destruction: Nationalist China in war and revolution*. Stanford, Calif.: Stanford University Press.

Evans, Peter B., Dietrich Rueschemeyer, and Theda Skocpol. 1985. On the road toward a more adequate understanding of the state. In *Bringing the state back in*, ed. Peter B. Evans, Dietrich Rueschemeyer, and Theda Skocpol. New York: Cambridge University Press.

Feuerwerker, A. 1977. Economic trends in the Republic of China, 1912–1949. *Michigan Papers in Chinese Studies*, no. 31. Ann Arbor: University of Michigan, Center for Chinese Studies.

Gereffi, G. 1990. Big business and the state: East Asia and Latin America compared. *Asian Perspective* 14 (1):5–12.

Gereffi, G., and D. Wyman, eds. 1990. *Manufacturing miracles: Paths of industrialization in Latin America and East Asia*. Princeton, N.J.: Princeton University Press.

Gold, T. 1986. *State and society in the Taiwan miracle*. Armonk, N.Y.: M. E. Sharpe.

Haggard, S. 1990. *Pathways from the periphery: The politics of growth in the newly industrializing countries*. Ithaca, N.Y.: Cornell University Press.

Hillman, A. L. 1989. *The political economy of protection*. Chur, Switzerland: Harwood.

Hintze, O. 1975. *The historical essays of Otto Hintze*. Edited by F. Gilbert. New York: Oxford University Press.

Ho, Samuel P. S. 1978. *Economic development of Taiwan, 1860–1970*. New Haven, Conn.: Yale University Press.

Hou, C. -M. 1965. *Foreign Investment and Economic Development in China, 1840–1937*. Cambridge, Mass.: Harvard University Press.

———. 1988. Relevance of the Taiwan Model of development. In CIER 1988.

Hou, C. -M., and T. -J. Chen. 1989. The Taiwan economy: Problems and prospects. Taipei: Chung-Hua Institution for Economic Research. Typescript.

Jacoby, Neil H. 1966. *U.S. aid to Taiwan: A study of foreign aid, self-help, and development*. New York: Praeger.

Kerr, G. H. 1965. *Formosa betrayed*. Boston: Houghton Mifflin.

Koen, Ross. 1974. *The China lobby in American politics*. Reprint. New York: Harper & Row.

Koo, H. 1987. The interplay of state, social class and world system in East Asian development: The cases of South Korea and Taiwan. In Deyo 1987a.

Krasner, Stephen D. 1978. *Defending the national interests: Raw materials, investments and U.S. foreign policy.* Princeton, N.J.: Princeton University Press.

———. 1984. Approaches to the state: Alternative conceptions and historical dynamics. *Comparative Politics* 16 (January): 223–46.

Krueger, A. 1978. *Liberalization attempts and consequences*. Cambridge, Mass.: Ballinger/NBER.

Kuo, K. -M., and C. L. Wea. 1988. Access to the world market and the growth of foreign trade. In CIER 1988.

Kuo, S. W. Y. 1983. *The Taiwan economy in transition*. Boulder, Colo.: Westview.

Kuo, S. W. Y., and J. Fei. 1985. Causes and roles of export expansion in the Republic of China. In *Foreign trade and development: Economic development in the newly industrializing countries,* ed. W. Galenson. Madison: University of Wisconsin Press.

Lane, F. 1958. Economic consequences of organized violence. *Journal of Economic History* 18:401–417.

Lee, T. H., and K. -S. Liang. 1982. Development strategies in Taiwan. In *Development strategies in semi-industrial economies,* ed. B. Balassa et al. Baltimore: Johns Hopkins University Press.

Li, K. T. 1988. *The evolution of policy behind Taiwan's development success*. New Haven, Conn.: Yale University Press.

Liang, K. -S., and C. H. Liang. 1982. Trade and incentive policies in Taiwan. In *Experiences and lessons of economic development in Taiwan,* ed. K. T. Li and T. S. Yu. Taipei: Academia Sinica.

———. 1988. Strategies for the development of foreign trade in the Republic of China. In CIER 1988.

Lin, C. Y. 1973. *Industrialization in Taiwan, 1946–1972: Trade and import-substitution policies for developing countries*. New York: Praeger.

Marks, S., and J. McCarthur 1990. Empirical analyses of the determinants of protection: A survey and some new results. In *International trade policies: Gains from exchange between economics and political science,* ed. J. Odell and T. Willett. Ann Arbor: University of Michigan Press.

Mendel, D. 1970. *The politics of Formosan nationalism*. Berkeley: University of California Press.

Nelson, Douglas. 1988. Endogenous tariff theory: A critical survey. *American Journal of Political Science* 3:796–837.

———. 1989. Domestic political preconditions of U.S. trade policy: Liberal structure and protectionist dynamics. *Journal of Public Policy* 9 (1): 83–108.
———. 1990. The state as a conceptual variable: Another look. Department of Economic, Syracuse University. Typescript.
Peng, M. -M. 1972. *A taste of freedom: Memoirs of a Formosan independence leader.* New York: Holt, Rinehart & Winston.
Richardson, J. David. 1991. U.S. trade policy in the 1980s: Turns—and roads not taken. NBER Working Paper no. 3725. June.
Schive, Chi. 1990. The next stage of industrialization in Taiwan and South Korea. In Gereffi and Wyman 1990.
Scitovsky, T. 1986. Economic development in Taiwan and South Korea, 1965–1981. In *Models of development,* ed. L. Lau. San Francisco: ICS.
Tien, H. -M. 1989. *The great transition: Political and social change in the Republic of China.* Stanford, Calif.: Hoover Institution.
Tilly, C. 1990. *Coercion, capital, and European states,* A.D. *990–1990.* Oxford: Blackwell.
Tsiang, S. C. 1984. Taiwan's economic miracle: Lessons in economic development. In *World economic growth,* ed. A. Harberger. San Francisco: ICS.
Wade, R. 1990. *Governing the market: Economic theory and the role of government in East Asian industrialization.* Princeton, N.J.: Princeton University Press.
Winckler, E. 1981. Roles linking state and society. In *The anthropology of Taiwanese society,* ed. E. Ahern and H. Gates. Stanford, Calif.: Stanford University Press.
———. 1984. Institutionalization and participation on Taiwan: From hard to soft authoritarianism. *China Quarterly,* no. 99: 481–99.
———. 1987. Statism and familism on Taiwan. In *Ideology and national competitiveness: An analysis of nine countries,* ed. G. Lodge and E. Vogel. Boston: Harvard Business School Press.
———. 1988. Elite political struggle, 1945–1985. In Winckler and Greenhalgh 1988.
Winckler, E., and S. Greenhalgh, eds. 1988. *Contending approaches to the political economy of Taiwan.* Armonk, N.Y.: M. E. Sharpe.
Yergin, D. 1977. *Shattered peace: The origins of the cold war and the national security state.* Boston: Houghton Mifflin.
Young, A. 1971. *China's nation-building effort, 1927–1937: The financial and economic record.* Stanford, Calif.: Stanford University Press.

Comment Koichi Hamada

This paper is a lucid, systematic account of political economy on both sides of the Pacific—in the United States and the Republic of China (ROC). Methodologically, the study of the supply side of public goods is as important as the demand side. Just to say that the state is the supply side is oversimplistic. Political entrepreneurship, leadership, and exploitation should be explicitly analyzed. Also, one should not neglect the intricate structure of trade conflicts

Koichi Hamada is professor of economics at Yale University and a research associate of the National Bureau of Economic Research.

because trade conflicts can be regarded as a layer of games at both the international and the domestic levels. As Robert Putnam emphasizes (see Putnam and Bayne 1987), international economics can be analyzed as a two-level game. The interaction between international conflict and domestic conflict is tighter in trade disputes than in the macroeconomic coordination attempts that he focuses on because losers and winners in trade disputes are quite distinct groups of people. As illustrated in figure 11C.1, the game of trade issues between the United States and the ROC is of the two-level type, level 1 being international negotiations between representatives and level 2 domestic economic conflicts between groups within a country. Export industries in a country share the same interests with consumers in the other country. Since the countervailing power of consumers is weak, the outcome of the political interplay of domestic producer interests is often a protectionistic world trade regime.

Let us look at the game at the international level. When the United States held full hegemony over the world, it could serve as a leader in multilateral worldwide decisions relying on the rule of established international organizations. However, with its declining hegemony—the United States in the Gulf War was like *samurai* (warriors), who had military authority and leadership but no economic power during the late Edo period before the Meiji Restoration, and Japan was like *chonin* (merchants), who had money but no leadership—the United States cannot afford to rely exclusively on a multilateral approach. Thus, the bilateral approach to VERs (voluntary import restraints) or OMAs (orderly marketing agreements) as well as the regional approach to the North American Free Trade Area (NAFTA) came to the surface.

At the domestic level, the description of the power balance between the U.S. Congress and the president is illuminating. I understand that the U.S. Constitution sets a stage for the balance-of-power game between the legislative branch and the executive branch. This political structure gives the U.S. trade representative the power to threaten its trading partners that the Congress

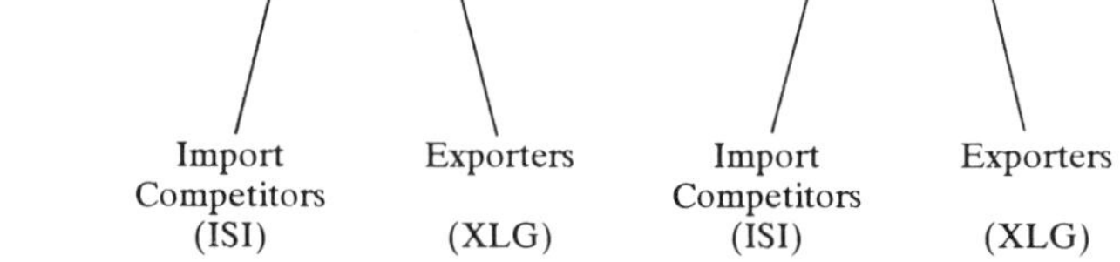

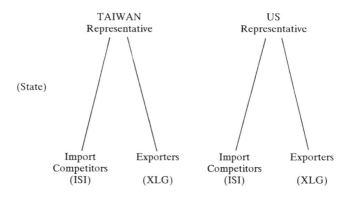

Fig. 11C.1 Structure of a two-level game

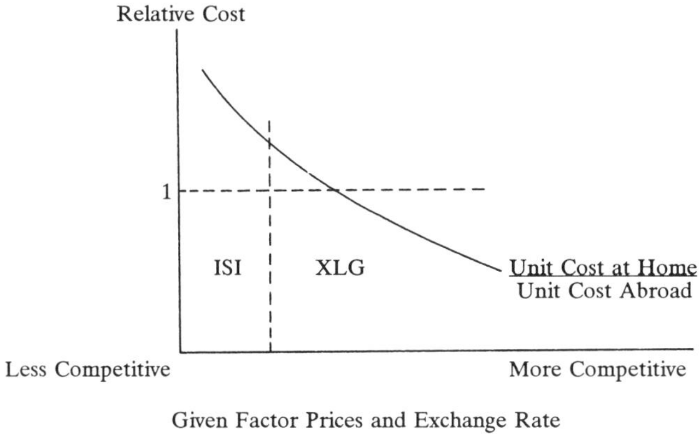

Fig. 11C.2 ISI vs. XLG policy

will retaliate unless the partner accepts U.S. proposals, and it allows U.S. trade policy to be free of foreign pressure.

For Taiwan, I have two questions. The first is, Why did the corrupt KMT turn into a rather disciplined, honest institution? Incidentally, the success of the power elite in civil society reminds me of the success of occupational reform by the supreme commander of the Allied power in the Occupation period in postwar Japan. The second is, Given the fact that the government cannot subsidize all industries, how can you draw the line between ISI (import-substituting industrialization) policy and XLG (export-led growth) policy? Figure 11C.2 ranks on the horizontal axis the relative competence of industries in the fashion that the Dornbusch-Fischer-Samuelson version of the Ricardo model would indicate. ISI policy protects the least competent or incompetent in the future. XLG policy is to subsidize the most competent or the most promising in the future. With limited resources, the government must choose some pattern of protection or subsidization. I wonder if there is some optimal pattern for conducting this and if indeed the ROC followed such a policy.

Reference

Putnam, Robert, and Nicholas Bayne. 1987. *Hanging together.* Cambridge, Mass.: Harvard University Press.

Comment Richard H. Snape

I found this paper very instructive on the course of Taiwan's trade policy and on U.S.-Taiwan relations.

The paper opens with an emphasis on the "supply" of trade policies, as distinct from demand, and argues that the role of the state (politicians, bureaucrats, etc.) in supplying trade policies that address collective goals has been ignored in political economy models. I think that there could be more consideration of this *supply* of collective goals and their relation to demand. Presumably, these collective goods are demanded by the electorate in some manner—voters, funders, and lobby groups certainly include defense and, in the United States and Taiwan, anti-Communism in their demands. Politicians seeking legitimacy and hence retention of their positions can lead, follow, or anticipate public opinion. Following opinion is obviously responding to demand. Leading or anticipating is also demand oriented, although to future rather than present demand—just like any product innovator. A product innovator hopes to convert people to his product—if he does not get the demand, he fails; a visionary politician hopes to convert people to his vision—if he does not get the demand, *he* fails. In some situations, demanders may be the military rather than the voters.

In describing and analyzing U.S. policy, four key changes are identified: (1) a shift to "fair" trade (about 1970); (2) greater use of unilateral/bilateral/plurilateral policies (1982); (3) discriminatory nontariff barriers (from the early 1960s but momentum in late 1970s and the 1980s); and (4) the greater role of Congress (from 1974). This list is generated by a focus on manufacturing industry. If agriculture were to be included, things would look a bit different. The first point—fair trade—would remain. With respect to points 2 and 3, unilateral and bilateral policies and plurilateral restrictive agreements came much earlier. At the insistence of the United States, the original GATT contained provisions for import quotas when there was domestic agricultural price support combined with production limitations—as in the postwar United States. In the 1950s, there was the GATT waiver for many U.S. agricultural products, and sugar quotas, for example, clearly discriminated among suppliers on foreign policy grounds. Finally, on the fourth point, the role of Congress in trade policy, Congress was right in there from 1951 at least. An amendment of the Trade Agreements Extension Act of 1951 provided that "no trade agreement . . . shall be applied in a manner inconsistent with the requirements of this section," those requirements in fact being inconsistent with GATT (Gardner 1980, 375; Dam 1970, 260). Thus, the focus could be broadened to include agriculture in the story, even though it is not particularly relevant to Taiwan as such, and one could then see how the story with agriculture included meets the hypotheses.

Richard H. Snape is professor of economics at Monash University, Melbourne, Australia.

On the switch of responsibility for countervailing duty and anti-dumping from Treasury to Commerce, I would suggest that it is not just that Treasury deals with *international* finance but rather that Treasury has an overview role with a general constituency, whereas Commerce is a client department with a specific constituency.

There is one irony in the paper that perhaps should not be passed unnoticed in view of Ken Flamm's paper. The United States targeted Taiwan for using "constructed values" for calculating import tariffs, just when it was using constructed values for antidumping purposes for semiconductors. Also, it was less than a decade after the United States had, in the Tokyo Round, been induced to give up the American selling price as a basis for duty calculation and the highly protective "wine gallon."

It would be instructive to compare changes in Taiwan's policy in the 1970s, and indeed all the time after 1960, with Korea's. Taiwan adopted the "second" import-substitution policy at about the same time as Korea implemented its heavy and chemical industry policy and abandoned it at about the same time as Korea switched back to less discriminatory support. It would be interesting to see whether the changes were related.

References

Dam, Kenneth W. 1970. *The GATT: Law and international organization.* Chicago: University of Chicago Press.

Gardner, Richard N. 1980. *Sterling-dollar diplomacy in current perspective.* Expanded ed. New York: Columbia University Press.

12 The Political Economy of Trade Protection in the Republic of China on Taiwan

Tain-Jy Chen and Chi-ming Hou

The Republic of China on Taiwan (ROC) has consistently adopted both an export-expansion policy and an import-substitution policy concurrently. While the export-expansion policy has been widely scrutinized and generally regarded as an important driving force behind Taiwan's economic success, the import-substitution policy has received relatively little examination, especially with regard to how it was formulated and its effects on economic development. This paper has the limited purpose of analyzing some aspects of the principal instruments of import substitution, namely, tariff policy and import controls.

12.1 Tariff and Nontariff Policies

12.1.1 Tariff Rates

Table 12.1 shows both the nominal tariff rates and the "average tariff burden" in Taiwan. The nominal tariff rate is the average rate of all tariff items in the tariff schedule. The average tariff burden is the ratio of total tariff revenue to total value of merchandise imports before tariffs and hence does not take into account the effect of prohibitive tariff rates. The nominal rates (simple average) remained around 40 percent throughout the 1950s, 1960s, and 1970s. In 1974, the average nominal tariff rate reached a high of 55.7 percent. Thereafter, it began to decline gradually, reaching 39.1 percent in 1979.

Tain-Jy Chen is a research fellow at the Chung-Hua Institution for Economic Research, Taipei. The late Chi-ming Hou was a visiting senior research fellow at the Chung-Hua Institution for Economic Research and Charles A. Dana Professor of Economics at Colgate University.

The authors wish to express their sincere thanks to Meng-chun Liu for his work in the construction of the models used in this paper. Liu is an assistant research fellow at the Chung-Hua Institution for Economic Research.

Table 12.1 Tariff Rates and Tariff Revenue: Taiwan

Year	Nominal Tariff Rates (%)		Average Tariff Burden (%)	Tariff Revenue as % of Total Tax Revenue
1955	47.0		20.9	14.6
1961	38.8		12.8	17.3
1965	35.4		14.8	20.8
1971	39.1		11.3	19.3
1974	55.7		10.1	27.6
1975	52.7		11.4	23.8
1976	49.1		10.6	23.5
1977	46.2		10.8	23.3
1978	43.6		11.3	24.2
1979	39.1		10.6	23.6
	Column I	Column II		
1980	36.0	31.2	8.1	20.1
1981	36.0	31.2	7.5	17.6
1982	36.0	31.0	7.3	16.2
1983	36.0	31.0	7.7	17.4
1984	36.0	30.8	8.0	17.8
1985	32.8	26.5	7.7	16.0
1986	31.8	22.8	7.8	17.2
1987	. . .	19.4	7.0	15.2
1988	. . .	12.6	5.8	13.3
1989	. . .	9.7	7.0	13.2
1990	. . .	9.7	5.4	9.5

Source: Nominal tariff rates are adopted from Mao and Tu (1991, table 7). Average tariff burden and tariff revenue as percentages of total revenue are the authors' calculations based on *Yearbook of Tax Statistics, Republic of China* (various issues).

It continued to decline after 1980, when the two-column tariff schedule was enacted. Column I tariffs applied to the countries that did not grant preferential tariffs (most-favored nation [MFN] treatment) to the ROC and hence had to pay higher tariffs for their commodity exports to Taiwan, while Column II tariffs applied to the countries that granted a preferential trade status to Taiwan. In practice, except for the Communist states, virtually all free-world trade partners were categorized as Column II countries. Nevertheless, the average nominal tariff rate in that category did not fall below 30 percent until after 1985. For Column I countries, the average nominal tariff rate remained above 35 percent before 1985. Significant import liberalization has taken place since 1985, and, consequently, the average nominal tariff rate has been substantially reduced.

A similar pattern of evolution can be observed for the average tariff burden. It was above 12 percent in the 1960s and began to decline in the 1970s. It was

11.3 percent in 1971 and reached 7.5 percent in 1981. Thereafter, it remained at nearly 8 percent until 1986. By 1988, it was down to 5.8 percent. According to the four-year (1989–92) tariff reduction plan announced by the government in November 1988, the average tariff burden will be reduced to 3.5 percent in 1992, about the same level as the average of the industrialized members of the OECD. The average nominal tariff rate, according to the plan, will be reduced to 7 percent by 1992.

12.1.2 Import Controls

In Taiwan, direct import controls are as important as tariffs in regulating the flow of trade. Importable commodities may be subject to three types of controls: (i) commodities that cannot be imported at all by private importers; (ii) commodities that may be imported, but under strict controls; and (iii) commodities that are imported but where the consent of certain branches of the government is required or restrictions on the qualifications of importers or countries of origin may be imposed. Over the years, the number of items under the first category (i.e., prohibited) has been reduced from 4.8 percent of all importable items in 1956 to 0.03 percent in 1987. The number of items under the second category (i.e., controlled) has been reduced from 46 percent of all importable commodities in 1956 to 1.6 percent in 1987. The number of items under the third category (i.e., restricted) has also been reduced.

It should be noted that many import restrictions are imposed for reasons of national defense, environmental protection, and sanitation and health as well as for the protection of government monopolies and the agricultural sector. Restrictions on countries of origin are designed sometimes to correct trade imbalances (e.g., restrictions on imports from Japan, with which Taiwan has had large trade deficits) and sometimes to fend off products from competitive countries.

These import controls are regarded by many as more restrictive than high tariffs. In the 1950s and 1960s, almost half of importable items were classified in prohibited or controlled categories. Dramatic liberalization took place in the 1970s and 1980s. Today, less than 2 percent of the importable commodities are still prohibited or controlled. But other restrictive measures, such as those imposed on the sources of imports and the eligibility of importers, are still commonplace. The various branches of the government whose consent for certain imports is necessary are often those whose job it is to protect the interests of the import-competing industries.

12.1.3 Changes in Trade Policy

The government of the ROC began the reconstruction and development of Taiwan after the island was retroceded to China in 1945. Economic difficulties abounded, and there was rampant inflation, budgetary deficits, trade deficits, a shortage of foreign exchange, a lack of infrastructure, and low living standards. To deal with all these economic ills, the government adopted a host of policies, among them high tariff barriers, quantitative import restrictions, exchange controls, and currency overvaluation. All these policies were highly fashionable then in certain circles of the economic profession and were generally labeled as import-substitution policies. Government officials believed that these policies not only could solve all the current economic problems but could also nurture the infant industries and bring about economic development. Thus, in the 1950s, high tariff rates and import controls were instituted to protect industries such as textiles, flour, sugar, plywood, plastics, cement, and paper that the government wanted to develop. Import restrictions and high tariffs were also imposed on luxury goods to save foreign exchange.

This import-substitution policy did have the effect of promoting domestic production, but the home market was soon saturated. By 1959, capacity utilization rates in a broad spectrum of industries had fallen to very low levels. From 1958 to 1961, a series of measures such as currency devaluation, provision of export incentives, establishment of tax-free export-processing zones, etc. were adopted to promote exports. In fact, the export expansion strategy can be said to have begun in July 1955, when provisions were made for the rebate of import duty, the defense surtax, and the commodity tax in order to encourage the processing of imported materials for export.

Despite the export-promotion strategy, import substitution as a key economic policy was not discontinued. Import controls and protective tariff rates remained in effect. Some products, such as textiles and certain agricultural products, which had already grown to be the main sources of exports, continued to be protected.

High tariffs, coupled with controls on nearly half the import items, successfully suppressed imports during the course of export expansion. Under the pegged exchange rate, a trade surplus began to develop and grow. The surplus amounted to U.S. $105 million in 1970 and U.S. $766 million in 1973. The successive trade surpluses forced the Central Bank to neutralize the exchange market by injecting a flood of new money. The surging money supply threatened price stability and forced the government to switch policies. Bold import liberalization measures were undertaken in 1972 and 1974. The measures brought the controlled and prohibited import items to less than 3 percent, and that proportion stayed virtually unchanged until the mid-1980s, when a trade surplus reemerged and grew to a very high proportion of GNP.

More extensive import liberalization and deeper tariff cuts were undertaken in the 1980s owing to political pressure from the U.S. government as well as swelling trade surpluses. The United States has been Taiwan's major trade partner, and the ballooning trade imbalance in Taiwan's favor produced a strong American demand that Taiwan open its domestic market. As a result, tariff concessions were successively made, and nontariff trade barriers were removed one after another. In fact, since 1980, the ROC government has been forced to revise its tariff schedule virtually every year.

12.2 Empirical Models of Trade Protection

In his survey of the literature regarding the political economy of tariff protection, Baldwin noted the "widespread disagreement as to which of the various competing hypotheses best explains the structure of protection within industrial democracies" (Baldwin 1984, 573). The disagreement may be even more widespread when we come to discuss a developing country lying between democracy and dictatorship. Nevertheless, in our empirical modeling of Taiwan's trade protection, we shall examine two models to see their relevance for the analysis of Taiwan's tariff and nontariff protection measures.

The first model is the interest group model. This model views the government as "intermediates who balance the conflicting interest of various groups in society in order to maximize their likelihood of remaining in power" (Baldwin 1984, 573). In a democratic society, these interest groups are tied to voting power or campaign effectiveness, which eventually decide the election outcome. In that scenario, political decisions depend on the preferences of voters and interest groups, with the state having little independent influence. This view is exemplified in Olson (1965) and Brock and Magee (1978).

The second model, the national interest model, holds the opposite point of view. It views the state as an autonomous decision maker, formulating policies in line with the "national interest." National interest may cover broad areas of concern, such as national security, price stability, rapid economic growth, equity, national prestige, etc. The model seems to be a natural portrait of an authoritarian regime. It is also called the "bureaucratic authoritarian" model by Findlay and Wellisz (1982). The difference between the two models is obvious, and they represent two contrasting styles of policy-making. In the interest group model, the government responds to the demands of the pressure groups with the sensitivity of responses in line with the group's political leverage. In essence, the structure of tariffs is set in a political "market" where equilibrium is reached when demand for protection matches the state's willingness to supply it. In contrast, in the national interest model, the government behaves according to certain "principles" that it applies irrespective of the amount of pressure (Lavergne 1983, 3).

In the real world, both models may find a certain explanatory power. Hence, they are not mutually exclusive. Even in an apparent "autonomous" state like Taiwan, pressure groups may find ways and means to influence political decisions. In order to consolidate its power base, the state used economic interests to glue together its loyalists (Chu 1989). This includes Mainland entrepreneurs who made the exodus to Taiwan with the Nationalist government, local business conglomerates that maintain an intimate relation with the party, etc. In an autonomous regime, these favored constituents may act as de facto pressure groups.

In the following study, we shall examine the explanatory power of both models when applied to Taiwan's structure of trade protection in 1981 and 1986, the most recent years for which input-output tables provide the necessary data. In the 1980s, the state's degree of autonomy had been considerably lessened from previous years, and democratic elements had begun to emerge in society. The ruling KMT party started to face real challenges from independent politicians in elections; political pluralism was taking shape, climaxing in the formation of an opposition party in 1986. Taiwan also emerged as one of the world's major trading countries in the 1980s, and surging trade surpluses made it susceptible to international protectionism. In sum, the autonomous state gradually dissolved in the 1980s, and we expect the patterns of protection in 1981 and 1986 to reveal some of the changes in the political arena.

We shall examine the protection structure in terms of both tariff and nontariff barriers. The nontariff barriers are presumably the protection measures favored by the executive branch of the government for they afford the bureaucrats more discretionary power. While any revision of the tariff schedule, including reclassification of import items among permissible, controlled, and prohibited categories, must be approved by the legislative branch, the imposition of the aforementioned administrative restrictions on permissible imports was in the power of the executive branch.

How to measure the degree of protection provided by nontariff barriers is an unresolved issue. Various indexes have been proposed in the literature. In this paper, in addition to adopting an aggregated index, we shall also employ a disaggregated measurement for analysis. First, according to the classification in Taiwan's tariff schedule, all import items fit into one of the following six nontariff barrier (NTB) categories in accordance with its administrative regulations, or lack thereof:

1. Controlled or prohibited (denoted NTB1);
2. Facing a producer-only import restriction (denoted NTB2);
3. Facing a public-enterprise-only import restriction (denoted NTB3);
4. Facing a sources-of-import restriction (denoted NTB4);
5. Facing a special-agency-licensing restriction (denoted NTB5);
6. Freely importable (denoted NTB6).

The objects of our study are the four-digit industry sectors laid out in the input-output tables, each sector containing a number of seven-digit tariff items defined in the Customs Import Tariff (Schedule) of the Republic of China. Each item fits into one of the above NTB categories, and the distribution of these items is a fair representation of the structure of protection in each industry sector. Dividing the number of import items in each category by the total number of import items in the whole industry, we obtain a percentage distribution across six NTB categories, with the percentages always summing to unity. Our task is to see how the above-stated models explain this distribution, which is a disaggregated representation of trade protection.

Note that analyzing the fraction of the industry subject to each kind of protection differs from the traditional probit-model approach to the analysis of nontariff barriers. While the probit model classifies each industry as protected or nonprotected, our approach looks beyond the yes-or-no question by examining the methods of protection. Through joint estimation of the distribution of import controls, we will understand not only how the relevant explanatory variables affect the existence of nontariff barriers but also how these variables determine the composition of barriers. The approach is analogous to the share equation analysis of the choice of inputs.

In the second step, we will follow the traditional approach in formulating an aggregate index to represent nontariff barriers. The index will then enter the two models along with the tariff in a simultaneous-equations setting to examine their goodness of fit. In doing so, we basically view nontariff measures and tariffs as two policy options open simultaneously to policymakers. The choices may be made simultaneously as the policymakers choose the policy mix that minimizes the cost of protection, or maximizes their likelihood of remaining in power, or fits into whatever objective function they may adhere to. The choices may also be made sequentially, as in Ray (1981), where U.S. policymakers were depicted as choosing tariffs first and complementing them with nontariff protection measures when necessary.

We largely follow Chang (1986) in choosing the explanatory variables. The interest group model comprises the following explanatory variables:

CR4: Four-firm concentration ratio. It measures the market power of the dominant firms. The public choice theory predicts that the firms in an oligopolistic industry have a lower cost in exercising their political influence and hence are more effective in obtaining protection.

DPAR: Dummy variable for KMT party–affiliated industries. DPAR takes the value of 1 for the industry where one or more KMT party–affiliated firms exist and they are also among the top 500 firms in the China Credit Information Service (CCIS) annual survey. It takes the value of 0 otherwise.

DPE: Dummy variable for public enterprises. DPE takes the value of 1 for the industry where one or more public enterprises exist and they are also among the top 500 firms in the CCIS annual survey. It takes the value of 0 otherwise.

DFDI: Dummy variable for foreign direct investment. DFDI takes the value of 1 for the industry where one or more foreign-owned firms exist and they are also among the top 500 firms in the CCIS annual survey. It takes the value of 0 otherwise.

The four variables are designed to capture the influences of party-affiliated enterprises (by DPAR), public enterprises (by DPE), and local private enterprises (by CR4, which includes the effects of others). Labor unions are conspicuously missing as an explanatory variable, for, until 15 July 1987, the right to strike was suspended, and labor unions were little more than organizers of employees' pastime activities.

The national interest model comprises the following variables:

LAB: Labor intensity, measured by the ratio of labor input to capital input in each sector. Both include the direct inputs as well as the indirect inputs embodied in intermediate goods. The variable is designed to see whether the protection favors labor or capital.

RMK: Producer-goods ratio, measured by the proportion of imports used by producers as raw materials, intermediate goods, or capital goods. In other words, it is the proportion of the sector's imports designated for industrial usage, as opposed to consumption. It is typical in a developing country that producer goods are given preference over consumer goods to be imported.

IP: Import-penetration ratio, measured by the ratio of imports to total demand in each sector. It indicates the market share taken by imports. A higher import-penetration ratio alerts the government to award more protection to the endangered industry if the government is protectionist oriented. In this case, there exists a positive correlation between the import-penetration ratio and the degree of protection. If the government is apathetic to the industry threatened by imports, a higher import-penetration ratio may simply reflect the result of slack protection. In this case, the correlation is negative.

EXSH: Export share, measured by the ratio of exports to the value of production. The export share normally indicates its international competitiveness. We expect a higher EXSH to be correlated with a lower level of protection.

CRIM: Import-concentration ratio, measured by the ratio of imports in each sector to total imports. It indicates the extent to which the sectoral imports drain foreign exchange. This variable matters particularly when the government is concerned with its foreign exchange position.

DKEY: Dummy variable for key sector. This variable takes the value of 1 for the industry that is designated as a strategic mining or manufacturing industry under the Statute for the Encouragement of Investment, the law that regulates investment promotion. If the government resorts to tariff or nontariff barriers to protect the strategic industry, we should expect a positive correlation between DKEY and the degree of protection.

PESH: Public enterprises' share in output, measured by the ratio of the output of public enterprises to the output of the whole industry. It attempts to capture the possible trade preferences given to public enterprises.

DAGR: Dummy variable for the agricultural sector. This variable takes the value of 1 for the forestry, fishing, and farming sectors. It takes the value of 0 otherwise.

12.3 Empirical Results

The distribution of nontariff barriers (NTB) is estimated first. Since the percentage associated with each NTB category is interrelated, the disturbance term associated with each regression equation may also be intercorrelated, and we adopt the seemingly unrelated regression method to conduct the estimation. Furthermore, since the six variables (NTB1–NTB6) always sum to unity, their disturbance terms are indeed perfectly correlated. Hence, we drop one of the variables (NTB2) to form a five-equation model. The estimation results for the interest group model are reported in tables 12.2–12.3 and those for the national interest model in tables 12.4–12.5.

Then a *K*-class model is employed to jointly estimate the tariff and an aggregated index of nontariff barriers (NTB). The NTB index is formulated by a weighted average of nontariff protection measures, with controlled and prohibited items given a weight of 1, public-enterprise-only and special-agency-licensing restrictions given a weight of 0.75, sources-of-imports restrictions given a weight of 0.5, producer-only restrictions given a weight of 0.25, and, finally, freely importable items given a weight of 0. The weighting scheme, albeit arbitrary, is assigned in accordance with the order of the degree of restriction imposed by each type of regulation. The estimation results from the

Table 12.2 Interest Group Model of Nontariff Barriers, 1981

	NTB1	NTB3	NTB4	NTB5	NTB6
Constant	.0139	−.0702**	.0272*	−.0120	1.0158**
	(.84)	(2.93)	(1.51)	(.95)	(25.78)
CR4	.0004	.0018**	.0002	.0003	−.0027**
	(1.45)	(4.63)	(.73)	(1.45)	(4.29)
DPAR	−.0109	−.0546	−.0490*	.0873**	.0589
	(.45)	(1.55)	(1.85)	(4.70)	(1.02)
DPE	−.0403*	.2016**	−.0392*	−.0058	−.0963*
	(1.72)	(5.97)	(1.55)	(.33)	(1.74)
DFDI	−.0152	.0146	.0836**	.0226	−.0953
	(.60)	(.40)	(3.05)	(1.18)	(1.59)
		N = 280, weighted R^2 = .0846			

Note: NTB1 = controlled or prohibited; NTB3 = facing a public-enterprise-only restriction; NTB4 = facing a sources-of-import restriction; NTB5 = facing a special-agency-licensing restriction; NTB6 = free of restrictions. Numbers in parentheses are *t*-statistics.

*Significant at the 10 percent level.

**Significant at the 5 percent level.

Table 12.3 Interest Group Model of Non-tariff Barriers, 1986

	NTB1	NTB3	NTB4	NTB5	NTB6
Constant	.0317	−.0362**	−.0037	.0340	.9736**
	(1.57)	(2.43)	(.73)	(1.05)	(24.4)
CR4	−.0002	.0007**	.0001*	.0009*	−.0017**
	(.55)	(3.05)	(1.68)	(1.79)	(2.61)
DPAR	−.0031	−.0223	−.0020	−.0297	.0582
	(.14)	(1.33)	(.48)	(.81)	(1.29)
DPE	.0431**	.1304**	.0055	.0154	−.1771**
	(2.05)	(8.40)	(1.42)	(.46)	(4.26)
DFDI	−.0201	.0043	.0017	.0644**	−.0468
	(1.71)	(.34)	(.55)	(2.34)	(1.38)
			N = 297, weighted R^2 = .1033		

Note: See table 12.2.
*Significant at the 10 percent level.
**Significant at the 5 percent level.

Table 12.4 National Interest Model of Nontariff Trade Barriers, 1981

	NTB1	NTB3	NTB4	NTB5	NTB6
Constant	.0626**	.1390**	.0848**	.0418**	.7850**
	(2.51)	(3.48)	(2.57)	(2.08)	(14.15)
LAB	−.0001	−.0018	.0008	.0016	.0035
	(.07)	(.58)	(.32)	(1.02)	(.80)
RMK	−.0214	−.1162**	−.0361	.0475**	.1451**
	(.88)	(2.97)	(1.12)	(2.41)	(2.67)
IP	−.0119	−.0556	−.0471	.0534**	−.0088
	(.38)	(1.11)	(1.14)	(2.12)	(.13)
EXSH	−.0444	−.1719**	−.0066	−.0588**	.1809**
	(1.58)	(3.82)	(.18)	(2.60)	(2.89)
CRIM	−.1469	3.3498**	.1954	−.1378	−2.9494**
	(.30)	(4.30)	(.30)	(.44)	(2.73)
DKEY	−.0239	−.0740**	−.0415**	−.0099	.0928**
	(1.28)	(2.46)	(1.67)	(.65)	(2.22)
PESH	−.0411	.4999**	−.0582	−.0191	−.4101**
	(1.36)	(10.33)	(1.46)	(.78)	(6.10)
DAGR	−.0365*	−.0134	−.0386	−.0320*	.0414
	(1.69)	(.39)	(1.35)	(1.84)	(.86)
			N = 336, weighted R^2 = .1123		

Note: See table 12.2.
*Significant at the 10 percent level.
**Significant at the 5 percent level.

Table 12.5 **National Interest Model of Nontariff Trade Barriers, 1986**

	NTB1	NTB3	NTB4	NTB5	NTB6
Constant	.0331	.0697**	.0592**	.223**	.9452**
	(1.33)	(3.73)	(5.65)	(4.79)	(31.24)
LAB	.0002	−.0012	−.0020**	.0053	−.0009
	(.13)	(.79)	(2.43)	(1.44)	(.38)
RMK	−.0125	−.0688**	−.0453**	−.1533**	.0167**
	(.52)	(3.80)	(4.46)	(3.40)	(.57)
IP	−.0477	−.0287	−.0028	.0993*	−.0868**
	(1.58)	(1.26)	(.22)	(1.75)	(2.36)
EXSH	−.0297	−.0702**	−.0207*	−.1831**	.0636*
	(1.09)	(3.43)	(1.80)	(3.59)	(1.92)
CRIM	.2003	3.0376**	.1638	1.4048	−1.2422
	(.20)	(4.11)	(.40)	(.76)	(1.04)
DKEY	−.0084	−.0193	−.0065	−.0249	.0127
	(.38)	(1.17)	(.71)	(.61)	(.48)
PESH	.0098**	.2472**	−.0128	−.0559	−.1507**
	(3.35)	(11.23)	(1.04)	(1.02)	(4.23)
DAGR	.0130	−.0004	−.0213**	.2988**	−.1050**
	(.63)	(.02)	(2.45)	(7.70)	(4.17)
		N = 372, weighted R^2 = .1743			

Note: See table 12.2.
*Significant at the 10 percent level.
**Significant at the 5 percent level.

interest group model are reported in tables 12.6–12.7 and those from the national interest model in tables 12.8–12.9.

It appears that the national interest model explains the structure of protection better than the interest group model, especially when tariff and nontariff measures are jointly considered. In the determination of nontariff barriers, the effect of explanatory variables pertaining to the interest group model is sporadic. Only the four-firm concentration ratio (CR4) and public enterprise dummy (DPE) show a consistent effect on distribution. A higher concentration ratio is shown to reduce the sector's likelihood of being categorized as freely importable (shown by a smaller percentage for NTB6) and to increase its likelihood of being subject to the public-enterprise-only import constraint. Presumably, the more oligopolistic sectors are also dominated by public enterprises. In 1986, a high concentration ratio also leads to sources-of-import and special-agency-licensing constraints.

However, it is the public enterprises that indicate the strongest effect on NTB protection, judged by its highest significant coefficient estimates. The existence of major public enterprises reduces the sector's chance to conduct free trade and increases its chance of being classified as controlled or prohibited or of being subject to public-enterprise-only and sources-of-import con-

Table 12.6 Interest Group Model of Protection, 1981 (*K*-class Estimates, *K* = .7)

	NTB	TF
Constant	−.0277	27.627**
	(.55)	(13.8)
TF/NTB	.0003	1.842
	(.00)	(.22)
CR4	.0019**	.0621*
	(4.07)	(1.71)
DPAR	−.0130	−9.525**
	(.30)	(3.24)
DPE	.0574	−15.153**
	(1.25)	(5.17)
DFDI	.0285	−.488
	(.69)	(.16)
Adjusted R^2	.0624	.0981

Note: NTB = nontariff barrier index; TF = tariff rate.
*Significant at the 10 percent level.
**Significant at the 5 percent level.

Table 12.7 Interest Group Model of Protection, 1986 (*K*-class estimates, *K* = .7)

	NTB	TF
Constant	.0229	38.718**
	(.38)	(14.17)
TF/NTB	.0003	1.022
	(.15)	(.15)
CR4	.0011**	−.057*
	(2.11)	(1.72)
DPAR	−.0414	.437
	(1.11)	(.19)
DPE	.1415**	−.742
	(4.12)	(.32)
DFDI	.0305	−.363
	(1.09)	(.21)
Adjusted R^2	.0972	−.0017

Note: See table 12.6.
*Significant at the 10 percent level.
**Significant at the 5 percent level.

straints (the latter for 1981 only). In addition, the presence of multinational enterprises is shown to invite the sources-of-import constraint in 1981 and the special-agency-licensing constraint in 1986. The presence of major party–affiliated enterprises is shown to increase the likelihood of special-agency-licensing and sources-of-import restriction in 1981, but this influence disappeared in 1986. It suggests that KMT enterprises' ability to manipulate the

Table 12.8 National Interest Model of Protection, 1981 (*K*-class estimates, *K* = .7)

	NTB	TF
Constant	.3208**	51.049**
	(3.75)	(11.59)
TF/NTB	−.0012	−7.191
	(.89)	(.89)
LAB	−.0015	−.515
	(.36)	(1.64)
RMK	−.2108**	−25.331**
	(3.63)	(6.53)
IP	−.0116	5.104
	(.20)	(1.16)
EXSH	−.2128**	−4.123
	(3.85)	(.91)
CRIM	2.0595**	−139.694**
	(2.30)	(2.04)
DKEY	−.1070**	−7.569**
	(3.03)	(2.80)
PESH	.2589**	−7.574
	(4.02)	(1.44)
DGR	−.0821*	−2.506
	(1.89)	(.75)
Adjusted R^2	.1462	.2190

Note: See table 12.6.
*Significant at the 10 percent level.
**Significant at the 5 percent level.

licensing scheme and to divert the source of imports in favor of particular suppliers (e.g., the United States) had subsided by 1986. Except for the switching preference in the forms of protection by major multinational firms, for which no obvious explanation is at hand, the results are largely in conformity with a priori expectations.

As for the national interest model, virtually all explanatory variables exert some influence over NTB distributions. Producer goods are shown to be favored by free import. A higher RMK is shown to reduce the likelihood of public-enterprise-only restrictions and special-agency licensing, and it reflects the government's proindustry policy. A higher EXSH exerts exactly the same influence, indicating the government's proexport stance. The estimates for DKEY are rather counterintuitive, however. We would normally expect the government to protect the strategic sectors, which are often synonymous with infant industries. The key to this puzzle lies in the fact that Taiwan's concept of strategic industries is an unconventional one. It views the industries with good export potential as strategic, and the protection of such industries does not require import control measures for there is little domestic market for

Table 12.9 **National Interest Model of Protection, 1986 (*K*-class estimates, *K* = .7)**

	NTB	TF
Constant	.3601**	41.744**
	(4.09)	(14.90)
TF/NTB	−.0017	−4.650
	(.92)	(.92)
LAB	.0021	.305
	(.57)	(1.58)
RMK	−.2490**	−22.963**
	(4.13)	(9.05)
IP	−.00002	−8.566**
	(.00)	(2.98)
EXSH	−.2360**	−3.920
	(4.74)	(1.38)
CRIM	3.5478**	−21.020
	(2.00)	(.22)
DKEY	−.0500	−3.484*
	(1.25)	(1.68)
PESH	.2366**	5.314*
	(4.29)	(1.73)
DAGR	.2492**	2.525
	(6.44)	(1.07)
Adjusted R^2	.2194	.3856

Note: See table 12.6.
*Significant at the 10 percent level.
**Significant at the 5 percent level.

them. Instead, the government resorts to other fiscal incentives, such as tax reduction, interest subsidies, and duty-free import of machinery and equipment, to assist the industries.

Public enterprises, again, exert a consistent and powerful effect on protection. Their market share is positively correlated with the likelihood that they receive protection in the form of the exclusive right to import (NTB3). The import-concentration ratio (CRIM) also shows a consistent effect on protection. A higher ratio reduces the likelihood of free trade in favor of state-only import restriction. It suggests a government attempt to put itself in firm control of the "essential" import items. Meanwhile, a higher import-penetration ratio (IP) increases the likelihood of special-agency licensing. But licensing seems to be a substitute for other forms of protection without reducing the proportion of freely importable items. Perhaps the government believes that licensing is more effective in curtailing imports when foreign products have made deep inroads into the domestic market. IP is shown to be positively associated with the proportion of free import in 1986. This correlation seems to indicate a causation running from protection to market share; that is, a freer import arrangement leads to a higher degree of import penetration. It suggests that the government became apathetic to import competition in 1986. The agricultural sector (DAGR) shows a conflicting effect on protection. It shows a negative effect on the likelihood of special-agency licensing (NTB5) in 1981 and a positive effect on the same variable in 1986. This reflects the fact that the import liberalization measures undertaken in 1981–86 were mainly directed toward the industrial sector, leaving the agricultural sector relatively more protected as a result. The related evidence is that DAGR exerts a negative influence on the proportion of free import in 1986 but not in 1981.

Now let us turn to the joint estimation of tariffs and nontariff barriers by the *K*-class method. It is obvious that the interest group model is outperformed by the national interest model, judging by the adjusted R^2, especially for the year 1986. In the interest group model, the four-firm concentration ratio (CR4) and state enterprise dummy variable continued to show an influence on the overall measure of nontariff barriers to trade. The other variables ceased to produce significant coefficients, probably because aggregation conceals some micro effects on individual NTB measures.

On the tariff side, the estimation results indicate the inadequacy of the interest group model. In 1981, the four-firm concentration ratio (CR4) has a positive effect on tariff rates, a result in conformity with our prior expectations. What seems surprising is that both Party-affiliated and public enterprises (DPAR and DPE) show a strong and negative effect on tariff rates. It indicates that these politically influential groups resort to specific forms of nontariff measures to protect themselves, thereby earning themselves exclusive rights to import and making their imports subject to a lower rate of tariff. Thus, the lower tariffs actually enhance the degree of protection for these enterprises, rather than lowering it. In 1986, the four-firm concentration ratio (CR4) and public-enterprise dummy variable (DPE) again show positive effects on the nontariff barriers index. But the interest group model as a whole performs poorly in explaining the tariff structure, with the adjusted R^2 taking a negative value. The only slightly significant coefficient appears in front of CR4, with the sign contradictory to the theory. It may simply indicate that the model totally falls apart in explaining tariff protection.

On the other hand, the national interest model performs well in both years. The effects of the producer-goods ratio, export share, import-concentration ratio, key-industry consideration, and public enterprises on the overall index of NTB are largely in conformity with their effects on free import proportions (NTB6) shown in tables 12.4 and 12.5. A notable difference between 1981 and 1986 can be observed for the agriculture dummy (DAGR), where DAGR is shown to have a negative effect on NTB in 1981 and a positive effect in 1986.

The structure of tariffs is also well explained by the national interest model. In both years, the producer-goods ratio (RMK) shows the strongest effect on tariffs, indicating that tariffs were designed to favor imports of raw materials, intermediate goods, and capital goods for industrial production. Note that it is also the most powerful variable in explaining the NTB scheme. Strategic industries (DKEY) were also shown to be favored by low tariffs in addition to low NTBs. Public enterprises' market share in the industry is positively correlated with nontariff protection in addition to tariff protection in 1986. A higher import-penetration ratio is correlated with a lower tariff rate in 1986, indicating that lower tariffs are favorable for the performance of imported goods and that protectionist measures to curtail import penetration were apparently lacking. Meanwhile, high import-concentration ratios were likely to be associated with low tariffs (at least in 1981), but they were usually accompanied by nontariff barriers.

In both models, tariff and nontariff barriers show little correlation. The decisions made on them seem to be independent of each other. There is no evidence indicating that the policy tools have been viewed either as substitutes or as complements in protecting domestic industries.

12.4 Concluding Remarks

This paper has adopted an interest group model and a national interest model to explore the determinants of Taiwan's tariff and nontariff barriers. In general, the national interest model has outperformed the interest group model in its portrait of Taiwan's structure of protection, especially in the area of tariffs. The results support the thesis that Taiwan has been an autonomous state in the formulation of trade policies. Even in the second half of the 1980s, when a democratic society gradually took shape, the state's autonomous power did not appear to subside.

The structure of protection closely reflects the state's proindustry, proexport development strategy. Raw materials, intermediate goods, and capital equipment were consistently favorable imports. On the other hand, labor benefits from neither tariff protection nor nontariff barriers. Instead, labor's rapidly rising income has been mainly derived from the rapidly growing export sectors, which are relatively labor intensive. The results also show that Taiwan did not resort to trade protection as a measure to boost "strategic industries." On the contrary, the strategic industries were likely to be the low-tariff industries. The government opted for fiscal incentives to nourish these industries.

The most powerful interest group, in the determination of tariff and nontariff barriers, was that of public enterprises. They often benefited from being the sole importers of the goods that were directly substitutable for their own products or could be used to produce such substitutes. The active role played by public enterprises in production as well as trade indicates that Taiwan is not entirely a capitalist state. Before privatization takes hold, it is likely that only external pressure can force a trade liberalization that would strip the public enterprises of their vested interests.

In retrospect, it is not hard to understand why the national interest model explains Taiwan's tariff protection better than the interest group model. Until recently, government economic policy was dictated by a small group of government officials under the leadership of the late presidents Chiang Kai-Shek and Chiang Ching-Kuo. These officials were largely engineers by training, arriving in Taiwan from the Mainland without personal wealth and without connections to local business groups. The political environment was such that they could pursue virtually whatever policy they wanted as long as such policies had the backing of the top leadership. They did not have to bow to pressure from vested interest groups.

Nonetheless, in view of the emerging political pluralism and the visible U.S. pressure in the 1980s, we have expected, a priori, an increase in the receptiveness of the state to pressure groups during the 1980s. But the protection structure fails to reveal any significant policy shift between 1980 and 1986. Instead, national interest concerns still seemed to prevail. Perhaps we need to wait a few more years to witness the change. In a sense, the slowness of change also reflected the resistance from the vested interest groups that had been protected in the name of national interest, such as state-owned enterprises.

References

Baldwin, Robert. 1984. Trade policies in developed countries. In *Handbook of international economics,* vol. 1, ed. Ronald Jones and Peter Kenen. Amsterdam: North-Holland.

Brock, W. A., and Stephen Magee. 1978. The economics of special interest politics: The case of tariffs. *American Economic Review* 68:246–50.

Chang, Jui-Meng. 1986. The determinants of trade policies in Taiwan. Ph.D. thesis, Columbia University. (Also published as Economic Monograph no. 18, Chung-Hua Institution for Economic Research, Taipei.)

Chu, Yun-Han. 1989. Oligopolistic economy and authoritarian state (in Chinese). In *Monopoly and Exploitation.* Taipei: Taiwan Research Foundation.

Findlay, Ronald, and Stanislaw Wellisz. 1982. Some aspects of the political economy of trade restriction. Working Paper no. 125. Columbia University, Department of Economics.

Lavergne, R. 1983. *The political economy of the U.S. tariffs: An empirical analysis.* New York: Academic.

Mao, Yu-Kang, and Chaw-Hsia Tu. 1991. Agricultural development and policy adjustments in Taiwan, ROC. Paper presented at the Sino-European Conference on Economic Development: Globalization and Regionalization, 23–24 May Chung-Hua Institution for Economic Research, Taipei.

Olson, Mancur. 1965. *The logic of collective action: Public goods and the theory of groups.* Cambridge, Mass.: Harvard University Press.

Ray, Edward. 1981. The determinants of tariff and non-tariff trade restrictions in the United States. *Journal of Political Economy* 89:105–21.

Comment Kenneth Flamm

This is a very interesting paper. It documents some extraordinary shifts in trade policy and attempts to explain them in terms of a "political economy" framework that has increasingly been used to address questions of this sort. My background in this particular framework is nil, and for this reason I am going to squeeze their exposition into the more conventional microeconomic framework of supply and demand that I am accustomed to using in analyzing markets. In this case, the market is for a rather unconventional commodity called "protection."

I will address three issues. First, what exactly are the authors estimating? My somewhat critical comments on this question probably apply to much of the work in this area, including other papers presented at this conference, so they should not be interpreted as a specific indictment of their work but rather as a more general set of questions about all work adopting this framework. There may be little that they can do to fix some of the specification problems that trouble me. Second, I will make some specific comments about their econometrics, focusing on estimation issues. Third, I want to raise some flags about testing and inference questions.

To begin, when we talk about a market, even one as ill defined as the one for "protection," my first impulse is to draw supply and demand curves. The quantity axis of my diagram should clearly specify units of "protection." After some thought, I decided that one reasonable choice for the "price" axis would be "net price" to the politicians or bureaucrats of protection, that is, votes or payoffs or whatever, net of the political costs of the inefficiency that protection created. The demand curve naturally slopes downward, and, ceteribus paribus, I would expect it to be shifted by the efficiency or competitiveness of the sector; more efficient sectors should value protection less than inefficient sectors.

I would expect the supply curve to slope upward or perhaps be vertical—if, for example, national interest places value on a sector that is insensitive to economic considerations. My diagram refers to a single sector. Multisectoral data allow one to estimate the location of some "generic" supply curve as it is shifted by industry-specific factors.

Chen and Hou identify two theories of the supply side: one, the "interest group" theory, discusses relative changes in supply in terms of factors that make it easier for interest groups to act on the state. Thus, for example, a more concentrated industry, or an industry associated with a powerful political party, might face a greater supply of protection for given price. They also identify a "national interest" theory of supply (which one might also call the "autonomous state" theory), which argues that visionary—or stubborn—bu-

Kenneth Flamm is senior fellow in the Foreign Policy Studies Program at the Brookings Institution, Washington, D.C.

reaucrats supply protection based on criteria that are independent of the blandishments, or the ability to supply blandishments, of the industry in question. To my way of thinking, this supply curve should probably rise vertically. They see it shifted by such factors as labor intensity, orientation toward production (rather than consumption) goods, and import penetration.

Now, in general, we will observe actual industry outcomes generated by shifts in both supply and demand, and we have to ask whether we can identify supply or demand. Unfortunately, it seems to me that the factors identified as shifting supply under the "national interest" hypothesis also determine competitiveness and therefore shift the demand for protection; this raises the serious question of whether we can identify this "supply curve" econometrically. One seeming way out would be to estimate a reduced-form equation giving the equilibrium quantity of protection, rather than a structural equation, and test for hypotheses concerning the supply curve by means of exogenous variables included in this reduced form. However, if the demand curve contains the same exogenous variables as arguments, this approach still will not work.

The interest group theory of supply faces other problems. Some of its determinants—notably industry concentration and the presence of foreign investment—are clearly caused by, as well as possibly causing, the level of protection. Therefore, this requires the use of statistical models that provide for their endogeneity, which the authors, unfortunately, do not use.

Next, let me turn to estimation issues. The authors use a seemingly unrelated regression model to estimate the supply of different types of nontariff barriers. Why not also include tariff levels in this system? Also, as previously mentioned, some of their explanatory variables are almost certainly endogenous.

For some unspecified reason, the authors decide to use a K-class estimator for an alternative model, which includes equations explaining both tariff and aggregate nontariff barriers. For even less clear reasons, they choose a value of $K = .7$, which guarantees that their coefficient estimates are inconsistent. Why not simply use two-stage least squares (i.e., $K = 1$)? The only justification for such another choice of K (other than the root of a determinantal equation, which gives the limited information maximum likelihood estimator) that I can think of would revolve around possible small sample characteristics of the distribution of the estimator, and I see no such justification given here. Also, since the K-class estimator is a limited information estimation technique, I surmise that they are "stacking" the two equations and not attempting to estimate cross-equation covariances. Thus, the only sense in which they are using a "joint" estimation technique is that they presume identical variances for the disturbance terms in each of the two equations. Some discussion of their variables and equation structure justifying the techniques they have chosen to use would have been desirable.

The last issue I must mention is that of specification testing. With seemingly unrelated regressions (because you are transforming variables using an estimated covariance matrix), R^2 cannot be used as a test of goodness of fit for alternative specifications. In fact, the only context in which R^2 measures something that is directly and appropriately interpretable as a transformation of a meaningful specification statistic is for ordinary least squares, which they are not using. One way in which they might construct a meaningful specification test is to include both sets of variables, then constrain subsets to equal zero and calculate a Wald statistic, which is easily done in most econometric packages.

In conclusion, I would offer the following suggestions for further work. Estimate reduced-form equations, using all the exogenous variables discussed in this paper. Then constrain those associated with the "interest group" theory of supply to equal zero and construct a Wald test for this hypothesis, which will allow you to accept or reject the interest group theory hypothesis. Unfortunately, you will not be able to use an analogous procedure with the "national interest" theory because the exogenous variables playing a potential role in supply may also be expected to affect the demand for protection.

Comment Ching-huei Chang

This is an interesting and stimulating paper, and I enjoyed reading it very much. In this paper, Tain-Jy Chen and Chi-ming Hou attempt to determine whether Taiwan's tariff and nontariff trade policy can be better described by an interest group model or a national interest model. For that purpose, they formulate some aggregate and disaggregate indexes according to the degree of protection provided by nontariff barriers. These indexes and tariff levels are then fitted into several regression equations, using different explanatory variables under different hypotheses, for the years 1981 and 1986. From the results obtained, they conclude: "In general, the national interest model has outperformed the interest group model in its portrait of Taiwan's structure of protection, especially in the area of tariffs."

I do not have any doubts about the adequacy of their estimation, and the conclusion they reach seems to me not surprising. However, I would like to see some discussion about how the demand and supply of protection works to determine the levels and structure of tariffs and nontariff barriers. The political "market" in Taiwan is markedly different from that in the United States or other advanced nations. It is close to a monopolistic market, even after 1985, when the first opposition party was formed. Compared with the ruling KMT party, the major opposition party, the Democratic Progressive party (DPP), is quite weak in every aspect. Because administrators, including the president,

Ching-huei Chang is a research fellow of Sun Yat-sen Institute for Social Sciences and Philosophy, Academia Sinica, Taiwan.

the vice president, prime ministers, and a large proportion of parliamentary members, are not elected by citizens of the society, they do not have the intention of taking actions in line with the will or preference of the people. Here we have a divergence between the government objective function and the social welfare function (however it is defined), even though the decision makers may rationalize these actions in terms of national security, national prestige, or national interest. However, because there still exists a potential threat of competition from the opposition party, these decision makers may restrain their behaviors in order not to lose market shares to DPP or other parties. Summing up, Taiwan is not a democratic country, nor is it a dictatorship. Therefore, whether a national interest model or an interest group model can be applied to explain Taiwan's protection policy is questionable.

Another point should be made. There are interest groups existing in Taiwan that exercise their influence, not through lobbying or any other open actions found in advanced nations, but through under-the-table operations (like bribery or seeking a good connection with some power "elite"). For example, one of the automobile companies used to be protected from foreign competition by tariff and nontariff barriers because its owner had close connections with the late President Chiang Kai-shek. Finally, there exists pressure from the United States and some other countries that may have some effect on the demand for, or supply of, protection.

At any rate, we need a new theoretical model that fits into the framework of Taiwan's political situation. This suggestion may be consistent with the results of Chen and Hou's regression analyses reported in their tables 12.2–12.9. In most of these regression equations, adjusted R^2 is quite small, and the estimated value of the constant term is significantly different from zero. Obviously, some important variables are missing in these equations.

13 The Political Economy of Protection Structure in Korea

Yoo Jung-ho

There have not been many empirical studies of the determination of the protection structures in developing countries. Korea is no exception. Alikhani and Havrylyshyn (1982) (as quoted in Amelung [1989]) and Jwa (1988) are examples of the few studies of Korea's protection. The empirical part of Jwa investigates the determinants of the import liberalization that took place in the mid-1980s. This paper attempts to explain the political economy of the determination of protection levels.

Section 13.1 presents three different measures of nominal protection in Korea for 1978, 1982, and 1988, the years for which data are available. The section also presents estimates of the effective rates of protection for 1978 and 1982. It should be noted that nominal and effective protective rates are estimated only for domestic sales, not for total sales, as export sales cannot be protected. The section also discusses the salient features of the protective structure and changes over time.

Section 13.2 considers whether the political economy discussion of the protection structure can be profitably applied to a developing country, in particular, to Korea, where the influence of elected representatives on trade policy matters has not been as strong as in the industrial democracies. Section 13.3 estimates simple regression models of the determination of the nominal and effective protection structures and reports the results. Section 13.4 provides a brief summary and conclusion.

13.1 The Protection Structure in Korea

13.1.1 The Structure of Nominal Protection

In tables 13.1–13.3, tariffs, actual tariffs, and nominal rates of protection (NRPs) are presented by primary sector and manufacturing three-digit KSIC

Yoo Jung-ho is a senior fellow at the Korea Development Institute.

Table 13.1 The Structure of Nominal Protection in 1978 (%)

	Tariffs	Actual Tariffs	NRP
Agriculture	25.8	20.6	50.0
Forestry	13.8	13.1	3.9
Fishing	34.7	22.2	1.4
Mining	17.7	1.8	1.3
Manufacturing	40.8	25.1	19.7
Food	39.4	30.0	18.5
Beverage	125.0	18.1	12.9
Tobacco	150.0	127.1	19.3
Textiles	49.2	29.8	10.9
Clothing	60.0	39.3	32.9
Footwear, leather	47.9	44.0	29.1
Wood	30.0	19.8	2.4
Furniture	60.0	3.6	22.8
Pulp, paper	36.4	26.3	18.1
Printing	8.1	3.5	8.5
Industrial chemicals	23.6	16.4	17.5
Other chemicals	35.9	34.6	27.9
Oil refining	20.4	7.4	5.8
Petrol., coal products	20.4	.5	15.1
Rubber products	50.0	27.3	5.2
Plastic products	60.0	29.8	6.1
Pottery, china	60.0	20.8	14.3
Glass	45.5	32.4	13.2
Other nonmetal min. prods.	30.6	21.9	8.2
Iron & steel	20.8	13.6	15.5
Nonferrous metal	21.0	17.5	24.8
Fabricated metal	39.8	23.5	14.5
Nonelectrical mach.	23.6	13.3	30.8
Electrical mach.	36.5	27.3	36.7
Transport. equip.	45.6	25.7	34.5
Prof., scien. equip.	34.5	28.1	40.5
Miscellaneous mfg.	63.2	25.9	8.6
All industries	36.3	22.6	22.3
	(38.1)	(22.9)	(17.4)
Standard deviation	21.4	17.9	20.9
	(22.1)	(17.7)	(18.5)

Note: Tariffs are the rates applied to trade from July 1978 to June 1979. Actual tariffs were computed for 1978. NRPs are based on the price survey conducted in 1982. The figures in parentheses refer to "all industries" excluding the agricultural sector.

(Korea Standard Industrial Classification) industry. These sectors and industries are aggregates of the more detailed industries in the *Input-Output Tables* that the Bank of Korea estimated.[1] The three different rates of nominal protec-

1. The bank publishes the tables at different levels of aggregation. The ones used in this paper have about 160 industries, of which about 120 are producing tradable goods (the number differs for different years).

Table 13.2 **The Structure of Nominal Protection in 1982 (%)**

	Tariffs	Actual Tariffs	NRP
Agriculture	18.7	14.8	72.3
Forestry	17.2	12.0	.5
Fishing	29.7	28.4	5.6
Mining	4.2	3.2	.3
Manufacturing	32.9	21.2	17.2
Food	21.4	19.0	11.7
Beverage	126.7	24.1	8.4
Tobacco	150.0	143.9	16.3
Textiles	40.3	29.3	8.5
Clothing	60.8	14.0	29.0
Footwear, leather	51.4	38.8	28.3
Wood	25.8	22.3	8.6
Furniture	58.9	3.8	.2
Pulp, paper	37.8	22.9	18.3
Printing	11.0	1.5	1.2
Industrial chemicals	18.7	11.9	24.3
Other chemicals	31.9	30.7	33.0
Oil refining	6.2	4.0	22.7
Petrol, coal products	4.2	.3	3.0
Rubber products	47.0	26.7	13.6
Plastic products	60.0	33.2	16.3
Pottery, china	60.0	20.1	12.7
Glass	42.4	32.6	13.0
Other nonmetal min. prods.	23.5	23.2	22.7
Iron & steel	14.7	10.5	12.9
Nonferrous metal	22.4	16.0	13.0
Fabricated metal	35.5	22.6	9.8
Nonelectrical mach.	18.1	9.6	22.2
Electrical mach.	38.6	22.5	26.2
Transport. equip.	53.8	25.3	31.9
Prof., scien. equip.	29.5	21.6	26.4
Miscellaneous mfg.	58.5	30.2	6.4
All industries	30.8	20.2	22.0
	(32.1)	(20.8)	(16.4)
Standard deviation	23.4	18.3	24.6
	(23.8)	(18.2)	(14.7)

Note: Tariffs are the rates applied to trade from July 1981 to June 1982. Actual tariffs were computed for 1981. NRPs are based on the price survey conducted in 1982. The figures in parentheses refer to "all industries" excluding the agricultural sector.

tion for a sector or KSIC industry shown in the tables are weighted averages of the respective rates for the input-output industries belonging to the sector or industry, the weights being the domestic sales evaluated at border prices.

The tariff for an industry in the *Input-Output Tables* is an unweighted, simple average of the tariffs on imported products classified as belonging to the industry. The actual tariff for an input-output industry, in contrast, is the ratio of the tariff revenue to the imports of the products belonging to the in-

Table 13.3 **The Structure of Nominal Protection in 1988 (%)**

	Tariffs	Actual Tariffs	NRP
Agriculture	23.1	14.4	103.9
Forestry	15.3	10.9	15.3
Fishing	19.8	11.9	11.9
Mining	5.7	4.5	2.3
Manufacturing	18.3	12.4	12.7
Food	15.2	9.9	10.8
Beverage	80.0	56.1	25.5
Tobacco	70.0	49.2	70.0
Textiles	19.0	11.7	8.1
Clothing	28.7	17.4	15.9
Footwear, leather	19.9	9.8	9.8
Wood	17.1	13.7	8.2
Furniture	19.5	9.2	4.2
Pulp, paper	18.2	14.4	8.4
Printing	3.1	4.2	3.1
Industrial chemicals	15.9	10.1	11.5
Other chemicals	19.4	14.6	25.8
Oil refining	9.8	8.5	9.9
Petrol, coal products	.7	.8	3.0
Rubber products	18.6	12.2	10.5
Plastic products	18.6	13.4	20.1
Pottery, china	25.5	18.9	7.7
Glass	19.3	12.2	11.1
Other nonmetal min. prods.	17.9	13.5	8.9
Iron & steel	11.6	7.0	2.3
Nonferrous metal	18.1	12.3	7.0
Fabricated metal	20.1	12.6	7.6
Nonelectrical mach.	18.5	10.1	20.5
Electrical mach.	19.9	20.4	20.6
Transport equip.	18.8	7.8	13.5
Prof., scien. equip.	21.0	10.7	22.0
Miscellaneous mfg.	21.5	10.5	13.0
All industries	18.4	12.4	20.1
	(18.0)	(12.2)	(12.5)
Standard deviation	12.0	11.2	54.8
	(11.6)	(10.4)	(14.9)

Note: Both tariffs and actual tariffs are for 1988. NRPs are based on the survey conducted in 1990. The figures in parentheses refer to "all industries" excluding the agricultural sector.

dustry less the imports of the products for export production. The latter imports were subtracted from the denominator because they were exempted from tariffs by the Tariff Act and their inclusion will understate the extent to which an industry's domestic sales are protected by tariffs.

An NRP is estimated, first, for an industry in the *Input-Output Tables,* by selecting one among the following three candidates: tariff, actual tariff, and the tariff equivalent of the price differential between the domestic and the international price, which is also called the implicit tariff. In the selection, such things were taken into account as whether the products of an industry were being exported or were import competing, how large imports were compared to domestic demand, and whether there were nontariff barriers.[2] It should be noted that the three candidates for the 1988 NRPs were tariffs and actual tariffs in 1988 and the tariff equivalents obtained from a price survey conducted in 1990.

In obtaining the averages presented in tables 13.1–13.3, the industries' domestic sales evaluated in border prices (which were in turn obtained by deflating the domestic sales by the NRPs) were used as weights. Thus weighted, the average rates indicate the extent by which the price of a basket of goods that are domestically produced and sold by an aggregate industry would increase as the result of import restrictions of one form or another.

The Differences among the Three Nominal Rates of Protection

An interesting feature of the protection structure for 1978 and 1982 is that tariffs were generally much higher than actual tariffs and that the latter in turn tended to be higher than the NRPs. In table 13.1 for 1978, mining products provide an extreme example, where the actual tariff was less than 2 percent, while the tariff was nearly 18 percent, and the NRP was still smaller than the actual tariff. The average tariff for manufactured goods was 41 percent, the average actual tariff was 25 percent, and the average NRP was 20 percent. An important exception to this feature was the agricultural sector, for which the NRP was much higher than the actual tariff.

Korea's Tariff Act allowed tariff exemptions and rebates on imported inputs for export production. However, this was not the reason why actual tariffs were substantially lower than tariffs. Tariff-exempted imports for export production were not counted in calculating the reported actual tariffs, as mentioned earlier. The Tariff Act also allowed tariff exemptions for the intermediate inputs used by defense industries and others that "lead the technological development" in the rest of the economy. Use of tariff quotas could also be one of the reasons why actual tariffs were lower than tariffs.

The obvious reason why NRPs tended to be lower than actual tariffs is that, for some products, the tariff equivalent implicit in the domestic to border price ratio was lower than the actual tariffs. Such a thing cannot happen if the domestic and foreign products were identical. A domestic price lower than the border price plus tariff will prevent the product from being imported. Hence, no tariffs would be collected, and no actual tariff would be available. However, since most products can only be defined to include a spectrum of differ-

2. The tariff equivalents were estimated on the basis of a detailed survey of domestic and international prices in 1982. The domestic to international price ratios were extrapolated backward to obtain the tariff equivalents for 1978. In the extrapolation, domestic and foreign price indices were used. Korea Development Institute (1982) reports the actual tariffs and NRPs for 1978 and 1982. The tariffs, actual tariffs, and nominal rates of protection in table 13.3 are newly estimated.

entiated products, it can happen that imported goods at one end of the spectrum have after-tariff prices that are higher than the average price of the products in the domestic market.

An interesting question raised by the observed difference between tariffs and NRPs is why tariffs are maintained at levels "higher than necessary." One possible explanation, related to external trade relations, would be that tariffs are the outer wall protecting the ability to protect domestic industries, with the difference between the tariffs or actual tariffs and NRPs constituting a buffer. Another likely explanation would be the internal one that the government maintains a considerable degree of discretionary power to intervene in the market and to allocate favors between groups in the private sector. These hypotheses cannot be fully explored in this paper, but its investigation will be directed to the related issue of how interindustry differences in protection came into being.

The tendency for tariffs to exaggerate the level of actual protection did not hold in the late 1980s, and the tendency had important exceptions in 1978 and 1982. In the agricultural sector, the average NRP was higher than the average tariff, and the same was true for a number of individual industries in the manufacturing sector, most notably for the machinery industries. An NRP of a product will exceed the tariff or actual tariff if there are nontariff barriers (NTBs) in addition to tariffs.

This suggests that NTBs have been important policy instruments in protecting industries of low comparative advantage. Korea's comparative advantage is very low in the agricultural sector even though that sector still accounts for a large proportion of the labor force, 38 percent in 1978 and 20 percent in 1989. The comparative advantage is also low in the production of machines. Imports of all kinds of machinery have been the major reason for trade deficits, which the country longs very much to get rid of. If NTBs were indeed important in protecting the sectors and industries with low comparative advantage, this suggests that, in Korea, the policymakers and bureaucrats in the administrative branch of the government were playing a very influential role in determining the structure of protection, for the administration of NTBs generally involves a greater degree of discretion than the administration of tariff barriers.

Changes Over Time

The three tables presented above cover a period of about ten years from the late 1970s to the late 1980s. During that period, there was a sharp decline in tariffs. As a comparison of tables 13.1 and 13.3 reveals, the average tariff for all industries was halved from 36 percent to about 18 percent. This largely reflected the decline in the average tariff for the manufacturing sector from 41 percent in 1978 to 18 percent in 1988 since the sector has much larger domestic sales than the other sectors.

The average of actual tariffs for all industries was also halved from 23 percent to 12 percent during the same period. Here again, the decline largely reflects what happened to the actual tariffs in the manufacturing sector, which declined from 25 percent to 12 percent. A major part of the decline took place since 1982.

In contrast to this trend in tariffs and actual tariffs, there was little change in the average NRP for all industries for the ten-year period. This was due mostly to the trends in the NRPs for the agricultural and manufacturing sectors offsetting each other. On the one hand, the average NRP doubled from 50 percent to more than 100 percent in the agricultural sector. On the other hand, it declined from 20 percent to 13 percent in the manufacturing sector, roughly in line with what happened to tariffs and actual tariffs.[3]

The variations in tariffs and actual tariffs tended to decline. At the bottoms of tables 13.1–13.3 are shown the standard deviations of the three protective rates for about 120 industries in the *Input-Output Tables*. The standard deviation of the tariffs was roughly halved between 1978 and 1988, and that of the actual tariffs also declined sharply, although not as rapidly. In contrast, the standard deviation of the NRPs rose steeply during the same period. Here again, the reason was the rise in the standard deviation of the NRPs for the agricultural sector. With that sector excluded, the standard deviation of the NRPs declined, although the pace was the slowest among the three rates of protection.

13.1.2 The Structure of Effective Protection

Table 13.4 presents estimates of the effective rates of protection (ERPs) for 1978 and 1982 at the same level of industry aggregation as the ones used for nominal protection. To obtain these estimates, the NRPs were applied to the *Input-Output Tables*, after indirect taxes were subtracted from interindustry transactions and all inputs were reevaluated in domestic prices, and the "Corden method" (suggested in Corden [1966]) was followed. At the time of estimation, the latest *Input-Output Table* available was that for 1978, and this was used in estimating the 1982 ERPs as well as the 1978 ERPs.[4]

The main features of the effective rates presented in table 13.4 are that the ERPs were high for the agricultural and manufacturing sectors and that, within the manufacturing sector, the chemical and machinery industries enjoyed high ERPs.

The relation between the structure of effective protection and the compara-

3. The NRPs for a number of manufacturing industries show somewhat erratic fluctuations, especially for furniture, oil refinery, petroleum and coal products, rubber products, and plastic products, between 1978 and 1982. The sharp decline in the NRP for furniture seems to reflect import liberalization. Kim (1988) notes that, in 1980, all items in the industry were under some kind of quantitative import restriction, although restrictions were lifted for over 60 percent of the items in 1983. The sharp increase in NRP for oil refining seems to reflect the rapid rise in the energy price from 1978 to 1982, which was faster inside Korea than in the international market. For other industries, no ready explanation seems available. In the cases of rubber products and plastic products, the big increases in NRPs are likely to be the results of changes in product composition in the industries.

4. The method of estimating the effective rates of protection is discussed and reported in Yoo (1982), and the estimates are reported in Korea Development Institute (1982).

Table 13.4 The Structure of Effective Protection (%)

	1978	1982
Agriculture	64.6	85.7
Forestry	.4	−.1
Fishing	−.5	−.5
Mining	−1.5	−1.5
Manufacturing	24.4	31.5
Food	−28.8	−27.6
Beverage	4.8	−4.1
Tobacco	73.7	50.0
Textiles	5.5	5.3
Clothing	75.2	93.8
Footwear, leather	−6.1	−2.4
Wood	−9.3	6.5
Furniture	46.6	−2.1
Pulp, paper	36.2	22.9
Printing	−3.6	−11.7
Industrial chemicals	42.2	65.8
Other chemicals	45.4	35.9
Oil refining	26.1	681.9
Petrol., coal products	121.6	−.2
Rubber products	−9.6	2.0
Plastic products	−3.9	−6.5
Pottery, china	23.1	15.4
Glass	15.4	8.8
Other nonmetal min. prods.	10.9	40.1
Iron & steel	24.7	31.5
Nonferrous metal	31.6	23.6
Fabricated metal	12.8	.0
Nonelectrical mach.	44.2	22.0
Electrical mach.	105.4	44.8
Transport equip.	30.4	12.4
Prof., scien. equip.	102.6	42.8
Miscellaneous mfg.	5.9	−7.1
All industries	31.6	37.2
	(20.5)	(27.8)
Standard deviation	76.7	312.8
	(79.3)	(323.6)

Note: The figures in parentheses refer to "all industries" excluding the agricultural sector.

tive advantage ranking seems worth mentioning. Since Korea is a resource-poor country and therefore depends heavily on imports for its supply of raw materials, it does not appear surprising that the effective protection is near zero for forestry, fishing, and mining. However, if comparative disadvantage were the reason for little or no protection for the primary sectors, the agricultural sector should also receive low effective protection. Instead, its protection was very high.

In the manufacturing sector, the effective protection was higher for the heavy and chemical industries, in which Korea had relatively low comparative advantage. In contrast, most of the so-called light industries producing consumer goods had low or negative effective protection. The major exceptions were tobacco, which was under government monopoly, and clothing. Other light industries such as furniture and paper also had greater-than-average ERPs, but theirs were not exceptionally high. In the light industries with low or negative protection, Korea's comparative advantage was high until the early 1980s. These industries used to account for more than half of all exports—and they still do if electrical machinery, which mainly produces consumer electronics products, is regarded as a light industry.

These features of the interindustry structure of effective protection were common in 1978 and 1982. The change between the years was that ERPs became larger on average, but at the same time there was some noticeable decline in the effective protection rate for the machinery industries. The entries in table 13.4 for 1982 appear to suggest that the variation of ERPs among the industries diminished over the years. However, at the level of aggregation at which the regression analysis was conducted in this paper—namely, where there are 120 or so tradable-goods-producing input-output industries—there was a tremendous rise in the standard deviation from 1978 to 1982.

13.2 The Political Economy of Protection and the Demand and Supply Conditions in Korea

The political economy discussion of the protection structure refers mostly to industrial countries with parliamentary democracy. As Baldwin (1982) notes, the discussion usually postulates a political marketplace where elected representatives are regarded as the suppliers of protection and producers as the demanders. In the market, the effective demand for protection is expressed in ballot box votes rather than dollar votes. Thus, the question arises whether the political economy of protection is relevant to a developing country where a democratic tradition is not firmly established.

What makes the political economy discussion useful is that the demand for protection exists and is transmitted in some form to the people who can provide it. The institutional feature that the suppliers are the elected representatives seems to be of incidental importance. In a developing country, the suppliers could be authoritarian rulers or government bureaucrats. In the following sections, the demand and supply conditions of protection in Korea will be discussed.

13.2.1 The Demand Conditions of Protection

An Industry's Demand for Protection

The basic logic underlying the collective action expounded by Mancur Olson (1965) would differ little across countries. In particular, the ease or difficulty of organizing a group and having it take collective action does not depend mainly on whether a country has a long-established tradition of parliamentary democracy. Insofar as the objective that collective action attempts to achieve has the nature of a public good, the free-rider problem exists in any country.

As there are no professional lobbyists in Korea, industry associations tend to play that role to a certain extent, and the industrialists themselves attempt to influence trade and other policies. In any case, the contribution of one's own time and money to a collective cause would be more easily forthcoming if the beneficiaries were few in number. Hence, the higher an industry's concentration ratio, the more likely that there will be collective action for protection.

In addition to the likelihood of collective action, how great an effort will actually be made will depend on the expected reward. What may be safely disregarded in a large economy, but not in a smaller one, are exports. In Korea, exports are about one-third as large as the country's GNP. Since protection of an industry obviously cannot increase its export sales, an industry would not be much interested in lobbying for protection if its output is mostly exported.

Demand for Protection by Politicians and the Government

Elected representatives are usually portrayed as the suppliers of protection. But it seems appropriate to view them as the demanders. Compared to the benefits they get in the form of ballot box votes, the costs they incur seem small. What works as the constraint on the provision of protection is the opposition to it. The stronger the opposition, the harder it is to obtain protection. Thus, one may say that society as a whole is the supplier of protection and that the supply cost is expressed in the form of opposition.

Similarly, the government (mainly the executive branch) can also be regarded as the demander. According to the adding machine model as referred to in Caves (1976), the government tries to gain as many votes as possible in setting tariffs or other barriers to maximize the probability of reelection. Although the model assumes a democratically elected government, it is not difficult to see that the model can also be applied to less democratic countries, once we recognize that no government can be effective, however authoritarian it may be, if it turns the majority of the population against it. People's confidence in a government would depend a great deal on whether it appears to be protecting their interests. Thus, the number of workers in an industry is a variable that would be duly considered in decisions on trade policy.

An important related factor that would be most relevant in this regard is the sympathy given by the general public to a particular group of workers, namely, the farmers. It seems universal that the plight of rural people gets sympathy from the rest of the country. That sympathy seems to be exceptionally strong in Korea. Because of the rapid urbanization that accompanied

Korea's rapid economic growth, more than three-quarters of urbanites are first-generation migrants from rural areas, where their parents, brothers, and sisters are still working. They seem no less offended by the suggestion of opening the agricultural market than rural workers are. Hence, the government cannot afford to appear to be turning its back on the farmers.

The Government's Own Agenda

The governments of many developing countries assume the role of development state, and Korea is an exemplary case. Since the late President Park took power in a military coup and the next president, Chun, similarly lacked constitutional legitimacy, the governments of these two presidents attempted to obtain legitimacy on the basis of economic performance. The political elite maintained a strong economic bureaucracy and protected it from interest-group politics. This meant that the ideas and initiatives of the bureaucrats in various economic ministries mattered a great deal. In this regard, the political economy of protection in Korea seems substantially different from that in industrial democracies in that the economic ministries are not mere implementers of the decisions made by somebody else but should be viewed rather as the important decision makers themselves. They have their own agenda for the economy, independent of ballot box politics.

Korean bureaucrats seem to be heavily influenced by the Japanese model. Geographic proximity and cultural affinity, coupled with the fact that Japan was once a latecomer to economic development, tend to make the Japanese experience appear highly relevant to Korea. Since Japan's economic success is often attributed, rightly or wrongly, to its protectionist trade policy and industrial targeting policy, the adoption of similar policies is often believed to be a shortcut to rapid growth.

On the other hand, Korea's own experience with the so-called heavy and chemical industry policy of the 1970s convinced many policymakers of the need to liberalize the trade regime. The policy, a typical industrial targeting policy, attempted to promote the development of selected industries through heavy protection, a strongly biased credit and interest rate policy, and tax incentives. It gave rise to excess investments in the policy-favored industries, rapid inflation, and a deterioration of economic performance. The policy is understood to have been one of the main causes of the real decline in exports in the late 1970s and the negative economic growth in 1980. The fact that the policy was discontinued in the spring of 1979 by the same government that launched it is evidence that there were many in the government who believed the policy to be a mistake.[5]

5. Some support to the views expressed in this paragraph may be found in Yoo (1990), which discusses the background of the heavy and chemical industry policy and attempts to evaluate the effects on resource allocation among the manufacturing industries and on the industries' export performance.

Out of these two conflicting lessons, Japanese and Korean, arose the order of import liberalization that has been followed in the 1980s. The government liberalized those industries first that were either strongly competitive in international markets or not competitive at all. The industries in the middle of this competitiveness ranking (although it is not clear how the ranking was determined) were given a few more years of protection in the hope that they would become more competitive in the meantime. The policy was a sort of infant industry protection. Thus, the relation between competitiveness and the order of liberalization was not "linear."

13.2.2 The Supply Condition of Protection: The Opposition

Protection necessarily implies higher prices, lower quality, or a combination of both to users of the imports and their domestic substitutes. The adversely affected users have the incentive to oppose the protection. Just as successful lobbying by producers provides a collective good, protection, so does successful opposition by users, no protection. Whether and how much the opposition succeeds will depend on the ability of users to take collective action. Thus, there seems to be the same issue of collective action on the user side.

Opposition would be least likely if the protection is for a consumer good. In general, it would be difficult to organize a group and take collective action when the benefit from doing so is thinly and widely spread. This is typical of most consumer goods. Thus, an industry's lobby for protection is less likely to be opposed and more likely to succeed if its output is a consumer good.

The opposition to protection can come from the industries that use as inputs the protected goods. Amelung (1989) proposes to measure it by the index of forward linkage opposition. The index incorporates the importance of a protected industry's output as an input to the user industries and the latter's concentration ratios. He also develops a measure for an industry, say, industry A, that indicates how strong those industries' demand for protection will be that produce the inputs that the industry uses, the index of backward linkage opposition.

In the previous subsection, the Korean government was seen as a demander of protection. It assumes the role of opponent, too. For decades, one of the primary concerns of the economic ministries has been export expansion. The late President Park and the whole government gave the highest policy priority to ensuring that export performance was the best it could be, and the general public also used to be highly concerned with export performance. This attitude has changed little. Given the national concern, it would not be surprising if the economic ministries paid attention to the negative effects of raising protective barriers on export performance. Under the circumstances, exporters would be more effective than otherwise in persuading the economic ministries of the need to reduce or eliminate protection on the intermediate inputs they use.

13.3 Estimation of a Regression Model

This section investigates the determination of the interindustry difference in protection by estimating simple regression models on the basis of the discussion in the last section. It first describes the independent variables to be used and discusses the estimation results.

An "observation" in the regression analysis is an industry in the *Input-Output Tables* of the Korean economy for the nearest year estimated by the Bank of Korea. The unit of observation was convenient because the *Input-Output Tables* can supply data on industry characteristics that may be used as independent variables.

13.3.1 Independent Variables

While the nominal rates of protection (NRPs) and the effective rates (ERPs) discussed above were used as the dependent variables, the independent variables to be included in the regression analysis were chosen on the basis of the discussion in the previous section.

The concentration ratio (CR) is included as a determinant of the likelihood for an industry to take collective action for protection and the intensity of that action. Unpublished estimates of CRs by KDI researchers were available for five-digit KSIC manufacturing industries. The estimated CR for an industry represents the proportion of shipments accounted for by the three largest firms. As the five-digit KSIC industries are more disaggregated than the input-output industries of this study, the value of shipments was used as a weight to obtain an average CR for an input-output industry. The CRs for industries in the agricultural, forestry, fishing, and mining sectors were assumed to be zero.

Other determinants of collective action that were used as independent variables were the proportion of value added (VA) and the proportion of exports in the industry's output (EO). The smaller the VA, the greater the effective protection to an industry, given a protective measure on the output. Also, how much an industry would be interested in securing protection for itself is likely to be negatively correlated to EO. The VAs and EOs were obtained from the *Input-Output Tables*. The benefit to a protected industry will also depend on the elasticity of the domestic supply. However, the elasticity estimates were not available and could not be included.

The variables chosen to represent the politicians' and the government's interests in ballot box votes were the number of workers in an industry (L) and a dummy variable for the agricultural sector (AG). Representing the government's own agenda for the Korean economy, a dummy variable (HCI) was included to distinguish from others the favored industries: iron and steel, nonferrous metal, fabricated metal, all kinds of machinery industries, industrial chemicals, and oil refining.

As mentioned in the last section, in the trade liberalization of the 1980s the government lifted protection first from the most and least competitive industries. To represent this policy of infant industry protection, it was hypothesized that the level of protection first rises and then falls as the import dependency ratio (MD) increases from zero to one, MD being the proportion of domestic demand met by imports. To capture the nonlinear relation, MD and its square (MD^2) were included in the regression model. MD was obtained from the *Input-Output Tables* by taking the ratio of imports to domestic absorption of the relevant products.

As a variable representing the opposition to protection, or the lack of it, the directly consumed proportion of an industry's output (C) was included as an independent variable in the regression with the expectation that it would be positively correlated with the level of protection.

The ability of other industries to oppose the protection of a given industry is represented by the index of forward linkage opposition (FL). Hence, the higher FL is for an industry, the lower the industry's protection level. The index was computed using the input-output coefficients and the CRs mentioned above, as suggested by Amelung (1989). The index of backward linkage opposition (BL) is also computed. BL for an industry represents the combined abilities to obtain nominal protection for themselves of the producers of the inputs that the industry uses, and it is supposed to adversely affect the industry's effective protection. The formulas for FL and BL are the following:

$$FL_i = \Sigma_j a_{ij} \, CR_j, \quad \text{for } i \neq j,$$
$$BL_j = \Sigma_i a_{ij} \, CR_j, \quad \text{for } j \neq i,$$

where a_{ij} stands for the input from the ith industry for a unit output of the jth industry and CR_j for the concentration ratio of the jth industry.

The opposition to protection can come from within the government itself. In view of the fact that the export performance has been the national concern in Korea, the effects of protection on the export industries could have been given due consideration in the decision-making process on tariff and nontariff measures. Thus, it may be hypothesized that the inputs into export production would have low protection, other things being equal. Thus, the following measure of indirect exports (IE) was obtained from the *Input-Output Tables* and included in the regression:

$$IE_i = \Sigma_j r_{ij} E_j, \quad \text{for } i \neq j,$$

where r_{ij} is the ijth element in the inverse matrix of $[I - A]$, A being the input-output coefficient matrix, and E_j is exports by the jth industry.

Finally, the intensities in physical capital (PK) and human capital (HK) are included. They are the measures of industrial characteristics in the tradition of the factor proportions theory of international trade. An empirical study of Korea's protection structure by Alikhani and Havrylyshyn (1982) found the human capital intensity to have a significant positive correlation with the level of protection. Following Balassa and Bawens (1988), the "flow" measures of the two intensities were obtained as follows:

$$\mathrm{PK}_i = v_i - w_i,$$
$$\mathrm{HK}_i = w_i - uw_i,$$

where v_i, w_i, and uw_i stand for the value added per worker, the average wage rate, and the wage rate of unskilled workers in industry i. As uw_i's were not available, the minimum of the average wage rates among all industries was used in its place. Thus, HK is statistically little different from the average wage rate, w_i, in the regression analysis that follows.

13.3.2 The Estimation Results

The Determination of Nominal Rates of Protection

The regression models, estimated by the ordinary least squares method of determination of NRPs for 1978, 1982, and 1988, are presented in table 13.5.

According to the results for 1978, the regressors whose estimated coefficients turned out to be statistically significant and have the expected signs were the proportion of exports in an industry's output (EO) in the group of the determinants representing the industry's demand for protection, the number of workers (L) representing the politician's demand, the dummy (HCI) for the government-favored heavy and chemical industries and import dependency (MD) representing the government's agenda, and the proportion of output purchased by the consumers (C) representing the lack of opposition to protection.

Thus, the government appears to have been an active force behind protection. Because of political considerations, a higher level of protection was given to the industries where the number of workers was large, and the government protected those industries that it was promoting under the so-called heavy and chemical industry policy during the 1970s.

The private sector appears to have been an inactive bystander. Of the determinants representing the industry's demand for protection, the concentration ratio (CR) and the proportion of value added in output (VA) had expected signs but were not statistically significant. And the protection was higher if the protected was more of a consumer good, a high C, or if the industry was less interested in securing protection, a high EO.

The reason why the industry was inactive may have been that lobbying for protection was not rewarding enough during the 1970s, when the government was strongly pushing the heavy and chemical industry policy. As the estimation result indicates, what mattered most in determining the protection level one can enjoy was whether one belonged to the industries favored by the policy.

The estimation for 1982 portrays a somewhat different picture. Of the group of regressors representing the government's agenda for the economy, the coefficients of the variables for infant industry protection (MD and MD^2) became significant with the expected signs, replacing the dummy for HCI, and the coefficient of the flow measure of human capital (HK) showed a positive sign of high significance. Thus, the estimation results seem to reflect the fact that,

Table 13.5 Determinants of Nominal Rates of Protection

Regressors	1978	1982	1988
Constant	8.90	−13.02	−20.11
	(8.18)	(8.63)†	(18.40)
CR (+)	5.61	21.83	38.40
	(8.36)	(9.23)*	(20.20)*
EO (−)	−.14	−.06	−.01
	(.08)*	(.10)	(.20)
VA (−)	−.11	−.05	.67
	(.14)	(.16)	(.33)*
AG (+)	5.88	18.48	114.12
	(7.97)	(9.42)*	(24.86)**
L (+)	.037	.11	.031
	(.012)**	(.016)**	(.043)
HCI (+)	12.57	.31	4.36
	(4.15)**	(4.85)	(10.58)
MD (+)	.36	.36	.11
	(.22)†	(1.44)**	(.58)
MD^2 (−)	−.0029	−.0019	.002
	(.0026)	(.001)*	(.007)
C (+)	.29	.16	.14
	(.07)**	(.07)**	(.18)
FL (−)	−4.35	6.85	54.03
	(10.10)	(11.23)	(24.42)*
IE (−)	−.76	−8.28	−26.86
	(29.3)	(11.87)	(11.89)*
HK (+)	−2.55	4.48	−6.17
	(3.85)	(2.20)**	(5.14)
PK (?)	.12	(.44)	.42
	(.76)	(.35)	(.58)
$\bar{R}^2$	.32	.42	.48
df	115	105	105

Note: In the parentheses following the names of the regressors are shown the expected signs of the estimated coefficients. Each column of the table represents one regression. Each entry gives the estimated regression coefficient (and its standard error in parentheses). The level of statistical significance is indicated by † (10 percent), * (5 percent), and ** (1 percent).

by 1982, the government had discontinued the heavy and chemical industry policy. However, the government still appears to have been the active force behind protection, promoting the development of infant industry and protecting the human capital–intensive industries.

To be noted parenthetically is the implication of the magnitudes of the estimated coefficients for MD and MD^2. Import dependency (MD) was expected to have such a diminishing influence on protection that, as MD rises, the protection level goes up, reaches a peak, and declines. This expectation was not met. The coefficient of MD^2 was negative, but its magnitude was not large enough for the protection level to decline. That is, as MD increases, the rise in the protection level indeed decelerated, but not rapidly enough. The estimated magnitudes indicate that MD's influence peaked when it was slightly bigger than 100 percent, the theoretical maximum for MD.

Compared to 1978, the influence of politics on protection seems to have become stronger in 1982. Not only the number of workers (L) but also the dummy for agriculture (AG) became significant with the expected signs.

The private business sector appears to have become more active in 1982. The concentration ratio (CR), which became significant, indicates that, the more concentrated an industry, the higher the protection level for that industry.

Thus, in determining the 1982 protection structure, the influence of the government's agenda does not appear to be as dominant as it was in 1978 but had to compete with ballot box politics and with more assertive private business interests.

The estimated results for 1988 were very different from those for 1978 or 1982 and difficult to interpret. First, the proportion of value added in output (VA) and the index of forward linkage opposition (FL) had coefficients of unexpected signs with high statistical significance. Three independent variables had coefficients of expected signs with statistical significance. They were the concentration ratio (CR), the dummy for agriculture (AG), and indirect exports (IE).

In the estimation result for 1988, the government does not appear to have been active. Although IE was estimated to be a statistically significant variable, the influence of the government represented by it is a passive one, as it represents its resistance to the private sector's demand for protection. This is no match to the influence it had in earlier years, when it was implementing the heavy and chemical industry policy (represented by the HCI dummy), or to the promotion of infant industries and human capital–intensive industries (represented by MD and MD^2). Thus, insofar as the estimated results reflect reality, the influence of the government having its own agenda for the economy was not apparent in the late 1980s.

However, it cannot be said that the finding is beyond any reasonable doubt. As noted at the outset, tariffs were from 1988, and the tariff equivalents from which the NRPs were chosen came from 1990. Thus, a new estimation with a more accurate set of data may produce a different finding.

Determination of the Effective Rates of Protection

The regression model for the determination of effective rates of protection included all the independent variables used for nominal rates of protection and an additional one representing the backward linkage opposition (BL), which affects the ERPs but not the NRPs. The estimation results for 1978 and 1982 are presented in table 13.6. Interpretation of the estimation results needs to refer to the estimation of the determination of NRPs since an industry's ERP is determined by the relative sizes of the NRPs given to the output of and the inputs into the industry.

Table 13.6 Determinants of Effective Rates of Protection

Regressors	1978	1982
Constant	−63.90	−123.4
	(36.05)*	(38.67)**
CR (+)	37.74	106.4
	(35.22)	(42.2)**
EO (−)	−.09	.30
	(.32)	(.42)
VA (−)	.93	1.60
	(.58)†	(.68)**
AG (+)	−3.87	7.19
	(33.23)	(41.08)
L (+)	.033	.13
	(.050)	(.07)*
HCI (+)	52.3	22.4
	(17.7)**	(21.1)
MD (+)	.53	.18
	(.93)	(.63)
MD^2 (−)	−.004	−.004
	(.011)	(.004)
C (+)	.81	.23
	(.31)**	(.32)
FL (−)	−24.0	50.4
	(43.1)	(49.6)
BL (−)	88.38	32.6
	(56.72)†	(63.2)
IE (−)	62.41	40.4
	(123.7)	(54.3)
HK (+)	−23.95	3.64
	(16.12)†	(9.64)
PK (?)	4.79	.14
	(3.24)†	(1.61)
$\bar{R}^2$	.31	.09
df	114	104

Note: See the note to table 13.5.

In the model estimated for 1978, only the dummy variable for heavy and chemical industries (HCI) and the proportion of output purchased by consumers (C) had coefficients with the expected signs with high statistical significance. These coefficients were also estimated to have statistically significant, expected signs in the 1978 regression for the NRPs. Thus, the tendency of higher effective protection for the heavy and chemical industries and for those industries producing consumer goods seems to be the "intended results."

Other regressors, such as the proportion of value added in output (VA), backward linkage opposition (BL), and human capital intensity (HK), had coefficients with "wrong" signs with high significance. The interpretation is not straightforward. On the one hand, since the coefficient of VA in the NRP determination model had an insignificant but expected minus sign, the estimation in the ERP determination model appears to be a result, neither expected nor intended, that merely shows the net effect of protecting inputs and outputs at different rates.

On the other hand, the coefficient of HK was estimated to have the same, negative sign in both models of NRP and ERP determination. What does the statistical significance in the latter model mean? Does it mean that the estimated results reflect the intentions of lobbyists, politicians, or government officials? Or is it merely a spurious statistical correlation? Without additional independent information, the answer is not clear.

In the estimation of the 1982 ERP determination model, the same problem occurs with regard to VA. CR and L were the only two independent variables that had coefficients of expected sign that were statistically significant. Their coefficients had expected signs of statistical significance, too, in the NRP determination model. Thus, it appears that business interests and political considerations had a significant influence on the determination of ERPs in 1982. HCI was not a significant factor in the 1982 determination of ERPs, as it ceased to be one in the NRP determination.

It is interesting to note that MD and HK, which represent the government's own agenda, were estimated to be significant factors in the NRP determination but not in the ERP determination. Insofar as the data used in the estimation were correct, the results of the two estimations seem to indicate that the industry structure of ERPs that the government intended to bring about through import restraints was not achieved.

13.4 Summary and Conclusion

The tariff structure across industries hardly supplies sufficient information for the protection structure in Korea. Tariffs were much higher than actual tariffs or estimated nominal rates of protection. Also, variation across industries in tariffs is very much different from variation in NRPs. This difference suggests that NTBs are an important factor in determining the protection structure, and the importance of NTBs in turn suggests that the executive branch of the government has been influential in determining nominal protection.

Between 1978 and 1988, tariffs and actual tariffs substantially declined, but the average NRP for all industries rose owing to a steep rise in the rate for the agricultural sector. For other sectors, the NRPs declined, but more slowly than tariffs or actual tariffs. Thus, the buffer between tariffs and NRPs has diminished. The tendency for NRPs to exceed tariffs or actual tariffs for the agricultural sector and the machinery industries changed little during the ten-year period covered in this paper.

In the determination of nominal protection, the political consideration represented by either the agriculture dummy (AG) or the number of workers (L) was found to have a significant influence. The government's own agenda for the economy had a strong influence on the protection structure in the late 1970s and in the early 1980s, but it appears to have become insignificant later. In contrast, the influence of private interests represented by CR was not apparent in the late 1970s but became stronger in later years.

The opposition to protection had an influence on the protection structure in the passive sense that consumer goods tended to be protected more heavily. The forward and backward linkage opposition (FL and BL) standing for an industry's opposition to the protection of the producers of its inputs were not found to be significant. The exporters' opposition to protecting the producers of its inputs, represented by IE, was found to be significant in the late 1980s.

The proportion of value added in output (VA) was not found to be significant, except that it was once estimated to be significant, but with a coefficient of unexpected sign. Physical capital (PK) as an industrial characteristic was not found to have any significant correlation with the nominal protection structure.

The structure of effective protection seems similar to that of nominal protection in that agriculture and the machinery industries were the major beneficiaries and the light industries producing consumer goods were the victims. Notable exceptions to this in the light industries were tobacco, which was under government monopoly, and clothing.

The estimation of the effective protection determination was less satisfactory than that of the nominal protection determination. In the late 1970s, the heavy and chemical industry policy was estimated to have had a strong influence on the effective protection structure. Effective protection also tended to be higher for those industries for which the proportion of output purchased by the consumers was high. In the early 1980s, the concentration ratio and the number of workers had a significant, positive influence on effective protection. Besides these variables, however, most of the others were found to have little influence, while the coefficients of a few regressors were estimated to have unexpected signs with high statistical significance.

The fact that the estimated results of the regression models were statistically more significant for the structure of nominal protection than for that of effective protection makes one wonder whether the effective or the nominal protection structure better reflects the political economy of protectionism, especially in the context of a developing country. The only reason why one may expect the structure of effective protection to better reflect the forces of political economy seems to be that the value added should be what ultimately matters to those who attempt to obtain protection.

However, effective rates of protection can be affected only through nominal rates of protection. Thus, efforts would first be directed toward gaining nominal protection for oneself and opposing nominal protection for the producers of the inputs that one needs. The effective rate of protection is the net results of countless such efforts by many. Thus, less information would be contained in the effective rates than in the nominal rates of protection about the political economy of protection.

Moreover, when the government pushes its own agenda for the economy, what the final outcome of lobbying efforts will be is less predictable. If the government merely implemented what is determined by interest group politics, for example, lobbyists and interest groups would understand sooner or later what produces the most desired results and act accordingly. Government intervention in effect introduces noise in this feedback process. Hence, it seems that the structure of nominal protection is a better object to investigate than that of effective protection for the study of the political economy of protection.

Finally, an interesting question, as Korean society is becoming more democratic, is what will happen to the protection structure? The significance of democratization for the subject of this paper would be that the influence of politicians and industries rises relative to the economic ministries and their technical bureaucrats. In terms of the discussion presented above, on the one hand, it will imply that the influence of such variables as the agricultural dummy and the number of workers in an industry will become more pronounced. On the other hand, interest groups are likely to become more active, raising the influence of such variables as the concentration ratio on the determination of the protection structure.

To some extent, these changes seem to have already been taking place, as the regression results indicated. Despite the changes, however, the pattern of protection across industries does not appear to have substantially changed. As mentioned earlier, besides the agricultural sector, the machinery industries had consistently enjoyed higher than average NRPs during the ten-year period considered in this study. Since nontariff barriers are the important factor in determining NRPs and the barriers are administered by the executive branch of the government, the apparent consistency in the protection structure seems to indicate that the strength of government influence on the protection structure was not substantially affected.

Whether it will remain strong in the future is a question that no one can answer with certainty. Moreover, the pressure from the international community for an opening of Korean markets has been and will continue to be strong. Thus, the government has to compete with politicians, industrialists, and the international community for influence on the protection structure.

References

Alikhani, Iradj, and Oli Havrylyshyn. 1982. The political economy of protection in developing countries: A case study of Colombia and South Korea. Working Paper no. 1892–4. Washington, D.C.: World Bank, International Trade and Capital Flows Division.

Amelung, Torsten. 1989. The determinants of protection in developing countries: An extended interest-group approach. *Kyklos* 42 (4): 515–32.
Balassa, B., and L. Bawens. 1988. *Changing trade patterns in manufactured goods: An economic investigation*. Amsterdam: North-Holland.
Baldwin, Robert E. 1982. The political economy of protectionism. In *Import competition and response*, ed. Jagdish N. Bhagwati. Chicago: University of Chicago Press.
Caves, R. E. 1976. Economic models of political choice: Canada's tariff structure. *Canadian Journal of Economics* 9 (May): 278–300.
Corden, W. M. 1966. The structure of a tariff system and the effective protective rate. *Journal of Political Economy* 74 (June): 221–37.
Jwa, Sung-hee. 1988. The political economy of market-opening pressure and response: Theory and evidence for the case of Korea and the U.S. *Seoul Journal of Economics* 1 (4): 387–415.
Kim, Kwang-suk. 1988. *The economic effects of import liberalization and industrial adjustment policy* (in Korean). Seoul: KDI Press.
Korea Development Institute. 1982. *The basic task of industrial policy and the reform proposals of the industrial assistances* (in Korean). Seoul: KDI Press.
Olson, M. 1965. *The logic of collective action: Public goods and the theory of groups*. Cambridge, Mass.: Harvard University Press.
Yoo, Jung-ho. 1982. Estimation of effective protective rates: Methodology (in Korean). *Korea Development Review* 4 (Winter): 30–52.
———. 1990. The industrial policy of the 1970s and the evolution of the manufacturing sector in Korea. Working Paper no. 9017. Seoul: KDI Press.

Comment Anne O. Krueger

This is an excellent paper, one that greatly increases our understanding of the political economy of protection in developing countries. Yoo has done a thoroughly professional and careful job with the data he could obtain. As always with a newly explored area, however, a good analysis raises more questions than it answers. These comments are therefore largely devoted to raising additional considerations and, as such, to asking for further work in yet other papers.

A first question concerns the political economy of differences between tariffs, actual tariffs, nominal rates of protection, effective rates of protection, and nontariff barriers to trade. In Yoo's paper, as elsewhere in the political economy literature, it is always taken for granted that the determinants of these different rates may be different. Yet, if political economy questions are the focal point of analysis, it seems that there should be at least some indication as to *why* politicians choose the protective instruments that they do and a theory as to why there should be differences between these different rates—especially between various versions of nominal tariff rates.

Anne O. Krueger is Arts and Sciences Professor of Economics at Duke University and a research associate of the National Bureau of Economic Research.

A second question arises from Yoo's discussion of the importance of export performance in the Korean context. From other work, there has been considerable emphasis on the divergence between Korean rates of protection for the home market and for export. Yoo notes that account should have been taken of the negative effects of protection on exports. Yet, as is well known, protection to some is deprotection to others. And, in Yoo's data, all industries received positive protection. Surely something is missing. Could the data consist of averages of protection for the domestic market and protection for export? Does it make sense to examine only the rates of protection for one?

This is not a criticism of Yoo because these questions remain unanswered throughout the literature on political economy. It would be interesting to see if Yoo could extend his analysis to effective rates of subsidy for exports and contrast the results to those he obtains with his present estimates.

A third question pertains to the data and the inferences drawn with respect to changes over time. Yoo has three data points: 1978, 1982, and 1988. It is interesting to note how individual rates fluctuate between these points, especially if one examines effective rates (which are perhaps the most economically meaningful in the absence of a theory as to why nominal rates are of concern). Examination of table 13.4 suggests very large changes in rates in just four years. The most glaring cases that leap out are oil refineries, whose ERP is estimated at 26 percent in 1978 and 682 percent in 1982! However, the most significant change between 1978 and 1982 is in the much greater standard deviation of rates in the later year.

These observations raise several questions. First, how much "noise" is there in year-to-year changes in ERPs? This phenomenon has been observed in other studies and is not unique to Korea. If, however, noise is substantial, it may be dangerous to use point observations four, or even ten, years apart as a basis for inferences about changes in political economy. Given the evolution of Korean trade policies over the past forty years, one would conjecture that major changes occurred in the early 1960s, in the early 1970s, and then again in the late 1980s. Why one would expect much change between 1978 and 1982 is not clear. And, before analysis of changes to 1988 can be reliable, questions about the variance of ERP rates from year to year need to be addressed.

There is one final comment—and that is that 1978 and 1982 were years during which Korean economic policy was still managed almost entirely by technocrats. Considerations of economic growth and maintaining the export drive were highly important in their decision-making process. By 1988, the Korean government had become much more responsive to democratic forces. It was probably too early in 1988 for interest groups to have built up in support of or opposition to protection, but one would expect these forces to operate differently than they did under the earlier regime. An interesting question for political economy will be to examine and analyze the differences in the determinants of protection in Korea in the 1990s from those factors that influenced protection levels in the late 1970s and early 1980s.

Comment Chia Siow Yue

This is an excellent paper, providing much information on and an analysis of industrial protection in Korea.

I have four comments about Yoo's presentation of measures of nominal and effective rates of protection. First, the data show tariffs, actual tariffs, and nominal rates of protection. Yoo states that NTBs seem to have been an important factor in protecting the industries of low comparative advantage such as agriculture and machinery. It is not clear from the paper what NTBs are used in Korea. Second, subsidies appear to be missing in the computations. Yet it is well known that Korea makes liberal use of subsidies to promote its industries, in particular, preferential credit provided by the state-controlled banking system. Third, the data for nominal protection are for 1978, 1982, and 1988, and the data for effective protection are for 1978 and 1982. The analysis of the changes over time appears incomplete. The major import liberalization efforts in Korea took place only in recent years, and the effects would be felt mainly after 1988. It would have been highly informative if more recent data were available to show the extent of import liberalization that has taken place to date. Fourth, Yoo states that the effective rates of protection tended to be minimal or negative for the industries of high comparative advantage, except for clothing and electrical machinery. It would be instructive if there were measures of the effective rates of subsidies in these industries as well.

I have four comments on Yoo's examination of the political economy of protection. First, I agree with his argument that the political economy of protection in industrial democracies is different from that in developing countries like Korea, where the democratic tradition is not as firmly established and/or where the government assumes the role of the developmental state. In such countries, the suppliers of protection could be authoritarian rulers or government bureaucrats, and the demand for protection could come not only from industrialists, workers, and farmers but also from the government itself, namely, the economic ministries and bureaucrats. The regression results for 1978 did indicate that the most important determinant of the protection level was whether the industry is one favored by government industrial policy. Second, except for agriculture, the demand for protection in countries like Korea is determined by the desire to promote industrialization, protect infant industries, and hasten the emergence of dynamic comparative advantage, whereas in the industrial democracies it is usually determined by the desire to protect sunset industries losing their competitive edge. It is a well-known fact that the Korean government is active in industrial targeting and picking winners. Third, the political economy of protection may vary between the import-

Chia Siow Yue is associate professor in the Department of Economics and Statistics, National University of Singapore.

substitution and the export-orientation phases. Under the former, the demand is for tariff and nontariff protection, but, under the latter, the demand is for subsidies to promote export performance. Fourth, the political economy of import liberalization may be different from that of protection. Yoo seems to indicate that, convinced of the mistake of promoting heavy and chemical industries in the 1970s, Korean policymakers moved toward import liberalization in the 1980s. My question is, Was it a unilateral decision of Korean policymakers, or was there external pressure as well? It would appear that U.S. pressure has had some effect on the import liberalization schedule in Korea.

14 Government Policy and Strategic Industries: The Case of Taiwan

Ya-Hwei Yang

Governments of less developed countries (LDCs) usually adopt policies that will stimulate economic growth in their countries. The effects of these policies, therefore, should be evaluated. In its process of economic development, Taiwan has adopted several different economic strategies. In the 1950s, an import-substitution policy was followed to reconstruct the economy after the Second World War. In the 1960s, an export-promotion policy was put forward to stimulate exports and to speed up economic growth. At that time, labor-intensive industries were comparatively advantageous and became the key industries that gained the support of the government. After the oil crises of the 1970s, capital intensive and technology-intensive industries became the new key industries. In the 1980s, because higher wages resulted in a loss of comparative advantage in the production of labor-intensive products, and because the technology level of Taiwan was still far behind that of the developed countries, bottlenecks occurred in Taiwan's development. So, in order to promote industrial development and improve the country's industrial structure, the concept of "strategic industries" was adopted as one of the means to overcome these bottlenecks. (For reviews of Taiwan's economic development, see Li and Yu [1982] and Kuo [1983].)

Preferential policies for strategic industries began to be introduced in 1982, and six criteria were adopted that the strategic industries must meet. The six criteria are as follows: high linkage effect; high market potential; high technological intensity; a high degree of value added; a low energy coefficient; and a low level of polluting emissions. Most of the selected products have been in the mechanical products, information, and electronics sectors. The list of selected products has been changed four times, and a few products in the biochemical and material industries were included after 1986.

Ya-Hwei Yang is a research fellow at the Chung-Hua Institution for Economic Research, Taipei.

Taiwan's government offers two preferential measures to subsidize the strategic industries: preferential loans and technology and management assistance. Preferential loans are administered through two channels: the pool of funds administered by the Bank of Communications and that administered by the Medium Business Bank of Taiwan. The funds for both are partially supplied by the government's Development Fund. The funds managed by the Bank of Communications were disbursed in four phases, from 1982 to 1989, with 10 billion New Taiwan dollars (NT $) having been put in the pool in the first phase and NT $20 billion in each of the following phases. The funds issued by the Medium Business Bank were disbursed in three phases, with NT $8 billion having been put in the pool in the first and second phases and NT $12 billion in the third phase. The preferential loan rates are 1.75–2.75 percent lower than the prime rate of general commercial banks. The funds can be used for several purposes besides new investment projects, such as the purchase of automated equipment, domestically produced machines, the pollution-prevention equipment, the production of exports, and the development of new products, as shown in table 14.1. Of the preferential loans, 32.14 percent actually go to strategic industries. These strategic loans are the focus of this paper.

As for technology and management assistance, the Ministry of Economic

Table 14.1 **Preferential Medium- and Long-Term Loans, 31 December 1988 (NT $thousand)**

	Bank of Communications	Medium Business Bank of Taiwan	Total
Investment project for strategic industries	4,866,252 (20.28)	29,238,576 (35.609)	34,104,828 (32.142)
Investment project for automated equipment	7,045,254 (29.36)	26,575,925 (32.366)	33,621,179 (31.686)
Investment project for domestically produced machines	8,700,725 (36.26)	21,584,814 (26.288)	30,285,539 (28.542)
Investment projects for environmental protection and pollution-prevention program	. . .	4,146,611 (5.050)	4,146,611 (3.908)
GMP projects	. . .	41,930 (.052)	41,930 (.040)
Cooperative exports and new product development	3,385,215 (14.10)	. . .	3,385,215 (3.190)
Projects supported by CEPD	. . .	521,764 (.635)	521,764 (.492)
Total amount	23,997,446 (100.00)	82,109,620 (100.00)	106,107,066 (100.00)

Note: CEPD = Council for Economic Planning and Development; GMP = Good Manufacture Product. Figures in parentheses are percentages.

Affairs asked six governmental consulting institutions to advise local firms. The government also subsidized 60 percent of the total consulting expenses of the firms, up to a total of NT $1 million.

In 1991, a new preferential plan for strategic industries was promulgated. The total amount of the plan is NT $30 billion. This plan will be executed by the Bank of Communications (Central Development Bank). By law, the difference between the preferential interest rate and the prime rate of the Bank of Communications must be smaller than 2 percent. The selected industrial items include investments in pollution-prevention equipment, the establishment of plants, energy-saving equipment, public parking lots, mass transportation equipment, and automation equipment. In addition, the idea of "star industries" was adopted by the government in 1989. In the Six-Year National Development Plan for Taiwan, which got under way in 1991, the development of "new industries" was stated to be one of the plan's targets. The criteria for new industries are similar to those for strategic industries.

Generally speaking, governments always want to stimulate economic growth by speeding up the development of certain specific industries. No matter whether the industries are called key industries, strategic industries, or new industries, industrial promotion is one of the main policies of governments. Furthermore, this type of policy is common in the LDCs.

Although preferential policies for strategic industries in Taiwan have been used for over eight years, no in-depth or thorough evaluation has been done on this subject. The purpose of this study is to provide an evaluation framework to investigate the effects of the strategic industry preferential policy, especially the effects of the preferential loan policy, and of the program for technology and management assistance.

Scholars have different viewpoints as to the effects of industrial policy. Scholars supporting the balanced growth theory believe that all sectors should develop simultaneously under an equilibrium between demand and supply (see Nurkse 1953; and Yotopoulos and Nugent 1973). Scholars supporting the unbalanced growth theory recommend a "disequilibrium development strategy" requiring the government to intervene in the market and select key industries in order to pull along the growth of the whole economy (see Hirschman 1953). Infant industry protection is usually employed in the beginning stage of economic development in order to help the growth of infant industries by lessening foreign competition (see Dervis and Page 1984). Also, after Adam Smith propounded the value of the invisible hand, the development of a free economy has become the target of the developed countries. However, market failure theory agrees that governments may intervene in the marketplace in the case of market failure, that is, when the market mechanism fails to reflect the true cost of resources or fails to use resources efficiently, such as in the case where an externality exists (see Pigou 1918).

Comparing the different theories, developing countries tend to accept the infant industry protection theory and the unbalanced growth theory.

It is still not certain how to identify key industries under these criteria.[1] The government of Taiwan has established six criteria for industries to meet in order to be classified as strategic. Shea (1983) points out that these criteria contradict each other. He proposes that a product that contains a large amount of value added probably has a low linkage effect. Wu, Lee, and Yu (1988) comment that some criteria, such as market potential and pollution, are hard to measure by econometric indexes. They try to identify what industries would be selected under each individual criterion. They find that different industries would be selected under each individual criterion. Almost no industries meet all the criteria.

14.1 Theoretical Framework and Empirical Approach

To evaluate the effects of preferential policies, the following questions need to be answered:

1. Is the selection of strategic industries (which receive preferential treatment) necessary for stimulating economic growth?
2. Are the criteria used for selecting strategic products suitable for achieving the role of key industries?
3. Are the process of and measures for executing policy effective in improving the investment position and performance of firms?

The complete framework for evaluation can be summarized as in figure 14.1. There are two main areas that are evaluated: policy execution and policy direction. If preferential loans can really help economic growth, they probably work through various types of channels. The effectiveness of each channel should be tested. To evaluate the effectiveness of these channels, the following null hypotheses and alternative hypotheses should be tested:

NULL HYPOTHESIS 1. Preferential loans provide a stable source of funds and lessen the cost of capital.

ALTERNATIVE HYPOTHESIS 1A. Even without preferential loans, firms could still find other sources of funds.

ALTERNATIVE HYPOTHESIS 1B. The decrease in interest burden provided by the preferential loans is not important in the firms' investment decisions when compared to the total expenses of the firms.

NULL HYPOTHESIS 2. With low-cost funds, the subsidized firms increase their investments.

ALTERNATIVE HYPOTHESIS 2. Other factors play a more important role in the investment decision process of firms, such as market potential, profitability, etc.

1. For discussions of the criteria, especially linkage effects, see, e.g., Laumas (1975, 1976) and Yotopoulos and Nugent (1973, 1976).

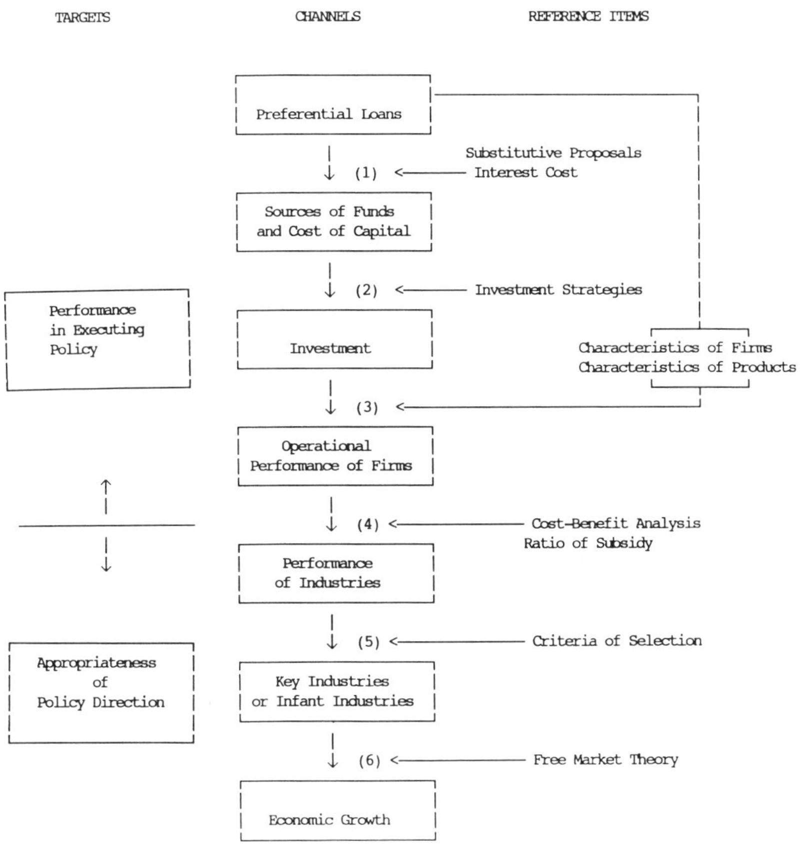

Fig. 14.1 Evaluative framework for effects of preferential loans on the strategic industries

NULL HYPOTHESIS 3. A high level of investment using preferential loans results in better operational performance.

ALTERNATIVE HYPOTHESIS 3. A good company with a high frequency of investment and a sound financial situation maintains a high level of operational performance, whether subsidized or not.

NULL HYPOTHESIS 4. The subsidized firms drive the growth of the whole industry.

ALTERNATIVE HYPOTHESIS 4A. Even though preferential policy results in better performance in the subsidized firms, the opportunity cost of moving the funds away from others is greater.

ALTERNATIVE HYPOTHESIS 4B. The number of subsidized firms is too small to influence the whole industry.

NULL HYPOTHESIS 5. The subsidized industries play the role of key industries or infant industries and drive the whole economy.

ALTERNATIVE HYPOTHESIS 5. If the criteria for selecting key or infant industries are inappropriate, there is resource distortion.

NULL HYPOTHESIS 6. Preferential policies for strategic industries help the economy grow faster.

ALTERNATIVE HYPOTHESIS 6. If the government does not intervene in the market and just lets the invisible hand of the market play its role, then the economy as a whole would be more efficient.

This study tests these hypotheses and examines the strength of each channel shown in figure 14.1. As for technology and management policy, its effect is tested following an approach similar to the one used to study the effect of preferential loan policy.

The ratio of subsidized firms should also be looked at. Both the number of firms and the amount of assistance are used as the measure indexes. The numbers of the firms receiving preferential loans from the Bank of Communications and the Medium Business Bank of Taiwan are 568 and 876, respectively. The number of firms receiving consultation assistance from the Ministry of Economic Affairs is 364. The total number of firms in the mechanical industry and the information and electronics industry is 17,796. Therefore, the preferential loan ratio is 8.1 percent (i.e., [568 + 876]/17,776). The consultation assistance ratio is 2.0 percent (i.e., 364/17,796).

The ratio of preferential loans can now be observed. Taking the amount of preferential loans to strategic industries as the numerator and the loans to privately owned metal products as the denominator, we can calculate the ratio of 22.6 percent at the end of 1988. Taking the same numerator and the medium- and long-term loans to the metal products and machinery industry extended by financial institutions as the denominator, the ratio is 63.7 percent.

The date given above reveal the following phenomenon. The ratio of preferential loans is much higher than the ratio of the number of subsidized firms. A small number of firms in selected industries have acquired a big portion of medium- and long-term loans.

Questionnaires were sent to firms in the mechanical products and the information and electronics industries. The sample includes (1) those firms that acquired strategic preferential loans provided by the Bank of Communications and by the Medium Business Bank of Taiwan; (2) those firms that acquired technical and management assistance provided by the Industry Development Bureau, Ministry of Economic Affairs; (3) those firms that applied for preferential loans but were rejected; and (4) those firms that did not apply for preferential loans.

The questionnaire format is described in figure 14.2. The analytic framework of the questionnaire is divided into several sections. First, the surveyed firms are asked whether they understand the preferential policy. This question

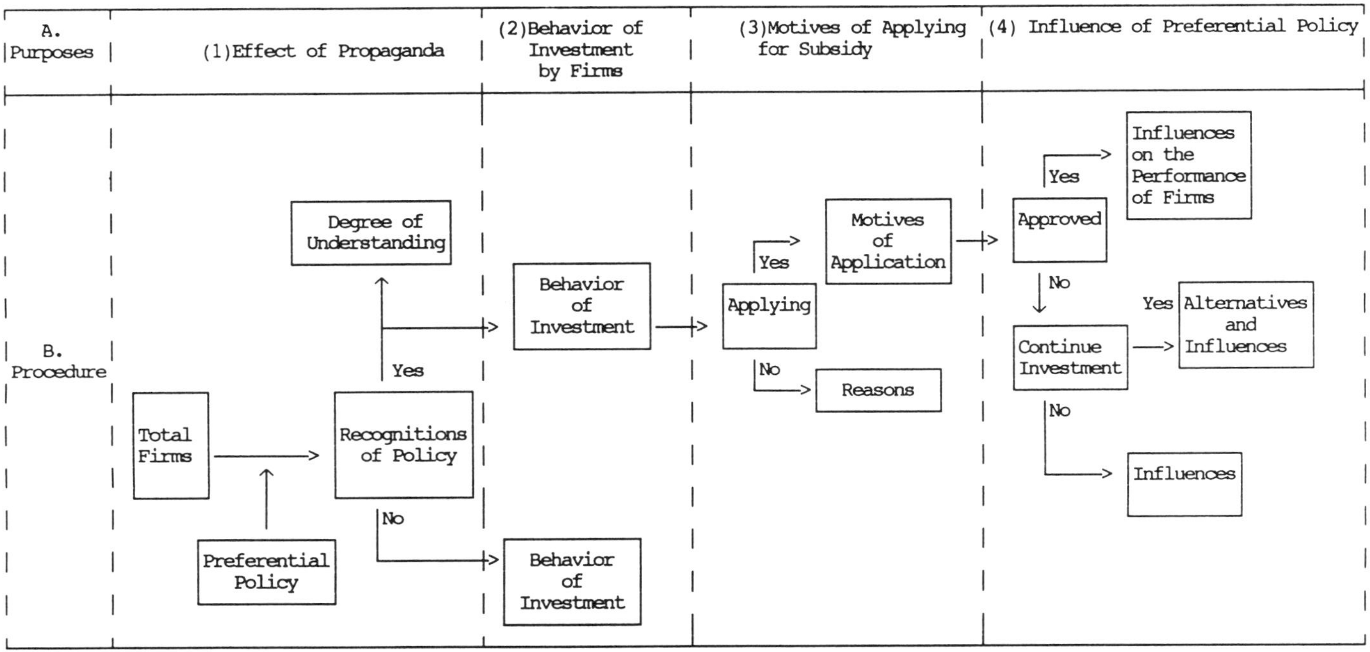

Fig. 14.2 Analytic framework of questionnaires

is used to measure the effect of propaganda. Second, questions regarding the decision process that is used in the firms' investment decisions are posed to analyze the firms' behavior in making investments. Third, firms are asked to explain why they did or did not apply for preferential loans. Finally, those firms that acquired preferential loans are asked to answer some questions about their operations. Those firms that did not acquire preferential loans are also asked whether they continued with their investment plans using an alternative source.

To evaluate the influence of preferential loans on the operation of firms, a "path analysis" was conducted. This approach is shown in figure 14.3. Suppose that an effective preferential loan policy has three effects: (1) a decrease in interest burden;[2] (2) an increase in fixed capital growth; and (3) improvement in operational efficiency (i.e., an increase in sales, profitability, or the productivity of capital and labor). The degree of these three factors might also be influenced by the characteristics of the individual firms. The characteristics of the firms include the industry that it is in, its scale of production, its technology level, its investment mood, and its credibility. Since the possible channels are so numerous, the degree of influence of each channel must be tested by path analysis.

The number of questionnaires distributed and returned is shown in table 14.2. In all, 3,033 questionnaires were distributed at the end of 1988; of these, the returned ratio was 11.7 percent, and the valid ratio was 10.6 percent.

The structure of valid samples can be described as follows (table 14.3).

1. In the valid sample, 58 percent of the firms are in the mechanical industry (i.e., 186/322), and 42 percent are in the information and electronics industry (i.e., 136/322).

2. In the valid sample, 15.8 percent of firms acquired preferential loans from the Bank of Communications, 32.6 percent of firms acquired preferential loans from the Medium Business Bank of Taiwan, and 8.4 percent of firms acquired assistance in technology and management from the Ministry of Economic Affairs. The other 43.2 percent of the sample did not receive either preferential loans or consultation assistance from the government.

3. A firm can be called a small or medium-sized business when its capital is less than NT $40 million or its number of employees is less than two hundred, according to the government definition. Usually, the customers of the Medium Business Bank are small and medium-sized businesses. In our survey, 65 percent of the valid sample are small and medium-sized businesses, and 35 percent are big businesses. In terms of the number of employees, 75.2 percent of the valid sample are small and medium-sized businesses. The mechanical industry has a higher ratio of small and medium-sized businesses than the information and electronics industry has.

2. The interest burden is measured by the ratio of interest cost over total expenses.

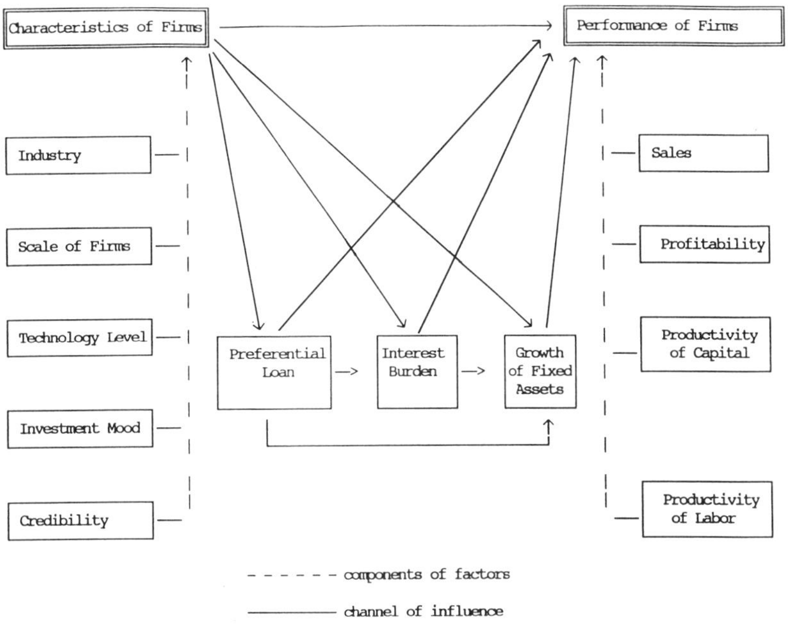

Fig. 14.3 Path analysis of influential factors on the performance of firms

Table 14.2 Ratio of Return and the Ratio of Valid Questionnaires

Category of Samples	No. Distributed	No. Returned	Return Ratio (%)	No. Obsolete	No. Valid	Valid Ratio (%)
Finance from the Bank of Communication	257	57	22.1	6	51	19.8
Finance from the Medium Business Bank of Taiwan	614	105	17.1	0	105	17.1
Guidance of technology and management	189	27	14.3	0	27	14.3
No finance and no guidance	1,973	168	8.5	29	139	7.1
Total	3,033	357	11.7	35	322	10.6

14.2 The Effect of a Preferential Loan Policy

Several topics are dealt with in this section. First, the effectiveness of preferential policy information programs is analyzed (table 14.4). Surveyed firms were asked how much they understand about this policy? It was found that 59 percent of the surveyed firms have little understanding of the government's

Table 14.3 Structure of Samples (No. of firms)

	Mechanical Industry	Information and Electronics Industry	Total
Kind of subsidy:			
Finance from Bank of Communications	27	24	51
	(14.5)	(17.6)	(15.8)
Finance from Medium Business Bank of Taiwan	80	25	105
	(43.0)	(18.4)	(32.6)
Assistance of tehnology and management	6	21	27
	(3.2)	(15.4)	(8.4)
No subsidy	73	66	139
	(39.2)	(48.5)	(43.2)
Total	186	136	322
	(100.0)	(100.0)	(100.0)
Size of firms (A):			
Capital < NT $40 million	136	68	204
	(75.1)	(51.1)	(65.0)
Capital ≥ NT $40 million	45	65	110
	(24.9)	(48.9)	(35.0)
Total	181	133	314
	(100.0)	(100.0)	(100.0)
Size of firms (B):			
No. of employees < 200	163	76	239
	(89.1)	(56.3)	(75.2)
No. of employees ≥ 200	20	59	79
	(10.9)	(43.7)	(24.8)
Total	183	135	318
	(100.0)	(100.0)	(100.0)

Note: Figures in parentheses are percentages.

Table 14.4 Effect of Propaganda (no. of firms)

	Industry			Size of Firms		
	Mechanical Products	Information and Electronics	Total	Big	Medium and Small	Total
Deep understanding	44	34	78	46	32	78
	(23.7)	(25.6)	(24.5)	(42.6)	(15.6)	(24.9)
A little understanding	112	74	186	58	126	184
	(60.2)	(55.6)	(58.3)	(53.7)	(61.5)	(58.8)
Little understanding	29	23	52	4	44	48
	(15.6)	(17.3)	(16.3)	(3.7)	(21.5)	(15.3)
No understanding	1	2	3	. . .	3	3
	(.5)	(1.5)	(.9)		(1.5)	(1.0)
Total	186	133	319	108	205	313
	(100)	(100)	(100)	(100)	(100)	(100)

Note: Figures in parentheses are percentages.

preferential policies. The degree of understanding of the large firms is generally more extensive than that of the medium-sized and small firms.

As far as investment behavior is concerned, surveyed firms were asked to rank the six most important factors in the investment decision. These factors are shown in table 14.5. The market potential was ranked as the number one factor in a firm's investment decisions. The factors of financial cost and credit availability were ranked fifth and sixth, respectively. Kendall's coefficient of concordance was then used to test whether the rank given by each firm is consistent. The hypothesis of concordance was supported. This result reveals that the finance factor does not dominate other factors in the investment decision–making process of the firms.

The question of what a firm would have done had it not acquired the preferential loan was then raised with the subsidized firms. Table 14.6 shows the results of this question. In all, 53.7 percent of the firms answered that they would have continued with their investment projects by finding another source of funds without delay, and 38.8 percent of the firms would have continued their investment projects with perhaps a few years of delay. The average delay period mentioned is two years.

Some of the reasons given for why firms did not apply for preferential loans are also observed. Other available sources of funds and no understanding of the policy were the two major factors for the firms that did not apply.

Next, a path analysis is used to test the following four hypotheses:

THEME 1. The characteristics of the firms influence the probability of their receiving preferential loans.

THEME 2. Strategic preferential loans help decrease the interest burden of firms.

Table 14.5 Rank of Importance of Factors Influencing Investment and Kendall's Coefficient of Concordance

	Criterion for Investment					
Industry	Market Potential	Short-Run Profitability	Promotion of Technical Level	Competitive Situation	Credit Availability	Cost of Capital
Total Firms	1	3	2	4	5	6
	Kendall's $W = .3632$, $\chi^2 = 493.93$, $p = .0$*					
Mechanical products industry	1	3	2	5	4	6
	Kendall's $W = .3288$, $\chi^2 = 254.81$, $p = .0$*					
Information and electronics industry	1	3	2	4	6	5
	Kendall's $W = .4187$, $\chi^2 = 240.73$, $p = .0$*					

*Kendall's W is significant at the 5 percent level.

Table 14.6 Questions on the Possibility of Receiving Alternative Sources of Funds Answered by Those Who Received Strategic Loans

	No. Surveyed that Received Financing from:		
Possible Decisions	Bank of Communications	Medium Business Bank of Taiwan	Total (ratio)
Continuing investment projects using other financial sources	28	51	79 (53.7)
Postpone the execution of the investment project for a few years	15	42	57 (38.8)
Stop the investment project	2	9	11 (7.5)
Total	45	102	147 (100.0)

THEME 3. Strategic preferential loans cause a greater level of fixed asset accumulation in subsidized firms than in nonsubsidized firms.

THEME 4. Strategic preferential loans increase the operational performance of subsidized firms compared to that of nonsubsidized firms.

For the empirical part of this study, some factors must be quantified. (*a*) First we must consider the characteristics of firms:

1. *Scale of firms:* the paid-in capital of firms at the end of 1988;
2. *Technology level:* the ratio of engineers and technical persons to total employees;
3. *Financial status:* the financial status required for maintaining the firm's current capacity level and for enlarging its capacity;[3]
4. *Investment mood:* evaluated using the following categories: the frequency of a firm's investments, the depth of the evaluation employed in the investment decision–making process, the importance of the investment to the firm's growth, and the understanding of the technology by the employees who are responsible for the firm's investment activities;[4]
5. *Credibility:* evaluated in the following areas: the availability of short-term credit to the firm and the availability of medium- and long-term credit to the firm.[5]

3. There are two questions in the questionnaires regarding financial status: the degree of the firm's ability to maintain the current capacity based on the current financial status and the degree of the firm's financial sufficiency to expand its capacity. The answer to each question was reported on an ordinal scale ranging from 1 to 5. This method is used to quantify variables so that mathematical computation can be executed.

4. The method used for quantifying variables is the same as that mentioned in n. 3 above.

5. The answer to each question regarding the firm's investment mood and credibility is reported on an ordinal scale ranging from 1 to 5.

(*b*) Then we must consider the decision of the firms whether to acquire preferential loans. The to-acquire case is represented by the dummy variable 1 and the not-to-acquire case by the dummy variable 0. (*c*) The interest burden is the ratio of the average interest cost to the total expenses of the firm in the years from 1985 to 1988. (*d*) The fixed asset formation is: The average growth rate of fixed capital from 1985 to 1988. (*e*) Four variables are used to determine the performance of firms for the years from 1985 to 1988:

1. *Growth of sales;*
2. *Profitability:* the ratio of profits to revenues;
3. *Productivity of capital:* the ratio of average sales to capital;
4. *Productivity of labor:* the ratio of average sales to the number of employees.

The combining of several variables to represent each characteristic of the firms, that is, to form a representative variable, is achieved using a principal components analysis.[6] The growth of sales and profitability are combined to form a term to represent operational performance. The variables of productivity of capital and of labor are combined to form a term to represent productivity performance. The following discriminate equation and regression equations are then tested. This method is called path analysis:

(1) $$X6 = a_{11}X1 + a_{12}X2 + a_{13}X3 + a_{14}X4 + a_{15}X5,$$

(2) $$X7 = a_{21}X1 + a_{22}X2 + a_{23}X3 + a_{24}X4 + a_{25}X5 + a_{26}X6,$$

(3) $$X8 = a_{31}X1 + a_{32}X2 + a_{33}X3 + a_{34}X4 + a_{35}X5 + a_{36}X6 + a_{37}X7,$$

(4) $$X9 = a_{41}X1 + a_{42}X2 + a_{43}X3 + a_{44}X4 + a_{45}X5 + a_{46}X6 + a_{47}X7 + a_{48}X8,$$

(5) $$X10 = a_{51}X1 + a_{52}X2 + a_{53}X3 + a_{54}X4 + a_{55}X5 + a_{56}X6 + a_{57}X7 + a_{58}X8,$$

where X1 is the technology level, X2 is the scale of firms, X3 is sufficiency of funds, X4 is the investment mood, X5 is credibility, X6 is subsidized or not, X7 is the interest burden, X8 is growth of fixed capital, X9 is operational efficiency (sales and profitability), and X10 is production efficiency (productivity of capital and labor).

The results are shown in table 14.7. The following conclusions can be drawn:

1. From equation (6) (see table 14.7), the most significant item influencing the availability of preferential loans is the firm's investment mood. The other factors are not important in the issuance of preferential loans.

6. For further information on the principal components analysis, see Judge et al. (1980).

Table 14.7 **Path Analysis Regression of All the Surveyed Firms (N = 289)**

Explained Variable	Explanatory Variable									
	X1	X2	X3	X4	X5	X6	X7	X8	$\bar{R}^2$	F
(6): X6	.065	−.173	.141	.984	−.114				***	2.4298**
	(.294)	(.209)	(.301)	(26.80)*	(.180)					
(7): X7	.004	.004	−.171	.019	.019	−.015			.0403	1.9633
	(.832)	(.131)	(−2.988)*	(−.024)	(−.024)	(−.329)				
(8): X8	−.051	−.060	.000	.193	−.055	.040	.000		.050	1.9869
	(−.801)	(−.961)	(−.013)	(3.012)*	(−.887)	(.627)	(.003)			
(9): X9	.136	.196	.065	.231	−.052	−.038	.024	.235	.1833	7.0119**
	(2.282)*	(3.355)*	(1.029)	(3.840)*	(−.882)	(−.673)	(.283)	(3.973)*		
(10): X10	−.008	.093	−.094	−.014	−.068	.039	−.061	−.071	.0288	.9262
	(−.136)	(1.454)	(−1.461)	(−.219)	(−1.079)	(.601)	(−.965)	(−1.105)		

Note: t-statistics are given in parentheses.

*Significant coefficient at the 5 percent level.

**Goodness of fit is acceptable.

***p = .0015.

2. From equation (7), it is found that preferential loans do not significantly influence interest burden.[7]

3. From equation (8), it is found that preferential loans do not stimulate fixed capital formation significantly.

4. From equation (9), it is found that preferential loans have no close relation with operational performance. Also, those firms that have a higher level of technology, a more active investment mood, a larger scale of production, and more capital have better operational performance.

The effect of preferential loans on various industries was also tested. The regressions on firms in the mechanical products industry are shown in table 14.8. The regressions on the firms in the information and electronics industries are shown in table 14.9. Similar results are obtained in both cases: preferential loans do not significantly influence interest burden, investment, or operational performance. Investment mood probably plays more of a role in a firm's investment activities.

14.3 The Effect of Assistance in Management and Technology

The Ministry of Economic Affairs provided strategic-product-producing firms with technology and management assistance, through six relevant institutions. Financial support to defray the cost of the assistance was given to the firms, covering up to 60 percent of the total expense, with a ceiling of NT $1 million. The effects of the assistance are analyzed in this section.

A firm can obtain management and technology assistance from one or more sources: the government, academic institutions (e.g., universities), parent companies, private consulting companies, or foreign companies. Most firms (i.e., 54 percent of those surveyed) said that they would continue to ask for consultation whether or not they obtained financial support from the Ministry of Economic Affairs, as shown in table 14.10.

In the questionnaire, some questions regarding the degree of satisfaction of the assistance-receiving firms were asked; the answers are expressed by ordinal rank. The measures of the correlation coefficients between the level of satisfaction, the amount of financial support, and the ratio of financial support to total expenses are shown in table 14.11. All the coefficients are nonsignificantly negative. Therefore, the amount and the ratio of financial support do not seem to play an important role in the technology and management improvement activities of the firms.

The degree of satisfaction, as regards the various assistance areas, can be further analyzed. From figure 14.4, it can be seen that the government-assisted firms are more satisfied than the others in the area of technology,

7. Not all the equations of path analysis have satisfying goodness of fit. However, the key purpose of this study is to emphasize the influence of preferential policies. Other factors influencing the behavior of firms are not analyzed in depth.

Table 14.8 **Path Analysis Regressions for the Mechanical Products Industrys (N = 168)**

Explained Variable	Explanatory Variable									
	X1	X2	X3	X4	X5	X6	X7	X8	$\bar{R}^2$	F
X6	−.028	.242	.151	.974	.015				***	2.5745**
	(.032)	(.888)	(.450)	(21.95)*	(.037)					
X7	−.033	−.045	−.168	.102	−.099	−.110			.0643	1.9643
	(−.197)	(−.596)	(−2.392)*	(.817)	(−1.333)	(−1.363)				
X8	−.008	−.033	−.074	.228	−.152	.055	−.027		.0861	2.0034
	(−.099)	(−.390)	(−.911)	(2.672)*	(−1.838)	(.647)	(−.323)			
X9	.114	.132	.026	.263	.019	−.101	.002	.224	.1612	3.4346**
	(1.466)	(1.674)*	(.262)	(3.090)*	(.220)	(−1.204)	(−.091)	(2.789)*		
X10	.038	.027	−.078	.000	.008	.014	−.095	−.066	.0973	1.9877
	(.471)	(1.091)	(−.976)	(−.003)	(.105)	(.171)	(−1.174)	(−.814)		

Note: t-statistics are given in parentheses.

*Significant coefficient at the 5 percent level.

**Goodness of fit is acceptable.

***p = .0007.

Table 14.9 **Path Analysis Regression for the Information and Electronics Industry ($N = 119$)**

Explained Variable	Explanatory Variable									
	X1	X2	X3	X4	X5	X6	X7	X8	$\bar{R}^2$	F
X6	−.340	−.176	.097	.946	−.059				***	1.1432**
	(.997)	(.001)	(.038)	(8.441)*	(.284)					
X7	.082	.036	−.170	−.100	.089	.078			.1204	1.9887
	(.806)	(.339)	(−1.725)*	(−1.015)	(1.944)	(.748)				
X8	−.077	−.148	.134	.127	.039	.043	.041		.1981	1.7337
	(−.759)	(−1.438)	(1.298)	(1.243)	(.382)	(.419)	(.397)			
X9	.218	.243	.144	.169	−.165	.106	.057	.250	.2502	4.0467**
	(2.356)*	(2.614)*	(1.509)	(1.826)*	(−1.810)	(1.082)	(.553)	(2.734)		
X10	−.158	−.011	−.051	.037	−.118	−.043	.075	−.079	.0515	.6590
	(−1.544)	(−.109)	(−.486)	(.352)	(−1.150)	(−.423)	(.726)	(−.774)		

Note: t-statistics are given in parentheses.

*Significant coefficient at the 5 percent level.

**Goodness of fit is acceptable.

***$p = .0473$.

Table 14.10 **Answers of Surveyed Firms Regarding Whether Financial Support Obtained from the Government (no. of firms)**

	Large Firms	Small and Medium Firms	Mechanical Products Industry	Electronics and Information Industry	Total
Continue project, regardless of obtaining preferential support or not, to pay for assistance	6 (35.3)	17 (68.0)	17 (54.8)	6 (54.5)	23 (54.8)
Preferential policy speeds up the guidance project	8 (47.1)	5 (20.0)	10 (32.3)	3 (27.3)	13 (31.0)
Preferential policy determines the guidance project	3 (17.6)	3 (12.0)	4 (12.9)	2 (18.2)	6 (14.3)
Total	17	25	31	11	42 (100)

Note: Figures in parentheses are percentages.

Table 14.11 **Correlation Coefficient between the Firms' Level of Satisfaction and Financial Support**

	Degree of Satisfaction	Amount of Financial Support	Ratio of Financial Support
Degree of satisfaction	1.0000		
Amount of financial support	−.1832	1.0000	
Ratio of financial support	−.3000	−.0997	1.0000

especially with regard to research and automation. Consulting companies, making up the greatest part of nongovernment-assigned institutions, seem to give firms a greater degree of satisfaction in the areas of financial management and marketing.

In evaluating the effects of technological and management assistance on the firms' operational performance, a path analysis is used. The results are reported in figures 14.5 and 14.6. It is found that assistance promotes a greater level of production performance. Higher-tech firms usually do not ask the government for support but do ask other types of consultation institutions for assistance. It is also revealed that the government does aid in the dissemination, but not the upgrading, of technology. However, whether a firm obtains assistance through the government or through other institutions is not a key factor influencing production performance.

Empirical studies of the mechanical products and the information and elec-

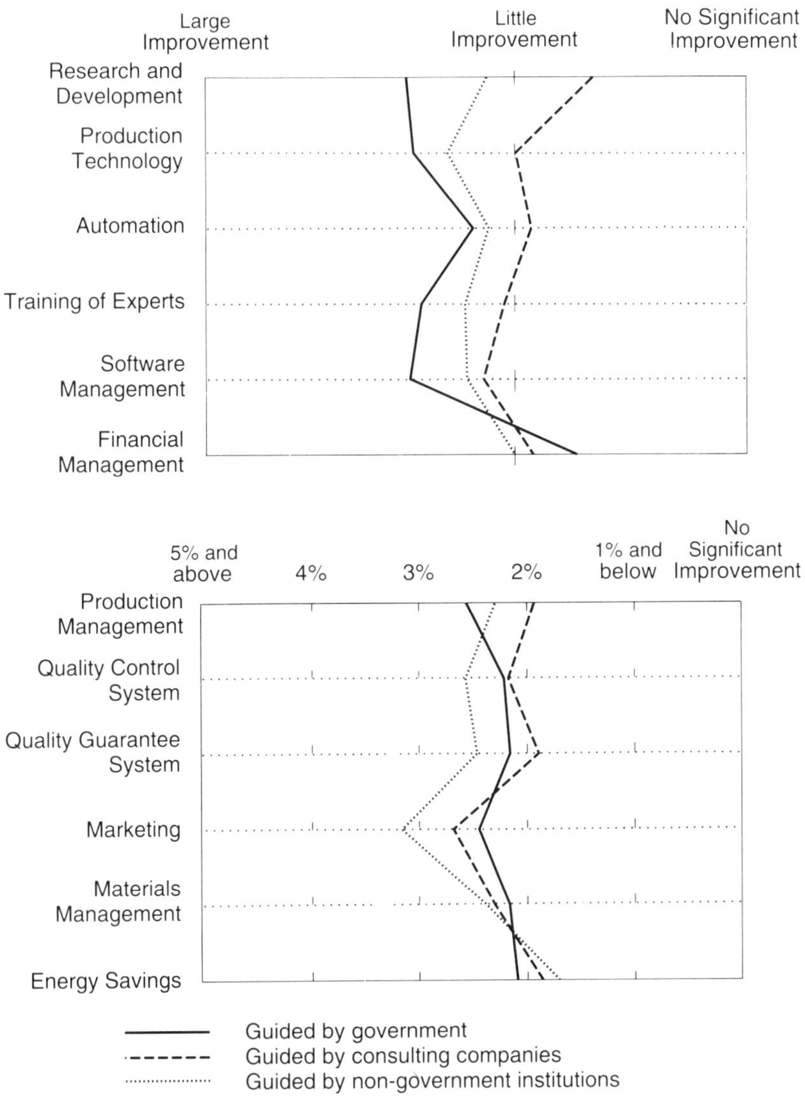

Fig. 14.4 Effects of different types of guidance items

tronics industries were also conducted using a similar approach, and similar results were obtained. The larger mechanical products firms tend to ask for more management and technology assistance, and they also display better production performance. Whether a firm obtains consultation through the government or through other institutions does not, however, seem to make any difference. Production performance increases in both cases.

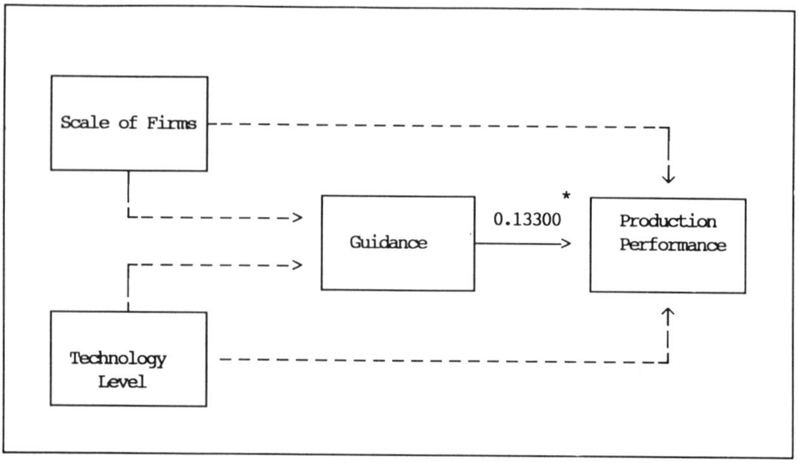

Fig. 14.5 Path analysis of the effects of guidance policy.

Note: The variables are defined as follows: X1 = scale of firms; X2 = technology level; X3 = dummy variable (X3 = 1 if obtained guidance, 0 otherwise); and X4 = production performance. Sample N = 300. * α = .05. The regressions are the following:

$$(1)\quad X3 = \underset{(.365)}{.80641}\,X1 + \underset{(.257)}{.70456}\,X2,\quad R^2 = .04883,\ F = .70899,$$

$$(2)\quad X4 = \underset{(.130)}{.07696}\,X1 - \underset{(-.332)}{.01966}\,X2 + \underset{(2.265)^{*}}{.13300}\,X3,\quad R^2 = .01475,\ F = 2.43238.$$

14.4 Conclusion

Preferential policies for strategic industries were introduced in 1982. Their effects were evaluated in this study through the aid of a questionnaire. The study found that most subsidized firms would have continued with their investment projects and would have still asked for assistance from other institutions even if they had not obtained preferential support from the government. The results of a path analysis show that the Taiwanese government's preferential policy of low-interest loans does not significantly reduce the interest burden, increase the fixed capital formation, or improve the operational performance of the firms. Those firms that took advantage of technological and management consultation showed better performance in comparison to the situation where no consultation was provided. However, the resulting improvement in performance was the same regardless of whether the consultation was provided by the government or by other institutions.

The answers to the three questions mentioned in section 14.1 above can be briefly summarized as follows:

1. Is the selection of strategic industries (which receive preferential treatment) necessary for stimulating economic growth?

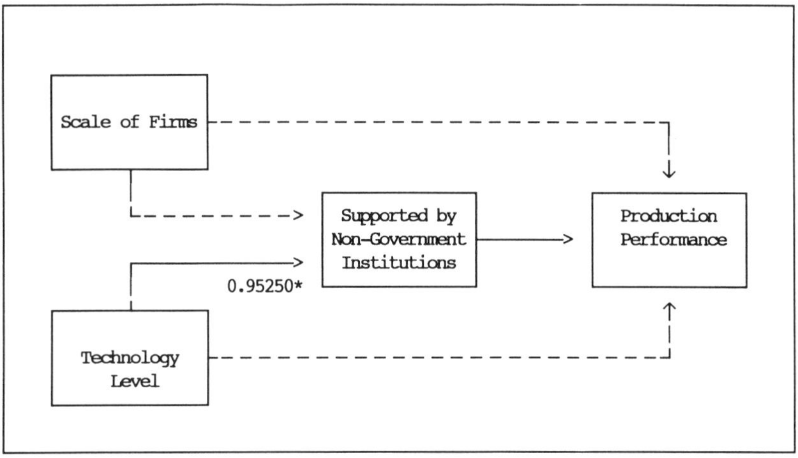

Fig. 14.6 Path analysis of the effects of guidance policy.
Note: The variables are defined as follows: X1 = scale of firms; X2 = technology level; X3 = dummy variable (X3 = 1 if obtained guidence, 0 otherwise); and X4 = production performance. Sample N = 118. * α = .05. ** = .01. The regressions are the following:

(1) $X3 = .48878\ X1 + .95250\ X2$, $R^2 = .24270$, $F = 6.97959$,**
(.835) (5.567)*

(2) $X4 = .15198\ X1 - .01901\ X2 - .11508\ X3$, $R^2 = .03565$, $F = 1.36770$.
(1.604) (−.197) (−1.203)

The unbalanced growth theory and the infant protection theory support the idea of key industries. The free economy theory and the balanced growth theory do not support this idea. Some scholars of the market failure theory agree that the government can intervene in the marketplace in the case of market failure.

2. Are the criteria used for selecting strategic products suitable for achieving the role of key industries?

Contradictions exist among different criteria, as is shown in Shea (1983) and Wu, Lee, and Yu (1988). Unless the government can clearly identify the social welfare objective and set definite weights for different criteria, arbitrarily selected criteria would not help economic development.

3. Are the process of and measures for executing policy effective in improving the investment position and performance of firms?

This paper provides empirical evidence that the preferential policy for strategic industries has not significantly improved the investment, financial situation, and operational performance of firms.

This study does have some limitations, however. Data on the surveyed firms before 1981 could not be obtained. The quantification of the qualitative variables used in the study may also be subject to criticism for its exactness. However, the method used in this study is a better approach than those used in other studies. As for the influence of the preferential policies studied, it could be the case that other policies (such as fiscal preferential policy) might have some effect on the decision-making processes of firms in Taiwan; however, these are not touched on here. Moreover, if the effects of preferential policies require more time to take effect, only future studies, given sufficient data, would be able to discover the actual effects.

References

Dervis, K., and J. M. Page, Jr. 1984. Industrial policy in developing countries. *Journal of Comparative Economics* 8: 436–51.
Hirschman, A. O. 1958. *The strategy of economic development*. New Haven, Conn.: Yale University Press.
Judge, G. G., W. E. Griffiths, R. C. Hill, and T. C. Lee. 1980. *The theory and practice of econometrics*. New York: John Wiley & Sons.
Kuo, Shirley W. Y. 1983. *The Taiwan economy in transition*. Boulder, Colo.: Westview.
Laumas, P. S. 1975. Key sectors in some underdeveloped countries. *Kyklos* 28 (1): 62–79.
———. 1976. Key sectors in some underdeveloped countries: A reply. *Kyklos* 29 (4): 767–69.
Li, Kwoh-ting, and Yu Tzong-shian, eds. 1982. *Experiences and lessons of economic development in Taiwan*. Taipei: Academia Sinica.
Nurkse, R. 1953. *Problems of capital formation in underdeveloped countries*. New York: Oxford University Press.
Pigou, A. C. 1918. *The economics of welfare*. London: Macmillan.
Shea, Jia-Dong. 1983. Industry upgrading, capital accumulation, and finance strategy (in Chinese). *Monthly Review of Money and Finance* 12 (May): 2–9.
Wu, H. L., S. F. Lee, and R. R. Yu. 1988. *The policy of industrial structure adjustment* (in Chinese). Taipei: Chung-Hua Institution for Economic Research.
Yotopoulos, P. A., and J. B. Nugent. 1973. A balanced-growth version of the linkage hypothesis: A test. *Quarterly Journal Economics* 87 (2): 157–71.
———. 1976. *Economics of development: Empirical investigation*. New York: Harper & Row.

Comment Yoo Jung-ho

The first thing that one would like to know in evaluating an industrial policy is whether it is prompted by a case of market failure that justifies government intervention of some form. If the market can do better acting alone than it can

Yoo Jung-ho is a senior fellow at the Korea Development Institute.

with government intervention, there is no justification for government intervention. However, market failure is a theoretical concept, the existence of which is very difficult to prove or disprove, and the question of market failure may be irrelevant for an industrial policy that is already implemented.

Another tack that one may take in evaluating a government policy is to consider whether the benefit of the policy to the society is larger than or at least as large as its opportunity cost. Yang's paper appears to take this approach in evaluating the Taiwanese government's industrial policy in the 1980s. The major support measures of the policy were preferential loans with interest rates lower than market rates and technical and management assistance. The paper hypothesizes that the effects will take place through a number of "channels" and estimates the effectiveness of the policy supports at each channel. The empirical investigation is based on a survey of firms in the industries in which the recipients of the policy supports were located. The industries were mechanical products and information and electronics.

It should be pointed out that the paper evaluates Taiwanese industrial policy by the effects on the firms that received some support from the policy. For a balanced evaluation, one should weigh the effects on the recipients of the policy supports against the negative effects experienced by others. Since no government can create something out of nothing, if the government gives assistance to some, that assistance inevitably entails some costs that must be borne by someone else in the economy, not the government.

Admittedly, a correct estimation of these costs is almost always impossible. This does not mean, however, that one may ignore the problem. The paper could have made a greater contribution to the understanding of the effects of industrial policy had it provided some information on, for example, what the provision of preferential policy loans meant to the firms in the industries not favored by the policy in terms of higher cost of capital or increased difficulty in obtaining the loans or in terms of investment opportunities foregone as a consequence.

Most likely, the firms in the industries not favored by the policy were even less aware of the industrial policy than those in the favored industries. It is also likely that no more statistically significant replies can be expected from the firms in the nonfavored industries to the questionnaires than those the author obtained in her survey from the firms in the favored industries. Thus, an analysis of survey returns may not be an effective way of evaluating industrial policy. It may have been better to examine the performance of two groups, favored and not favored by the industrial policy, either at the firm level or at the industry level.

The paper, however, deserves praise for its efforts to identify the paths through which the effects of an industrial policy take place. This kind of inquiry will increase our understanding of the interaction between government policy and business responses and will enable us to make a more informed judgment as to the desirability of industrial policy.

Comment Tan Eu Chye

Ya-hwei Yang presents a very useful analysis of the effectiveness of the strategic industrial preferential policy of Taiwan. Such an evaluation of government policies is definitely needed to ensure their efficacy. The following are points raised by the author that I feel call for specific comment.

1. *Taiwan's experience can be used as a reference for other developing countries' industrial policy.*

   To some extent this is true. But each country has its own economic, social, and political background. The Asian nations are a heterogeneous grouping. Hence, none of the newly industrialized countries (NICs) can be used as a model of economic development for Asian developing countries.

2. *The finance factor does not dominate the other factors in the investment decision-making process of the firms and their operational performance.*

   Apart from the reasons given by the author, this may also be due to the magnitude of the assistance extended given the fact that the preferential loan rates are only 1.75–2.75 percent lower than the prime lending rate of commercial banks and the low limit of NT $1 million that the government can subsidize on the consulting expenses of the firms as stated by the author. The finance factor may become a major factor if the magnitude of assistance is revised upward.

3. *The criteria adopted before industries can be designated as strategic may be in conflict with each other. For example, there is a conflict between a high degree of value added as one criterion and a high linkage effect as another.*

   There may be no conflict between the two depending on the level at which value added is defined. If it is defined at the national level, which I am more ready to believe, then high value addedness of an industry is consistent with strong linkages in the economy, particularly backward linkages.

4. *The government does not follow the criteria when identifying strategic industries.*

   The fact that the government arbitrarily chooses the industry to be granted such preferential treatment means that there is the attendant risk of making an inappropriate choice. It is a well-acknowledged fact that the public sector cannot respond more efficiently to market signals than the private sector. Rather than making an arbitrary choice, the government can always initiate a study of prospective industries, a study that approximates some social cost-benefit analysis. An environmental impact assessment (EIA) study of industries can also be launched.

Tan Eu Chye is a lecturer in economics at the University of Malaya, Kuala Lumpur, Malaysia.

5. *Government-assisted firms are satisfied in the area of technology, especially with regard to research and automation. And private consulting firms seem to give firms a greater degree of satisfaction.*
   This is not an unexpected phenomenon as it is common knowledge that private-sector-run establishments are generally more efficient than public-sector-run establishments.

Generally, the move by the Taiwanese government to designate certain industries as strategic is a step in the right direction, disregarding its practical aspect, so long as these industries are not lavished with tariff protection at the same time. Otherwise, it merely constitutes a "double" protection for these industries, and the effective rate of protection (EPR) can be very high. Industries that are heavily protected usually remain infant forever.

15 Export-Oriented Growth and Equity in Korea

Wontack Hong

Numerous literatures have documented that Korea's rapid growth since the early 1960s is owed almost entirely to its export-oriented growth strategy. According to Samuelson's static factor price equalization theorem, free trade with incomplete specialization can lead to the equalization of absolute factor returns among trading countries. In the early 1960s, Korea commenced its export-oriented growth by promoting exports of labor-intensive products on the basis of abundant cheap labor. By opening up and integrating its economy into the world market and trading directly with the most advanced countries in the world, the returns to the most abundant factor of production in Korea (i.e., the returns to labor) began to catch up with those of the advanced countries. Indeed, the average wage rate in the Korean manufacturing sector amounted to mere one-twenty-third of that of the U.S. manufacturing sector in 1960 ($2.30 per hour) but grew to one-seventeenth of the latter ($3.35 per hour) in 1970 and to one-quarter of the latter ($14.31) by 1989. Even after making due allowance for autonomous capital accumulation and technical progress, such a steady and rapid rise in the rate of return on labor suggests the enormous absolute magnitude of gains from trade that Korea has been reaping over time through an export-oriented growth strategy based on comparative advantage.

In the process of export-oriented growth in Korea (1962–91), the rapid expansion of productive employment opportunities and the steady rise in real wage rates of various labor groups did contribute positively to the reduction of inequality in the distribution of income. The Korean government, however, has pursued this export-oriented growth strategy without paying much attention to the distributional aspect of the growth process. Critics have accused the Korean government of promoting export expansion by using various

Wontack Hong is professor of international economics at Seoul University.

second-best or third-best policy measures that have generated all kinds of undesirable side effects, such as the concentration of production activities in the hands of a small number of big business groups (*Jae-buls*), worsening the distribution of income and wealth, proliferating unearned incomes, institutionalizing rent seeking, hostile and unstable labor relations, maintenance of a command economy for the banking sector, excessive dependence on the U.S. and Japanese economies, and so on. Presumably in order to take advantage of the scale economies in production activities, the government has deliberately concentrated economic power in the hands of a small number of *Jae-buls;* presumably in order to enhance national savings, it has minimized the taxation on capital gains and on incomes arising from the ownership of property and financial assets; and perhaps in order to take advantage of some kinds of scale economies that might arise from the concentration of wealth, it has minimized the effort to collect inheritance and gift taxes. Three decades of rapid economic growth seem to have generated politically powerful groups who have vested interests in the continuation of such an economic regime. Consequently, it is argued that, in spite of such a brilliant growth performance, Korea now experiences magnified internal conflicts and social unrest, making the prospect of its continued prosperity anything but a certainty.

The objectives of this paper are to examine the changing pattern of various published distributional statistics of Korea over the last three decades, the problems associated with such estimates, the government policies to concentrate economic power, the tax and public expenditure system, and the political economy of distribution policies. I conclude, first, that difficulties with Korea's income distribution are not the result of the export-oriented growth strategy itself and, second, that an export orientation alone, however, is not enough to result in a more equitable distribution of income and wealth.

15.1 Distribution Statistics on Income and Wealth

We may define the wage elasticity of productivity (WEP) as the percentage change in the wage rate (in manufacturing) divided by the percentage change in the average value added per employed person (of the whole economy). This index shows the relation between the speed of increase in the average labor productivity of the whole economy and the speed of increase in the average return to labor. The WEP amounted to 1.08 in 1965–70, 0.93 in 1970–76, 1.16 in 1976–80, 0.95 in 1980–85, and 1.22 in 1985–91. During 1965–91, labor productivity (i.e., value added per employed person) increased by about 4.3 times and the wage rate (in manufacturing) by about 5.8 times.[1]

1. The average annual wage rate in manufacturing amounted to $1,992 (in 1991 prices) in 1965, which became $11,500 in 1991. The value added per employed person amounted to $3,543 (in 1991 prices) in 1965, which became $15,116 in 1991. Data are from BOK, *Economic Statistics Yearbook;* MOF, *Fiscal and Monetary Statistics;* and BOK (1990).

The shift in the Gini coefficient from 0.344 in 1965 to 0.332 in 1970 may reflect the positive contribution to income distribution in the latter half of the 1960s of the rapid increase in employment opportunities that commenced after the early 1960s and the significant rise in real wages every year after 1965. The shift in the Gini coefficient to 0.391 in 1976 and 0.389 in 1980 may reflect the negative contribution to the distribution of income of the amplified concentration of economic power in the hands of big business groups and of the increased skewedness in wage rates among labor groups as well as of the increasing income disparity between farm households and urban households (during 1970–76). The shift in the Gini coefficient to (0.345 in 1985 and) 0.336 in 1988 may reflect the positive contribution of the active labor union movement in the late 1980s on labor's share of national income.[2] Studies by Choo and Yoon (1984) and Yoo (1990) show a similar trend of inequality over time.

It may not, however, be wise to attempt to explain changes in a Gini coefficient of 0.002 or 0.012 or even 0.053. All estimates tend to seriously underestimate the actual degree of inequality because the basic data for these estimates exclude most of the very rich and the very poor (particularly during 1965–76), do not report the income figures of self-employed households (such as private businessmen, doctors, and lawyers), do not include nonfarm households in rural areas and farm households in urban areas, and, while including various unrealized incomes in farm households associated with their production activities, do not properly cover capital gains, inheritance, and property income.[3] The size of Korea's underground economy is estimated to be very substantial, and of course its existence could not be taken account of in these estimates.

On the other hand, a sample survey by the Bank of Korea shows a Gini coefficient of 0.56 for financial asset ownership in 1988 compared to that of 0.30 for income distribution of the households included in the survey (see Kang 1989, 76). According to a sample survey conducted by the Korea Development Institute in May 1989, the Gini coefficient for financial assets was 0.77 and that for physical assets was 0.60, while the Gini coefficient for income distribution of the households included in the survey amounted to 0.40 in 1988 (see Soonwon Kwon 1990).[4] Including the imputed rents from owner-

2. Data are from EPB (1989, 101). In 1965, the income of the wealthiest 20 percent was about 2.2 times that of the poorest 40 percent. In 1970, the ratio fell slightly to about 2.0, but it rose to about 2.7 in 1976 and to about 2.8 by 1980. By 1985, the ratio had fallen to about 2.5 to 1.

3. Nor is the imputed income from owner-occupied housing included in each household's total income figure. Furthermore, the basic data report only the mean income of each income bracket instead of the income of individual families belonging to each bracket. Since these studies assume that the mean income is the representative of each income bracket, the results are bound to lead to the underestimation of the inequality in Korea.

4. Since the KDI sample survey includes a larger number of rich and poor households than the government sample survey, the degree of income inequality is greater than other estimates based on government survey data. Capital gains are not counted in household surveys.

occupied housing as well as capital gains arising from the increase in housing prices, the Gini coefficient for income distribution computed on the basis of KDI survey data amounted to 0.436 in 1988. According to the Securities and Exchange Commission, about 91.56 percent of total *listed* stocks in Korea were owned by 0.264 million (juridical and nonjuridical) persons as of December 1990.

As of 1988, the total number of people economically active in Korea was 17.3 million. According to the *Report* of the Land Committee (Land Committee 1989), as of June 1988 in Korea, 0.54 million persons (i.e., equivalent to 3.1 percent of the economically active population) owned 65.2 percent of total private land, and 1.08 million persons (i.e., the upper 6.2 percent group) owned 76.9 percent of private land. The Gini coefficient of land ownership, computed without including about 6.5 million adults who do not own any land at all, amounted to 0.85 (see Land Committee 1989, 4).

By the end of 1988, the most plausible estimate for total value of privately owned land in Korea amounted to about 8.1 times GNP, which became about 9.4 times GNP by the end of 1990 (see estimate C of table 15.1).[5] The average land price increased by about 7 percent in 1985 and 1986, 14.7 percent in 1987, 27.5 percent in 1988, 32.0 percent in 1989, and 20.6 percent in 1990.[6] The most plausible estimates of (realized plus unrealized) "real" capital gains (i.e., taking account of overall inflation) arising from land ownership were equivalent to about 99 percent of GNP in 1983, about 74 percent of GNP in 1987, about 137 percent of GNP in 1988, about 199 percent of GNP in 1989, and about 79 percent of GNP in 1990 (see table 15.1).

In 1988, about 66 percent of total land in Korea was owned by private citizens, about 24 percent by the public sector, and about 4 percent by corporations. Among the land owned by corporations, about 67 percent was owned by the largest 403 firms, and about 88 percent was owned by the 2,174 largest firms (see Land Committee 1989, 244–46). As of 1988, about 90 percent of property-tax payers in Korea owned land whose assessed value amounted to less than 11.8 million won (about $17,000) and paid less than 40,000 won (about $58.00) as property taxes per annum. On the other hand, less than 2 percent of property-tax payers owned land whose assessed value exceeded 31.1 million won (about $45,000) and paid more than 60,000 won (about

5. Estimates B are based on the facts that the total amount of land value assessed by the Ministry of Home Affairs for the purpose of local tax collection amounted to 84.2 trillion won as of 1 May 1989, that the average rate of increase in land price in 1989 was 32.0 percent ($\times$ 0.6666 = 0.21333), and that the average ratio of assessed value to market value estimated by the Korea Research Institute of Human Settlement amounted to 0.137 as of 1 January 1990.

6. The rapid increases in land price are often explained by the severe restrictions imposed on land use in Korea (such as the *absolute farmland* system), which inhibit land supply, and the fact that land itself became the object of speculative activities. One might, however, contend that the heavy protection of agricultural production in Korea has been the real cause of the rapid rise in land prices. This is because, with free trade in agricultural products, the rates of return on farming as well as the land prices themselves would be drastically driven down.

Table 15.1 **Increase in Stock and Land Prices and Associated Capital Gains**

	1983	1984	1985	1986	1987	1988	1989	1990
Rate of inflation (%)[a]	5.0	3.9	4.1	2.8	3.5	5.9	5.2	10.6
Increase in land price (%):								
Nominal rate (*n*)	18.5	13.2	7.0	7.3	14.7	27.5	32.0	20.6
Real rate (*r*)[b]	13.5	9.3	2.9	4.5	11.2	21.6	26.8	10.0
Estimates (in trillion won) of (year-end)								
Land value (A)[c]	139.8	158.2	169.1	181.4	216.2	275.7	363.9	438.9
Land value (B)[d]	297.2	336.4	360.0	386.2	443.0	564.9	745.6	899.2
Land value (C)[e]	538.6	609.7	652.3	700.0	802.9	1,023.6	1,351.2	1,614.5
Real capital gains (in trillion won):								
rA_{t-1}	15.9	13.0	4.6	7.6	20.3	46.7	73.9	36.4
rB_{t-1}	33.9	27.6	9.8	16.2	43.3	95.7	151.4	74.6
rC_{t-1}	61.3	50.1	17.7	29.4	78.4	173.4	274.3	135.1
GNP (current price in trillion won)	61.7	70.1	78.1	90.6	106.0	126.2	141.8	171.5
Land value/GNP:								
Estimate A	2.3	2.3	2.2	2.0	2.0	2.2	2.6	2.6
Estimate B	4.8	4.8	4.6	4.3	4.2	4.5	5.3	5.2
Estimate C	8.7	8.7	8.4	7.7	7.6	8.1	9.5	9.4
Capital Gains/GNP (%):								
Estimate rA_{t-1}	26	19	6	8	19	37	52	21
Estimate rB_{t-1}	55	39	13	18	41	76	107	44
Estimate rC_{t-1}	99	72	23	33	74	137	193	79

(continued)

Table 15.1 (continued)

	1983	1984	1985	1986	1987	1988	1989	1990
Increase in stock price (%)	4.7	3.3	5.3	64.0	83.3	66.0	32.5	−18.7
Paid-in assets (in trillion won)	3.2	4.3	4.7	5.7	7.6	12.6	21.2	24.0
Market value of stocks (in trillion won)	3.5	5.2	6.6	12.0	26.2	64.5	95.5	79.0
Stock value/GNP (%)	5.7	7.4	8.5	13.3	24.7	51.1	67.4	46.1
Capital gains in stock (in trillion won)	.1	.6	1.1	4.4	12.3	33.3	22.4	−19.3
Capital gains/GNP (%)	.2	.9	1.4	4.9	11.6	26.4	15.8	−11.3

Sources: MOF, *Fiscal and Monetary Statistics;* Land Committee (1989); Jin Soon Lee (1990, 45, 63); Ministry of Home Affairs, *Yearbook of Local Tax Administration: 1990;* and Bank of Korea, *Monthly Bulletin.*

[a]Rate of change in GNP deflator each year.

[b]The difference between the rate of increase in land price and that of GNP deflator each year.

[c]Figures for 1984–87 were obtained from Land Committee (1989, 238), and figures for other years were obtained by applying the rates of change in nominal land price.

[d]Total land value at the end of 1989 was estimated by using the total assessed value of land as of 1 May 1989 (i.e., 84,185.6 billion won), the average rate of increase in land price in 1989 (32.0 percent × 0.666 = 0.21333), and the average ratio of assessed value to market value as of 1 January 1990 (13.7 percent). Earlier data were obtained from Ministry of Home Affairs, *Yearbook of Local Tax Administration: 1990,* and the Korea Research Institute for Human Settlements.

[e]Total land values at the end of 1989 and 1990 were estimated by the Ministry of Construction and announced on 28 October 1991.

$87.00) as property taxes per annum (see Kang 1989, 163). In 1990, only 3.43 percent of property-tax payers (334,806 out of 9,732,001 persons) paid more than $140 under the new global land tax system (see Tae Dong Kim 1990, 36). This may imply that land ownership by value is more concentrated than land ownership by area.

15.2 Concentration of Economic Power in Production Activities

As of 1985, the largest thirty big business groups (*Jae-bul*) produced 40 percent of Korea's total manufacturing value added (see Young Ki Lee 1990, 327), and, as of 1989, the largest fifty big business groups comprising 520 companies produced 16 percent of Korea's GNP (see KIS 1990, 58). In 1985, the thirty largest business groups (comprising 270 firms) possessed 40 percent of total tangible fixed assets and hired 17.6 percent of total employees in the Korean manufacturing sector (see Cho 1990, 138, 143). These thirty largest business groups contributed 38.5 percent of Korea's total commodity exports in 1977 and 41.3 percent in 1985 (see EPB 1989, 238).[7]

As of 1991, about 47 percent of the stocks of the thirty largest business groups are apparently owned directly or indirectly (through the intragroup cross shareholdings) by the major owner families of each group (see Yoo 1992). In Korea, however, the listed stocks can be purchased anonymously or in someone else's name; hence, should we take account of hidden ownership, most of the owner families are likely to own much more than 50 percent of the stocks of each group on average. Including the stocks owned by the nonprofit foundations that are controlled by *Jae-bul* families, studies of stock ownership show that the share of the major owner family of each *Jae-bul* group amounted to about 39–61 percent in 1985–86 (see Cho 1990, 399–400).[8]

Since conglomerates enjoy greater financial resources and market dominance, their behavior makes entry by new firms difficult and inhibits the growth of small and medium-sized firms. The corporate empires of big business groups dominate markets not only for manufacturing but also for sales, trade, finance, and real estate by taking advantage of superior financing ability and information resources. Such domination results in abuse of market power, collusive action, and excessive monopolistic profits, reducing the gains of

7. Throughout the period 1962–91, these highly diversified *Jae-buls* have been expanding rapidly in terms of aggregate sales volume and value added, yet their share in total manufacturing employment has been declining since the beginning of the 1980s owing to their active participation in capital and technology-intensive industries.

8. Young Ki Lee (1990, 334) notes that "cross-holding of shares among member companies of a group is one common means of interlocking member companies, thus reinforcing the controlling power of the owner [without requiring additional equity contribution]. In the mid-1980s, the share of equity shares exchanged among affiliated companies within a group was, on average, close to 50 percent of the total outstanding shares of the group."

production specialization.[9] The market domination of large firms is revealed by the fact that competitive markets, defined as those in which the three largest firms account for less than 60 percent of total shipment value, amounted to only 22.3 percent of all commodity items and 37.8 percent of total shipment value as of 1985 (see PCER 1989, 72–73).

During the period 1961–79, bureaucrats led by President Park enforced the export-oriented growth strategy in Korea, but the core agents who actually executed the investment and production activities were the individual entrepreneurs. The bureaucracy and business both had to recruit the necessary manpower among the existing pool of labor. Owing to the scarcity of qualified manpower, the rent for the people with the proper educational background and managerial talent rapidly increased. Although economic power in Korea had mostly been concentrated in the hands of a small number of successful entrepreneurs through investment licensing and credit rationing, a large number of decision-making politicians and bureaucrats as well as people with managerial talents could also claim a substantial share of economic power.

The overambitious investment plans of the Korean government induced not only large inflows of foreign capital but also chronic inflation. Inflation not only perpetuated the negative bank interest rate regime that discouraged household savings but also constantly pushed up land prices and encouraged real estate speculation. The real estate speculation generated large windfall wealth in the hands of individuals who, in many cases, did not possess any entrepreneurial ability and consequently resulted in a waste of resources. On the other hand, a large number of privileged entrepreneurs has been actively involved not only in curb market lending activities but also in real estate speculation on a massive scale with bank loans that were officially earmarked for productive investment activities. This helped accelerate wealth accumulation in the hands of a privileged few businessmen in Korea.

The government believed that taxing the interest income of large-scale curb market lenders and exposing their identities would disrupt the operation of entire curb markets and hence greatly jeopardize the national economy. In Korea, most interest and dividend income has not been subject to the progressive global income tax, all kinds of capital gains have been almost free from formal taxation, and profit income has enjoyed extensive tax-exemption privileges. Government revenue has been raised mostly through regressive indirect taxes.

9. Perhaps because of the snowballing effect of wealth accumulation, there has been an extreme concentration of economic power in the hands of a small number of big business groups that goes well beyond the limits justified by scale economies. Extreme overextension of a given entrepreneurial talent implies poor management of the extended group's business activities and frequent cases of failure on a gigantic scale. In Korea, the entrepreneurial ability of the chosen few businessmen has been unreasonably exaggerated, and a tremendous waste of resources in the hands of some of these chosen few has often occurred.

15.3 Most Favorite Tax Treatment for Unearned Incomes

As of 1989, the total (central and local) government tax revenue amounted to 18.6 percent of GNP, and only about 39 percent of this revenue was raised from various direct taxes, including corporation income tax (12 percent), global income tax (2.8 percent), and withheld income tax on wages and salaries (5.8 percent). Taxes on various asset incomes amounted to only about 10.6 percent of the total tax revenue: 2.5 percent from the property tax (including the city planning tax and defense surtax), 3.0 percent from the capital gains tax on individual real estate transactions (including the inhabitant tax and defense surtax), 0.4 percent from the corporate special additional tax (the corporate capital gains tax) on corporate real estate transactions, 3.8 percent from withheld income taxes on interest and dividends (including the defense and education surtaxes and inhabitant taxes), and 0.7 percent from the inheritance tax.[10] Quite a few tax experts contend that many of the so-called direct taxes are transferred to consumers and hence should be regarded as indirect taxes.

According to Kwack and Lee (1991, 14–15), "As of 1987, less than 2 percent of GDP was collected as personal income tax, while in most Western countries the level is around 10 percent. With this low share of the personal income tax it is impossible to significantly affect the size distribution of income through tax policies. . . . First, though the marginal tax rate is very high and progressive, the exemption level is also very high. . . . Second, most interest income and about half of dividend income is taxed separately at a low flat rate. Third, capital gains from financial asset transactions are completely untaxed and those from real asset transactions are known to be undertaxed. Probably most importantly, the general level of income tax compliance and administration is very low. In particular, proprietors' income is notorious for escaping taxation."[11]

Capital gains arising from stock transactions were not subject to income tax, while the estimated (realized and unrealized) capital gains from the price increases of listed stocks amounted to about 19–38.4 trillion won in 1988 (i.e., 15–31 percent of GNP). Most of the interest and dividend income was separately assessed from global income and subject to a separate taxation of

10. Allegedly in order to encourage financial savings, the military government introduced a system in 1961 under which financial transactions in fictitious names were allowed. In 1982, a law barring financial transactions in fictitious names was passed in the National Assembly, but actual implementation of the law was suspended indefinitely.

11. "An unincorporated firm whose annual sale is below 36 million won is eligible for the *special taxation* program of the VAT (2 percent of total sales). . . . This sales information is also used in estimating the firm's income tax base by applying the *standard income ratio*. If the ratio is 10 percent, monthly taxable income of such business owner is only 300 thousand won which is even lower than the starting salary of a typical highschool-graduated worker. About 70 percent of the unincorporated firms in Korea are covered under the special tax program. As a result about 65 percent of proprietors belong to the zero (income tax) bracket" (Kwack and Lee 1991, 14–15).

16.75–17.75 percent (including defense and education surtaxes and the inhabitant tax), withheld at source, while the maximum global income tax rate applied to income exceeding 50 million won amounted to 63.75 percent (including a 10–20 percent defense surtax and a 7.5 percent inhabitant tax). The Korean government still does not enforce the use of real names in financial transactions and allows the ownership of savings accounts in financial institutions, stocks, and bonds in false or borrowed names, effectively placing this income beyond the reach of the global income tax system and rendering the inheritance and gift tax system ineffective. It is estimated that only 11.8 percent of rent income in 1983 and only 33.4 percent of interest income and 36–54 percent of dividend income in 1987 were subject to tax and that the rest escaped any kind of taxation. Among those incomes captured by tax authority, 99.1 percent of interest income and 63.6 percent of dividend income were subject to separate taxation withheld at the source in 1987 (see FKI 1988, 1:21; and Kwack and Lee 1988, 194, 198).

The typical property tax rate that was applied to most land in Korea had been 0.3 percent of the assessed value.[12] Since, according to government statistics, the assessed value amounted to about 32.9 percent of market value in 1988, the real average property tax rate should have amounted to less than 0.1 percent of the market value of land.[13] Tax statistics show that the real average property tax rate on land could not have exceeded 0.04 percent in 1987. The nominal capital gains tax amounted to 51–76.5 percent of assessed capital gains, including the defense surtax and inhabitant tax, implying approximately 16.8–25.2 percent of real capital gains arising from land transactions. However, owing to extremely unrealistic assessment of land values and various tax exemption clauses, the ratio of capital gains tax actually collected to actual (realized plus unrealized) capital gains from land ownership could not have exceeded 1 percent in 1987.[14] It is not very difficult for corporations to make capital gains arising from real estate transactions look like those arising from stock transactions, which are tax exempt (see Hong 1990b).

In the face of growing public sentiment against enormous windfall gains arising from land speculations, the Korean government introduced in 1990 a series of reform measures such as a more realistic assessment of land prices for tax purposes, a global land tax system, a progressive capital gains tax on land transactions, an upper limit on the size of dwelling sites, taxes on unreal-

12. The typical nominal rate of property tax became 0.56 percent of the assessed value if we include the city planning tax (0.2 percent) and defense surtax (0.06 percent). In Korea, the base date of assessment of land value is 1 May each year. In Taiwan, the basic rate of property tax amounted to 1.5–3.0 percent, and the assessed property value amounted, on average, to about 50 percent of market value. In Japan, the basic property tax rate amounted to 1.4 percent (see FKI 1988, 2:104–35; and Jene K. Kwon 1990, 25).

13. As a percentage of GNP, property tax revenue amounted to 0.5 percent in Korea in 1989, 1.1 percent in Taiwan, 3.4 percent in Japan, 3.1 percent in the United States, and 4.7 percent in the United Kingdom in 1988. Data are from the Korean Ministry of Finance FKI (1988, 1:26, 47), and OECD (1991, 73).

ized capital gains generated by land price increases, and a levy on land development profits arising from land price increases. The government target for a realistic assessment of land prices for tax purposes is to raise them from 32.9 percent, that is, supposedly the average level of assessed land price compared to the real market price in 1988, to the level of 48 percent of market value by 1994, that is, to apply 60 percent of the unified land prices assessed by the government (the so-called publicly announced land price that amounts to approximately 80 percent of market values) as the tax basis by 1994.[15] Even if this target is achieved by 1994, however, the government will collect only about 0.54 percent of market value per annum from those who own as much as $3 million worth of land purely for speculative purposes (such as forest and dry and paddy fields) through the new global land tax system.[16] The upper limit on dwelling sites is enforced only in the six largest cities in Korea. The 50 percent tax on unrealized capital gains (in excess of normal gains) arising from increased land prices (the so-called excessive land profit tax) is to be applied only in very limited cases and anyway harbors all the problems inherent in taxing unrealized gains. The 50 percent special levies on land development profits are imposed only on a small number of large land development firms, and the base price of land in computing the rate of increase in land prices is the price at the beginning date of development instead of the real acquisition price. Furthermore, the government is to continue to maintain the system that tolerates land ownership in someone else's name, although such an act is subject to nominal fines. This system dilutes the effectiveness of the global land tax. The government also wants to maintain the system that defines a factory lot (which is subject to the flat 0.3 percent rate of property tax) on the basis of the size of the factory's ground structure irrespective of its scale of productive activities (i.e., value added).

In 1991, the separate tax rate on interest and dividend income (including the inhabitant tax) was merely raised from 16.75 percent (or 17.75 percent for income exceeding 8.4 million won) to 21.5 percent. The hitherto tax-exempt capital gains realized from stock transactions became subject to a proportional tax as far as the capital gains arising from the transactions of unlisted stocks

14. The magnitude of the capital gains tax on land transactions amounted to about 0.5 percent of GNP in 1989 in Korea and about 3.0 percent of GNP in 1988 in Taiwan.

15. According to the Korea Research Institute for Human Settlements, the assessed value amounted to 13.7 percent of market value on average for the whole nation as of 1 January 1990. Then the assessed value amounting to 32.9 percent of market value may more likely correspond to that for, say, January 1985 rather than that for 1988. Under the new global land tax system in 1990, the average effective rate of property tax on land amounted to 0.04 percent, while that in Taiwan amounted to about 0.2 percent (in 1988), in Japan to about 0.2 percent (in 1985), and in the United States and the United Kingdom to about 1.4 percent (in 1985).

16. Since the maximum capital gains tax on land transactions became 64.5 percent of the publicly announced land price (owing to the abolition of the defense surtax in 1991), the maximum effective rate of the capital gains tax on land transactions will be 51.6 percent. Increases only in the capital gains tax while very low property tax rates on land ownership are maintained are likely to result in, first, a *lock-in effect* (reduced supply of land) and, consequently, a shifting of most tax burdens to buyers.

of closed corporations are concerned: 20 percent for those of large corporations and 10 percent for those of small corporations. The effective rates of these capital gains taxes are, however, even lower than the previous taxes on retained earnings that were replaced by these.

15.4 Subsidized Credit Rationing to Selected Sectors and Firms

This section examines credit rationing, one of the major economic policy instruments adopted by the Korean government for the sake of the country's export-oriented growth, and the consequences of such a policy measure. Although the Korean government has reached far down into the activities of individual entrepreneurs with its manipulation of incentive schemes, the Korean economy in general has been far from a command economy. The most conspicuous exception was the banking sector. Until the early 1980s, the government was the single major shareholder in all nationwide commercial banks. By the early 1980s, these banks were privatized, placing a ceiling of 8 percent on individual shareholdings. The activities of the so-called privatized commercial banks as well as the government-owned specialized banks, however, continued to be subject to tight government control. Indeed, the banking activities are still those of a command economy in Korea.

Since the early 1960s, the Korean government has emphasized the need to mobilize domestic household savings as much as possible. The government indeed had enforced an interest rate reform in 1965 that was designed to mobilize household savings through formal monetary financial institutions essentially by maintaining significantly positive real interest rates on time deposits. There arose tremendous increases in bank savings as well as in the money/GNP ratio itself, implying an increased supply of loanable funds through the formal financial institutions. The period 1965–72 is called the high interest rate era for the Korean economy. However, the government soon came under heavy pressure from the privileged entrepreneurs, who had been using large bank loans, to reduce their financial costs by lowering the real interest rates on bank loans. The government eventually succumbed to this pressure on 3 August 1972 and resumed the negative real interest rate regime. Perhaps the decree of 3 August constituted the point of departure for the Korean economy from what is called the Taiwan model. There arose enormous disparities between the negative bank interest rates and the positive curb market rates. Except for a limited amount of captive bank savings, household savings tended to stay away from the banking institutions as much as possible, and the curb loan markets flourished.[17] Loanable funds in banks stopped growing rapidly.

17. The real interest rate on one-year time deposits jumped from −8 percent per annum on average in 1961–64 to about 11 percent in 1965–71 and then fell to about −5 percent per annum on average in 1972–81. The M2/GNP ratio rose from about 0.12 in 1961–65 to 0.35 in 1972 but was still about 0.34 in 1981. During 1982–89, however, the real interest rate on time deposits was maintained at about 5 percent per annum, and the M2/GNP ratio (on a year-end basis) rose to 0.41 by 1989.

The available loanable funds were mostly rationed to selected sectors and firms at negative real interest rates.

The average ratio of net worth to total assets of the fifty largest business groups was 23.6 percent in 1989 without taking account of intragroup cross shareholdings and about 20 percent taking account of cross holdings (see KIS 1990, 61, 73).[18] On the other hand, as of 1990, the thirty largest business groups absorbed 41.6 percent of total credits provided by commercial banks, specialized banks, provincial banks, and foreign bank branches and about 43.6 percent of the credits provided by the nonmonetary financial institutions such as investment and finance companies and insurance companies.[19] The nonbank financial institutions are mostly controlled by *Jae-buls*. The ratio of direct financing (i.e., net working capital raised by issuing stocks divided by total net working capital raised) by the thirty largest business groups amounted to only about 10.7 percent as of 1987 (see Cho 1990, 156). It was only after 1988 that these highly leveraged big business groups in Korea started to raise large amounts of capital through direct financing in the stock market.

The negative bank interest rate regime discouraged the efforts of low-income households to increase their savings rates and moreover reduced the proportion of their savings that they put into bank deposits. According to Scitovsky (1985), "The absence of an attractive and reliable repository for personal savings may well be the main reason for the slowness with which the saving habit is taking root and spreading in Korea" (p. 252).[20] Scitovsky further contends that "growth Taiwanese-style kept business firms small and encouraged personal saving by the newly entering or about-to-enter small businessmen; growth Korean-style discouraged new entrants and their saving, and

18. Young Ki Lee (1990, 334) notes that "share cross-holding inflates the capital base of the companies involved without any corresponding increase in actual investment. Since book-value-based debt-equity ratios of borrowing firms are an important lending criterion used by banks, an inflated equity capital base will increase the borrowing limit of each company [creating additional fictitious borrowing capacity]." E. Han Kim (1990, 343) shows that the (market-value-based) mean equity to total value (equity plus debt) ratios for all nonfinancial firms listed on the Stock Exchange amounted to only 16.3 percent in Korea during 1977–86, while the comparable figures for Japan and the United States amounted to 44.2 percent and 45.3 percent, respectively. Furthermore, in Korea, the largest firms had the weakest financial structure. (During 1984–86, more than one-third of the largest 10 percent of listed firms in Korea had an equity ratio below 5 percent.) Similar figures based on book value show 21.4 percent for Korea, 29.4 percent for Japan, and 46.9 percent for the United States.

19. Excluding credits that are not subject to the credit management program, the share of the thirty largest business groups in total credits amounted to 16.81 percent by the end of 1990. Figures are those that were presented to the National Assembly by the superintendent of banks and published in the *Korea Economic Daily,* (2 February 1991), and the *Chosun Ilbo* (2 February 1991).

20. In 1980, the household saving rate in Korea (6.6 percent) amounted to 56 percent of that in Taiwan (11.9 percent) and 38 percent of that in Japan (17.3 percent), while the corporation saving rate in Korea (8.8 percent) amounted to 67 percent of that in Taiwan and 83 percent of that in Japan. By 1985, the corporation saving rate became similar in these countries, but the household saving rate in Korea (10.6 percent) still amounted to less than 70 percent of those in Taiwan and Japan (data from BOK 1988, 10).

made it easy for [already] established firms to grow without generating their own saving" (p. 248) through the government rationing of loans on concessionary terms.

The negative real interest rate policy was coupled with chronic and self-defeating inflationary development financing, resulting in cumulating foreign debt. Furthermore, the extreme disparities between the private rates of return on investment and the real interest rates on bank loans have generated a built-in incentive mechanism for the privileged entrepreneurs to maximize debt-equity ratios and minimize direct financing, critically weakening in the long run the financial status of the so-called leading business groups and amplifying out of proportion their dependence on government credit rationing policy.[21] The rationing of low-interest loans to privileged firms also encouraged them, by providing arbitrage profit opportunities, to smuggle out the low-cost funds into speculative activities in securities and real estate. After all, the income arising from such speculative assets has been receiving the most preferential treatment in the Korean tax system.

In Korea, the influential entrepreneurs seem to have been willing to surrender their decision-making power in the financial market without active resistance and to have willingly accepted the government as the ultimate unit of control in the financial market. This acquiescence was due to the fact that the chosen few, who turned out to be the existing group of influential big entrepreneurs, enjoyed access to very low-cost capital. Apparently, this low interest rate regime helped generate an investment climate that encouraged the privileged businessmen to expand their sphere of investment activities. On the other hand, the unprivileged small entrepreneurs had to depend on self-financing and informal curb market loans, and nonentrepreneurial households had to accept amplified risk taking in their savings activities (see Hong 1986). According to data filed by the superintendent of banks, about 51 percent of total bank loans in 1988 were provided without collateral or payment guarantees. For small and medium-sized firms, however, the proportion of loans without collateral amounted to a mere 7.8 percent of total bank loans in 1988 (see Kang et al. 1990, 48).

Since the late 1970s, there has been a rapid expansion of the nonmonetary financial institutions in the form of investment and finance companies, mutual savings and finance companies, merchant banking corporations, mutual credit facilities, life insurance companies, etc. In order to reduce the risk element, the curb market lenders actively utilized these new institutions in undertaking their informal lending activities. Thus, it has become extremely difficult to ascertain to what extent the activities of these institutions represent the curb lending activities in disguise. One may argue that the only significant development that has occurred in Korea's financial sector since the late 1970s is the

21. Furthermore, in Korea, corporate interest payments are tax deductible, whereas dividends are not.

tremendously reduced risk element in curb lending activities and more efficient intermediation of the curb markets through their alliance with the rapidly expanding nonmonetary financial institutions.[22] These nonmonetary financial institutions are mostly controlled by the *Jae-buls,* which have been seeking alternative outlets that can reduce their dependence on the government-controlled banks.

Under the negative real interest rate system in banking institutions, the typical saver was the low-income household, and the typical borrower was the privileged big businessman, so that negative interest rates enhanced the profits of the latter through income transfer from the former. In the high real interest rate curb markets, the typical lender was the rich capitalist, and the typical borrower was the unprivileged small businessman, so that the high interest rates favor what the Marxists call the "unproductive capitalist class" at the expense of the poor small entrepreneurs (see Scitovsky 1985).

Taking the difference between the estimated rate of return on capital and the weighted-average real interest rate on domestic bank loans to be the subsidy associated with credit rationing, Hong (1990c, 117–19) estimates the annual provision of interest subsidies in Korea to have amounted to about 3 percent of GNP in 1962–71 and about 10 percent of GNP in 1972–79, on average. The interest subsidies associated with foreign loan allocations are estimated to have amounted to about 6 percent of GNP each year on average in the 1970s.

The successful control of inflation by the Korean government during 1982–89 terminated the negative real interest regime, brought about a drastic increase in the domestic savings propensity (from about 28 percent of GNP in 1983 to about 36 percent in 1989), and generated surpluses in trade accounts during 1986–89. All these changes suggest that Korea had unnecessarily underutilized its savings potential before 1982 by adopting an improper set of policies.[23]

In the 1980s, the Korean government introduced various reform measures in the name of financial liberalization and internationalization. Yet the bank-

22. The M3/GNP ratio amounted to about 0.40 on average in 1971–76, while the M2/GNP ratio amounted to about 0.33. The M3/GNP ratio began to rise rapidly from 0.42 in 1977 to 0.49 in 1980, to 0.61 in 1981, and to 0.70 in 1985, reaching 1.18 by 1991, while M2/GNP still amounted to only 0.41 in 1991. That is, deposits in nonmonetary financial institutions (including debentures issued, commercial bills sold, commercial paper, and repurchase agreements) became 1.9 times larger than those in deposits at monetary institutions (data from BOK, *Economic Statistics Yearbook*). As of 1991, only about 22 percent of total financial saving (which amounted to 280 trillion won) took the form of savings deposits in banks, while 60 percent took the form of savings in nonbank financial institutions, 12 percent in stocks, 11 percent in corporate bonds, 7 percent in government bonds, and 15 percent in overlapping intersectoral transactions (double-counted) (data from MOF, *Fiscal and Monetary Statistics* [March 1992], 41–42).

23. The domestic savings ratio increased steadily from about 3 percent of GNP in 1961 to about 9 percent in 1963, about 15 percent in 1968, about 22 percent in 1973, and about 28 percent in 1979. However, Korea maintained net foreign capital inflows amounting to about 7 percent of GNP on average throughout the period 1961–81. The magnitude of foreign saving began to decline drastically only after 1982.

ing institutions are still tightly controlled, and the nonbank financial institutions are heavily manipulated by the government. The Korean government still does not show any visible intention of dismantling the credit rationing system or really modernizing the financial sector on the basis of the competitive market principle.

15.5 The Growth-Oriented Government Expenditure System and Labor Policy

During 1976–91, the ratio of gross tax burden to GNP amounted to 18 percent on average (fluctuating within the range of 16.3–19.7 percent), while the ratio of general government expenditure to GNP amounted to about 23 percent (fluctuating within the range of 20–26 percent). The ratio of general government expenditure on social security to GNP increased from 0.88 percent in 1977 to 1.63 percent in 1989, which still amounted to far below the average ratio in advanced countries, which exceeded 12 percent of GNP, and even below the average ratio in developing countries, which was close to 5 percent of GNP. As of 1986, the ratio of general government expenditure on health to GNP amounted to a mere 0.5 percent in Korea while that in advanced countries amounted to 5.4 percent on average (see MOF, *Fiscal and Monetary Statistics;* NTA, *Statistical Yearbook;* and Song and Kwon 1990, 72–77).[24] According to data provided by the Korea Education Development Institute, the ratio of general government expenditures on education to GNP amounted to 5.1 percent in 1991, while the individual household expenditure on education amounted to 5.5 percent.

The Korean government wanted by all means to prevent labor disputes, which would hinder economic growth and export expansion. However, it seems to have adopted a rather shortsighted approach by directly intervening and preventing actual and potential labor disputes on behalf of the entrepreneurs. As a result, Korean entrepreneurs developed a habit of delegating intrafirm labor-relations problems to the government and of devoting minimal efforts to reducing potential sources of labor disputes. Consequently, one often hears the argument that it is rare to find workers in Korean firms who really identify their personal welfare with the prosperity of the firm for which they work. Most of the workers do not seem to be convinced that a higher rate of return to the firm is by any means directly related to the improvement of the

24. The ratio of total social security expenditure to GNP in Korea increased from 0.89 percent in 1975 to 2.56 percent in 1987, and the government share in these social security expenditures increased from 49 to 64 percent. The social security expenditure level in other developing countries amounts to about 7 percent of GNP on average and, in advanced countries, to about 10–15 percent of GNP. In Korea, social security expenditures consist of social insurance, which in principle is financed by government subsidy, and the social welfare service, which is given little support by the government (see PCER 1988, 119–21).

welfare of the workers themselves. The fact that Korean products still suffer from a cursory handling at the final finishing process might reflect the absence of such an identification effect, which may be a crucial ingredient in generating devotion from the workers.

Under the authoritarian regimes, labor disputes could have been ruthlessly controlled. With the progress in democratization since 1987, however, the latent grievances of the workers have exploded into extremely violent and destructive disputes. Prior to 1987, the success or failure of an entrepreneur was unrelated to his ability to maintain peaceful intrafirm labor relations; the Korean government had enforced peaceful relations in each firm using naked power. Since late 1987, not only the success of individual entrepreneurs but also the growth performance of the Korean economy in general are determined by the development of nationwide labor disputes and the speed of learning-by-doing by the related parties. Employers, employees, and the government have yet to learn the advantages of free collective bargaining, how to handle disputes and grievances in an orderly fashion, and how to institutionalize harmonious labor-management relations.

15.6 A System of Government Picking the Winners

In Korea, the efficiency gains associated with the long process of opening up a semiautarkic economy to free trade have materialized not only in the form of rapidly rising real wages but also in the form of high rates of return on investment. These enhanced rates of return in turn seem to have generated vigorous investment activities in Korea over the past three decades. The big efficiency gains associated with the initial phase of the opening up to trade, however, must have been more or less exhausted.[25] In this sense, Korea might have to worry about the weakening vigor of entrepreneurs' investment activities in the 1990s. One may yet argue that, with the vast amount of positive experience and kinetic energy accumulated during the past three decades, the gains from "marginal" structural adjustment can be amplified continuously. For this purpose, however, Korea may have to pay more attention to "marginal" efficiency and the more active role of the competitive market mechanism in general (see Hong 1990a).

Ever since 1962, planning in Korea entailed essentially the setting up of aggregate as well as sectoral targets of outputs and exports and the setting up of construction targets for various social overhead capital (SOC) facilities. The execution of planning implied mostly the actual execution of investments

25. The commodity-export/GNP ratio reached a peak of 37 percent by 1987, but began to decrease afterward, reaching 26 percent in 1991. According to estimates of the Korea Foreign Trade Association, however, the import content of Korea's exports still amounted to 32 percent in 1991. In this sense, one might argue that there still exists substantial room to increase the net value-added content of exports in Korea.

for the planned (or supposedly planned) project "by all possible means" and, in the 1970s, through hand-picked entrepreneurs.[26] Indeed, the Korean government promoted the expansion of domestic production and the exports of selected industries by directly intervening in the market; however, this policy damaged the competitive market mechanism and the long-term allocative efficiency of the economy.[27]

Not only has the Korean government indulged in efficiency-damaging second-best policy measures, but it has almost completely ignored the equity aspect of export-oriented growth. It is high time to change the essential mode of planning and its execution. The highlights of planning should now become a set of concrete time-phased schedules to implement various efficiency-enhancing and equity-improving systems. Any system that is meant to enhance the equity and the efficiency of resource allocations, however, can seldom be enforced overnight. One cannot ignore the past and its legacy to the present. It takes time to implement a lasting, effective system. Therefore, five-year planning seems to be the ideal instrument to carry out such schemes. The prime objective of the government's five-year planning may have to become the step-by-step enforcement of an equitable tax system that can eliminate rampant unearned income, a self-sustaining market system that can select the correct industries and penalize inefficient entrepreneurs more efficiently, a financial system based on the market mechanism, a system conducive to peaceful labor relations that maximizes workers' devotion and entrepreneurial creativity, and so on.

If people believe in the fairness of the economic rules of the game, wealth accumulation can be seen as the result of the free market mechanism, and unequal distribution can be tolerated as a by-product.[28] However, many of the policy measures for export promotion in Korea, such as subsidized credit rationing and investment licensing, have been implemented by the government in such a way as to give the general public an impression of wanton favoritism. As a result, the wealth accumulated by successful entrepreneurs is often

26. As of 1991, one may readily say that, from now on, Korea will increasingly have comparative advantages in more physical and human capital–intensive goods and in more technology- (or knowledge-) intensive goods than before (see Hong 1987). As of the year 2000, or even in later years, we will be saying more or less the same thing. Armed with only such vague and catchall concepts, the government cannot continue selecting specific industries and the *right* entrepreneurs (to carry out the selected production activities) without repeating the late 1970s disaster.

27. Yet one may still say that Korea was extremely fortunate to make all kinds of policy mistakes in the name of export promotion and not in the name of import substitution and self-sufficiency. Had the Korean government instead pursued the Latin American–style import-substitution-oriented growth strategy, Korea might never have been able to escape the Lewis-type economy of massive disguised unemployment even by the 1980s, and the limited supply of physical and human capital would have exerted a critical constraint on rapid growth.

28. According to Krueger (1974, 302), government intervention in the market mechanism leads people to compete for rents, and "the existence of rent seeking surely affects people's perception of the economic system. If income distribution is viewed as the outcome of a lottery where wealthy individuals are successful (or lucky) rent seekers . . . the market mechanism is bound to be suspect."

regarded as a political reward rather than as the reward for Schumpeterian entrepreneurship. Consequently, the export-oriented growth strategy and even the market mechanism itself have become suspect for many Korean people. Unfortunately, most of the big businessmen themselves, who recently came to wield great political influence, do not seem to recognize that the private property system can prosper without intermittent violations only if the general public believes in the objectivity and fairness of the economic system and hence that it is in their long-term interest to help maintain a competitive market mechanism untainted by crony capitalism.

15.7 The Political Economy of Distribution Policies

In the name of export-oriented growth, the Korean government has concentrated production activities in the hands of a small number of big business groups through investment licensing and credit rationing. Although the government has always stated that the promotion of small firms is necessary in order to strengthen the foundation of the nation's economy and export base, it seems to have found relief in various sets of conspicuous but ineffective policy measures to promote small firms throughout the last three decades.

On the other hand, the magnitude of capital gains associated with the ownership of real estate and financial assets has recently been comparable to or greater than the magnitude of GNP each year. Furthermore, most of these capital gains have accrued to the upper 5 percent of the population and been taxed at extremely low rates. In spite of the popular clamor against this state of affairs, the Korean government has been very reluctant to initiate any fundamental reform of the existing system.

In Korea, it is not only the government but also political groups (including the national assemblymen of both the ruling and the opposition parties), business, and the press that have avoided taking up the equity issue seriously, not to mention making any concerted effort to initiate institutional reform. The members of these upper echelons in Korea (i.e., government officials, politicians, businessmen, and press people) seem to constitute the upper 5 percent who could have consolidated the political and economic power of the nation in their hands in the process of export-oriented growth, forming an intricate partnership among themselves and enjoying the existing system of prolific capital gains, economic rents, and wealth concentration.

On the other hand, the antiestablishment groups are so thoroughly indoctrinated with obsolete Marxist-Leninist-Maoist ideologies as to be unable to make any rational analysis of the real economy. The ideology of these antiestablishment groups has always been a variation on the theme of nationalization, central planning, autarky, and proletarian dictatorship. They have completely ignored the recent revolution in socialist countries and consequently have been unable to offer any realistic policy alternatives that can appeal to the unsophisticated masses.

In Korea, neither the establishment nor the antiestablishment seems to enjoy much popular support, yet the people are not able to find any effective means of initiating institutional reform, although they could cast out a dictator and produce the semblance of a democratic political system.

15.8 Conclusion

Korea has begun to experience extremely militant labor disputes and serious social unrest since its political democratization in 1988. Yet, during the 1990s, the Korean economy must transform its output and export composition, moving from the traditional simple labor-intensive consumption goods toward more capital intensive and more technology-intensive intermediate and investment goods (as well as high-quality durable consumption goods), waging fierce battles against the established Japanese manufacturers, who dominate the international market.

Korea has arrived at the stage that requires concentrated investment of human and physical resources in research and development and new high-technology export manufacturing activities in order to upgrade productivity and international competitive power. The Korean government, however, continues to maintain a tax system that provides the highest rate of return on financial assets and speculative real estate activities. The Korean tax system has been, intentionally or unintentionally, designed to provide the most preferential treatment for capital gains arising from stock transactions, the second most preferential treatment for capital gains arising from real estate transactions, and the third most preferential treatment for income from the ownership of financial assets such as interest and dividend income. The effect of such a distorted tax system has become very conspicuous since the beginning of the 1980s, from which time we can observe Korean entrepreneurs (as well as wealthy nonentrepreneurial families) being more active in speculative activities with financial assets and real estate than in the productive investment activities in research and development and export production that would be necessary to upgrade the productivity and international competitive power of Korean industries. If the Korean government does not enforce a fundamental reform, restructuring the rates of return on various economic activities so as to induce a more equitable distribution of income and wealth and at the same time induce most of the investment funds and human resources to flow into nonspeculative productive activities, the magnified internal conflicts and waste of resources will jeopardize Korea's long-term growth prospects.

Raising the relative rates of return on investment for, say, research and development and high-technology export manufacturing activities, while lowering the relative rates of return on, say, the simple ownership of financial assets and real estate transactions, will promote economic growth by channeling available human and physical resources in the country into productive activities; at the same time it will help achieve a more equitable distribution of income by providing relatively preferential treatment for wage and entrepreneurial income. In this sense, there is a need for the Korean government to actively implement *growth-promoting redistribution policies.*

We can conclude that difficulties with Korea's income distribution are not the result of the export-oriented growth strategy itself, but we can also conclude that export orientation alone is not enough to result in a more equitable distribution of income and wealth.

References

Bank of Korea (BOK). 1988. *Comprehensive bibliography of savings* (in Korean). Seoul.

———. 1990. *National income accounts.* Seoul.

———. Annual. *Economic statistics yearbook.* Seoul.

Cho, Dong-Sung. 1990. *A study of Korea's big business groups (Jae-buls)* (in Korean). Seoul: Mae-il Kyungje Shinmun-sa.

Choo, Hakchoong, and J. Yoon. 1984. Size distribution of income in Korea, 1982: Its estimation and sources of change (in Korean). *Korea Development Review* 6 (March): 2–18.

Economic Planning Board (EPB). 1989. *Major policy issues of the Korean economy* (in Korean). Seoul, June.

Federation of Korean Industrialists (FKI). 1988. *The direction of tax reform in BOP surplus economy* (in Korean). Vols. 1, 2. Seoul.

Hong, Wontack. 1986. Institutionalized monopsonistic capital markets in a developing economy. *Journal of Development Economics* 21:353–59.

———. 1987. A Comparative static application of the Heckscher-Ohlin model of factor proportions: Korean experience. *Weltwirtschaftliches Archiv* 123 (2): 309–24.

———. 1990a. Export-oriented growth of Korea: A possible path to advanced economy. *International Economic Journal* 4 (Summer): 97–118.

———. 1990b. Korea's land problem and policy direction (in Korean). *Kyong Je Hak Yon Gu* 38 (June): 253–68.

———. 1990c. Market distortion and polarization of trade patterns: Korean experience. In Kwon 1990.

Kang, Bong Kyun. 1989. *Economic development strategy and income distribution in Korea* (in Korean). Research Data 89–06. Seoul: KDI.

Kang, M. S., J. K. Park, D. S. Lee, S. H. Lee, and K. H. Cho. 1990. *Industrial adjustment of small and medium-sized firms and the direction to improve the measures to support small and medium-sized firms* (in Korean). Research Report no. 90–10. Seoul: KDI Press.

Kim, E. Han. 1990. Financing Korean corporations: Evidence and theory. In Kwon 1990.

Kim, Tae Dong. 1990. The socioeconomic implication of land price (in Korean). *Land Study* (*To-ji Yon-ku*) 1 (November–December): 29–39.

Korea Investors Service (KIS). 1990. *Report on analysis of big business groups (Jaebul), 1990* (in Korean). Seoul.

Krueger, Anne O. 1974. The political economy of rent-seeking society. *American Economic Review* 64 (June): 291–303.

Kwack, Tai-Won, and Kye Sik Lee 1988. *National budget and policy objectives* (in Korean). Seoul: KDI.
———. 1991. *Tax reform in Korea, 1991*. Working Paper no. 9103. Seoul: KDI, January.
Kwon, Jene K., ed. 1990. *Korean economic development*. New York: Greenwood.
Kwon, Soonwon. 1990. *Korea: Income and wealth distribution and government initiatives to reduce disparities*. Working Paper no. 9008. Seoul: KDI.
Land Committee (To-ji Gong-gai-nyum Yon-gu Wi-won-whoi). 1989. *Research report of Land Committee* (in Korean). Seoul: Korea Research Institute for Human Settlements, May.
Lee, Jin Soon. 1990. The characteristics of land price formation in Korea (in Korean). *Land Study (To-ji Yon-ku)* 1 (November–December): 40–63.
Lee, Young Ki. 1990. Conglomeration and business concentration in Korea. In Kwon 1990.
Ministry of Finance (MOF). 1990. *Major statistical data on taxation* (in Korean). Seoul, May.
———. Monthly. *Fiscal and monetary statistics* (in Korean). Seoul.
National Tax Administration (NTA). Annual. *Statistical yearbook of national tax*. Seoul: MOF.
Organization for Economic Cooperation and Development (OECD). 1991. *Revenue statistics of OECD member countries: 1965–1990*. Paris.
Presidential Commission on Economic Restructuring (PCER). 1988. *Realigning Korea's national priorities for economic advance*. Report. Seoul: KDI.
Scitovsky, Tibor. 1985. Economic development in Taiwan and South Korea: 1965–81. *Food Research Institute Studies* 19 (3): 215–64.
Song, Dachee, and Soonwon Kwon, eds. 1990. *National budget and policy objectives* (in Korean). Research Report no. 90–12. Seoul: KDI Press.
Yoo, Jong Goo. 1990. Income distribution in Korea. In Kwon 1990.
Yoo, Seong-min. 1992. The ownership structure of Korea's big business conglomerates and its policy implications (in Korean). *Korea Development Review* 14 (Spring): 3–36.

Comment Motoshige Itoh

It is not clear to me what effects "export orientation" had on income distribution. Most of the phenomena discussed in the paper seem to be observable in many other countries (e.g., Japan) and to be explained by such domestic structures as taxes.

In order to make the discussion of the paper clearer, it is useful to compare the Korean experience with the Japanese experience, where the latter can be considered a typical case of domestic-market-oriented growth. (I must confess that I do not know much about the Korean economy.) In spite of the fact that the pattern of economic growth is quite different between the two countries, the phenomena discussed in Hong's paper can be observed in Japan.

I do agree with the author's point that some fundamental reforms are nec-

Motoshige Itoh is associate professor of economics at the University of Tokyo.

essary. But, to have more realistic future perspectives, it is constructive to consider the possibility that market forces will work to correct the various kinds of distortions in the Korean economy. The fact that there are serious distortions in the Korean economy reflects the fact that the economy is still closed (just like Japan's). If the economy becomes more open to the rest of the world, some parts of the distortion will be corrected.

Comment Richard H. Snape

This is an interesting paper, one that makes it point forcefully. It draws attention to socially destructive forces. However, in reading it I sometimes wondered which country I was reading about: "The overambitious investment plans . . . induced not only large inflows of foreign capital but also chronic inflation"; "large windfall wealth in the hands of individuals who, in many cases, did not possess any entrepreneurial ability and consequently resulted in unproductive waste of resources"; "entrepreneurs . . . more active in speculative activities with financial assets and real estate than in productive investment activities in research and development and export production . . . to upgrade the productivity and international competitive power"; "chronic and self-defeating inflationary development financing, resulting in cumulating foreign debt." Surely this is some highly inflationary, stagnant country, not a country that quadrupled its real per capita income over a twenty-year period.

Hong points to social unrest and resentment in Korea and sees it as threatening future growth. He sees many of the export-promotion measures as having been implemented in "such a way as to give the general public an impression of wanton favoritism. As a result, the wealth accumulated by successful entrepreneurs is often regarded as a political reward rather than as the reward for Schumpeterian entrepreneurship. Consequently, the export-oriented growth strategy . . . [has] become suspect for many Korean people."

This view of Korean attitudes contrasts with that reported by Hong twelve years ago: "Not only [do] the Korean exporters always get the immediate and close attention of the president, but the successful ones are regularly honored with honor medals. As a result, anyone who has accumulated wealth via export activities is almost considered a patriot and he is assured that he has the blessing of the government. This has an immense psychological impact in a society which still carries remnants of traditional Confucianism" (Hong 1979, 58). I would be interested to hear more of the reasons for this change in attitude of the Korean public—is it a high income elasticity of demand for equality?

The wage elasticity of productivity has been greater than one over the

Richard H. Snape is professor of economics at Monash University, Melbourne, Australia.

whole period, suggesting that the wage share of output has grown, so it would appear that the relative position of the employed has increased rather than decreased: I would be interested to hear more on which groups have lost in real or proportionate terms. I am not suggesting that the tax system does not have huge gaps, inequities, and inefficiencies, but are they overstated?

On more specific points, I do not think that a Gini coefficient of land ownership by area is informative. How would one compare a hectare of land on Manhattan with one hundred hectares in Nevada?

Land prices have increased rapidly in Korea, Japan, and elsewhere. The increase in Korea is no doubt associated with the tax system. But presumably there is a limit to this, just as tax-encouraged land booms in other countries have burst. At least some of this increase would be due to a high income elasticity of demand for space. One expects the price of land to increase in real terms in a rapidly growing economy, and I am surprised that it has not increased more rapidly: the increases relative to GNP (see table 15.1) on all three estimates are quite modest. Similarly, the capital gains on stocks reported in table 15.1 may not be out of line with many other countries. We might note also the 19 percent loss of value in 1990.

Hong mentions the market dominance and advantages of the conglomerates (*Jae-buls*). Without questioning his statements regarding their favored access to credit (and even that they may not always use the funds for the purposes specified), are there not also diseconomies of scale and opportunities for small enterprises among these huge, favored, corrupt (perhaps) giants? Have small entrepreneurs in fact entered Korean industry and grown large?

Some smaller points: I do not think it wise to attempt to explain changes in a Gini coefficient of .002 or .009. Why should the law on the upper limit of dwelling sites be enforced? Some people like big cars, others big houses; one does not fix income or wealth distribution by restricting the quantity or quality of one item of expenditure.

Finally, in note 25 Hong seems to suggest that Korea should encourage the domestic content of exports—that is, it should import final rather than intermediate products. It is not clear why Korea should want to do this.

Reference

Hong, Wontack. 1979. *Trade, distortions and employment growth in Korea*. Seoul: Korea Development Institute.

Contributors

Robert E. BALDWIN
Department of Economics
University of Wisconsin
1180 Observatory Drive
Madison, WI 53706

Ching-huei CHANG
Sun Yat-sen Institute for Social Sciences and Philosophy
Academia Sinica
Nankang, Taipei, Taiwan 11529
The Republic of China

Tain-Jy CHEN
Chung-Hua Institution for Economic Research
No. 75 Chang-Hsing Street
Taipei, Taiwan 10671
The Republic of China

CHIA Siow Yue
Department of Economics and Statistics
National University of Singapore
10 Kent Ridge Crescent
Singapore 0511

Kenneth FLAMM
The Brookings Institution
1775 Massachusetts Avenue, NW
Washington, DC 20036–2188

Koichi HAMADA
Economic Growth Center
Yale University
27 Hillhouse Avenue
New Haven, CT 06520–1987

Kaori HATANAKA
Graduate Student
Faculty of Economics
University of Tokyo
7–3–1 Hongo, Bunkyo-ku,
Tokyo 113
Japan

Wontack HONG
Department of International Economics
College of Social Sciences (Rm. 14–410)
Seoul University
Seoul 151–742
Korea

Masayoshi HONMA
Department of Economics
Otaru University of Commerce
3–5–21 Midori
Otaru-shi, Hokkaido 047
Japan

Takatoshi ITO
Institute of Economic Research
Hitotsubashi University
Kunitachi, 186 Tokyo
Japan

Motoshige ITOH
Faculty of Economics
University of Tokyo
7–3–1 Hongo, Bunkyo-ku
Tokyo 113
Japan

Anne O. KRUEGER
Department of Economics
Duke University
227 B Social Sciences Bldg.
Durham, NC 27706

Kuo-shu LIANG
Chairman
Bank of Communications
91, Hen-Yang Road
Taipei, Taiwan
The Republic of China

Bih Jane LIU
Department of Economics
National Taiwan University
21 Hsu-chuo Road
Taipei, Taiwan
The Republic of China

Chong-Hyun NAM
Department of Economics
Korea University
1, 5-Ga, Anam-dong, Sungbuk-Ku
Seoul 136–701
Korea

Douglas NELSON
Department of Economics
Syracuse University
202 Maxwell Hall
Syracuse, NY 13244–1090

Gary R. SAXONHOUSE
Department of Economics
University of Michigan
Ann Arbor, MI 48109

Richard H. SNAPE
Department of Economics
Monash University
Melbourne
Australia

Yun-Wing SUNG
Department of Economics
The Chinese University of Hong Kong
Shatin, Hong Kong
The Republic of China

TAN Eu Chye
Faculty of Economics and Administration
University of Malaya
Lembah Pantai
59100 Kuala Lumpur
Malaysia

TRAN Van Tho
School of International Studies
Obirin University
3758 Tokiwa-cho Machida-shi
Tokyo 194–02
Japan

Shujiro URATA
Department of Economics
Waseda University
1–6–1, Nishiwaseda
Shinguku-ku, Tokyo 169
Japan

Alberto VALDÉS
The World Bank
Room I-4019
1818 H Street, NW
Washington, DC 20433

Ya-Hwei YANG
Chung-Hua Institution for Economic Research
No. 75 Chang-Hsing Street
Taipei, Taiwan
The Republic of China

YOO Jung-ho
Senior Fellow
Korea Development Institute
P.O. Box 113
Chongnyang, Seoul
Korea

Joachim ZIETZ
Economics and Finance Department
Middle Tennessee State University
Box 129
Murfreesboro, TN 37132

Author Index

Adachi, Fumihiko, 251
Aliber, Robert Z., 301
Alikhani, Iradj, 361, 374
Amelung, Torsten, 361, 372, 374
American Iron and Steel Institute, 208t
Amsden, A., 320n9
Amundsen, Chris B., 68
Anderson, K., 110t
Anderson, Kym, 116, 117, 121, 125, 126n12
Ashton, Peter K., 68

Baker, James A., III, 8
Balassa, Bela, 323n13, 374
Baldwin, Richard E., 56
Baldwin, Robert E., 126, 307n1, 313, 317, 343, 369
Bank of Korea, 418t, 425n20
Barichello, Richard R., 127, 135
Bark, Taeho, 208t
Barrett, Richard E., 322n11
Baumol, William, 150, 151
Bautista, Romeo M., 120
Bawens, L., 374
Bayne, Nicholas, 334
Bhagwati, Jagdish, 9, 14, 26n2, 44
Blackman, Sue Anne, 150, 151
Bowen, Harry P., 161, 175
Brock, W. A., 343

Carter, Colin A., 120n7
Cavallo, Domingo, 120
Caves, R., 296n10, 370
Chang, Jui-Meng, 345
Chee, Peng Lim, 262
Chen, Edward K. Y., 255n6, 265
Chen, T.-J., 323n12, 326n18, 328n22
Cho, Dong-Sung, 419, 425
Choo, Hakchoong, 415
Christ, Carl F., 170n19
Chu, Y.-H., 323n12, 343
Chung, Ching-Fan, 162n15
Clements, Kenneth W., 128
Coble, P., 320
Condliffe, J. B., 9
Cooper, Richard N., 9, 154
Copland, D. B., 17n8
Corden, W. Max, 367
Crafts, N. F. R., 155
Culbert, Jay, 17n7

Dam, Kenneth W., 336
Davis, Forrest, 312n4
Deardorff, Alan V., 49n3, 50n5, 53
De Long, J. Bradford, 151n2
Dervis, K., 389
Destler, I. M., 11
Deyo, F., 323n12
Dick, Andrew R., 55n12, 68n27, 80n38
Diebold, William, Jr., 17
Dixit, Avinash K., 54n11
Domenech, Roberto, 120
Dore, Ronald, 152
Dornbusch, Rudiger, 11, 15
Dorosh, Paul, 120
Downs, Anthony, 112, 126
Drysdale, Peter, 19n10, 20

Eastman, L., 319n7, 321
Economic Planning Board (EPB), Korea, 184t, 415n2, 419
Egan, Thomas P., 68
Emerson, Michael, 19
Evans, Peter B., 311

Federation of Korean Industrialists (FKI), 422
Fei, J., 323n12, 325
Feuerwerker, A., 320n8
Finan, William F., 68
Findlay, Ronald, 343
Finger, J. Michael, 183, 189
Flamm, Kenneth, 51n8, 53n9, 54n11, 68, 80n37, 81n40
Fleming, Wendell H., 84n41, 85n42
Freeman, Richard B., 153n3
Fudenberg, Drew, 50n5

Garcia, Jorge Garcia, 120
Gardiner, Walter H., 120n7
Gardner, Richard N., 336
Garnaut, Ross, 19n10, 20
General Agreement on Tariffs and Trade (GATT), 20n11
Gereffi, G., 323n12
Gerschenkron, Alexander, 265
Gold, T., 320n9, 321, 323n12
Goldberger, Arthur S., 162n15
Goldin, Ian, 115
Greene, William H., 162n15
Grubel, Herbert C., 157

Haggard, S., 323n12, 326n18
Hall, H. Keith, 189
Hamada, Koichi, 170
Hansen, Alvin H., 176n20
Harding, William E., 66n21
Hart, O., 231n2
Hathaway, Dale E., 130n18
Havrylyshyn, Oli, 361, 374
Hayami, Y., 99, 100t, 101, 104, 116, 117, 126, 134, 162n14
Helpman, Elhanan, 56n13, 156, 157, 158n6, 159n10
Hemmi, K., 99
Hill, Hal, 256n9
Hillman, A. L., 307n1
Hintze, O., 308n3
Hirata, A., 291n6
Hirschman, Albert O., 157, 389
Ho, Samuel P. S., 313, 323n12
Holmstrom, B., 231n2
Hong, Wontack, 422, 426, 427, 429, 430n26, 435
Honma, M., 104, 126, 134, 162n14
Horlick, Gary N., 47
Hou, C.-M., 320n8, 323n12
Hudec, Robert E., 130, 139
Hufbauer, Gary, 39
Hunter, Robert A., 312n4
Hutcheson, Dan, 66n22

Integrated Circuit Engineering (ICE), 70n34
International Business and Economic Research Corporation, 207n18
International Monetary Fund (IMF), 32t, 189, 273n1
Islam, Nurul, 118
Itoh, M., 231nn2,3
Iwata, Kazumasa, 159t

Jackson, John H., 13
Jacoby, Neil H., 312–13
Janes, C. V., 17n8
Japanese Ministry of Agriculture, Forestry, and Fisheries, 96t
Japan External Trade Organization (JETRO), 251, 256, 285, 295n9
Johnson, D. Gale, 99, 103, 137n26, 138n27
Judge, G. G., 399n6
Jwa, Sung-hee, 361

Kang, Bong Kyun, 415, 419
Kang, M. S., 426
Katz, Lawrence, 176
Kerr, G. H., 321
Keynes, John M., 155
Kim, Chungsoo, 198, 209
Kim, E. Han, 425n18
Kim, Kwang-suk, 367n3
Kim, Tae Dong, 419
Kindleberger, Charles, 9
Knudsen, Odin, 115
Koen, Ross, 311, 312n4
Koo, Bohn Young, 259n10
Koo, H., 323n12
Korea Development Institute, 365n2, 367n4
Korea Foreign Trade Association, 185t, 187–88t, 197t, 201t, 203t, 205t
Korea Investors Service (KIS), 419
Kosai, Yutaka, 266
Krasner, Stephen D., 311
Kreinin, Mordechai E., 288, 302
Kreps, D. M., 50n6, 57–58n14
Krishna, Kala, 56

Krueger, Anne O., 116, 120, 126, 129n17, 132, 135, 136, 325n16, 430n28
Krugman, Paul R., 56, 156, 157n6, 159n10, 176
Kuo, K.-M., 323n12, 325
Kuo, Shirley W. Y., 387
Kwack, Tai-Won, 421, 422
Kwon, Jene K., 422n12
Kwon, Soonwon, 415, 428

Lancaster, Kelvin, 84n41
Land Committee, Korea, 416, 418t
Lane, F., 308n3
Lardinois, P., 99
Laumas, P. S., 390n1
Lavergne, R., 343
Lawrence, Robert Z., 158n9, 164n17
Leamer, Edward E., 158n8, 160, 161
Lee, Jin Soon, 418t
Lee, Kye Sik, 421, 422
Lee, S. F., 390, 407
Lee, T. H., 323n12
Lee, Young Ki, 419, 425n18
Leitmann, George, 83
Li, K. T., 323n12, 387
Liang, C. H., 323n12
Liang, K.-S., 323n12
Lin, C. Y., 323n12
Lindert, Peter H., 116
Lipsey, Robert E., 157
Lloyd, P. J., 157
Lopez, M., 95, 117t, 131

McCarthur, J., 307n1
McCormick, Garth P., 84n41
McCulloch, Rachel, 271
McElroy, M. B., 164n16
Maddison, Angus, 150, 151, 152, 154tt, 157t
Magee, Stephen, 343
Mao, Yu-Kang, 340t
Marks, S., 307n1
Mendel, D., 321
Messerlin, Patrick A., 127, 209n21
Micron Technology, 47n2
Milgrom, Paul, 50n6, 51n8
Miner, William M., 130n18
Ministry of Finance, Japan, 250t, 280t
Ministry of Home Affairs, Korea, 418t
Ministry of International Trade and Industry (MITI), Japan, 247, 248n4, 249, 251, 252n5, 284t, 285t, 293n7
Ministry of Finance, Korea, 418t, 422n13, 428

Moon, Pal-Young, 129
Morkre, Morris E., 209
Mundlak, Yair, 120

Nam, Chong-Hyun, 183, 193, 207n17
National Tax Administration (NTA), Korea, 428
Nelson, Douglas R., 189, 307n1, 311, 330n24
Nivola, Pietro S., 47n1
Nogues, J. Julio, 31, 183
Noyce, Robert N., 66n21
Nugent, J. B., 389, 390n1
Nurske, Ragnar, 389

Ogawa, Eiji, 246
Ohkawa, Kazushi, 151, 152, 156
Olechowski, Andrzej, 183
Olson, Mancur, 126, 343, 369
Oman, Charles, 245
Ordover, Janusz A., 50n4, 51n7
Organization for Economic Cooperation and Development (OECD), 34t, 36t, 37t, 95, 116, 422n13
Otsuka, K., 99, 125

Page, J. M., Jr., 389
Park, Yung Chui, 16n6, 18n9, 29n6
Patrick, Hugh T., 9, 26n2
Peng, M.-M., 321
Penn, R., 95, 117t, 131
Petit, Michel, 132n22
Petri, Peter, 160n11
Pigou, A. C., 389
Presidential Commission on Economic Restructuring (PCER), 420, 428n24
Putnam, Robert, 334

Ramstetter, Eric D., 256, 259
Ranis, Gustav, 153
Ray, Edward, 345
Rhe, Sungsup, 260t
Richardson, J. David, 315
Rishel, Raymond W., 84n41, 85n42
Roberts, J., 50n6
Robertson, Dennis, 155
Rosen, Howard, 28n3
Rosenberg, Nathan, 261
Rosovsky, Henry, 152, 156
Rueschemeyer, Dietrich, 311
Ruttan, V. W., 104

Saloner, Garth, 50n4, 51n7
Saxonhouse, Gary R., 153, 158nn6,7,8, 160, 161, 162, 164, 168n18, 170, 175, 195
Scheinkman, J. A., 57–58n14
Schiff, Maurice W., 116, 120, 126, 129n17, 132, 135, 136
Schive, Chi, 323n12
Schott, Jeffrey J., 13, 15, 25–26n1, 39, 189
Scitovsky, Tibor, 323n12, 425, 427
Sekiguchi, Sueo, 246n3, 261n11
Shapiro, Carl, 54n11
Shea, Jia-Dong, 390, 407
Sjaastad, Larry A., 128
Skocpol, Theda, 311
Snape, Richard H., 12, 19, 117n4
Sombart, Werner, 154–55
Somsak, Tunbunlertchai, 251
Song, Dachee, 428
Spence, A. Michael, 52, 56
Srinivasan, T. N., 170
Stern, Paula, 191
Stern, Robert M., 158n7
Summers, Lawrence, 176
Sveikauskas, Leo, 161

Takeuchi, K., 238, 291n6
Tarr, G. David, 207, 209
Teece, David J., 263
Thee, Kian Wie, 259, 262
Thomas, Mark, 155
Tien, H.-M., 328n22
Tilly, C., 308n3
Tirole, Jean, 50nn5,6, 51n7
Torrens, Robert, 154
Tran Van Tho, 247, 248, 256n8, 261n11, 262, 267
Tsiang, S. C., 323n12
Tsushosangyosho, 159t
Tu, Chaw-Hsia, 340t
Tyers, Rod, 116, 126n12
Tyson, Laura, 160n12, 162

Umemura, Mataji, 151
UNCTAD, 190n2
United Nations, 33n14
United Nations Centre on Transnational Corporations (UNCTC), 245n2
U. S. Congress, 66n21
U. S. Council of Economic Advisers, 28nn3,4, 33, 36–37n17
U. S. Department of Agriculture, 122t, 124t
U. S. Department of Commerce, 294n8
U. S. Department of Labor, Bureau of Labor Statistics, 34n15
U. S. International Trade Commission, 39t, 130, 131n19
U. S. Trade Representative, 118, 119t, 135t, 137t
Urata, Shujiro, 274n2

Valdés, Alberto, 115, 116, 120, 126, 129, 129n17, 132, 135, 136, 138n28
Vernon, Raymond, 261n11
Vincent, David, 125
VLSI Research, 66n22, 69

Wade, R., 323n12
Waller, Larry, 54n10
Wea, C. L., 323n12
Webb, A. J., 95, 117t, 131
Webbink, Douglas W., 66n21
Wechsler, Andrew, 191
Weitzman, Martin, 153n3
Wellisz, Stanislaw, 343
Williamson, Jeffrey, 150n1
Williamson, Oliver E., 231n2
Wilson, Robert W., 50n6, 68
Winckler, E., 323
Winters, L. Alan, 183
Wolff, Edward, 150, 151
Wonnacott, Ronald J., 16n6, 17–18, 29n6, 30n9
World Bank, 151
Wright, Gavin, 152, 155, 156
Wu, H. L., 390, 407

Yamazawa, Ippei, 156
Yellen, Janet, 271
Yergin, D., 322
Yokota, K., 291n6
Yoo, Jong Goo, 415
Yoo, Jung Ho, 16n6, 18n9, 29n6, 367n4, 371n5
Yoo, Seong-min, 419
Yoon, J., 415
Yotopoulos, P. A., 389, 390n1
Young, A., 320n8
Yu, R. R., 390, 407
Yu, Tzong-shian, 387

Zermaño, Mayra, 36–37n17
Zietz, Joachim, 115, 116, 129, 138n28
Zysman, John, 160n12

Subject Index

Agricultural Basic Law (1961), Japan, 97–98
Agricultural sector: estimates of protection levels, Japan, 95–97, 103–8; financing of support for, 116; growth of protection for, 115; loss of comparative advantage, 118–20; predicted productivity in Latin America, 136–37; reorientation of policy for, 145; response to loss of comparative advantage, 120–34; support price and subsidies in Japan for, 97–98, 99
Antidumping (AD) duties, United States, 309
Antidumping (AD) investigations, United States: administration under GATT, 189–94; effect on Korean exports, 212; of Korean exports, 202–4; against Taiwan, Korea, and Brazil, 317; use of, 131
Antidumping (AD) laws, United States: design and effect of, 191–92; enforcement of, 317–18; Korean exports under, 198, 201
ASEAN countries: absorption of Japanese FDI by, 249, 252; Japanese FDI in, 276, 279, 281–82; Korean foreign direct investment in, 256, 259–60; local procurement in, 287–89; manufacturing sector in, 243; Taiwanese investment in, 255–57
Asian Pacific region: changes in factor endowments in, 343–44; countries as technology transmitters, 255–60; defined, 244; Japanese foreign direct investment in, 275–76; Japanese technology transfer to, 249–55; as market for new technology, 260–63; trends in economic development in, 263–66. *See also* East Asian countries
Asia-Pacific Economic Conference (APEC), 222
Asia Pacific Economic Cooperation (APEC) initiative, 20

Balanced growth theory, 389, 407
Border protection: as alternative to tariffs, 130–31; in Japan, 98–99
Business groups (*Jae-bul*), Korea: power and dominance of, 419–20

Cairns group, 140, 141t
Canada: intrahemisphere trading patterns of, 31–34
Chile: potential for U.S. free trade with, 16, 30; uniform tariff system of, 138
China: foreign direct investment in, 263; Japanese technology transfer to, 252–53; U.S. policy toward Communists in, 311–12
Closed economy: effect of Korea's, 435
Closer Economic Relations agreement, Australia–New Zealand, 14
Coase theorem, 23–24
Commerce: Japanese foreign direct investment in; 275
Commodities: in Asian trade with Japan, 293–96; composition of Canada's export, 33; with high income elasticities of demand, 120–21; protection in Japan for agricultural, 98–99. *See also* Subsidies

Comparative advantage: Canada's, 33; decline in Japan's agricultural, 95–97, 110–11; effect of agricultural protection on, 129; of Latin American countries in agriculture, 136–37, 141; relation to protection levels of agricultural, 102–3; responses to loss of agricultural, 120–34
Competitiveness: Japanese loss of, 275; in U.S. agricultural production, 121
Compulsory import expansions (CIEs), 23
Consumer subsidy equivalents (CSEs), 117
Cost concepts (product life cycle), 70–75
Countervailing duties (CVD), United States, 191–94, 309
Countervailing duty (CVD) investigations, United States, 131, 189, 202–4, 317
Countervailing duty (CVD) law, United States: design and effect of, 191–93; enforcement of, 317–18; Korean exports under, 198
Credit market: rationing in Korean, 424–28
Curb market, Korea, 420

Decoupling concept, 145
Demand elasticities: motivation for agricultural commodities with, 120
Developed countries: share of Japanese FDI in, 276, 277
Developing countries: in GATT framework, 139, 145–46; Japanese FDI in, 276–79; special and differential treatment of, 139, 145–46; trend of agricultural protection in, 137–40
Discrimination, price: under GATT rules, 191–92
Discrimination, trade: effect of preferences, 19; factors contributing to, 9; in free trade environment, 7–9; in hub-and-spoke trade agreements, 17–18; provisions in U.S. law for, 9
Division of labor, international: in Japanese firms, 282–83
DRAM. *See* Dynamic random access memory (DRAM) chips
Dumping: cost test for, 79–80; probability over product life cycle of, 59–60. *See also* Antidumping (AD) investigations, United States; Fair value; Foreign market value (FMV); Product life cycle; Semiconductor product life cycle
Dynamic random access memory (DRAM) chips: dumping of, 47–48; estimated demand for 1M, 68–69; 1M and 256K, 48

East Asian countries: exports under MFA, 38; Western Hemisphere trade with, 33–35
Economic performance: of Asian Pacific region, 263; convergence of U.S. and Japanese, 150–52; growth of South Korean, 184
Economic policy: reform in Mexico for, 28–29
Education: requirement for, 137–38
Educational levels, Asian Pacific region, 261, 262t
Effective rates of protection (ERPs): hidden, 112; in Korea, 367–69, 373, 377–79, 380–81, 383
Employment, nonfarm, 125
Engel's law, 127–28
Enterprise for the Americas, 26, 30
Environmental issues: as factor in resistance to protection, 128
Erasable programmable read only memory (EPROM) chips, 48
Export-led growth (XLG) policy, Taiwan, 324–27
Export-processing zones, 286
Export promotion policy, Taiwan, 324–25, 342, 387
Exports: from Asian countries to Japan, 291–92; decline in Korea-to-United States, 212–16; from Korea to United States, 184–88, 197–98; from Korea under administered U.S. protection, 198–216; share of Korean under import restrictions, 197

Factor endowments: changes in developing country, 243–44; in estimating interindustry trade, 162–69; Japanese, 181–82; theory of intraindustry trade with, 158–62
Factor price equalization theorem, 413
Fair value, 48. *See also* Less than fair value (LTFV) cases
FDI. *See* Foreign direct investment (FDI)
Firms: Asian affiliates of Japanese, 283–98; influence in Korea of, 370; trade behavior of Japanese affiliate, 302. *See also* Business groups (*Jae-bul*), Korea; Interfirm trade; Interindustry trade; Intrafirm trade; Intraindustry trade; Multinational corporations (MNCs); Strategic industries concept, Taiwan
FMV. *See* Foreign market value (FMV)
Food Control Law (1942), Japan, 97–98, 99

Foreign direct investment (FDI): as channel of technolgoy transfer, 245–46, 248–49; expansion and pattern of Japanese, 249, 274–82; expansion of, 273–74; features of, 249–52; of Korea, 256, 259–60; motivation and strategy for Japanese, 279, 281, 282–89, 291–96; by Taiwan, 255–57; in Vietnam, 256
Foreign market value (FMV): construction of, 49–51; derivation of, 48–49
Foreign policy: linked to trade policy, 9
Foreign pressure: effect of, 97, 129–30, 144
Forward pricing: in models of semiconductor product life cycle, 55–58
Free trade agreements (FTAs): Australia-New Zealand, 14–15; effect of Western Hemisphere, 26–28; hub-and-spoke, 16–19, 21; proposed U.S.-Mexico, 26, 27; of United States, 8. *See also* U. S.-Canada Free Trade Agreement; U. S.-Israel Free Trade Agreement; U. S.-Mexico Free Trade Agreement (proposed)
FTAs. *See* Free trade agreements (FTAs)

General Agreement on Tariffs and Trade (GATT): Article III, 194; Articles I and XXIV on preferential trading arrangements, 12–14, 43–44; Articles VI and XVI, 191–92; Article XIX (escape clause), 190, 217; contribution of, 25; discipline of, 138–39; discriminatory mechanisms in, 7–9; equalization of treatment under, 138–39, 145–46, 216, 218, 222; exemptions for developing countries under, 145–46; interpreting U.S. AD and CVD laws under, 191–94; laws not covered by, 196; proposal for Taiwan's entrance into, 44; proposed Pacific Round, 20; protection by, 15; unfair trade practices in, 314–15; VERs escape from, 196, 218. *See also* Tokyo Round; Uruguay Round
Generalized System of Preferences (GSP): effect on Japanese FDI decisions, 275–76; ineligibility of Korea for, 221
Government intervention: circumstances for, 389; to protect Japanese agriculture, 97–98; requirement to change policy of assistance, 145; to support agricultural prices, 131–34; to support loss of comparative advantage, 125–26
Government role: as development state in Korea, 371–72; motivation in setting trade barriers, 370–71; in Taiwan's trade policy, 327–30

Imports: of Asian affiliates of Japanese firms, 292; controls in Taiwan for, 341; protection levels for, 134–37; U.S. actions to curtail, 317–18; U.S. share of Korean, 185–88. *See also* Compulsory import expansions (CIEs)
Imports, Japan: of food, 95–96; of manufactured goods, 149–50, 224; manufactured goods as ratio of all, 224–26; quotas on, 98
Import-substituting industrialization (ISI), Taiwan, 323–27, 387
Industrialization, Asian Pacific region, 263–67
Industrial policy: Korea, 370–72; Taiwan, 387–89, 409
Information: on costs and benefits of protection, 144–45
Intellectual property rights, 194, 216, 318
Interest groups: Taiwan, 349–51, 352, 354–55, 359
Interfirm trade, 296
Interindustry specialization, Japan, 176–77
Interindustry trade, 156–58, 177, 293
International procurement offices (IPOs), 283
Interprocess trade: between Japan and its Asian affiliate firms, 286, 293–94
Intrafirm production arrangement, 283
Intrafirm trade, 294–96
Intraindustry trade: beneficial, 177; factor-endowment-based theory of, 158–62, 176; growth of, 156–58; horizontal and vertical, 293–94; indices of, 157–58, 159t, 175–76; Japanese, 150, 177, 180, 181–82, 282–83; between Japanese firms and Asian affiliates, 293–96
Investment: in land infrastructure, Japan, 99. *See also* Foreign direct investment (FDI)
ISI policy. *See* Import-substituting industrialization (ISI)
ITC. *See* U. S. International Trade Commission (ITC)

Japan: distribution system in, 227–36; geographic location of, 149–50, 180, 182; procurement by affiliate firms in Asia, 287–89; technology transfer from, 247–55; trade patterns of, 170–77, 180

Korea: CVD and AD cases against, 317; economic performance of, 184–85; exports from, 184–88, 197–216; foreign direct investment by, 256, 259–60; Japanese direct investment in, 251; less than fair value cases against, 202–4; trade policy of, 361–67, 373, 375–77, 379–83, 435
Kuomintang (KMT) party: political role in Taiwan, 327–29; role in Taiwan of, 319–323; role in Taiwan's trade policy, 323–27

Land ownership, Korea, 416, 419
Land resources: as factor in agricultural productivity, 121–24; as factor in protection decision, 135; in Latin America, 136–37
Large-Scale Retail-Store Law, Japan, 224, 233–34, 237, 238–39
Latin America: agricultural products of, 136–37; Japanese FDI in, 276; potential for free trade with, 30–31, 38–40
Latin American: trade liberalization in, 136
Learning curve: approximation of, 61–63; elasticities of, 66–68
Learning economies: definition and function of, 52; in semiconductor industry model, 56–57; specification of, 80–81, 87–89
Less than fair value (LTFV) cases, 191, 202–4. *See also* Antidumping (AD) investigations, United States; Countervailing duty (CVD) investigations, United States
Licensing arrangements, 245, 252
Long Term Arrangement on Cotton Textiles (LTA), 198
LTFV cases. *See* Less than fair value (LTFV) cases

Manufacturing sector: direct investment in Asia of Japanese, 249–55; economic performance of Korean, 185; increase of imports to Japan, 224; Japanese FDI in Asian, 279
Market failure theory, 389, 407
Market system: nonpersonal transactions in, 9; for protection, 356. *See also* Political market
Mexico: as competitor in free trade, 34–38; initiative for free trade with United States, 28–29; potential for trade agreements with, 16, 17–18; trading patterns of, 31–35. *See also* U. S.-Mexico Free Trade Agreement (proposed)
MNCs. *See* Multinational corporations (MNCs)
Multifiber Arrangement (MFA): effect of free trade agreements on, 27; effect of quotas, 208–9; quotas under, 198, 200; U.S. imports under, 38, 39f. *See also* Wool textile industry
Multilateral trading system: costs of agreements in, 23; U.S. commitment to, 25
Multinational corporations (MNCs): issues in transfer of technology, 247–48; as suppliers of technology, 245

Natural resource sector: Japanese foreign direct investment in, 275; Japan's endowment in, 150, 152; U.S. endowment in, 152
Newly industrialized economies (NIEs): heterogeneity of, 410; Japanese FDI in, 249, 252, 275, 278–79, 281; local procurement in, 287–89; manufacturing sector in, 243; transfer of managerial resources by, 255
NIEs. *See* Newly industrialized economies (NIEs)
Nominal protection coefficient (NPC), agricultural, 103–4, 105–8, 110–11
Nominal rates of protection (NRPs): in analysis of Japanese protection levels, 112–13; country comparison showing, 100–101, 102–3; Korea, 361–67, 373, 375–77, 379–81
Nonmanufacturing sector: Japanese FDI in, 277; Japanese FDI in Asian, 279
Nontariff barriers (NTBs): in advanced industrialized countries, 183; analysis of Taiwan's, 344–45, 347–54, 357–58; commodities protected by, 118; hidden nature of, 144; Korea, 379, 384; Korean exports under, 197–222; protective levels of Taiwan's, 366; of United States, 309. *See also* Antidumping (AD) laws, United States; Countervailing duty (CVD) law, United States; Voluntary export restraints (VERs)
NPC. *See* Nominal protection coefficient (NPC)

OEM. *See* Original equipment manufacturing (OEM)
Omnibus Trade and Competitiveness Act

(1988), United States: effect of, 9, 189, 194, 195; Section Super-301, 309, 316–17
Optimal technological gap concept, 265–66
Orderly market agreements (OMAs), 23, 190, 191
Original equipment manufacturing (OEM), 245, 252, 261

Pacific Economic Cooperation Conference (PECC), 222
People's Republic of China. *See* China
Political activity: costs of, 144–45; liberalization of Taiwan's, 327–29; to offset loss of comparative advantage, 125, 144
Political market: as determinant of agricultural protection, 101–2, 110–11, 126, 129–30, 144; international scope of, 144; in Taiwan, 327–30
PRC. *See* China
Preferential systems: changing focus of, 7; create discrimination, 19; under GATT, 12–13; mechanisms for, 9–10; negative, 8–9; with nondiscriminatory trade, 9; U.S. role in free trade, 7–8; in U.S. trade law, 9. *See also* Special and differential treatment (S&D)
Prices: elasticity of demand for DRAMs, 68–70; regulation in Japan of rice, 97. *See also* forward pricing
Price stabilization programs, Japan, 99
Privatization, Mexico, 29
Producer subsidy equivalent (PSE), 112, 116–17, 144
Product differentiation strategy, 283
Production process: cooperation in, 252; differentiation in division of, 282–83, 292–96
Productivity, agricultural: motivation to raise, 120, 121; predictions for Latin American, 136–37
Productivity growth: changing levels of U.S., 150–52; of Japan, 149, 151–54, 181; United States, 150–52
Product life cycle: cost concepts in analysis of, 70–75; costs, prices, and revenues over, 59–64; Hirschman-Herfindahl index of concentration in, 71–78; in models of semiconductor product life cycle, 53–58; production levels over, 60–79. *See also* Learning curve; Learning economies
Product subsidy equivalent (PSE), Korea and Taiwan, 125
Protection: demand and supply conditions for, 126–30, 369–72; demand in Japan for, 102; devices in Japanese economy for, 98–99; effect on Korean exports of U.S., 204–16; hidden measures of, 144; of infant industry, 389; of intellectual property rights, 194, 216; levels in Latin America, 136–37; motivation for East Asian country, 117–18; motivation for EC, 117; trend in, 130–31, 134–37, 183, 189; visible costs of, 144–45. *See also* Border protection; Nominal rates of protection (NRPs); Nontariff barriers (NTBs); Quotas; Subsidies; Trade barriers
Protection, agricultural: decisions on forms of, 130–31, determinants of, 101–3; effect of, 128–29; effect of foreign pressure on, 129–30, 144; estimates of levels of, 103–10; factors influencing resistance to, 128–29; in Japan, 95–97, 98–99; with loss of comparative advantage, 119–20, 125–34; proposals to constrain spread of, 137–40; trends in, 134–37. *See also* Commodities; Subsidies

Quantitative restrictions, 136. *See also* Quotas; Voluntary export restraints (VERs)
Quotas: on Japanese imports, 98

Republic of China (ROC). *See* Taiwan
Resource base: as determinant of agricultural productivity, 121–22. *See also* Land resources; Natural resources
ROC. *See* Taiwan

Safeguard actions: of United States, 189–90
Safeguard investigations: initiated by United States, 189
Section 232. *See* Trade Expansion Act (1962), U.S.
Section 301. *See* Trade Act (1974)
Section 307. *See* Trade Act (1984), United States
Section 337. *See* Tariff Act (1930), U.S.
Section 201 (escape clause). *See* Trade Act (1974), United States
Section Super-301. *See* Omnibus Trade and Competitiveness Act (1988), United States

Self-sufficiency, food, 95–96
Semiconductor product life cycle: Baldwin-Krueger model, 56–57; Flamm's model, 53–54, 57–58; Spence's model, 54–56, 57–58
Semiconductor Trade Arrangement (1986), 79
Short Term Cotton Textile Arrangement (STA), 198
Small and medium-sized firms (SMSFs): in Asian newly industrialized economies, 265–66; as channels for technology transfer, 271; as Japanese FDI projects, 251, 267, 281
Special and differential treatment (S&D), 139, 145–46, 216, 218, 222
Steel Import Stabilization Act, U.S., 200
Strategic industries concept, Taiwan: effects of preferential policies on, 390–405; policy and subsidies for, 387–90
Structural Impediments Initiative (SII): issues of, 223–24; pressure on Japan by, 153, 180, 181
Subsidies: countervailing of export, 192; defined in GATT, 193; as form of protection for agriculture, 99; political aspect of agricultural, 126. *See also* Consumer subsidy equivalents (CSEs); Producer subsidy equivalent (PSE)
Supply: factors shifting protection, 127–30; increased off-farm labor, 125
Support levels: for agriculture in Indonesia, 135; setting and adjusting, 131

Taiwan: foreign direct investment of, 255–57; import substitution in, 323–27, 387; industrial policy of, 387–405, 409; Kuomintang (KMT) party in, 319–27; political market in, 327–30; recent economic and political history of, 319–323; trade policy of, 323–27, 339–43, 347–55, 357–58, 365–67; U.S. trade policy toward, 308–18
Tariff Act (1930), U.S.: effect of, 11, 191nn4,5; Section 337, 194, 198, 201–2, 206, 212, 214t
Tariffs: alternatives to, 130–31; analysis of Taiwan's, 353–54, 357–58; protective levels of Taiwan's, 365–67; rates in Taiwan, 339–41, 342; reductions as bilateral agreements, 23; requirement of policy change to, 138
Tax system, Korea, 432
Technology: Asian Pacific region as market for, 260–63; defined, 244; effect of flows of, 264–65; public and private channels of transfer, 244–49; types of, 246–47. *See also* Optimal technological gap concept
Technology transfer: Asian NIEs as channels of, 255–59; effect of cost on location of, 263; forms of Japanese, 252–55; types in Asian Pacific countries of, 263–64; types of, 246. *See also* Foreign direct investment (FDI); Multinational corporations (MNCs); Small and medium-sized firms (SMSFs)
Textile and clothing industry: Korea, 198, 200; Multifiber Agreement effects on, 208–9; U.S.-Taiwan agreement for, 317–18
Tokyo Round, 314–15
Trade: factors influencing Japanese-Asian, 223–40; inter- and intraindustry, 156–58, 175–76, 182, 293–96; interprocess, 286, 293; intra- and interfirm, 294–96; with technological change and capital accumulation, 155–56; U.S.-Korean bilateral, 185–86
Trade, international: effect of Japanese FDI on Asian, 296; factors in importance of, 156–58; growth for industrialized countries, 153–54; intraindustry, 156–58; pattern in Japanese-Asian, 283–96; predictions of declining importance of, 154–55; role in Japan and United States of, 155–56. *See also* Interindustry trade; Intraindustry trade
Trade Act (1974), United States, 189, 319; Section 301, 195–96, 309, 316, 318; Section 201 (escape clause), 190–91, 200, 217
Trade Act (1979), United States, 317
Trade Act (1984), United States, 316; Section 307, 318
Trade Act (1988), United States. *See* Omnibus Trade and Competitiveness Act (1988)
Trade Agreement Act (1979), U.S., 193nn9,10
Trade agreements, bilateral, 23
Trade Agreements Extension Act (1951), United States, 336
Trade barriers: decisions to reduce, 11–16; in developing countries, 192; elimination as

bilateral agreement, 23; to Japanese imports, 227–32; preferences in manipulation of, 9–10
Trade Expansion Act (1962), U.S.: Section 232 (national security clause), 194–95, 198, 201–2, 206, 314
Trade Expansion Act (1988), U.S., 44
Trade laws. *See* Antidumping (AD) laws, United States; Countervailing duty (CVD) law, United States
Trade monopolies, Japan, 98–99
Trade policy: development of Taiwan's, 323–27; evolution of U.S. (1945–91), 308–18; liberalization in Latin American countries, 136; liberalization in Taiwan, 324–25, 326, 329–30, 341–42; politicization of Taiwan's, 327–29; pressure on Japan to liberalize, 97; protection decision making in, 97, 129–34, 144; protectionism in U.S., 189–97; of Reagan administration, 8; reform in Mexico for, 28–29. *See also* Preferential systems
Trade policy, Taiwan: export-promotion strategy of, 342; import-substitution aspect of, 341–42
Trade preferences. *See* Preferential system
Trade protection: interest group model of Taiwan's, 343, 347–55; national interest model of Taiwan's, 343, 349, 351–55
Trigger-price system (TPS), 200

Unbalanced growth theory, 389, 407
United States: in hub-and-spoke trade agreements, 16–19; intrahemisphere trading patterns, 31–34
U. S.-Canada Free Trade Agreement, 1, 16, 26, 28, 29
U. S. Department of Commerce (DOC), 193–94, 202, 204
U. S. International Trade Commission (ITC), 190, 202, 206
U. S.-Israel Free Trade Agreement, 8, 14, 28
U. S.-Japan Semiconductor Trade Arrangement (STA), 48
U. S.-Mexico Free Trade Agreement (proposed), 1–2, 28–31, 41–42
U. S. Trade Representative (USTR), 195–96
Uruguay Round: motive for, 317; objective of, 129–30; role of developing countries in, 139

Vietnam, 256, 267
Voluntary export restraints (VERs): function of, 23; Korea exports to United States under, 198, 200–202; maintained by United States, 189; under Multifiber Arrangement (MFA) quotas, 198; rise in, 131; trend and effect of, 196–97, 206–8; of United States on iron and steel products, 200–201. *See also* Trigger-price system (TPS)

Wafer starts, 53
Western Hemisphere: effect of free trade agreements in, 26–28; trading patterns of, 31–34. *See also* Canada; Latin America; Mexico; United States
Wool textile industry: production and trade structure of, 227

XLG. *See* Export-led growth (XLG) policy, Taiwan